IMPACTS OF RECENT COMPUTER ADVANCES ON OPERATIONS RESEARCH

PUBLICATIONS IN OPERATIONS RESEARCH SERIES
Saul I. Gass, *Editor*

Volume 1
MANPOWER PLANNING MODELS
  Richard C. Grinold and Kneale T. Marshall

Volume 2
FIRE DEPARTMENT DEPLOYMENT ANALYSIS
  The Rand Fire Project

Volume 3
QUEUEING TABLES AND GRAPHS
  Frederick S. Hillier and Oliver S. Yu

Volume 4
ADVANCED TECHNIQUES IN THE PRACTICE OF OPERATIONS RESEARCH
  Harvey J. Greenberg, Frederic H. Murphy, and Susan H. Shaw, *Editors*

Volume 5
IMPACTS OF MICROCOMPUTERS ON OPERATIONS RESEARCH
  Saul I. Gass, Harvey J. Greenberg, Karla L. Hoffmann,
  and R. Warren Langley, *Editors*

Volume 6
A MATHEMATICAL ORGANIZATION THEORY
  R. F. Drenick

Volume 7
FACILITIES LOCATION: MODELS AND METHODS
  Robert F. Love, James G. Morris, and George O. Wesolowsky

Volume 8
ENGINEERING DESIGN: BETTER RESULTS THROUGH OPERATIONS RESEARCH METHODS
  Reuven R. Levary, *Editor*

Volume 9
IMPACTS OF RECENT COMPUTER ADVANCES ON OPERATIONS RESEARCH
  Ramesh Sharda, Bruce L. Golden, Edward Wasil, Osman Balci,
  and William Stewart, *Editors*

IMPACTS OF RECENT COMPUTER ADVANCES ON OPERATIONS RESEARCH

Editors:

Ramesh Sharda
College of Business Administration
Oklahoma State University
Stillwater, Oklahoma, U.S.A.

Bruce L. Golden
College of Business and Management
University of Maryland
College Park, Maryland, U.S.A.

Edward Wasil
Kogod College of Business Administration
The American University
Washington, D.C., U.S.A.

Osman Balci
Department of Computer Science
Virginia Polytechnic Institute and State University
Blacksburg, Virginia, U.S.A.

William Stewart
School of Business
College of William and Mary
Williamsburg, Virginia, U.S.A.

NORTH-HOLLAND
New York • Amsterdam • London

No responsibility is assumed by the Publisher for any injury and/or damage to persons or property as a matter of products liability, negligence or otherwise, or from any use or operation of any methods, products, instructions or ideas contained in the material herein.

© 1989 by Elsevier Science Publishing Co., Inc. All rights reserved.

This book has been registered with the Copyright Clearance Center, Inc. For further information, please contact the Copyright Clearance Center, Salem, Massachusetts.

This book is printed on acid-free paper.

Published by:
Elsevier Science Publishing Co., Inc.
655 Avenue of the Americas, New York, New York 10010

Sole distributors outside the United States and Canada:

Elsevier Science Publishers B.V.
P.O. Box 211, 1000 AE Amsterdam, The Netherlands

Library of Congress Cataloging in Publication Data

Impact of recent computer advances on operations research / editors, Ramesh Sharda...[et al.].
    p. cm. — (Publications in operations research series; v. 9)
    Includes index.
    1. Operations research—Data processing.   I. Sharda, Ramesh.   II. Series.
T57.6.I483 1989
658.4'034—dc20   89-11653
ISBN 0-444-01492-6   CIP

Current Printing
10 9 8 7 6 5 4 3 2 1

Manufactured in the United States of America.

CONTENTS

Preface   xi

I. PLENARY PAPER

Decomposition Techniques for Large-Scale Electric Power Systems Planning Under Uncertainty   3
George B. Dantzig

II. PARALLEL ALGORITHMS FOR MATHEMATICAL PROGRAMMING

A Parallel Auction Algorithm: A Case Study in the Use of Parallel Object-Oriented Programming   23
Richard S. Barr and Michael G. Christiansen

A Comparative Study of Some Parallel Bin Packing Algorithms   33
Judith O. Berkey and Pearl Y. Wang

SIMD Knapsack Approximation Algorithms   44
Thomas E. Gerasch, Pearl Y. Wang and Scott T. Weidman

A Vectorized Dual Algorithm for Generalized Network Problem   57
Anand R. Joshi and Der-San Chen

Vectorization of Transportation Network Equilibrium Assignment Codes   71
Hani S. Mahmassani and Kyriacos C. Mouskos

A Flexible Parallel Algorithm for Block-Constrained Optimization Problems   82
G.L. Schultz and R.R. Meyer

Supercomputers and Global Optimization   92
Regina Hunter Mladineo

Evaluation of a Parallel Hedging Algorithm for Stochastic Network Programming   106
John M. Mulvey and Hercules Vladimirou

Parallel Solution of Dynamic Programming Equation Using Optimistic Evaluation   120
David M. Nicol

Parallel Branch and Bound Algorithms for Unconstrained Quadratic Zero-One Programming   131
Panos M. Pardalos and Gregory P. Rodgers

A Supercomputer Algorithm for the 0-1 Multiknapsack Problem 144
  Gerard Plateau and Catherine Roucairol

Implementing an Interior Point LP Algorithm on a Supercomputer 158
  Matthew J. Saltzman, Radhika Subramanian and Roy E. Marsten

Expriences with Large Scale Network Optimazitation on the
Connection Machine 169
  Cindy Phillips and Stavros A. Zenios

III. GRAPHICS IN OPTIMIZATION

Application of Interactive Computer Graphics to Linear Programming 183
  Irvin Lustig

A PC-Based Interactive Network Design System for Fiber Optic
Communication Networks 190
  Clyde L. Monma and David F. Shallcross

IV. MICROCOMPUTERS IN OPERATIONS RESEARCH

Personal Computer Version of Nearly Triangular Leontief LP Solution 205
  E. Gelman and M. A. Pollatschek

Optimizing Exchange Agreements in the Refining Industry 217
  Terry P. Harrison and Jack L. Martin

Nonprocedural Implementation of Mathematical Programming Algorithms 226
  James K. Ho

Closed Queueing Network Analysis of Indirect Labor Requirements 238
  Robert Terry, David DeBald and Ramesh Chikkala

A Microcomputer-Based Marine Geographic Information System with
Marketing Application 248
  Maria Luisa Villanueva, Nancy A. Wittpenn,
  C. Bruce Austin and Edward Baker

Mathematical Programming Software for the Microcomputer: Recent Advances
Comparisons and Trends 263
  Edward Wasil, Bruce Golden and Ramesh Sharda

Project Management Software for the Microcomputer: Recent Advances
and Future Directions 273
  Edward Wasil and Arjang Assad

V. ARTIFICIAL INTELLIGENCE AND EXPERT SYSTEMS

Artificial Intelligence Based Approaches for Solving Hierarchical
Optimization Problems 289
G. Anandalingam, R Mathieu, C. L. Pittard and N. Sinha

Impact of Neurocomputing on Operations Research 302
James W. Denton and Gregory R. Madey

Neural Networks for an Intelligent Mathematical Programming System 313
Harvey J. Greenberg

The Computer as a Partner in Algorithmic Design: Automated
Discovery of Parameters for a Multi-Objective Scheduling Heuristic 321
*Michael R. Hilliard, Gunar E. Liepins, Mark Palmer
and Gita Rangarajan*

Flexible Systems for the Design of Heuristic Algorithms in Complex
OR Domains 332
Jean-Yves Potvin and Stephen F. Smith

VI. VEHICLE ROUTING AND SCHEDULING APPLICATIONS

SCAN: A Decision Support System for Railroad Scheduling 347
Dejan Jovanovic and Patrick T. Harker

An Interactive Decision Support System for Vehicle Routing 361
Kendall E. Nygard, Paul Juell and Kadaba Nagesh

Vehicle Routing and Scheduling for Home Delivery 373
Joanne R. Schaffer and Pamela K. Pearl

VII. SIMULATION

Simulation Model Development: The Multidimensionality of the Computing
Technology Pull 385
Osman Balci and Richard E. Nance

Locating P Mobile Servers on a Congested Network: A Simulation Analysis 396
Rex K. Kincaid, Keith W. Miller and Stephen K. Park

The Design and Development of an Analyzer for Discrete Event
Model Specifications 407
  Robert L. Moose, Jr. and Richard E. Nance

Visual Simulation: Seeing is Believing? 422
  Ray J. Paul

Simulating a Marine Container Terminal on the Macintosh II 433
  Michael B. Silberholz, Bruce L. Golden and Edward K. Baker

VIII. MODEL DEVELOPMENT AND ANALYSIS SYSTEMS

Mathematical Programming Modeling Project - Overview 447
  Gordon H. Bradley

Optimization with Constraint Programming Systems 463
  R. G. Brown, J. W. Chinneck and G. M. Karam

Concept and First Experiences with an Object-Oriented Interface for
Mathematical Programming 474
  Manfred Grauer, Stephan Albers and Martin Frommberger

Tools for Modelling Support and Construction of Optimization Applications 484
  Gautam Mitra

The GRG2 Model Builder 497
  Allan D. Waren, Michael Pechura and Leon S. Lasdon

On the Use of Advance Architecture Computers via High-Level
Modelling Languages 507
  Stavros Zenios, Soren S. Nielsen and Mustafa Pinar

IX. TELECOMMUNICATIONS

Evaluation and Design of Voice Telecommunications Network 521
  Anthony J. Perticone, James P. Jarvis and Douglas R. Shier

X. NUMERICAL ANALYSIS

Interval Arithmetic Methods for Nonlinear Systems and Nonlinear
Optimization: An Outline and Status 533
  R. Baker Kearfott

Polynomial Continuation 543
  Alexander P. Morgan

Modern Homotopy Methods in Optimization ... 555
Layne T. Watson

Index ... 567

PREFACE

Over the last four years, the operations research (OR) community has witnessed a phenomenal growth in computer technology that has dramatically impacted the way in which decision problems are modeled and solved. Sophisticated languages now enable analysts to model large-scale linear and nonlinear problems easily and efficiently. Powerful multiprocessor supercomputers using state-of-the-art algorithms can solve problems quickly. High-performance graphics workstations can help researchers study the geometry of mathematical programs while complex systems can now be simulated on the microcomputer. Neural networks are being used to design intelligent mathematical programming systems.

In early January 1989, nearly 160 computer science and OR practitioners and researchers from industry, government, academia, and the military gathered in Williamsburg, Virginia to report on recent computer hardware and software advances and to discuss new opportunities and outline new challenges for the OR profession. The conference on **Impacts of Recent Computer Advances on Operations Research** was sponsored by the Computer Science Technical Section of the Operations Research Society of America.

This volume chronicles the proceedings of the conference and includes forty-six refereed papers that survey important computer developments and applications. The plenary paper by George Dantzig reports on a recent large-scale mathematical programming application in the electric power industry. The remaining papers are clustered into 9 categories that represent areas of significant research and real-world application over the last four years: Parallel Algorithms, Graphics, Microcomputers, Artificial Intelligence and Expert Systems, Vehicle Routing and Scheduling, Simulation, Model Development and Analysis, Telecommunications, and Numerical Analysis. We believe that researchers, practitioners, and students alike will find these papers interesting, useful, and provocative.

The organizing committee for the meeting consisted of the editors and the following individuals: Harvey Greenberg, Mary Magrogan, and Gautam Mitra. The editors thank them for their help. The organizing committee thanks the College of Business Administration, Oklahoma State University and the School of Business, College of William and Mary for financial support of this conference. We also appreciate the help from the following individuals who contributed to the meeting by either reviewing papers or by helping with various arrangement details. Their help was invaluable in making the meeting a success:

John R. Armendariz, Jerry Banks, Golgen Bengu, Alice Birnac, Lawrence Bodin, Gordon Bradley, Aunshumali Chahande, Dalen Chiang, Ann Conty, Cihan H. Dagli, Robert Dauffenbach, Susan Fineagan, Saul Gass, Patrick T. Harker, Benjamin Harrison, Michael R. Hilliard, James K. Ho, Ruth B. Hofstra, Srinath Jagannathan, Anand Joshi, Rex Kincaid, Donald H. Kraft, Elton Li, John Llewellyn, S. Mandala, Roy Marsten, Clyde L. Monma, Wayne Meinhart, Pat Morris, Rajendra Patil, Charles M. Parks, Ramesh Parmar, Allan Ross, Robert A. Russell, Dean Robert Sandmeyer, Smaeel M. Sarsalari, Usha Sharda, Douglas Shier, George Schell, Eui-Ho Suh, Leonard Tashman, Shirley Tey, Michael G. Thomason, Pearl Y. Wang, Layne T. Watson.

The referees rejected nearly one half of the conference submissions and ensured a high level of quality for accepted manuscripts. The contributors to this volume also deserve special thanks for their cooperation and help in assembling their papers for publication.

The Editors

Ramesh Sharda
Bruce Golden
Edward Wasil
Osman Balci
William Stewart

ptimization # I.
PLENARY PAPER

DECOMPOSITION TECHNIQUES FOR LARGE-SCALE ELECTRIC POWER SYSTEMS PLANNING UNDER UNCERTAINTY

GEORGE B. DANTZIG

Department of Operations Research, Stanford University
Stanford, CA 94305

ABSTRACT

Resource planning for large-scale electric power systems under uncertainty by mathematical programming, parallel processors, and importance sampling is central to our approach to solving the basic problem: Given a large multi-area electric power system, determine a mix of various types of generation and transmission capacities to the planning horizon that will meet future demand and reliability requirements and such that the total discounted capital and operating costs are minimized. The power system can consist of a single utility's service area, or a whole geographical region served by interconnected multiple utilities. In order to take properly into account the effects of long lead times for installation of new technologies, the planning horizon of the model will typically be quite long — say 30 - 40 years.

Planning over such a long time span must necessarily be under uncertainty concerning future values of many parameters of the system. Consequently, the certainty that there will be future contingencies must be taken into account in developing a good plan. The proper treatment of uncertainty in the planning process turns the representation of the problem from an ordinary linear (or nonlinear) program, that can be solved by available software into a stochastic mathematical program whose solution requires the application of techniques such as decomposition as well as the use of improved computer technologies such as parallel processors and importance sampling.

1. INTRODUCTION

Electric power system planning under uncertainty is only one example of the more general problem of multiperiod resource planning under uncertainty. Other examples of planning are long-term fleet planning by airlines, or long-term asset allocations by financial institutions. Such problems can be readily modelled as multiperiod stochastic linear (or nonlinear) programs. Solution of such models in the general case is, however, impractical since the size of the problem grows exponentially with the number of periods. Fortunately, for the multiperiod electric power system planning problem under uncertainty, the size of the problem need not grow exponentially. Hence this type of problem is amenable for solution.

This paper reviews research presented in Dantzig (1988), Dantzig and Glynn (1988) and research under way in the System Optimization Laboratory of the Operations Research

Published 1989 by Elsevier Science Publishing Co., Inc.
Impacts of Recent Computer Advances on Operations Research
Ramesh Sharda, Bruce L. Golden, Edward Wasil, Osman Balci, William Stewart, Editors

Department at Stanford University on long-term expansion of electric power systems. Those participating in the latter effort are Mordecai Avriel, Marc Bellovin, Peter Glynn, Robert Entriken, Marvin Nakayama, John Stone, and the author.

2. FORMULATION OF DYNAMIC LINEAR PROGRAMS

I begin with the deterministic case of multi-period planning in order to point out why the general problem grows exponentially in size with the number of periods when we extend the formulation to include stochastic effects. I then restrict the extension to certain important type of investment or resource planning problems. For this class, the size need not grow exponentially with the number of time periods T. Applications include systems having a vector of capacities being considered for expansion.

Lower block-triangular matrix structures are typical for planning problems modelled as linear programs because activities initiated in period t have input and output coefficients in periods $t, t+1, \ldots$. For example, for $T = 3$ periods, the coefficient matrix has submatrix blocks of coefficients displayed in (1) below:

$$\begin{bmatrix} A_{11} & & \\ A_{21} & A_{22} & \\ A_{31} & A_{32} & A_{33} \end{bmatrix} \begin{bmatrix} X_1 \\ X_2 \\ X_3 \end{bmatrix} = \begin{bmatrix} b_1 \\ b_2 \\ b_3 \end{bmatrix} \qquad (1)$$

where A_{ij} are submatrices, $X_t \geq 0$ the vector of activity levels in period t, and b_t are the specified vectors of inputs and outputs of the system being modelled.

By the introduction of in-process inventories and other devices, linear programs of lower block-triangular type are mathematically equivalent to *staircase* or *multistage* problems of the form: *Find $\min Z$ and vectors $X_t \geq 0$, such that*

$$\begin{aligned}
b_1 &= A_1 X_1 \\
b_2 &= -B_1 X_1 + A_2 X_2 \\
&\vdots \qquad \ddots \\
b_t &= \qquad\qquad -B_{t-1} X_{t-1} + A_t X_t \\
&\vdots \qquad\qquad\qquad\qquad \ddots \\
b_T &= \qquad\qquad\qquad\qquad -B_{T-1} X_{T-1} + A_T X_T \\
(\min) Z &= c_1 X_1 + \cdots + c_t X_t + \cdots \qquad\qquad + c_T X_T
\end{aligned} \qquad (2)$$

where matrices A_t, B_t and vectors b_t, c_t are given.

A number of promising methods for solving dynamic deterministic linear programs are known. Some references are [Dantzig 1963], [Dantzig and Wolfe 1960], [Glassey 1973], [Ho and Manne 1974], [Dantzig and Perold 1979], [Ho and Loute 1980], [Fourer 1982, 1983, 1984], [Nishiya 1983], [Jackson and Lynch 1982]; for a general reference, see [Dantzig, Dempster, and Kallio, eds. 1981].

For a very general class of stochastic planning problems, the values of $b_t, B_{t-1}, A_t,$ c_t for $t > 1$ are not known to the planner with certainty at the start of stage 1 but become known to him at some later time τ. The value τ itself could be a random variable and there could be a different τ for every element of the matrices and vectors. While the values of these matrices may not be known, their probability distributions could be given and this we assume.

In such problems, the planner wants to make a decision X_1; let random events happen; make a decision in period $t = 2$; let random events happen; make a decision in period $t = 3$, etc. He may wish to make the choice X_1 so that the expected value of Z is minimum. We now give reasons why this very general class of stochastic problems is likely to remain intractable in the foreseeable future with existing conventional (serial) computers or even with the availability of parallel processors. We will then discuss a less general, but very important class of stochastic programs which up to the present have not been practical to solve on serial mainframes but could become so using parallel processors.

3. TWO-STAGE STOCHASTIC PROGRAMMING

We begin with the simplest *two-stage case* first studied in [Dantzig 1955] and subsequently developed by [Wets 1966, 1984]:

$$\begin{aligned} b_1 &= A_1 X_1, & (X_1, X_2) &\geq 0, \\ b_2 &= -B_1 X_1 + A_2 X_2 \\ (min)\, Z &= c_1 X_1 + c_2 X_2 \end{aligned} \qquad (3)$$

where the first stage parameters (b_1, A_1, c_1) are known with certainty while those of the second stage can take on possibly a continuum of values $(b_2(\omega), c_2(\omega), B_1(\omega), A_2(\omega))$ with probability (density) distribution $p(\omega)$ for ω in Ω, or a discrete probability distribution $p(\omega)$ where $\omega = 1, 2, \ldots, K$. The range of ω in Ω may therefore be continuous or it may be discrete, finite or infinite.

For the purposes of the computational approach outlined in this proposal, we require that Ω be discrete with a finite number of elements. Practically speaking, this is no restriction since any distribution may be approximated by a probability mass function concentrated on a finite set of points. Then, assuming we label the sample points ω using the integers $\{1, 2, \ldots, k\}$, the random vectors and matrices (b_2, c_2, B_1, A_2) take on the value $(b_2(\omega), c_2(\omega), B_1(\omega), A_2(\omega))$, $(1 \leq \omega \leq K)$ with known probability $p_2(\omega)$.

We now illustrate the approach for $K = 3$. The two-stage stochastic program of minimizing expected costs under uncertainty then has *as its certainty equivalent* the deterministic linear program of the following form:

Find $min\, Z$, $X_1 \geq 0$, $X_2(\omega) \geq 0$, $\omega = 1, 2, 3$: **(4.0)**

$$b_1(1) = A_1 X_1 \tag{4.1}$$

$$\begin{aligned}
b_2(1) &= -B_1(1)X_1 + A_2(1)X_2(1) \\
b_2(2) &= -B_1(2)X_1 \hspace{3.5cm} + A_2(2)X_2(2) \\
b_2(3) &= -B_1(3)X_1 \hspace{7cm} + A_2(3)X_2(3)
\end{aligned} \tag{4.2}$$

$$min\ Z = c_1 X_1 + p_2(1)\ c_2(1)X_2(1) + p_2(2)\ c_2(2)X_2(2) + p_2(3)\ c_2(3)X_2(3) \tag{4.3}$$

To simplify the discussion that follows, we assume a bounded optimal solution exists. It follows that we can always find $\pi_2(k)$ to multiply constraints corresponding to $b_2(k)$ above and subtract from the objective so that the adjusted $c_2(\omega) \geq 0$. Therefore we can assume without loss of generality $c_2(\omega) \geq 0$. Except as noted otherwise, we assume B_1 is independent of ω, i.e., $B_1(\omega) = B_1$.

Typically this problem is solved using Benders decomposition algorithm (see [Benders 1962]). The key idea is to replace the objective function contribution of the second period variables by a scalar θ_2, and to replace the second period (stage) constraints — those shown in (4.2) between the dashed lines — by a set of inequalities expressed in terms of X_1 and θ_2 only. These are called "cuts" and are *necessary conditions* which are satisfied by all feasible and optimal solutions to (4). These cuts are added sequentially ($\ell = 1, 2, \ldots$) to the first period problem, $A_1 X_1 = b_1(1), X_1 \geq 0$; and these together with a modified objective $c_1 X_1 + \theta_2$ constitute the *restricted master problem* whose $min\ Z$ is a lower bound estimate for $min\ Z$ of (4). Cuts are added to the restricted master problem until they become *sufficient* to solve (4). This happens when the current value of the objective Z for a feasible solution to (4) equals the lower bound estimate of $min\ Z$. In practice the iterative process is stopped when this difference is judged to be "small enough".

The restricted master and subproblem for Benders' decomposition method have the form:

The Master Problem

$$\text{FIND}\ min\ Z,\ X_1 \geq 0,\ \theta_2 \geq 0, \tag{5.0}$$

$$b_1 = A_1 X_1, \tag{5.1}$$

$$\text{CUTS:}\quad g_1^\ell \leq -G_1^\ell X_1 + \delta_2^\ell \theta_2, \quad \ell = 1, \ldots, L \tag{5.2}$$

$$min\ Z = c_1 X_1 + \theta_2 \tag{5.3}$$

The Sub Problem For each $\omega = 1, \ldots, K$, find $min\ Z_2(\omega), X_2(\omega) \geq 0$,

$$\begin{aligned}
A_2(\omega)X_2(\omega) &= b_2(\omega) + B_1 X_1^* &&: \pi_2(\omega) \\
p_2(\omega) \cdot c_2(\omega)X_2(\omega) &= Z_2(\omega)(min) &&
\end{aligned} \tag{6}$$

Dual Prices

where $\delta_2^\ell = 0$ for "feasibility" cuts if the subproblem from which it was derived is infeasible, and $\delta_2^\ell = 1$ for "optimality" cuts if the subproblem (6) is feasible.

The optimal solution $X_1 = X_1^*$ to (5) is then "tested" to see if it is the first period component of an optimal solution (X_1, X_2) for (4) by solving the set of subproblems (6) to see (i) if the contribution $B_1 X_1^*$ from the first period implies for the second period a feasible solution for every choice of ω, and (ii) if it together with the set of optimal solutions to the second period for every ω provides a global optimum to the original problem. Global optimality is easily tested by checking whether the lower bound estimate for $\min Z$ is equal to the value of Z for the current feasible solution. If the answer to (i) or (ii) is negative, the optimal $\pi_2(\omega)$ to (6) is substituted in formula (7.1) or (7.2) below in order to generate cut $L + 1$ which is then added to the L already generated in (5.2).

The optimal dual "prices" if (6) is feasible, or "infeasibility weights" if not feasible are computed and used as follows: If any subproblem ω is infeasible, its infeasibility weights are used to generate a "feasibility" cut (7.1) with $\delta_2^{\ell+1} = 0$:

$$g_1^{\ell+1} = \pi_2(\omega) b_2(\omega); \quad G_1^{\ell+1} = \pi_2(\omega) B_1(\omega) . \tag{7.1}$$

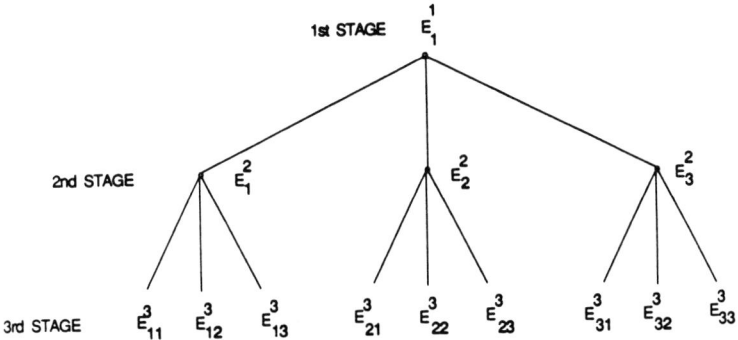

(8)

(Later when the concept of a "reliable" system is discussed, this strict notion of infeasibility will be relaxed somewhat.) If feasible for all $\omega \in \Omega$, then X_1^* is tested for optimality by comparing the lower bound estimate of θ from the master problem with $\sum_\omega Z_2(\omega)$. If the test fails (i.e. $\theta_2 \neq \sum_\omega Z_2(\omega)$), the *expected values*

$$g_1^{\ell+1} = \sum_\omega \pi_2(\omega) b_2(\omega); \quad G_1^{\ell+1} = \sum_\omega \pi_2(\omega) B_1(\omega) . \qquad (7.2)$$

are used to generate new "optimality" cut conditions to augment those of (5.2) with $\delta_2^{\ell+1} = 1$. Note that (7.2) are actually expected values because $\pi_2(\omega)$ as defined by (6) are weighted by the probabilities $p_2(\omega)$ appearing in the objective.

4. MULTI-STAGE STOCHASTIC PLANNING PROBLEM

The two-staged stochastic program (4) just discussed is one amenable to solution using parallel computers. The corresponding "reduction" to the equivalent deterministic linear program, for the general multi-staged case, however, becomes intractable due to the exponential increase in the number of possible outcomes, see (8) below for the case of $T = 3$ where the various contingencies in the third stage $E_{11}^3, \ldots, E_{22}^3$, etc. depend on the various contingencies E_1^2 or E_2^2 that preceed them in the second stage.

It is now easy to see why, for large K, the proliferation of cases quickly becomes out of hand as the number of stages increases. Even if large numbers of inexpensive parallel processors were available, it does not seem to lead to a practical way to solve stochastic problems in general. In order to make headway with this fundamental problem, we propose to consider a certain restricted class of relevant problems which is tractable. In this proposal, we focus on a subclass of multi-stage uncertainty problems whose dynamic deterministic part, once fixed, is assumed unaffected by stochastic events. Its "event tree" is displayed in (9).

In the resource planning context, the planner is confronted with the problem of planning system resources for T periods. The decision variables can be divided into two major groups: The *design* variables, that are determined by taking into account future uncertainties, but whose values, once determined, will not be affected by stochastic events. For example, the installed capacities of generation units and transmission lines are such design variables. The second group of variables are the *production* variables, or operating variables. In solving the multi-stage planning problems these variables may take on several values, corresponding to the outcomes of the stochastic events. For example, the actual power generated by the various generation units is a production variable, clearly affected by such stochastic events as demand variability and equipment failure.

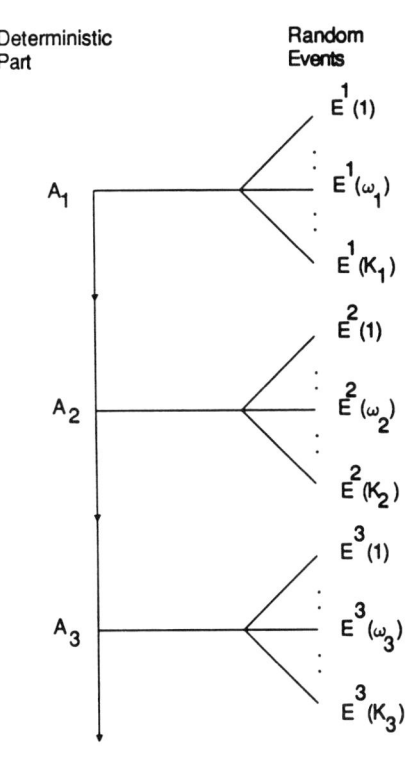

4.1 Mathematical Formulation of the Multi-stage Resource Planning Problem

The multi-stage resource planning problem can be generically stated as follows: Given a finite number of periods, find the levels of the design and the production variables that will minimize the total expected costs of building and operating the resources up to the planning horizon.

Let us formulate now this problem as a multi-stage stochastic mathematical program. To simplify the presentation, we consider the two-period case first. For this case we assume the random events occurring in stage (period) 1 are independent of those occurring in stage (period) 2. Moreover, we assume that within a stage, there are random events concerning supply availability and random events concerning demand levels, and these two types of random events are independent of each other. Let $\tilde{\omega}_t, \bar{\omega}_t$ denote the random events in stage t corresponding to supply availability and demand levels, respectively. The two period problem then has the form:

Find $min\ Z$, *"design" vectors* $X_t \geq 0$, *and "production" vectors* $U_t(\omega_t) \geq 0$, *corresponding to each point* $\omega_t = (\tilde{\omega}_t, \bar{\omega}_t)$ *in* Ω_t *such that*

$$\begin{aligned}
b_1 &= A_1 X_1 \\
0 &= -F_1(\tilde{\omega}_1) X_1 & & & +D_1 U_1(\omega_1) \\
d_1(\bar{\omega}_1) &= & & & +E_1 U_1(\omega_1) \\
b_2 &= -B_1 X_1 & +A_2 X_2 \\
0 &= & & -F_2(\tilde{\omega}_2) & & +D_2 U_2(\omega_2) \\
d_2(\bar{\omega}_2) &= & & & & +E_2 U_2(\omega_2) \\
Z &= c_1 X_1 & +c_2 X_2 & +\mathcal{E} f_1 U_1(\omega_1) & +\mathcal{E} f_2 U_2(\omega_2)
\end{aligned} \qquad (10)$$

where $\mathcal{E}$ *denotes expectation over* $\omega_t = (\tilde{\omega}_t, \bar{\omega}_t) \in \Omega_t$.

Here A_1 and b_1 have to do with the initial conditions of the resources at the beginning of the planning horizon and are known with certainty. $F_t(\tilde{\omega}_t)$ and D_t relate supply availability with operating levels in stage t. $d_t(\bar{\omega}_t)$ and E_t relate uncertain demands with operating levels in stage t, and B_1, A_2 relate the levels of the design variables in stages 1 and 2 (addition of new resources, retirement of old ones). Note that our formulation implies a "here and now" type decision, discussed in [Dantzig and Madansky 1961].

More specifically, the solution of how much resources to have in the future takes the form of a decision we make *here and now* of what our resource development path will be over time, and not a decision of what branches to take depending on what different contingencies may arise in the future such as: "If there is a high demand in year t, increase capacity in year $t+1$ because this implies a higher expected demand in year $t+1$."

Whether or not a "here and now" decision is realistic depends on a number of factors: For many industries, such as electric power, resource planning is a major undertaking involving raising capital, and making long-term contractual arrangements that results in a great deal of built-in inertia to stick to a course of action for several years once a commitment is made. For such situations, our "here and now" assumption may not be a bad one.

In practice, of course, planners often act as if they are making a decision here and now of what resources they plan to have on hand in the future, even though they know that later on they are likely to change their mind. It probably would be better in such situations for planners to incorporate into their decision model the possibility of making some "**in course**" future corrections. From a computational point of view, there is no difficulty extending our approach to allow for some branching provided the number of branches is kept down to a few, say two or three, major ones. More branches than that could create computational difficulties. How to generalize the model to allow for stochastic events that are correlated from one period to the next will be described in greater detail later.

The mathematical structure for the deterministic part of the resource planning problem would be the same as in (2), namely:

$$b_t = -B_{t-1}X_{t-1} + A_t X_t, \quad \text{for } t = 1,\ldots,T \text{ and } B_0 X_0 \equiv 0, \qquad (11)$$

where $X_t \geq 0$ are the planned design variables (to be determined) for period t at a cost $= \Sigma c_t X_t$ where b_t, A_t, B_t, c_t are all known with certainty. The subproblem for period t is defined for some $X_t = X_t^*$ by first finding the level of design variables available for use in period t:

$$F_t(\tilde{\omega}_t) X_t^*, \quad \tilde{\omega}_t \text{ in } \tilde{\Omega}_t, \qquad (12)$$

which depends on X_t^* and a random variable $\tilde{\omega}_t$ measuring the uncertain proportion of unavailable X_t^* requiring repair. The probability distribution of $\tilde{\omega}_t$ is assumed known. Letting $d_t(\bar{\omega}_t)$ be the uncertain demand we then solve for the dual multipliers and Z_t that solves (13) below for each random choice of right-hand side, i.e., for $\tilde{\omega}_t$ in $\tilde{\Omega}_t$ and $\bar{\omega}_t$ in $\bar{\Omega}_t$, in order to determine the expected values of the cuts generated by (14) below. If the number of discrete values of $\tilde{\omega}_t, \bar{\omega}_t$ are small, this can be done exactly. If large, then their expected values have to be estimated by an importance sampling procedure described later. Let $\omega_t = (\tilde{\omega}_t, \bar{\omega}_t) \in \Omega_t$. The sub-subproblems are:
Find $U_t(\omega_t) \geq 0$ and $\min Z_t(\omega_t)$, $\omega_t = (\tilde{\omega}_t, \bar{\omega}_t) \in \Omega_t$:

$$\begin{aligned} D_t\, U_t(\omega_t) &= F_t(\tilde{\omega}_t)X_t^*, & \bar{\omega}_t \text{ in } \tilde{\Omega}_t, & \quad : \tilde{\pi}_t(\omega_t) \\ E_t\, U_t(\omega_t) &= d_t(\bar{\omega}_t), & \bar{\omega}_t \text{ in } \bar{\Omega}_t, & \quad : \bar{\pi}_t(\omega_t) \\ f_t U_t(\omega_t) &= Z_t(\omega_t) \quad (min), & & \end{aligned} \qquad (13)$$

Dual Prices shown on the right.

where corresponding dual prices are shown on the right. The samples are used to estimate expected cuts $\ell = 1, 2, \ldots$ of the form

$$g_t^\ell \leq G_t^\ell X_t + \delta_t^\ell \theta_t; \qquad (14)$$

where, in case the subproblems are all feasible,

$$g_t^\ell = \sum_{\omega_t} p_t(\omega_t)\bar{\pi}_t(\omega_t)d_t(\bar{\omega}_t); \quad G_t^\ell = \sum_{\omega_t} p_t(\omega_t)\tilde{\pi}_t(\omega_t)F_t(\tilde{\omega}_t) \qquad (15)$$

and a cost form

$$Z = \sum_t (c_t X_t + \theta_t). \qquad (16)$$

which, together with (9), form the MASTER PROBLEM (17) below.

Several parallel processors could be assigned to each stage. The processors receive X_t^* as inputs from the Master Program, generate random $\tilde{\omega}_t$, $\bar{\omega}_t$ and solve the subproblems, and finally give back to the MASTER approximate cuts (14) obtained by sampling. These cuts are then used to augment those obtained earlier.

4.2 Master Problem.

FIND $min\ Z,\ X_t \geq 0,\ \theta_t \geq 0$:

$$\begin{aligned}
b_1 &= A_1 X_1 \\
b_2 &= -B_1 X_1 & +A_2 X_2 \\
g_1^{\ell_1} &\leq G_1^{\ell_1} X_1 & +\delta_1^{\ell_1} \theta_1 \\
g_2^{\ell_2} &\leq & G_2^{\ell_2} X_2 +\delta_2^{\ell_2} \theta_2 \\
min\ Z &= c_1 X_1 & +\theta_1 & +c_2 X_2 +\theta_2
\end{aligned} \qquad (17)$$

where $\ell_1 = 1, \ldots, L_1,\ \ell_2 = 1, \ldots, L_2$.

Note that the Master Problem has the form of a deterministic staircase system which can be solved directly; or, if too large, can be solved by using the dual nested decomposition approach, see for example [Abrahamson 1983], and [Wittrock 1983]. Entriken (1988) has developed a version for parallel processors. The advantage of the dual-decomposition approach is that the parallel processors at each stage can be used effectively to provide information in the form of X_{t+1}^* to the stage below and to pass back cuts generated in stage t to stage $t-1$.

4.3 Partial Interperiod Dependence of Random Events

As noted earlier, there may be situations where our previous assumptions on interperiod independence of the stochastic events may not always be appropriate. At the other extreme, when there is complete dependence as in (8) the exponential growth of cases with number of periods, makes such stochastic planning problems in general too costly to find a numerical solution. However, based on ideas due to Modecai Avriel (verbal communication), it would be practical to solve a model when there is a limited amount of stochastic dependence between periods. This idea we propose to develop. The contingent events occurring in the planning horizon (for $K = 3$) would have an event tree like that depicted in (18) where, note, *we force the consolidation of some of the stochastic events, like E_{12}^3 and E_{21}^3, into a single composite event.*

Such a consolidation is an approximation which, if acceptable causes the number of possible outcomes (in the example) to increase by two from one stage to the next one, instead of the exponential growth as in the case of the total dependence. Suppose, for example, that the demand for electricity can either grow, remain the same, or decline by a fixed amount from one period to another. If demand is, say, 100 at the beginning of the planning horizon, and can either grow by 10 units, remain the same, or decline by 10 units, we have:

$E_1^1 = 110$;

$E_1^2 = 90, \ E_2^2 = 100, \ E_3^2 = 110;$

$E_{11}^3 = 80, \ E_{12}^3 = E_{21}^3 = 90, \ E_{13}^3 = E_{22}^3 = E_{31}^3 = 100, \ E_{23}^3 = E_{32}^3 = 110, E_{33}^3 = 120.$

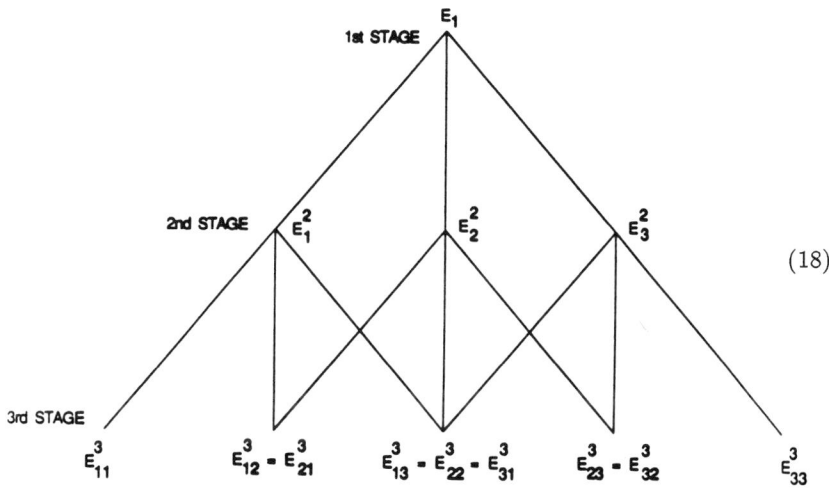

(18)

Incorporation of this type of partial interperiod dependence into a multi-period resource planning framework requries new formulations and perhaps also new decomposition techniques, subjects that we propose to investigate.

4.4 Solution Methods Based on Sampling

The decomposition algorithm described earlier is clearly only practical when K is small. When K is large, it is proposed that parallel processors be used as high-speed sampling or quadrature devices to effectively solve such problems. One idea is to have a processor at the Master level serve as an *integrator* which sequentially receives as input estimates of the cuts (5.2). The Master Problem is then solved to optimality with the estimates it has received so far, and is used to generate as output revised $X_1 = X_1^*$ that are sent to other parallel processors which are busy solving (6) for various choices of ω. This process also provides a *lower bound* estimate for $min\ Z$ which monotonically increases with each solution of the master problem.

The amount of space needed to store the generated cuts in the computer memory need not be large. Assuming B_1 is independent of ω, no more than $L \leq m_2$ of the cuts will be tight on any major iteration, where m_2 is the number of rows in B_1. This is so because G_1^ℓ, generated by linear combinations of the rows of B_1, has rank $\leq r$ where $r \leq m_2$ is the rank of B_1. The remainder may be dropped (possibly to be regenerated on some later iteration).

Several parallel processors could be at the Sub level, each having as input the latest value of X_1^* and solving (6) in dual form for many random or stratified choices of ω. When c_2, A_2 are the same for all ω, the dual of (6) is a linear program with only the dual objective $b_2(\omega)$ changing. By judiciously stratifying the random sampling of Ω we hope to use the optimal basic dual feasible solution for one choice of ω to find quickly the optimal one for the next ω. To provide cuts for the Master, the parallel processors are to be used to determine the expected values $g_1^{\ell+1}$ and $G_1^{\ell+1}$ defined by (7.2) or to approximate them by means of a large enough "importance sample".

If it is practical to solve (6) for all ω, the set of solutions to (6) would generate a valid cut and a correct *upper bound* estimate for $min\ Z$. In that case, the difference between the lower bound and upper bound estimates can be used to test optimality of X_1^* for the original problem. When Z, according to some specified tolerance, is close enough to the lower bound estimate for $min\ Z$ the iterative process is stopped and X_1^* is declared "optimal".

A major methodological problem to be solved is the choice of the sampling strategy. A more detailed discussion based on ideas due to Glynn will be found in Dantzig and Glynn (1988) from which the material below is drawn.

For the cases where K is large, it is no longer possible to solve (6) for all ω. Instead, we propose to use random sampling to choose a set of ω's for which (6) will be solved. This solution strategy will need to overcome several problems:

a) development of an efficient sampling rule,

b) development of an efficient stopping rule.

By a), we refer to the fact that naive sampling will tend to be an inefficient computational tool, in the sense that a large number of ω's will typically be needed to obtain a reasonable degree of solution accuracy. The reason is that within the class of applications that we wish to consider, certain ω's will play a particularly important role in the solution. For example, in an electric power system planning problem, the ω's corresponding to generator failure, while comprising only a small portion of the total sample space ω, are significant enough to force the utility to "hedge". Hence, it is important to design sampling schemes which concentrate an appropriate level of computational effort on these "rare" ω's. We use two basic ideas, from Monte Carlo simulation, to accomplish this task: *stratification* and *importance sampling*.

In stratification one pre-assigns a certain proportion of the total sample to each of (say) m subsets partitioning the sample space Ω. This increases the efficiency of the sampling procedure by reducing the clustering effects typical of a conventional sampling scheme. For example, in naive random sampling, the entire sample could (with small probability, of course) fall into one subset. We also consider a variant of stratification called pre-stratification, that may permit simpler programming implementations, see [Cochran 1977].

The second concept that we exploit is importance sampling. Within each subset of the stratification partition described above, we design our sampling procedure so that we sample not according to the original probability mass function (or, more precisely, the original mass function conditioned on ω belonging to the particular subset), but rather according to a mass function which assigns more weight to the "important" elements of the sample space. By "important", we mean those elements which contribute significantly to the average value of the dual variables. The estimator needs to be appropriately adjusted to account for the new sampling mechanism, but this is easily done see [Hammersley and Handscomb 1964]. We use both theory and exploratory data analysis to guide us in developing efficient importance sampling algorithms.

As for problem (6) described above, we need to develop a stopping rule (hopefully sequential) which meshes appropriately with the mathematical programming ideas described elsewhere. Specifically, the stopping rule should ensure that a sufficient accuracy is obtained at each iteration of the sampling procedure so as to impart useful information to the optimization loop of the routine. We expect the basic structure of the stopping rule to be of Chow-Robbins type, see [Chow and Robbins 1965].

We believe in the sampling approach for two reasons, one historical and the other prospective. First, the dimension of the sample space over which expectations need to be computed is large. The historical experience of numerical analysis suggests that Monte Carlo sampling is typically the most efficient way to calculate such expectations (i.e., random sampling is the method of choice for integrating functions in high-dimensional spaces). The second reason is that Monte Carlo methods are easy to extend to the parallel computing environment, and the speed-ups are significant. The reason, of course, is that

Monte Carlo methods are based on replication and replication with minor variation is trivial to distribute over parallel processors. We believe that Monte Carlo ideas, in conjunction with the mathematical programming concepts described earlier, form a promising avenue for development of efficient solution algorithms for complex stochastic resource planning problems.

4.5 Reliability Considerations

An important aspect of electric power system planning models has to do with introducing constraints that guarantee the system is reliable. A 100% reliable system would be too costly to build. What is done in practice is to tolerate some failure not to exceed a specified upper bound on the amount of expected failure to supply the demand. We use a constraint of the form

$$\sum_{\omega \in \Omega_t} p_t(\omega) g_t \, \tilde{U}_t(\omega) \leq \alpha_t$$

which sets an upper bound α_t on the expected amount of unserved demand. Here $\tilde{U}_t(\omega)$ denotes unserved energy in period t.

Adding such a constraint means that the subproblem no longer decomposes into separate subproblems for each $\omega \in \Omega_t$. In order not to lose this feature, we form a primal decomposition of the problem into relations (19) and (20) corresponding to a "high-level" Master Problem in the sense of the Dantzig-Wolfe primal decomposition approach:

$$\sum_t c_t(X_t) + \sum_t \sum_{\omega \in \Omega_t} p_t(\omega) f_t \tilde{U}_t(\omega) = min \, Z \qquad (19)$$

$$\sum_{\omega \in \Omega_t} p_t(\omega) g_t \tilde{U}_t(\omega) \leq \alpha_t, \qquad t = 1, \ldots, T \,, \qquad (20)$$

All remaining constraints are treated as the constraints of the "high-level" subproblem. This essentially is a systematic way of assigning "penalty" prices ρ_t to the reliability constraints which are then used to replace the coefficients f_t of (19) by $\bar{f}_t = f_t - \rho_t g_t$. The subproblem of this new problem is in exactly the same format as the problem we discussed earlier without reliability constraints. In this formulation infeasibility constraints no longer need to be generated because all the sub-subproblems (6) can now be formulated in such a way that they are always feasible.

Part of our research concerns the best way to order the flow of information to the dual masters to form the cuts of various periods and to the primal master to adjust $\bar{f}_t = f_t + \rho_t g_t$.

Robert Entriken has tested some key aspects of the research just outlined on parallel computers at Oak Ridge National Laboratories and has more recently run tests on equipment available at Stanford. He has already developed as part of his Ph.D. thesis a multi-stage decomposition algorithm for a deterministic model.

5. DEMONSTRATION OF THE RESEARCH METHODOLOGY ON ACTUAL POWER SYSTEMS

The results of the methodological developments in this research is undergoing test on a realistic resource planning problem. We have constructed for this purpose a prototype model of the combined power system of six supply regions of Western U.S. and Canada. Details can be found in Mathematical Decomposition Techniques for Power System Expansion Planning, Uses of Parallel Computers for Multi Area Planning. [EPRI EL-5299, Volume 5, Project 2473-6, Final Report Feb. 1988.] Our most recent formulation (July 1988) contains substantial extensions, improvements and updates.

REFERENCES

Cohen, K.J. and S. Thore (1970). "Programming Bank Portfolios Under Uncertainty," *J. of Bank Research*, Vol. 1, No. 1, 42–61.

Abrahamson, P.G. (1983). "A nested decomposition approach for solving staircase linear programs," Report SOL 83-4, Department of Operations Research, Stanford University, Stanford, Ca.

Beale, E.M.L., Dantzig, G.B. and R.D. Watson (1986). "A First Order Approach to a Class of Multi-Time-Period Stochastic Programming Problems," *Mathematical Programming Study* 27, pp. 103-117.

Benders, J.F. (1962). "Partitioning procedures for solving mixed-variable programming problems," *Numerische Mathematik* 4, pp. 238-252.

Birge, J.R. (1984). "Aggregation in Stochastic Linear Programming," *Mathematical Programming* 31, pp. 25-41.

Birge, J.R. and S.W. Wallace (1988). "A Separable Piecewise Linear Upper Bound for Stochastic Linear Programs," *SIAM J. Control and Optimization* 26 No. 3.

Birge, J.R. and J.B. Wets (1986). "Designing Approximation Schemes for Stochastic Optimization Problems, in Particular for Stochastic Programs with Recourse," *Mathematical Programming Study* 27, pp. 54-102.

Bratley, P., Fox, B., and L. Schrage (1983). *A Guide to Simulation*, Springer-Verlag, New York.

Brodt, A.I. (1984). "International Bank Asset and Liability Management," *J. of Bank*

Research, Vol. 15, No. 2, 82–94.

Chow, Y.S. and H. Robbins (1965). "On the Asymptotic Theory of Fixed Width Sequential Confidence Intervals for the Mean," *Ann. Math. Stat.* 36, pp. 457-462.

Cochran, W.G. (1977). *Sampling Techniques*, John Wiley, New York.

Cohen, K.J. and S. Thore (1970). "Programming Bank Portfolios Under Uncertainty," *J. of Bank Research*, Vol. 1, No. 1, 42–61.

Dantzig, G.B. (1955). "Linear programming under uncertainty," *Management Science* 1, pp. 197-206.

Dantzig, G.B. (1963), *Linear Programming and Extensions*, Princeton University Press, Princeton.

Dantzig, G.B. (1982). "Time-staged methods in linear programs," In *Studies in Management Science and Systems, Vol. 7 Large- Scale Systems*, Y.Y. Haims (ed.). North Holland Publishing Company, Amsterdam, pp. 19-30.

Dantzig, G.B. (1988). "Planning under uncertainty using parallel computing," *Annals of Operations Research*, in press.

Dantzig, G.B., Dempster, M.A.H. and M.J. Kallio (Eds.) (1981). *Large-Scale Linear Programming (Volumes 1, 2)*, IIASA Collaborative Proceedings Series, CP-81-51, IIASA, Laxenburg, Austria.

Dantzig, G.B. and P.W. Glynn (1988). "Parallel Processors for Planning Under Uncertainty," Technical Report SOL 88-8, Department of Operations Research, Stanford University. To appear in *Annals of Operations Research*.

Dantzig, G.B. and M. Madansky (1961). "On the Solution of Two-Staged Linear Programs under Uncertainty," In *Proceedings Fourth Berkeley Symposium on Mathematical Statistics and Probability I*, J. Neyman (ed.), pp. 165-176.

Dantzig, G.B. and M.V.F. Pereira, et al. (1988). Mathematical Decomposition Techniques for Power System Expansion Planning, EPRI EL-5299, Volumes 1 - 5, Electric Power Research Institute, Palo Alto, Ca.

Dantzig G.B. and A.F. Perold (1979). "A basic factorization method for block triangular linear programs," Report SOL 78-7, Department of Operations Research, Stanford University, Stanford, Ca.; *Sparse Matrix Proceedings*, 1978, Iain S. Duff and G. W. Steward, Eds. SIAM, pp. 283-312.

Dantzig, G.B. and P. Wolfe (1960). "The decomposition principle for linear programs," *Operations Research* 8, pp. 110-111.

Emoliev, Y. (1983). "Stochastic Quasigradient Methods and Their Applications to Systems Optimization," *Stochastics* 9, pp. 1-36.

Entriken, R. (1988). "A Parallel Decomposition Algorithm for Staircase Linear Programs," Oak Ridge National Laboratory Report ORNL/TM 11011, November 1988.

Fourer, R.H. (1982). "Solving staircase linear programs by the simplex method, 1: Inversion," *Mathematical Programming* 23, pp. 274-313.

Fourer, R.H. (1983). "Solving staircase linear programs by the simplex method, 2: Pricing," *Mathematical Programming* 25 pp. 251-292.

Fourer, R.H. (1984). "Staircase matrices and systems," *SIAM Review* 26, pp. 1-70.

Glassey, R. (1973). "Nested decomposition and multi-stage linear programs," *Management Science* 20, pp. 282-292.

Glynn, P.W. and W. Whitt (1988). "Efficiency of Simulation Estimates." Submitted for publication.

Glynn, P.W. and D.L. Iglehart (1988). "Importance Sampling for Stochastic Simulation." Submitted for publication.

Hammersley, J.M. and D.C. Handscomb (1964). *Monte Carlo Methods*, Mathuen, London.

Ho, J.K., Tak, C. and R.P. Sundarraj (1988). "Decomposition of linear programs using parallel computation (revised)," Invited paper at the Symposium on Parallel Optimization, Madison, Wis.

Ho, J.K. and E. Loute (1980). "An advanced implementation of the Dantzig-Wolfe decomposition algorithm for linear programming," Discussion Paper 8014, Center for Operations Research and Econometrics (CORE), Belgium.

Ho, J.K. and A.S. Manne (1974). "Nested decomposition for dynamic models," *Mathematical Programming* 6, pp. 121-140.

Jackson, P.L. and D.F. Lynch (1982). "Revised Dantzig-Wolfe Decomposition for Staircase-Structured Linear Programs," Technical Report 558, School of Operations Research and Industrial Engineering, Cornell University (revised 1985). To appear in *Mathematical Programming*.

Kall, P. (1979). "Computational Methods for Solving Two-Stage Stochastic Linear Programming Problems," *Z. Angew. Math. Phys.* 30, pp. 261-271.

Lavenberg, S.S. and P.D. Welch (1981). "A perspective on the use of control variables to increase the efficiency of Monte Carlo simulation." *Management Science* 27, pp.

322-335.

Louveaux, F.V. (1986). "Multistage stochastic programs with block-separable recourse," *Mathematical Programming Study* 28, pp. 48-62.

Nazareth, L. and R.J-B. Wets (1986). "Algorithms for Stochastic Programs: The Case of Nonstochastic Tenders," *Mathematical Programming Study* 28, pp. 1-28.

Niederreiter, H. (1986). "Multidimensional numerical integration using pseudo random numbers," *Mathematical Programming Study* 27, pp. 17-38.

Nishiya, T. (1983). "A basis factorization method for multi-stage linear programming with an application to optimal operation of an energy plant," (draft report).

Prekopa, A., (1978). "Dynamic Type Stochastic Programming Models," In *Studies in Applied Stochastic Programming*, A. Prekopa, Ed. Hungarian Academy of Science, Budapest, pp. 179-209.

Strazicky, B. (1980). "Computational Experience with an Algorithm for Discrete Recourse Problems," In *Stochastic Programming*, M. Dempster, Ed. Academic Press, London, pp. 263-274.

Wets, R.J. (1984). "Programming under uncertainty: the equivalent convex program," *J. SIAM Applied Math.* 14 (1), pp. 89-105.

Wets, R.J. (1984). "Large-scale linear programming techniques in stochastic programming," In *Numerical Methods for Stochastic Optimization*, Y. Ermoliev and R. Wets, Eds. Springer-Verlag. IIASA WP-84-90.

Wets, R.J. (1985). "On Parallel Processor Design for Solving Stochastic Programs," In *Proceedings of the 6th Mathematical Programming Symposium*, Japanese Mathematical Programming Society, Tokyo, pp. 13-36.

Whittrock, R.J. (1983). "Advances in a nested decomposition algorithm for solving staricase linear programs," Report SOL 83-2, Department of Operations Research, Stanford University, Stanford, Ca.

II.

PARALLEL ALGORITHMS FOR MATHEMATICAL PROGRAMMING

A PARALLEL AUCTION ALGORITHM: A CASE STUDY IN THE USE OF PARALLEL OBJECT-ORIENTED PROGRAMMING

RICHARD S. BARR AND MICHAEL G. CHRISTIANSEN
School of Engineering and Applied Sciences, Southern Methodist University
Dallas, Texas 75275

ABSTRACT

This paper discusses the design of a parallel implementation of Bertsekas' auction algorithm for the linear cost assignment problem. Unique to this work is the application of parallel object-oriented (O-O) programming to the implementation. The O-O programming paradigm readily supported the development of this application, added in parallel task partitioning, and was shown to be useful in rapid prototyping. The algorithm's implementation on a shared memory multiprocessor is discussed and computational results presented.

1. OVERVIEW

This paper describes an experiment with object-oriented programming as a means of expressing and implementing a parallel algorithm for solving assignment problems. The objectives are: (1) to study the effectiveness of O-O programming for prototyping a serial algorithm's implementation and for parallel task organization, (2) to investigate modifications required, if any, to obtain an efficient code, and (3) to perform a computational study of the parallel implementation's solution speed.

To be studied is an asynchronous variant of Bertsekas' "auction" algorithm for linear cost assignment problems. The test environment is a Sequent S81, a shared-memory, multiple-instruction-multiple data (MIMD) parallel computer system. The implementation language is C++, chosen for its efficiency relative to other O-O languages and its ability to access the shared memory and parallel processsing features of the Sequent.

2. OBJECT-ORIENTED PROGRAMMING

A key element of object-oriented programming is the notion of a user-defined *abstract data type*, which consists of a data type and an associated set of operations. A class definition defines an abstract data type by describing its underlying data structure (*instance variables*) and all operations (*methods*) which may be performed on the data. An *object* is a particular instance of a specific class. The process of invoking a method is termed *passing a message* to the object, and a message may include calling parameters. An object's instance variables and methods are designated to be public or private; private data and methods may only be used "internally" by the object's methods, while public entities are also accessible by other objects or program elements. The value of this partitioning is discussed below. Once defined, new data types become part of the extensible language.

For example, Figure 1 illustrates a partial class definition for a "Counter" data type. A Counter object X is a particular instance of the class "Counter." Once defined, a program may invoke the methods to initialize, increment, decrement, or obtain the current value of X. By the same token, a user may define data types for complex and rational arithmetic, vectors, matrices, chess pieces, credit histories, and binary trees, each with different types of instance variables and methods.

The values stored in each object's instance variables define the local state of the object. This state is *persistent*, in the sense that it is maintained between method calls.

The set of methods provided by an object's class form an interface between an instance of the object and the other objects in the application. Many object-oriented languages will not allow direct access to the local state of an object by external objects, who must then indirectly access the values through message-passing. This restriction enforces the *encapsulation* of each object in the design, lowers the likelihood that errors in the application will occur from unseen dependencies, and reduces design complexity by enforcing a partition between units. But this restriction reduces the runtime efficiency by forcing an otherwise-simple operation into a method call with its accompanying overhead. To address this problem, some languages allow the programmer to define certain instance variables to be public.

```
class Counter
    private
        data value
    public
        method initialize()
        method increment()
        method decrement()
        method getValue()
```

Figure 1. Depiction of class "Counter"

The encapsulation and persistence facilities provide the ability to consider each object as an independent entity in the application. In the O-O design methodology, the process of developing an application can be thought of as defining the behavior of a set of interacting objects, a notion with natural extensions to parallel work partitioning.

3. PARALLEL OBJECT-ORIENTED PROGRAM DESIGN

In the previous section we described the object as an independent unit that contains its own local state information, and provides an interface through which other objects interact. The natural extension of these ideas is to supply each object with its own local thread of execution, that is, allow multiple objects to execute simultaneously. This forms the basis for the design and implementation of parallel applications.

In this section we discuss categories of parallel processing machines and explore three key issues in parallel program design: interprocess communication, task partitioning, and process synchronization.

3.1 Distributed Versus Shared-Memory Multiprocessors

The use of the object paradigm has been extensively applied to the development of *distributed multiprocessing systems* and applications. In these multiprocessing systems, each processing element is disjoint from the others (no shared memory), and each has access to a common interprocess communication medium (e.g. Ethernet network). In this processing environment the message-passing and encapsulation provided by the traditional object paradigm maps well onto the constraints of this class of multiprocessing system. These constraints include the lack of shared memory, and the relatively slow interprocess communication channels.

We have applied a different approach in our application of the object paradigm, by using a *shared memory multiprocessing system* to implement our designs. In such a system, multiple processors share a common primary storage, allowing the programmer to designate data structures as accessible by either a single processor or by many — an attractive alternative to message-passing communications. Hence the shared memory scheme provides a substantially-faster communication channel between processing elements than a distributed system. But the channel has a heavier workload, since it is used for most memory references, and can thus become a bottleneck as the number of processors increases. Current channel technology can support about 30 processors.

3.2 Work Partitioning Schemes for Parallel Machines

The primary objective of parallel processing is the reduction of real time required for completion of a body of work. To achieve this objective, a parallel application developed for either shared-memory or distributed systems must partition its work into a series of tasks and assign them to separate processors for simultaneous execution.

The most common approaches to task partitioning are domain decomposition and functional partitioning. *Domain decomposition* involves creating multiple identical processes and assigning a portion of the application's data to each processor. *Functional partitioning* involves the creation of multiple processes which apply different operations to a shared data set. The newer approach of task *partitioning by objects* resembles domain decomposition when multiple instances of the same class are active, while functional partitioning occurs when different types of objects execute simultaneously.

When attempting to develop an application on a distributed system, the task partitioning is especially important. The amount of interprocessor communication cannot exceed the limits imposed by the speed of the communications channel. The object paradigm readily supports distributed processing through the nature of its own inter-object message-passing mechanisms, and provides a conceptual framework for partitioning the application into cooperating tasks.

In many ways, designing an application for a shared memory multiprocessor is simpler than for a distributed system, since data can be stored efficiently and shared between processing elements in familiar data structures such as variables, arrays, linked lists, etc. This reduces the importance of the task partitioning in the design in that each process can have unrestrained access to shared information.

But allowing unrestrained access to shared data can cause problems, since some operations must be performed atomically. For example, the updating of a shared variable might require that the updates be performed sequentially so that two processes do not overlap the update operation. A common solution to this *mutual exclusion access problem* is to restrict access to shared data when necessary. This is often implemented using a *locking mechanism* that is designed to allow access by a single process at any instant. That is, if two or more processes attempt to gain ownership to a lock concurrently, only a single process will succeed. The other processes will either be rejected, or blocked, depending on the lock implementation. When the process owning the lock has finished accessing the program's *critical section*, it releases the lock, allowing other waiting processes to continue. We will show how O-O designs can incorporate such interprocess synchronizations and make them transparent to the programmer.

To test the practicality of these software design concepts, we applied them to a new optimization algorithm which appeared to be ready-made for both object-oriented organization and parallel implementation.

4. THE AUCTION ALGORITHM FOR ASSIGNMENT PROBLEMS

A classic model in operations research is the *linear cost assignment problem*. The problem may be envisioned as a set of n items which are to be assigned to n persons. Each person i associates a numerical preference a_{ij} with each item j. The objective is identify a one-to-one mapping of persons to items that maximizes the sum of the preferences in the n assignment pairs.

Mathematically the assignment problem may be stated as following linear program. Given the set of all persons, $I \equiv \{1,...,n\}$, and the set of all items, $J \equiv \{1,...,n\}$,

$$\text{maximize} \quad \sum_{i \in I} \sum_{j \in J} a_{ij} x_{ij},$$

subject to: $\sum_{j \in J} x_{ij} = 1,$ for all $i \in I,$

$\sum_{i \in I} x_{ij} = 1,$ for all $j \in J,$ and

$x_{ij} \geq 0,$ for all $i \in I,$ and $j \in J.$

Because of basis triangularity and the constraints, if a feasible solution to the problem exists, there exists an optimal feasible solution in which all x_{ij} are either zero or one. In this manner we say that person i is assigned item j only if $x_{ij}=1$. The constraints ensure that all persons are assigned one item and each item is assigned to only one person.

While a variety of algorithms exist for solving the assignment problem, one relatively new approach appears to have much promise for efficient implementation in a parallel environment. The process has the metaphor of an auction where competing persons bid against each other for assignment to items. What follows is a variant of the methods developed by Bertsekas and presented in [Bertsekas and Tsitsiklis 1989]. In it there is a price p_i associated with each of the n items, and a queue of unassigned persons.

Auction Algorithm:

Step 1.* Set $p_j = 0$, for all $j \in J$, and place all persons $i \in I$ in the queue.

Step 2. Perform the following until the queue remains empty:

    a.* Take person i from the front of the queue.

    b. Compute a bid b_{ij*} as follows, and send bid to item $j*$.

        1. Define the "current value" of each object j as: $v_{ij} \equiv a_{ij} - p_j$.

        2. Identify a "best" item $j* \in \{j : v_{ij} = \max_{j \in J}\{v_{ij}\}\}$.

        3. Compute bid for item $j*$ as: $b_{ij*} = a_{ij*} - \max_{j \in \{J-j*\}}\{v_{ij}\} + \varepsilon^{\dagger}$.

    c. If $b_{ij*} \leq p_{j*}$, return person i to the end of the queue.

    d.* If $b_{ij*} > p_{j*}$, item $j*$ accepts the bid.

        1. Set $p_{j*} = b_{ij*}$.

        2. Assign person i to item $j*$.

        3. Place any person previously assigned to $j*$ at the end of the queue.

---

†For optimality to be assured, $0 < \varepsilon < 1/n$.

A chaotic parallel version of this algorithm may be implemented by executing step 2 in parallel asynchronously, but treating steps marked with a "*" as critical regions that may only be executed by one process at a time.

The "auction" embodied in the algorithm proceeds as follows. An item is assigned to the person making the highest bid, shown as the current price. Initially all persons and items are unassigned and prices are zero. Then, an unassigned person chooses an item, based on preferences and prices, and submits a bid for it that is higher than its current price. If an item receives a bid that is higher than its current price, the item is assigned to the bidder and any previous owner becomes unassigned. The bidding process continues with another unassigned person until all persons, and therefore all items, are assigned.

In the serial (one processor) case, bids are always accepted, hence the auction metaphor is more descriptive of the multiprocessor version where several persons are bidding simultaneously, sometimes for the same item. The algorithm's critical regions ensure sequential processing of the bids, low bids based on "old" prices are rejected, and the monotonically-increasing prices assure convergence.

5. PARALLEL OBJECT-ORIENTED IMPLEMENTATION

The auction algorithm was implemented on Southern Methodist University's Sequent Symmetry S81, a 12-processor MIMD computer with 32 megabytes of sharable memory. Each processor is rated at three million operations per second.

In choosing an implementation language, many were available with object-like constructs. Interpreted languages, like Smalltalk, were considered too slow for our application. The superior runtime performance of compiled languages, like C++ and Ada, led us to use C++ (C Plus Plus) [Stroustrup 1986] in our development of the parallel programming environment and the auction code. C++ provides all of the O-O features mentioned previously, has the runtime efficiency of its parent language C [Weiner and Pinson 1988], and permits the use of shared memory, multitasking, and public data.

5.1 Auction Objects' Class Descriptions

The auction algorithm has a natural expression as a set of interacting person and item objects, as described in Figure 2. In addition, a queue object sequences the bidding persons and a scheduler object pairs bidders and processors.

The objects interact as follows. The scheduler removes a person from the queue and invokes that person's makeBid() method. As a result, a bid is computed and sent to an item's takeBid() method, with acceptance assumed by the bidding person. If the item rejects the bid, the bidder is sent a reject() message which results in his (or her) return to the end of the queue. If the bid is accepted, the item updates its price and sends a reject() message to the

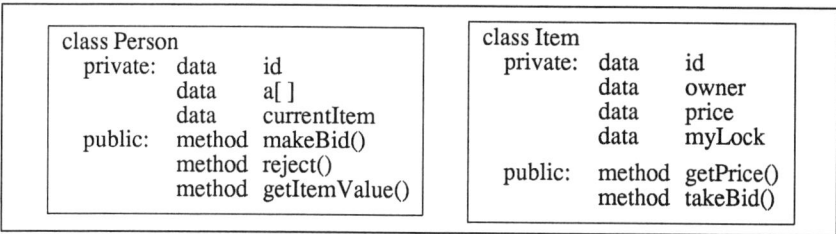

Figure 2. Depictions of "Person" and "Item" Classes

previous owner, if any. The thread of control returns to the scheduler who continues to schedule persons from the queue until none are available. Figure 3 illustrates the thread of control for a person whose bid is accepted by a previously-owned item. In the parallel version, the scheduler assigns different bidders to each available process.

5.2 Shared and Active Objects

In the construction of our parallel programming environment, we identified two new class categories. The *shared class* of objects defines data structures such as variables, stacks, queues, linked lists, etc., which can be accessed by multiple processes concurrently. The key feature of these objects is that the needed locking is incorporated into the object's interface methods, and is transparent to the users of the data structures. This provides a useful level of abstraction and results in less-cluttered source code.

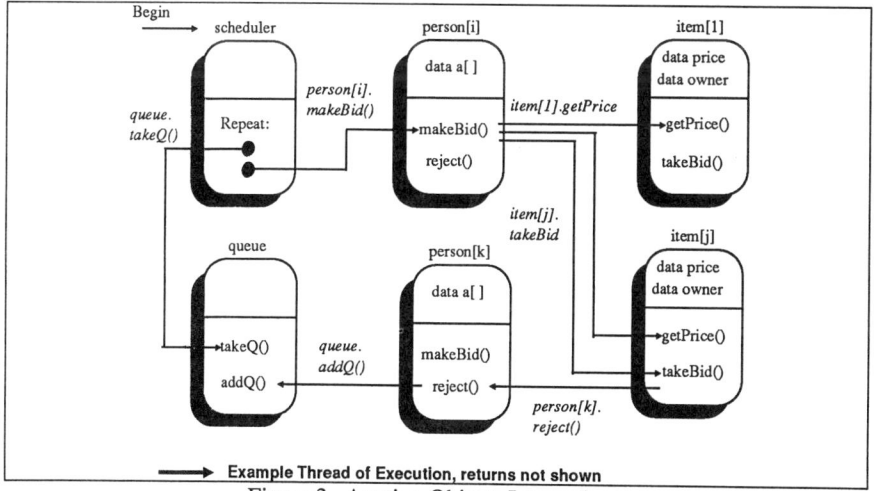

Figure 3. Auction Objects Interactions

The class of shared objects can be seen as passive entities that can be acted upon by multiple processes, but are not themselves actively processing data or generating results. *Active objects* are the objects that act upon data and perform some useful function in the application. In terms of multiprocessing, these objects are designed to execute concurrently. Ideally, each active object is assigned to a single processing element. If more objects than processors exist, active objects must be scheduled to processors.

5.3 Inter-object Coupling

A feature offered by shared-memory systems is the ability to couple objects with varying levels of interdependence. We define the coupling between objects in terms of the access scheme for their instance variables. Two objects are *tightly coupled* if one is able to directly access the data structures of the other. Although tightly-coupled objects provide fast interactions, they can be dangerous in developing applications. This is because the accessing object may be defective and corrupt the accessed object's internal data structures.

Two objects are *loosely coupled* if all interactions occur through methods. Methods provide the ability to define runtime checks, and generally produce systems that are more robust that ones without such checks. On the other hand, such checks are time-consuming and a tradeoff is made between security and speed.

The approach we have taken is to prototype the system using loosely-coupled objects and, once the implementation is operational, tighten the interface between objects to enhance performance. A major performance gain was made by the creation of a shared object of item prices, which allowed the substitution of array references for millions of method calls.

6. COMPUTATIONAL TESTING RESULTS

The serial and parallel versions of the object-oriented auction code were tested on two sets of eight randomly-generated problems. The values of problem size, n, were 500, 1000, 1500, and 2000, and the preferences, a_{ij}, were uniformly distributed in the ranges of 1 to 100 and 1 to 1000. These were "totally dense" problems in that all person-item combinations were included, hence the largest models consisted of 4000 linear constraints and four million decision variables.

As shown in Table 1, each problem was solved using one to six processors, and real ("wall clock") time recorded for problem solution, exclusive of input and output but inclusive of array initializations and any parallel process creations. All reported times are the average of four runs, since times varied even with a lightly-loaded computer system.

These results indicate that serial run times are significantly affected by the objective function coefficient range, although not in a consistent manner. On large problems with narrow preference ranges, solution times remain small since a solution with all preferences

Problem Size, n	Pref. Range	Problem Set	Number of Processors					
			1	2	3	4	5	6
500	1-100	A	446.45	225.85	151.78	151.31	151.34	151.36
		B	468.29	236.26	234.72	234.70	234.73	234.44
	1-1000	A	89.44	59.90	50.95	47.63	47.07	46.56
		B	37.31	15.11	11.21	9.31	8.05	7.83
1000	1-100	A	14.80	10.28	9.04	8.58	8.00	7.71
		B	14.07	10.08	8.87	8.70	7.89	7.66
	1-1000	A	562.53	412.64	372.85	366.91	343.24	344.45
		B	818.94	604.56	545.24	499.90	482.64	459.25
1500	1-100	A	34.85	25.69	22.57	20.90	21.55	20.64
		B	33.87	23.63	20.55	18.82	18.60	17.78
	1-1000	A	277.27	149.27	126.24	83.32	64.36	58.08
		B	1831.54	943.34	872.72	775.04	738.86	728.23
2000	1-100	A	58.25	42.43	37.45	33.54	32.18	31.45
		B	58.00	41.79	38.19	36.10	34.59	35.12
	1-1000	A	4131.95	1720.09	1061.04	428.79	223.37	40.90
		B	3352.21	2186.41	1126.46	993.25	921.26	849.40

Table 1. Mean Solution Times for Totally Dense Assignment Problems (in seconds on a Sequent Symmetry S81, each time an average of four runs, $\varepsilon = 1/(n+1)$)

Problem Size, n	Pref. Range	Problem Set	Number of Processors					
			1	2	3	4	5	6
500	1-100	A	1.00	1.98	2.94	2.95	2.95	2.95
		B	1.00	1.98	2.00	2.00	1.99	2.00
	1-1000	A	1.00	1.49	1.76	1.88	1.90	1.92
		B	1.00	**2.47**	**3.33**	**4.01**	4.64	4.76
1000	1-100	A	1.00	1.44	1.64	1.72	1.85	1.92
		B	1.00	1.40	1.59	1.62	1.78	1.84
	1-1000	A	1.00	1.36	1.51	1.53	1.64	1.63
		B	1.00	1.35	1.50	1.64	1.70	1.78
1500	1-100	A	1.00	1.36	1.54	1.67	1.62	1.69
		B	1.00	1.43	1.65	1.80	1.82	1.91
	1-1000	A	1.00	1.86	2.20	3.33	4.31	4.77
		B	1.00	1.94	2.10	2.36	2.48	2.52
2000	1-100	A	1.00	1.36	1.56	1.74	1.81	1.85
		B	1.00	1.39	1.52	1.61	1.68	1.65
	1-1000	A	1.00	**2.40**	**3.89**	**9.64**	**18.50**	**101.01**
		B	1.00	1.53	2.98	3.37	3.64	3.95

Table 2. Mean Relative Speedups for Totally Dense Assignment Problems (based on Table 1 times, an average of four runs, superlinear values in boldface)

of one is available. With a wider preference range, times tended to grow exponentially with problem size.

In order to view the effect of parallel processing, Table 2 displays mean solution time speedups, relative to the single processor case, computed as:

$$\text{Relative speedup, } S(p) \equiv \frac{\text{Mean solution time with one processor}}{\text{Mean solution time with } p \text{ processors}}.$$

Linear speedup, where $S(p) = p$, is typically considered indicative of an ideal division of work among the processors. While reasonably good speedups are obtained with two processors (mean $S(2) = 1.67$), the average rate of improvement drops off quickly as the number of processors in increased (mean $S(4) = 2.67$). Note that in a few instances *superlinear speedup*, $S(p) > p$, occurred. This may be the result of the inevitable differences in timing of events in the unsynchronized parallel algorithm, occasionally leading the search procedure to uncover alternate, more direct paths to an optimal assignment. The surprising superlinear results could not be replicated on similar problems.

From further analysis, we found that the auction algorithm is very parallel when it begins a problem, but a significant portion of the time is spent in the "end game" where a few persons are unassigned and there is little or no parallelism. Hence the modest results for larger numbers of processors are due to the algorithm, rather than the programming scheme.

7. CONCLUSIONS

Object-oriented program design provided a natural expression of the auction algorithm, as well as a convenient and efficient means of parallel task partitioning. These same concepts could be applied to a variety of mathematical programming algorithms and management science applications. (For example, in an O-O generalized network code, a basis-subtree object could and could be scheduled in parallel to price its incident nonbasic arcs, and perform pivots either on itself or with another cooperating object.) Hence we feel this object paradigm is an effective means of both prototyping and implementing new applications in serial and parallel settings.

REFERENCES

Bertsekas, D.P. and J.N. Tsitsiklis (1989), *Parallel and Distributed Computation: Numerical Methods*, Prentice-Hall, Englewood Cliffs, N.J.

Stroustrup, B. (1986), *The C++ Programming Language*, Addison-Wesley, Reading, Mass.

Wiener, R.S. and L.J. Pinson (1988), *An Introduction to Object-Oriented Programming and C++*, Addison-Wesley, Reading, Mass.

A COMPARATIVE STUDY OF SOME PARALLEL BIN PACKING ALGORITHMS

JUDITH O. BERKEY and PEARL Y. WANG
Department of Computer Science, George Mason University
Fairfax, Virginia 22030-4444

ABSTRACT

This paper compares several parallel algorithms that obtain approximate solutions to the one-dimensional bin packing problem. The majority of these algorithms are parallelizations of well-known sequential approximation algorithms and are designed for two distinct models of parallel computation: a MIMD distributed memory, message-passing model, and a SIMD exclusive-read, exclusive-write (EREW) shared memory model. The algorithms examined are implemented on two representative parallel computers- an Intel iPSC/2 Computer and a Connection Machine System. The implementations are compared both in execution times and in the efficiency of the packing solutions for several data sets. The advantages and limitations of the two parallel models are also summarized.

1. INTRODUCTION

In the one-dimensional bin packing problem, a set of n pieces, each having size in the interval $(0,1]$ is to be packed into a minimum number of unit size bins. A feasible packing is an allocation of all n pieces to a set of N bins, subject to the bin size restriction. The goal is to determine the packing that requires the minimal number N^* of bins. Since this problem is NP-Complete, many sequential algorithms have been developed which obtain approximate solutions. Worst case error bounds and several quantitative studies of these serial algorithms have appeared in the literature. (See [Coffman et al. 1984] for a recent survey.)

In this paper, we first present parallelizations of some sequential bin packing approximation algorithms. A MIMD bin packing heuristic and two parallel packing heuristics designed for the SIMD model of computation are also proposed. In the next part of the paper, quantitative studies of these parallel methods are presented. The results of executing the MIMD algorithms on an Intel iPSC/2 hypercube and the SIMD algorithms on a Connection Machine System for large data sets (n=8192, 16384) are reported and compared. The last section of the paper presents some observations concerning these implementations. The results indicate that solutions to one-dimensional bin packing problems can often be efficiently approximated by using parallel algorithms. The advantages and limitations of the two models of computation when used to solve this type of optimization problem are also summarized.

2. SOME SEQUENTIAL PACKING ALGORITHMS

Several well-known one-dimensional packing heuristics have appeared in the literature. These are the Next Fit (NF), First Fit (FF), Best Fit (BF), First Fit Decreasing (FFD), Best Fit Decreasing (BFD), Refined First Fit (RFF), Harmonic (H) and Refined Harmonic (RH) packing methods. The worst-case behavior of these algorithms has been established in [Baker 1985; Johnson et al. 1974; Yao 1980; Lee and Lee 1985]. Petal Fit (PF) is an alternative one-dimensional packing heuristic which has been determined to perform well in practice [Berkey 1986].

The Next Fit algorithm packs pieces sequentially into a single bin. When the bin's capacity is exceeded, it is considered full and eliminated as a candidate for further packing. The packing proceeds in a new empty bin, and the process is repeated until all pieces are packed. First Fit and Best Fit pack pieces sequentially using an indexed list of bins. FF places pieces into the lowest indexed bin in which they fit. Best Fit places each piece in the bin whose remaining capacity is the smallest of all bins in which the piece fits. First Fit Decreasing and Best Fit Decreasing presort the pieces into non-increasing order and then use the FF and BF packing rules, respectively.

The Refined First Fit algorithm puts each piece into one of four infinite classes: A-pieces, B_1-pieces, B_2-pieces and X-pieces. With m a fixed integer, the pieces are then assigned to bins sequentially. A piece is put by first fit into a bin in Class 1 if it is an A-piece, a bin in Class 2 if it is a B_1-piece, a bin in Class 3 if it is a B_2-piece (but not the mi^{th} B_2-piece seen so far for any integer i), or a bin in Class 4 if it is an X-piece. If a piece is the mi^{th} B_2-piece, it is placed into the first bin containing an A-piece in which it can fit; otherwise, it is put in a new bin of Class 1.

The Harmonic algorithm also packs the bins by classfying each piece into a harmonic partition consisting of M subdivisions of the unit interval: I_k for $k = 1 .. M$. A piece is an I_k-piece if its size is in the I_k interval, and a bin designated to pack only I_k-pieces is called an I_k-bin. As the pieces are sequentially considered, each I_k-piece is packed using the NF rule into I_k-bins. Only M bins have to be maintained in this algorithm. The Refined Harmonic packing algorithm is similar to the Harmonic scheme, except that 22 partitions are used: J_a, J_b, and J_k for $k = 1 .. 20$. As before, J_a-bins contain J_a-pieces, J_b-bins contain J_b-pieces, J_k-bins contain J_k-pieces, but J_{ab}-bins contain one J_a-piece and one J_b-piece, and J_{bb}-bins contain two J_b-pieces. Pieces are packed using the

NF rule and the details of the full algorithm appear in [Lee and Lee 1985].

The Petal Fit heuristic partitions partially filled bins into classes by considering the remaining capacities of the bins. Each successive piece is allocated by selecting the first bin in a class that most closely corresponds to the size of the piece. After a piece is packed into a bin, the bin's capacity decreases and hence it moves into another class. New bins are created only if there are no bins in any class into which the next piece can be packed. In practice, this heuristic was determined to have a worst-case behavior that was similar to FF, but has a computing time of $O(n \log c)$ for c between 0 and 1.

3. MIMD PARALLEL PACKING ALGORITHMS

For the MIMD parallel bin packing algorithms discussed below, a coarse-grained model of parallelism is used in which the processing elements execute independently on their separate data sets. Communication between processors is accomplished only by passing data messages over a network. One of the processing elements acts as a "host" node and oversees the execution of the algorithm.

The host process in the parallel Next Fit MIMD implementation (ParNF$_M$) distributes the set of pieces evenly among the available processors (nodes). The node processes operate concurrently using the sequential NF algorithm to pack the pieces. When a node has finished packing its pieces, it sends the bin count to the host node. The host accumulates the total bin count from the participating nodes and terminates the node processes when all pieces have been packed. The nodes operate asynchronously; no communication is required between nodes during the packing operation. The time complexity of the algorithm is $O(n/k)$ where n is the size of the problem and k is the number of processors available.

The MIMD First Fit algorithm (ParFF$_M$) utilizes a pipelined parallel processing approach. The processing nodes are interconnected in a ring topology with the host node acting as an input conduit. The set of pieces is again divided evenly among the processing nodes. The host initiates the packing procedure by sending a bin to the first node in the ring. If that node can pack one or more pieces into the bin, it does so and then sends the bin to the next node in the ring. The second node attempts to pack pieces in the bin while concurrently, the first node is receiving another bin from the host. Each bin is initiated by the host and is passed around the ring of node processes. The last node in the topology sends the packed bin back to the host. Packing continues in this fashion until the host receives a bin that has travelled the ring and remains empty. This signals the host that there are no more pieces to pack. The time required by ParFF$_M$ is $O(n/k)$. However, the time complexity is affected by the inter-node communication efficiency of the system since the latter is significant. If the set of n pieces is sorted first and ParFF$_M$ is applied, then a MIMD implementation of FFD (ParFFD$_M$) is obtained.

The sequential Harmonic algorithm can be adapted into a perfectly parallel MIMD algorithm (ParH$_M$). Each node process corresponds to an interval I_k as specified in the sequential algorithm. A host process initiates the node processes by broadcasting the set of pieces to the nodes. Each node process receives only the pieces that fall within its specified interval. The processors pack the pieces by concurrently executing the sequential NF algorithm. A process is terminated when it sends its total bin count to the host. The total processing time for all processes will be determined by the longest running process and is dependent upon the distribution of the pieces. If pieces are uniformly distributed, then one processing node will receive approximately $n/2$ pieces and the workload distribution will cause that node to require significantly more processing time than the other node processes. Since $n/2$ pieces are packed using the NF rule, the average time for the parallel algorithm will be $O(n/2)$. The worst case occurs when all pieces fall in the interval *(1/2,1]*. The time required for the algorithm is then $O(n)$.

In the MIMD parallel version of Refined First Fit (ParRFF$_M$), the host process divides the pieces into the classes specified in the sequential algorithm and distributes them over the processing nodes so that each node packs only pieces of one class. Depending upon the number of nodes available, several nodes may be assigned to pack the pieces of a class. The node processes use a first fit packing rule to pack the pieces they receive. They send the completed bins to the host, where bin and piece totals are accumulated. Since each class is packed independently, no communication is required between processes that pack different classes. The total processing time is dependent upon the piece distribution and the number of processing nodes that are used. ParRFF$_M$ requires time $O(n/4)$ if the pieces are evenly distributed over the interval *(0,1]*.

The sequential Petal Fit heuristic partitions bins into classes based on their remaining capacity. These classes correspond, in the MIMD parallelization of the algorithm (ParPF$_M$), to the processing nodes. The set of pieces is divided among the processors by mapping each piece to a processing node according to its size. Pieces are broadcast by the host process. The processing nodes that contain pieces with size greater than or equal to 0.5 initiate bins, pack their piece list, one piece to a bin, and then send the bin to the node that corresponds to the remaining capacity in the bin. The receiving node process packs additional pieces in the bin if possible. If it cannot pack a piece in the bin, it sends the bin to the next smaller class. Bin counts are sent to the host when all pieces have been packed. The time complexity of ParPF$_M$ is $O(n/c)$ where c is the number of processor nodes that are used. ParPFD$_M$ and PARPFI$_M$ are obtained by presorting the pieces into non-increasing and non-decreasing order, respectively.

4. SIMD PARALLEL PACKING ALGORITHMS

For the SIMD parallel bin packing algorithms discussed below, a fine-grain organization of processing element nodes is assumed. A host computer sequentially broadcasts each instruction to all the nodes at the same time. Selected nodes may choose not to participate in the execution of the instruction. In addition, each processor is assumed to know its unique "self-address" in the collection of all processing elements. This model of computation is also referred to as the EREW PRAM shared memory model of computing where processors may only read from or write to distinct locations in memory at one time.

The list of partially filled bins is maintained as an array of memory locations in the SIMD machine. These locations correspond to one memory location in each processing element. In the following algorithms, the final packing arrangements, as well as the number of bins required by each packing, can be displayed.

To implement a SIMD algorithm which produces a NF packing, all of the pieces are distributed to the processors, one piece per processing element. If the processors are viewed as an array, a *prefix* summation operation is performed, where each processor gets the sum of the piece values of its predecessors. Those processors whose sum values do not exceed the bin capacity then represent the pieces that are packed using the NF rule into a single bin. These processors are "turned off" and the process is repeated: the summation operation is executed on the remaining processing elements and the next bin is packed. If the summation operation requires time $t(n)$ for n processing elements, the entire packing takes time for ParNF$_S$ is $O(n\ t(n))$. No space is required for maintaining the capacity of the bin currently being packed, but each processor (piece) does store a number corresponding to the bin number in which it was packed.

In the SIMD parallelization of the First Fit algorithm (ParFF$_S$), both the list of pieces and the list of partially filled bins are distributed to the processors, one piece and one bin per processor. The algorithm iterates over the n processors so that pieces can be packed sequentially. The parallelism in ParFF$_S$ is evident when the bin to be packed must be determined. The size of the piece being packed is broadcast to all bins. Each bin determines if the piece will fit in it, and the piece is then packed in the bin with the least index (processor self-address). The capacity of that bin is reduced, and packing proceeds with the next piece. If the determination of the least-indexed processor requires time $T(n)$, then the overall time of the parallel algorithm is $O(n\ T(n))$. As in the sequential FFD algorithm, the parallel First Fit Decreasing algorithm (ParFFD$_S$) presorts the pieces and then performs the FF packing. If $S(n)$ is the time needed to perform a parallel sort on the n pieces, then ParFFD$_S$ requires time $O(nT(n)) + S(n)$.

The SIMD version of the Best Fit algorithm (ParBF$_S$) is similar to that for the FF algorithm. Pieces are distributed to the processors and each processor also represents a partially packed bin. Each piece is broadcast to all bins and packed in the bin that has the best fit. The determination of the best bin also requires $O(T(n))$ time so that the overall time for ParBF$_S$ is $O(n\, T(n))$. Similarly, ParBFD$_S$ requires $O(nT(n) + S(n))$ time.

The parallel version of RFF (ParRFF$_S$) requires that pieces first be labeled as belonging to one of four classes: A-piece, B_1-piece, B_2-piece, X-piece. Every mi^{th} piece is then relabeled as an A-piece. These steps require $O(1)$ time on a SIMD machine if each processor contains one of the pieces to be packed. After these four classes are obtained, the ParFF$_S$ algorithm is applied four times, once for each class. This produces sets of bins that are disjointly packed and identical to the Class 1-4 type bins that are produced in the sequential version of the algorithm. The total time for ParRFF$_S$ is $O(4nT(n))$.

The parallel Harmonic algorithm (ParH$_S$) works in the same manner. First, pieces are distributed one to a processor. Then each piece (or processor) is labeled as an I_k-piece where $k = 1\ ..\ M$. The labeling process requires $O(1)$ time. For each set of I_k-pieces, the ParNF$_S$ algorithm is applied, resulting in the I_k-bins of the sequential algorithm. The time complexity of the parallel algorithm is $O(Mn\, t(n))$, the same as for ParNF$_S$.

In the sequential version of Refined Harmonic algorithm, pieces are labeled as belonging to one of 22 classes: J_a, J_b, and J_k for $k = 1\ ..\ 20$. The J_k classes are packed using the NF rule into J_k-bins, and the others are packed into J_{a^-}, J_{b^-}, J_{ab^-}, or J_{bb^-} bins. In the SIMD parallelization of this algorithm (ParRH$_S$), the pieces are labeled ($O(1)$ time) and the J_k-pieces are packed using the ParH$_S$ algorithm. The remaining pieces are sequentially packed into one of the other four bin types. The determination of which one of the bins is to be chosen is done in parallel using a technique similar to that used in ParFF$_S$. The total computing time for ParRH$_S$ is $O(22n\, t(n))$.

Each of the above algorithms is a SIMD algorithm which produces the same number of bins and the same packing arrangement as would have been obtained by the serial versions of the algorithms. In parallelizing these algorithms, it was evident that the task of dividing the pieces into subgroups is a simple and inexpensive procedure to carry out on a SIMD machine. In the next two parallel packing heuristics, this subgrouping technique is employed.

Parallel Segment Fit (ParSF$_S$) requires the use of a parameter, s which is used to define the length of a segment, or collection of processing elements. The pieces are initially distributed, one to a processor, and each is labeled as belonging to one of $S = n/s$ segments. The prefix summation operation is carried out in parallel within these S segments of processors. This is like using the NF rule to pack a single bin in each segment, and so S bins and at least S pieces will be packed. The heuristic continues by packing the remaining pieces using the ParFF$_S$ algorithm, using these partially filled bins, and creating new ones when needed. The overall execution time of the algorithm will then be $O(t(n)+(n-S)T(n-S))$.

Parallel Match Fit (ParMF$_S$) is a heuristic which requires dividing pieces into subgroups based on their sizes. An attempt is then made to match subgroups together. The heuristic consists of four steps. If the pieces are assumed to be integers in $(0, B]$ and B is also the bin size, then the first step packs all pieces of size B into bins. The second step of the algorithm consists of an iteration of i from 1 to $B/2$. For each iteration, pieces of size i are matched with pieces of size $B-i$, using as many of each group as is possible. If $T(n)$ is the time required to count the number of pieces of a given size, then this step requires time $O(B\ T(n))$. In the third step of the heuristic, the remaining pieces are examined and an iteration of i from $B/2$ to $B-1$ is performed. For each iteration, a loop similar to that used in step 2 is performed to find pairs of pieces which fit exactly into the remaining capacity $B-i$. This requires time $O(B^2\ T(n))$. The first three steps of the algorithm then determine packings which fill each bin exactly. The last step of the heuristic packs any remaining pieces using the best fit rule. The total time for the procedure is $O((B+B^2+n)\ T(n))$.

For the above analyses, the times $t(n)$ and $T(n)$ are of complexity $O(logn)$, while $S(n) = O(log^2n)$. Thus all algorithms, except for PARFFD$_S$ and PARBFD$_S$, have time complexity $O(nlogn)$. PARFFD$_S$ and PARBFD$_S$ both have time complexity $O(nlogn+log^2n)$. The number of processors required by each SIMD algorithm is n.

5. QUANTITATIVE RESULTS

The parallel algorithms discussed above were implemented on two respective parallel computers. The MIMD algorithms were executed on a 16-node Intel iPSC/2 hypercube computer, and the SIMD algorithms were executed on a Connection Machine System with both 8K and 16K processors. No attempt was made in either case to optimize the code. The objective in executing the parallel algorithms on these two machines was to test the proposed parallelizations of the serial algorithms and to verify their relative performance as parallel bin packing methods.

For the MIMD experiments, the set of pieces was transmitted from the cube manager to the processing elements, and execution times reflect this transmission time. In the SIMD experiments, the set of n pieces was transferred from an array on the host to the n processors, one piece per processor. The SIMD execution times reported below do not include this data transmission time. The total time required to transfer 8,192 pieces to 8K processors was 1 second and the time needed to send 16,384 pieces to the same number of processors was 1.5 seconds. For the parallel FFD and BFD algorithms, the set of n pieces was sorted in parallel before the algorithms were executed. For the SIMD algorithms, the average time required to sort 8,192 pieces using a parallel sort was .03 seconds while the average time to sort 16,384 pieces was .04 seconds. The sorting times are also not reflected in the reported results.

ALGORITHM	N		User Time		Total Time	
n	8192	16384	8192	16384	8192	16384
N* lower bound	4032	8154				
ParNF$_M$	5353	10854	8.3	18.5	63	124
ParFF$_M$	4127	8329	9.1	19.0	77	153
ParFFD$_M$	4066	8232	9.0	19.2	76	153
ParRFF$_M$ (m=7)	5110	10345	7.5	15.3	21	50
ParH$_M$ (M=12)	5191	10512	7.9	14.9	21	37
ParPF$_M$	4367	8790	8.0	15.6	22	46
ParPFD$_M$	4973	9057	7.7	15.2	24	48
ParPFI$_M$	4879	9513	7.7	15.6	26	50

MIMD Implementations (B=100)
Table 1

ALGORITHM	N		User Time		Total Time	
n	8192	16384	8192	16384	8192	16384
N* lower bound	4066	8266				
ParNF$_M$	5437	11003	9.4	19.3	64	126
ParFF$_M$	4197	8437	9.8	21.3	78	161
ParFFD$_M$	4140	8354	9.9	20.9	77	160
ParRFF$_M$ (m=7)	5186	10468	7.8	16.7	22	51
ParH$_M$ (M=12)	5277	10649	8.1	15.9	22	36
ParPF$_M$	4385	8812	8.6	16.2	23	47
ParPFD$_M$	4766	8928	7.9	15.4	25	48
ParPFI$_M$	4792	9007	8.2	16.1	25	49

MIMD Implementations (B=1000)
Table 2

The results of executing the parallel MIMD packing algorithms on an Intel iPSC/2 computer for four representative data sets are summarized in Tables 1 and 2. The results of executing the SIMD packing algorithms on a Connection Machine System for four similar data sets are summarized in Tables 3 and 4. In these tables, an instance of the bin-packing problem is defined by a set of n (uniformly distributed) integers between 1 and B with a bin size of B. The number of bins packed and the amounts of time needed to execute each algorithm are reported along with an estimate on the minimum number of bins required to pack the respective data sets.

In the MIMD implementations, the time estimates are from the XENIX operating system. The User Time is the time spent in execution of processes outside of the kernel and Total Time measures the elapsed time. For the SIMD executions, CM Time measures the time needed by the parallel processors while Total Time includes both CM and Vax time for executing the algorithm. All timings are given in seconds and are averaged over three executions of each algorithm on the same data set.

ALGORITHM	N		CM Time		Total Time	
n	8192	16384	8192	16384	8192	16384
N^* lower bound	4047	8235				
ParNF$_S$	5379	10959	5.4	11.1	10.9	21.2
ParFF$_S$	4161	8379	6.6	13.2	19.5	38.2
ParBF$_S$	4123	8309	8.1	16.3	24.4	47.8
ParFFD$_S$	4071	8245	6.6	13.2	19.5	38.2
ParBFD$_S$	4071	8245	8.1	16.2	24.6	47.1
ParRFF$_S$ ($m=7$)	5110	10392	6.5	13.1	20.1	40.2
ParH$_S$ ($M=12$)	5197	10563	5.3	10.8	10.5	20.7
ParH$_S$ ($M=20$)	5198	10565	5.3	10.8	10.9	20.7
ParRH$_S$	5168	10505	5.0	10.1	10.5	20.0
ParSF$_S$ ($s=4$)	4205	9016	3.8	7.7	12.2	23.4
ParSF$_S$ ($s=8$)	4250	8660	5.2	10.5	16.5	31.9
ParMF$_S$	4074	8247	0.8	1.0	2.4	2.8

SIMD Implementations (B=100)
Table 3

ALGORITHM	N		CM Time		Total Time	
n	8192	16384	8192	16384	8192	16384
N^* lower bound	4158	8143				
ParNF$_S$	5535	10876	5.4	11.1	11.9	21.5
ParFF$_S$	4306	8341	6.6	13.3	20.5	38.4
ParBF$_S$	4265	8262	8.2	16.3	25.4	47.3
ParFFD$_S$	4185	8161	6.7	13.5	20.7	39.6
ParBFD$_S$	4185	8161	8.2	16.7	25.5	49.4
ParRFF$_S$ ($m=7$)	5270	10338	6.5	13.3	21.7	41.5
ParH$_S$ ($M=12$)	5363	10516	5.4	10.8	11.6	21.5
ParH$_S$ ($M=20$)	5366	10519	5.4	10.8	11.6	21.6
ParRH$_S$	5334	10458	5.1	10.2	11.3	20.8
ParSF$_S$ ($s=4$)	4569	8929	3.9	7.7	12.8	23.8
ParSF$_S$ ($s=8$)	4399	8571	5.3	10.6	17.3	32.8
ParMF$_S$	4251	8218	35.7	27.7	114.5	84.8

SIMD Implementations (B=1000)
Table 4

6. SUMMARY

In both the MIMD and SIMD versions of the algorithms, the parallelizations of First Fit Decreasing (and similarly, Best Fit Decreasing in the SIMD case) yield the best packings but require the most time. The parallel versions of Next Fit require slightly less time and produce the worst packings. These results were expected for they reflect the behavior of the sequential versions of FF, BF and NF.

In the MIMD case, the parallel version of Petal Fit made communication demands which proved to be a problem. The heuristic was implemented in a modified form that reduced this demand and correspondingly reduced the packing efficiency. However, it still performed better than the parallel Refined First Fit and Harmonic algorithms, and was much faster than Next Fit or First Fit. When the pieces were sorted into non-increasing or non-decreasing order, the performance of the Petal Fit heuristic deteriorates. It appears to be a good method for on-line packing, however, and we feel its packing efficiency can be improved by further modification.

In the SIMD case, the time and packing performance of the Segment Fit heuristic reflected the fact that it employs both the NF and FF packing approachs. The Match Fit heuristic attempts to capitalize on the parallelism of the SIMD model and the assumption that the pieces are uniformly distributed between 1 and B. As expected, it produced packings comparable to ParFFD$_S$ and PARBF$_S$ using much less computing time when the sizes of the pieces and bins is small. The reduction in computing times for n=8192 to 16384 is due to the fact that fewer left-over pieces are packed using the best fit rule. The behavior of Match Fit also supports the belief that parallelizations of sequential approximation algorithms may not always be as efficient as algorithms specifically designed with models of parallel computing in mind. Recent theoretical results concerning parallel bin packing [Anderson et al. 1988] also support this belief.

The parallel algorithms examined in this paper form the basis of our initial study in designing parallel solution strategies for solving one-dimensional bin-packing problems. The algorithm implementations show that significant execution speedups can be obtained in practice, even by parallelizing algorithms that are considered to be inherently sequential in nature. This study has provided the authors with useful insight towards the design of new and efficient parallel bin packing algorithms.

ACKNOWLEDGEMENTS

This research was partially supported by the Army Research Office, contract DAAL03-87-k-0087. The authors would also like to thank the Naval Research Laboratory in Washington D.C. for providing access to the Connection Machine System.

REFERENCES

Anderson, R.J, E.W. Mayr, and M.K. Warmuth (1988), "Parallel Approximation Algorithms for Bin Packing," Computer Science Technical Report STAN-CS-88-1200, Stanford University, Ca.

Baker, B.S. (1985), "A New Proof for the First-fit Decreasing Bin-Packing Algorithm," *Journal of Algorithms*, 6, 49-70.

Berkey, J.O. (1986), *Two-dimensional Bin Packing Algorithms*, M.S. Thesis, Dept. of Computer Science, George Mason University, Fairfax, Va.

Coffman, E.G. Jr., M.R. Garey, and D.S. Johnson (1984), "Approximation Algorithms for Bin-Packing - an Updated Survey," In *Algorithm Design for Computer System Design*, G. Ausiello, M. Lucertini, P. Serafini, Eds. Springer, New York, pp. 49-106.

Johnson, D.S., A. Demers, J.D. Ullman, M.R. Garey, and R.L. Graham (1974), "Worst-case Performance Bounds for Simple One-Dimensional Packing Algorithms," *SIAM Journal of Computing*, 3, pp. 295-325.

Lee, C.C. and D.T. Lee (1985), "A Simple On-line Bin-packing Algorithm," *Journal of the ACM*, 32, 562-572.

Yao, A. (1980), "New Algorithms for Bin Packing," *Journal of the ACM*, 27, 207-227.

SIMD KNAPSACK APPROXIMATION ALGORITHMS

THOMAS E. GERASCH	PEARL Y. WANG	SCOTT T. WEIDMAN
SPARTA, Inc.	*Dept. of Computer Science*	*MRJ, Inc.*
7926 Jones Branch Drive	*George Mason University*	*10455 White Granite Drive*
McLean, Virginia 22102	*Fairfax, Virginia 22030*	*Oakton, Virginia 22124*

ABSTRACT

In this paper, we present several parallel approximation algorithms for the 0/1 integer knapsack problem. These algorithms are designed for a shared memory SIMD model of computation where processors access memory in exclusive-read, exclusive-write fashion. A discussion of these algorithms and their theoretical behavior is presented. The performance of the methods when implemented on a Connection Machine System for various data sets (including examples with tens of thousands of items) is compared using execution times and profits obtained.

1. INTRODUCTION

The 0/1 integer knapsack problem is defined by a set of n objects having positive integer profits p_i and weights w_i, and a positive integer knapsack capacity M. The problem is concerned with maximizing the profit $P=\sum_i x_i p_i$ subject to a weight constraint $\sum_i x_i w_i \leq M$ with x_i in $\{0,1\}$ for $i=0,1,...,n$. An instance of the knapsack problem consists of an assignment of values for the profits, weights and the capacity. A feasible solution to a problem instance is a set of x_i values which satisfy the capacity constraint by indicating whether an item is to be included in the knapsack. This well-known optimization problem is NP-Complete [Garey and Johnson 1979] and, consequently, considerable interest has been generated in developing algorithms which obtain approximate solutions [Lawler 1979; Horowitz and Sahni 1978; Ibarra and Kim 1975; Sahni 1975].

There has been a growing interest in parallel computation and in the parallelization of optimization techniques and algorithms. Recent parallel approximation algorithms for the knapsack problem include a MIMD solution for hypercubes [Lee et al. 1987] and a SIMD algorithm [Gopalkrishnan et al 1986]. The SIMD algorithm is based on some of the refinements given by Lawler [1979] for the algorithm presented by Ibarra and Kim [1975].

In the second section of this paper, a basic model of SIMD computation is described. The programming paradigm that is followed is an EREW paradigm with scan operations added.

The third section of the paper discusses three SIMD parallelizations of knapsack approximation strategies. The algorithms that are described are a straightforward greedy algorithm, a parallelization of [Sahni 1975] for limited numbers of combinations of items (and hence of replicates of the instance), and a new parallelization of the Ibarra and Kim [1975] algorithm. An analysis of these algorithms is given in Section 4.

In the fifth section, the performance of the algorithms when implemented on a Connection Machine System is presented. The actual run times and processor requirements for various problem instances are compared, and some discussion of performance in terms of relative profit error is provided. Problem instances include problem sizes of up to tens of thousands of items.

The final section of the paper summarizes the results of the quantitative study with respect to the algorithm analyses presented. In addition, general observations are made as to the suitability of applying parallel processing for solving large integer knapsack optimization problems.

2. PARALLEL PROGRAMMING MODELS

The basic programming model used for the parallel knapsack algorithms is that of a collection of processors executing in a SIMD fashion. A single controller issues the instructions and is a serial computer. The processors then execute the same instruction in lock-step fashion under the direction of the controller. Processors may choose not to participate in the execution of an instruction on the basis of a conditional test. It is also assumed that the processors share access to a common memory, but that no two processors may read or write simultaneously to the same memory location. This model of computation is also referred to as the EREW PRAM (Exclusive-Read, Exclusive-Write Parallel Random Access Machine). Further, processors are uniquely numbered and are aware of their processor numbers.

In the implementations of the algorithms to be discussed, the data items are represented in arrays. If the indices for the array elements are between 1 and n, then it will usually be assumed that there are n processors manipulating the data, one processor per array index. If some data items need not be manipulated, then there will be a test by the processors which are monitoring those data items so that they will decide not to participate in the manipulations. To insure that data is accessed in an exclusive-read, exclusive-write fashion, all processors which are actively participating in a computation step will reference the data using a uniform addressing scheme. For example, each active processor i will reference the data item $i+k$ whose offset is the fixed distance k from its own index i. Such indexing requirements are necessary to guarantee an EREW model. To indicate identical statements in an algorithm that can be executed in parallel, the statements will be enclosed in a **for all** statement.

Algorithms are also presented using *scan*, or parallel prefix operations [Kruskal et al. 1985; Blelloch 1987]. A scan operator takes an associative operator ⊕ and a sequence of elements $[a_1, a_2, ..., a_n]$, and returns the sequence

$$[a_1, (a_1 \oplus a_2), ..., ((a_1 \oplus a_2 \oplus ... \oplus a_{n-1}) \oplus a_n)].$$

The scan operations used in the algorithms will be *plus_scan*, which uses addition to obtain the sequence of partial sums, *copy_scan* to replicate a data item a specified number of times (a *plus_scan* with all items but the first contributing *0*), and *max_scan* to find the maximum of *n* items. A scan operation can also be run in parallel on subsequences of an array, and will be called a *segmented scan* operation. *Scan* operations take $O(\log n)$ time using $O(n)$ processors in the EREW PRAM model.

3. PARALLEL KNAPSACK APPROXIMATION ALGORITHMS

3.1 Parallel Greedy Algorithm

A greedy algorithm in the EREW model uses *n* processors to perform a parallel sort, and then proceeds in a serial fashion in considering the items. The algorithm shown in Figure 1 is a straightforward parallel version employing scan operations, of a simple greedy strategy for the knapsack problem.

> **sort** the items by nonincreasing profit/weight densities
> **while** (there are active items and capacity > 0) **do**
> *plus_scan* active profit values into a profit_sum array
> *plus_scan* active weight values into a weight_sum array
> determine the segment of the weight_sum array for which each
>   weight_sum[i] ≤ capacity; let *last* denote the largest index for
>   which this is true
> capacity ← capacity - weight_sum[*last*]
> profit ← profit + profit_sum[*last*]
> knapsack ← active i for which i ≤ *last*
> **if** (i ≤ *last*) **then** set i to inactive **endif**
> **if** (i is active and weight[i] > capacity)
>   **then** set i to inactive
> **endif**
> **endwhile**

Parallel Greedy Algorithm Using Scans
Figure 1.

This algorithm repetitively does *plus_scan* operations over the items which remain active, with inactive items contributing *0* to the scan. Initially, all items are active. The active items in each *plus_scan* whose sum of weights will fit into the remaining knapsack capacity are taken. These items then become inactive in the next scan and the remaining knapsack capacity is adjusted. The use of scan operations introduces additional time complexity; they are present to reflect their use in the algorithm's implementation for the Connection Machine System, on which scan operations execute relatively quickly.

3.2 Parallel ε-Approximation

The second algorithm to be presented is a parallel version of a well-known pseudo-polynomial ε-approximation algorithm [Sahni 1975; Horowitz and Sahni 1978]. The algorithm presented in Figure 2 is guaranteed to provide approximate solutions to knapsack problem instances which are within $min\{1/(k+1), p'/P\}$ of the optimal solutions, where p' is the $(k+1)^{st}$ largest profit and P is the total profit of the algorithm's computation. Actual performance of the algorithm may be better, but is not guaranteed. The algorithm works with replicates of the initial knapsack problem instance. Each replicate initially holds a combination of up to k of the items. The algorithm is considered to be a pseudo-polynomial approximation algorithm because the time requirement for the serial algorithm is $O(kn^{k+1})$ [Sahni 1975]. The space requirement for the parallel version which is presented here is $O(kn^k)$ since the parallel algorithm requires one processor for each knapsack replicate.

```
sort the items by nonincreasing profit/weight densities
initialize each of the N knapsack replicates to contain a combination of
        items; each replicate must know the items with which it was initialized
for j = 1 to n do
        {test item j for all replicates in parallel}
        for all i, 1 ≤ i ≤ N do
                if (item j is not in replicate i)
                        and (rem_cap[i] + weight[j] ≤ capacity)
                then  {item j goes into knapsack replicate i}
                        rem_cap[i] ← rem_cap[i] - weight[j]
                        p_sum[i] ← p_sum[i] + profit[j]
                endif
        endfor
endfor
max_p_sum ← max_scan of p_sum[1...N]
m ← max_scan of i for which p_sum[i] = max_p_sum
create a knapsack problem instance from the original with replicate m's items
        removed and with the capacity reduced by the sum of replicate m's initial
        items; run the parallel greedy algorithm on the knapsack instance derived
        from replicate m; add the items which were used to initialize replicate m
```

Parallel ε–Approximation Algorithm
Figure 2.

The main portion of the algorithm tracks the profits and remaining capacities of each of the replicates in two arrays, $P\_sum[1...N]$ and $rem\_cap[1...N]$ where N denotes the total number of combinations of n items taken up to k at a time. Each replicate will be maintained by a single processor. The indices of those items which are placed into a replicate are recoverable from the processor number. After all items have been considered by all of the replicates, the winning replicate is selected and the items which actually contributed to its profit are reconstructed using the parallel greedy algorithm. (When N is small, i.e. $N<1000$, a contents list may be constructed for each replicate during the main portion of the algorithm, obviating this reconstruction step.)

As can be seen by inspection, the algorithm in Figure 2 is a straightforward parallelization of the original serial algorithm. The parallelism occurs in the maintenance of the knapsack replicates. Since the number of replicates, and hence the number of processors required, depends on N, this algorithm can quickly become difficult to implement on most existing parallel computers. The algorithm will be analyzed in Section 4 only for the special case where $k=2$. This case can be reasonably programmed on many of the massively parallel computers that are currently available. No attempt has been made to efficiently parallelize the initialization phase of the algorithm beyond the $k=2$ case.

3.3 Parallel ε-Approximation Scheme

The last knapsack approximation algorithm to be parallelized is the ε-approximation scheme of Ibarra and Kim [1975]. This serial algorithm accepts a knapsack instance and an ε $(0<\varepsilon<1)$ as input and produces an ε-approximation for the problem instance with time and space complexity that is polynomial in the instance's size and in $1/\varepsilon$. The approximate solution is obtained by first separating the items into two sets of relatively "large" items and relatively "small" items. The item separation is performed using scaling and threshold factors which ensure that one-half of the relative approximate error is allocated to each of the two calculation stages. These stages correspond to computations involving each of the two sets of items [Lawler 1979]. The threshold and scale factors are determined by using an estimate P_0 of the optimal profit value for the knapsack instance. This estimate satisfies $P_0 \le P^* \le 2P_0$, where P^* denotes the optimal profit value for the problem instance.

The large item computation uses a dynamic programming approach to find an optimal solution to a knapsack instance that consists of the items with scaled large profit values and has capacity equal to the original capacity. To restrict the growth of the number of feasible solutions during the large item computation, the following dominance relation is used. Let S_1 and S_2 be two feasible solutions (i.e. sets of elements whose weight sums do not exceed the knapsack capacity). The solution S_2 *dominates* S_1, written $S_2 > S_1$, if $P(S_1) \le P(S_2)$ and $W(S_1) \ge W(S_2)$, where $P(S) = \sum_{i \in S} p_i$, and $W(S) = \sum_{i \in S} w_i$. It should be noted that if $S_j > S_i$ and if S_k is a set of indices disjoint from both S_i and S_j, then $S_j \cup S_k > S_i \cup S_k$.

During the large item computation, a sequence of feasible solutions is maintained whose profit and weight sums are in increasing order and for which no solution is dominated by any other in the sequence. As each item is considered, the dominance rule is applied to preserve the properties of the sequence of feasible solutions. The last solution in the sequence is actually the optimal solution to the scaled large item problem instance. At the end of the large item computation, the entire sequence of feasible solutions is retained, not just the last in the sequence.

Each of the feasible solutions from the large item computation has its remaining capacity augmented by small items. This augmentation of the solutions is done using a greedy approach. The ε-approximate solution to the problem instance is the one with greatest profit value after the large and small item computation stages.

Figure 3 provides a general outline of the algorithm for an ε-approximation scheme. The first step in the parallel algorithm can be accomplished by sorting the items into nonincreasing profit/weight ratios so that $p_1/w_1 \geq p_2/w_2 \geq ... \geq p_n/w_n$, and next determining the largest m such that $p_1 +...+ p_m \leq C$ but $p_1+...+p_m+p_{m+1} > C$. P_0 is then taken to be $max\{p_1+...+p_m, max\{p_i: m<i\leq n\}\}$ [Lawler 1979]. The rearrangement of the items in the item separation phase is accomplished by first using n processors to enumerate the items in each set. An enumeration can be obtained using parallel prefix summation (*plus_scan*) operations. The rearrangement is an easy matter given the enumerations.

In the third step of the ε-approximation scheme, the choices of the scale and threshold factors guarantee that $q_i \geq 2/\varepsilon$ and that no more than $(8/\varepsilon^2)/q_i$ items with scaled profit value q_i can fit in any feasible solution to the scaled large item problem [Lawler 1979]. It can also be shown that the largest possible scaled profit obtainable is $8/\varepsilon^2$ and that the maximum number of items in any scaled solution is $4/\varepsilon$.

The rearrangement of the large items for the purpose of selecting a minimal set of large item candidates can be performed by first sorting the large items using the values $\{(8/\varepsilon^2)-q_i\}W+w_i$ as the sort keys. Here, W is the maximum of the weights w_i of the large items. After the rearrangement, the items in all scaled profit groups can be enumerated in parallel so that items will know if they are to be actual large item candidates from their group. Such an enumeration of the items in the groups can be performed in parallel using an additive parallel prefix operation in which group identifiers are also carried along with the partial sums during the prefix operation.

The key to this SIMD parallelization of the algorithm is the representation of the feasible solutions during the dominance-based optimization on the large items. The feasible solutions in the large item computation are indexed by the possible profit values in the scaled problem. The largest scaled profit obtainable is $8/\varepsilon^2$. Also, since the maximum number of items in any of the scaled large item solutions is $4/\varepsilon$, the feasible solutions in the large item computation can be maintained in $8/\varepsilon^2$ sections of an array with each section being of length $4/\varepsilon$.

> Find P_0 such that $P_0 \leq P^* \leq 2P_0$, set the scale factor $K=(\varepsilon/2)^2 P_0$ and the
> threshold factor $T=(\varepsilon/2)P_0$
> {item separation}
> **for all** items **do**
>   **if** $p_i > T$
>   **then** item i is a *large* item
>   **else** item i is a *small* item
>   **endif**
> **endfor**
> Arrange the items so that each set of items occupies contiguous blocks of
>   locations in the profit and weight arrays
> **for all** *large* items **do**
> $q_i = \lceil p_i/K \rceil$ {scaled profit values for *large* items}
> **endfor**
> {select a minimal set of *large* candidates}
> **for all** scaled profit values q_i **do**
>   arrange those *large* items with scaled profit value q_i into nondecreasing
>   order of weight
>   select the first $(8/\varepsilon^2)/q_i$ items of each group as candidates
> **endfor**
> {*large* item computation}
> Perform a dominance-based optimization on the minimal set of *large* item candidates
>   to produce a sequence of feasible solutions whose profits and weights are
>   nondecreasing (and consequently for which no solution dominates another)
> {*small* item augmentation of *large* item solutions using greedy approach}
> sort the *small* items into nonincreasing order of p_i/w_i ratios
> **for each** *small* item **do**
>   **for all** feasible solutions from the *large* item computation **do**
>   if the *small* item fits in the feasible solution then add the profit and
>   weight of the *small* item to the profit and weight sums for the solution
>   (not remembering the *small* item's index)
>   **endfor**
> **endfor**
> Select the feasible solution with the greatest profit value as the ε-approximate
>   solution to the knapsack instance, rerun a greedy algorithm to augment the
>   *large* item feasible solution, remembering the indices of *small* items taken

Outline of Parallel ε-approximation Scheme
Figure 3.

During the computation, each of these feasible solutions consists of the indices of the large items actually placed into the solution, as well the location of the next position in the feasible solution's section which is to obtain a new item's index, if the item meets the dominance criterion. The general form of the large item computation is shown in Figure 4. This algorithm is based directly on the dominance-based optimization originally given by Ibarra and Kim [1975]. For convenience, a feasible solution is denoted by $F(s)$ and its weight by $W(s)$, where the scaled profit s of the feasible solution is its index. When an item can be added to a feasible solution and the resulting new solution dominates another in the list, the dominated solution is replaced in a single step by using $4/\varepsilon$ processors. Also, all dominated feasible solutions are replaced in parallel.

```
for each large item candidate do
    let i' denote the index of the item
        for all s such that 0≤s≤(8/ε²)-qᵢ' and F(s)≠∅ and W(s)+wᵢ'≤C do
            if F(s+qᵢ')=∅ or W(s+qᵢ')>W(s)+w then
                replace F(s+qᵢ') by F(s), add index i', add wᵢ' to W(s+qᵢ')
            endif
        end for
endfor
```

Outline of Parallel Dominance-Based Optimization
Figure 4.

The implementation of the small item augmentation of the feasible solutions in Figure 3 is carried out in two steps. In the first step, all large item feasible solutions consider each small item, but do not actually remember small items taken; this is meant to avoid storage costs for maintaining many lists of indices in our SIMD model. After the feasible solution with the largest profit over both the large and small items is selected, a greedy algorithm is again performed on the small items, this time remembering the indices of the small items to be taken.

4. COMPLEXITY

In the complexity analysis which follows, the time to perform parallel sorting will be included. In the EREW PRAM model, the time to sort n items using n processors is taken to be $O(log^2 n)$. This can be obtained by modifying the bitonic merge sorting algorithm for the EREW computation model. In the literature, some authors use a time estimate of $O(log n)$ for n processors that is based on the algorithm in [Atjai et al. 1983]. As pointed out by Leighton [1984], the limit obtained in [Atjai et al. 1983] is an asymptotic limit and the constant of proportionality is so large that this sorting strategy becomes infeasible from a technological standpoint. For this reason, the more realistic time estimate for sorting of $O(log^2 n)$ using n processors is used here.

4.1 Parallel Greedy Algorithm

It has already been mentioned that the EREW model greedy algorithm uses parallelism only for the sorting step, and proceeds in a serial fashion in its item selection.

The performance of the greedy algorithm in the EREW model is summarized by the following theorem.

THEOREM 1. The parallel greedy knapsack algorithm takes $O(log^2 n+n)$ time using n processors in the EREW PRAM model if parallel prefix operations are not used.

The obvious implementation of the greedy algorithm in the EREW model has no apparent speed-up due to the inherently serial nature of the greedy processing. The primary speed-up in the algorithm is due to the parallelization of the sorting step in the algorithm.

4.2 Parallel ε-Approximation

For the parallel ε-approximation algorithm, we consider only the special case where $k=2$, i.e. where there are replicates of the problem for each combination of n items taken up to two at a time. This specialization results in an $\varepsilon=1/3$ approximation for which $(n^2+n)/2$ processors are required. It can be shown for the general algorithm that the error estimate is $(P^*-P)/P^* \leq min\{1/(k+1), p'/P\}$, where P is the profit value produced by the algorithm and p' is the $(k+1)^{st}$ largest profit value of the items [Sahni 1975]. This error estimate will be used in the discussion of the implementation results in Section 5. For $k>2$, the processor requirements of the approach adopted here quickly exceed the current processor technologies when n exceeds several hundred items, since the approach presented requires a processor for each replicate. The algorithm could be implemented with a fixed number of processors by iterating through collections of combinations, but this would result in higher time requirements.

The central **for** loop of the parallel ε-approximation algorithm requires n steps for the EREW model of computation. The parallel prefix operations require $O(log(n^2+n)/2)) = O(log\ n)$ operations in the EREW model. The sorting step can be incorporated into the use of the greedy algorithm at the end of the algorithm. Since k is fixed at 2, the sort and greedy steps require $O(log^2 n+n)$ time and n processors in the EREW model.

Conceptually, one can imagine the n knapsack items placed along the diagonal of an n×n matrix. The elements above and along the diagonal represent the knapsack replicates. The elements along the diagonal are copied along their respective rows to the right of the diagonal so that item i is in position (i,j) for $i \leq j \leq n$. Now the elements along the diagonal are each copied along the column above the diagonal element. Each diagonal position i can now discard one of the two copies of item i which it possesses. Each position (i,j), $i<j \leq n$, in the upper triangular region has both items i and j. Such a scheme in the EREW model is possible using a linear addressing method for the non-zero portions of the triangular matrix that uses $(n^2+n)/2$ indices, and hence the same number of processors. Consecutive rows are represented in consecutive array segments with a diagonal element's position being the starting position of an array segment. For the column copy, the items can easily be

rearranged into a column-segment arrangement, again with diagonal elements at the starting positions of the segments. These rearrangements can be performed in constant time. The copy operations require $O(\log n)$ time.

THEOREM 2. For $k=2$, the parallel $1/(k+1)$-approximation algorithm can be performed using $(n^2+n)/2$ processors and requires $O(n+\log^2 n+\log n)$ time in the EREW PRAM model.

4.3 Parallel ε-Approximation Scheme

Since there are n items, at least n processors are needed by this parallel ε-approximation scheme. The estimate of P_0 is obtained using a sort and several max operations, which require $O(\log^2 n + \log n)$ time in the worst case in the EREW model.

The item separation and rearrangement can be done using constant time operations together with a sorting operation. The selection of the minimal set of large item candidates is done by sorting the large items on a composite key and then enumerating the items in the scaled profit segments in parallel using segmented *plus_scan* operations. The time requirements are of the same order as those of the previous steps. The large and small item computations will iterate over $O(n)$ items in the worst case.

The key to the parallel algorithm is the large item optimization problem. It is also the primary contributor to the final number of processors required by the algorithm. The large item computation iterates over at most $min \{n, (8/\varepsilon^2) \log(4/\varepsilon)\}$ candidates as the number of candidate items cannot exceed n. The number of processors needed for the large item computation is $(4/\varepsilon)(8/\varepsilon^2-2/\varepsilon)$ since there are a maximum of $4/\varepsilon$ items in each feasible solution and the feasible solutions are indexed by scaled profit values. $8/\varepsilon^2$ is the maximum obtainable scaled profit, while $2/\varepsilon$ is the smallest possible scaled profit value because of the scaling and threshold factors.

During the large item optimization procedure all processors which are managing index positions in a feasible solution's representation can test the dominance criterion in parallel (all processors managing a feasible solution can have copies of the profit taken and capacity used). The dominance rule and the uniform, maximum length of the feasible solutions, together with a copy of profit and capacity information for each processor, ensures that EREW memory references are possible.

THEOREM 3. The parallel ε-approximation scheme presented takes $O(n+\log^2 n+\log n)$ time and requires $max\{n, (4/\varepsilon)(8/\varepsilon^2-2/\varepsilon)\}$ processors.

This ε-approximation scheme is a direct implementation of the dominance-based optimization presented by Ibarra and Kim [1975]. In contrast, the parallelization discussed in [Gopalkrishnan et al. 1986] is a recursive algorithm requiring $n^{2.5}/\varepsilon^{1.5}$ processors in the worst case. By current technological standards, the approximation scheme outlined in this paper is more suitable for implementing large knapsack proglem instances with moderate values of ε. For example, if $n=10,000$ and $\varepsilon=.5$, then 10,000 processors would be required for the scheme presented here, while the algorithm of [Gopalkrishnan et al. 1986] would need $2^{3/2} \, 10^{10}$ processors, in the worst case.

5. EXPERIMENTAL RESULTS

The three parallel knapsack approximation algorithms described above were coded in *Lisp and executed on a Connection Machine System. The CM is a massively parallel, SIMD computer on which the scan operations execute as fast as interprocessor memory references. The algorithms were implemented in an EREW interprocessor memory reference fashion. Table 1 summarizes the run times that were obtained. In general, the timings for each trial were quite close to the means displayed in the table. An exception occurs for the $n=256$ case where one data set took twice as long to run (except for algorithm 3.2 with $k=2$), thus inflating the mean values.

The profit values for the trials were uniformly distributed integers in [20,120] and weights were coupled to their respective p_i: $w_i = p_i$-$19+x_i$, where x_i is a random integer in [0,39]. The knapsack capacity used was w'_i (15.5-$log_2 n$) where w'_i is the average value of the w_i, except when $n=65,536$ for which the capacity was $w'_i/2$. These capacities were empirically derived to force the dynamic programming portion of the ε-approximation scheme to be invoked. For many problem instances, the dynamic programming routine was bypassed, resulting in the application of only the parallel greedy algorithm.

# of items	Greedy	Pseudo-polynomial k=1	k=2	ε-approx. scheme $\varepsilon = 0.25$
64	0.228	0.89	0.737	1.10
128	0.245	1.18	1.07*	1.42
256	0.328	1.96	2.18*†	1.92
512	0.252	2.11	-	2.03
1024	0.264	3.32	-	2.28
4096	0.306	10.6	-	5.08
8192	0.359	20.4	-	8.10
16384	0.443*	39.8*	-	14.3*
65536	1.27*†	157.*†	-	66.9*†

* These runs with 16384 processors; all others with 8192
† Each physical processor acts as four virtual processors

**Mean Run Times in Seconds for 3 Trials Each
Table 1**

The executions performed with capacity $\sum_i w_i/2$ were reported in [Gerasch and Weidman 1988] for the parallel greedy and pseudo-polynomial ($k=1$) algorithms. Those performance and run times are very similar to the case at hand, so our choice of a small capacity is not biasing. The execution times for the greedy algorithm in the earlier paper were less than those appearing in Table 1 because sorting times were not previously included. The sorting times are included here for consistency with the other two approximation algorithms.

6. SUMMARY

For large instances of uniformly distributed profits and weights, all the algorithms perform nearly as well in terms of accuracy. The best profit total was always found by the pseudo-polynomial ε-approximation algorithm with $k=2$, or with $k=1$ when $n>256$. However, the greedy result is never more than 3.3% below that value. In fact, over the 27 trials, the greedy profit total averaged just 99.3% of the best of all tested algorithms. For the instances described, the pseudo-polynomial algorithm output has accuracy generally guaranteed to be within 13-14% of optimal. Therefore, the greedy algorithm produces good results with minimal execution time required.

The ε-approximation scheme with $\varepsilon=.25$ never produced a higher profit total than the greedy algorithm, and tended to be 1-5% lower in profit total for small problem instances. In practical terms, the algorithm does not appear to be a good choice, except perhaps for particularly troublesome distributions of profits and weights.

In three of the nine trials that compared the $k=1$ and $k=2$ cases of the pseudo-polynomial algorithm, the latter case exceeded the former's best profit total. However, this improvement was only 0.3% and would be less if the zero change trials are averaged in. Run times for the $k=2$ case will generally be longer than those where $k=1$. This does not happen in Table 1 because the $k=2$ algorithm kept a running tally of knapsack replicate contents, whereas the $k=1$ version had to reconstruct the contents in an additional operation. This is necessary for larger n values, but could have been dropped for $n<512$ to show the $k=1$ program in a more favorable light.

In conclusion, we have demonstrated that existing knapsack approximation algorithms are amenable to SIMD parallelization. Further, these parallel algorithms are implementable on existing massively parallel architectures subject to reasonable constraints on the desired percentage of error. Of the three parallel algorithms, the greedy approach exhibited the fastest execution behavior, while the pseudo-polynomial algorithm with $k=2$ had the best performance behavior.

ACKNOWLEDGEMENTS

The authors would like to acknowledge the support of the Perkin-Elmer Advanced Development Center in Oakton, VA and the Naval Research Laboratories in Washington, DC for providing Connection Machine time.

REFERENCES

Atjai, M., Komlos, J., and Szemeredi, E. (1983), "An O(NlogN) Sorting Network," In *Proceedings of the 15th ACM Symposium on the Theory of Computing* (Boston, Mass., Apr.), ACM, N.Y.C., pp. 1-9.

Blelloch, G. (1987), "Scans as Primitive Parallel Operations," In *Proceedings of the 1987 International Conference on Parallel Processing* (St. Charles, Ill., Aug. 17-21), Penn State Press, University Park, Penn., pp. 355-362.

Garey, M., and Johnson, D. (1979), *Computers and Intractability: A Guide to the Theory of NP-Completeness*, W. H. Freeman, San Francisco, Calif.

Gerasch, T., and Weidman, S. (1988), "Massively Parallel Computing Applied to 0/1 Knapsack Problems," In *Proceedings of the Third International Conference on Supercomputing,* Volume II (Boston, Mass., May), International Supercomputing Institute, St. Petersburg, Fla., pp. 448-451.

Gopalkrishnan, P., Ramakrishnan, I., and Kanal, L (1986), "Parallel Approximate Algorithms for the 0/1 Knapsack Problem," In *Proceedings of the 1986 International Conference on Parallel Processing* (St. Charles, Ill., Aug. 19-22), IEEE, Washington, D.C., pp. 444-451.

Horowitz, E., and Sahni, S. (1978), *Fundamentals of Computer Algorithms*, Computer Science Press, Potomac, Md.

Ibarra, O., and Kim, C. (1975), "Fast Approximation Algorithms for the Knapsack and Sum of Subsets Problems," *Journal of the ACM* 22, 4 (Oct.), pp. 463-468.

Kruskal, C., Rudolf, L., and Snir, M. (1985), "The Power of Parallel Prefix," In *Proceedings of the 1985 International Conference on Parallel Processing* (St. Charles, Ill., Aug. 20-23), IEEE, Washington, D.C., pp. 180-185.

Lawler, E. (1979), "Fast Approximation Algorithms for Knapsack Problems," *Mathematics of Operations Research* 4, 4 (Nov.), pp. 339-356.

Lee, J., Shragowitz, E., and Sahni, S. (1987), "A Hypercube Algorithm for the 0/1 Knapsack Problem," In *Proceedings of the 1987 International Conference on Parallel Processing* (ST. Charles, Ill., Aug. 17-21), Penn State Press, University Park, Penn., pp. 699-706.

Leighton, T. (1984), "Tight Bounds on the Complexity of Parallel Sorting," In *Proceedings of the 16th Annual Symposium on the Theory of Computing* (Washington, D.C., April 30 - May 2), ACM, N.Y.C., pp. 71-80.

Sahni, S. (1975), "Approximate Algorithms for the 0/1 Knapsack Problem," *Journal of the ACM* 22, 1 (Jan.), pp. 115-124.

A VECTORIZED DUAL ALGORITHM FOR GENERALIZED NETWORK PROBLEM

Anand R. Joshi and Der-San Chen
Department of Industrial Engineering, The University of Alabama
Tuscaloosa, Alabama 35487

ABSTRACT

The generalized network problem considered here is a minimum cost flow problem with gains and losses imposed on arcs. This paper presents modifications and implementation of a dual algorithm on the CRAY X-MP. Data structures and computational results on the benchmark problems are included.

1. INTRODUCTION

Most algorithms for solving network problems are sequential in nature. The advent of the parallel computers have stimulated the designs of new algorithms to improve the computational efficiency. This paper presents modifications and implementation of a dual algorithm for the generalized network problem on a vector supercomputer. Data structures, vectorization and computational results are discussed.

1.1 The Generalized Network Problem

The generalized network problem (GNP) is a minimum cost flow problem with gains and losses represented by a multiplier associated with each arc. It can be formulated as a special class of linear programming problem with each column having only two nonzero elements. The problem is to minimize the total cost of flow subject to the conservation of flow at each node and an upper bound constraint for each arc.

$$\text{Minimize} \quad \sum_{j=1}^{n} \sum_{i=1}^{n} c_{ij} f_{ij}$$

$$\text{subject} \quad \sum_{k=1}^{n} (m_{ki} f_{ki} - f_{ik}) = b_i \quad \text{for } i=1,\ldots n$$

$$f_{ij} \leq u_{ij} \quad \text{for } i,j=1,\ldots n$$

$$f_{ij} \geq 0 \quad \text{for } i,j=1,\ldots n$$

Where f_{ij} is the decision variable representing the flow in the arc joining nodes i and j; c_{ij},

m_{ij} and u_{ij} respectively are the cost per unit flow, multiplier and upper bound associated with an arc from node i to j. The multiplier either amplifies ($m_{ij} \geq 1$) or attenuates ($m_{ij} \leq 1$) the flow passing through an arc which implies that the flow entering an arc is not necessarily the same as leaving that arc. The value of b_i is negative if it is a supply node, is positive if it is a demand node, and 0 otherwise. In the current paper, the lower bounds are assumed to be 0 as otherwise they can be easily transformed.

The generalized network problem has many applications in the fields of cash flow management [Crum 1977], water resource management [Bhaumik 1973], scheduling [Wagner 1979] and air traffic control [Zenios 1986], to name a few. And very often it is also formulated as a subproblem to larger problems like warehouse location, facility planning or a nonlinear network problem [Zenios 1986] etc.

1.2 Literature Review

Several algorithms, which have been developed to solve the GNP, are based on the primal and dual simplex algorithm for the linear programming by taking advantage of the special structure of the network model. This section reviews the existing sequential and parallel algorithms.

1.2.1 Sequential Algorithms

A solution method similar to the out-of-kilter algorithm was developed to solve the generalized network problem with capacitated arcs [Jewell 1962], which was later modified to guarantee the finite termination [Minieka 1972]. Later, few data structures were designed to represent the basis network in a three pointer system [Johnson 1966]. This system was then used to implement the generalized network algorithms [Glover et al. 1973]. An algorithm based on primal simplex was developed and implemented to solve pure network problems [Bradley et al. 1977], which was further extended to the generalized network [Brown and McBride 1984]. It resulted in a commercial software package entitled GENNET, which is claimed to be the fastest code on the sequential computers to date. An algorithm based on dual incremental approach was developed for the generalized network problem [Jensen and Bhaumik 1977], which was later modified to improve its computational efficiency [Jensen and Barnes 1980]. Recently a new class of algorithms for pure and generalized networks was developed based on relaxation procedures [Bertsekas and Tseng 1986]. The above mentioned algorithms are suitable for sequential computers.

1.2.2 Parallel Algorithms

To date, a couple of attempts have been made to modify and implement the currently available algorithms in parallel environment. An attempt was made to vectorize and implement the primal algorithm on CRAY computer systems [Zenios 1986]. He had difficulty in reaching his goals due to the currently available data structures to store the basis network. These data structures do not allow the updating of the basis network efficiently in a vector processing environment due to complicated indirect indexing. As a result, the algorithm was implemented in the scalar mode. A modified version of the primal algorithm was implemented on CRYSTAL multicomputer systems at University of Wisconsin [Chang et al. 1986]. Maximum efficiency was achieved for multiperiod generalized network problem with a speedup linear to the number of processors. In addition, few simple network flow algorithms were implemented on BALANCE 2000 computer, which works in a multiple instruction multiple data parallel environment [Helgason and Stewart 1987].

2. DUAL ALGORITHM

In this section, the algorithm selected for the vectorization is presented along with the modifications and its features from the point of view of vectorization. Because of the failure in vectorizing a primal based algorithm, a dual algorithm is considered. The dual algorithm requires arc scanning procedures with bulky computations to select the incoming arc into the basis. These computations are attractive from the point of view of vector processing. In addition, the computations in the updating procedures of the dual variables and basis network also support the vectorization features of the algorithm. All these above factors stand favorably for the dual algorithm to be vectorized.

2.1 Existing Dual Algorithm

The dual algorithm, to be discussed is presented in its original form here [Jensen and Barnes 1980]. It employs the procedure of flow augmentation at the minimum possible cost. The details of the algorithm are as follows.

Step 1 : A shortest route algorithm, e.g. Dijkstra algorithm , is employed to determine the shortest routes from the super source to all the other nodes [Jensen and Barnes 1980]. The only modification from the original Dijkstra algorithm is the introduction of arc multipliers, m_{ij} in the computation of dual variables.

$$v_j = (v_i + c_{ij})/m_{ij}$$

where v_j and v_i are dual variables associated with nodes j and i respectively. Compute γ_j, the node gain factor, for every node by the following formula,

$$\gamma_j = 1/\prod_{i=1}^{n} m_i$$

where 1 to n is the sequence of the arcs in the flow path.

Step 2 : The flow is augmented, in the shortest route traced, as much as possible until a forward arc (arc present in the basis in its original direction) reaches its upper bound or a reverse arc (arc present in the basis in the reverse of its original direction) reaches 0. The computation of the maximum flow augmentation, Δf is carried out as follows,

$$\Delta f = \min \{u_{ij}\gamma_i \text{ for forward arcs}; (u_{ij}-f_{ij})/\gamma_j \text{ for reverse arcs}\}$$

The saturated arc is made nonbasic. If more than one arc is saturated then the one farthest from the super sink is made nonbasic as this would mean that at most n, where n is the number of nodes in the network, degenerate iterations would occur before any flow augmentation. No flow augmentation at all signifies a degenerate iteration. The nodes are divided into two sets, N_1 and N_2. Set N_1 represents the nodes connected to the super sink in the basis and N_2 represents the remaining nodes.

Step 3 : The arcs originating in N_2 and terminating in N_1 are scanned for forward arcs if the flow is below the upper bound. The arcs originating in N_1 and terminating in N_2 are scanned for reverse arcs if the flow is positive. The arcs originating and terminating in N_1 are scanned for forward or reverse arcs and are subjected to above flow conditions, where the arcs satisfying the flow conditions are termed as admissible. The cycle factor, β which is the product of the multipliers of all the arcs in a cycle, has to be more than 1 for the inclusion of either reverse or forward arc. The computations of cycle factor and d_a, the increment in the dual variable of the super sink node, are as follows,

$$\beta = \gamma_j m_{ij}/\gamma_i$$

$d_a = ((v_i + c_a)/m_a - v_j)\gamma_i$ for $a(i,j)$ admissible, $i \in N_1, j \in N_2$

$d_{-a} = (v_j m_a - c_a - v_i)\gamma_i$ for $-a(i,j)$ admissible, $i \in N_2, j \in N_1$

$d_a = \beta/(\beta-1)((v_i + c_a)/m_a - v_j)\gamma_i$ for $a(i,j)$ admissible, $i,j \in N_1$

$d_{-a} = \beta/(\beta-1)(v_j m_a - c_a - v_i)\gamma_i$ for $-a(i,j)$ admissible, $i,j \in N_1$

Step 4 : Select the arc with the minimum d_a, denoted by d_a^{min}. If no arc can be found, then the maximum flow in the network has been obtained, otherwise admit the arc in the basis. Check that all the arcs in the new path to the super sink, originating either at the super source or a flow generating cycle, are admissible. Update the node gain factors, γ_j, and dual variables v_j for the nodes in set N_1. If all the arcs are admissible then go to Step 2, otherwise remove the inadmissible arc from the basis and go to Step 3. The inadmissibility of any arc in the flow path leads to a degenerate iteration. The dual variables are updated as follows,

$$v_j^{k+1} = v_j^k + d_a^{min} \gamma_j$$

where the superscripts k and k+1 etc. represent the number of iterations.

2.2 Modifications

Two modifications in the existing dual algorithm are made in order to improve its efficiency and conform it to the vector processing environment. These modifications are based on the special structures of the basis network, which are often encountered in its update. They are as follows.

1. If the arc leaving the basis, i.e. the saturated arc, is the same as the one that entered the basis then the basis network does not require any changes. In addition, the arc scanning operations for the subsequent iteration are greatly reduced as the d_a^{k+1} for the iteration k+1, where k is the current iteration, is updated by subtracting d_a^{min} from the d_a^k of all the candidate arcs of the kth iteration. This can be proved as follows. The arc entering the basis alters the dual variables of the nodes only in the set N_1 as per the formula stated in Step 4 of the existing dual algorithm. Substituting these updated dual variables in the formulae for the computations of d_a in Step 3 of the dual algorithm, one can prove that the difference between the d_a's of the consecutive iterations is only d_a^{min}. The candidate arcs for both the iterations also remain the same, except the one entering and leaving the basis, as the sets N_1^k and N_1^{k+1} are identical.

2. If the set N_1^{k+1} is a subset of N_1^k then the set of candidate arcs for the iteration k+1 is a subset of the set of candidate arcs for the iteration k. This again greatly reduces the scanning operations and can be proved as follows.

As N_1^{k+1} is a subset of N_1^k, N_2^k must be subset of N_2^{k+1}, as they are complimentary sets. The set of candidate arcs for entry into the basis, C can be divided into three mutually exclusive subsets such as,

$C_1 = \{a_{ij} | i \in N_2, j \in N_1\}$

$C_2 = \{a_{ij} | i \in N_1, j \in N_2\}$

$C_3 = \{a_{ij} | i,j \in N_1\}$

Similarly, the set C_3^k, for the kth iteration can be divided into three mutually exclusive sets such as,

$C_{31}^k = \{a_{ij} | i \in N_2^{k+1}, j \in N_1^{k+1}\}$

$C_{32}^k = \{a_{ij} | i \in N_1^{k+1}, j \in N_2^{k+1}\}$

$C_{33}^k = \{a_{ij} | i,j \in N_1^{k+1}\}$

As seen from the above conditions and the definitions, C_1^{k+1} is a subset of $C_1^k+C_{31}^k$ and C_2^{k+1} is a subset of $C_2^k+C_{32}^k$ and C_{33}^k is identical to C_3^{k+1} by its definition. As $C_1^{k+1}+C_2^{k+1}+C_3^{k+1} = C^{k+1}$, it is concluded that C^{k+1} is a subset of C^k.

This modification is a particularly great improvement as the dual algorithm is prone to degenerate iterations which lead to very time consuming scanning operations without any flow gain. Degenerate iterations lead to the situation described above due to the policy adopted in the selection of an arc to be removed from the basis in case of the ocurrence of multiple saturated arcs in a flow path.

3. IMPLEMENTATION OF THE ALGORITHM

The dual algorithm discussed in the previous section is implemeted on CRAY X-MP/24. The following sections discuss the data structures designed for the storage of the basis network and other network variables, the vectorization procedures with the computational experiments and the performance evaluation.

3.1 Data Structures

The data structure design is the first stepping stone in the implementation of any algorithm in an efficient manner. To start with, the network is stored in a forward star notation [Jensen and Barnes 1980]. That is, a node length vector IARC2 points to

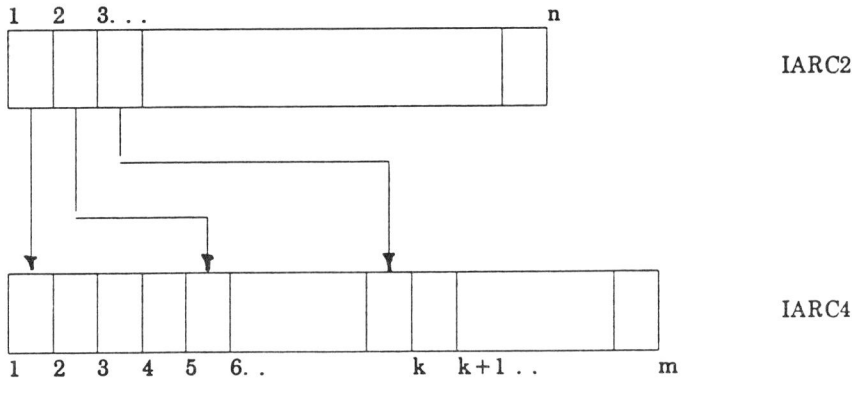

Figure 1 Forward Star Notation

the starting location of the arcs in an arc length vector IARC4, originating from the node corresponding to that position. This procedure stores the network in a very compact manner and even the computational operations are easy to perform. The arc parameters such as cost per unit flow, upper bound and multiplier are stored in three arc length vectors ARC5, ARC6 and ARC7 respectively. The flow corresponding to each arc is stored in an arc length vector AFLO. A node length vector VOLT1 stores the dual variables for each node and another two node length vectors IVOLT2 and IVOLT4 store the preceding node and the arc in the basis for that node. The path from the super sink to the super source is traced back and is stored in vectors ITRAL1 and ITRAL2, for nodes and arcs respectively, which can at most be of node length size. A node length vector TRAL8 stores the node gain factors. To differentiate between the nodes in set N_1 and N_2 an indicator system is developed which requires two node length vectors IVOLT and ITP.

In addition to the above vectors, a few others are required for the scanning operations. An arc length vector FR stores the computed d_a for each candidate arc entering the basis. Vector IND stores the indicator for each arc, computed from the vectors IVOLT , ITP and few other parameters. ARC12, an arc length vector stores the cycle factor associated with each candidate arc, if that arc is entered in the basis. Few additional vectors are required in the GATHER and SCATTER operations. Many of these vectors gather the information from the larger data structures, as required, to perform the necessary computations for the scanning operations. Totally, about 15 node length and 15 arc length vectors are required in the implemented code. As the CRAY X-MP/24 has a large amount of memory, speed is prioritized over the memory requirements.

3.2 Vectorization

The dual algorithm is coded in CFT(CRAY FORTRAN). It starts with the computation of the shortest path tree. These computations are vectorized with the help of the vectors IARC2 and IARC4. A temporary vector TEMP of arc length is introduced to store the temporary dual variables associated with the head of each arc. Once the node is permanently labeled all the arcs terminating at it are disabled by assigning a very large negative value to its temporary dual variable. At the same time the preceding arc and node of the permanently labeled node are also recorded. All these operations are performed in one sweep and at most n-1 DO loop iterations are required to complete the computations. The flow path from the super sink to the super source is traced back by using information in IVOLT2 and IVOLT4. The tracing operation is totally scalar but is not very time consuming as it is performed only once in the algorithm. Similarly the shortest path computations are also performed only once in subroutine SHORTD.

The execution of the above step is followed by the computation of the maximum possible flow augmentation in the basis network. Using the traced flow path, the arc multipliers are gathered for the arcs in the path to compute the node gain factors.

Using the formula stated in Step 2 of the dual algorithm the maximum flow augmentation is computed. This operation is conditionally vectorized by using a compiler directive CVMGT. The flows in the arcs are updated by multiplying the augmented amount of flow by the node gain factor of their head nodes and adding that up to the previous flows.

The nodes in set N_1 have to be segregated from the rest of the nodes. Based on the three cases of whether N_1^{k+1} is a subset, superset or identical to N_1^k, a segregation procedure is performed. The nodes are totally scanned and segregated only for the very first iteration. Subsequently, the nodes are either deleted or added to N_1 depending on the case. All these operations are conditionally vectorized and only in the worst case one might perform n^2 computations. The updating of the indicators, denoting the status of that node in set N_1, and the node gain factors is also integrated with these operations. Initially, these operations were grouped in a separate subroutine but were found to have overbearing overheads in the transfer of the arrays and hence were merged with the mainstream subroutine DUAL.

An indicator system is developed to segregate the candidate arcs from the rest. The candidate arcs have to satisfy various conditions such as flow requirements depending on the orientation status and cycle factor requirement, as stated earlier. To start with, all the out-of-basis arcs joining sets N_1 and N_2 and within N_1 are separated using the indicator arrays IVOLT and ITP. Then these arcs are tested for their flow requirements as stated in Step 3 of the dual algorithm. The indicators are updated to segregate the admissible ones from the inadmissible ones. The cycle factors are computed if that arc lies completely in set N_1. The arcs with a cycle factor 1 are discarded from the candidate arcs list. Then the information such as dual variables, node gain factors is gathered for the tail and head nodes of the candidate arcs. The computations of the d_a are carried out by employing the formulae in Step 3 of the dual algorithm. The arc with the minimum d_a is entered in the basis. These operations are conditionally vectorized using the indicators associated with each arc and are performed in one sweep.

A few computational experiments are performed to take advantage of the special cases, as discussed earlier. The filtering of the candidate arcs can be carried out in stages requiring fewer GATHER and SCATTER operations. To shed some light on this, the first stage filters out all the arcs present in the basis and the ones in set N_2 from the set of candidate arcs. The second stage removes all the arcs which do not satisfy the respective flow conditions, as mentioned earlier, whereas the third stage deletes the arcs with cycle factors between 0 and 1, both inclusive. This procedure improved the solution time at the cost of extra memory as the information from one stage to another needs to be carried forward. The first modification is easily implemented with one vectorized DO loop. The second one is partly integrated with the node segregation operations and partly with the filtering operations. The dual increment, d_a, of the candidate arcs in sets C_1^k, C_2^k and

C_{33}^k are updated in a manner similar to the first modification and is integrated with the node segregation operation. In addition to the above, the arcs in sets C_{31}^k and C_{32}^k need filtering as some of them become ineligible for the candidate list.

The entry of a new arc in the basis requires the updating of the basis tree, node gain factors and dual variables for the nodes in set N_1. The updating of the basis tree is similar to the node segregation operations and carried out in a similar fashion. The difference arises due to formation of a flow generating cycle, but it can be taken care of with a small modification in the previous procedures. These operations are also vectorized in a similar way to node segregation operations. The updating of the node gain factors requires the gathering of the multipliers of the arcs in the new flow path to carry out the operation. The dual variables are updated by employing the formula in step 4. It is easily vectorized using the vectors VOLT1, TRAL8 and TRAL9. But before augmenting the flow again, the new path is checked for the admissibility of all the arcs. Again an indicator system, similar to the previous one, is employed to carry out the operations in one sweep.

Most of the dual algorithm with modifications is implemented in a vector mode. The memory requirement is almost double the one for any primal or dual simplex code on sequential computers due to large usage of arrays in vector processing. But, CRAY systems have equally large memory capacity to deal with and it is justifiable at the gain of large computational speed.

3.3 Computational Results

The performance of the vectorized code is evaluated by solving benchmark problems generated by NETGEN [Klingman et al. 1974]. Its performance is compared with that of GENNET, as it is claimed to be the fastest code on the sequential computers [McBride and Brown 1984]. Another reason for this comparison is that no vectorized code for the generalized network is available so far.

The NETGEN problems are converted to generalized networks by incorporating the arc multipliers as unity. NETGENG is another code to generate generalized network problems [Glover et al. 1976], but its unavailability required us to adopt the above strategy. Out of 40 standard problems, first 10 are transportation problems, the next 5 are assignment problems and the remaining ones are transshipment problems with and without capacitated arcs. As more efficient specialized algorithms are available for the assignment and the transportation problems, they are not utilized in this evaluation of the vectorized code. The vectorized dual algorithm is coded in CRAY FORTRAN, a modification of FORTRAN 77 with some additional functions, and is implemented using the compiler CFT 1.15.

The solution times for the vectorized dual algorithm and GENNET are gathered using the FLOWTRACE option. These times are listed in Table 1. Analyzing the solution times for the vectorized algorithm it can be infered that the solution times are proportional to both the number of arcs and nodes, but for fixed number of nodes they seem to have an increasing trend with the number of arcs. The explanation of these trends is based on the facts that the arc scanning procedure and the related computations are the most time consuming portions of the algorithm and the time consumed is obviously proportional to the total number of arcs. But, the shortest path computations, basis tree update and node segregation procedures are a function of the total number of nodes, so even though these operations do not consume as much as the arc scanning operations, they do seem to increase the solution time for groups of problems with increasing number of nodes. This is evident from the three groups of problems with 400, 1000 and 1500 nodes respectively. Among the groups, percent of capacitated arcs and range of upper bounds also influence the solution times as more capacitated arcs with lower upper bounds imply more constraints, resulting in more iterations. These trends are not very pronounced in the solution times of GENNET except the fact that the problem size, in general, does have an effect on its performance.

Comparing the performance of the vectorized code and GENNET, problems 16 to 19 have a high performance ratio, where performance ratio is defined as the ratio of GENNET solution time to vectorized algorithm's solution time. Among these four problems, the ratio has deteriorated for the problems with a greater number of arcs. Problems 20 to 23 have higher percentage of capacitated arcs and the performance ratio has plumeted, especially for problems 21 and 23 which have a larger number of arcs also. Problems 24 to 27 have regained superiority over GENNET with a rise in performance ratio even though the percent of capacitated arcs is higher. But, the total number of arcs are comparatively lower than in the problems 20 through 23, which may have brought about the change. The two problem groups 28 through 31 and 32 through 35, have shown a decline in the performance ratio. Problems 36 through 40 are large problems and have substantially large solution times. Due to some unknown reasons GENNET terminated these problems as infeasible ones. The solution times of 36 and 37 are substantially greater than the remaining three and are attributed to large amount of supply, which requires more iterations. The number of arcs and nodes have increased substantially over the past sets of problems but the problems are totally incapacitated. The behavior of the performance ratio is an irregular one and this irregularity can be explained by the fact that the two algorithms operate in entirely different fashions. So the organization of the problem has different effects on the performance of the two codes.

Another measure of performance for the vectorized code is the number of

NETGEN Problem	Solution times, seconds		Performance Ratio	Objective Function
	Vectorized Code	GENNET		
16	0.193	0.587	3.041	64152588
17	0.331	0.813	2.456	35832837
18	0.161	0.574	3.565	61241753
19	0.294	0.662	2.251	35187351
20	0.170	0.600	3.529	56978634
21	0.538	0.861	1.600	39632257
22	0.165	0.583	3.624	54345977
23	0.459	0.826	1.799	38627263
24	0.301	1.194	3.966	132625937
25	0.392	1.014	2.586	54073398
26	0.170	0.660	3.882	103006170
27	0.300	0.783	2.610	49407575
28	0.999	1.884	1.885	142590546
29	1.214	1.965	1.618	116502592
30	1.770	2.087	1.179	90199932
31	1.523	2.111	1.386	79587259
32	2.544	2.941	1.156	188897997
33	2.453	3.088	1.258	214412840
34	2.726	3.350	1.228	167085049
35	2.976	3.152	1.059	149118111
36	94.494	DNR	...	1010922256
37	95.662	DNR	...	363662156
38	59.548	DNR	...	87428534
39	73.663	DNR	...	521601882
40	53.569	DNR	...	189285494

DNR- did not run

Table 1. SOLUTION TIMES

MFLOPS achieved. PERFTRACE option is used in measuring the MFLOPS for the vectorized code. The SHORTD subroutine, which contributes about 10% of the total time, has achieved a steady performance of 45 to 50 MFLOPS for all the problems solved. This is considered to be an average performance by previous investigators [Zenios and Mulvey 1987] and one can claim that the shortest path computations are successfully vectorized. The DUAL subroutine has a peak performance in excess of 54 MFLOPS, but has wider fluctuations than SHORTD. Its performance is very much dependent on the size of the problem, with greater MFLOPS achieved with larger problems. DUAL has quite a few GATHER and SCATTER operations, which have a peak performance of 30 MFLOPS, and they seem to be influencing the performance of the smaller problems much more than the relatively larger ones.

The vectorized dual algorithm is only tested with the problems having arc multipliers as unity but, the only difference between these problems and the ones with nonunity arc multipliers, is the ocurrence of a flow generating cycle. The basis management is affected by the ocurrence of a cycle but is taken care of with little modification. This particular change does not alter the performance of the code in a drastic manner and one can claim that the current testing of the problems is adequate to conclude its performance.

4.CONCLUSION

The vectorized dual algorithm is implemented on a CRAY X-MP/24 and its performance is evaluated using NETGEN and GENNET. The vectorized code always maintains its superiority over GENNET, even though the performance ratio fluctuates widely. The peak speed in excess of 54 MFLOPS is certainly a satisfactory one for the dual algorithm. Based on this performance one can claim to have the dual algorithm successfully vectorized. As GENNET is superior to the original dual algorithm on sequential computers, we are reasonably certain that the performance of the vectorized code would have been much superior to the original dual algorithm.

This research is an attempt to modify a currently available algorithm and implement it in vector mode. Still, a 'truly' parallel algorithm, either for the vector or multiprocessor environment is yet to be developed. The advent of new supercomputers will be a major motivation to proceed in this direction. In addition, no one can claim that this is the optimum performance of the vectorized dual code and one can certainly improve it by designing new data structures or by developing new modifications. The same can also be true for the primal algorithm. All these developments can also stimulate the formulation and implementation of larger practical problems.

ACKNOWLEDGMENT

The supercomputer time of this work was provided by National Science Foundation Engineering supercomputer Initiation Grant ECS-8515804 and Alabama Supercomputer Network. Other supporters include the College of Engineering and the Research Grants Committee of the University of Alabama.

REFERENCES

The Alabama Supercomputer Center (1988), *Alabama Supercomputer Network User's Manual*, 1st Edition, Boeing Computer Services, BCSASN01, Feb.

Bertsekas, D.P. and P. Tseng (1986), "Relaxation Methods for Minimum Cost Ordinary and Generalized Network Flow Problems," Technical Report LIDS-P- 1462, Laboratory for Information and Decision Systems and the Operations Research Center, M.I.T., Cambridge, Mass., Sept.

Bhaumik, G. (1973), *Optimum Operating Policies of a Water Distribution System with Losses*, Ph.D. dissertation, The University of Texas at Austin, Tex.

Bradley, G.H., G.G.Brown and G.W.Graves (1977), "Design and Implementation of Large Scale Primal Transshipments Algorithms," *Management Science 20*, 1 (Sept.), 1-32.

Brown, G.G., and R.D. McBride (1984), "Solving Generalized Networks," *Management Science 30*, 12 (Dec.), 1497-1523.

Chang, M.D., M. Engquist, R. Finkel and R.R. Meyer (1987), "A Parallel Algorithm for Generalized Networks," Technical Report 642, Department of Computer Science, University of Wisconsin, Madison, Wis., Mar.

Crum, R. (1977), "Cash Management in the Multinational Firm: A Constrained Generalized Network Approach," Working Paper, The University of Florida, Gainsville, Fla.

Glover, F., D. Klingman, and J. Stutz (1973), "Extensions of the Augmented Predecessor Index Method to Generalized Network Problems," *Transportation Science 7*, 4 (Nov.), 377-384.

Glover, F., J.Hultz, D.Klingman and J.Stutz (1976), "A New Computer-Based Planning Tool," Research Report CCS289, Center of Cybernetic Studies, Univ. of Texas at Austin, Tex., Dec.

Helgason, R.V. and D.B.Stewart (1987), "Implementing Simple Network Flow Algorithms on Parallal Computers," ORSA Conference, St.Louis, Mo., Oct.

Jensen, P.A., and G. Bhaumik (1977), " A Flow Augmentation Approach to the Network with Gains Minimum Cost Flow Problem," *Management Science 23*, 6 (June),

631-643.

Jensen, P.A., and J.W. Barnes (1980), *Network Flow Programming*, John Wiley & Sons, New York, N.Y.

Jewell, W.S. (1962), "Optimal Flow Through Network With Gains," *Operations Research 10*, 4 (July-Aug.), 476-499.

Johnson, E. L. (1966), "Networks and Basic Solutions," *Operations Research 14*, 10 (July-Aug.), 619-623.

Klingman, D., A. Napier and J.Stutz (1974), " NETGEN: A Program for Generating Large Scale Capacitated Assignment, Transportation, and Minimum Cost Flow Problems," *Management Science 20*, 5 (Jan.), 814-821.

Minieka, E. (1972), "Optimal Flow in a Network with Gains," *INFOR 10*, 2 (June), 171-178.

Wagner, H. (1979), *Principles of Operations Research*, Prentice-Hall, Inc., Englewood Cliffs, N.J.

Zenios, S.A. (1986), *Sequential and Parallel Algorithms for Convex Generalized Network Problems and Related Applications*, Ph.D. dissertation, Civil Engineering Department, Princeton University, Princeton, N.J.

Zenios, S.A., and J.M. Mulvey (1987), " Vectorization and Multitasking of Nonlinear Network Programming Algorithms," Report 87-03-03, Civil Engineering Department, Princeton University, Princeton, N.J., Mar.

VECTORIZATION OF TRANSPORTATION NETWORK EQUILIBRIUM ASSIGNMENT CODES

HANI S. MAHMASSANI AND KYRIACOS C. MOUSKOS
Department of Civil Engineering, The University of Texas at Austin
Austin, Texas 78712

ABSTRACT

Network equilibrium problems occupy a central role in transportation science and transportation planning applications, and are an essential component of solution procedures for the combinatorial network design problem. This paper assesses the potential of supercomputers to address large scale problems with enhanced realism and greater detail in system representation. Codes for the solution of two network equilibrium formulations (Frank-Wolfe algorithm for the single-class user equilibrium problem, and the diagonalization algorithm for multiple user classes with asymmetric interactions) are vectorized and tested on a CRAY X-MP/24 supercomputer. Only local vectorization by limited recoding of existing programs is performed. Computational tests are performed on actual as well as on randomly generated networks. Significant improvements are achieved relative to the unvectorized performance on the CRAY and on large mainframes, with encouraging implications for large-scale applications as well as for future developments on the dynamic assignment and the network design problems.

1. INTRODUCTION

The network equilibrium assignment problem arises in connection with a variety of transportation planning activities, including the evaluation of capital improvement projects and the analysis of operational strategies in transportation networks. It has seen considerable theoretical, methodological and computational advances in the past two decades, leading to efficient algorithms, and increasingly realistic tractable problem formulations. However, further developments and wider application of the available algorithms have been hampered by several limitations that affect:

1) The size of the networks that can be addressed, as multimodal urban transportation networks typically consist of several thousand nodes and links.

2) The level of detail in system representation; often, considerable effort is expanded on aggregating features of a physical network in order to reduce the computational requirements, usually at the expense of accuracy and policy sensitivity.

3) The realism of the assumptions underlying the problem formulation; problems with multiple user classes and asymmetric link interactions are notoriously more demanding computationally than the basic single class formulation with no interactions.

4) The extent of scenario testing and sensitivity analysis performed in actual applications, which is of particular concern given the political elements present in the context in which planning decisions are made and debated.

5) Solution of the network design problem, which is an np-hard combinatorial problem. The network assignment routine is repeatedly executed in the search processes in both exact algorithms and heuristics for this problem.

Developments in computing hardware and system architectures provide opportunities for advances in methodologies for the analysis and design of large-scale networks and enhance our ability to overcome the above limitations. The CRAY X-MP series of supercomputers, widely available to the US academic community, offers a dimension of parallelism achieved by vector or matrix operations of an algorithm (vectorization). Descriptions of its hardware aspects that are pertinent to a programmer of OR applications are given in [Chen 1983; Zenios and Mulvey 1986]. Compilers are available to "vectorize" a particular code, by identifying those portions that can be executed in parallel. Understandably, compilers are risk averse, and do not at present possess sufficient knowledge to identify essentially vectorizable operations that have been programmed using constructs that could contain dependencies. As such, the typical FORTRAN code for network analysis is likely to substantially underutilize available supercomputer capabilities. It is usually possible to take fuller advantage of the latter by modifying, or vectorizing the code. Three levels of vectorization can be distinguished, in order of increasing effort [Zenios and Mulvey 1986]: 1) local software vectorization, where the program is re-examined only in its parts and subroutines; 2) global software vectorization, affecting algorithm implementation and data structures; and 3) overall algorithm vectorization, where the solution algorithm itself is conceived to take advantage of the machine architecture.

The principal objective of our effort is to test the performance of vectorized codes for network equilibrium problems, and assess the computational improvements that can be achieved by local vectorization. The results have implications for research and practice, in terms of the size and complexity of problems that can be addressed, and for the future development of solution approaches to the network design problem. As such, the relevance of the results should not be limited to the transportation domain, but also include network problems in telecommunications, and spatial equilibrium problems in economics.

2. THE NETWORK EQUILIBRIUM PROBLEM AND ALGORITHMS

Two problem classes are addressed in this work: 1) the basic formulation of the network User Equilibrium (UE) problem with a single class of users; and 2) the more general UE problem with multiple user classes and asymmetric interactions. A very brief description of these problems and their solution algorithms is given below; see Friesz [1985] for a recent review and Sheffi [1985] for a textbook presentation.

2.1 Single Class UE Problem and F-W Algorithm

Given a known matrix of origin-destination flows, a network of directed links connecting nodes, and link performance functions that describe the (usually nonlinear) dependence of link costs on the corresponding link flows, this problem consists of finding the flows (and travel times) on the individual links of the network so as to achieve certain equilibrium conditions, namely that no driver can improve her travel time by unilaterally switching routes. Exact solution algorithms for this problem are based on Beckman's equivalent mathematical programming formulation. The most widely used solution algorithm is based on the Frank-Wolfe or convex combinations method, which is well documented elsewhere [Sheffi 1985].

At each iteration, the algorithm finds a search direction by solving a linearized approximation, then solves for the optimal move size along that direction. The direction finding step is equivalent to an all-or-nothing assignment, where all flow between an origin and a given destination is assigned to the shortest path in between, which requires repeated application of a one-node-to-all-nodes shortest path routine. An additional source of computational cost is the line search to find the optimal move size, and the evaluation of the nonlinear travel cost (link performance) functions. Letting $t_a(.)$ denote the link performance function for link a, the principal steps of the algorithms are:

STEP 0: Initialization. Perform all-or-nothing assignment based on free flow travel times.
STEP 1: Update. Set $t_a^n = t_a(X_a^n)$, $\forall a$.
STEP 2: Direction finding. Perform all-or-nothing assignment based on $\{t_a^n\}$. This yields a set of (auxiliary) link flows $\{y_a^n\}$.
STEP 3: Line search. Find optimal move size α_n.
STEP 4: Move. Set $X_a^{n+1} = X_a^n + \alpha_n (y_a^n - X_a^n)$, $\forall a$.
STEP 5: Convergence test. If a convergence criterion is met, STOP (the current solution is the set of equilibrium link flows); otherwise, set n = n+1 and GO TO STEP 1.

In the code, the characteristics of the problem are input in TRAFASN. STEP 0 takes place in subroutine UE, which controls the main steps of the algorithm. Following initialization of all paths to zero flows, subroutine AON is called to initialize link flows to zero. All travel time computations are performed by calling function COSTFN. Given the travel times, subroutine SHPATH is called, as many times as the number of origins, to identify the shortest path for each O-D pair, so as to perform all-or-nothing assignment. The calculation of the travel times and the allocation of the flows to the links correspond to STEP 1 and STEP 2, respectively. STEP 3 is controlled by subroutine BISECT, where the move size is determined using the bisection line search method. This move size is used in STEP 4, followed by the convergence test (STEP 5), in subroutine UE. Program output is controlled by subroutine DUMP.

2.2 Asymmetric Interactions and the Diagonalization Algorithm

In this problem, the travel cost t_a on link a is a function not only of the flow on link a, but of the entire vector x of link flows. The problem arises when several classes of users (e.g. cars, trucks and buses) share the use of the physical right-of-way, and is therefore important to the evaluation of truck-related infrastructure improvements [Mahmassani et al. 1987]. A direct algorithm known as the diagonalization algorithm is the most common approach for its solution [Abdulaal and Leblanc 1979]. At each iteration, it requires that all cross-link effects be fixed at their current levels for each link, resulting in a tractable single class UE subproblem (with no interactions). Because several F-W iterations are required to solve the diagonalized subproblem, the algorithm's computational demands are high, seriously hampering its use in practice. The computer code for this algorithm, especially its streamlined versions [Sheffi 1985; Mahmassani and Mouskos 1988], is comprised of the same subroutines as the single class code, modified to take into account the division of traffic into classes. The previously listed subroutines and functions are renamed, in the respective order previously mentioned, as UETRDIA, UED, AONUED, TRCOST, SHPUED, BISUED, and DUMPUED. In this paper, computational results for this code are reported only for one network, but the results of the experiments with the single class UE code are almost directly applicable to it.

3. APPLICATION OF VECTORIZATION GUIDELINES TO UE CODES

We highlight here some of the more effective steps followed in modifying the codes to enhance vectorized performance, and summarize the results obtained in the initial tests performed on a medium-sized network with 182 O-D pairs, 128 nodes, and 336 links, similar to one used in earlier experiments with the diagonalization algorithm [Mahmassani and Mouskos 1988]. A maximum of 500 iterations were allowed before the algorithm was terminated for any run with this network. All runs were executed on the CRAY X-MP/24, using the CFT77 FORTRAN compiler (written in PASCAL), which we found to be superior to the other available compiler (CFT, written in CRAY assembly language).

Table 1 presents the execution time summary for the single class UE code on the test network with and without compiler vectorization, revealing an overall reduction of 32% without any program modification. The same problem required 79 secs on a CYBER CDC 170/750 mainframe, yielding ratios of 5.3:1 and 7.7:1 (mainframe to CRAY without and with compiler vectorization, respectively). More relevant to local vectorization efforts is the relative reduction for each subroutine. The reductions for functions COSTFN and FINT were less than 5%, whereas the shortest path routine vectorized quite well. Thus most of our effort was directed at the obvious opportunities in COSTFN, BISECT and FINT (TRAFASN did not vectorize well either, but does not contain any algorithmic steps, so was not addressed in this effort). Local modifications of the shortest path routine did not

SUBROUTINE	No Compiler Vectorization	With Compiler Vectorization	Modified Code With Compiler Vect.
AON	2.559 (17.07)	0.917 (8.99)	0.847 (25.66)
BISECT	2.412 (16.09)	1.517 (14.87)	0.641 (19.43)
COSTFN	6.115 (40.79)	5.785 (56.72)	* *
DUMP	0.202 (1.35)	0.201 (1.97)	0.206 (6.23)
FINT	0.521 (3.47)	0.487 (4.78)	--- ---
SHPATH	2.827 (18.86)	1.055 (10.34)	1.056 (31.99)
TRAFASN	0.050 (0.33)	0.048 (0.47)	0.048 (1.47)
UE	0.304 (2.03)	0.191 (1.87)	0.505 (15.23)
Total Execution Time	14.990 (100%)	10.199 (100%)	3.301 (100%)

*Note that COSTFN was placed on line in BISECT in the modified code

Table 1. Summary of Execution Times, in seconds, (and Percent of Total Execution Time) for the Single Class UE Code.

yield significant improvement; more global effort may be required. Further confirmation of the relative vectorizing performance of the compiler was subsequently obtained on two of the large random networks described in the next section (Table 2).

To improve the targeted subroutines, dependencies that inhibit vectorization were removed, especially in the evaluation of the link performance functions. These were placed on line in BISECT and elsewhere instead of repeated calls to COSTFN as such calls in a loop may inhibit vectorization. Further dependencies were removed by including in the same equation the calculation of its various terms (instead of separate equations), replacing repetitive divisions by multiplications (computationally less demanding on the CRAY), removing several IF THEN ELSE and GO TO statements, and subdividing some loops into smaller ones [UT CHPC 1987; Mouskos and Mahmassani 1989].

The execution time summary on the test network after these changes is shown in Table 1. Remarkably, the combined time for BISECT and COSTFN (the latter now folded into the former) dropped by 91%, total execution time by 68% relative to the unmodified but compiler vectorized code (78% relative to non-compiler vectorized). The speedup relative to the CDC becomes of the order of 24:1. As noted, local improvements were not

	Random Net 9 (1000 Nodes, 4266 Links, 100 Centroids)			Random Net 19 (4500 Nodes, 18908 Links, 300 Centroids)		
SUBROUTINE	No Comp. Vect.	With Comp. Vect.	% Reduction	No Comp. Vect.	With Comp. Vect.	% Reduction
AON	10.653	4.323	59.4	85.533	35.355	58.7
BISECT	2.838	1.814	36.1	11.096	7.451	32.8
COSTFN	7.482	6.927	7.4	29.877	28.278	5.4
DUMP	0.078	0.037	52.6	0.348	0.166	52.3
FINT	0.649	0.590	9.1	2.601	2.422	6.9
SHPATH	47.404	20.144	57.5	455.189	194.889	57.2
TRAFASN	1.430	1.388	2.9	10.086	9.957	1.3
UE	0.371	0.221	40.4	1.477	0.920	37.7
Total Time	70.905	35.445	50.0	598.207	279.439	53.3

Table 2. Summary of Execution Times, in Seconds, for Unmodified Single Class UE Code on Two Random Test Networks with and without Compiler Vectorization.

SUBROUTINE	No Compiler Vectorization	With Compiler Vectorization	Modified Code With Compiler Vect.
ANOUED	0.949 (4.89%)	0.448 (3.45%)	0.299 (5.18%)
BISUED	2.795 (14.40%)	1.983 (15.25%)	0.795 (13.76%)
DUMPUED	0.257 (1.32%)	0.136 (1.04%)	0.187 (3.24%)
SHPUED	8.429 (43.41%)	3.712 (28.56%)	3.647 (63.11%)
TRCOST	5.945 (30.62%)	5.865 (45.13%)	-*- -*-
UED	0.239 (1.23%)	0.084 (0.64%)	0.084 (1.45%)
UETRIA	0.802 (4.13%)	0.770 (5.92%)	0.766 (13.26%)
Total Execution Time	19.414 (100%)	12.998 (100%)	5.779 (100%)

*Note that COSTFN was placed on line in BISECT in the modified code

Table 3. Summary of Execution Times in Seconds, (and Percent of Total Effort) for the Diagonalization Code on Two-Class Test Network.

successful for the shortest path routine, which was otherwise vectorizing relatively well. The overall improvement will depend on the extent to which this routine is called in a particular problem.

Similar modifications of the diagonalization code were tested with two classes of vehicles (cars and trucks). A separate copy of the physical network is created for each class; the interactions between classes sharing a physical link are represented through the link performance functions in the individual copies [Mahmassani et al. 1987]. The resulting network has 364 O-D pairs, 1400 nodes, and 3912 links. A total of 25 iterations were allowed before the code was terminated for all runs. The results, summarized in Table 3, indicate a non-vectorized to vectorized ratio in excess of 336%. The code executed in 126 seconds on the CDC mainframe, for a ratio of about 22:1. Greater improvement was achieved for the targeted subroutines BISUED and TRCOST.

The above test networks are realistic networks developed in previous transportation applications, but they do not provide a sufficient basis for generalization. This motivated the experiments on randomly generated networks described in the next section.

4. EXPERIMENTS ON RANDOM NETWORKS

For a given number of nodes and O-D pairs, the generator developed for this study randomizes the topology of the network and the characteristics of its links (length, capacity, speed limit, and parameters of the link performance functions). An essential feature of a transportation network is that it be connected, i.e., with at least one path between any two of its nodes. This was achieved by a path connecting all nodes from 1 to N consecutively, by specifying directed links from node n to nodes n-1 and n+1, for n=2,...,N-1, in addition to links from node 1 to node 2 and from N to N-1[†].

Two groups of 10 networks each were generated. The first consists of networks 1-10, each with 1000 nodes and 100 centroids (9900 O-D pairs), and the second of

---

[†] A more general approach would be to generate a random path by "shuffling" the nodes from 1 to N.

networks 11-20, with 4500 nodes and 300 centroids (89700 O-D pairs). O-D flows for the first group ranged from 10 to 500 vehicles, and from 5 to 100 for the second. These were set so as to produce reasonable volume to capacity ratios (an index of congestion) on the links. The number of links in the resulting networks ranged from 4266 to 4352 for the first group, and 18898 to 19026 for the second.

The main objectives of the tests are to assess the effectiveness of the code vectorization improvements and identify the levels and variability of execution times for large-scale networks. Given the high computational requirements of these experiments, only the single-class UE code is tested here, though the results are expected to transfer to the diagonalization code as well. Each network was solved to convergence using the original and the modified codes (with compiler vectorization in both cases). The results of the two sets of runs are shown in Tables 4 and 5, respectively, for the 1000-node networks, and in Tables 6 and 7, and for the 4500-node networks. Each table includes: execution times (for each subroutine, and overall, for each network, as well as the average and standard deviation over all networks in a particular group), number of generated links, number of F-W iterations until convergence, and CPU per iteration.

In Tables 5 and 7, the percent improvement in execution time due to the code modifications (i.e. relative to the results in Tables 4 and 6, respectively) is reported for the overall execution time and for the targeted subroutines (BISECT and COSTFN). The results are consistent with those of the previous section. The targeted subroutines exhibit the same remarkable 92.6 percent reduction . Of course, as the relative importance of the shortest path routine increases with network size and with the number of O-D centroids, the reduction in overall execution time will suffer. This reduction is 23.6% on average for the 1000-node networks (Table 5), and only 11.7% for the 4500-node networks (Table 7). Relative to the unmodified code without compiler vectorization, and using Networks 9 and 19 as examples (from Table 2), the percent reductions are 61.6% and 53.3%, respectively.

Much of the variability in total execution time across the networks in each group is due to the different number of iterations to reach convergence. The CPU per iteration is reported in Tables 4-7 (only subroutines AON, BISECT and SHPATH for the improved code and AON, BISECT, COSTFN and SHPATH for the non-improved code are used in the calculation because the other routines are not included in the iterative process of the algorithm). The average CPU/iteration are 1.52 and 12.1 seconds, respectively for the first and second network groups.

In summary, the local code modification has achieved its objective, replicating for the random networks the same percent improvement in the targeted subroutines as in the initial test network. The impact on overall performance depends on network size and number of O-D centroids, which affect the frequency of execution of the shortest path

SUBROUTINE	Net 1	Net 2	Net 3	Net 4	Net 5	Net 6	Net 7	Net 8	Net 9	Net 10	Average	S.D.	% Effort
AON	5.138	4.154	4.712	4.216	4.803	4.668	3.447	3.558	4.323	4.251	4.327	0.534	11.9
BISECT	2.524	1.884	2.149	1.929	2.265	2.117	1.419	1.558	1.814	1.911	1.957	0.326	5.4
COSTFN	9.289	6.957	8.110	7.209	8.437	7.838	5.468	5.822	6.927	7.114	7.317	1.156	20.1
FINT	0.781	0.591	0.686	0.612	0.715	0.666	0.470	0.499	0.590	0.606	0.622	0.094	1.7
DUMP	0.039	0.039	0.037	0.038	0.038	0.038	0.037	0.038	0.037	0.038	0.038	0.001	0.1
SHPATH	23.941	20.674	22.140	20.032	22.133	21.903	17.465	16.837	20.144	19.432	20.471	2.193	56.3
TRAFASN	1.417	1.414	1.396	1.394	1.406	1.403	1.400	1.406	1.388	1.401	1.402	0.009	3.8
UE	0.304	0.230	0.262	0.236	0.275	0.257	0.176	0.191	0.221	0.233	0.239	0.038	0.6
TOTAL	43.432	35.943	39.491	35.781	40.073	38.890	29.881	29.910	35.445	34.986	36.383	4.305	
No. Links	4338	4324	4322	4320	4326	4310	4352	4318	4266	4292	4316.8	23.8	
Iterations	28	21	25	22	26	24	17	18	22	22			
CPU/Iteration	1.46	1.60	1.48	1.52	1.45	1.52	1.64	1.54	1.51	1.49	1.52	0.06	

Table 4. Summary of Execution Times, in seconds, and Network Characteristics for the First Group of Random Networks (1000 Nodes, 100 Centroids) for the Unmodified Single Class UE Code with Compiler Vectorization

SUBROUTINE	Net 1	Net 2	Net 3	Net 4	Net 5	Net 6	Net 7	Net 8	Net 9	Net 10	Average	S.D.	% Effort
AON	4.951	4.028	4.574	4.096	4.655	4.526	3.366	3.450	4.216	4.124	4.199	0.508	15.1
BISECT	0.839	0.635	0.751	0.681	0.783	0.722	0.518	0.542	0.656	0.661	0.679	0.100	2.4
DUMP	0.077	0.077	0.077	0.077	0.078	0.077	0.078	0.077	0.076	0.077	0.077	0.000	0.3
SHPATH	23.840	20.674	22.235	20.032	22.746	22.486	18.071	17.280	20.797	19.970	20.820	2.083	74.9
TRAFASN	1.388	1.385	1.400	1.403	1.402	1.400	1.409	1.405	1.395	1.401	1.399	0.007	5.0
UE	0.782	0.592	0.701	0.619	0.733	0.676	0.482	0.506	0.613	0.614	0.632	0.094	2.3
TOTAL	31.877	27.474	29.139	27.158	30.396	29.886	23.924	23.261	27.753	26.847	27.772	2.719	
% Overall Improvement	26.6	23.6	26.2	24.1	24.1	23.2	19.9	22.2	23.1	23.3	23.6	1.9	
% Targeted Improvement	92.9	92.8	92.7	92.5	92.7	92.8	92.5	92.7	92.5	92.7	92.7	0.02	
No. Links	4338	4324	4322	4320	4326	4310	4352	4318	4266	4292	4316.8	23.8	
No. Iterations	28	21	25	22	26	24	17	18	22	22			
CPU/Iteration	1.06	1.21	1.10	1.13	1.08	1.20	1.29	1.18	1.17	1.12	1.15	0.07	

Table 5. Summary of Execution Times, in seconds, and Network Characteristics for the First Group of Random Networks (1000 Nodes, 100 Centroids) for the Modified Single Class UE Code

SUBROUTINE	Net 11	Net 12	Net 13	Net 14	Net 15	Net 16	Net 17	Net 18	Net 19	Net 20	Average	S.D.	% Effort
AON	30.919	30.698	35.831	35.343	37.065	30.697	32.536	32.262	35.355	32.248	33.295	2.379	12.5
BISECT	6.507	6.563	7.467	7.390	7.864	6.212	6.606	6.603	7.451	6.660	6.932	0.553	2.6
COSTFN	24.434	24.508	28.296	28.278	29.734	23.921	25.426	25.399	28.278	25.377	26.365	2.064	9.9
FINT	0.166	0.169	0.163	0.170	0.166	0.164	0.161	0.163	0.166	0.168	0.166	0.003	0.1
DUMP	2.100	2.108	2.420	2.424	2.536	2.054	2.196	2.173	2.422	2.180	2.261	0.171	0.8
SHPATH	175.412	171.683	201.723	196.644	206.179	172.335	184.572	180.580	194.889	180.135	186.415	12.537	70.0
TRAFASN	9.976	9.964	9.948	9.995	9.907	9.964	9.879	9.941	9.957	9.954	9.949	0.034	3.7
UE	0.800	0.810	0.917	0.918	0.962	0.766	0.829	0.815	0.920	0.816	0.855	0.067	0.3
TOTAL	250.315	246.503	286.774	281.161	294.414	246.114	262.205	257.993	279.439	257.481	266.240	17.706	
No. Links	18976	19010	18962	18984	18898	18950	19026	18942	18908	18944	18960.0	40.7	
No. Iterations	17	17	20	20	21	17	18	18	20	18	18		
CPU/Iteration	13.9	13.7	13.7	13.4	13.4	13.7	13.8	13.6	13.3	13.6	13.6	0.2	

Table 6. Summary of Execution Times, in seconds, and Network Characteristics for the Second Group of Random Networks (4500 Nodes, 300 Centroids) for the Unmodified Single Class UE Code with Compiler Vectorization.

SUBROUTINE	Net 11	Net 12	Net 13	Net 14	Net 15	Net 16	Net 17	Net 18	Net 19	Net 20	Average	S.D.	% Effort
AON	30.487	30.312	35.423	34.903	36.662	30.347	32.195	31.883	34.917	31.866	32.899	2.363	14.0
BISECT	2.254	2.268	2.655	2.653	2.780	2.248	2.395	2.380	2.640	2.373	2.465	0.198	1.0
DUMP	0.351	0.355	0.351	0.354	0.350	0.350	0.351	0.348	0.348	0.355	0.351	0.002	0.1
SHPATH	175.266	172.574	202.472	197.159	207.166	172.703	185.456	181.114	195.340	180.460	186.971	12.688	79.6
TRAFASN	9.965	10.078	9.980	9.985	9.964	9.955	9.963	10.009	10.007	9.953	9.986	0.038	4.2
UE	2.111	2.136	2.488	2.489	2.610	2.109	2.243	2.226	2.470	2.233	2.312	0.185	1.0
TOTAL	220.433	217.724	253.369	247.544	259.531	217.712	232.60	227.960	245.722	227.241	234.984	15.408	
% Overall Improvement	11.9	11.7	11.6	11.9	11.8	11.5	11.3	11.6	12.1	11.7	11.7	0.2	
% Targeted Improvement	92.7	92.7	92.6	92.6	92.6	92.5	92.5	92.6	92.6	92.6	92.6	0.00	
No. Links	18976	19010	18962	18984	18898	18950	19026	18942	18908	18944	18960.0	40.7	
No. Iterations	17	17	20	20	21	17	18	18	20	18	18		
CPU/Iteration	12.2	13.8	12.0	11.7	11.7	12.1	12.2	12.0	11.6	11.9	12.1	0.6	

Table 7. Summary of Execution Times and Network Characteristics for Second Group of Random Networks (4500 Nodes, 300 Centroids) for the Modified Single Class UE Code.

routine. The latter vectorized quite well with the compiler without modification. However, for large problems, it would be worthwhile to consider global vectorization of this routine.

5. CLOSURE

The above results provide an indication of the magnitude of the reductions in execution time of network assignment codes on the CRAY X-MP/24 that can be achieved by code vectorization, and also relative to mainframe computers. The results confirm that off-the-shelf codes for network analysis originally developed to maximize efficiency on mainframes are not likely to run very efficiently on supercomputers with vector processing capabilities. However, it was demonstrated that relatively simple local modifications can have significant impacts on their performance. In this study, we did not go beyond the local level of code vectorization. It is quite possible that additional improvements can be achieved through more efficient data structures, or different algorithms for the overall problem or any of its parts.

The implications for practice and research are significant. The limitations identified in the first section become virtually non-existent in the kind of computing environment offered by supercomputers. Rapidly evolving hardware and innovative architectures promise comparable computing power at a fraction of the present cost. One can then address very large problems, afford greater realism in modelling and network representation (e.g., multiple user classes, asymmetric interactions, simultaneous models, land use-transportation interactions). Enhanced computing power should also contribute to alleviating the reluctance, in practice, to perform sensitivity analyses, which are so important in controversial areas such as transportation planning. Nevertheless, to keep matters in proper perspective, everyday applications of network equilibrium models, generally to small subsectors of an area, or to evaluate the effects of actions unlikely to affect but a small portion of a network, are and should continue to be more appropriately performed in a microcomputing environment. However, for serious large-scale applications, where issues of behavioral realism and modelling detail and accuracy are essential, the results presented here are quite encouraging.

Supercomputer capabilities also hold the promise for breakthroughs in two subjects of current interest to researchers and of importance for practice: dynamic assignment problems, and the network design problem. The latter, which is np-hard, requires codes for the UE problem to evaluate the objective function, along with codes for the System Optimal (SO) assignment problem, which serves as a lower bound. The structures of the SO and UE codes are very similar; thus similar changes will produce similar results for the SO code. The interest for network design problems remains one of finding good heuristics; however, better heuristics are likely to result from more frequent application of the assignment procedures.

ACKNOWLEDGEMENTS

Principal funding for this study came from a grant from Cray Research Inc. Computing resources were provided by the University of Texas System Center for High Performance Computing (CHPC). The contributions of Spiros Vellas to the vectorization of the codes and Marios Pattichis to the network generator are gratefully acknowledged. The single-class UE code used in this study is a modified version of one initially provided by Dr. Fred Mannering, presently at the University of Washington, who modified a program originally supplied by Dr. Stella Dafermos at Brown University. The authors of course are solely responsible for the content of this paper.

REFERENCES

Abdulaal M. and L.J. Leblanc (1979), "Methods for Combining Modal Split and Equilibrium Assignment Models," *Trans. Sci.* 13, 4, 292-314.

Buzbee, B.L. and D.H. Sharp (1985), "Perspectives on Supercomputing," *Science*, 227, 591-597.

Chen, S.S. (1983), "Large-Scale and High-Speed Multiprocessor System for Scientific Applications," *High Speed Computation*, NATO ASI Series F, 7, Springer-Verlag, Berlin.

Friesz, T.L. (1985), "Transportation Network Equilibrium, Design and Aggregation: Key Developments and Research Opportunities," *Trans. Res.*, 19A, 413-427, 1985.

Mahmassani, H.S. and K.C. Mouskos (1988), "Some Numerical Results on the Diagonalization Network Assignment Algorithm with Asymmetric Interactions between Cars and Trucks," *Trans. Res.*, 22B, 4, 275-290.

Mahmassani, H.S., K.C. Mouskos, and C.M. Walton (1987), "Application and Testing of the Diagonalization Algorithm for the Evaluation of Truck-Related Highway Improvements," *Trans. Res. Rec.* 1120, 24-32.

Mouskos, K.C. and H.S. Mahmassani (1989), "Guidelines and Computational Results for Vector Processing of Network Assignment Codes on Supercomputers," forthcoming in *Trans. Res. Rec.*

Sheffi, Y. (1985),*Urban Transportation Networks.*, Prentice-Hall, Englewood Cliffs, N.J.

UT CHPC (1987), "CRAY FORTRAN Optimization and Performance Analysis," Ctr. for High Performance Computing User Services, Univ. of Texas at Austin.

Zenios S.A. and J.M. Mulvey (1986), "Nonlinear Network Programming on Vector Computers: A Study on the CRAY X-MP," *Oper. Res.* 34, 667-682.

A FLEXIBLE PARELLEL ALGORITHM FOR BLOCK-CONSTRAINED OPTIMIZATION PROBLEMS

G. L. SCHULTZ   R. R. MEYER

University of Wisconsin, Madison, WI

ABSTRACT

A method is developed for solving optimization problems with block-structured constraint sets. The value of this method is that the amount of work done at each iteration is flexible so that the algorithm may be tailored to suit a variety of parallel computing environments.

1. THE PROBLEM

Suppose the sets $\Omega_k \subset \mathbf{R}^N$ for $k \in \{1, \ldots, K\}$ are polyhedral sets. Let the product set

$$\Omega := \{X | X_k \in \Omega_k \text{ for } k = 1, \ldots, K\} \subset \mathbf{R}^{N \times K}$$

be the feasible region for the optimization problem

$$minimize \ F(X) \text{ subject to } X \in \Omega. \tag{1}$$

In this paper, we consider F to be a convex, C^1 function on some open set containing Ω. Also we assume that $\Omega \cap \{X | F(X) \leq \alpha\}$ is bounded for any α. (This assumption is made to guarantee that a monotonic algorithm which generates feasible points will always have accumulation points.) The collection of variables X_k is referred to as the kth block of variables.

An example of an important problem class of this form is the nonlinear multi-commodity network flow problem, where A (an $M \times N$ matrix) is a node-arc-incidence matrix, T and L (both $N \times K$ matrices) are upper and lower bounds on the variables, and the columns of B (an $M \times K$ matrix) are the divergences of the different commodities. Then we have

$$\Omega_k := \{X_k | AX_k = B_k; L_k \leq X_k \leq T_k\} \text{ for } k \in \{1, \ldots, K\}, \text{ and}$$
$$\Omega := \{X | AX = B; L \leq X \leq T\}.$$

---

[1]This research was supported in part by the National Science Foundation under grant CCR-8709952 and by the Air Force Office of Scientific Research under grant AFOSR-86-0194.

Copyright 1989 by Elsevier Science Publishing Co., Inc.
Impacts of Recent Computer Advances on Operations Research
Ramesh Sharda, Bruce L. Golden, Edward Wasil, Osman Balci, William Stewart, Editors

Let the set $\Gamma \subset \Omega$ be the set of optimal solutions to the problem (1). The goal of this paper is to define a general class of parallel algorithms that generate sequences of feasible points, with accumulation points in Γ. This class of algorithms is interesting because the amount of work done by each processor may be modified dynamically. Thus, different strategies would be used in different computing environments.

Some notation used throughout the paper is presented here.

- e_k is the kth unit vector in $\mathbf{R}^K$.

- $\{X^i\}$ is the sequence of iterates produced by the algorithm.

- The $N \times K$ matrix U will be used to denote a proposed *update* to the current point.

- If $X, Y \in \mathbf{R}^{N \times K}$ are matrices, then

$$\langle X, Y \rangle := \sum_{n=1}^{N} \sum_{k=1}^{K} X_{nk} Y_{nk}.$$

That is, matrices are viewed as vectors in $\mathbf{R}^{N \times K}$ in the context of inner products.

- If $w \in \mathbf{R}^K$ is a vector, then the matrix $\Lambda(w)$ is the diagonal $K \times K$ matrix with diagonal elements w_k for $k = 1, \ldots, K$. In particular, if U is an $N \times K$ matrix, then $U\Lambda(w)$ is a weighted collection of the columns of U.

- If $\{X^i\}$ is a sequence then $acc\{X^i\}$ is the set of accumulation points of the sequence.

- The symbol ∇_k denotes the components of the gradient associated with the kth block.

- Throughout this paper, the iteration number is always represented as a *superscript*, and the *subscript* k denotes the block index.

2. BATCHES OF SUBPROBLEMS

To solve the problem, the block structure of the constraint set will be exploited. This may be done by constructing block separable approximations to F, i.e., a function in which each term depends on *only one* block of variables. Thus, at the ith iteration we would use an approximation

$$S^i(U) := \sum_{k=1}^{K} g_k^i(U_k) \approx F(X^i + U) - F(X^i).$$

With this type of approximation, the resulting problem decomposes into independent subproblems corresponding to the blocks. Since the goal of the algorithm is computational efficiency in parallel computing environments, we provide for load balancing by dealing with subproblems in groups termed *batches*.

Definition 1 *A batch $\beta^i \subset \{1, \ldots, K\}$ is a subset of the block indices.*

The subproblems in a batch will be done in parallel with a coordination step that guarantees improvement in the original objective. This, therefore, is *coarse grain parallelism*, in which each subtask itself is a complex optimization problem. In this case the communications tasks (corresponding to sharing optimal solutions) become relatively small as the problem size becomes large. This approach is well-suited to parallel systems with a modest number (on the order of 100 or fewer) of powerful processors with shared or distributed memory, as opposed to massively parallel systems of less powerful processors. For the latter architectures, fine grained relaxation methods (e.g., [Bertsekas and Eckstein 1988], [Zenios and Lasken 1988], and [Mangasarian and DeLeone 1987]) applied to suitable relaxations are more appropriate. One batch of subproblems is solved per iteration.

Definition 2 *The recurrence $\rho = \rho(\{\beta^i\})$ of the sequence $\{\beta^i\}$ of batches is the smallest integer such that the union of any ρ consecutive batches is equal to the entire set of block indices. In symbols;*

$$\rho(\{\beta^i\}) := min\{\rho | \bigcup_{j=0}^{\rho-1} \beta^{s+j} = \{1, \ldots, K\} \text{ for } s = 0, 1, \ldots\}.$$

The above definition will be used to guarantee that by doing ρ iterations, we will have solved a subproblem corresponding to each block at least once.

3. A CLASS OF PARALLEL ALGORITHMS

3.1 Notation
The following notation will be used in the description of the algorithm.

- $\psi \in (0, 1]$ denotes a constant.

- The functions g_k^i are approximations to the objective function about the current point. (More will be said about these in a later section.)

- $\{U^i\}$ is a corresponding sequence of proposed updates. Each column of each U^i is obtained by solving a subproblem.

- The scalar μ^i corresponds to the best improvement resulting from any single block update. (A formal definition is given below.)

- The vector w^{i+1} is the set of weights assigned to the columns of the proposed updates U^i to produce the new iterate $X^{i+1} = X^i + U^i \Lambda(w^{i+1})$. (They are computed by solving an optimization problem defined below.)

The "coordination" phase of the algorithm combines subproblem solutions to generate weights w^{i+1}. This is done by optimizing the function c^i, given by

$$c^i(w) := F(X^i + U^i \Lambda(w)),$$

over the region

$$H^i := \{w | X^i + U^i \Lambda(w) \in \Omega\}.$$

The letter H is used to denote the feasible region because the constraint $w \in H^i$ reduces to a hyperrectangle in $\mathbf{R}^K$.

Also, for a given function F, we let the function $\mu(X, U)$ be any function which satisfies the following condition:

Condition 3 *For any $X, U \in \mathbf{R}^{N \times K}$, $\mu(X, U) \leq 0$, and there is some $\bar{w} \in [0, 1]^K$ such that*

$$F(X + U\Lambda(\bar{w})) - F(X) \leq \mu(X, U).$$

Thus, μ corresponds to a bound on the improvement achievable via the updates U. If U^{i+1} corresponds to a feasible update (i.e., $X^i + U^{i+1} \in \Omega$), note that $[0, 1]^K \subset H^i$, by the convexity of the feasible set.

3.2 The FLEX Algorithm

The basic idea of the algorithm described below is that, at every iteration, we solve some batch of subproblems and simultaneously coordinate the previous updates, producing a new point. (See figure 1.)

- Choose a constant $\psi \in (0, 1]$, a sequence of batches $\{\beta^i\}$ with finite recurrence ρ, and some scheme for choosing g_k^i

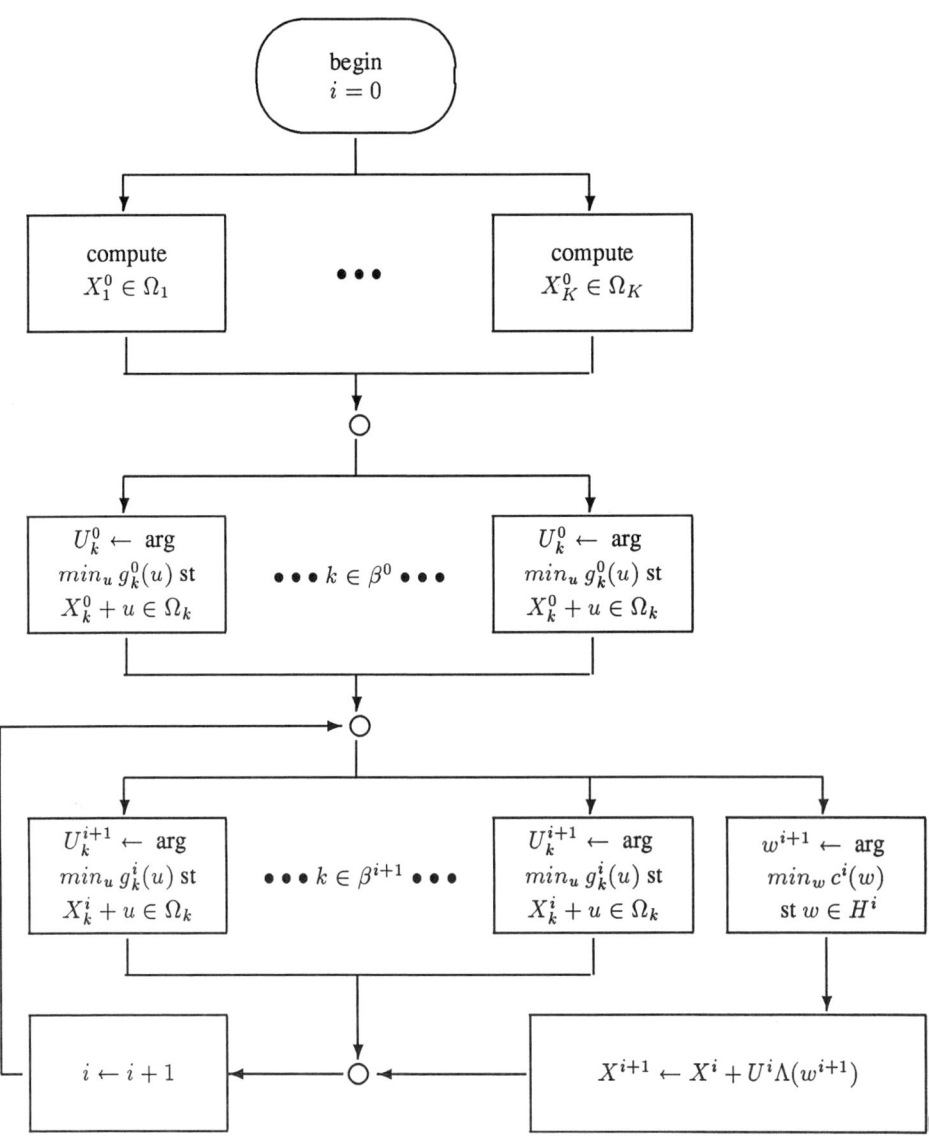

Figure 1: Flowchart of FLEX

- $X^0 \leftarrow$ an initial feasible solution

- In parallel, do:

  - For each $k \in \beta^0$: $U_k^0 \leftarrow u$ where u is a solution of

  $$minimize\ g_k^0(u)\ \text{subject to}\ X_k^0 + u \in \Omega_k$$

- $\mu^0 \leftarrow \mu(X^0, U^0)$

- For $i \leftarrow 0$ to ∞, do:

  - In parallel, do:

    - *(Parallel Subproblem Solution)* For each $k \in \beta^{i+1}$: $U_k^{i+1} \leftarrow u$ where u is a solution of

    $$minimize\ g_k^i(u)\ \text{subject to}\ X_k^i + u \in \Omega_k$$

    - *(Non-batch Blocks)* For $k \notin \beta^{i+1}$: $U_k^{i+1} \leftarrow 0$
    - *(Improvement Bound)* $\mu^{i+1} \leftarrow \mu(X^i, U^{i+1})$
    - *(Coordination Step)* $w^{i+1} \leftarrow$ solution of

    $$minimize\ c^i(w)\ \text{subject to}\ w \in H^i$$

    If

    $$F(X^i + U^i \Lambda(w^{i+1})) - F(X^i) \leq \psi \mu^i < 0 \qquad (2)$$

    then $X^{i+1} \leftarrow X^i + U^i \Lambda(w^{i+1})$ otherwise $X^{i+1} \leftarrow X^i$.

This algorithm, in order to prevent the coordination step from being a serial bottleneck, *overlaps* the coordination and subproblem solution phases. Consequently, X^i is used simultaneously as the basepoint for the generation of the "new" updates U^{i+1} as well as in the coordination phase of the "old" updates U^i (which were generated relative to X^{i-1}).

3.3 Convergence

If the approximations used in the subproblems guarantee a sufficient objective function value decrease, then convergence to an optimal solution may be demonstrated.

Lemma 4 (Monotonicity) *For any two consecutive iterates X^i and X^{i+1} of the above algorithm, $F(X^i) \geq F(X^{i+1})$.*

Proof: In the only case in which $X^{i+1} \neq X^i$, we have a strict decrease by the inequality(2). ∎

The following lemma is used to guarantee that a non-null update will eventually be carried out at a non-optimal solution.

Lemma 5 *Suppose that $\mu(X,U)$ satisfies condition (3). Suppose $\mu^i < 0$ and the inequality (2) is not satisfied. Let b be the next iteration number such that $\mu^b < 0$. Then the inequality(2) is satisfied at iteration b.*

Proof: By condition 3, there is some $\bar{w} \in [0,1]^K \subset H^{b-1}$ for which the following holds:

$$\begin{aligned}
& F(X^b + U^b \Lambda(w^{b+1})) - F(X^b) \\
\leq\ & F(X^b + U^b \Lambda(\bar{w})) - F(X^b) \\
=\ & F(X^{b-1} + U^b \Lambda(\bar{w})) - F(X^{b-1}) \\
\leq\ & \mu^b \leq \psi \mu^b.
\end{aligned}$$

∎

Lemma 6 *If the objective function F is bounded from below on the feasible set Ω, then $\liminf \mu^i = 0$.*

Proof: Suppose $\liminf \mu^i < 0$. Then, because of lemma 5, the inequality (2) says that $F(X^i) \to -\infty$, which is a contradiction. ∎

The results of the lemmas are collected into the following theorem.

Theorem 7 *Suppose that the objective function F is bounded from below on the feasible set Ω. Suppose further that the sequence of objective functions of the subproblems $\{g_k^i\}$ and the batch sequence $\{\beta^i\}$ are chosen so that $\liminf \mu^i = 0$ only if the set of accumulation points of $\{X^i\}$ are in Γ. Then any accumulation point of the algorithm is in Γ.*

Proof: Since F bounded below on Ω and $\mu^i \leq 0$ for all i, lemma 6 says that $\liminf \mu^i = 0$. By hypothesis then, $acc\{X^i\} \subset \Gamma$. ∎

This result may be viewed as a condition on the subproblems which produce the μ^i. These issues will be taken up in the next sections.

4. TYPES OF APPROXIMATIONS

4.1 Linearization

The simplest block structured (and separable) approximation to F is the linear approximation. With this approximation and a line search in the coordination phase, the FLEX algorithm becomes a variant of the well known algorithm of Frank and Wolfe [1956]. Lawphongpanich and Hearn [1983] consider a restricted simplicial decomposition algorithm in which linearization is used at every iteration for the subproblems and a multidimensional search is done over the simplex defined by a bounded number of subproblem solutions. This approach differs somewhat from the FLEX algorithm in that it does not overlap the subproblem and coordination tasks and uses a more general set of "old" updates in the coordination phase. However, FLEX could be similarly generalized to allow the inclusion of additional prior updates in the coordinating step. (See section 5 for further details.)

4.2 Piecewise-Linear Approximation

A nonlinear block separable approximation is obtained by fixing all variables not in the block. If the resulting separable g_k^i are further approximated by piecewise-linear functions, s_k^i, then the subproblems may be reduced to linear programs. Feijoo and Meyer [1984] (see also [Feijoo 1985]) developed this approach.

4.3 Nonlinear Approximation

One may use appropriate quadratic approximations about the current basepoint. Suppose F is C^2. Note that simply doing a standard second order approximation will lead to difficulties, since there will, in general, be coupling between the blocks. However, by modifying the second order approximation to remove coupling between blocks, the convergence properties considered above may be obtained. (See [Toint and Tuyttens 1988] for a discussion of partitioned quasi-Newton updating methods.)

5. DIRECTIONS FOR FUTURE RESEARCH

Research is currently under way to determine the best choices for the batch sequence $\{\beta^i\}$ from the standpoint of convergence rate and efficient use of the computing resources available. The extreme cases have already been done by Chen [1987], without the multi-dimensional coordination step. The case where $\beta^i = \{1, \ldots, K\}$ for each i is analogous to the *parallel block Jacobi method*, and the case where $\beta^i = \{i \bmod K\}$ for each i is similar to the *parallel block Gauss-Seidel method*.

Another promising idea is to solve as many subproblems as possible while the coordination step is in progress. It is also possible that early termination of the subproblems may lead to increased efficiency without destroying the convergence properties of the algorithm. An important research issue here is to find a way to allow the algorithm to efficiently determine the batch sequence *at run time*.

Note that the coordination step does not need to work with only one previous set of updates. FLEX may be extended to the case where any number of previous updates are used. The only formulae which are affected are the definitions of c^i and H^i and the formula from which X^{i+1} is calculated. The H^i will generally no longer be hyperrectangles in the case where more than one update is considered for a given block.

REFERENCES

Bertsekas, D. P. and J. Eckstein (1988), "Dual Coordinate Step Method for Linear Network Flow Problems," *Mathematical Programming*, Series B, to appear.

Chen, R. J. (1987), "Parallel Algorithms for a class of Convex Optimization Problems," Ph.D. Thesis, Computer Sciences Department, University of Wisconsin–Madison. Also appeared as technical report number 731, Dec.

Chen, R. J. and R. R. Meyer (1986), "A Scaled Trust Region Method for a class of Convex Optimization Problems," Technical Report 675, Computer Sciences Department, University of Wisconsin–Madison, Madison, Wis. 53706, Dec.

Chen, R. J. and R. R. Meyer (1987), "Parallel Optimization for Traffic Assignment," Technical Report 732, Computer Sciences Department, University of Wisconsin–Madison, Madison, Wis. 53706, Dec.

Feijoo, B. (1985), "Piecewise-Linear Approximation Methods and Parallel Algorithms in Optimization," Ph.D. Thesis, Computer Sciences Department, University of Wisconsin–Madison. Also appeared as technical report number 598, May.

Feijoo, B. and R. R. Meyer (1984), "Piecewise-Linear Approximation Methods for Nonseparable Convex Optimization," Technical Report 521, Computer Sciences Department, University of Wisconsin–Madison, Madison, Wis. 53706, Dec.

Frank, M. and P. Wolfe (1956), "An Algorithm for Quadratic Programming," *Naval Research Logistics Quarterly*, 3, 2, 95–110.

Lawphongpanich S. and D. W. Hearn (1983), "Restricted Simplicial Decomposition with Application to the Traffic Assignment Problem", Technical Report 83-8, Industrial and Systems Engineering Department, University of Florida, Gainesville, Fla. 32611, Sep.

Mangasarian, O. L. and R. DeLeone (1987), "Parallel Successive Overrelaxation Methods for Symmetric Linear Complementarity Problems and Linear Programs," *Journal of Optimization Theory and Applications*, Vol. 54, No. 3, Sep.

Toint, Ph. L. and D. Tuyttens (1988), "On Large Scale Nonlinear Network Optimization," Report 88/19, Department of Mathematics, Facultés Universitaires de Namur, Belgium, Aug.

Zenios, S. A. and R. A. Lasken (1988), "Nonlinear Network Optimization on a Massively Parallel Connection Machine," *Annals of Operations Research*, 14, to appear.

SUPERCOMPUTERS AND GLOBAL OPTIMIZATION

REGINA HUNTER MLADINEO
Rider College, Lawrenceville, New Jersey

ABSTRACT:

This paper describes the evolution of a global optimization algorithm as it was implemented for the CYBER-205 vector processor and CYBER software which emulates the ETA-10 parallel processor. Algorithmic and program code changes for vectorization and multitasking are discussed and test results presented.

1. INTRODUCTION

1.1 Global Optimization

Research in global optimization (g.o.) has been attempted sporadically for only about twenty years and within the last few years has been given a large impetus by developments within the field and by availability of faster computers. Within the broad classes of deterministic methods, which guarantee convergence to a global optimum, and stochastic methods, which converge to a point with an associated probability of being the global optimum, there are various approaches. See [Pardalos and Rosen 1986; Rinnooy Kan 1987] for complete bibliographies of research in this area. The aim of each of these diverse algorithms is to find the global optimum as accurately and as quickly as possible. However, the problem is inherently computation bound. If the algorithm saves time in function evaluations (iterations), then it needs much computation time in intermediate steps between iterations. Thus there is much more research needed in improving the efficiency of existing algorithms. Parallelization is an increasingly attractive route toward this goal.

Global optimization has applications in many areas. For example, in molecular modeling used in drug design, the global minimum of bond strain energy is desirable, though currently in such systems only some relative minima are obtained. As g.o. algorithms are becoming refined and useful, other problems such as technical design problems have been formulated as g.o. problems. Cost minimizations where the cost function is multimodal fall naturally into this formulation [Dixon and Szego 1978].

The author's previous work in this area has consisted of developing, implementing and testing a deterministic algorithm for optimizing an arbitrary Lipschitz continuous function. More precisely, the algorithm solves the problem:

$$\text{Max } f \text{ subject to } x \in I^N$$

where I^N is an N-cube in R^N and satisfies the strict Lipschitz condition that, for all x, y in I^N,

$| f(x) - f(y) | \leq k \parallel x - y \parallel$,

k a real positive constant, $\parallel \parallel$ Euclidean distance.

The computer-implemented algorithm has been tested using standard functions and results obtained in convergence and timing comparable to other known algorithms [Dixon and Szego 1978]. The Pijavskii-Shubert-Mladineo (P-S-M) algorithm [Mladineo 1986], an N-dimensional generalization of the Pijavskii-Shubert algorithm [Pijavskii 1972; Shubert 1972], guarantees convergence to the global optimum (maximum) by obtaining successively closer piecewise differentiable approximations of the objective function.

1.2 The Supercomputers

The serial, scalar code (originally implemented on a VAX 11-780) was first rewritten using vector Fortran code for execution on a CYBER 205 supercomputer (see acknowledgements). The CYBER 205 has two vector arithmetic pipelines which each can process vectors of 64K words. It has a cycle time of 20 nanoseconds and can perform up to hundreds of megaflops (millions of floating point arithmetic operations per second) when vector operations on long vectors are being executed. For example, to add two vectors of length 100 words would take 101 cycles (start-up time of 51 cycles plus 50 cycles using two vector pipelines) whereas a loop with 100 iterations and scalar addition would take more than 1000 cycles.

The CYBER 205 has 32 megabytes of CPU memory and 14.4 gigabytes of disk storage. Since its operating system uses virtual memory, program sizes are limited only by disk space.

This machine and others like it give the researcher an opportunity to test problems or solve real problems that previously were considered too large. For example, part of the speedup achieved in going from the VAX to the CYBER was simply a decrease in page fault time (fewer page faults as well as faster data transfer). Furthermore, the limit imposed on the number of iterations in testing on the VAX was precisely because memory was too small, causing even modest-sized test problems to take an inordinate amount of time.

The testing of the parallelized algorithm was done using CYBER software which emulates the ETA-10 multi-tasking (parallel processing) system. This software was used because although at the time of this writing, the ETA-10 was in place, its four processors were not running in parallel.

The ETA-10, with MIMD architecture (multiple instruction, multiple data), is designed to have eventually eight CPU's operating in parallel, each having local memory (CPM) of 32 megabytes and access to shared memory of 2 gigabytes. Each of these processors is a supercomputer similar to the CYBER, with a cycle time of 10.5 nanoseconds which will be

7.0 nanoseconds when fully upgraded.

The architecture of the ETA-10 is in distinct contrast to that of SIMD (single intruction multiple data) massively parallel machines such as the Connection Machine (CM) [Zenios and Lasken 1987]. The latter has 64K microprocessors which can be connected as needed like the corners of a N-cube. Clearly the philosophy in programming for the CM is vastly different from that for the ETA-10 and the types of problem which can be efficiently solved on each fall into two separate categories. The P-S-M algorithm, as will be shown, falls clearly into the MIMD variety, whereas many matrix operations are efficiently implemented on SIMD machines.

2. THE SERIAL ALGORITHM

2.1 Description

Given a nonlinear objective function f of N simply-bounded variables, assume f satisfies a Lipschitz condition with Lipschitz constant K. We wish to find the global maximum. The mathematics of the serial algorithm [Mladineo 1986] can be described geometrically as follows.

Step 0. Initially, f is evaluated at some arbitrary point x_0 in the domain. The approximating function F_0 is defined, whose graph, $gr(F_0)$, is an N-cone with vertex at x_0 and whose slope is K. Thus the maximum of f, max(f), is less than $max(F_0)$.

Step 1. Suppose we have defined the jth approximating function F_j. Then $gr(F_j)$ is made up of $gr(F_{j-1})$ intersected with the cone C_j at x_j, the current iterate. We find M_j, the maximum of F_j, which will be located at some corner formed by the cone intersections making up $gr(F_j)$. The computations to find each new corner consist of plane parameters for pairs of cone intersections, then the solution of a system of N linear equations and a quadratic equation [Mladineo 1986].

Step 2. The location of M_j found in step 1 is x_{j+1}. The objective function is evaluated at this point and convergence is tested. Step 1 and 2 are repeated until M_j-$f(x_j)$ becomes accept bly small or until the preset number of iterations has been performed. Note that at each successive step, F_j is a better approximation to f and thus the sequence M_j converges to max(f).

2.2 Feasibility of Parallelization

Prerequisites for efficient use of vector processors are large vectors, i. e. sets of contiguous data, and program loops operating on this data in which the iterations are independent. (Recursions can also be translated to vector operations, but not all will be more efficient than the scalar versions.) The above-described algorithm has large arrays, such as MLIST, the list of corners of the approximating surface, which are the actual iterates, and

PL, the list of plane parameters which changes each iteration. The two most time-consuming routines are **corner computations** and **surface checking**. (The cone at the current iterate is intersected with cones at each of the previous iterates; some of these points clearly lie above the graph of F_j, or are outside the feasible region, so are discarded). These routines operate on large portions of these arrays in such a manner that the iterations of the routine are independent of each other, i. e. corners can be computed independently and checked for feasibility independently. Vectorizing the program and subdividing it for multitasking were straight-forward, as will be described below.

3. VECTORIZATION

3.1 Technical considerations

There are three approaches one can take in converting scalar code to vector code: clean up loops so that vector pre-compilers (software that converts scalar loops to vector statements) can convert most of one's program loops, recode all appropriate loops into vector code, or use a combination of the first two approaches. The first option has the advantage of making the program transportable from one vector machine to another but may not result in as efficient a program as the second option produces. The third option is a compromise in transportability but not in efficiency and is what this author chose to do. All simple, easily converted loops were left as such, for a pre-compiler run to convert. Loops that were not translatable by a pre-compiler or that the pre-compiler's generic routines may render inefficient were converted "by hand".

Another major consideration is how arrays of more than one dimension are to be stored. MLIST, for example, contains N coordinates for each of up to thousands of points, depending on the limit on the number of iterations. This array is accessed both by column and by row in several routines. Suppose the algorithm has reached the Jth iteration. A time-consuming subroutine PLANES computes J-1 sets of plane parameters using MLIST. If MLIST is stored with the ith coordinate as column i (column-wise) then PLANES performs vector arithmetic on N long vectors with no gathering of data into contiguous vectors. On the other hand, another long routine GEN which computes the corner coordinates (an intervening routine has eliminated most unnecessary planes) accesses MLIST row-wise, so must do a periodic gather, then scatter, of the N coordinates into or from a vector. The gathers alone for say N=4, J=1000 and an average of 30 corners would take about 1320 machine cycles:

$$30 * (\text{startup of } 39 + 4/.8).$$

Suppose, instead, MLIST was stored row-wise, then the longer PLANES would have to do periodic gathers of columns of coordinates which would take

$$4 * (39 + 1000/.8) = 5156 \text{ machine cycles.}$$

Furthermore, this latter number would increase each iteration whereas the gather time for

GEN stays relatively fixed. The foregoing analysis was the main factor in determining the column-wise storage of MLIST and similar considerations dictated the storage of most arrays. The idea of storing two versions of MLIST was briefly considered and discarded, the assumption being that in the future when larger problems are solved, storage requirements would be prohibitive.

3.2 Initial Results

The initial conversion to vector code for the CYBER involved no algorithmic changes and was tested using small runs in order to compare results and timings to those obtained on the VAX. Table 1 shows the CPU times and speedup ratios obtained from maximizing several functions. All but GR1 and GR3 are standard test functions used for testing global optimization algorithms and found in [Dixon and Szego 1978]. GR1 and GR3 are due to Griewank [Snyman 1984] and each has many (5 or more) local optima in the unit cube, unlike the other test functions. All test runs were limited to 600 iterations because of elapsed time on the VAX.

Table 2 shows the global maxima obtained and the number of functions evaluations in each case. All functions are scaled to
$$0 \leq x \leq 1, -1 \leq f(x) \leq 1.$$
The differences between the results obtained with scalar code and vector code are because some changes in order of corner generation occurred when a routine was vectorized.

Table 1. CPU Time in Seconds and Speedup Ratios

Function	scalar code VAX11-780 T_1	vector code CYBER 205 T_2	T_1/T_2	CYBER205 T_v	T_2/T_v	T_1/T_v
GOLDPR	503	21	24	8.4	2.5	60
GR1	1058	38	28	7.6	4.9	139
GR3	1290	44	29	7.6	5.8	170
RCOS						
K = 20.0	458	21	22	8.0	2.6	57
K = 50.0	513	20	26	8.8	2.3	58
HART	842	56	15	21.2	2.6	40
SQRIN	965	71	14	36.8	1.9	26

3.3 Algorithmic Changes - the Sphere Heuristic

A major revision to the algorithm was to enable it to handle more than five variables, since before implementation on super-computers it was not feasible to test problems larger than that. The routine PLANES which selected N planes and calculated the intersection used

Table 2. Locations of Global Maxima

Function actual global max	scalar code global max	f.e.[1]	vector code global max	f.e.
GOLDPR(.5,.25,1.0)	(.5132,.2478,.999992)	259	(.4762,.2427,.99998)	237
GR1 (.44,.44,1.0)	(.4426,.4473,.9976)	286	(.4426,.4473,.9976)	226
GR3 (.1<u>6</u>,.1<u>6</u>,1.0)	(.1161,.1672,.99997)	289	(.1668,.1662,.99998)	232
RCOS(.5428,.1350,1.0)				
(.1239,.8017,1.0)	(.1204,.8334,.9997)[2]	264	(.1166,.8334,.9991)	235
(.9617,.1500,1.0)	(.9504,.1588,.9979)[2]	263	(.5424,.1511,1.00003)	246
HART(.2317,.5,.<u>8</u>,1.0)	(.5409,.5509,.8465,.8791)	120	(.3823,.5785,.8110,.8173)	104
SQRIN(.4,.4,.4,.4,1.0)	(.5,.5,.5,.5,-.8849)	59	(.4999,.5,.5,.5,-.8849)	46

1. Function evaluations.
2. Lipschitz constants 20.0, 50.0, respectively.

---

simply a set of nested loops, clearly unsatisfactory for arbitrary numbers of variables. Nor was it feasible, though algorithmically possible, to have a routine to calculate all possible combinations of N planes from an arbitrarily large list. Consequently, the following routine was developed which, in essence, identifies the points around the current iterate which form a topological sphere and groups spherically "close" points whose cones are then intersected to form new corners of the approximating surface.

Let x_* be the current iterate and v any previous cone point. the spherical cordinates for v are determined as follows:

We may safely assume x_* is the origin.

Let $proj_i(v) = (v_1, v_2, ...v_i, 0, ...,0)$ be the projection of $v = (v_1,....,v_N)$ onto R_i, Euclidean space.

Let $d = \| x_* - v \| = \| v \| = d_{N-1}$.

project v to R_{N-1}. The angle $\theta_{N-1} = \arcsin(v_n / d_{N-1})$, has possible full range $0 \leq \theta_{N-1} \leq 2\pi$, determined by the sign of the $N - 1$ component. Similarly project $proj_{i+1}(v)$ to R_i to obtain θ_i. we have

$v = (d_0, d1sin\theta_1,.....,d_{N-1}sin\theta_{N-1})$, and also,

$d_{i-1} = d_i \cos\theta_i$.

To include bounadry planes among those determining cone interseçtions, we determine spherical coordinates for the projections of x_* on each boundary plane.

An array of N-1 lists of 0_i are sorted. Then N contiguous points (according to each 0_i) are selected, then another N until as many points have been selected as the length of the list. Initially a heuristic is used to generate points, because in initial iterations with many boundary planes the possible intersections are an exponential function of N.

Table 3 shows the results of longer runs using these heuristics for functions of more than two variables.

Table 3. Results Using Sphere Heuristic

Function	Global Max.	CPU sec.[1]	f. e.
HART	(.3329,.5398,.8458.9233)	520	1045
SQRIN	(.3889,.3605,.3756,.3745,-.2835)	780	1211
GR15[2]	(.4409,.4341,.4423,.4488,.4340,.9821)	1700	1623

1. All runs were 4000 iterations.
2. All functions GR1N have global maximum 1.0 at x_i = .44..., i=1,...N.

4. MULTITASKING

4.1 Partitioning into Tasks

Timing analysis software used during CYBER runs of the vector code revealed that 94% or more of the execution time was spent in subsets of the routines PLANES and GEN. The analysis was done for functions of 2 and 3 variables and it is clear that this percentage increases with the number of variables.

The multitasking effort was concentrated on those two subroutines. It was easy to identify the program loops which took up the time in these routines and furthermore to determine that they could be simply "strip-mined" for multitasking. The term strip-mining is borrowed from its use in vectorizing loops and here means that P roughly equal portions of the serial loop can be executed by P processors (see Figure 1) while preserving data integrity; i. e. there is no recursion to prevent this simple approach. Furthermore this could be done without disturbing the vectorization already in place. A portion of the multitasked code for calculating the plane parameters of cone intersections follows; the multitasking language has been simplified for illustration. NCPU is the number of CPU's, DIFF1 and DIFF2 are vectors of length J, XBIT is a bit vector of length J and Q8- - - indicates a library vector function.

```
    STRIP = J/NCPU
    TOP = STRIP*NCPU - 1
    DO 299 I=0,TOP,STRIP
        LOWER = I
        UPPER = I + STRIP - 1
        MTRUN PLANES (J,LOWER,UPPER)    ←—starts the task PLANES on any
```

```
299 CONTINUE                                available CPU.
    WAIT until counter = J
------------------------------------                                         (1)
    TASK PLANES(J,UPPER,LOWER)
    :       (data transfer from shared memory)
    CALL PL2 (J,LOWER,UPPER)
    :       (data transfer to shared memory)
    ADD to counter                                                           (2)
    TASKEND
------------------------------------
    SUBROUTINE PL2 (J,LOWER,UPPER)
    DO 979 NJ=LOWER,UPPER
        DIFF2 = 0.0
        DO 969 I=1,N
            DIFF1 = MLIST(0,I;J) - B(NJ,I)
            DIFF1 = DIFF1*DIFF1
            DIFF2 = DIFF1 + DIFF2
969     CONTINUE
        DIFF2 = XK*VSQRT(DIFF2;J) + MLIST(0,N+2;J)                           (3)
        DIFF2 = DIFF2 + TINY*(1.0+VABS(DIFF2;J))
        XBIT = ((ZVAL(NJ).GT.DIFF2).AND.FLBIT(0;J))
        NS = Q8SCNT(XBIT)
        IF (NS.GT.0)  PL(N2+NJ,N+2) = LN                                     (4)
979 CONTINUE
    RETURN
```

The routine GEN is much longer and more complex, but is strip-mined similarly.

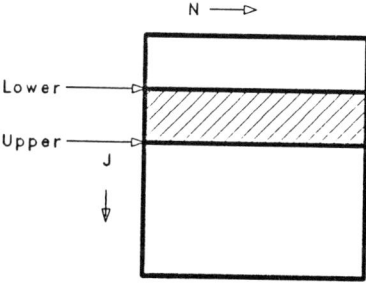

figure 1: Matrix PL

4.2 Dynamic Task Scheduling

Assigning a task to a CPU for execution is the function of task scheduling. In this particular case the only feasuble approach is to allow the system to dynamically assign tasks to available CPU's. The running program has no need to preassign tasks to CPU nodes. See [Zenios and Lasken 1987] for an example of a predefined mapping of tasks to CPU nodes.

Another consideration involved in deciding between predefined or dynamic task scheduling is how the ETA-10 (or other such system) will be used: allowing multiple users on the machine or dedicating the entire machine to one user at a time. In fact, the intention is to have both approaches available, so a highly parallel, efficient problem will use the dedicated ETA-10, whereas several users whose problems, though benefitting from multitasking, do not require or use efficiently the entire system can share the CPU's and global memory. In this latter environment, dynamic task scheduling is prescribed.

4.3 Synchronization and Communication

In designing a multitasked program, the largest problems are encountered in deciding what data needs to be where at what time. Since several tasks may be using and changing the same data simultaneously, tasks must be synchronized - some control or partial ordering established - and each task must have a private copy of data used and communicate the changed data back to shared memory. Tasks can be synchronized by use of semaphores, counters, or critical regions [Andrews and Schneider 1983] - whereby a task waits for a signal to tell it to proceed, that the correct data is available or that it may proceed to change sensitiver data. As will be seen, the strip-mining approach to multitasking assures a simple solution to data communication and task synchronization concerns.

The two multitasked routines of the P-S-M algorithm are treated alike, so again we will look at only the PLANES routine. Referring to the Fortran code above, we see that copies of the task PLANES are sent to different processors to begin execution. The preceding code, not reproduced here, has updated the arrays MLIST and PL in shared memory. Each copy of PLANES reads a private copy of all or part of these arrays. Each task uses all of MLIST (3) but updates only its unique part of PL (4). The separate tasks write back to shared memory separate and distinct portions of PL. Thus the tasks can finish in any order and data integrity is preserved.

The next step in the program, however, requires that all PLANES tasks be done, so that it has a fully updated version of PL available. This is satisfied by use of a shared counter. Each task adds to the counter (2) (a library call) and the calling program waits (1) for the counter to reach the required limit before proceeding to the next step. Control of this counter is under system software so its integrity is not the concern of the application programmer. Details of protocols etc. are in [Andrews and Schneider 1983].

4.4 Results and Measures of Performance

Test runs of the multitasked P-S-M algorithm were made using software emulating the ETA-10, with varying numbers of CPU's and various objective functions. The global optima obtained after 4000 iterations were the same as for the serial program.

There are many advantages to using an emulator instead of the expensive real thing while designing a multitasked program but one disadvantage is that the timings obtained are approximate. Thus it seems inappropriate to use measures such as elapsed time and work - CPU charges - as in [Zenios and Mulvey 1987] until these can be obtained more accurately. However, the relative measures discussed below are useful while designing the program. In fact, one of the advantages to using the emulation software on the CYBER is that one can inexpensively measure the effects of parameter changes in the program, for example the number of CPU'S.

4.4.1 Speedup

The speedup measured here (Figure 2 and Figure 5) is the ratio of CPU time for the serial code to CPU time for the multitasked code:

$$s = T_1 / T_p,$$

where P = number of processors. In Figures 5 and 6 eight processors were used. The emulation software measures the CPU time (not wall-clock time) used on all CPU's, which gives the serial time T_1 and uses the longest time accumulated on any on the CPU's as T_p. (Similar statistics will be available on the ETA-10.) Amdhal's Law [Amdhal 1967] gives T_p as a weighted average of T_1 and T_1 / P :

$$T_p = (1-f)T_1 + f(T_1 / P),$$

where f = fraction of program executed in parallel. Assuming that in converting PLANES and GEN to strip-mined multiple tasks we have achieved at least 94% parallelism, then Amdhal's Law gives a speedup of 5.6 for 8 processors, while test runs give a speedup of 4.0. Similarly for P < 8, actual speedups are less than those given by Amdhal's Law. This is due to the high overhead spent in multitasking library routines, mostly data transfers between CPM and shared memory. It is clear, both theoretically and in practice, that as the number of variables N increases the speedup will improve, up to some (unknown) upper limit (usually < P) reached when the array sizes challenge both the size and transfer rate of shared memory.

4.4.2 CPU Utilization

The percent CPU utilization (Figure 3 and Figure 6) gives a measure of how much the program uses the resources. It is calculated as

$$100 * (L + T_1) / (T_p * P),$$

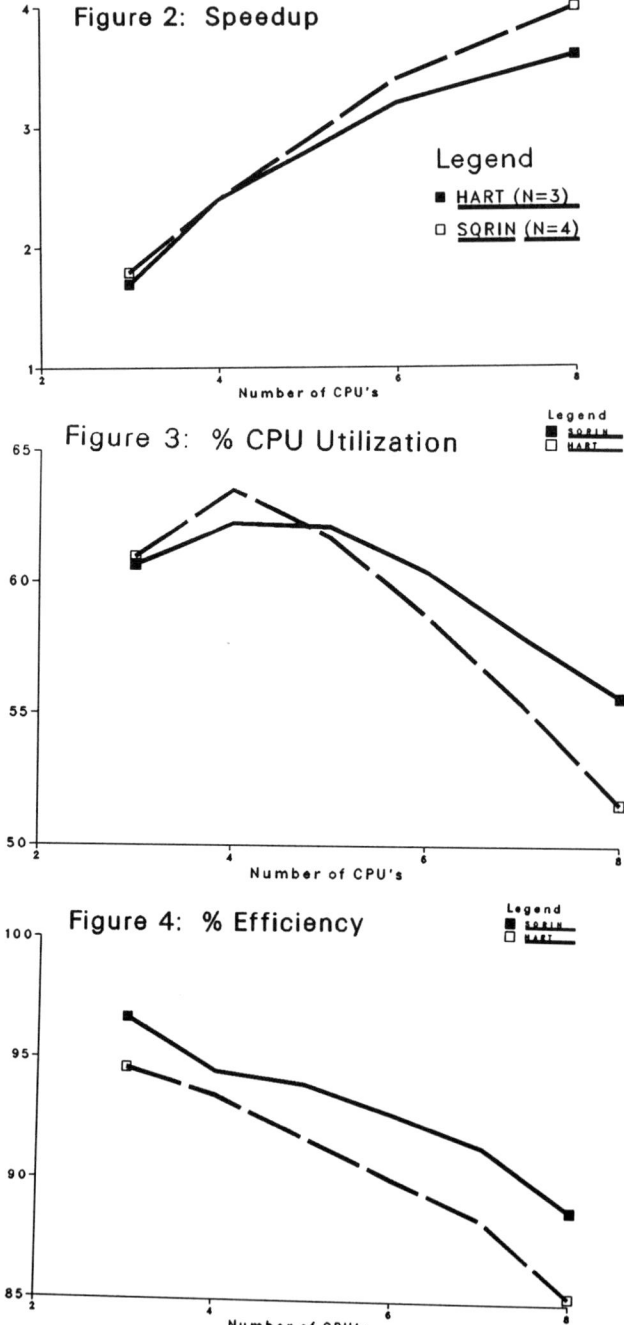

103

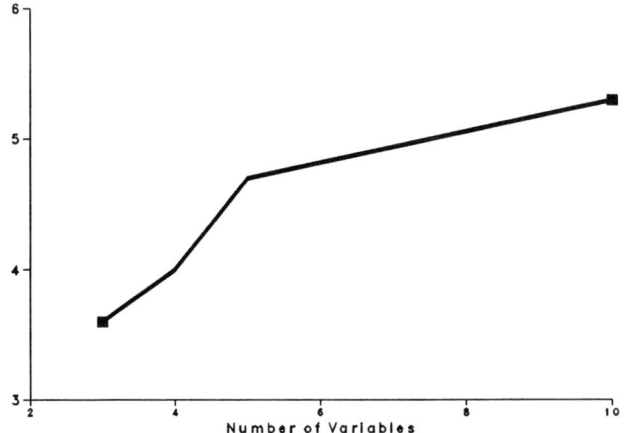

Figure 5: Speedup by Number of Variables

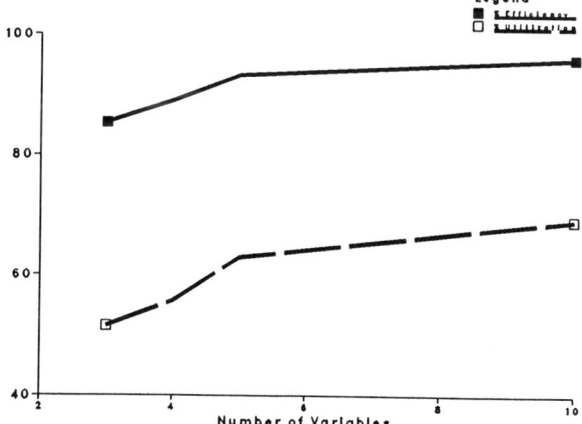

Figure 6: % Efficiency and % Utilization by Number of Variables

where L = library time. This would be a crucial statistic if the ETA-10 were to be dedicated to a problem. In a multi-user environment, it is not so important. This problem, for small N, will not run on a dedicated system. However, for larger N, this percentage will be higher, since it increases with speedup.

4.4.3 Efficiency

Efficiency can be judged in many different ways. Here (Figure 4 and Figure 6) it is a measure of the amount of CPU time used in problem solving as opposed to multitasking library functions such as data transfer.

$$\% \text{ Efficiency} = T1 / (L + T1).$$

An inefficient program, according to this measure, is one which uses an inordinate amount of library time to achieve multitasking. In fact, if one assumes

$$TP > (T1 + L) / P, \text{ then}$$
$$s < P * T1 / (T1 + L).$$

Thus a 50% efficient program achieves a speedup of no more than half the number of processors.

ACKNOWLEDGEMENTS

This work was done on the CYBER 205 at the John von Neumann National Supercomputer Center in Princeton, New Jersey under grant number NAC 27001 for computer time.

The original code (serial, scalar version) was implemented on the VAX 11-780 at Rider College, Lawrenceville, New Jersey.

The author thanks L. Feeney and L. Warren for invaluable help with the word processing, printing, and graphics.

REFERENCES

Amdhal, G. (1967) "The Validity of Single Processor Approach to Achieving Large Scale Computing Capabilities", *AFIPS Proceedings 30*, 483-485.

Andrews, G.R. and F.B. Schneider (1983), "Concepts and Notations for Concurrent Programming", *Computing Surveys 15*, 1-43.

Dixon, L.C.W. and G.P. Szego (1978), <u>Towards Global Optimisation 2</u> North- Holland, Amsterdam.

Mladineo, R.H. (1986) "An Algorithm for Finding the Global Maximum of Multimodal, Multivariate Function", *Mathematical Programming 34,* 188-200.

Pardalos, P. and J.P. Rosen (1986), "Methods for Global Concave Minimization: A Bibliographical Survey", *SIAM Review*.

Pijavskii, S.A. (1972), "An Algorithm for Finding the Absolute Extremum of a Function", *USSR Computational Mathematics and Mathematical Physics, 57-67*.

Rinnooy Kan, A.H.G. and G.T. Timmer (1986), "Global Optimization", *Report 8612/A, Econometric Institute, Erasmus University, Rotterdam.*

Shubert, B. (1972), "A Sequential Method Seeking the Global Maximum of a function", *SIAM Journal of Numerical Analysis 9 (3),* 379-388.

Snyman, J. (1985), "A Multistart Global Minimization Algorithm with Dynamic Search Trajectories", *Technical Report 39, University of Pretoria, Republic of South Africa.*

Zenios, S.A. and R.A. Lasken (1987), "Nonlinear network optimization on a massively parallel Connection Machine", *technical report 87-08-03, The Wharton School,* University of Pennsylvania, Philadelphia.

Zenios, S.A. and J.M. Mulvey (1987), "Vectorization and Multitasking of Nonlinear Network Programming Algorithms", *Technical Report 87-03-03* .The Wharton School, University of Pennsylvania, Philadelphia.

EVALUATION OF A PARALLEL HEDGING ALGORITHM FOR STOCHASTIC NETWORK PROGRAMMING [1]

JOHN M. MULVEY AND HERCULES VLADIMIROU

Department of Civil Engineering and Operations Research
School of Engineering and Applied Science
Princeton University, Princeton, N.J. 08544

ABSTRACT

Problems in finance, transportation planning and engineering design can be modeled as nonlinear generalized networks. Inherent uncertainties in these models give rise to large-scale stochastic programs, imposing severe computing requirements. Parallel computing provides a promising means of coping with the computational needs of programs in this class. Recently developed algorithms based on ideas of scenario aggregation allow the decomposition of multistage stochastic programs for concurrent execution on multiprocessors. We address the design of a parallel hedging algorithm for stochastic nonlinear and generalized network programs. The algorithm's performance is evaluated by means of simulations on a sequential computer.

1. INTRODUCTION

Many important planning problems can be modeled as linear or nonlinear generalized networks with stochastic elements. Stochastic network models arise in such diverse areas as logistics planning, utility service scheduling, personnel management and financial planning under uncertainty [Dembo et al. 1988]. While the need to account for uncertainties in these problems has long been recognized, real-world applications have, generally, been restricted to deterministic models despite their known limitations. Deterministic analysis based on point forecasts or "worst case" values of uncertain quantities in mathematical models often leads to decisions which vary significantly from the optimal solution to the underlying stochastic problem [Birge 1982]. Yet, deterministic analysis has been employed, out of necessity, as a computationally tractable surrogate for stochastic programming.

The main obstacle to the development of effective stochastic optimization software has been the size and complexity of stochastic programs. Explicit consideration of the deterministic equivalent models leads to very large programs, not practically solvable with

---

[1] Research partially supported by National Science Foundation Grant #CCR-861-4057 and IBM Grant #5785.

general purpose optimizers. The size of dynamic stochastic programs grows exponentially with the number of time periods in the planning horizon and the number of discrete outcomes of the uncertain parameters at each stage of the program [Dantzig 1988; Mulvey and Vladimirou 1988a; Varaiya and Wets 1988]. Moreover, special structures in the underlying stochastic model are destroyed in the explicit representation of the deterministic equivalent program.

Despite computing limitations, stochastic programming has remained a fertile area of research in the last thirty years. For overviews of developments in the field see Dempster [1980], Wets [1983] and Varaiya and Wets [1988]. Emphasis has been placed on special problem classes, but until recently limited testing of algorithms had been done on realistic size problems. The advent of vector and parallel computers, more sophisticated algorithms and the growing awareness of the limitations of deterministic models dictate a reevaluation of our capabilities to cope with stochastic programs. Already promising decomposition methods with potential for execution in parallel environments have been proposed for multistage stochastic programs (e.g. Noel and Smeers [1987] and Ruszczynski [1988]). The progressive hedging algorithm proposed by Rockafellar and Wets [1987] based on ideas of scenario analysis falls in the same class. Decomposition approaches are being investigated as means of coping with the size explosion in dynamic stochastic programs, while parallel computing promises to meet the computational needs of these programs.

We focus on the design and evaluation of parallel versions of the hedging algorithm. In §2 we examine the structure of two-stage stochastic network programs. A brief description of the progressive hedging algorithm is given in §3, while in §4 we present parallel versions of the algorithm representing different task scheduling strategies for multiprocessing. The parallel processing potential of the algorithm is examined in §5 based on the results of simulations on a sequential computer. Conclusions and directions for further research are discussed in §6.

2. TWO-STAGE STOCHASTIC NETWORK PROGRAMS

Often discretization of the probability space of the random parameters in a stochastic problem is applied, leading to multi-scenario formulations. Each postulated realization of the uncertain quantities in the model yields a deterministic scenario subproblem. Scenario analysis, as it was practiced until now, involved an ad-hoc examination of the subproblem solutions to identify similarities and trends on which a satisfactory solution to the overall problem could be based. It was not until Rockafellar and Wets [1987] (see also Wets [1988]) recently introduced the *progressive hedging algorithm* that a systematic procedure that combines the scenario solutions to a robust decision policy became available.

We consider stochastic nonlinear generalized networks in which some or all of the following parameters are uncertain: arc multipliers, node supply/demand values and arc flow cost function coefficients. For simplicity in notation and brevity of exposition we describe here only two-stage stochastic network programs. Dynamic multistage formulations of stochastic networks can be found in Mulvey and Vladimirou [1988a]. Note that "stages" do not necessarily refer to time steps, but rather correspond to stages in the decision process. Hence, two-stage programs can be used to describe some multiperiod decision problems. Such programs arising in portfolio management under uncertainty are described in Mulvey and Vladimirou [1988b].

Let Ω be a discrete, finite sample space with elementary outcomes ω and associated probabilities π_ω. Each elementary outcome $\omega \in \Omega$ determines a specific realization of the uncertain quantities in the stochastic network model. Denote by $x_1 \in \Re^{n_1}$ the decisions that must be made before the values of the uncertain parameters are observed and aggregate in $x_2(\omega) \in \Re^{n_2}$ all the decisions to be made after a realization $\omega \in \Omega$ of the uncertain quantities is revealed. The explicit representation of the deterministic equivalent program becomes:

$$[MSP] \qquad min \sum_{\omega \in \Omega} \pi_\omega f_\omega(x_1, x_2(\omega))$$

subject to

$$A_1 x_1 \qquad\qquad\qquad = b_1$$
$$A_2(\omega) x_1 + B_2(\omega) x_2(\omega) = b_2(\omega) \quad \forall \omega \in \Omega$$

$$l_1 \leq x_1 \leq u_1, \ l_2 \leq x_2(\omega) \leq u_2 \quad \forall \omega \in \Omega.$$

$f_\omega(.)$ is a convex objective function of the arc flows; $b_1 \in \Re^{m_1}$, $b_2(\omega) \in \Re^{m_2}$ are the supply/demand values; $A_1 \in \Re^{m_1 \times n_1}$, $A_2(\omega) \in \Re^{m_2 \times n_1}$, $B_2(\omega) \in \Re^{m_2 \times n_2}$ specify the generalized node-arc incidence matrix under scenario $\omega \in \Omega$.

Generalized networks with stochastic arc multipliers involve uncertainties in the coefficient matrices $A_2(\omega)$ and $B_2(\omega)$ of the second stage constraints. The constraint coefficient matrix of program [MSP] clearly has a dual block diagonal structure, but the network form of the underlying stochastic model is destroyed with the repetition of the second stage constraints for each possible scenario $\omega \in \Omega$. The constraint coefficients in a multistage program form an arborescent structure which can not be easily exploited in procedures that directly address the deterministic equivalent.

Each realization $\omega \in \Omega$ yields a deterministic scenario subproblem:

$$[SP_\omega] \qquad min \qquad f_\omega(x_1(\omega), x_2(\omega))$$
$$subject\ to \quad (x_1(\omega), x_2(\omega)) \in \mathcal{C}_\omega.$$

$\mathcal{C}_\omega = \{ x_1(\omega), x_2(\omega) : \omega \in \Omega, A_1 x_1(\omega) = b_1, A_2(\omega)x_1(\omega) + B_2(\omega)x_2(\omega) = b_2(\omega),$
$l_1 \leq x_1(\omega) \leq u_1, l_2 \leq x_2(\omega) \leq u_2 \}$ is the polyhedral feasible region generated by the generalized network constraints and bounds under scenario $\omega \in \Omega$.

Each scenario subproblem has its own set of first stage decisions $x_1(\omega)$. The network structure of the underlying stochastic model is preserved in all scenario subproblems. Hence, the constraint coefficient matrix of [SP$_\omega$] corresponds to a generalized node-arc incidence matrix. The topology (nodes, arcs and connectivity) of the network remains the same for all scenarios; only the arc multipliers, supply/demand values and cost function coefficients may differ between scenarios.

The scenario subproblems [SP$_\omega$] provide a series of solutions none of which necessarily coincides with the optimal solution to the overall problem stated in [MSP]. The total problem requires that all scenarios be taken into consideration and that non-anticipativity (independence from hindsight) be met by the solution. The logical requirement of non-anticipativity dictates that the first stage decisions be the same regardless of the scenario (i.e. $x_1(\omega_1) = x_1(\omega_2) = x_1, \forall \omega_1, \omega_2 \in \Omega, \omega_1 \neq \omega_2$).

The progressive hedging algorithm blends the solutions of appropriate versions of the scenario subproblems and iteratively imposes the non-anticipativity restriction by means of augmented Lagrangian functionals. Thus, subproblems of significantly smaller size than the deterministic equivalent program are iteratively solved. The preservation of the network structure of the subproblems allows the use of specialized algorithms in their solution to achieve computational efficiency; we use the nonlinear network optimizer GENOS [Mulvey and Zenios 1987] to solve the scenario subproblems. The independence of disjoint scenario subproblems indicates a coarse level of parallelism in the algorithm which can be exploited for concurrent execution on parallel multiprocessors; this issue is addressed in §4.

3. THE PROGRESSIVE HEDGING ALGORITHM

Rockafellar and Wets [1987] proposed a decomposition algorithm which iteratively solves appropriate variants of the constituent scenario subproblems as a means of coping with the rapid increase in program size with the number of discrete outcomes of the uncertain quantities. Aggregations of the scenarios at each stage are employed to reflect the manner in which information evolves; scenarios sharing the same information history up to a particular stage are grouped in the same bundle. In order to avoid dependence on hindsight subproblems corresponding to scenarios in the same bundle at a certain stage must yield the same values for the decisions of that stage. Iterative adjustments are made to the solutions of cost-modified versions (linear-quadratic perturbations) of the scenario subproblems to adapt to the information structure and yield a non-anticipative solution representative of the scenario probabilities. With the iterative solution of subproblem variants and adaptive "blending" of the successive solutions based on the scenario aggregation structure, the solution to the overall problem is obtained. The procedure can be viewed as a decomposition method drawing heavily from the theory of augmented Lagrangians and the proximal point algorithm [Rockafellar 1976].

A detailed description of the algorithm for multistage stochastic programs and convergence proofs are given in Rockafellar and Wets [1987]. An implementation for dynamic stochastic network programs and computational results are presented in Mulvey and Vladimirou [1988a]. We describe here the simplest form of the algorithm as it applies to the two-stage stochastic programs introduced in §2.

The Progressive Hedging Algorithm
Step 1
Initialize the iteration counter $\nu \leftarrow 0$ and the price vectors $p^\nu(\omega) = 0$, $\forall \omega \in \Omega$.
Solve each scenario subproblem $[SP_\omega]$ ($\forall \omega \in \Omega$) to obtain $(x_1^0(\omega), x_2^0(\omega))$.

$$[SP_\omega] \qquad min \quad f_\omega(x_1(\omega), x_2(\omega)) \qquad s.t. \quad (x_1(\omega), x_2(\omega)) \in \mathcal{C}_\omega.$$

Step 2
Blend the first stage decisions according to:

$$\hat{y}^0(\omega) = \sum_{\omega \in \Omega} \pi_\omega x_1^0(\omega) \qquad \forall \omega \in \Omega.$$

Note that although $(\hat{y}^0(\omega), x_2^0(\omega))$ satisfy the nonanticipativity restriction they are not necessarily feasible in the scenario subproblems $[SP_\omega]$.

Step 3
Solve the modified versions of the scenario subproblems for ($x_1^{\nu+1}(\omega), x_2^{\nu+1}(\omega)$).

$$[SP_\omega^\nu] \qquad min \quad f_\omega(x_1(\omega), x_2(\omega)) + p^\nu(\omega) \cdot x_1(\omega) + \frac{r}{2} \| x_1(\omega) - \hat{y}^\nu(\omega) \|^2$$

$$subject\ to \quad (x_1(\omega), x_2(\omega)) \in \mathcal{C}_\omega$$

where $r > 0$ is a penalty parameter.

Step 4
Again, blend the first stage decisions by:

$$\hat{y}^{\nu+1}(\omega) = \sum_{\omega \in \Omega} \pi_\omega x_1^{\nu+1}(\omega) \qquad \forall \omega \in \Omega$$

and update the multiplier vectors

$$p^{\nu+1}(\omega) = p^\nu(\omega) + r\left(x_1^{\nu+1}(\omega) - \hat{y}^{\nu+1}(\omega)\right) \qquad \forall \omega \in \Omega.$$

Step 5

Increment the iteration counter $\nu \leftarrow \nu + 1$.

If the termination criteria are satisfied exit, else use the new blended solutions and prices to modify the augmented Lagrangian functionals of the scenario subproblems and return to Step 2.

An appropriate convergence norm is given by:

$$\delta_r^\nu = \left[\sum_{\omega \in \Omega} \pi_\omega \left\{ \| \hat{y}^\nu(\omega) - \hat{y}^{\nu-1}(\omega) \|^2 + \| x_1^\nu(\omega) - \hat{y}^\nu(\omega) \|^2 \right\} \right]^{\frac{1}{2}}.$$

4. PARALLEL VARIANTS OF THE HEDGING ALGORITHM

The solution of the scenario subproblems (Step 3) required at each iteration of the algorithm constitutes the most computationally intensive part of the procedure. However, the separability and independence between the scenario subproblems allows for their concurrent solution. This feature can be exploited in algorithmic implementations for execution on MIMD multiprocessor computers.

Concurrent processes involve solving independent subproblems, requiring minimal communication with a central controller. This coarse level of granularity makes the algorithm suitable for implementation on tightly coupled, shared memory systems, as well as loosely coupled, message passing multiprocessors. The network structure of a scenario subproblem is passed from the controller to each individual processor, with the solution being reported back upon completion of the process. The constraints of a subproblem remain unchanged during the solution process; only the coefficients of linear-quadratic perturbations to the objective function are modified from one iteration to the next. Hence, parallel processes can be easily scheduled using a data partitioning framework. Process synchronization is required only once in each iteration.

We view the projection operations, price updating and the convergence checks (Steps 2, 4 and 5) as the serial parts of the algorithm. Microtasking or vector processing can be applied in these operations to further enhance the parallel potential of the algorithm. However, here we ignore this option for exploiting low level parallelism. As the computational results indicate, the serial parts require only a marginal fraction of the total execution time (typically less than 1%). Hence, near linear speedup could be expected in parallel implementations of the hedging algorithm.

We examine two parallel versions of the hedging algorithm corresponding to alternative task scheduling schemes besed on data partitioning. The first version represents a straightforward application of static task prescheduling.

4.1 Static task scheduling

Consider a symmetric multiprocessor system with N identical processors. For each processor k a static task queue Q_k is constructed as follows:

$$Q_k = \{\, ord(\omega) : \omega \in \Omega,\, mod(ord(\omega), N) = k,\, \} \quad k = 1, \ldots, N-1;$$
$$Q_N = \{\, ord(\omega) : \omega \in \Omega,\, mod(ord(\omega), N) = 0,\, \}.$$

A subset of the scenario subproblems is preassigned to each processor. Clearly, this is just one possible scheme for static task allocation; other static partitions of the subproblem set among the processors can be easily devised. In Step 1 of the initial iteration and Step 3 of all subsequent iterations, each processor k solves in sequence the scenario subproblems in its own queue (i.e. SP_ω^ν; $ord(\omega) \in Q_k$) before reaching the synchronization barrier. When all processors finish solving the subproblems in their respective queues, the resulting solutions are averaged as described in Step 4 and the price vectors are updated before continuing with concurrent execution of the scenario subproblems in the next iteration. By convention, we assume that all serial computations are carried out by processor 1.

The issue of load balancing among processors — a prerequisite to achieve high speedup — is critical in designing task scheduling schemes for multiprocessors, because different scenario subproblems may require unequal solution times. Proper task scheduling is particularly important when the number of scenarios is not divisible by the number of processors, because processors are then assigned unequal numbers of subproblems. Obviously, static task scheduling can not take into consideration the relative solution times of different scenario subproblems; as a result, it can not be expected to produce even load distribution among all processors.

4.2 Dynamic task scheduling

We turn to dynamic task scheduling, in which assignment of scenario subproblems to individual processors is decided at run time, as an alternative to improve load balance among processors and achieve higher speedup.

The scenario subrpboblems are assumed to be ordered in a job queue. Each processor removes a subproblem from the queue, solves it and returns for more work. The dynamic task scheduling scheme can be summarized as follows:

1. Each free processor after obtaining a lock on the job queue, searches for unsolved subproblems. If the job queue is empty, the processor releases the lock and becomes idle until the queue is reconstructed; otherwise it removes the next available subproblem from the top of the queue, releases the lock and starts a process to solve the newly assigned subproblem;

2. When processor 1 finds the job queue empty it starts executing the projection and price updating operations that constitute the serial part of the algorithm. It then reconstructs the job queue to signal the beginning of a new iteration.

Clearly, dynamic task scheduling distributes computing load more evenly because no processor becomes idle while there are still unsolved subproblems during a given iteration. Although dynamic task scheduling is the preferred procedure in shared memory systems, in loosely coupled multiprocessors static task scheduling can help reduce data transfer overhead. With static task assignments the fixed data associated with a subproblem (i.e. constraint information and objective function parameters) need only be transferred once to the local memory of the individual processor to which the corresponding subproblem is assigned. Only minimal data, involving the scaled solutions and price updates will then need to be transferred from the central controller to the other processors in all subsequent iterations. Therefore, the architecture of computer hardware and the tradeoff between communication overhead and computing load balance on different systems become important considerations in selecting an appropriate task scheduling procedure when implementing a parallel version of the hedging algorithm on a true multiprocessor computer.

5. SIMULATION RESULTS

In this section we examine the performance of the two parallel variants of the hedging algorithm described in §4. Assessments on the algorithm's parallel potential are based on the results of simulations performed on a sequential computer. All tests were run on a Silicon Graphics IRIS4D/70 compute station. Our test problems represent two-stage stochastic nonlinear generalized network programs corresponding to portfolio management problems [Mulvey and Vladimirou 1988b].

The performance of the progressive hedging algorithm in sequential mode is compared in Table 2 with the solution of the deterministic equivalent nonlinear programs; MINOS [Murtagh and Saunders 1983] was used to solve the deterministic equivalents. Although decomposition procedures are not expected to be competitive when the explicit programs can be directly solved, the progressive hedging algorithm fared rather well against a state of the art nonlinear optimizer. Considering the rate of increase in the size of the deterministic equivalents with the number of scenarios, in many applications decomposition might be the only viable alternative. It should be noted that the convergence performance of the algorithm can be influenced with appropriate selection of algorithmic parameters (e.g. r) and other internal tactics; an investigation of such issues is considered in Mulvey and Vladimirou [1988a]. The algorithm generally exhibits a rapid initial rate of convergence, which is an attractive property when approximate solutions are satisfactory.

		Problem Size			
PROBLEM	# of	Scenario Subproblems		Deterministic Equivalent	
	scenarios	# nodes	# arcs	# constraints	# variables
A	21	45	116	725	1996
B	_1	45	116	725	1996
C	21	45	118	725	1998
E	25	45	116	861	2372
F	29	45	118	997	2750
N	39	67	178	2195	6106

Table 1: Test Problems

	MINOS Solution		Hedging Algorithm Solution			
PROBLEM	objective	time	objective	% from	time	Efficiency
	value	(sec)	value	optimality	(sec)	
A	0.61150203	132.96	0.61171827	0.035	356.10	2.68
B	-0.41916295	170.80	-0.41916295	0.000	376.72	2.21
C	-0.40800157	148.27	-0.40769031	0.076	109.68	0.74
E	0.65734476	243.78	0.65734476	0.000	116.34	0.48
F	-0.43504628	269.98	-0.42209584	2.977	174.52	0.65
N	-0.66431372	1431.31	-0.66431372	0.000	428.95	0.30

Table 2: Comparison of the Sequential Progressive Hedging Algorithm with MINOS

To assess the parallel potential of the hedging algorithm we need to establish some evaluation measures. The realized speedup of the parallel versions of the algorithm can be compared against the upper bound provided by Amdahl's law:

$$Speedup = \frac{T_1}{T_N} \leq \frac{s+p}{s+p/N} .$$

N is the number of available processors; s, p are the fractions of serial and parallel work in the algorithm; T_k is the execution time with k processors. Amdahl's law provides an upper bound on achievable speedup because it is based on the assumption that the parallel work in the algorithm can be evenly distributed among all available processors. This is generally unattainable even if all scenario subproblems could be solved in identical times, because the number of scenario subproblems is not always divisible by the number of processors. For the same reason realized speedup in our parallel hedging procedures is not necessarily

STATIC TASK SCHEDULING							
# of Processors	Observed Speedup						
	A	B	C	E	F	N	Average
1	1.000	1.000	1.000	1.000	1.000	1.000	**1.000**
2	1.902	1.927	1.870	1.898	1.916	1.919	**1.905**
3	2.790	2.844	2.800	2.705	2.701	2.826	**2.778**
4	3.341	3.590	3.312	3.415	3.569	3.586	**3.469**
6	4.609	4.841	4.629	4.644	4.998	5.106	**4.804**
7	5.679	5.880	5.861	5.617	5.656	5.871	**5.761**
8	5.912	6.083	5.675	5.975	6.246	6.650	**6.090**
10	7.178	7.027	6.459	7.030	7.189	8.009	**7.149**
12	7.929	8.299	7.687	7.342	7.429	8.428	**7.852**
DYNAMIC TASK SCHEDULING							
# of Processors	Observed Speedup						
	A	B	C	E	F	N	Average
1	1.000	1.000	1.000	1.000	1.000	1.000	**1.000**
2	1.948	1.955	1.956	1.957	1.960	1.964	**1.957**
3	2.852	2.861	2.850	2.834	2.809	2.897	**2.851**
4	3.685	3.653	3.614	3.707	3.744	3.778	**3.697**
6	5.084	5.102	5.140	5.185	5.242	5.481	**5.240**
7	5.797	6.100	5.923	5.867	5.955	6.256	**5.983**
8	6.351	6.543	6.396	6.590	6.505	7.035	**6.570**
10	7.614	7.372	7.350	7.731	7.625	8.665	**7.726**
12	8.695	8.779	8.459	8.574	8.477	9.964	**8.825**

Table 3: Performance of the Parallel Hedging Algorithm

increasing monotonically with the number of processors, because in some configurations equal distribution of subproblems among the processors is not possible (see Table 3).

Consequently, we use a modified version of Amdahl's law to obtain a more realistic estimate of expected speedup, as follows:

$$Speedup = \frac{T_1}{T_N} \approx \frac{\sum_{k=1}^{N} \gamma_k}{\sum_{k=1}^{N} \gamma_k / k} \cdot$$

γ_k is the fraction of work to be executed at level of parallelism k. In applying this formula we set $\gamma_1 = s$, $\gamma_m = m(p/N)$; $m = mod(card(\Omega), N)$, and $\gamma_N = (p - \gamma_m)/N$. This again assumes that even load distribution can be achieved at a certain level of parallelism. Although the expected speedup estimate provided by the above formula is more realistic, it is no longer an upper bound.

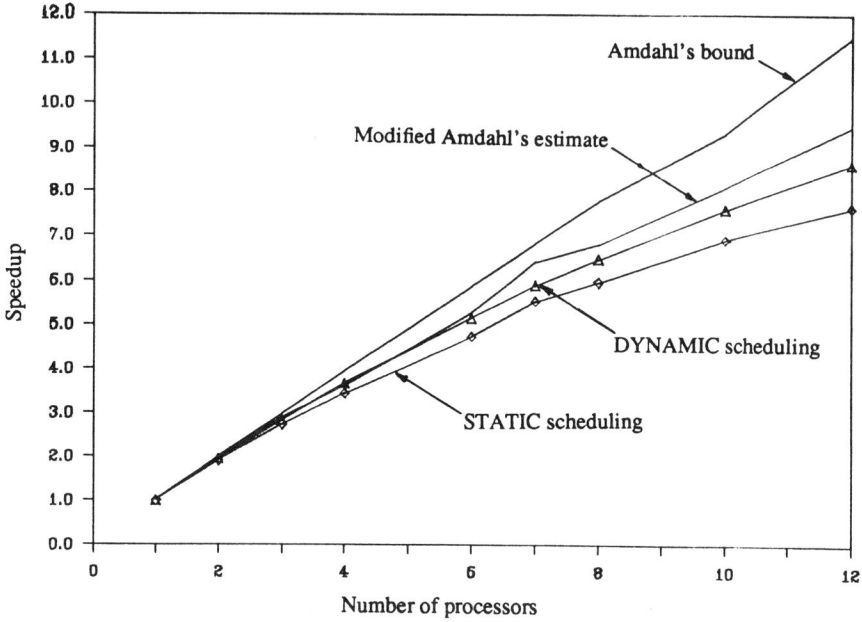

Figure 1: Estimated and Observed Speed of Parallel Heding Algorithm

In terms of realized speedup, dynamic task scheduling clearly outperforms static task scheduling (see Table 3); this is the result of more even load balancing by dynamic task scheduling as indicated in Tables 4 and 5 for a sample problem. However, the selection of an appropriate task scheduling scheme could also be influenced by other factors such as communication overhead which are system depended. In Figure 1 we compare the observed speedup with the speedup estimates averaged over all the test problems. As these results indicate, near linear speedup can be achieved with increasing number of processors for parallel versions of the hedging algorithm.

N	Busy time for each processor (sec)												Total time (sec)	Speedup
	p1	p2	p3	p4	p5	p6	p7	p8	p9	p10	p11	p12		
1	824.61												824.61	1.000
2	427.03	397.58											429.69	1.919
3	284.95	269.50	270.15										291.80	2.826
4	216.06	210.19	210.42	187.94									229.98	3.586
6	152.26	143.16	148.26	132.17	126.34	122.41							161.50	5.106
7	122.90	127.00	122.27	130.33	103.48	114.37	104.25						140.44	5.871
8	115.17	111.56	107.74	106.35	100.70	98.35	103.07	81.45					124.01	6.650
10	91.01	87.69	90.61	83.43	80.72	82.86	80.29	81.61	83.88	62.49			102.96	8.009
12	93.66	82.02	83.77	64.55	57.88	59.93	58.43	61.05	64.13	68.39	68.61	62.18	99.86	8.428

Table 4. Workload Distribution Among Processors, STATIC TASK SCHEDULING (Problem N)

N	Busy time for each processor (sec)												Total time (sec)	Speedup
	p1	p2	p3	p4	p5	p6	p7	p8	p9	p10	p11	p12		
1	824.61												824.61	1.000
2	413.86	410.75											419.80	1.964
3	275.24	273.05	276.32										284.65	2.897
4	207.73	205.61	206.69	204.58									218.24	3.778
6	139.71	133.77	138.97	136.73	138.78	136.66							150.46	5.481
7	120.62	118.13	117.22	116.45	116.95	118.42	116.81						131.81	6.256
8	106.56	101.83	103.97	103.65	103.74	101.10	102.47	101.18					117.21	7.035
10	82.91	80.77	82.07	80.13	82.97	80.62	82.91	83.95	84.54	83.75			95.16	8.665
12	68.69	66.60	69.45	69.09	68.60	68.98	71.17	71.53	66.71	67.26	69.96	66.58	82.76	9.964

Table 5. Workload Distribution Among Processors, DYNAMIC TASK SCHEDULING (Problem N)

6. CLOSING REMARKS

Parallel computers have been recognized as suitable vehicles for the solution of large-scale stochastic programs. This study demonstrates that substantial benefits can be derived by specializing stochastic programming algorithms for execution on multiprocessor systems. Parallel variants of the hedging algorithm were shown to be capable of achieving near linear speedup. Although our results were obtained with simulations on a sequential uniprocessor, they clearly demonstrate the parallel potential of a promising decomposition algorithm for stochastic programming. Undoubtedly, the best performance of parallel optimization software can be observed through tests on true multiprocessor computers. Nevertheless, our simulation results help put current expectations in the right perspective. Once the parallel potential of the algorithm is being established, implementation software can be streamlined to the architecture of available parallel computer systems.

Investigation of parallel decomposition algorithms that can take advantage of advanced computer technology will undoubtedly continue. As a first step, the adaptation of existing algorithms for execution on parallel multiprocessors is being examined. In the case of the hedging algorithm, its parallel potential can be further enhanced by utilizing vector processing or microtasking in the projection and price updating operations which now constitute the serial part of the procedure. Additionally, low level parallelism can be exploited by using microtasking in the specialized algorithms that solve the individual scenario subproblems, when processors become available at the late stages of each iteration. For example, vector and parallel versions of the nonlinear optimizer GENOS [Mulvey and Zenios 1987], which we use to solve the scenario subproblems, were shown to achieve superior performance in solving generalized network programs [Zenios and Mulvey 1986; 1987].

Modifications of the hedging algorithm may also be considered as means of improving its parallel performance. An attractive possibility would be to solve some of the scenario subproblems inexactly, in a controlled fashion that preserves the algorithm's convergence properties, so as to achieve even load balance. Alternatively, asynchronous versions of the algorithm may be possible which could allow the achievement of even higher speedup.

REFERENCES

Birge, J.R. (1982), "The value of the stochastic solution in stochastic linear programs with fixed recourse," *Mathematical Programming*, 24, 314-325.

Dantzig, G.B. (1988), "Planning under uncertainty using parallel computing," in *Annals of Operations Research*, 14, Special volume on *Parallel Optimization on Novel Computer Architectures*, R.R. Meyer and S.A. Zenios, eds.

Dembo, R.S., J.M. Mulvey and S.A. Zenios (1988), "Large scale network models and their application," *Operations Research*, (to appear).

Dempster, M.A.H., ed. (1980), *Stochastic Programming*, Academic Press, 1980.

Mulvey, J.M. and S.A. Zenios (1987), "GENOS 1.0 user's guide: A generalized network optimization system," Technical Report 87-12-03, Decision Sciences Dept., University of Pennsylvania, Philadelphia, Penn., Dec.

Mulvey, J.M. and H. Vladimirou (1988a), "Solving multistage stochastic networks: An application of scenario aggregation," Technical Report SOR-88-1, Dept. of Civil Engineering and Operations Research, Princeton Univ., Princeton, N.J., Feb.

Mulvey, J.M. and H. Vladimirou (1988b), "Stochastic network optimization models for investment planning," Technical Report SOR-88-2, Dept. of Civil Engineering and Operations Research, Princeton Univ., Princeton, N.J., Sept.

Murtagh, B.A. and M.A. Saunders (1983), "MINOS 5.0 user's guide," Report SOL-83-20, Dept. of Operations Research, Stanford University, Stanford, Calif., Dec.

Noel, M.C. and Y. Smeers (1987), "Ns decomposition of multistage nonlinear programs with recourse," *Mathematical Programming*, 37, 131-152.

Rockafellar, R.T. (1976), "Monotone operators and the proximal point algorithm," *SIAM Journal of Control and Optimization*, 14, 877-898.

Rockafellar, R.T. and R.J.-B. Wets (1987), "Scenarios and policy aggregation in optimization under uncertainty," WP-87-119, IIASA, Laxenburg, Austria, Dec.

Ruszczynski, A. (1988), "Parallel decomposition of multistage stochastic programming problems," Working Paper, Institute of Automatic Control, Warsaw Institute of Technology, Warsaw, Poland, July.

Varaiya, P. and R.J.-B. Wets (1988), "Stochastic dynamic optimization approaches and computation," WP-88-87, IIASA, Laxenburg, Austria, Sept.

Wets, R.J.-B. (1983), "Stochastic programming: Solution techniques and approximation schemes," in A. Bachem and B. Korte, eds., *Mathematical Programming: The State of the Art*, Springer-Verlag, Berlin, 507-603.

Wets, R.J.-B. (1988), "The aggregation principle in scenario analysis and stochastic optimization," Working Paper, Dept. of Mathematics, University of California, Davis, Calif., Sept.

Zenios, S.A. and J.M. Mulvey (1986), "Nonlinear network programming on vector supercomputers: A study on the CRAY X-MP," *Operations Research*, 34, 5, 667-682.

Zenios, S.A. and J.M. Mulvey (1987), "Vectorization and multitasking of nonlinear network programming algorithms," Technical Report 87-03-03, Decision Sciences Dept., University of Pennsylvania, Philadelphia, Penn., Mar.

PARALLEL SOLUTION OF A DYNAMIC PROGRAMMING EQUATION USING OPTIMISTIC EVALUTION

DAVID M. NICOL [1]

Department of Computer Science
The College of William and Mary
Williamsburg, VA 23185

ABSTRACT

The availability of parallel computers offers the potential for quickly solving large computational problems in operations research. However, it is often a non-trivial task to effectively use parallel computers. Solution methods must sometimes be reformulated to exploit parallelism; the reformulations are often more complex than their slower serial counterparts. We illustrate these points with a simple example: solution of the one dimensional dynamic programming equation

$$V(j) = C_j + \min_{L(j) \leq i \leq j} \{V(i-1)\}.$$

The process of solving this equation appears to be inherently serial, as the value of $V(j)$ depends on the value of $V(j-1)$. However, it is possible to formulate a parallel solution by *optimistically* assuming that the index which defines the min term is not "near" j. This allows the function to be computed in parallel at indices which are "close"; of course, if the optimism is unwarranted we need to recompute some function values. This paper describes the solution method, sketches an expected complexity argument that gives conditions for the speedup to to be proportional to the number of processors used, and presents empirical data demonstrating that significant speedups are realized when using up to sixteen processors.

1. INTRODUCTION

The availability of parallel computers offers the potential for quickly solving large computational problems in operations research. However, to exploit parallelism it may

---

[1] This research was supported in part by the National Aeronautics and Space Administration under NASA contract NAS1-18107 while the author was in residence at ICASE, Mail Stop 132C, NASA Langley Research Center, Hampton, VA 23665.

Copyright 1989 by Elsevier Science Publishing Co., Inc.
Impacts of Recent Computer Advances on Operations Research
Ramesh Sharda, Bruce L. Golden, Edward Wasil, Osman Balci, William Stewart, Editors

be necessary to reformulate the solution algorithm; the construction of effective parallel algorithms is still an art in its infancy. Parallel solutions may be more complex than their serial counterparts, and may rely on insights not generally called for in serial algorithms. To illustrate these points we consider a simple dynamic programming equation which arises in the partitioning of chains. We have a chain of m nodes; node i has non-negative weight w_i, and shares edges with nodes $i-1$ and $i+1$ (unless i is at the end of the chain). The edge connecting nodes i and $i+1$ has a non-negative cost C_i. We are given some threshold T; we are to find an optimal partitioning of the chain into contiguous subchains so that the sum of node weights in any subchain does not exceed T. The cost of a partitioning is the sum of the weights on the "cut" edges. For example, if a five node chain is partitioned into subchains $(1)(2\ 3)(4\ 5)$, the cost of the partitioning is $C_1 + C_3$. This problem was orginally solved by Kernighan [1971] who optimally divides a computer program into segments; more recently the problem has arisen in a parallel scheduling context discussed by Nicol [1988]. The problem is solved using dynamic programming. Let $V(j)$ be the minimized cost of partitioning nodes 1 through j, given that a cut is placed directly after node j. For every j we let $L(j)$ be the smallest integer such that $\sum_{i=L(j)}^{j} w_i \leq T$; then the principle of optimality states that

$$V(j) = C_j + \min_{L(j) \leq i \leq j} \{V(i-1)\}. \tag{1}$$

The index which defines the min term identifies the last node in the next-to-the-last subchain in the optimal partitioning of nodes 1 through j. Once all values of V are found, the optimal partitioning is discovered in the usual way by backtracking.

At a glance it would seem that this equation can only be solved serially, since $V(j)$ may be equal to $C_j + V(j-1)$. However, if we knew that $V(j)$'s min term is **not** equal to $V(j-1)$ then we could compute $V(j)$ in parallel with $V(j-1)$. Since this prescience is lacking, we propose to compute $V(j)$ *optimistically*, under the assumption that none of the values near it (say $V(j-1)$, $V(j-2)$, $V(j-3)$) define its min term. If we have n processors, we will optimistically compute a block of n adjacent values in parallel. A simple check reveals whether the optimism was justified. If not, the incorrectly computed values are recomputed serially.

This paper explores the idea of using optimistic evaluation by (i) developing the algorithm sketched above, (ii) by providing analytic conditions under which we can expect the algorithm to perform well, and (iii) by presenting significant, measured speedups using 2, 4, 8, and 16 processors. Although equation (1) is very simple, the concept of optimistic evaluation is one that may be used to solve other dynamic programming problems.

2. SERIAL ALGORITHM

This study was motivated by an application where we sought to partition a chain of m software modules for execution on a parallel computer with n processors. In our solution, equation (1) is repeatedly solved with varying values of the threshold T, until the smallest value of T yielding an optimal partition with n or fewer partition elements is discovered. By changing T we potentially change the value of $L(j)$ for each j. An effective serial solution employs a heap whose elements point to known V values. The heap is organized so that the least element is at the top. Elements are compared by two keys—the major key is the element's V value while the minor key is its domain position.

To compute $V(j)$ we must first identify $L(j)$, and then use the heap to find $V(j)$'s min term. Once computed, a pointer to $V(j)$ is placed in the heap. Details of this method are given below.

1. For every j, compute $S(j) = \sum_{i=1}^{j} w_i$; initialize priority heap with a pointer to $V(0) = 0$; set $j = 1$;

2. Find the range of $V(j)$'s min term. This is accomplished with a binary search on $S(1), \ldots, S(j-1)$ that finds the smallest k such that $S(j) - S(k-1) \leq T$. $L(j)$ is equal to this k.

3. Discard items from the heap until the top item points to some $V(i)$ such that $L(j) \leq i$. Compute $V(j) = C_j + V(i)$, and insert an entry for $V(j)$ in the heap.

4. $j = j + 1$; if $j \neq n + 1$ goto 2.

The complexity of this algorithm is $O(m \log m)$ since the searching and heap operations have logarithmic cost.

The bulk of this computation lies in the binary search, and in the heap manipulations. If we are to achieve good speedups we will either have to effectively parallelize searching and heap operations, or we will have to allow concurrent searchs and heap operations for different values of j. We have chosen the latter option, described in the following section.

3. PARALLEL ALGORITHM

Our problem is to solve equation(1) for $j = 1, \ldots, m$, using n processors $P_1, \ldots, P_n$. We assume that each processor has its own local memory, and that processors have access to a common memory. As illustrated in figure 1a for $n = 8$, our parallel algorithm divides for $n = 8$ the domain $[1, \ldots, m]$ into m/n blocks of adjacent domain points. We denote the sequence of blocks as $B_1, B_2, \ldots, B_{m/n}$. The function values are computed one block at a time; all points within a block are computed in parallel, with each processor being responsible for exactly one value. The workload assignment is trivial: in block B_k processor P_i computes $V((k-1)n + i)$. The fundamental problem is that the min term of the value computed by P_i when $i > 1$ includes values which are being concurrently computed by $P_1, \ldots, P_{i-1}$. We circumvent the problem by optimistically assuming that the min term is not defined by any of the values being concurrently computed. This idea is illustrated by figure 1b.

The general form of the parallel algorithm is as follows. To compute a function value, a processor executes a modification of the serial algorithm described above. The computation is optimistic in that the min term is taken without considering function values within the current block. Once all processors have computed their tentative function values they cooperatively compute the least function value v_b within the block. As illustrated by figure 2a, v_b can be computed in parallel by constructing a combining tree. We will later see that this construction is quite important. A simple test performed in one processor determines whether all of these tentative values are correct. If so, every processor modifies its heap to include a pointer to v_b and the algorithm proceeds to the next block. If the test fails then some of the block's points will have to be recomputed serially.

Each processor maintains a heap in its local memory, but with a significant difference: every heap entry points to the minimum value within an entire block. This allows the algorithm cost due to heap manipulation to scale proportionally with the number of processors—a necessary condition for good speedups. It is somewhat more complex to find min terms; to see this let a and b be the least and greatest domain points in $L(j)$'s block, respectively. If the minimum value for that block lies at c when $a \leq c < L(j)$, then the heap pointer to c is of no use to us. To correctly consider terms in $L(j)$'s block the processor must find the minimum over $[L(j), b]$, an interval we call a *fractional block*. To construct $V(j)$'s optimistic min term the processor then manipulates its heap to see if the fractional block minimum is less than the minimum value among all complete blocks between $L(j)$'s and j's.

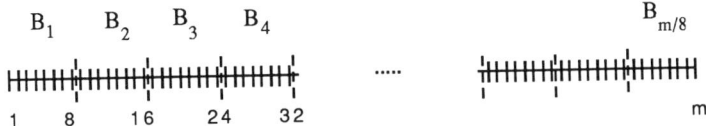

(a) Domain partitioned into blocks of eight elements

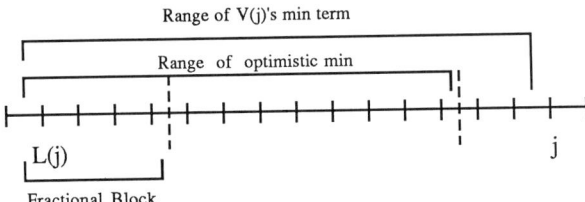

(b) V(j)'s min term may be defined outside of V(j)'s block

Figure 1: Domain divided into blocks for parallel solution

We have not yet resolved the problem of efficiently finding the fractional block minimum. If n is small a simple linear scan of $V(L(j)), \ldots, V(b)$ will suffice. This method does not scale well as the number of processors increases. An efficient method is possible if the combining tree constructed for $L(j)$'s block is left in memory. As illustrated by figure 2b, it is possible to find the minimum value over $[L(j), b]$ by comparing no more than $\log n$ values.

The parallel algorithm used to compute the points of block B_k is given below.

1. *Serial Step:* P_n determines whether it is feasible to compute B_k's points in parallel. A necessary condition is that $L(kn)$ be outside of B_k. If not, the block's points are computed serially, and the algorithm advances to the next block.

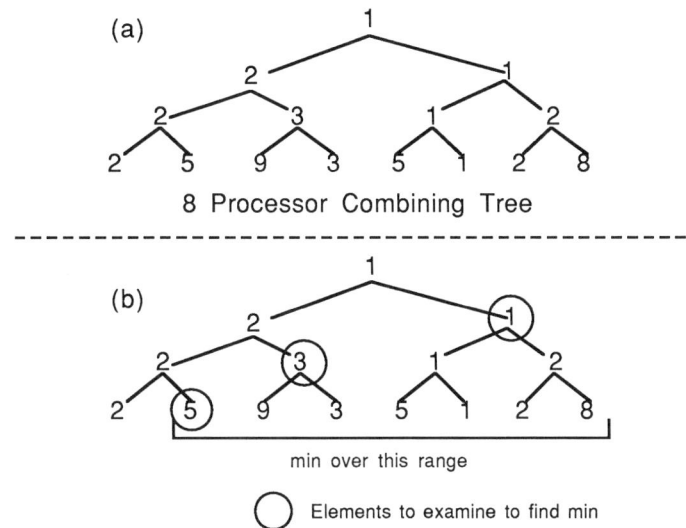

Figure 2: Combining tree to compute and find minimums

2. *Parallel Step:* P_j is responsible for computing $V((k-1)n+j)$. P_j uses a binary search to find $L((k-1)n+j)$, and then identifies the minimum $v_f(j)$ of that point's fractional block. P_j then iteratively discards the top element of its heap until the top element points to a point within a block between $L((k-1)n+j)$'s block and $((k-1)n+j)$'s block. Letting $v_h(j)$ be the value of that point, P_j optimistically computes

$$V((k-1)n+j) = C_{(k-1)n+j} + min\{v_f(j), v_h(j)\}.$$

3. *Parallel Step:* The processors cooperatively build a combining tree to find the minimum tentative value in the block, called v_b.

4. *Serial Step:* P_n checks to see if $v_b < min\{v_f(n), v_h(n)\}$. If so, the function values

in the block are recomputed serially. Otherwise the algorithm advances to the next block.

4. COMPLEXITY ANALYSIS

We next turn to a study of the parallel algorithm's complexity. Worst case bounds are of little use, since it is possible that every block is serially computed, yielding no performance benefit from parallel processing. Instead we present an expected complexity analysis based on quantifying the probability that a block computation is serialized. The expected complexity is then a weighted combination of the algorithm's serial complexity and its parallel complexity. We first consider the complexity in the absence of serialization.

Step (1) requires $O(\log m)$ time, since identifying $L(kn)$ requires a binary search. P_j's cost of performing step (2) includes an $O(\log m)$ cost to identify $L((k-1)n + j)$, and an $O(\log n)$ cost to identify $v_f(j)$. The cost of finding $v_h(j)$ is a little more delicate to quantify, as an unknown number of heap elements are discarded. However, every processor is discarding almost the same set of heap elements, so that the processors' behavior at this step is highly correlated. Amortized over the entire computation, the expected cost of finding $v_h(j)$ can be shown to be $O(\log(m/n))$. Step (3) requires $O(\log n)$ time, and step (4) takes constant time. The dominating term is $O(\log m)$ from step (2); taken m/n times we see that the full complexity is $O((m/n)\log m)$.

The complexity of a serialized solution is $O(m \log m)$. If p is the probability that a block serializes, then the expected complexity is $O(pm \log m + (1-p)(m/n)\log m)$. Consequently, if p is as low as $O(1/n)$, then the expected complexity is the same as the pristine parallel complexity. We turn next to the problem of identifying situations where p is low.

We must base the probability of serialization on stochastic assumptions about the node and arc weights. We assume simply that the node weights are independent and drawn from a common distribution with mean μ and finite variance; likewise we assume that the arc weights are independent and drawn from another (possibly different) common distribution with finite mean and variance.

The first opportunity the algorithm has for serialization is step (1). There we serialize if the range of $V(kn)$'s min term falls entirely within block B_k. A necessary and sufficient condition for this to occur is that the sum of the n node weights associated with the block is less than T. By appealing to Chebychev's inequality (e.g. see Larson and Shubert [1979]), it is possible to prove the following lemma:

Lemma 1 *Let p_1 be the probability of serialization at step (1). If $T \geq 2n\mu$, then $p_1 = O(1/n)$.*

Now let p_2 be the probability that the min term of some point in block B_k is defined at a point in B_k. We will again see that if T is large enough, p_2 will be $O(1/n)$. Towards this end we state the following lemma, whose proof is found in Nicol [1988].

Lemma 2 *Let $V(i), V(i+1), \ldots, V(i+N-1)$ be a consecutive sequence of V values, $N > n$. Then the probability that the minimum occurs in one of the last n sequence elements is no greater than n/N.*

The sense of this lemma is that given a sequence of V values, the minimum one is more likely to have a low index than a high index. Of course, this is exactly what our algorithm is exploiting, that a point's min term is not defined within the point's block. For a given block B_k, the value N is the number of values encompassed within the range of $V(kn)$'s min term. As such, N is a random variable. To drive $p_2 = n/N = O(1/n)$, we seek conditions under which $E[n/N] = O(1/n)$. Also shown in Nicol [1988] is that when $T > n^2\mu/2$, then $E[n/N] = O(1/n)$. This proves the final lemma:

Lemma 3 *Let p_2 be the probability that the min term of some point in a block is defined at some other point in that block. If $T \geq n^2\mu/2$, then $p_2 = O(1/n)$.*

The probability that a block serializes is no greater than $p_1 + p_2$; consequently lemmas (1) and (3) give us the type of result we seek: when the threshold T is large enough, the probability of serialization is $O(1/n)$, and the expected complexity of the algorithm is $O((m/n)\log m)$.

5. PERFORMANCE RESULTS

Our parallel algorithm has overheads that are not suffered by a serial code. For example, its calculation of a point's min term is somewhat more complex than in the serial case, the processors cooperatively compute the minimum over a block, and the processors globally synchronize after step (1) (to see if the block must serialize) and after step (4) (to ensure that every processor is working on the same block). Consequently, our parallel algorithm cannot be n times faster than the best serial implementation. The best we can hope for is that the algorithm have acceptable performance, and that its speedup scale up linearly as the problem and number of processors increases. Our complexity results suggest that the algorithm achieves linear speedup asympotically, but such results often have little bearing on the performance of actual implementations. We have coded our parallel algorithm on a shared-memory multiprocessor, and have very promising initial performance measurements.

The algorithm is implemented on the Flex/32 (see Matelan [1985]) at the NASA Langley Research Center. The Flex/32 has twenty processors; two of these serve as multiprocessing hosts, and the remainder serve as a parallel array. Each processor has 4 Mb of local memory, and can access a 16 Mb common memory over a local bus. At present the CPU's are based on the National Semiconductor 32032 chip.

We are interested in two facets of performance. Foremost, can we **ever** achieve significant speedups? *Speedup* is measured as the time required by an optimized serial algorithm divided by the time required by a parallel version. An isomorphic notion is that of *efficiency:* speedup divided by the number of processors employed, and represents the fraction of time that an average processor spends performing useful work (additional overhead is considered to be non-useful work, however necessary). We will use both speedup and efficiency to describe raw performance. The second facet of interest is the ability of the analytic model to predict good performance. We will see that good performance is possible, and that the analytic results are reasonable in their estimation of that performance.

The first graph in figure 3 plots average measured speedups for an ensemble of randomly generated problems where $\mu = 20$, and $m = 2048$. For 2,4,8, and 16 processors we plot speedup as a function of T; we assume that $T = 10 \times 2^i$ and label the horizontal axis with values of i from 1 to 8. The empirical results support both intuition and the analytic results: performance improves as T gets larger. The limiting efficiencies are 70%, 63%, 54%, and 41% for 2,4,8, and 16 processors, respectively. These numbers are quite good, considering the parallel code's additional overheads. For each processor performance curve we have marked with a diamond the T value where $T = n^2 \mu / 2$. Our analytic model suggests that good performance is achieved for T larger than this threshold; the model predictions are borne out in the measurements. The second graph illustrates the frequency of serialization as a function of T for these same runs. As expected, the performance degradation seen under low values of T is due to block serialization.

6. SUMMARY

The availability and promise of parallel processing suggests that we develop parallel algorithms for solving computational problems in operations research. The field of parallel

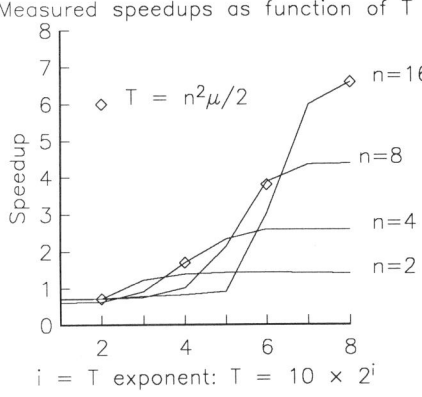
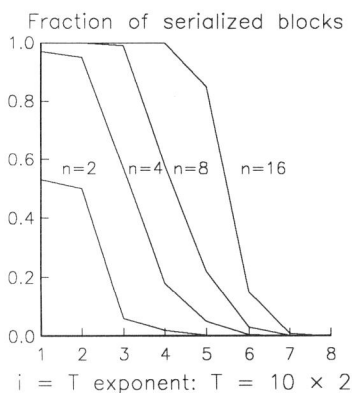

Figure 3: Performance as function of T, where $m = 2048$ and $\mu = 20$

algorithm development is still very young, and is open to new methods of finding and exploiting parallelism. In this paper we introduce the concept of *optimistic evaluation* as a means of exploiting parallelism in problem that is seemingly serial. The problem is the solution of a simple one-dimensional dynamic programming equation, but optimistic evaluation can clearly be attempted in more complex problems. We have derived conditions under which our algorithm achieves expected linear speedup asymptotically; we have also measured our algorithm's performance on a multiprocessor, using up to 16 processors. The performance values are quite good: for appropriately sized problems we achieve efficiencies of 70%, 63%, 54%, and 41% for 2,4,8, and 16 processors respectively.

REFERENCES

Kernighan, G. (1971) "Optimal Sequential Partitions of Graphs", *Journal of the ACM* *18*,1,(Jan.), 34-40.

Larson, H., Shubert, B. (1979) *Probabilistic Models in Enginee ring Sciences Vol. 1*, Wiley, New York.

Matelan, N. (1985) "The Flex/32 Multicomputer", In *Proceedin gs of the 12th International Symposium on Computer Architecture*, Computer Society Press, pp. 209-213.

Nicol, D. (1988) "Parallel Algorithms for Mapping Pipelined and Parallel Computations", ICASE Tech Rep. 88-2, NASA Langley Research Center, Hampton, VA.

PARALLEL BRANCH AND BOUND ALGORITHMS FOR UNCONSTRAINED QUADRATIC ZERO-ONE PROGRAMMING

PANOS M. PARDALOS AND GREGORY P. RODGERS †

Department of Computer Science, Pennsylvania State University

University Park, Pennsylvania 16802

ABSTRACT

We propose and implement branch and bound algorithms for unconstrained quadratic zero-one programming on various parallel computers. The algorithms are able to vary the *granularity* for tuning on a particular architecture. Furthermore, by using depth-first search and avoiding the use of a shared data structure, implementation on a distributed memory multiprocessor is possible. Algorithms have been implemented on two distributed memory multiprocessors, a 32 node iPSC/1 hypercube and a 16 node iPSC/2 hypercube, and two shared memory multiprocessors, the Cray X-MP/48 and the IBM 3090-600E.

1. INTRODUCTION

Unconstrained zero-one programs have the form:

$$\min f(x), \quad x \in \{0,1\}^N$$

If $f(x)$ is linear, the problem is trivial. However, when $f(x)$ is nonlinear the problem may be extremely difficult. In general, quadratic zero-one programming is NP-complete. The indefinite unconstrained quadratic zero-one programming problem is formulated as follows:

$$\min f(x) = c^T x + \frac{x^T A x}{2}, \quad x \in \{0,1\}^N \qquad \text{(QP)}$$

where A is an $N \times N$ rational matrix and c is a rational vector of length N. It has been shown that any nonlinear zero-one programs can be reduced to a quadratic program [Hansen 1979]. Other reductions can be found in [Pardalos and Rosen 1987]. Algorithms for solving QP on various parallel computers are considered in this paper.

One approach to solving QP is a branch and bound algorithm [Rodgers and Pardalos 1988]. This method implicitly enumerates all possible solutions. For zero-one variables this is done by traversing a binary tree where each level represents a different variable. Separate branches represent values of 0 or 1 for the variable at that

---

† Permanent Address: IBM Corporation, General Technology Division, Burlington Vermont 05452.

level. A path from the root to a leaf represents a complete assignment of zero-one values. For unconstrained problems any assignment of values is feasible. However, it may be determined that some branches of the tree may yield suboptimal solutions. In which case, those branches are not searched. This is referred to as pruning.

Branches of the search tree can be considered as independent subproblems which can be evaluated in parallel. Roucairol [1987] parallelizes a branch and bound algorithm for the quadratic assignment problem on the Cray XM/P. The algorithm uses shared memory to store the expanded nodes of the search tree in a heap. This heap also allows for multiple searching strategies. However, this method is limited by the storage capacity for the heap. Boehning, Butler, and Gillett [1988] and Lavellee [1987] also use a shared data structure to store subproblems for parallel execution.

Abdelrahman and Mudge [1988] proposed two parallelization methods on a distributed memory multiprocessor. The first method maintains a centralized list of subproblems and a manager. The second method outperforms the first by distributing the list of subproblems and balancing the load among neighboring processors. When all neighboring processes are idle the algorithm "guesses" to terminate. Their method is also capable of incorporating multiple searching strategies.

We eliminate the problem of storing large numbers of subproblems by using depth-first search. Details of our sequential algorithm are given in [Rodgers and Pardalos 1988]. Depth-first search uses a stack to store the subproblems. The last-in-first-out (LIFO) operation of the stack only requires a maximum depth of N. Depth-first search is frequently used in constrained programs to yield a feasible solution quickly. However, this is *not* the case in unconstrained optimization since all values are feasible. For unconstrained optimization we supplement the branch and bound process with an initially applied heuristic to find a "nearly" optimal solution to use as the branch and bound incumbent. A good initial incumbent reduces the need for best-first searching strategies since there is little chance of improving the incumbent enough to significantly reduce the size of the branch and bound tree. In fact, if the initial incumbent is the optimal solution and the branch and bound process is executed merely to verify that it is optimal, then the searching strategy will not affect the size of the branch and bound tree since the incumbent will not change.

In this paper we present algorithms for two computer architectures. In section 2 the general parallel algorithm is discussed. Considerations for shared memory architectures and distributed memory architectures are given in sections 3 and 4 respectively. Computational results are given in section 5 followed by further results of an improvement to the algorithm in section 6.

2. OVERVIEW OF PARALLEL ALGORITHM

The parallel algorithm is based on the idea of splitting the branch and bound tree into exactly as many subproblems as there are processors. The subproblems are then allowed to execute for a specified number of vertices of the branch and bound search tree. If a subproblem completes its search within the allotted number of vertices then an unfinished subproblem is split and assigned to a free processor. Algorithm 2.1 gives the general outline of our approach.

Algorithm 2.1

```
1     Assign initial problem to processor 1
2     while ( any processor is not assigned a subproblem ) do
2.a       Find a juncture for an active subproblem
2.b       Split the subproblem at the juncture
2.c       Assign new subproblem to a free processor
      endwhile
3     (Re)start depth-first branch and bound processes in parallel. These will
      terminate after a specified number of vertices have been visited (MAXV).
4     wait for all processors to finish their subproblems
      or exceed MAXV vertex evaluations.
5     Obtain the best minimum of all subproblems and provide
      this value to all subproblems as the new best minimum.
6     if ALL subproblems are unfinished goto step 3
7     if ANY subproblems are unfinished goto step 2
8     STOP
```

In depth-first search subproblems are removed from the top of the stack when a terminal vertex is encountered. A location in the tree where a branch exists is called a *juncture*. Each stack location defines a juncture. Hence, depth-first search removes junctures from the bottom of the tree which are at the top of the stack. However, splitting a subproblem involves removing the subproblem from the *bottom* of the stack and assigning it to a free processor (step 2). If the stack is empty the branch and bound process must be restarted to find a juncture. In summary, parallelism is applied to the breadth of the branch and bound tree while sequentially a depth-first search is performed.

The *parallel phase* of the algorithm (step 3) is asynchronous. However, the algorithm can be described as synchronous in the sense that each processor waits for all other processors to finish (step 4) before proceeding with the *synchronization phase* (steps 4, 5, 6, 7 and 2). Each pass through the parallel phase is defined as a *cycle*.

The selection of *MAXV* is a critical part of the algorithm. This control variable is actually the processing *granularity*. It has also been referred to as the "chunking factor" in [Cray 1986, p. 5-25] If *MAXV* is chosen too large, the result will be poor processor utilization because of ineffective load balancing due to large variations in the size of subproblems. If *MAXV* is chosen too small, the processing required for the synchronization phase will overcome the useful work being done in step 3.

The synchronization phase is important for efficient parallelization. It must be done quickly to achieve good processor efficiency. Furthermore, it is important to split the larger subproblems to assist in balancing the workload. This phase is handled quite differently for shared memory systems than it is for distributed memory systems. The implementation details vary depending on the computer architecture. On a hypercube the entire splitting process can be done in $\log_2 p$ steps, where p is the number of processors. This is done efficiently by taking advantage of the hypercube topology. Global communication and synchronization are also accomplished at the same time allowing for the broadcast of any new minimizer and for the detection of a correct termination condition.

3. SYNCHRONIZATION ON SHARED MEMORY MULTIPROCESSORS

We implemented our algorithm on two shared memory computers, the IBM 3090-600E and the Cray X-MP/48. The IBM has six processors while the Cray has four. For details on IBM multitasking see [IBM 1987a; IBM 1987b] and for Cray multitasking see [Cray 1986]. Both computers have the capability for asynchronous multitasking. Access to multitasking is achieved in FORTRAN by making calls to FORTRAN library routines which use the operating system's multitasking facilities to implement *fork* and *join* primitives. See [Quinn 1987] for a discussion of these operations. The fork operation is used to implement step 3 of algorithm 2.1 while the join operation is used for step 4.

The implementations on the two computers were identical except for name and syntax of the fork and join primitives. The fork primitive on the IBM is a VS FORTRAN library routine called DSPTCH while on the Cray the library routine is called TSKSTART. These routines start the parallel execution of a designated subroutine on another processor if another processor is available. These subroutines are called *child processes*. The main program which calls DSPTCH and TSKSTART is called the *mother process*. There is only one mother process. For efficiency the mother process may act like a child process while it is waiting for the other children to finish. The join primitive on the IBM is a library subroutine called SYCHRO while on the Cray it is called TSKWAIT. Join is only executed by the mother process to wait for the completion of child processes that were started by the fork primitive.

Since the IBM and the Cray are multiuser systems, other user processes may use idle processor time that may be introduced by improper load balancing. However, to obtain correct speedup measures, contention for CPU's must be eliminated by acquiring CPU dispatching priority higher than any other user processes on the system. Both of the installations that we used for our experiments provided this type of service as an exception to its normal operation. Indeed, after obtaining this priority, CPU time measurements on these systems were very close to elapsed time measurements when using one processor.

4. SYNCHRONIZATION ON DISTRIBUTED MEMORY MULTIPROCESSORS

Distributed memory multiprocessors communicate through message passing channels. This allows practical architectures with considerably more processors than shared memory multiprocessors. We have implemented our algorithm on two separate Intel iPSC hypercube multiprocessors. The first was a 32 node (D5) first generation iPSC which used ethernet communications with Intel 80286 microprocessors. The other was a 16 node (D4) second generation iPSC which used Intel's own protocol for faster communications. The second generation iPSC uses Intel 80386 microprocessors which are substantially faster than the predecessor 80286 microprocessors. The following discussion assumes some knowledge of the interconnection scheme for the hypercube architecture. For a description of this architecture see [Colley et al. 1986].

Defining a mother task as we did with the shared memory multiprocessors would cause a communications bottleneck. This is because more splitting and subproblem transmission is required when there are more processors resulting in excessive communication. Abdelrahman and Mudge [1988] experienced a similar bottleneck when they implemented their centralized list algorithm. Another disadvantage is that subproblems would have to execute on processors that are not connected directly to the mother process causing further communication delays. Hence, we consider a slightly different algorithm that distributes the splitting process (algorithm 4.1).

Algorithm 4.1 is executed as a single process on each processor in the hypercube. Hence, there is no mother-child relationship as there are in the shared memory implementations. Processes are independent except for the fact that a process may suspend itself while waiting to communicate with another processor. The initial problem is sent to processor 0. All processors have a busy status called *My_status*. Initially, processor 0 is marked busy (*My_status*=BUSY) and all other processors are marked free.

Algorithm 4.1

```
1   if (My_id=0) then
2       Receive the original problem.
3       Initialize subproblem.
4       My_status ← BUSY
5   else
6       My_status ← FREE
7   endif
8   call SYNC(My_status) "algorithm 4.2"
9   if (My_status =BUSY) then
10      (Re)start subproblem for MAXV vertices.
11      if (Subproblem was solved) then
12          My_status ← FREE
13      endif
14      goto step 8
15  endif
16  STOP
```

Algorithm 4.2

```
1   for i=1 to d
2       N_id ← XOR(My_id,2^(i-1))
3       Communicate with N_id to get N_status
4       if (My_status ≠ N_status) then
5           if (My_status = BUSY) then
6               Locate juncture
7               Split subproblem
8               Send subproblem to neighbor
9           else
10              Receive subproblem
11              My_status ← BUSY
12          endif
13      endif
14  endfor
```

The call to subroutine SYNC (algorithm 4.2) in step 8 performs all synchronization and subproblem splitting. The following two assumptions can be made about subroutine SYNC to show that this algorithm will terminate correctly.

Rule 4.1 SYNC may only change My_status from FREE to BUSY. When this happens SYNC has acquired a subproblem from another processor.

Rule 4.2 If any process has My_status=BUSY before calling SYNC then all processes will have My_status=BUSY after calling SYNC.

By these rules, the initial call to SYNC will cause the initial problem in processor 0 to be split amongst all processors in the cube. Hence each processor's call to SYNC will set My_status to BUSY. Then, each processor simultaneously starts/resumes its subproblem (step 10). This is equivalent to the cycle that occurs in step 3 of algorithm 2.1. After the cycle, each processor returns control (step 14) to SYNC to perform any necessary splitting or determine if a termination condition exists. It is easy to see that if SYNC follows the above rules, termination will occur for all processors after they all solve a subproblem in a simultaneous cycle.

We now discuss the details of subroutine SYNC to show that it follows rules 4.1 and 4.2. Our objective was to make SYNC perform very quickly by exploiting the hypercube architecture. Algorithm 4.2 was implemented using 2 or 3 synchronous messages per neighbor. Each processor only communicates with its d neighbors where $d = \log_2 p$ is the cube dimension and p is the number of processors. The exclusive OR (XOR) operation in step 2 is used to identify the id of the neighbor (differing by one bit) with whom to communicate next. The communication at step 3 is used to obtain the status of the neighbor as well as exchange minima. The lower of the two minima is kept by each processor. If one processor is free, it will initiate a split of its subproblem. Hence, both global communication and subproblem distribution are done in $\log_2 p$ steps. In the shared memory implementation there were potentially $p-1$ steps since that is how many splits might be required by the mother process to activate free processors. The tradeoff is that the shared memory algorithm is able to choose the largest subproblem to split.

It is easy to see that rule 4.1 holds because *My_status* is only changed in step 11 to BUSY after it receives a new subproblem. To show rule 4.2 holds, consider the propagation of "BUSY" processors from just one of the processors that was "BUSY" before entering SYNC. After the first step, two processors will be busy, the original and its neighbor whose id differs in the first bit. In the next step, those two processors will propagate the busy state to two more processors whose ids differ in the second bit. After each step, 2^i processors will be busy. Therefore, after d steps, all $2^d=p$ processors will be busy. Sometimes the process of finding a juncture will actually solve the subproblem because the branch and bound procedure must be restarted if no juncture exists. This is more likely to occur when subproblems are very small. When this happens two *phantom* subproblems are created, one for the original subproblem and one for the process requesting a subproblem. There is no actual work to do on phantom subproblems. This condition is created only to preserve the busy status which will ensure rule 4.2. If a process tries to split a phantom subproblem it creates another phantom subproblem for the requesting process.

5. NONPREEMPTIVE COMPUTATIONAL RESULTS

In this section results from implementations of the parallel algorithms are given. The term *nonpreemptive* is used because each processor is allowed to finish its search of *MAXV* vertices regardless of what happened to other processes in the cycle. To calculate speedup we had to first run the branch and bound algorithm on one processor of the respective systems. To ensure the best sequential time we set *MAXV*, the granularity, to infinity to eliminate unnecessary overhead resulting from interruption. The time to perform the initial heuristic was included in all of our elapsed time measurements below. However, this heuristic phase was not parallelized since the time was insignificant. Speedup is defined as T_1 divided by T_p where T_p is the elapsed time in seconds to solve the problem on p processors. Efficiency is defined as speedup divided by p.

To show how granularity affected speedup we chose one rather difficult problem of dimension $N=100$ and ran it with different values of *MAXV* and varied the number of processors. This problem was min $f(x)=x^T A x$ where A was a 100×100 integer matrix that had off diagonal elements generated randomly from the interval [-50, 50]. The diagonal coefficients were selected randomly from the interval [-2500, 2500].

The results of these experiments are given in figure 5.1 through 5.4. When *MAXV* =infinity the problem is forced to be solved in one cycle. That is, after the initial distribution of subproblems, all subproblems were solved on the first cycle without preempting regardless of how long each subproblem took. Notice that for *MAXV* =10, speedup was consistently worse than *MAXV* =100 and *MAXV* =1000. In this case synchronization overhead resulted in poor speedup. The erratic curves for *MAXV* =10000 and *MAXV* =infinity are the result of poor workload balancing and luck. By chance, the initial splitting and distribution of subproblems may be nearly perfectly matched to the number of processors.

Much of the literature on parallel branch and bound methods discusses computational anomalies. For example see [Lai and Sahni 1984]. An anomaly occurs when more or less total computation is required to solve the problem when more processors are applied *without* considering synchronization overhead. This occurs in branch and bound algorithms because the discovery of new incumbents varies unpredictably with different numbers of processors. Our example typically illustrates that with a good initial incumbent, computational anomalies are insignificant. In this example, the initial heuristic did not find the global minimum. However, the heuristic did find a minimum whose function value was -54208 while the actual global minimum was -54382. Hence, the heuristic value is within .3% of the global minimum. By using this solution as the branch and bound incumbent, anomalies in the number of vertices visited in the branch and bound tree are significantly reduced. Table 5.1 gives the number of vertices found in the branch and bound tree at the various numbers of processors and granularities for the iPSC/1. The numbers vary, albeit slightly, due to changes in the time when new incumbents are discovered. This chart shows that both "good" and "bad" anomalies can occur. But since the heuristic found a "close" solution, the anomalies (differences) are very small and thus do not affect the computational requirements significantly. Anomalies also occur due to the frequency of global data exchange which occurs once each cycle. With larger values for *MAXV* the incumbent is updated less frequently resulting in larger search trees.

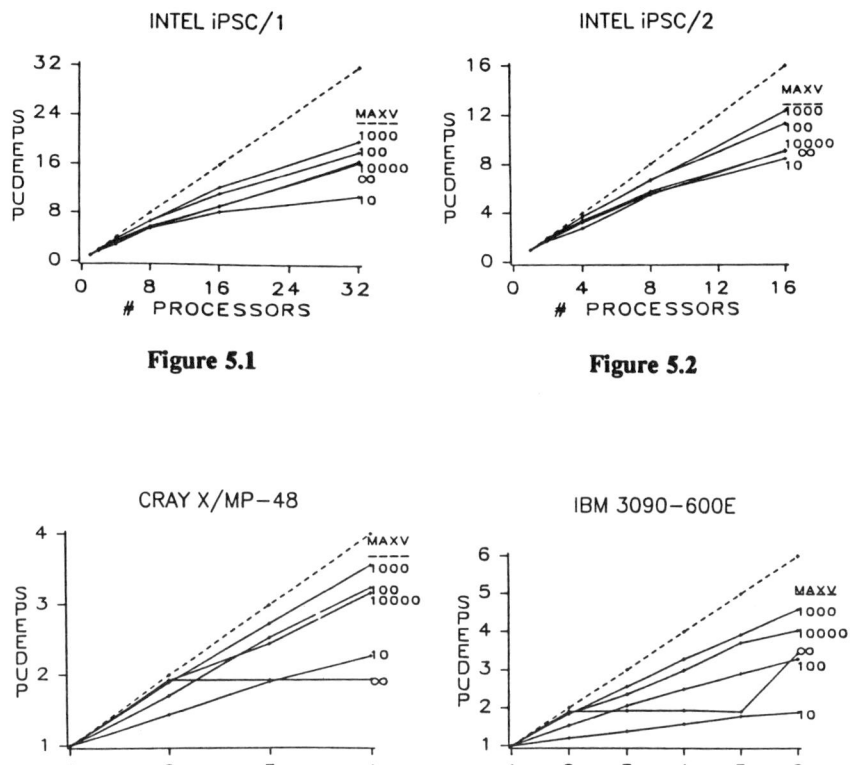

Figure 5.1

Figure 5.2

Figure 5.3

Figure 5.4

Table 5.1

Number of Vertices at Varying Granularities

P	10	100	1000	∞
1	183220	183220	183220	183220
2	183546	183548	183551	183894
4	183620	183622	183629	183983
8	183355	183361	183431	183983
16	183907	183045	183112	183984

6. A PREEMPTIVE ALGORITHM

It was observed that early in the algorithm, after the initial distribution of subproblems, many synchronizations occurred with NO splittings especially for low values of *MAXV*. This prompted us to consider a preemptive version of the algorithm. In the preemptive version no synchronization is done until at least one processor finishes its subproblem or a new incumbent is discovered. In other words, splitting is done on demand instead of testing if splitting is required at regular intervals. The first processor to solve its subproblem would request the preemption of all of its neighbors. Its neighbors in turn would stop their work and preempt their neighbors and so on. On a shared memory multiprocessor all processors are considered neighbors and preempting can be accomplished by updating a shared variable. On a distributed memory multiprocessor preempting is accomplished by message passing and probing. The definition of the granularity control *MAXV* was also changed to *limit* excessive preemption. Now, at least *MAXV* vertices must be visited before preemption unless the search terminates.

When this approach was implemented, we observed that much of the processing occurred with no synchronization. However, as expected, termination became very slow if *MAXV* was set too low. This is due to excessive preempting near the bottom of the branch and bound tree. If *MAXV* was set too high, the preemptive algorithm becomes the nonpreemptive algorithm and thus experiences the same load balancing problems. The best performance was achieved for all of the tested architectures when *MAXV* was greater than 100 and less than 1000. Variation in that range was minimal.

Table 6.1 compares the timings in seconds obtained on the four systems tested in our study. Note that the IBM does integer arithmetic in 32 bit precision while the Cray does 64 bit integer arithmetic. The iPSC/1 used the Intel 80286 microprocessor and the iPSC/2 used the improved 80386 microprocessor. This explains the disparity between the sequential times of the two hypercubes. It is interesting to note that the iPSC/2 with half as many processors was more than twice as fast as the iPSC/1. The largest common number of processors was 4 which is what was available on the Cray XMP/48. Comparisons of the speedup and efficiencies using 4 processors are given on the right side of the table.

The shared memory algorithms for the IBM and the Cray were identical. The reason for the difference in the efficiencies was traced to the cache management policy on the IBM. Cache segments are loaded in 128 byte increments. If two processors update data within the same 128 byte segment then the processors must continually refresh the cache. The branch and bound process in each processor managed a separate variable *lev* which was constantly changing within the subproblem. Our program stored the separate values for *lev* in an array which was indexed by the processor number. This affected the performance because FORTRAN stores contiguous array elements in contiguous memory. The obvious solution is to separate the appropriate read/write variables across 128-byte boundaries.

Table 6.1
Benchmark Timings for Various Multiprocessors

Computer	T_1	p	T_p	Speedup	Effic.	T_4	Speedup	Effic.
			p Processors				4 Processors	
Cray XMP/48	17.52	4	4.61	3.80	.95	4.61	3.80	.95
IBM 3090-600E	15.48	6	2.97	5.22	.87	4.35	3.56	.89
Intel iPSC/1	1903.35	32	95.32	19.97	.62	512.94	3.71	.93
Intel iPSC/2	428.26	16	35.10	12.20	.76	112.66	3.80	.95

It is clear from table 6.1 that the algorithm for the hypercubes were nearly as efficient as the shared memory algorithms. Even with four processors the distribution of the splitting process is key to improved efficiency. As a result, consideration should be given to implementing the distributed memory algorithm on the shared memory machine or at least the concept of distributing the splitting process. Methods by other authors which use a shared data structure to store active subproblems, solve this splitting problem at the expense of performing the necessary storage management and synchronization for that data structure.

It can now be shown that as the difficulty of problems increase, it becomes more efficient to use parallel processing. Thus far, we have shown the results of one problem with a large diagonal run many different ways. In [Rodgers and Pardalos 1988] it is shown that problems with a dominating diagonal are easier to solve. If all elements of the matrix are chosen randomly in a symmetric interval about zero, problems of degree larger than 35 become very difficult to solve. In the following experiment many random problems were generated with all elements including the diagonal chosen from the interval [-50, 50]. We ran 10 different problems for dimension $N = 10, 15, 20, 25, 30$, and 35. Due to practical reasons only one problem of size 35 was run on the iPSC/1. The averages of the results from the iPSC/1 and the iPSC/2 are given in table 6.2 and table 6.3 respectively. The column labeled "Vertices" is the average number of vertices in the branch and bound tree. Figures 6.1 and 6.2 plot the speedup curves for the two machines at the various problem sizes. It is clear from these figures that as the problem size grows based on number of vertices, a larger percentage of the CPU time is spent in the parallel portion of the algorithm.

Table 6.2
iPSC/1 Results

Dimension	Vertices	T_1	T_{32}	Speedup	Efficiency
10	55	0.1	.2	.53	.02
15	599	1.2	.4	3.08	.09
20	3679	9.2	1.0	9.00	.28
25	50417	146.4	7.7	19.03	.59
30	584266	1934.2	74.1	26.11	.82
35	5462093	16193.4	556.9	29.08	.91

Table 6.3
iPSC/2 Results

Dimension	Vertices	T_1	T_{16}	Speedup	Efficiency
10	55	0.02	.03	.76	.05
15	599	0.26	.09	2.78	.19
20	3679	2.01	.28	7.11	.44
25	50417	33.00	2.76	11.96	.75
30	584266	449.16	31.37	14.32	.89
35	5264634	4207.27	278.60	15.10	.94

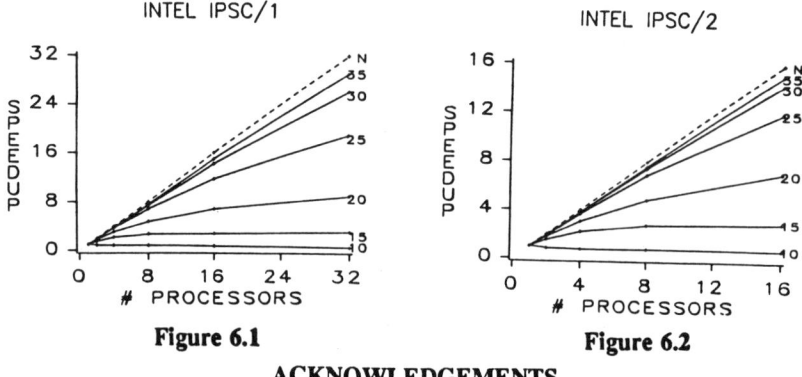

Figure 6.1 Figure 6.2

ACKNOWLEDGEMENTS

The authors are thankful to the Department of Computer Science at The University of Colorado for the use of the Intel iPSC/1. Instruction on the use of the iPSC/1 was given at the University of Colorado during a parallel processing workshop funded in part by the National Science Foundation. The authors are also indebted to Cray Research for a grant to use of the Cray X/MP-48 at the Pittsburgh Supercomputer Center. Access to the IBM 3090-600E was provided by the IBM Corporation Essex Junction, VT. Research by the second author is funded by IBM through the IBM Resident Study Program.

REFERENCES

Abdelrahman, T.S., and T.N. Mudge (1988), "Parallel Branch and Bound Algorithms on Hypercube Multiprocessors", In *3rd Conference on Hypercube Concurrent Computers and Applications*, JPL/Caltech, Calif. Jan.

Boehning, R.L., R.M. Butler, and B.E. Gillett (1988), "A Parallel Integer Linear Programming Algorithm", *European Journal of Operational Research*, 34 (Apr.), 393-398.

Cray Research Inc. (1986), *Multitasking User Guide*, Publication SN-0222, Cray Research Inc, Bloomington, Minn.

Hansen, P. (1979), "Methods of Nonlinear 0-1 Programming", In *Annals of Discrete Mathematics 5*, P.L. Hammer, E.L. Johnson and B.H. Korte, Eds. North-Holland, Amsterdam, pp. 53-70.

Colley S., J.P. Hayes, T.N. Mudge, J. Palmer, and Q.F. Stout (1986), "Architecture of a Hypercube Supercomputer", In *1986 International Conference on Parallel Processing*.

IBM Corporation (1987a), *VS FORTRAN Version 2 Language and Library Reference*, SC26-4221-2, San Jose, Calif.

IBM Corporation (1987b), *VS FORTRAN Version 2 Programming Guide*, SC26-4222-2, San Jose, Calif.

Lai, T. and S. Sahni (1984), "Anomalies in Parallel Branch and Bound Algorithms", *Communications of the ACM 27*, 6 (Jun.), 594-602.

Lavellee, I. (1987), "Algorithmique Combinatorire sur Ordinateurs Paralleles", Research Report 637, Institut National de Recherche en Informatique et en Automatique, Domaine de Voluceau Rocquencourt, France, Mar.

Pardalos, P.M. and J.B. Rosen (1987), *Constrained Global Optimization: Algorithms and Applications*, Lecture Notes in Computer Science 268, G. Goos and J. Hartmanis, Eds. Springer-Verlag, New York, N.Y.

Quinn, M.J. (1987), *Designing Efficient Algorithms for Parallel Computers* (McGraw-Hill, New York, 1987).

Rodgers, G.P. and P. Pardalos (1988), "Computational Aspects of a Branch and Bound Algorithm for the Indefinite Quadratic 0-1 Programming Problem", Technical Report CS88-04, Department of Computer Science, The Pennsylvania State University, Jan.

Roucairol C. (1987), "A Parallel Branch and Bound Algorithm for the Quadratic Assignment Problem", *Discrete Applied Mathematics*, 18, 211-255.

A SUPERCOMPUTER ALGORITHM FOR THE 0-1 MULTIKNAPSACK PROBLEM

Gérard PLATEAU
University Paris-Nord -
CSP
Département de
Mathématiques
et Informatique
Avenue Jean-Baptiste
Clément
91430 Villetaneuse,
France

Catherine ROUCAIROL
University Paris 6, and,
INRIA-Rocquencourt
BP. 105
78153 Le Chesnay Cédex,
France

ABSTRACT

The characteristics of parallel machines (vectorization, multiprocessing) are exploited in order to solve the 0-1 multiknapsack problem :
- in a first phase, a lot of test are performed in parallel in order to reduce this size of the problem (fixation of variables, elimination of constraints)
- in a second phase, a parallel branch and bound algorithm allows to get an optimal solution.

Our parallel algorithm has been implemented on the asynchronous multiprocessor machine CRAY 2. Computational results are reported and compared with those obtained in a sequential approach.

1. INTRODUCTION

Although NP-Hard, the 0-1 knapsack problem is well solved in a sequential way for many classes of instances. Exact algorithms in literature include implicit enumeration procedures with an experimental linear time complexity (see for example [Balas and Zemel 1980 ; Fayard and Plateau 1982 ; Martello and Toth 1978 and 1988 ; Plateau and Elkihel 1985]). Sizes up to several thousand variables are easily reached for some instances which are randomly generated from a uniform distribution.

On the other hand, optimal solutions of the 0-1 multidimensional knapsack problem are classically reached for instances with strongly limited sizes : about ten constraints and one hundred variables [Fleisher 1976 ; Freville and Plateau 1986 and 1987 ; Gavish and Pirkul 1985 ; Petersen 1967 ; Plateau 1976 ; Senju and Toyoda 1968 ; Shih 1979 ; Weingartner and Ness 1967].

Up to now, parallel algorithms devoted to the knapsack problem have only been designed for the one dimension case [Gopalashnan et al. 1987 ; Karnin 1984 ; Klein et al. 1983 ; Yao 1982; Lee, Schragowitz and Sahni 1988]. In addition, most of these works are based upon the use of theoretical models of parallel computation (PRAM with a polynomial - even exponential in the input size - number of processors).

The aim of our work is to describe an efficient parallel algorithm for solving 0-1 multiknapsack problem and to implement it on an actual supercomputer whose number of processors is obviously independent of the input size.

The solution of the 0-1 multiknapsack problems includes two main phases :
- the reduction of the size : computations of lower bounds (heuristic methods) and upper bounds (Lagrangean and surrogate relaxations) allow to fix variables at these optimal values and to drop redundant constraints,
- the implicit enumeration of the reduced problem.

The basic idea of this paper is to exploit first the speed of supercomputers in order to perform much more work than in a sequential way and thus to improve the size reduction (that is to increase the number of fixed variables and eliminated constraints).

In addition, a parallel branch and bound algorithm including this reduction scheme is designed by exploiting previous studies for various combinatorial optimization problems [Lavallée and Roucairol 1985 ; Roucairol 1987a and 1987b]. It allows to speed up the implicit enumeration of the tree search nodes.

2. PROBLEM STATEMENT

The following 0-1 multiconstraint knapsack problem (B) is considered :
$$\max \ cx \text{ subject to } Ax \leq b \ ; \ x \in V,$$
whose data are such that $c \in \ddot{E}_*^n$, $b \in \ddot{E}_*^m$, A is a mxn dense non-negative integer matrix

and where $V = \{x \in \mathcal{R}^n | x_j = 0 \text{ or } 1, j=1,2,...,n\}$.

3. NOTATIONS

Given an optimization problem (P) :
- $v(P)$: optimal value of (P) ;
- $\bar{v}(P)$ (resp. $\underline{v}(P)$: upper (resp. lower) bound on $v(P)$;
- $(P \mid x \in X)$: (P) with the added constraint $x \in X$.

4. REDUCTION TESTS

The use of a preprocessing reduction algorithm improves the efficiency of exact methods by decreasing the size of the problem (fixation of variables and elimination of constraints) (see [Freville and Plateau 1986 and 1987]).

The classical concept of surrogate constraints introduced by Glover [1965] allows to generate reduction tools with expected linear time complexities (see [Fayard and Plateau 1977 and 1982, Freville and Plateau 1986])).

Before giving the statement of these duality based reduction tests, the simple following ones allow the construction of a so-called *well-stated* problem.

4.1. The well-stated problem

This problem is obtained by dropping obviously redundant constraints and fixed variables

if there exists an index $j \in \{1,2,n...\}$ and an index $i \in \{1,2,...,m\}$ such that

(R_1) $a_{ij} > b_i$

then the variable x_j must be fixed at 0.

if there exists an index $i \in \{1,2,...,m\}$ such that :

(R_2) $\sum_{j=1}^{n} a_{ij} \leq b_i$

then the constraint i must be eliminated.

if there exists an index $j \in \{1,2,...,n\}$ such that :

(R_3) $A^j = 0$

then the variable x_j must be fixed at 1.

4.2. Duality based tests

For a well-stated problem (B) with n variables and m constraints, given a multiplier $w \in \mathcal{R}_+^m$ (generated or not by the solving of the Lagrangean (or surrogate) dual of (B)), let us consider :

- the associated surrogate relaxation (0-1 knapsack problem derived from (B)) :
  $(B^0(w))$,   max cx s.t. $wAx \leq wb$; $x \in V$
- for each q in $\{1,2,...,m\}$, the following 0-1 knapsack problem
  $(B^q(w))$ max $A_q x$ s.t. $wAx \leq wb$; $x \in V$

4.2.1 Fixation of variables

With the aim of finding a solution with a value greater than a given lower bound $\underline{v}(B)$ on $v(B)$, the fixation of variables at their optimal values is realized as follows :

Theorem 1.

If there exists an index $j \in \{1,2,...,n\}$ and $\varepsilon \in \{0,1\}$ such that $\bar{v}(B^0(w) \mid x_j = \varepsilon) \leq \underline{v}(B)$

then the variable x_j must be fixed at the value $1-\varepsilon$.

Proof : see [Freville and Plateau 1986 ; Plateau 1976].

4.2.2 *Elimination of constraints*

The following result gives a sufficient condition for dropping redundant constraints

Theorem 2.

If there exists an index q in $\{1,2,.........,m\}$ such that $\bar{v}(B^q(w)) \leq b_q$

then the constraint $A_q x \leq b_q$ can be eliminated.

Proof : see [Freville and Plateau 1986, Plateau 1976].

4.3. Main features of the serial reduction algorithm

The serial reduction system FPR83 realized by Fréville and Plateau includes three main phases :

(i) computation of an upper bound on the optimal value by using Lagrangean and surrogate relaxations.

(ii) computation of a lower bound by using the so-called AGNES heuristic methods.

(iii) size reduction by the conjunction of tests applied to 0-1 knapsack problems derived from (B) as described in theorems 1 and 2.

This serial algorithm FPR83 is extensively described in [Fréville and Plateau 1986 and 1987] with the actual chain of reduction tests and additional details about the selected options for its implementation.

It has been tested on a CII HB IRIS 80 with twenty concrete problems [Fleisher 1976 ; Petersen 1967 ; Plateau 1976 ; Senju and Toyoda 1968 ; Weingartner and Ness 1967] and thirty randomly generated problems [Shih 1979]. These computational results prove the quality of performance of heuristic AGNES and the decrease in the running times for exact methods including this preprocessing reduction system FPR83.

For example, for the seven problems due to Petersen [1967], table 1 details for each of them their original and reduced sizes, and the running times (in second) for their exact solving by Shih's code [1979] respectively without (original size) and with (reduced size) the inclusion of FPR83.

original size	time (second)	reduced size	time reduction	global
10 x 6	.2	0 x 0	1.2	1.2
10 x 10	.5	1 x 3	2.3	2.3
10 x 15	1.9	5 x 8	4.8	4.8
10 x 20	1.8	2 x 8	5.7	5.8
10 x 28	9.2	2 x 9	5.4	5.5
5 x 39	>25	4 x 28	7.5	25
5 x 50	>25	4 x 38	7.7	28.8

Table 1

5. HIGH-LEVEL DESCRIPTION OF THE PARALLEL ALGORITHM

5.1. Reduction phase

Instead of constructing the optimal dual multiplier w^* of (B), the aim of our parallel algorithm is to generate two sets W_1 and W_2 of dual multipliers which allow to produce a set of 0-1 knapsack problems :
- fixation of variables :
    $(B^0(w))$ max cx   s.t. $wAx \leq wb$; $x \in V, w \in W_1$
- elimination of constraints : $q \in \{1,...,m\}$
    $(B^q(w))$ max $A_q x$ s.t. $wAx \leq wb$; $x \in V, w \in W_2$.

This idea is motivated by the two following observations.

First, it is not proved that the use of the unique 0-1 knapsack problem $(B^0(w^*))$ leads to the best results as concerns the number of fixed variables and eliminated constraints. In addition, the relation $\bar{v}(B^0(w)) \leq \bar{v}(B^0(w'))$ $w, w' \in \mathbb{R}_+^m$ does not imply necessarily for any variable x_j and $\varepsilon \in \{0,1\}$

$\bar{v}(B^0(w) \mid x_j = \varepsilon) \leq \bar{v}(B^0(w') \mid x_j = \varepsilon)$.

Second, from a computational time point of view, it is not realistic to consider serially sets of tool knapsacks $(B^0(w))$, $w \in W_1$ and $w \in W_2$. However, this kind of approach had been used by Hansen and Plateau (in Plateau [1976]) in order to test experimentally its robustness.

Obviously, due to parallelism, it is possible to work concurrently with several tool knapsacks and to apply a sequence of reduction tests for each of them.

The distributed work is the following :
- fixation of variables :
    given a multiplier $w \in W_1$, perform the usual sequence of tests on $(B^0(w))$.
- elimination of constraints :

given a constraint $q \in \{1,2,...,m\}$ candidate for elimination, use of another sequence of tool knapsacks $(B^q(w))$, $w \in W_2$.

In fact, the 0-1 knapsack problems $(B^0(w)) \mid x_j = \varepsilon)$ and $(B^q(w))$ are not exactly solved, but with respect to theorems 1 and 2 these different kinds of relaxations are used :
- Lagrangean relaxations
- the associated linear programs.

This parallel reduction algorithm is an extended version of a previous algorithm denoted by PR^{2}87 [Plateau and Roucairol 1987].

5.1.1   Fixation of variables

Namely, the following results are applied : given a tool knapsack $(B^0(w))$, $w \in W_1$, let us define its Lagrangean relaxation associated with a multiplier $\lambda \in \mathcal{R}^+$:

$(LR(\lambda))$ max $cx + \lambda(wb-wAx)$ s.t. $x \in V$

Theorem 3.

(i) the function $\lambda \to v(LR(\lambda))$ is a convex piece-wise linear function.

(ii) the breakpoints of this function are $\lambda_j = c_j/wA^j$, $j=1,2,...,n$.

Due to theorems 1 and 3, this result is deduced :

Corollary :

For the fixation of any variable of (B) by Lagrangean relaxation, it is sufficient to consider the finite set $(LR(\lambda), \lambda \in \Lambda = \{0,\lambda_1,...,\lambda_n,+\infty\})$.

Proof :   see [Hammer, Padberg and Peled 1975].

One more time, instead of constructing the optimal Lagrangean dual multiplier λ^* of $(B^0(w))$, we generate the set Λ of multipliers ; this leads to an obvious vectorizable reduction structure.

Let us recall that for each λ in Λ, by denoting :

$J^+(\lambda) = \{j \in \{1,...,n\} \mid c_j - \lambda wA^j > 0 \}$; $J^-(\lambda) = \{j \in \{1,...,n\} \mid c_j - \lambda wA^j < 0\}$

then $v(LR(\lambda)) = \lambda wb + \sum_{j \in J^+(\lambda)} (c_j - \lambda wA^j)$

and for j in $J^+(\lambda)$: $v(LR(\lambda) \mid x_j=1) = v(LR(\lambda))$; $v(LR(\lambda) \mid x_j=0) = v(LR(\lambda)) - (c_j - \lambda wA^j)$

and for j in $J^-(\lambda)$: $v(LR(\lambda) \mid x_j=0) = v(LR(\lambda))$; $v(LR(\lambda) \mid x_j=1) = v(LR(\lambda)) + (c_j - \lambda wA^j)$

Thus, for each variable x_j, $j \in J^+(\lambda) \cup J^-(\lambda)$, it is sufficient to exploit the comparison of these two vectors : $(|c_j - \lambda wA^j|)_{\lambda \in \Lambda}$ and $(v(LR(\lambda)) - \underline{v}(B))_{\lambda \in \Lambda}$

Moreover, it is important to point out the following result :

Theorem 4.

The set of fixed variables by using all the Lagrangean multipliers is equal to the set that could be obtained by solving the linear programs associated with the knapsack problems

$$(B^0(w) \mid x_j = \varepsilon), \ \varepsilon \in \{0,1\}.$$

5.1.2   Binary relations

The previous results can be improved by using binary relations in the following way [Fayard and Plateau 1977, Jaumard 1986]. Given

$$\bar{\lambda} \in \Lambda, \ k \in \{1,...,n\} \ \text{and} \ \varepsilon = \begin{cases} 0 \ \text{if} \ k \in J^+(\bar{\lambda}) \\ 1 \ \text{if} \ k \in J^-(\bar{\lambda}) \end{cases}$$

we first search all the fixed variables by using the other Lagrangean multipliers when x_k is fixed at ε.

It means that these sets are constructed :

$$X_1 = \{j \mid \exists \ \lambda \in \Lambda \ - \bar{\lambda} : v(LR(\lambda) \mid x_k = \varepsilon \ ; x_j = 0) \leq \underline{v}(B))$$

and

$$X_0 = \{j \mid \exists \ \lambda \in \Lambda - \bar{\lambda} : v(LR(\lambda) \mid x_k = \varepsilon \ ; x_j = 1) \leq \underline{v}(B)).$$

Then we can strengthen the previous reduction results by comparing these two bounds :

$$v(LR(\bar{\lambda} \mid x_k = \varepsilon \ ; x_j = 1 \ \forall \ j \in X_1 \ ; x_j = 0 \ \forall \ j \in X_0) \ \text{and} \ \underline{v}(B).$$

5.1.3   Elimination of constraints

Finally, as concerns the elimination of constraints, we solve linear programs associated with $(B^q(w))$, $w \in W_2$ by applying the expected linear time complexity algorithm described in [Fayard and Plateau 1977 and 1982].

5.2.   Branch and Bound phase

Our parallel Branch and Bound algorithm includes the reduction scheme and exploits previous studies for various combinatorial optimization problems. [Lavallée and Roucairol 1985 ; Roucairol 1987a and b].

It is an asynchronous parallel algorithm based upon the case of a bounded number of processes which are to be dealt with concurrently. The distribution of the work among the different processes is done by giving access to a shared list which contains information about every node which is to be expanded. This list is implemented as a heap in order to use fast algorithms to insert, sort and remove items. As a best first strategy is used, every active process finds at the top of the list (node with the best upper bound) the node it is going to expand (i.e. to branch following the value of the basic variable of the continuous surrogate knapsack associated with this node and to evaluate the created successors).

In the shared list, insertion of items is done whenever the expansion of a node generates several successors whose evaluation is greater than the best know lower bound (feasible solution) ; these successors are then inserted in the list.

The best known lower bound (BKLB) is a shared variable which is updated whenever a local lower bound (llb), greater than BKLB, is found at a node to be expanded. Items are suppressed either at the beginning or at the end of the list. The former case occurs whenever an inactive process looks for a new job, the latter case occurs whenever a llb is greater than BKLB : every node whose evaluation is less than llb is eliminated because it cannot lead to an optimal solution.

The algorithm terminates whenever the list is empty and all the processes are inactive.

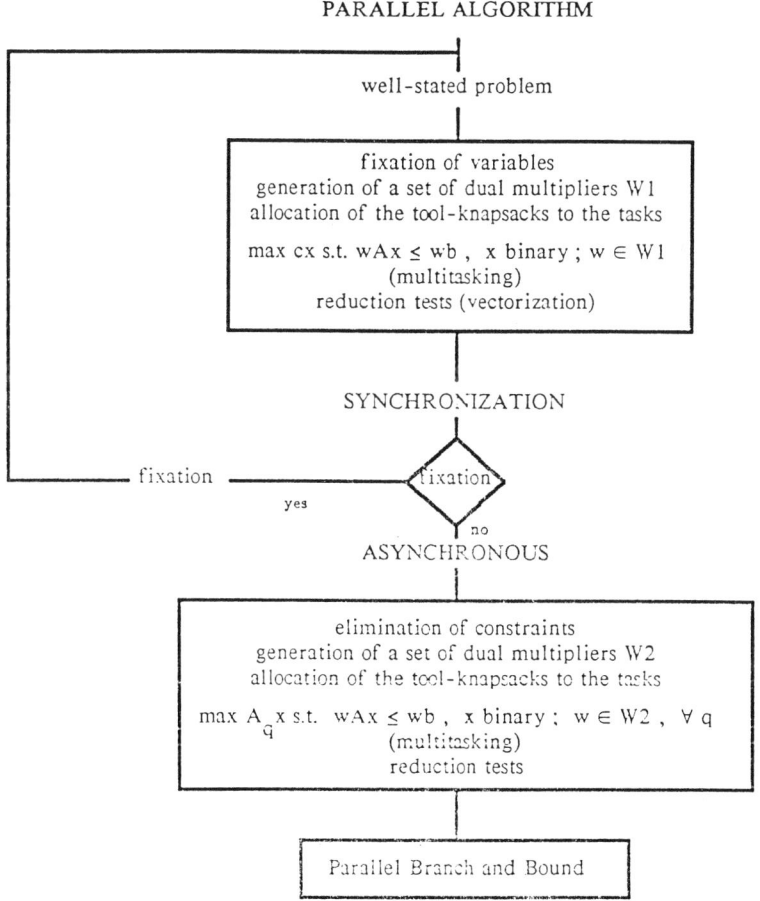

PARALLEL ALGORITHM

6. EXPERIMENTAL RESULTS

6.1. Implementation

Our algorithm has been implemented on the asynchronous multiprocessor CRAY2. Its four vector processors communicate by simultaneous reading or exclusive writing on a shared central memory (32Mega words, CPU cycle time 4 ns for vector operations).

The code has been written in Fortran 77 [Plateau, Roucairol and Gachet 1988] and the multitasking library of CRAY has been used for synchronization and communication operations.

6.2. Numerical results

Computational results are summarized by considering a lot of test problems including the fifty problems from literature reported in table 2, in order to realize comparisons with the sequential algorithms.

Author	Number of problems	Size	
		from	to
Shih	30	5 x 30	5 x 90
Ness, Weingartner	8	2 x 28	2 x 105
Petersen	7	10 x 10	10 x 28
		5 x 39	5 x 52
Senju, Toyoda	2	30 x 60	30 x 90
Hansen, Plateau	2	4 x 28	4 x 35
Fleisher	1	10 x 20	10 x 20

Table 2

Tables 3 and 4 contain comparisons of the number of variables fixed by our parallel algorithm denoted by PR^288 and the sequential algorithm FPR83.

Problem	Size	Size after reduction	
		FPR 83	PR^2 88
Petersen	10 x 6	0 x 0	0 x 0
	10 x 10	1 x 3	1 x 3
	10 x 15	5 x 8	5 x 8
	10 x 20	2 x 8	2 x 7
	10 x 28	2 x 9	2 x 6
	5 x 39	4 x 28	4 x 27
	5 x 50	4 x 38	4 x 36
Ness	2 x 28	1 x 4	1 x 4
Weingartner	2 x 28	1 x 5	0 x 0
	2 x 28	2 x 19	2 x 14
	2 x 28	1 x 5	1 x 5
	2 x 28	0 x 0	0 x 0
	2 x 28	2 x 7	2 x 5
	2 x 105	2 x 12	2 x 12
	2 x 105	2 x 29	2 x 28
Hansen	4 x 28	4 x 27	4 x 26
Plateau	4 x 35	4 x 34	4 x 34
Senju	30 x 60	30 x 40	30 x 40
Toyoda	30 x 60	30 x 37	26 x 33

Table 3

Our algorithm is always better or at least as good as the sequential one.

Problem	Size	Size after reduction	
		FPR 83	PR^2 88
	5 x 30	5 x 14	5 x 12
	5 x 30	1 x 5	0 x 0
	5 x 30	4 x 11	4 x 7
	5 x 30	1 x 2	0 x 0
	5 x 30	0 x 0	0 x 0
	5 x 40	3 x 11	2 x 10
	5 x 40	3 x 11	3 x 8
	5 x 40	2 x 10	2 x 5
	5 x 40	1 x 3	1 x 3
	5 x 50	3 x 18	3 x 7
Shih	5 x 50	2 x 12	2 x 12
	5 x 50	1 x 5	1 x 5
	5 x 50	3 x 15	0 x 0
	5 x 60	3 x 11	3 x 11
	5 x 60	2 x 8	2 x 8
	5 x 60	1 x 14	0 x 0
	5 x 70	3 x 13	3 x 11
	5 x 70	1 x 2	1 x 2
	5 x 70	3 x 9	3 x 9
	5 x 70	1 x 7	1 x 5
	5 x 80	3 x 29	3 x 10
	5 x 80	2 x 13	2 x 13
	5 x 80	3 x 20	3 x 20
	5 x 80	3 x 10	3 x 9
	5 x 90	3 x 30	0 x 0
	5 x 90	2 x 7	2 x 7
	5 x 90	2 x 8	0 x 0
	5 x 90	2 x 9	0 x 0
	5 x 90	0 x 0	0 x 0

Table 4

We are now conducting experiments for the global algorithm, several previous problems have been already exactly solved in very short computer time. The time ratio is about one hundred as compared with FPR83 ran on a CII HB IBIS 80 computer.

We report below the results obtained on one of the most difficult problem from the literature [Fleisher 1976].

The table 5 shows some problems of granularity due to the small sizes of literature's instances. In order to balance the load of each processor, we decided to define a priority rule for accessing the shared list of node. Namely, a process is allowed to treat a node if its current load does not exceed t% of the mean load. The running times are in seconds. For the best result, a gain of 41% is obtained for t equals 50.

	t%	Processors				global time
		1	2	3	4	
N	0	79	123	89	67	3.29
p		25%	34%	22%	19%	
N	10%	92	86	91	89	2.51
p		26%	24%	25%	25%	
q		2	2	24	3	
N	30%	84	95	87	92	2.113
p		23%	27%	24%	26%	
q		0	2	0	10	
N	50%	95	95	80	88	1.93
p		26,5%	26,5%	22%	25%	
q		0	3	0	0	

Table 5 - Granularity problem on Fleisher's example
(N number of nodes treated by a processor, p percentage of work done by a processor,
q number of times a processor waits)

7. CONCLUSION

The results of our first experiments show the various advantages of the use of parallel computing for combinatorial optimization :
- to perform much more work than in a sequential way in order to get more information and to improve the size reduction,
- to accelerate the search of an optimal solution in a Branch and Bound tree.

It is clear that multiprocessors machine will be much more attractive for instances with a number of variables and contraints greater than those of literature. This will be the future direction of our work.

REFERENCES

Balas, E. and Zemel, E. (1983), "An algorithm for Large Zero-One Knapsack Problem", *Operations Research*, 28, 1130-1154.

Fayard, D. and Plateau, G. (1982), "An algorithm for the Solution of the 0-1 Knapsack Problem", *Computing* 28, 269-287.

Fayard, D. and Plateau, G. (1977), "Reduction algorithm for single and multiple constraints 0-1 linear programming problems", *Proceeding off the Congress Methods of Mathematical Programming*, Zakopane, Poland.

Fleisher, J. (1976), *Sigmap Newsletter* 20.

Fréville, A. and Plateau, G. (1986), "Heuristics and reduction methods for multiple constraints 0-1 linear programming problems", *EJOR* 24, 206-215.

Fréville, A. and Plateau, G. (1987), "Hard 0-1 multiknapsack test problems for size reduction methods", *Research Report* 72, Université Paris-Nord.

Gavish, B. and Pirkul, H. (1985), "Efficient algorithms for solving multiconstraint zero-one knapsack problems to optimality", *Mathematical Programming* 31, 78-105.

Glover, F. (1965), "A multiphase dual algorithm for the 0-1 integer programming problem", *Operations Research* 13, 879-919.

Gopalakrishnan, P.S., Kanal, L.N. and Ramakrishnan, I.V. (1987), "Approximate algorithms for the Knapsack problem on Parallel computers", *IBM Report* RC 12549, 1-34.

Hammer, P.L., Padberg, M.W., and Peled, U.N. (1975), "Constraint pairing in integer programming", *INFOR - Canadian Journal of Operational research and Information Processing* 13, 68-81.

Jaumard, B. (1986), "Extraction et utilisation de relations booléennes pour la résolution des programmes linéaires en variables 0-1", *Thèse de Doctorat*, ENSET,France.

Karnin, E.D. (1984), "A parallel algorithm for the knapsack problem, *IEEE Trans. on Computers* C-33, 404-408.

Klein, P. and Meyer auf der Heide, F. (1963), "A lower time bound for knapsack problem on random access machine", *Acta Informatica* 19, 385-395.

Lavallée, I. and Roucairol, C. (1983), "Parallel branch and bound algorithms", *EURO VII Congress, Research Report MASI* 112, Université Paris 6.

Martello, S. and Toth, P. (1978), "Algorithm for the solution of the 0-1 single knapsack", *Computing* 21, 81-86.

Martello, S. and Toth, P. (1988), "A new algorithm for the 0-1 knapsack problem", Management Science 34, 633-644.

Petersen, C.C. (1967), "Computational experience with variants of the Balas algorithm applied to the selection of R and D projects", *Management Science* 13 (9), 736-750.

Plateau, G. (1976), "Réduction de la taille des problèmes linéaires en variables 0-1", *Research Report* 71, UST Lille 1.

Plateau, G. and Elkihel, M. (1985), "A hybrid method for the 0-1 knapsack problem", *Methods of Operations research* 49, 277-293.

Plateau, G. and Roucairol, C. (1987), "Algorithm PR^{2}87 for the parallel size reduction of the 0-1 multiknapsack problem", *First Colloquium on Boolean methods for combinatorial optimization*, Chexbres.

Plateau, G., Roucairol, C. and Gachet, S. (1988), "Algorithm PR^{2}88 for the parallel resolution of the 0-1 multiknapsack problem", *Research Report INRIA*, to appear.

Roucairol, C. (1987a), "A parallel branch and bound algorithm for the quadratic assignment problem", *Discrete Applied Mathematics* 18, 211-225.

Roucairol, C. (1987b), "Du sequentiel au parallèle : la recherche arborescente et son application à la programmation quadratique en variables 0-1", *Thèse d'Etat*, Université Paris 6.

Roucairol, C. (1988), "Parallel Computing in Combinatorial Optimization", *Proceedings of Numerical Methods for parallel vector computers*, North Holland, to appear 1989.

Senju, S. and Toyoda, Y. (1968), "An approach to linear programming with 0-1 variables", *Management Science*15(4), 196-207.

Shih, W. (1979), "A branch and bound method for the multiconstraint 0-1 knapsack problem", *Journal of the Operational Research Society* 30(4), 369-378.

Weingartner, H.M. and Ness D.N. (1967), "Methods for the solution of the multidimensional 0-1 knapsack problem", *Operations Research* 15 (1), 83-103.

Yao, A.C. (1982), "On parallel computation for the knapsack problem", *JACM* 29 (3), 898-903.

IMPLEMENTING AN INTERIOR POINT LP ALGORITHM ON A SUPERCOMPUTER

MATTHEW J. SALTZMAN, RADHIKA SUBRAMANIAN AND ROY E. MARSTEN

Dept. of Management Information Systems, University of Arizona
Tucson, Arizona 85721

ABSTRACT

We describe an implementation of the dual affine interior point algorithm for linear programming on a supercomputer. The notable aspect of this implementation is that it exploits the key features of the supercomputer, namely the vector pipeline and the shared-memory multiprocessor architecture. The key data structures and sub-procedures are described, and computational results are presented.

1. INTRODUCTION

Recent advances in linear programming (LP) solution methodology have focused on *interior point algorithms*. Unlike the simplex method, these algorithms transform the LP at each iteration so that the current solution is near the center of the interior of the feasible region, then move through the interior toward an optimum solution on the boundary.

Much more than the simplex method, the interior point algorithms offer opportunities to exploit parallel and vector computation to achieve significant performance improvements. In this paper we investigate these opportunities. In particular, we describe parallel and vector algorithms for solving large, sparse, symmetric, positive definite systems of linear equations, and we show how these methods can be integrated into the LP algorithm.

In Section 2 we describe the dual affine algorithm. In Section 3 we describe algorithms for solving positive definite linear systems. The solution of such a system is the heart of the interior point methods. We show that one particular form of the algorithm is superior for sparse systems, and is most suitable for parallel implementation. In Section 4 we describe the data structures to support the implementation of the solver, and we describe how vector processing can be exploited. We also describe our experience implementing the solver on an IBM 3090-600E, a shared-memory multiprocessor with six vector CPUs. Finally, in Section 5 we describe several open problems in the area of parallel solution of sparse positive definite systems, and parallel implementation of interior-point LP algorithms.

Copyright 1989 by Elsevier Science Publishing Co., Inc.
Impacts of Recent Computer Advances on Operations Research
Ramesh Sharda, Bruce L. Golden, Edward Wasil, Osman Balci, William Stewart, Editors

2. THE DUAL AFFINE ALGORITHM

The algorithm we implemented is that described in [Marsten, et al., 1988]. This is based on the dual affine algorithm of Adler, et al. [1987], and extended to handle bounded and free variables, among other features. In this section, we briefly recap this algorithm.

The LP to be solved is:

$$\min\{c^T x : Ax = b, \mathbf{0} \leq x \leq u\} \tag{1}$$

where A is $m \times n$. The dual of (1) is:

$$\max\{b^T y - u^T w : A^T y - w + z = c, \ w, z \geq \mathbf{0}\}. \tag{2}$$

Define $Z = \text{diag}(z_1, \ldots, z_n)$, $W = \text{diag}(w_1, \ldots, w_n)$ and $D^2 = (Z^2 + W^2)^{-1}$. Assume that y^0, w^0, z^0 are feasible for (2), and $w^0, z^0 > 0$. Let $0 < \gamma < 1$. An iteration of the algorithm consists of the following steps:

1. $d_y := (AD^2A^T)^{-1}(b - AW^2D^2u)$;
   $d_w := W^2D^2A^T d_y - Z^2W^2D^2u$;
   $d_z := d_w - A^T d_y$;

2. $x^{k+1} := -Z_k^{-2} d_z$;

3. $\alpha_z := \min\{z_j^k/(d_z)_j : (d_z)_j < 0, \ j = 1, \ldots, n\}$;
   $\alpha_w := \min\{w_j^k/(d_w)_j : (d_w)_j < 0, \ j = 1, \ldots, n\}$;
   $\alpha := \gamma \min\{\alpha_z, \alpha_w\}$;

4. $y^{k+1} := y^k + \alpha d_y$;
   $w^{k+1} := w^k + \alpha d_w$;
   $z^{k+1} := c - A^T y^{k+1} + w^{k+1}$;

5. $k := k + 1$;

The iterations are repeated until some stopping criteria are satisfied, usually that the improvement in the value of the dual objective is smaller than some tolerance. The primal solution x^k is the one that minimizes complementary slackness with respect to the current dual solution, with the constraints $0 \leq x \leq u$ relaxed. If x^k is feasible and the complementary slackness condition is exactly satisfied, then x^k is the optimal primal solution.

3. THE CHOLESKY DECOMPOSITION

The most computationally intensive step in each iteration of the dual affine algorithm (indeed, of any of the interior point algorithms) is the solution of $d_y := (AD^2A^T)^{-1}(b - AW^2D^2u)$ (or a similar system).[1] The matrix AD^2A^T is $m \times m$, symmetric and positive definite. In addition, for most realistic LP problems, A, and hence AD^2A^T, is sparse. Efficient implementation of the dual affine algorithm depends critically on efficient solution of this system.

Linear systems of the form $x = M^{-1}b$ are not usually solved by forming the explicit inverse of M. This is particularly true if M is sparse, since taking the inverse does not, in general, preserve sparsity. Instead, the system $Mx = b$ is solved directly, by decomposing M into lower- and upper-triangular factors L and U, such that $M = LU$. Then the triangular systems $Lx' = b$ and $Ux = x'$ can be solved efficiently by forward and backward substitution, respectively. If M is symmetric, positive definite, then M can be factored uniquely into symmetric triangular components $\hat{L}$ and $\hat{L}^T$. These matrices are the *Cholesky factors* of M. A slight variation on this theme computes $M = LL^T$, where $l_{jj} = 1$ for $j = 1, \ldots, m$, is a diagonal matrix and $\hat{L} = L^{1/2}$. This version has the advantage of not requiring the computation of square roots on the diagonal of $\hat{L}$, and it is the method that we use in our implementation.

3.1. Algorithms for Cholesky Decomposition

The formula for computing each element of L is given by

$$l_{ij} = (m_{ij} - \sum_{k=1}^{j-1} \delta_{kk} l_{jk} l_{ik})/\delta_{jj}. \tag{3}$$

Each element of is given by

$$\delta_{jj} = m_{jj} - \sum_{k=1}^{j-1} \delta_{kk} l_{jk}^2. \tag{4}$$

Note that in order to compute l_{ij} the values of δ_{kk}, l_{ik} and l_{jk} for $k < j$ and δ_{jj} must be known. Computing δ_{jj} requires l_{jk} and δ_{kk} for $k < j$.

As described in [George, et al., 1986a] the six permutations of the indices i, j and k in (3) and (4) naturally yield three different algorithms for performing Cholesky decomposition, and determine whether each algorithm applies to L stored in row- or column-major order. In *row Cholesky* (ijk and ikj), rows of L are computed successively; each element in the row is computed using the previously-computed rows and previously-computed elements in the same row. The *column Cholesky* algorithm (jik and jki) computes the

---

[1] In large problems or problems where the Cholesky factor of AD^2A^T is relatively dense, 80–90% or more of the computation time is spent in this step.

columns in succession, using previously-computed columns. *Submatrix Cholesky* (kij and kji) uses each column as it is computed to update all subsequent columns. If L is stored as a dense matrix, the algorithms are all essentially equivalent on a serial computer. On a shared-memory parallel computer, the precedence requirements for the updates and the pattern of processor utilization suggest the superiority of the jki form of the algorithm (column-major column Cholesky). For a detailed analysis, see [George, *et al.*, 1986a]. Suitability of these algorithms for sparse-matrix factorization is discussed in Section 4.

An important aspect of sparse matrix decomposition is the maintenance of sparsity in the resulting factors. In the case of Cholesky decomposition, the positions of nonzeros in the lower triangle of M are a subset of the positions of nonzeros in L. *Fill-in* (non-zeros in L corresponding to zero elements of M) is static, essentially independent of the values of the nonzeros in M, and highly dependent on the ordering of the rows and columns in M. If $M = AA^T$ then the permutation of rows and columns of M is determined by the permutation of rows of A. The Cholesky decomposition routines used up to now in implementations of the dual affine algorithm (see, *e.g.*, [Adler, *et al.*, 1987; Marsten, *et al.*, 1988]) have used graph-based heuristics such as *minimum degree* or *minimum local fill-in* [George and Liu, 1981] to order the rows of A so as to minimize fill-in. Although the problem of optimal row/column permutations for parallel computation involves additional considerations (see Section 5), research in this area is limited. We have implemented the *multiple minimum-degree* ordering heuristic of Liu [1985] for this paper. This heuristic is much faster than *minimum degree*, but gives results of comparable quality. The remaining discussion assumes that the row/column permutation of M, and hence the pattern of nonzeros in L, is fixed in advance.

4. IMPLEMENTATION

In the present application, the matrices A, AD^2A^T and L are all large and sparse. When the matrices are stored in sparse form, it becomes important that elements be accessed in sequential order. In particular, if the matrix is stored in column-major order, it is very difficult to locate the non-zero entries in a given row, and vice versa. This makes the ikj, jik and kij forms of the Cholesky algorithm (in which the matrix is stored in the order "opposite" that in which the computation is done) unattractive. Of the remaining forms, the ijk form is inferior on a sequential computer. The basic operation in this form is the sparse inner product, which is implemented as a merge of two ordered lists of column indices of nonzeros in a pair of rows; a nonzero contribution to the sum is made whenever two matching column indices are found. The difficulty with this operation is that it is possible that many non-overlapping indices will need to be tested. It is even possible that such a merge may discover no overlapping nonzeros!

Problem	m	n	Nonzeros in A	Nonzeros in L	Density of L
80bau3b	2,237	9,799	21,002	42,810	1.7%
plan02	2,733	5,734	25,242	72,384	1.9%
storm2	3,400	22,573	68,789	117,144	2.0%
aa1	823	8,904	72,965	226,809	67.0%

Table 1: Test problem parameters

The jki and kji forms do not suffer from this problem. The basic operation in both of these algorithms is a SAXPY, a sparse-vector computation of the form $\alpha x + y$ where α is a scalar and x and y are vectors. Furthermore, the update computation has the property that, if L_{*k} (the kth column of L) contains a nonzero in row j, then every nonzero in L_{*k} below row j contributes a nonzero value to the computation of L_{*j}. Thus, there are no multiplications by zero in an update computation. If L_{*k} contains a zero in row j, then there is no contribution from L_{*k} to the computation of L_{*j}. In the jki (column) form, an additional data structure is required in order to keep track of the columns required to update column j, and to avoid the need to search through column k to locate the entry in row j.

In preliminary tests, we compared implementations of the dual affine algorithm using row Cholesky and column Cholesky on a DEC VAX 8600. Solution times for several problems ranged from 10% to 30% faster overall for the column version over the row version. This improvement also carried over to our initial tests on a vector processor. Note that if the distribution of nonzeros in L is fairly uniform, it would be reasonable to expect that similar utilization patterns would result for parallel Cholesky algorithms in both the dense and sparse case. Also, the submatrix algorithm must contend with the problem of simultaneous updates of columns, whereas the column algorithm need not. Thus it appears that the column Cholesky algorithm is the best choice for parallel sparse implementation (see [George, *et al.*, 1986b]).

In the following discussion, computational results refer to tests on four problems: two NETLIB problems (*80bau3b* and *plan02*), an air cargo routing problem (*storm2*) and an airline crew scheduling problem (*aa1*). Their vital statistics are given in Table 1. All tests were run on the Cornell National Supercomputer Facility IBM 3090-600E using the IBM Parallel FORTRAN compiler. The CNSF machine runs IBM's VM/XA operating system. The tests were run using the EDAC facility for executing programs with very large memory requirements.

4.1. Data Structures

The principal data structure is a sparse, column-major representation of L. Three arrays are used: a double-precision array containing the values of all nonzeros in L, in order by column and within columns by row; an integer array containing the row indices of the nonzeros; and an m-array containing the index of the start of each column in the nonzero array. The diagonal matrix is stored in a separate m-array. This is a static structure that can be constructed once at the start of the dual affine algorithm, using a *symbolic factorization* procedure. The lower triangle of AD^2A^T can be stored in the same data structure, and the factorization done in place. Since the contents of D are altered at each iteration of the dual affine algorithm, AD^2A^T must be re-computed.

As we mentioned above, an additional data structure is required for column Cholesky, to link the columns that contribute to updating each column, and to locate the nonzero entry in the row corresponding to the column to be updated. This data structure is different depending on the algorithm in use. For serial (and vector) versions of the algorithm, Duff, *et al.* [1986] describe a set of non-overlapping linked lists, which can be maintained in three m-arrays. There is a list for each row of L. At the start of the algorithm, each column appears on the list corresponding to the row of the first nonzero in the column. As each column k on the list for row j is used to update column j, it is moved from the jth list to the list corresponding to the row of the next nonzero in column k. The list headers are contained in one m-array. Since each column appears on only one list at any given time, the lists themselves may be stored in a single m-array. Finally, for each column k on the list for column j, the index of l_{jk} in the array of nonzeros is stored in a third m-array. This allows the relevant portion of column k (those entries in row j and below), to be located directly without having to search the entire column.

4.2. Vectorization

In order to vectorize the SAXPY operation associated with the update of column j by column k for sparse matrix data structures, the target column j is "gathered" into a work array of length m, so that m_{ij} is stored in the ith position in the work array. The nonzeros in the work array are then updated using the values of nonzeros from the required columns directly from the sparse matrix structure (this is by far the single most-frequently executed code segment in the entire program). After updating with all columns, the work array is "scattered" back into the sparse matrix structure, dividing the entries by δ_{jj} before replacing them.

The loop that performs a column update contains an apparent *dependence relation* that prevents the FORTRAN compiler from automatically vectorizing the loop. The dependence is based on indirect indexing into the work array through the array of row indices. Since the row indices of the nonzeros in any column are distinct, the loop runs correctly when vectorized, but the compiler decision must be overridden explicitly.

	CPU seconds		
Problem	Auto	Manual	Improvement
storm2	186.49	121.91	34.6%
aa1	1056.32	488.80	53.7%

Table 2: Automatic *vs.* manual vectorization

Similarly, the loop that packs the work array back into the sparse data structure must be explicitly vectorized.

To illustrate the effect of careful vectorization, we solved problems *storm2* and *aa1* using code generated by the compiler with (*Manual*) and without (*Auto*) explicit vectorization directives. The total time spent in the Cholesky procedure is shown in Table 2. Although results are given only for the Cholesky procedure, loops with similar structure appear in many places in the dual affine code. These results indicate that care is required when porting serial code to vector machines; automatic vectorizing compilers are not a complete solution. Of course, this represents only a first step in the process of tuning the code for vector processing.

4.3. Parallelization

We implemented the column Cholesky algorithm in parallel as a subroutine in the dual affine algorithm. The particular scheduling discipline we chose is suggested in [Liu, 1986], and based on the *elimination tree model* of Jess and Kees [1982]. This discipline is described in [Liu, 1986] as a "large-grain" model. Each task is defined as the computation of a complete column, denoted $Tcol(j)$. This is contrasted with a "medium-grain" model, in which the individual tasks are column updates ($cmod(j,k)$) and division of a column by its diagonal ($cdiv(j)$), and a "fine-grain" model, where tasks are individual multiplications. The precedence relation, $Tcol(k)$ *precedes* $Tcol(j)$ indicates that $Tcol(k)$ must be completed before $Tcol(j)$, since completion of $Tcol(k)$ is required for $cmod(j,k)$. It is possible to begin $Tcol(j)$ before completing $Tcol(k)$, performing other updates as the required columns are completed. Nevertheless, the point of choosing a large-grain model is to reduce the synchronization requirements, so the scheduling discipline requires that $Tcol(j)$ not begin until all columns required for computation of column j have been computed. $Tcol(j)$ can then be scheduled, and once begun, can run to completion without synchronizing with any other tasks.

In order to allow multiple tasks to access the same column during their respective updates, the supporting data structure described in Subsection 4.1 must be modified. We use one m-array and two long arrays with entries for each nonzero in L. Each element of the m-array contains the head of a linked list of the nonzeros in a row of L. The lists themselves are kept in one of the long arrays, and the column number of each nonzero is stored in the second long array.

In IBM Parallel FORTRAN, the cost of creating and accessing a parallel resource (*e.g.*, a task or a lock) turns out to be fairly high, compared to the amount of work in $Tcol(j)$. Thus, in a problem with hundreds or thousands of columns in L, it is unreasonable to create and/or schedule a task for every column. We attempted to circumvent this problem by scheduling a task for each processor, and allowing the tasks to select columns to work on from a list of columns whose predecessors have all been completed. This process is managed by keeping count of the unfinished predecessors for each column. When a column is completed, the count for each of its successors is decremented, and when a count reaches zero, the corresponding column is put on the list of ready columns. The updating of the counts and the ready list, and the removal of a column from the ready list are all done within a critical section.

Results of computational tests are given in Table 3. The times reported are times spent in the Cholesky subroutine only, as we have not yet tested other parts of the algorithm in parallel. The best that can be said for these results is that the parallel implementation results in a marginal improvement over the serial (vector) version ($p = 1$), in terms of wall-clock time. The parallel implementation requires significantly more CPU time than the vector version. One conclusion is that the synchronization primitives (locking and freeing the locks on the critical sections) are still extremely expensive, compared to the cost of computing a column. The observation that wall-clock time does not decrease when six processors are used as compared to three may support this conclusion. It may also be due to the fact that the minimum-degree ordering of the rows of A can impose a fairly tightly constrained ordering of the computation of columns. Pictures of the non-zero structure of L for various problems indicate that the minimum-degree algorithm tends to concentrate the dense portion of L at the bottom and in the lower right corner. If a row near the bottom of L becomes completely dense, then the algorithm must compute each column in turn. The performance on *aa1* probably indicates that this approach is not effective on very dense problems, for the same reason. If the expense associated with the parallel primitives remains the bottleneck on other supercomputers, then indications are that parallel Cholesky algorithms will not transport well to supercomputers, unless the cost of the parallel primitives can be reduced significantly.

It should be noted that, although the tests were run in a controlled environment, they were not made on a standalone system. The IBM system provides a set of *virtual* processors, which are assigned dynamically to the physical processors. Thus, wall-clock times in particular are only approximate upper bounds on the true times.

		$p = 1$	$p = 3$	$p = 6$
80bau3b	W	80.6	69.4	75.3
	V	70.5	130.2	175.2
	R	71.3	143.8	212.6
plan02	W	74.6	58.1	58.8
	V	64.5	113.4	149.7
	R	65.0	124.4	183.5
storm2	W	162.1	149.4	168.9
	V	152.3	325.1	444.2
	R	152.9	363.0	559.3
aa1	W	469.1	499.7	547.0
	V	466.0	1126.4	1527.9
	R	466.9	1277.3	1966.9

Table 3: Parallel tests (times in seconds—W = wall-clock; V = virtual CPU; R = real (system) CPU; P = processors).

5. FUTURE RESEARCH

There are many open problems in implementing interior point algorithms on parallel computers. One obvious question is whether algorithms of the type described above are too fine-grained for implementation on supercomputer architectures in general (*i.e.*, shared-memory parallelism involving a small number of powerful processors), and are useful only for massively parallel architectures. If these algorithms are inappropriate for supercomputers, then are there more suitable algorithms? It is possible, for example, that Gaussian elimination is better suited for supercomputers since the individual tasks (row updates) require little synchronization, and the small number of processors implies that the decreasing workload over the course of the algorithm will not leave processors idle. Also, "block" Cholesky algorithms may admit coarser-grained tasks, tailored to the vector architecture of a supercomputer. On the other hand, more efficient implementation of synchronization primitives may be possible, which would make the Cholesky algorithms competitive in a supercomputer environment.

Even within the class of algorithms discussed above, there are open questions. For example, the scheduling of columns to be updated is an optimization problem in itself, namely the problem of scheduling tasks with different processing times and precedence constraints on multiple identical machines to minimize makespan. Static or dynamic application of heuristics for this problem, such as *shortest processing time* or *ranked positional weight* may give improved performance. (See also [Huang and Wing, 1979; Jess and Kees, 1982; Liu, 1985].) An alternative objective would be to schedule tasks in a way that would minimize synchronization requirements. Another critical question involves the optimal ordering of the rows of A, and the trade-off between minimizing fill-in and minimizing the strength of the precedence relations (maximizing parallelism), or developing algorithms that handle the dense portions of the matrices specially.

In addition to matrix factorization, other aspects of the interior point LP algorithms may be adapted for parallel architectures. In particular, the solution of the triangular systems resulting from the factorization (see, *e.g.*, [George, *et al.*, 1986b]), construction of the matrix to be factored, parallel execution of independent tasks within (and between) iterations, and parallel implementation of the algorithms in the preprocessor (static problem reduction [Adler, 1987; Marsten, *et al.*, 1988] and row reordering).

We have related here our experience with one shared-memory architecture. In addition to other shared-memory architectures, there are several classes of distributed architectures. Issues arising in implementation of these algorithms on distributed architectures are somewhat different from shared-memory implementation issues, since data and synchronization information are all communicated by passing messages rather than by sharing information in common memory (see, for example, [Geist and Heath, 1985]). Implementation of interior point LP algorithms on these architectures must still be investigated.

ACKNOWLEDGMENTS

This research was conducted using the Cornell National Supercomputer Facility, a resource of the Center for Theory and Simulation in Science and Engineering (Cornell Theory Center), which receives major funding from the National Science Foundation and IBM Corporation, with additional support from New York State and members of the Corporate Research Institute. We particularly wish to thank the CNSF consultants for their patience and assistance in this endeavor.

REFERENCES

Adler, I., N. Karmarkar, M. G. C. Resende and G. Veiga (1987), *An Implementation of Karmarkar's Algorithm for Linear Programming*, Report No. ORC 86-8, Operations Research Center, University of California, Berkeley, Calif.

Duff, I. S., A. M. Erisman and J. K. Reid (1986), *Direct Methods for Sparse Matrices*, Oxford University Press, New York, N.Y.

Geist, G. A. and M. T. Heath (1985), *Parallel Cholesky Factorization on a Hypercube Multiprocessor*, ORNL Technical Report ORNL-6190, Oak Ridge National Laboratory, Oak Ridge, Tenn.

George, A., M. T. Heath and J. W-H. Liu (1986), "Parallel Cholesky Factorization on a Shared-Memory Multiprocessor," *Linear Algebra and Its Applications 77*, pp. 165–187.

George, A., M. T. Heath, J. W-H. Liu and E. Ng (1986), "Solution of Sparse Positive Definite Systems on a Shared-Memory Multiprocessor," *International Journal of Parallel Programming 50*, 4, pp. 309–325.

George, A. and J. W-H. Liu (1981), *Computer Solution of Large Sparse Positive Definite Systems*, Prentice-Hall, Englewood Cliffs, N.J.

Huang, J. W. and O. Wing (1979), "Optimal Parallel Triangulation of a Sparse Matrix," *IEEE Transactions on Circuits and Systems, CAS-26*, 9 (Sept.), pp. 726–732.

Jess, J. A. G. and H. G. M. Kees (1982), "A Data Structure for Parallel L/U Decomposition," *IEEE Transactions on Computers, C-31*, 3 (Mar.), pp. 231–239.

Liu, J. W.-H. (1985), "Modification of the Minimum-Degree Algorithm by Multiple Elimination," *ACM Transactions on Mathematical Software 11*, 2 (June), pp. 141–153.

Liu, J. W-H. (1986), "Computational Models and Task Scheduling for Parallel Sparse Cholesky Factorization," *Parallel Computing 3*, pp. 327–342.

Marsten, R. E., M. J. Saltzman, D. F. Shanno, G. S. Pierce and J. F. Ballintijn (1988), *Implementation of a Dual Affine Interior Point Algorithm for Linear Programming*, CMI Working Paper WPS88-06, Department of Management Information Systems, University of Arizona, Tucson, Ariz.

EXPERIENCES WITH LARGE SCALE NETWORK OPTIMIZATION ON THE CONNECTION MACHINE

CINDY PHILLIPS

M.I.T. Laboratory for Computer Science and Thinking Machines Corporation, Cambridge, MA 02139

STAVROS A. ZENIOS

Department of Decision Sciences, The Wharton School, University of Pennsylvania, Philadelphia, PA 19104.

ABSTRCT

We summarize experiences with the solution of large scale network optimization problems using the massively parallel Connection Machine (CM). We discuss key features of the implementation of parallel algorithms for *assignment* and *strictly convex nonlinear network* problems and present results with numerical experiments.

1. INTRODUCTION

A network optimization problem is defined as follows:

$$\begin{aligned} \underset{x}{\text{Minimize}} \quad & F(x) \\ \text{subject to} \quad & A \cdot x = 0 \\ & l \leq x \leq u \end{aligned}$$

A is a node-arc incidence constraint matrix. The graph underlying this optimization model can be derived by associating rows of the constraint matrix with nodes $\mathcal{V} = \{1, 2, 3, \ldots, n\}$ and columns of A with directed edges $\mathcal{E} = \{(i,j) \mid i, j \in \mathcal{V},$ and some column of A has a +1 in row i and a -1 in row $j\}$. The model can be written in algebraic form as:

$$\begin{aligned}\text{Minimize}_{x_{ij}} \quad & \sum_{(i,j)\in\mathcal{E}} f_{ij}(x_{ij}) \\ \text{subject to} \quad & \sum_{(i,j)\in\mathcal{E}} x_{ij} - \sum_{(k,i)\in\mathcal{E}} x_{ki} = 0 \\ & l_{ij} \leq x_{ij} \leq u_{ij}\end{aligned}$$

The first set of constraints represents conservation of the flows x_{ij} at all nodes $i \in \mathcal{V}$, and the second imposes upper and lower bounds u_{ij}, l_{ij} on all edges $(i,j) \in \mathcal{E}$. In the *assignment problem* the set of vertices of the graph $\mathcal{V}$ is defined as $\mathcal{V} = P \bigcup O$, where $P = \{1,2,3,\ldots n\}$ and $O = \{1,2,3,\ldots n\}$. A typical modeling use of this problem is the one-to-one matching of persons from P to objects or tasks in O. Later we will be referring to P and O as persons and objects respectively. Edges in the network connect a node from P to a node in O. Each edge (i,j) has a weight v_{ij} which indicates the value of assigning person i to object j. The optimization problem is to choose the assignment that satisfies $Minimize_{x_{ij}} \sum_{(i,j)\in E} -v_{ij}x_{ij}$. The variable x_{ij} has the value 1 if person i is assigned to object j and zero otherwise. See Dembo et al. [1989] for a general reference on network problems.

Researchers have been turning recently to parallel computers as a possible way to solve very large network models. See Meyer and Zenios [1988] or Zenios [1989]. In this paper we report on the implementation of network optimization algorithms on the CM of Hillis [1985]. We discuss both assignment and nonlinear network optimization problems. A comprehensive discussion on the use of the CM for the solution of nonlinear network problems can be found in Zenios and Lasken [1988]. The experiences with the assignment problems are reported here for the first time.

2. NETWORK PROBLEMS ON THE CM

The basic component of the CM is an integrated circuit with sixteen processing elements (PE) and a *router* that handles general communication. A fully configured CM includes 4,096 chips — for a total of 65,536 PEs — wired together as a 12-dimensional hypercube. The concept of *virtual processors* (VP) allows an application to use more PEs than the number of physical elements available. A VP is specified by slicing the memory of a physical processor and then allowing the physical PE to loop over all the slices.

Using standard Gray coding the processors of the CM can be configured as an n-dimensional grid such that two processors that are neighbors in the grid are connected by a hypercube wire. Communication within a grid — called NEWS communication — is efficient since the required paths can be precomputed and the general router bypassed. General inter-processor communication is performed by the *routers*.

Programming languages on the CM are *LISP and C*. Parallel primitives that are relevant to our implementation are *Scans*, *PSet*, and *Global* operations. Scan is also known in the literature as parallel prefix. The $\otimes$-scan primitive, for associative, binary operator $\otimes$ takes a sequence $\langle x_0, x_1, \ldots, x_n \rangle$ and produces another sequence $\langle y_0, y_1, \ldots, y_n \rangle$ such that $y_i = x_0 \otimes x_1 \otimes \cdots \otimes x_i$. Options specified in the scan call allow the scan to be performed in reverse. A variation of the scan primitives allows their operation within *segments* of a parallel variable or VPs. These primitives are denoted as *Segmented-Scans*. They take as arguments a parallel variable and a set of segment bits which specify a partitioning of the processors into contiguous segments. Segment bits have a 1 at the starting location of a new segment and a 0 elsewhere. A *Segmented-Scan* operation re-starts at the beginning of every segment. When processors are configured as a NEWS grid, scans within rows or columns are special cases of segmented scans. *PSet* takes as arguments two parallel variables and a set of memory addresses and copies the first parallel variable to the second at the VPs given by the memory addresses. Because the communication pattern is arbitrary, this primitive uses the router. *Global* operations on parallel variables return a single value to the front end processor.

2.1 Representation of Dense Assignment Problems

Because we assume that the input graph is dense, we configured the CM as an $n \times n$ NEWS grid, where n is the number of people or, equivalently, the number of objects rounded up to the closest integer that is a power of 2. Row i is associated with person i and column j is associated with object j. In particular, processor (i, j) stores the value v_{ij} of object j to person i, local variables applicable to person i and local variables applicable to object j. Each processor will hold a parallel boolean variable called assigned-here. If assigned-here = True in processor (i,j) then person i is (perhaps temporarily) assigned to object j.

2.2 Representation of Sparse Network Problems

Figure 1 shows the representation of a small sparse network. Every arc in the network is associated with two processing elements (PH_{ij} and PT_{ij}) where PH and PT indicate processors at the *head* and *tail* of an arc respectively and the subscript indicates arc $(i,j) \in \mathcal{E}$. Processors corresponding to a node i are designated as a *segment* defined by $SEG_i = \{PT_{ij}, PH_{ki} \ \forall \ (i,j) \text{ and } (k,i) \in \mathcal{E}\}$.

The data stored at each processor PH_{ij} and PT_{ij} include: (1) arc data u_{ij}, l_{ij}, x_{ij} and the objective function $f_{ij}(x_{ij})$, (2) dual variables π_i and π_j, (3) deficit at the node associated with the processor, defined by

$$d_i = \sum_{(i,j)\in\mathcal{E}} x_{ij} - \sum_{(k,i)\in\mathcal{E}} x_{ki};$$

PH_{ij} stores d_j and PT_{ij} stores d_i, and (4) the address of the processor at the other end of the arc.

3. SOLUTION OF ASSIGNMENT PROBLEMS

We implemented the *auction algorithm* for assignment problems due to Bertsekas [1988]. Referring to the definition of the assignment problem, we see that in a globally optimal solution any given person may not be assigned to the object which is most valuable to him. For any optimal assignment it is possible to assign to each object j a *price* π_j such that if each person i views the *profit* of being assigned to object j as $v_{ij} - \pi_j$, then every person is assigned to the most profitable object. An assignment is ϵ-*optimal* if each person is assigned to an object that is no more than ϵ less profitable than its most profitable object.

The auction algorithm is performed as follows. We start with $\epsilon = max_{i,j} v_{ij}$ and find an ϵ-optimal assignment. Keeping the prices π generated in that round, we reduce ϵ and find a new assignment optimal for that ϵ, and so on until $\epsilon < 1/n$ where n is the number of people. At this point the assignment is optimal. In practice we scale all values by $n+1$ to allow integer calculations. Each inner loop (finding an ϵ-optimal assignment) can be

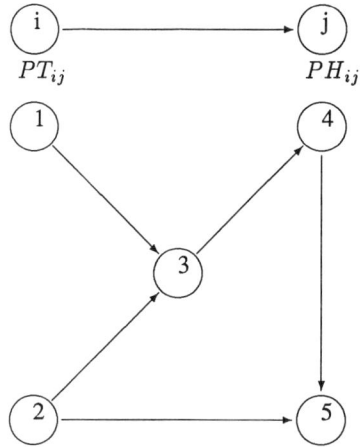

Processor	Address	Data Stored Locally
(P)	$ad(P)$	
PT_{13}	0000	$ad(PH_{13})$, d_1, π_1, π_3 and data for arc $(1,3)$
PH_{13}	0011	$ad(PT_{13})$, d_3, π_1, π_3 and data for arc $(1,3)$
PT_{23}	0001	$ad(PH_{23})$, d_2, π_2, π_3 and data for arc $(2,3)$
PH_{23}	0100	$ad(PT_{23})$, d_3, π_2, π_3 and data for arc $(2,3)$
PT_{25}	0010	$ad(PH_{25})$, d_2, π_2, π_5 and data for arc $(2,5)$
PH_{25}	1000	$ad(PT_{25})$, d_5, π_2, π_5 and data for arc $(2,5)$
PT_{34}	0101	$ad(PH_{34})$, d_3, π_3, π_4 and data for arc $(3,4)$
PH_{34}	0110	$ad(PT_{34})$, d_4, π_3, π_4 and data for arc $(3,4)$
PT_{45}	0111	$ad(PH_{45})$, d_4, π_4, π_5 and data for arc $(4,5)$
PH_{45}	1001	$ad(PT_{45})$, d_5, π_4, π_5 and data for arc $(4,5)$

$SEG_1 = \{PT_{13}\}$ $SEG_2 = \{PT_{23}, PT_{25}\}$
$SEG_3 = \{PH_{13}, PH_{23}, PT_{34}\}$ $SEG_4 = \{PH_{34}, PT_{45}\}$
$SEG_5 = \{PH_{25}, PH_{45}\}$

Figure 1: Representation of Sparse Network Problems.

viewed as an auction where all currently unassigned people bid on the most profitable object, the price of the object is raised to the highest bid and the object is temporarily assigned to the highest bidder. The auction algorithm is defined as follows:

Step 0: We keep a copy of ϵ in each processor. Using a global max operation and a broadcast, set $\epsilon \leftarrow (n+1) * max(v)$. In each processor set $\pi \leftarrow 0$ and assigned-here $\leftarrow$ False. We keep another boolean variable person-assigned which is True in all processors of row i if person i is assigned to an object. Set person-assigned $\leftarrow$ False. Also scale all values of v by $n+1$.

Step 1: Determine if everyone is assigned (global or of the person-assigned variable). If a person is unassigned proceed to Step 2. If every person is assigned to an object and $\epsilon \leq 1$ the algorithm terminates. If $\epsilon > 1$ reduce its value, unassign everyone whose current assignment is no longer ϵ-optimal for the new ϵ and proceed to Step 2.

Step 2: Select processors associated with unassigned people. Set profit $\leftarrow v - \pi$. Within each row i find the column index j_i of the most profitable object: form the concatenation of the profit and column number in each processor and do a grid max-scan. Set $best \leftarrow j_i$. Turning off processor $(i, best)$ use grid scan to find the profit p of the next best object and set $next - best \leftarrow p$. Person i bids on object $best$ by setting the variable bid in processor $(i, best)$. The value of the bid is computed as follows: Let $w_{(i,best)}$ be the maximum profit from all objects except $best$. The bid from i to $best$ is $v_{(i,best)} - w_{(i,best)} + \epsilon$.

Step 3: Using a max grid-scan within all columns, determine the maximum price bid on each object and update the prices π within the columns. For all objects bid upon, assign the object to the highest bidder by setting the assigned-here variable. Update the person-assigned variable using or grid-scans within the rows. Go to step 1.

At the start of each auction with a new ϵ, many people bid simultaneously, but the number of people bidding decreases monotonically during the auction. In our implementation we use an ϵ-scaling heuristic to reduce the tail-effect. For a given value of ϵ the auction terminates when $k\%$ people have been matched. k increases as ϵ decreases

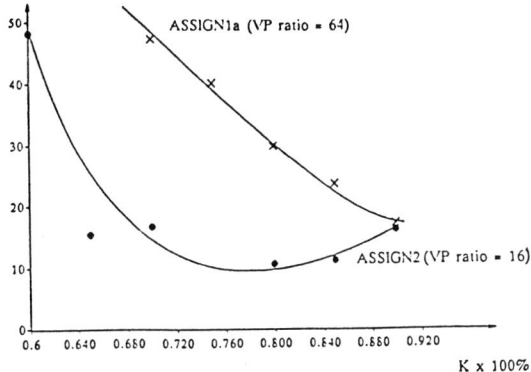

Figure 2: CM time with various values of k.

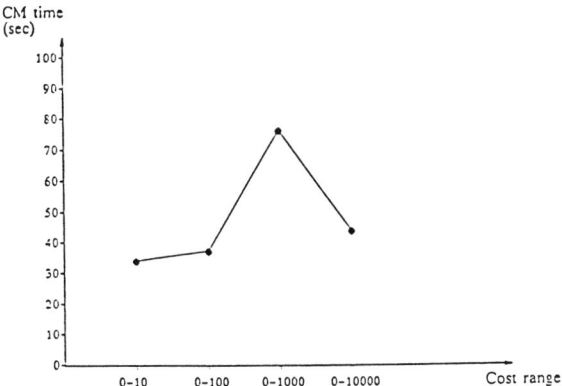

Figure 3: CM time with various cost ranges.

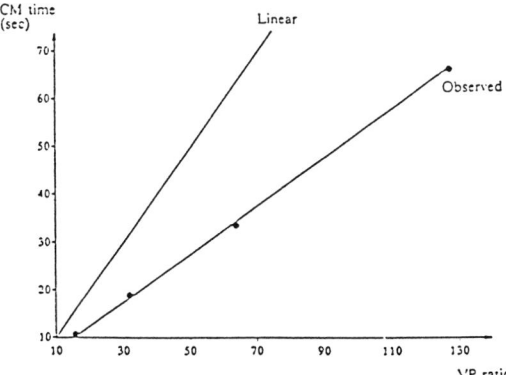

Figure 4: CM time with various VP ratios.

Problem	CM time	Best CM time		VP ratio	CM time Estimate
	$ndecr = 2, k = .9$	CM time	$ndecr/k$		on 64K CM
ASSIGN1	108.48	28.60	5/0.80	64	9.1
ASSIGN1a	53.88	33.77	5/0.80	64	10.7
ASSIGN1b	52.90	36.92	2/0.80	64	11.7
ASSIGN1c	223.08	76.25	2/0.95	64	24.1
ASSIGN1d	43.87	43.87	2/0.90	64	13.8
ASSIGN2	16.16	10.57	2/0.80	16	3.3

Table 1: Solution of Assignment Problems (CM time in sec).

until $k = 100\%$ when $\epsilon < 1$. ϵ is decreasing from its initial large value to less than 1 by dividing after each iteration by a parameter $ndecr$.

The auction algorithm was used to solve the assignment test problems shown in the Appendix. Observe from Figure 2 that significant savings in CM time are realized for suitable choice of the parameter k. Figure 3 indicates the performance of the algorithm for problems with increasing cost ranges. Figure 4 shows the solution time as a function of the VP ratio; it indicates the savings in solution time that can be anticipated if a larger machine is used. Table 1 summarizes the performance of the algorithm. All runs were performed on a CM–2 with 16K processors running at 6.69 MHz clock cycle. The solution time will improve by a factor of 3 with the use of a 64K machine. The estimated solution time on a 64K machine is summarized in the last column of the table.

4. SOLUTION OF NONLINEAR NETWORK PROBLEMS

A relaxation algorithm for strictly convex network problems proposed by Bertsekas, Hossein and Tseng [1987] was shown by Bertsekas and El Baz [1987] and Zenios and Mulvey [1988] to be well suited for massively parallel computations. Zenios and Lasken [1988] provide the first study of the algorithm on massively parallel hardware (the CM–1). Using the sparse representation of section 2.2 and the segmented-scan operations one iteration of the algorithm can be executed as follows:

Step 0: Choose starting prices $\pi^0 = \{\pi_1^0, \pi_2^0, \ldots, \pi_n^0\}$ (Fix one price to zero).

Step 1: Compute values of x_{ij} satisfying complementary slackness conditions:

$$x_{ij} = u_{ij} \quad if \quad \pi_i - \pi_j > \frac{\partial f_{ij}(x_{ij})}{\partial x_{ij}}\bigg|_{x_{ij}=u_{ij}} \quad (1)$$

$$x_{ij} = l_{ij} \quad if \quad \pi_i - \pi_j < \frac{\partial f_{ij}(x_{ij})}{\partial x_{ij}}\bigg|_{x_{ij}=l_{ij}} \quad (2)$$

$$x_{ij} = \hat{x}_{ij} \quad if \quad \pi_i - \pi_j = \frac{\partial f_{ij}(x_{ij})}{\partial x_{ij}}\bigg|_{x_{ij}=\hat{x}_{ij}} \text{ for } l_{ij} < \hat{x}_{ij} < u_{ij}. \quad (3)$$

This calculation is executed concurrently for all arcs $(i,j) \in \mathcal{E}$. PH_{ij} and PT_{ij} compute identical values for x_{ij}. Perform a *Segmented-Plus-Scan* operation over the flows of all processors to compute the deficit at all nodes. If the maximum deficit is less than some tolerance the algorithm terminates.

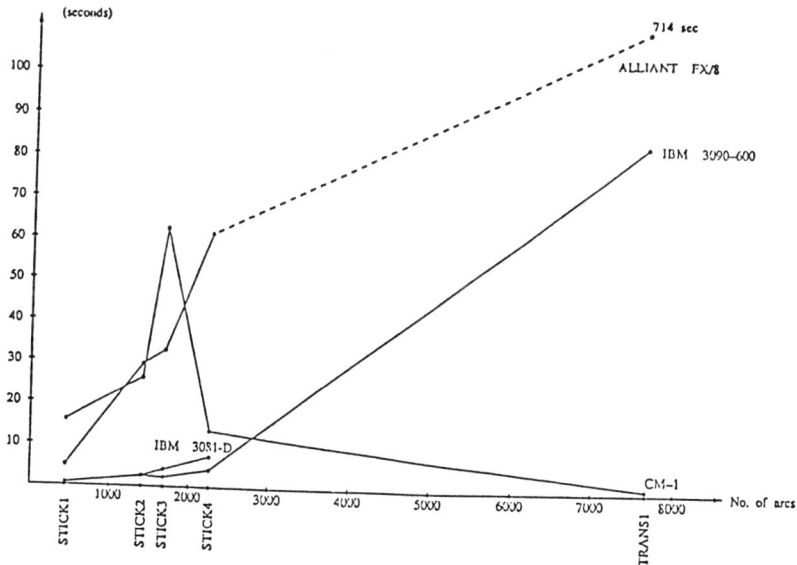

Figure 5: Benchmarks with the solution of nonlinear networks.

Step 2: The dual variable for all nodes is adjusted such that the flows corresponding to complementary slackness conditions result to zero deficit. This step is performed concurrently for all nodes by the last processor in every segment. (After the *Segmented-Plus-Scan* at Step 1 only the last processor in a segment has the correct value of the deficit.) A *Segmented-Reverse-Copy-Scan* operation copies the dual price to all processors in a segment. Finally each processor broadcasts its dual value to the processor at the other end of the arc using a $*PSet$ operation. Return to Step 1.

This algorithm run on a CM–1 and a CM–2 using the test problems of the Appendix. The same test problems were solved using the primal truncated Newton algorithm of Ahlfeld et al. [1987] on an IBM 3081–D, an IBM 3090–600/VF and an Alliant FX/8. On the last two machines significant effort went into modifying the software to take advantage both of the vector and parallel features of the hardware. Figure 5 summarizes the results.

5. CONCLUSIONS

We have seen how large scale network optimization problems can be represented and solved successfully on a Connection Machine. The results with the strictly convex nonlinear problems are impressive. The parallel relaxation algorithm on the CM outperforms significantly algorithms on supercomputers. The results with the assignment algorithm are very encouraging. Problems with 1M variables can be solved within 0.5 - 1 minute of CM time. The solution time can be brought down to a few seconds with a fully configured machine.

ACKNOWLEDGMENT

Part of the research reported here was completed while the authors were with Thinking Machines Corporation. The encouragement of Jill Mesirov is gratefully acknowledged. Research partially supported by NSF grants ECS–8718971, CCR–8811135, AFOSR grant 89–0145, DARPA grant N00014–87–K–0825 and awards from the Wharton School, University of Pennsylvania, Thinking Machines Corporation and IBM.

REFERENCES

D. P. Ahlfeld, R. S. Dembo, J. M. Mulvey, and S. A. Zenios (1987), Nonlinear programming on generalized networks. *ACM Transactions on Mathematical Software*, 13(4):350–368.

D. P. Bertsekas and D. El Baz (1987), Distributed asynchronous relaxation methods for convex network flow problems. *SIAM Journal on Control and Optimization*, 25(1):74–85.

D.P. Bertsekas (1988), The auction algorithm: a distributed relaxation method for the assignment problem. In R.R. Meyer and S.A. Zenios (eds.), Parallel Optimization on Novel Computer Architectures. *Annals of Operations Research*, 14.

D.P. Bertsekas, P. Hossein, and P. Tseng (1987), Relaxation methods for network flow problems with convex arc costs. *SIAM Journal on Control and Optimization*, 25:1219–1243.

G.E. Blelloch (1987), The scan model of parallel computation. In *Proceedings of the International Conference on Parallel Processing*.

R.S. Dembo, J.M. Mulvey, and S.A. Zenios (1986), *Large Scale Nonlinear Network Models and their Application.* Report EES–86–18, Civil Engineering and Operations Research, Princeton University.

W. D. Hillis. (1985), *The Connection Machine.* The MIT Press, Cambridge, Massachusetts.

J. L. Kennington and R. V. Helgason (1980), *Algorithms for Network Programming.* John Wiley, N. York.

R. R. Meyer and S. A. Zenios, editors (1988), *Parallel Optimization on Novel Computer Architectures.* Volume 14 of *Annals of Operations Research*, A.C. Baltzer Scientific Publishing Co., Switzerland.

S. A. Zenios and R. A. Lasken (1988), Nonlinear network optimization on a massively parallel connection machine. In R.R. Meyer and S.A. Zenios (eds.), Parallel Optimization on Novel Computer Architectures. *Annals of Operations Research*, 14.

S.A. Zenios (1989), Parallel numerical optimization: current status and an annotated bibliography. *ORSA Journal on Computing*, 1(1), (to appear).

S.A. Zenios and J.M. Mulvey (1988), A distributed algorithm for convex network optimization problems. *Parallel Computing*, 6:45–56.

Appendix: Test Problems

Problem	Nodes	Arcs	Comments
STICK1	209	454	Stick percolation
STICK2	650	1412	problems from
STICK3	782	1686	Ahlfeld et al. [?]
STICK4	832	2264	
TRANS1	2500	7668	Randomly generated transportation problem
Dense Assignment Problems			
ASSIGN1	2000	10^6	Cost range 1–10
ASSIGN1a	2000	10^6	Cost range 1–10
ASSIGN1b	2000	10^6	Cost range 1–100
ASSIGN1c	2000	10^6	Cost range 1–1000
ASSIGN1d	2000	10^6	Cost range 1–10000
ASSIGN2	1000	25×10^4	Cost range 1–1000

Problem ASSIGN1 was derived from a military application. The rest of the assignment test problems were randomly generated.

III.

GRAPHICS IN OPTIMIZATION

APPLICATIONS OF INTERACTIVE COMPUTER GRAPHICS TO LINEAR PROGRAMMING

IRVIN LUSTIG

Department of Civil Engineering and Operations Research
Princeton University
Princeton, NJ 08544

ABSTRACT

A system to display three-dimensional polytopes on a high-performance graphics workstation is described. Using special hardware and software graphics technology, these polytopes can be manipulated on the screen in real-time. The ability to interact with the graphics display is very powerful. Thus, one can easily study the geometrical structure of these polytopes and can also compare the solution paths of linear programming algorithms. The availability of these workstations for such applications enhances the researcher's understanding of the geometry of linear programming.

1. INTRODUCTION

"At their best, graphics are instruments for reasoning about quantitative information. Often the most effective way to describe, explore, and summarize a set of numbers—even a very large set—is to look at pictures of those numbers. Furthermore, of all methods for analyzing and communicating statistical information, well-designed data graphics are usually the simplest and at the same time the most powerful"

–Edward R. Tufte, *The Visual Display of Quantitative Information*

For many years, researchers in linear programming have studied the geometrical structure of the feasible region of linear programs. Consider the linear program,

$$\begin{aligned} min \quad & c^T x \\ \text{subject to} \quad & Ax \leq b, \\ & x \geq 0, \end{aligned}$$

where $A \in \Re^{m \times n}$, $c \in \Re^n$, and $b \in \Re^m$. It is well-known that the feasible region described by the set

$$P = \{\, x \in \Re^n \mid Ax \leq b,\ x \geq 0 \,\}$$

is a polytope with as many as $m + n$ faces. Given this description of a feasible region, the vertices of the polytope can be computed as well as the collection of edges connecting the set of vertices. Visually, the collection of vertices and edges of the polytope provide a geometric interpretation that is pleasing to the eye. Unfortunately, it is difficult for humans to visualize higher dimensional polytopes. While the display of higher dimensional objects would be ideal, the difficulty of projecting such an object onto a two-dimensional graphics screen restricts us to viewing three-dimensional objects. If $n = 3$, the edges can then be projected onto a two-dimensional graphics screen to depict the feasible region. To display the iterates of a linear programming algorithm, lines can be drawn between the iterates. Different colors can be used to emphasize the difference between two algorithms.

Because of the restricted dimensionality, the number of vertices and edges that need to be computed is small. If $n = 3$, the number of vertices v of P is bounded above by $2(m+1)$ [Chvátal 1983], while the number of edges e is bounded above by $2m(m+1)$ [McMullen 1970]. Previous computer technology has been able to display individual pictures of three-dimensional polytopes, but has been unable to provide the ability to dynamically change the viewing angle. The ability to move an object in real time and interact with the graphics display allows further understanding of the geometrical structure of the polytopes. Gay [1987] drew pictures of a polytope to demonstrate the solution path of Karmarkar's [1984] algorithm and other variants. His pictures, plotted with black ink on white paper, provided some insight into the new interior point methods for linear programming. However, pictures on paper are not sufficient to gain a full understanding. Gay remarked, "Nearly everyone who sees the pictures suggests making a movie ... I look forward to some future time when we'll all have workstations powerful enough to display such a movie in real time." Today, high-performance color graphics workstations, such as the Silicon Graphics 4D series, can provide these "movie" capabilities to the researcher interested in studying the structure of polytopes and the solution paths of linear programming algorithms.

In this paper, a system to compute the vertices and edges of three-dimensional polytopes is described. Section 2 describes the underlying geometry of three-dimensional polytopes. In Section 3, the algorithms used to compute the vertices and edges of the polytope are discussed. Section 4 describes the capabilities of the graphics software. This is followed by some conclusions in Section 5.

2. GEOMETRY OF THREE DIMENSIONAL POLYTOPES

Given the above linear program in inequality form with $n = 3$, let u be a vector of m slack variables so that $u = b - Ax$. We can then write the set P as

$$\bar{P} = \left\{ \bar{x} \in \Re^{m+n} \mid [A\ I]\bar{x} = b,\ \bar{x} \geq 0 \right\},$$

where $\bar{x} = [x\ u]$. The simplex method [Dantzig 1963] provides a useful characterization of vertices of the polytope $\bar{P}$. Let $\mathcal{B}$ and $\mathcal{N}$ be disjoint index sets such that

1. $\mathcal{B} \cup \mathcal{N} = \{1,\ldots,m+n\}$;
2. The cardinality of $\mathcal{N}$ is n; and,
3. The matrix B, which is formed by selecting the columns of $[A\ I]$ indexed by $\mathcal{B}$, is nonsingular.

Then $\bar{x} \in \Re^{m+n}$ is a vertex represented by $\mathcal{B}$ (or, equivalently, $\mathcal{N}$) if $B\bar{x}_{\mathcal{B}} = b$, $\bar{x}_{\mathcal{N}} = 0$, and $\bar{x} \geq 0$. (Note: $\bar{x}_{\mathcal{B}}$ are the components of $\bar{x}$ indexed by $\mathcal{B}$.) An edge of the polytope is characterized as the line between two vertices $\mathcal{B}^1$ and $\mathcal{B}^2$ with the property that the cardinality of $(\mathcal{B}^1 \cap \mathcal{B}^2)$ is exactly $m - 1$. It is easy to see that these properties define a graph $G(\bar{P})$, where the nodes of the graph correspond to vertices of $\bar{P}$ and the arcs of the graph correspond to edges of $\bar{P}$.

Let $\mathcal{B}$ correspond to some vertex of $\bar{P}$, with $B = [A\ I]_{\mathcal{B}}$. By definition, B^{-1} exists. The matrix $(B^{-1}[A\ I])$ will contain m unit columns corresponding to $\mathcal{B}$ and n other columns corresponding to $\mathcal{N}$. Let $\hat{A} = (B^{-1}[A\ I])_{\mathcal{N}}$. The feasible region described by P is then equivalent to the feasible region described by

$$\hat{P} = \left\{ \hat{x} \in \Re^n \mid \hat{A}\hat{x} \leq B^{-1}b,\ \hat{x} \geq 0 \right\}.$$

The sets P and $\hat{P}$ differ only by an affine transformation.

This equivalence has an important consequence when drawing polytopes. A choice must be made as to the variables that will be drawn. Consider the following feasible region, which is a cube with a corner cut out:

$$\begin{array}{rcl}
x_1 & \leq & 10, \\
x_2 & \leq & 10, \\
x_3 & \leq & 10, \\
x_1 + x_2 + x_3 & \leq & 25, \\
x_1,\ x_2,\ x_3 & \geq & 0.
\end{array}$$

Adding 4 slack variables, x_4, x_5, x_6, and x_7, produces the region

$$\begin{array}{rcl}
x_1 + x_4 & = & 10, \\
x_2 + x_5 & = & 10, \\
x_3 + x_6 & = & 10, \\
x_1 + x_2 + x_3 + x_7 & = & 25, \\
x_1,\ x_2,\ x_3,\ x_4,\ x_5,\ x_6,\ x_7 & \geq & 0.
\end{array}$$

This region is drawn in the space of x_1, x_2, and x_3 in Figure 1.

This region can also be draw in the space of x_4, x_5, and x_7, as in Figure 2. It is clear that the visual appearance of the region can change depending upon the variables that are chosen as axes.

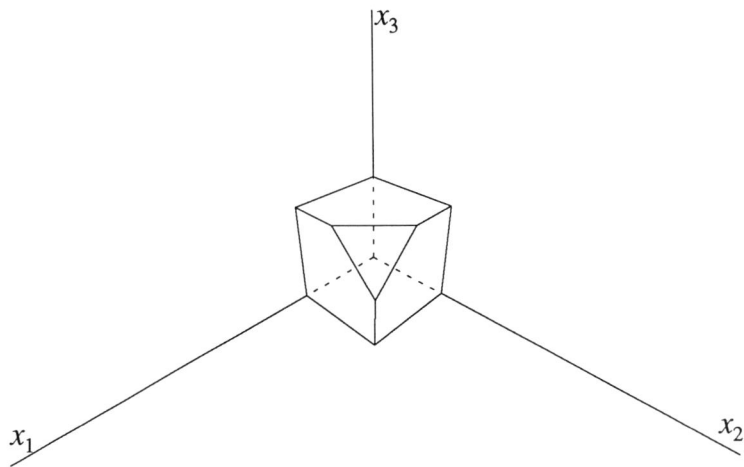

Figure 1. Region in x_1, x_2, x_3 coordinates

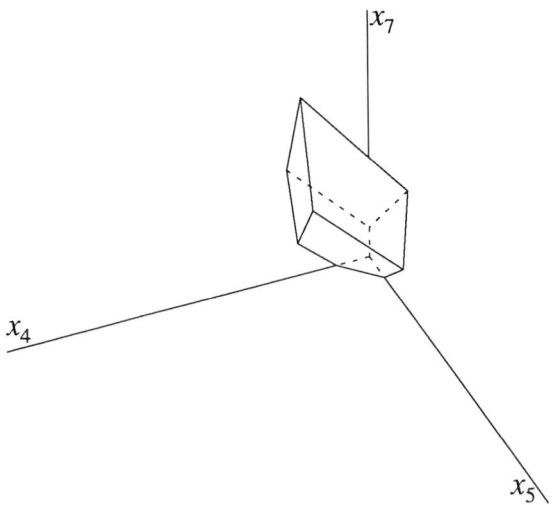

Figure 2. Region in x_4, x_5, x_7 coordinates

3. FINDING THE VERTICES, EDGES, AND FACES
OF A POLYTOPE

Chvátal (1983) describes a simple algorithm to find all the vertices of a polytope. The algorithm uses breadth-first search to build the graph $G(\bar{P})$. Let $\mathcal{B}^1$ index some known vertex. (Such a vertex can be found with Phase 1 of the simplex method.) The algorithm will build a list of vertices $\mathcal{B}^k$, $1 \leq k \leq M$ as follows:

$M \leftarrow 1; k \leftarrow 1;$
repeat
    for each neighboring vertex $\mathcal{B}$ of $\mathcal{B}^k$ **do begin**
        if $\mathcal{B} \neq \mathcal{B}^j$ for all $1 \leq j \leq M$ **then begin**
            $M \leftarrow M+1; \mathcal{B}^M \leftarrow \mathcal{B};$
        end
    end
    $k \leftarrow k+1;$
until $k > M;$

The neighboring vertices of $\mathcal{B}^k$ are discovered by applying the simplex method. Each of the indices $s \in \mathcal{N}^k$ is considered the index of a potential entering nonbasic variable. If the index s can be exchanged with some index $q \in \mathcal{B}^k$ so that $\mathcal{B} = ((\mathcal{B}^k \cup \{s\}) \setminus \{q\})$ indexes another vertex, then $\mathcal{B}$ is considered a neighbor of $\mathcal{B}^k$. An arc of $G(\bar{P})$ is then created between the two nodes $\mathcal{B}^k$ and $\mathcal{B}$, if it has not been previously created.

Once $G(\bar{P})$ is computed, it is desirable to compute the vertices that are on each face of $\bar{P}$. For each j, $1 \leq j \leq n+m$, a face is a cycle in $G(\bar{P})$ where each node in the cycle corresponds to a vertex $\mathcal{N}$ with the property that $j \in \mathcal{N}$. If $1 \leq j \leq m$, the jth face corresponds to the hyperplace $x_j \geq 0$. If $1 \leq i \leq m$, the $(n+i)^{th}$ face corresponds to the hyperplane $A_i.x \leq b_i$, where $A_i.$ corresponds to the ith row of A.

4. DRAWING THE POLYTOPE

After the graph $G(\bar{P})$ is computed, the polytope can be drawn. The Silicon Graphics 4D architecture easily supports the drawing of three-dimensional figures. A line segment in $\Re^3$ is drawn by specifying the coordinates in $\Re^3$. The graphics library software interface to the specialized hardware provides the mechanism of projecting this line onto the two-dimensional screen. Either mechanism is supported by the workstation hardware. A polytope can be drawn as a stick-figure or as a solid figure. The user is given the option of alternating between the two views easily. A stick-figure is drawn by specifying each edge of the polytope as a pair of three-dimensional coordinates. A solid figure is drawn by specifying the vertices of each face as the coordinates of a polygon in $\Re^3$. Care must be exercised in guaranteeing that the vertices are drawn in a counterclockwise order with respect to the normal vector to each face. When a solid figure is drawn, the workstation handles all aspects of lighting, z-buffering and shading as specified by subroutine calls to the graphics package.

Laur [1988] has developed a special *Viewer* package that allows user manipulation of three-dimensional images. The progammer simply provides a subroutine that draws the object in three dimensions. The Viewer package repetitively calls this subroutine to draw the object. As the user indicates a change in the viewing position with a mouse, the package computes a transformation matrix that is applied to each of the coordinates drawn by the subroutine. This transformation matrix describes the viewing angle of the object.

While in the package, a user can select (via pop-up menus) a number of different transformations to be done to the object. The primary capabilities are:

1. **Rotation.** The object can be rotated in any direction in order to be viewed from any angle.
2. **Zooming.** The point from where the object is viewed can be made closer to or farther from the object.
3. **Translation.** The object can be translated along the 3 axes independently.
4. **Scaling.** The object can be scaled along any of the three major axes.
5. **Depth Cueing.** Color can be used to make points that are farther away appear darker and nearer points appear brighter. This provides an excellent rendition of the depth of an object. This works well with the stick-figure rendition of the polytope.
6. **Field of View.** The width of the viewing cone can be changed to provide a wider or narrower view. This assists the user in zooming into a specific point.
7. **PostScript Output.** A black and white picture of the screen can be placed in a file as PostScript commands [Adobe 1985]. This file can then be sent to a PostScript printer to produce a hard-copy drawing on a two-dimensional page.

In addition, the capability of choosing the 3 variables for axes has been added. This allows the user to study the effects of affine transformations on the polytope. In order to study the solution paths of algorithms, the iterates of two algorithms can be input to the program and plotted in a different color to emphasize their difference.

When the user decides to draw the polytope as a solid object, the different faces are drawn in different colors. The user can then open another window on the screen and dynamically change the colors to emphasize different faces. With a palette of over 16 million colors, the capability of making such color changes can be very useful.

It should be mentioned that including figures (using black ink on white paper) in a report such as this does not provide the reader with a clear understanding of the capabilities of such a system. The ability to interact with the graphics display is the fundamental reason that this system is useful. Interested parties can obtain a demonstration copy of the software by contacting the author. A demonstration of the software will be provided at the conference.

5. CONCLUSIONS

Previously, a three-dimensional polytope could only be viewed by projecting a stick-figure onto a two-dimensional surface. Each projection was a computationally-intensive task. With the availability of high-performance three-dimensional color graphics workstations, these projections can be done quickly so that a user can manipulate the object in real-time and interact with the display. The ability to move an object on the graphics screen gives the user an excellent sense of the depth and shape of the polytope. In addition, color can be used to enhance understanding. The capabilities of dynamically changing the viewing angle and colors of the object is a very powerful tool. However, the positive or negative effects of such changes on the user's perception is not well understood. It remains to be seen if higher-dimensional polytopes can be studied using this graphics technology. These capabilities can provide a useful tool for the linear programming researcher who wishes to study the structure of polytopes and the performance of different algorithms on these structures.

ACKNOWLEDGEMENTS

The author would like to acknowledge the work of Charles Harkless, who did most of the software development for his senior thesis at Princeton University. In addition, David Laur of the Princeton Interactive Computer Graphics Laboratory provided assistance with the use of the Silicon Graphics workstations.

REFERENCES

Adobe Systems Incorporated (1985), *PostScript Language Reference Manual*, Addison-Wesley, Reading, Mass.

Chvátal, V. (1983), *Linear Programming*, W. H. Freeman and Company, New York, N.Y.

Dantzig, G. B. (1963), *Linear Programming and Extensions*, Princeton University Press, Princeton, N.J.

Gay, D. M. (1987), "Pictures of Karmarkar's Linear Programming Algorithm," Computing Science Technical Report No. 136, AT&T Bell Laboratories, Murray Hill, N.J., Jan.

Karmarkar, N.K. (1984), "A New Polynomial-time Algorithm for Linear Programming," *Combinatorica 4*, **4**, 373–395.

Laur, D. (1988), "Viewer Program," Private Communication.

McMullen, P. (1970), "The Maximum Number of Faces of a Convex Polytope," *Mathematika 17*, 179-187.

Tufte, E. R. (1983), *The Visual Display of Quantitative Information*, Graphics Press, Chesire, Conn.

A PC-BASED INTERACTIVE NETWORK DESIGN SYSTEM FOR FIBER OPTIC COMMUNICATION NETWORKS

CLYDE MONMA
DAVID F. SHALLCROSS
Bellcore
Morristown, New Jersey 07960

ABSTRACT

In this paper, we describe a PC-based Interactive Network Design System (INDS) tool developed at Bellcore for designing fiber optic communication networks. This tool makes extensive use of optimization heuristics, color graphics and user interaction. This allows the planner to evaluate many possible network designs in terms of costs and other measures before deciding on the best one. We illustrate the use of this tool, and describe computational results for particular real-world fiber network planning problems. This approach is shown to improve significantly upon methods currently used by network planners for designing fiber optic communications networks. These methods are being incorporated into a network planning system at Bellcore.

1. INTRODUCTION

In this paper, we describe a PC-based Interactive Network Design System (INDS) tool developed at Bellcore for designing fiber optic communication networks. This tool makes extensive use of optimization methods, color graphics and user interaction. The optimization methods are used to build and improve upon network designs and are incorporated into an interactive scheme to serve as an aid to the network planner. The planner sees a color graphics display of the current network solution and can compute various cost and "survivability" measures which will be described later. The planner can decide whether to accept a given solution, to modify it, or generate a completely new solution. In this way, the optimization methods incorporate the aspects of the problem which are easily modeled but which require a fast and accurate computer to evaluate, while the planner brings expert knowledge to the process which is not easily modeled and requires a human to evaluate. This allows the planner to evaluate many possible network designs in terms of costs and other measures before deciding on the best one.

We next describe the fiber network planning problem and formulate it as an optimization problem. In Section 2, we illustrate the use of the Interactive Network Design System (INDS) planning tool. In Section 3, we present computational results on some real-world fiber communication network problems. Concluding remarks are given in Section 4.

Recent work at Bellcore [Cardwell et al. 1988] has focused on the impact of fiber optic technology on telephone network design, and on methods for engineering fiber optic networks. One conclusion is that survivability against network failures is a particularly important issue for fiber optic networks. In particular, it was determined that a network topology should provide for at least two physically diverse paths between certain "special" offices, thus providing for protection against any single link or single node failure for traffic between these offices. These special offices represent high-revenue-producing offices and other offices which require a higher level of network survivability.

Survivability means the ability to restore network service in the event of a catastrophic failure, such as the complete loss of a link or the failure of a facility switch. Service can be restored by routing traffic through other existing facilities and switches, if the network design provides for this contingency. Survivability is a particularly important issue for fiber networks because the high capacity of fiber links results in much more sparse network designs than those which result when planning for copper facilities. This, in turn, increases the amount of traffic carried by a single link, and increases the potential disruption to network services and revenues due to even a single link or single switch failure. Although damage to network facilities occurs very infrequently, the result can be a loss of service to a large number of customers. This results in lost revenues and negatively impacts on customer goodwill. Since damaged facilities can be restored in a matter of hours or days, the likelihood of a second failure during this time frame is quite small. Thus, the so called "two-connected" topologies which allow for two physically diverse paths between certain offices is appropriate.

The problem considered here consists of central office switch locations, and potential links between offices where fiber facilities could be installed. These potential links correspond to pairs of offices between which conduit already exists or where fiber could be easily placed. Each link has an associated cost of installing the fiber facilities; this cost is (roughly) proportional to the length of the fiber facility along the route represented by the link. The goal is to design a network which minimizes the total installation cost subject to certain two-connected survivability constraints.

More precisely, the problem considered is as follows. We are given an undirected graph G=(V,E), where V represents the set of *nodes* or office locations, and E represents the set of *edges* or potential links. Associated with each edge (u,v) is an installation *cost* c_{uv}. Each node v has an associated *connectivity type* r_v. The overall network connectivity constraints require that there be at least min $\{r_v, r_w\}$ node-disjoint paths between every distinct pair of nodes v and w in the network. The goal is to design, from scratch, a network which minimizes the total cost subject to the network connectivity constraints. Related network design problems with connectivity constraints were considered in [Christofides and Whitlock 1981] and [Stiglitz et al. 1969].

For the fiber optic network design problem, all nodes are of connectivity type one or two, and are called ordinary and special offices, respectively. An example network is shown in Figure 1 with special offices indicated by squares and ordinary offices indicated by circles. Also shown in the figure are the potential links from which a network must be designed. A feasible network consists of a two-connected part containing all special nodes, in which every pair of nodes has at least two node-disjoint paths between them; this is illustrated by solid lines in Figure 2. The remaining nodes are linked into the two-connected part by spanning trees; this is illustrated by dashed lines in the figure.

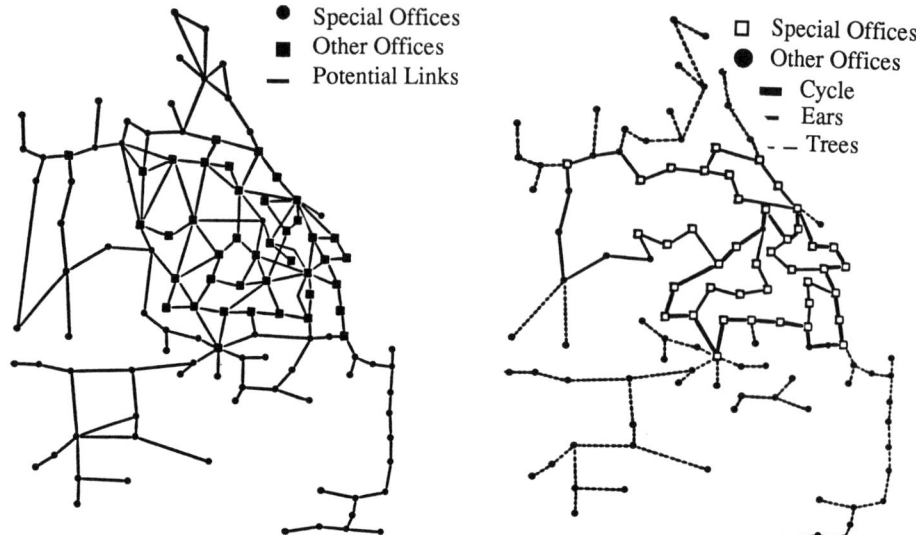

Figure 1. Example Network Design Problem   Figure 2. Example Feasible Network

2. INTERACTIVE NETWORK DESIGN SYSTEM (INDS)

In this section we describe the use of Interactive Network Design System (INDS) tool developed at Bellcore for designing fiber optic communication networks. INDS runs on an IBM PC with a color graphics monitor. The INDS display consists of a color graphics window on one side of the screen, and a menu/statistics window on the other side. Both windows are available at all times. A graphical display of the current problem or solution is displayed in the graphics window at all times. The user can select commands from the current menu using a single keyboard stroke; the menu is in the top left part of the screen. Statistics such as cost or other measures are displayed in the bottom right part of the screen. Commands include optimization methods for generating and improving network designs, computational procedures for calculating certain "diversity" and "survivability" measures, as well as commands for reading, writing or editing a current problem or solution. The optimization methods are all based on fast heuristics [Monma and Shallcross (1989)] so that they can be incorporated into an interactive scheme to serve as an aid to the network planner. The planner can decide whether to accept a given solution, to modify it, or generate a completely new solution. In this way, the optimization methods incorporate the aspects of the problem which are easily modeled but requires a fast and accurate computer to evaluate; the planner brings expert knowledge to the process which is not easily modeled and requires a human to evaluate. This allows the planner to evaluate many possible network designs in terms of costs and other measures before deciding on the best one.

Initially the Two-Connected Menu appears as shown below:

```
        TWO-CONNECTED

   p -  Problem
   b -  Build Solution
   i -  Improve Solution
   r -  Read Solution
   w -  Write Solution
   e -  Edit Solution
   z -  Statistics
```

This is the main menu which allows the user to access other menus for obtaining a new problem; building, improving, reading, writing or editing a solution for a problem; obtaining statistics about a solution, or quitting the INDS software to return to DOS. All of these menus can be accessed by a single keystroke corresponding to the letter shown in the menu.

The first step is to select "p" in the Two-Connected Menu to obtain the Problem Menu as shown below:

```
           PROBLEM

   r -  Read Problem
   w -  Write Problem
   e -  Edit Problem
   p -  Random Problem
   l -  Leave
```

The Problem Menu allows the user to read data from disk storage for a new problem, write data to disk storage for the current problem, edit the problem, generate a random problem, or leave the Problem Menu for the Two-Connected Menu. For example, selecting "r" prompts the user for the name of a problem file in disk storage. Typing "?" displays the names of all of the problem files. After entering the file name, the file is read and the graphics window displays the current network under consideration. Nodes are displayed as circles, or squares (offices are all green at this point), corresponding to type 1 and type 2 offices, respectively. The potential links which could be used in the network design are also displayed. See Figure 1 for an example showing a typical display. Also included in the problem data file are costs for each link, and (optionally) point-to-point traffic volumes.

The user may edit the current problem by selecting "e" in the Problem Menu. The edit function is controlled by keys in the keypad on the IBM PC keyboard. A summary of the keys and their editing functions are shown below:

Arrow keys -	Move the cursor ↑ ↓ → ←
Home key -	Moves cursor to vertex #1
Ins key -	Increases connectivity type
Del key -	Decreases connectivity type
PgDn key -	Positions inactive cursor, selects a link
PgUp key -	Removes active cursor and reactivates old cursor
End key -	Ends session, returns to Problem Menu

Initially, a (brown) circle is drawn around the "home" node, and data about the node is displayed, such as its number and name. Pressing the "PgDn" key selects this node and additional information about the node is displayed, such as its (x,y) plotting coordinates, and its connectivity type. Pressing the "Ins" key increases the connectivity type of a selected node while the "Del" key decreases the connectivity type. The arrow keys allow moving a (brown) arrow on the graphics display to other nodes. When the arrow lands on a node, it turns into a (brown) circle around that node which is now selected, displaying its node number and name. Pressing the "PgDn" key while encircling a second selected node displays information about this pair of nodes, such as their names, the amount of traffic between them, and the cost of the link between them (this cost is "infinite" if there is no such link). The user is given the option to input a new cost for this link. Selecting the "Ins" key adds a link between these nodes, and selecting the "Del" key deletes the edge. Selecting the "PgUp" key releases the selected nodes. Selecting the "Home" key returns the arrow to the initial "home" node with a circle around it. The "End" key returns control to the Two-Connected Menu.

The next step is to select "b" in the Two-Connected Menu in order to obtain the Build Solution Menu shown below.

BUILD SOLUTION
r - Random
g - Greedy
l - Leave

The Build Menu allows the user to construct an initial solution using either a random or greedy heuristic by selecting "r" or "g", respectively. Selecting "l" causes control to return to the Two-Connected Menu.

Both of the construction heuristics first build a two-connected network for the special nodes (and possibly some ordinary nodes as well), and then link in the remaining ordinary nodes with spanning trees. It is well-known that any two-node connected network can be constructed by starting with an initial cycle C, and repeatedly adding paths P, called ears, to the current partial solution which start at one node of the solution, run through nodes not yet on the solution, and end at a different node on the solution.

The "Random" heuristic randomly generates the cycle and ears, while the "Greedy" heuristic uses the cost information to greedily generate a cycle and and ears of low cost.

The greedy heuristic randomly selects a special node v, and then selects a special node w whose shortest path P to v is longest among all special nodes. Let node u be the node next to w on the path P. It now constructs a "short" cycle through the edge (u,w) by finding a shortest path from u to w not using the edge (u,w). (There must be such a path; if not, there would not be two node-disjoint paths between the special nodes u and w and so the problem would be infeasible.) The next step is to repeatedly add "short" ears to the current partial solution until all special nodes are on this two-connected network. This is done by first selecting a special node z not yet in the solution whose shortest path P to the partial solution is longest among all special nodes not yet included. It now finds another shortest path Q from z to the partial solution which does not use any edges of P and which terminates on the partial solution at a node w other than v. (Again, such a path must exist for the problem to be feasible.) The combination of paths P and Q must contain an ear which is added to the partial solution.

The random heuristic proceeds in a similar manner except that it selects a random cycle and a random ear at each stage rather than a short cycle or short ears. For more details on these and other construction heuristics, see [Monma and Shallcross 1989)].

The next step is to select "i" in the Two-Connected Menu in order to obtain the Improve Solution Menu as shown below:

IMPROVE SOLUTION	
2 -	2-Optimal Cycle
3 -	3-Optimal Cycle
p -	Pretzel Form
q -	Pretzel Remove
d -	Degree Reduction
1 -	1-Optimal
l -	Leave

The Improve Menu allows the user to apply one of several transformations to the network design, each of which is designed to reduce the overall network cost while preserving the network connectivity constraints. These transformations all make local improvements to the network and are designed to work in real-time. We briefly describe these improvement heuristics below. For more information about the details of these methods see [Monma and Shallcross (1989)]. Selecting "l" leaves the Improve menu for the Two-Connected Menu. It is also possible to save a solution to disk, read a previously-saved solution, and edit a solution using the Two-Connected menu.

Every two-connected network contains at least one cycle, and often is made up of many interconnected cycles. Furthermore, replacing the edges in a cycle C by edges forming a cycle C' on the same nodes, preserves the feasibility of a solution. So it is natural to draw upon the extensive research on the traveling salesman problem (see [Lawler et al. 1985]) for finding a near-optimal cycle. This is the basis of the two-optimal cycle and three-optimal cycle improvement heuristics. The pretzel, quetzel and degree improvement heuristics alter the structure of the two-connected part of the solution in less obvious ways. The one-optimal improvement heuristic alters the structure of the entire solution.

The two-optimal cycle heuristic attempts to interchange two edges, say edges (u,v) and (x,y), of a cycle C by two edges, say edges (u,y) and (v,x), to form a new cycle C' of lower cost. A two-optimal interchange is illustrated in Figure 3. The approach is to first randomly choose a cycle C in the current solution. (This can be done by forming a depth-first-search tree from a randomly-chosen node and randomly choosing an edge not in the tree to form a cycle C.) We then apply this interchange heuristic to the cycle C to obtain a locally-optimal cycle C' on the same set of nodes; we then replace C by C' in the solution.

The three-optimal interchange heuristic is similar in that it attempts to replace three edges of a cycle C by three other edges to form a new cycle C' of lower cost. These heuristics are repeated until no further improvements of these types are possible.

The two-optimal cycle and three-optimal cycle heuristics replace one cycle by another cycle on the same nodes, and so do not change the fundamental structure underlying the solution. We now describe a transformation which replaces one edge (u,v) of a cycle C with two "crossing" edges (u,y) and (v,x) to form a "pretzel" P as shown in Figure 4. The approach is to randomly choose a cycle C in the current solution, and apply this interchange heuristic to obtain a pretzel P of lower cost; we then replace C by P in the solution. The quetzel transformation is the reverse of the form pretzel transformation; that is, a pretzel P is replaced by a cycle C by removing two crossing edges (u,y) and (v,x), and adding an edge (u,v) as shown in Figure 4. These heuristics are repeated until no further improvements of these types are possible.

It can be shown [Monma et al. 1989], that if the costs satisfy the triangle inequality, then there is an optimal two-connected solution where all nodes are of degree two or three. The proof of this result implicitly contains the transformations necessary to reduce all degrees to two or three. We will not describe this transformation here.

All of the previous improvement heuristics operated only on the two-connected part of the solution. The one-optimal interchange heuristic considers the entire solution. This heuristic attempts to remove an edge (u,v) from the current feasible solution and replace it with another edge of the form (u,x) not currently in the solution. Such an interchange is made only if the resultant network is feasible and of lower cost. A one-optimal interchange is illustrated in Figure 5.

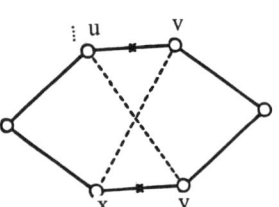
Figure 3. Two-Optimal Cycle Improvement Heuristics

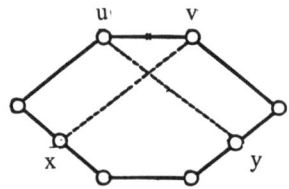
Figure 4. Pretzel and Quetzel Improvement Heuristics

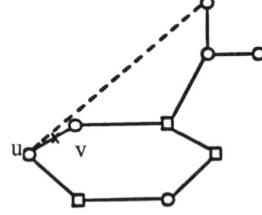
Figure 5. One-Optimal Improvement Heuristic

Selecting "z" in the Two-Connected Menu results in the Statistics Menu being displayed as shown below:

```
STATISTICS

d - Diversity
s - Survivability
l - Leave
```

It is possible to compute "diversity" and "survivability" statistics about the current solution so long as the current problem has the optional point-to-point traffic volumes as part of the problem data.

The *route diversity* of a network solution is the percentage of point-to-point traffic which has at least two node-disjoint paths in the given network (this represents the precent of traffic which could never be disrupted by any single link or node failure). This is computed by calculating all of the traffic between nodes on the two-connected part of the network and dividing by the total traffic in the network. Selecting "d" from the Statistics Menu results in a computation of the route diversity measure of the current solution as shown below:

```
Number of    Percent of
Routes       Traffic

One          20.4%
Two or more  79.6%
```

The *network survivability* is the percentage of point-to-point traffic which can still be carried after a particular single link or a particular single node failure. Four values are given for the survivability depending on whether we are concerned with a link or a node failure, and whether we are concerned with the worst possible failure or an average among all possible failures. This is computed by removing each link in turn and computing the percentage of traffic which can still be carried by the network. The lowest value over all links gives the worst-case value, and the average over all links gives the average-case value. Selecting "s" from the Statistics Menu results in the computation of the survivability measure for the current solution as shown below:

```
              Worst-Case     Average-Case
              Traffic Carried  Traffic Carried

Link Failure  96.9%          99.6%
Node Failure  72.8%          98.0%
```

3. COMPUTATIONAL RESULTS

In this section, we describe the effectiveness of the PC-based Interactive Network Design System (INDS) planning tool on three real-world fiber optic network design problems. These problems each represent particular real-world fiber optic network design problems. The underlying graphs for these types of problems are sparse and the link costs represent the length of a fiber routed through existing facilities along that link. These sparse problems are denoted by S100, S116, and S116f. Problem S100 is for a network with 100 nodes of which 15 are special nodes, and with 138 potential links. Problem S116 is for a network with 116 nodes of which 41 are special nodes, and with 239 potential links. Problems S116f is the same network with 116 nodes but with the additional constraint that 40 fiber links already exist and must be integrated into the final solution. These real-world problems correspond to a metropolitan area and surrounding region. For example, the Problem S116 is illustrated in Figure 1 with special offices indicated by squares and ordinary offices indicated by circles. Also shown in the figure are the potential links from which a network must be designed.

All of the computational results reported here were performed on an IBM PC/AT running at 6 MHz. The software package is implemented in complied BASIC using the IBM BASIC Compiler Version 2.0 running under DOS 3.00. The implementation includes the use of color graphics to show the animation of the heuristics. All CPU times are reported in seconds and include the time required to display the graphics.

The results of the computational tests on the three real-world problems are summarized in Tables I and II. For a more complete set of computational results including comparisons for each individual heuristic as well as results for randomly-generated problems see [Monma and Shallcross (1989)]. Table II compares the route diversity and network survivability of the various solutions generated for the real-world problems.

Table I gives the solution values and CPU times for the two heuristics which construct initial networks (random and greedy-ears), and for the combined result of using the various improvement heuristics with these two initial solutions. In all cases, the time required to improve the random initial solution is about two times more than the time required to improve the greedy-ears initial solution. For these problems, we show both the results of improving the first random initial solution, and the best improvement among five initial random solutions. The results show that this latter approach yielded the best solution in two cases, and nearly the best in the third case. This demonstrates the power of this local optimization search procedure for these real-world problems.

Table II gives the route diversity and network survivability of the solutions generated by our methods, and compares them to a minimum spanning tree solution shown in Figure 6. Each of these real-world problems have associated with them data on the amount of point-to-point traffic between pairs of nodes in the network. The route diversity of a network solution is the percentage of point-to-point traffic which has at least two node-disjoint paths in the given network. This represents the traffic on the two-connected part of the network which could never be disrupted by any single link or any single node failure. The network survivability is the percentage of point-to-point traffic which can still be carried after a particular single link or a particular single node failure. Four values are given for the survivability depending on whether we are concerned with a link or a node failure, and whether we are concerned with the worst possible failure or an average among all possible failures.

TABLE I. Solution Values and CPU Seconds

SPARSE PROBLEMS	INITIAL[a] GREEDY EARS	IMPROVED[a,b] GREEDY EARS	INITIAL[a] RANDOM	IMPROVED[a,b] RANDOM	BEST[a,c] RANDOM
S100	6,928 17.57	6,689 57.55	7,331 21.69	6,780 112.12	6,622 108.35
S116	8,776 67.06	7,549 79.81	8,824 53.77	7,526 153.90	7,484 118.31
S116 F	8,324 45.09	8,003 34.16	9,311 42.73	8,027 86.09	8,004 89.37

[a] Solution values and CPU seconds are given for each problem.

[b] Values given are for a local optimum found by the combined heuristics given the initial solutions.

[c] Values given are for best local optimum found after improvement of five initial random solutions.

TABLE II. Diversity And Survivability Measures

SPARSE PROBLEMS		SOLUTION VALUES	ROUTE[a] DIVERSITY	LINK SURVIVABILITY[b]		NODE SURVIVABILITY[b]	
				WORST	AVERAGE	WORST	AVERAGE
S100	Min Spanning Tree	6,405	0%	66.3%	95.2%	54.3%	94.2%
	Initial Greedy	6,928	39.4%	89.9%	98.7%	60.0%	96.9%
	Improved Greedy	6,689	48.1%	92.6%	98.8%	61.9%	97.0%
	Initial Random	7,331	66.9%	92.1%	99.5%	62.3%	97.7%
	Improved Random	6,780	60.7%	92.1%	99.4%	62.3%	97.5%
	Best Random	6,622	58.7%	92.1%	99.3%	62.3%	97.5%
S116	Min Spanning Tree	7,133	0%	70.1%	95.3%	62.0%	94.4%
	Initial Greedy	8,776	77.7%	96.9%	99.7%	72.8%	98.0%
	Improved Greedy	7,549	78.5%	96.9%	99.6%	72.8%	98.0%
	Initial Random	8,824	85.7%	97.1%	99.8%	72.8%	98.1%
	Improved Random	7,526	79.6%	96.0%	99.6%	72.8%	98.0%
	Best Random	7,484	81.3%	96.9%	99.7%	72.8%	98.1%
S116 F	Min Spanning Tree	7,422	0%	69.8%	96.7%	54.3%	95.8%
	Initial Greedy Solution	8,324	73.8%	96.9%	99.6%	72.8%	99.0%
	Improved Greedy	8,003	77.0%	96.9%	99.7%	72.8%	99.0%
	Initial Random	9,311	85.7%	97.1%	99.8%	72.8%	98.1%
	Improved Random	8,027	77.0%	96.0%	99.6%	72.8%	98.0%
	Best Random	8,004	77.0%	96.9%	99.6%	72.8%	98.0%

[a] Percentage of point-to-point traffic with two or more node-disjoint paths in the solution.

[b] Percentage of point-to-point traffic that can still be carried by the network after a single line (or single node) failure in worst case and average case.

It is clear that any tree network, such as the one shown in Figure 6, will have no route diversity since each pair of nodes has exactly one path between them. Also, a tree network will have low survivability since the removal of any node or link disconnects the graph into components which can no longer communicate with on another. For the real-world considered problems here, it is possible to gain a great deal of additional route diversity and network survivability with only a small additional cost over that of a tree network. Since the cost of a minimum spanning tree network is a lower bound on the cost of any network connecting the offices, it is also a (probably weak) lower bound on an optimal network for our problem. So the methods proposed here produce "near-optimal" solutions as well. For Problem S116, the optimal tree network is shown in Figure 6; the cost is 7,133 with 0% diversity, 70.1% worst-case link survivability, and 62.0% worst-case node survivability. The network satisfying the connectivity constraints which was generated by the methods described in this paper for Problem S116 is shown in Figure 2; the cost is 7,484 with 81.3% diversity, 96.9% link survivability and 72.8% node survivability. An additional 81.3% route diversity and an added 26.8% survivability is gained over the tree solution with an additional cost of less than 5%.

It is also worthwhile to compare the network produced by the methods proposed here with a network actually generated by network planners for Problem S116. This network was designed manually by a planner tracing solutions from a facility map, and is illustrated in Figure 7. The ad-hoc procedure works as follows. First, build a "protection" ring which includes some of the special offices and is "not too far away" from the other special offices; this is illustrated by dotted links in the figure. Next, link in the other offices to the ring by minimum spanning trees; this is illustrated by solid links in the figure. Finally, add links to ensure the two-connected survivability constraints for the special offices not on the protection ring; this is illustrated by the thick solid links in the figure. This network has about 8,375 total route miles. The network satisfying the connectivity constraints which was generated by the methods described here for Problem S116 is shown in Figure 2; the cost is 7,484 with 81.3% diversity, 96.9% link survivability and 72.8% node survivability. The network generated by the methods proposed here resulted in over a 10% reduction in the overall cost over the ad-hoc approach without sacrificing route diversity or network survivability.

We note that the network generated by INDS is the result of a person interacting with the system to generate several possible network design over a few hours. The planner generates and saves networks which are evaluated according to cost, diversity and survivability measures. These networks are also evaluated by the planner's understanding of the many aspects of the problems which are difficult to quantify. This approach provides the planner with a "what-if" planning tool rather than a single "take-it-or-leave-it" solution.

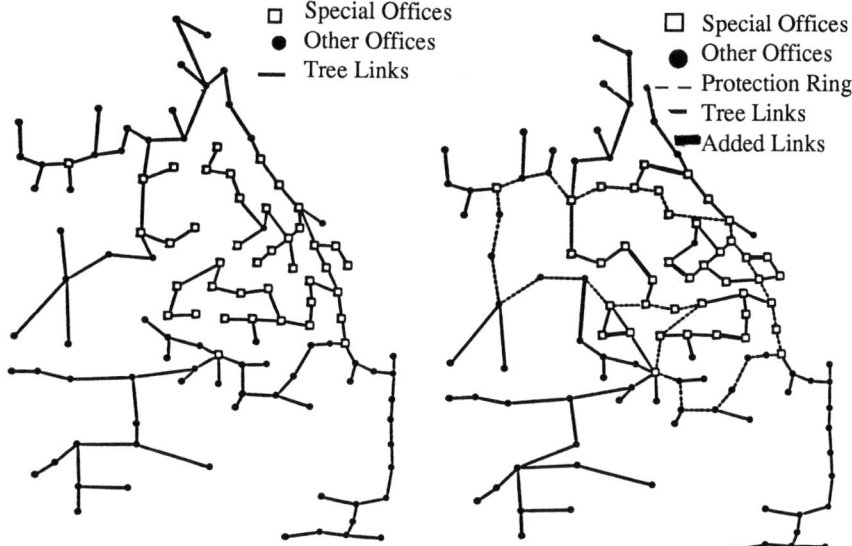

Figure 6. Example Tree Fiber Network Design

Figure 7. Example Ad-Hoc Fiber Network Design

4. CONCLUDING REMARKS

We have described a PC-based Interactive Network Design System (INDS) tool for designing fiber optic communications networks with certain two-connected survivability constraints. This approach of using optimization heuristics, color graphics and user interaction was shown to improve significantly upon methods currently used by Bellcore planners for designing fiber optic communications networks. As a result, these methods are being incorporated into a network planning system at Bellcore.

This work is a continuation of previous research on the structure of optimal two-connected spanning networks when the costs satisfy the triangle inequality [Monma et al. 1989]. Work is in progress to apply the polyhedral approach to obtain exact solutions to network design problems with more general connectivity constraints [Grötschel and Monma 1989].

REFERENCES

Cardwell, R. H., H. Fowler, H. L. Lemberg and C. L. Monma (1988), "Determining the impact of fiber optic technology on telephone network design," *Bellcore Exchange Magazine*, 27-32.

Christofides, N. and C. A. Whitlock (1981), "Network synthesis with connectivity constraints: a survey," in J. P. Brans (editor), *Operational Research '81*, 705-723.

Grötschel, M. and C. L. Monma (1989), "Integer polyhedra associated with certain network design problems with connectivity constraints," *SIAM Journal of Discrete Mathematics*, submitted.

Lawler, E. L., J. K .Lenstra, A. H. G. Rinnooy Kan and D. B. Shmoys (1985), *The Traveling Salesman Problem,* John Wiley, New York.

Monma,C. L., B. S. Munson and W. R. Pulleyblank (1989), "Minimum-weight two-connected spanning networks," *Mathematical Programming,* to appear.

Monma, C. L., and D. F. Shallcross (1989), "Methods for designing communications networks with certain two-connected survivability constraints," *Operations Research,* to appear.

Stiglitz,K., P. Weiner and D. J. Kleitman (1969), "The design of minimum-cost survivable networks," *IEEE Transactions on Circuit Theory CT-16*, 455-460.

IV.

MICROCOMPUTERS IN OPERATIONS RESEARCH

PERSONAL COMPUTER VERSION OF NEARLY TRIANGULAR LEONTIEF LP SOLUTION

E. GELMAN[1] AND M.A. POLLATSCHEK

Technion – Israel Institute of Technology
Faculty of Industrial Engineering and Management
Haifa 32000, Israel

ABSTRACT

The structure of LP in Production Planning appears to be Nearly Triangular. We use the last fact for drastic reduction of the memory requirements and acceleration of the common used LP algorithm such as Simplex. However, the solution of large scale LP via a "flexible" memory management is enabled on a personal computer.

1. INTRODUCTION

Often we solve a special structured problem [Poly1962] with a general method. Such an approach ignores the information of the problem structure. Hence, the general method performs worse than a special one, which utilizes the structure. The idea is not new and is used in many special linear programming (LP) techniques such as upper bounding, algorithms for networks and others cf. [Lasdon 1970, Murty 1983].

This paper is concerned with a solution of a special sparse structured linear programs called $NTLLP$, which appear in industrial planning and other areas. The most general features of them could be summarized as follows:

(1) Multi-period large scale problems, which consist of sparse Leontief (or pre-Leontief) matrices.

(2) The basis matrices are "nearly" upper triangular.

The closeness of a matrix structure to an upper triangular is measured by the number of columns with nonzero elements below the diagonal, without which the matrix would be triangular. Such columns are known as spikes. The lower triangular structures are dealt with

---

[1] Visiting at Colorado University at Denver, Computational Mathematics Group, Denver, CO 80204.

the same ease as the upper ones. Therefore, without lost of generality, in all the notations we will refer to the upper triangular structure. The mathematical characteristics of this type of problems could be found in [Gelman and Pollatschek 1986, 1987]. These results will be briefly discussed in the Section 2. Firstly, the problem was treated by [Dantzig 1954] and [Wagner 1954]. The following articles appeared later on, [Forrest and Tomlin 1972], [Gille and Loute 1981] and [Fourer 1981]. The latter has noted that the problem, which was known for a long time, is not easier to solve now, in spite of the research efforts spent on it.

We propose a method based on tearing principle [Kron 1963], which enables efficient solution of large scale structured linear programs on a most simple personal computer. The method belongs to the "Compact Inverse" family of algorithms. The following methods belong to the same family and are based on [Kron's 1963] principle without noting it explicitly: GUB Technique, [Bisschop and Meeraus 1977], [McBride 1980]. The basic ideas behind the tearing principle and the algorithm will be presented in Section 2. The special type of memory management for a mostly common used personal computer such as $IBM\ P.C.$ is discussed in Section 3. The Section 4 deals with different aspects of computational complexity for the proposed and other methods from the same family. Finally the summary and conclusions are given in Section 5.

2. THE GENERAL IDEA OF THE ALGORITHM

The presentation will begin with a detailed description of the underlying problems and their characterization in [Gelman and Pollatschek 1987]. The previously mentioned structured LP is a multi-period one, and has a Leontief type triangular or nearly triangular submatrix for each period. The closeness to triangular, as it was defined earlier, is measured by number of spikes, without which the matrix would be triangular. This is the source of the chosen term: $NTLLP \equiv$ Nearly Triangular Leontief Linear Program.

Besides these there exist other submatrices which express quantities of stored material passed from one period to another, unity submatrices for import, export, and other submatrices according to different constraints for each subsequent period. These multi-period problems are large scale tasks, the solution of which requires enormous memory and computational efforts. Even by using the well known sparse techniques several problems are "hard", because the sparsity could not be kept during the matrix inversion or LU factorization. The major reason for this "curse" is the so called "fill in" feature, i.e. appearance of new nonzero elements as a result of certain elementary matrix operations.

The following definitions will be used in the sequel.

Definition 1 Matrix A is *pre-Leontief* if and only if there is no more than one positive element in each of its columns.

Definition 2 Matrix A is *Leontief* if and only if

(a) there exists exactly one positive element in each column;

(b) there exists vector $x \geq 0 : Ax > 0$, (for square matrices the latter is equivalent to $A^{-1} \geq 0$.)

Definition 3 Matrix A is *Positively Pivoted* for a given vector $b \geq 0$, if and only if for a given constraints set $\{Ax = b, x \geq 0\}$, all the basis matrices are obtained by pivoting on the locations, which are defined by the positive elements of the original A only.

Using the results in [Gelman and Pollatschek 1986, 1987] and the definitions introduced above, the $NTLLP$ could be briefly characterized by the following statements:

(1) the constraints matrix is *Positively Pivoted*;

(2) there exists a "good" upper bound on number of the feasible extreme points;

(3) there exists a "good" upper bound on the number of spikes in the basis matrix, which turns to be nil for special cases.

These results gave us legitimization to use the tearing method during the solution of the Nearly Triangular Leontief LP. The research was inspired by [Kron's 1963] tearing principle and its application to general LP by [Bisschop and Meeraus 1977] and later on by [McBride 1980]. The proposed method is intended for a certain class of problems, for which the basis matrix is Nearly Triangular, i.e. the number of spikes is "low".

The structure of the underlying problem (for further details see Appendix A) can be schematically presented as follows:

	x	y	s	z		RHS
$\tilde{P}$	$-I_{mn}$	U	I_{mn}	0		b
U_1	0		$\tilde{U}_1$	0	I_{mk}	d_k
0	0		$\tilde{U}_2$	0	I_{ml}	d_l

where: m is the number of periods; $\tilde{P}$ is a Block Diagonal matrix; U is Unimodular matrix; $\tilde{U}_1$ or $\tilde{U}_2$ are vacuous according to XOR relation.

The basis matrix at each iteration is partitioned similar to [Kron 1963] and [McBride 1980], i.e.

$$B = \begin{bmatrix} B_T & B_2 & 0 \\ B_3 & B_V & 0 \\ M_T & M_V & I_M \end{bmatrix} \quad (1)$$

where: B_T is the triangular part. Several parts of the above partition could be vacuous. It is easy to show that

$$B^{-1} = \begin{bmatrix} B_T^{-1} + B_T^{-1}B_2\beta^{-1}B_3B_T^{-1} & -B_T^{-1}B_2\beta^{-1} & 0 \\ -\beta^{-1}B_3B_T^{-1} & \beta^{-1} & 0 \\ -M_TB_T^{-1} - (M_TB_T^{-1}B_2 - M_V)\beta^{-1}B_3B_T^{-1} & (M_TB_T^{-1}B_2 - M_V)\beta^{-1} & I_M \end{bmatrix} \quad (2)$$

where: $\beta = B_V - B_3B_T^{-1}B_2$.

Actually it is equivalent to the following proposition. B is non-singular if and only if B_T and β are non-singular. In other words B^{-1} could be expressed in terms of B_T^{-1} and β^{-1}.

Definition 4

(1) $T_r \equiv \{B_T \text{ rows set}\}$, $T_c \equiv \{B_T \text{ columns set}\}$, $|T_r| \equiv |T_c| \equiv |T|$.

(2) The B_V, I_M rows (columns) set is defined similar to these sets for B_T, i.e. the orders of V_r, V_c and M_r, M_c accordingly are $|V_r| \equiv |V_c| \equiv |V|, |M_r| \equiv |M_c| \equiv |M|$.

The idea of the algorithm is to preserve the form of the partition during the solution process. The tendency will be to keep the orders of B_T and I_M as big as possible or equivalently – the B_V order as small as possible. This type of partition invariance at all stages of the algorithm will cause ease in keeping track of the pivot coordinates (row, column) as $BB^{-1} = I$. The meaning of the latter related to a pivot choice due to the matrix partitions can be expressed as follows:

Columnn Partition	Row Partition
T_c	T_r
V_c	V_r
M_c	M_r

Generally for Revised Simplex the last result will not hold as $BB^{-1} = Q$, which is a permutation matrix. The updating of the basis takes into account the dimension changes of B_T, B_V, I_M. These changes will occur either if the new basic column affects the triangularity of the "old" B_T or as a result of row and column transferring from one part of B to another according to certain criteria. The partition member orders can increase, decrease or stay without change during the updating as shown below:

Cases	B_T	B_V	I_M	Pivot Row Partition
(1)	$|T| = |T| - 1$	$|V| = |V| + 1$	$|M| = |M|$	
(2)	$|T| = |T|$	$|V| = |V|$	$|M| = |M|$	T_r
(3)	$|T| = |T| + 1$	$|V| = |V| - 1$	$|M| = |M|$	
(1)	$|T| = |T|$	$|V| = |V|$	$|M| = |M|$	V_r
(2)	$|T| = |T|$	$|V| = |V| - 1$	$|M| = |M| + 1$	
(1)	$|T| = |T|$	$|V| = |V| + 1$	$|M| = |M| - 1$	M_r
(2)	$|T| = |T| + 1$	$|V| = |V|$	$|M| = |M| - 1$	

For example any change in B_T order will impose changes in B_2, B_3, M_T and therefore in M_V and B_V. This kind of interaction works vice versa as well.

It is clear now, that the main stages of the algorithm, i.e. solution of linear equations systems will be performed in terms of B_T^{-1} and β^{-1}. Current updating of the basis is executed by the "Rank One" transformations in terms of β^{-1}, which is kept in memory, and certain manipulations of linked lists (for details see next Section). This type of updating actually limits the appearance of the "fill in" only in β^{-1}, i.e. in a small matrix of the same order as B_V, although the main part of the basis still remains originally sparse. The stability is maintained periodically by an ordinary reinversion routine. The formal Pseudo-Code of the algorithm could be found in [Gelman and Pollatschek 1986].

3. ALLOCATION AND MEMORY MANAGEMENT – ADAPTATION FOR A MICRO COMPUTER

The special structure of the problem (see Appendix A) allows recovering of the whole problem from the following "generic" matrices: $P, U_1, \tilde{U}_1, \tilde{U}_2$, which will be stored in the memory together with β^{-1} and two other vectors – RHS and C (prices). The "generic" matrices will be stored row wise. From a certain level of sparseness (density) the maintenance of these matrices could bring a great reduction in memory requirements, compare to those, which are might be needed for storage of the whole constraints matrix.

It should be noted, that at different stages, there will be need in certain rows or columns of the partitioned basis matrix B, which on their turn, will be generated from the rows and columns of $P, U_1, \tilde{U}_1, \tilde{U}_2$.

The order of rows (columns) within the partitions of B could vary after the updating stage took place. The most efficient way of tracing this type of changes will be maintenance of a $Prede$- and a Suc-$cessor$ linked lists for rows (columns).

Example 1

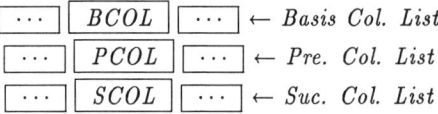

The meaning of the above for the partitioned matrix B is that, the appearance order of those three columns in a certain part of B, is: $\cdots, PCOL, BCOL, SCOL, \cdots$

According to (1), the most frequent step of the algorithm will be the solution of linear equations systems with matrix B involved. The solution will be expressed in terms of B_T^{-1} and β^{-1}, as determined previously. The dimension of the stored β^{-1}, which is periodically updated, could be changed from one iteration to another. Since the solution of triangular sparse linear systems is very efficient, there is no need in keeping B_T^{-1} in the memory.

The personal computer $IBM\ P.C.$ and the programming language $TURBO$-$PASCAL$ were chosen for illustration of the special algorithm features. The P.C. choice could be justified by the very wide and common use of these computer types in business and industry. Different manipulations with linked lists and pointer orientation are performed very efficiently in $TURBO$-$PASCAL$. For instance, in $FORTRAN$ this kind of operations are awkward.

Furthermore $TURBO$-$PASCAL$ allows a "flexible" Heap memory management, i.e. the top of the Heap is able to change its dimension. This kind of flexibility matches the needs of the algorithm for storage of β^{-1} matrix, dimension of which decreases or increases due to certain criteria. The memory, thus, is organized in a Heap as shown in Appendix B.

Assuming that the number of spikes ($|V|$) is small and the amount of rows in $\tilde{U}_1$ and $\tilde{U}_2$ are equal ($k = l$) the memory requirements for the whole Heap will be $6 \times (24mn + 28ml + 2nl + n^2)$ bytes.

The "performance" limits or maximal number of periods (m) as function of the P dimension (n) for different number of $\tilde{U}_1, \tilde{U}_2$ rows ($k = l$) are presented in Figure 1 below.

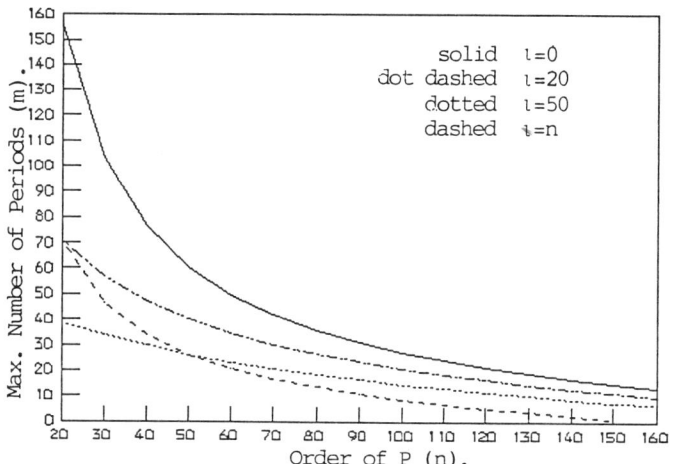

Fig. 1: Number of Periods as Function of P Order.

4. COMPUTATIONAL COMPLEXITY

Since multiplication is one of the most expansive computer operations, the number of multiplications at the main steps of the algorithm was chosen as a common used estimator for the total number of operations.

The estimation was performed under the following assumptions:

(a) The rows (columns) of the basis matrix are partitioned according to (1), i.e. $|T|+|V|+|M| = m(n + k + l)$.

(b) The density (d) of the constraints matrix, i.e. the percentage of nonzero elements in it, is low, as matrix is sparse.

(c) Three main stages of Simplex algorithm were taken into account.

The computational effort per iteration, whenever the previously introduced assumptions are satisfied is

$$A_1(|T|,|V|,|M|) = d(9|T|^2+10|T||V|+3|T||M|+3|V||M|+|T|+|M|)+6|V|^2+5|V|+3.$$

Similarly, for LU version of Revised Simplex the computational complexity per iteration will be

$$A_2(|T|,|V|,|M|) = 4(|T|+|T|+|V|)^2 + 2(|T|+|V|+|M|).$$

Assuming that $|T| = |M|$, the tearing version will be more efficient than the LU if the following condition will be satisfied:

$$\lim_{d \to 0} A_1(|T|,|V|,|M|) - A_2(|T|,|V|,|M|) \leq 0.$$

The latter is equivalent to $|V| \leq 0.8m(n+k+l)$. In other words as long as the number of spikes does not exceeds 80% of the total constraints amount, the tearing method is more efficient than the LU version of Simplex.

Similar results could be obtained for GUB Technique. Denote by $|T|$ the amount of the GUB constraints and by $|V|$ the rest of the constraints. Then the comparison between tearing method and GUB according to the criterion described previously shows that, $|V| \leq 0.8(|T|+|V|)$, which is similar to the one obtained for comparison of tearing with LU version. It means that the tearing method is more efficient than GUB, whenever at least 20% of the constraints are GUB type constraints.

It should be noted that the presented version of the algorithm is non-commercial and was ran mostly for the qualitative analysis of the algorithm. The following results were obtained for seven real life problems, which were formulated for a chemical production and refinery plants.

Table 1: **Numerical Results.**

Prob. No.	No.of Rows	No.of Columns	Density (%)	No.of Iterations	Max.Order of β
1	88	200	1.6	16	0
2	40	200	2.8	24	0
3	40	200	3.0	22	5
4	105	525	1.1	87	12
5	264	600	.6	238	0
6	192	960	.7	153	16
7	200	1000	.3	131	0

As it could be observed from the Table 1 for the underlying problems, the order of β is below 10% of the total number of rows.

5. CONCLUSIONS

Besides a brief mathematical characterization of the problems, we offer a solution procedure, which is theoretically better than others known for this type of LP. The memory requirements for the procedure are lower than those needed for similar methods. The last fact in addition to the flexible memory management enable the solution of real size LP on a personal computer with all data stored within the main memory.

The methods commonly used today for solution of sparse linear systems are mostly based on LU factorization. The structure and the sparsity of the basis matrices are destroyed in these methods as a result of their inversion.

The proposed method will almost always prevent these disadvantages. According to the tearing principle of [Kron 1962], there exists a square nonsingular submatrix (β) of the basis which has to be inverted. Of course, the inversion affects the structure, but the "main" part of the basis matrix still remains easy for solution.

However, the complexity of the procedure is dependent upon the order of the submatrix (β) which is small for certain class of problems, as shown in [Gelman and Pollatschek 1986, 1987].

The tearing method belongs to the family of "Compact Inverse" algorithms. Comparison, between the tearing and other methods from the same family, on the basis of two commonly used criteria – memory requirements and computational effort (complexity) – showed:

(a) The memory requirements of the proposed method are lower than those of other previously described. As matter of fact, there are no versions of them for personal computers.

(b) The tearing method is better than the GUB technique according to computational complexity, whenever at least 20% of the constraints are of GUB type. The computational effort of [Bisschop and Meeraus 1977] is similar the complexity of GUB technique. [McBride 1980] used a heuristic policy of [Hellerman and Rarick 1972] to make the matrix as close to triangular as possible. The latter problem was proven to be NP-complete. The method we used does not need such a technique, because for the problems it is intended, there exists an upper bound on the number of spikes, without which the basis matrix would be triangular. Numerical experience showed that the a order, which is defined by the upper bound on the number of spikes, is relatively small – at most 10% of the total number of constraints.

REFERENCES

Bisschop, Y. and A., Meeraus (1977), "Matrix-Augmentation and Partitioning in the Updating of the Basis Inverse," *Math. Prog. 13*, 241-254.

Dantzig, G.B. (1954), "Block Triangular Systems in Linear Programming," RAND Rep. RM-1273, The RAND Corporation, Santa Monica, Calif.

Forrest, J.J.H. and J.A. Tomlin (1972), "Updating Triangular Factors of the Basis to Maintain Sparsity in the Product Form Simplex Method," *Math. Progr. 2*, 263-278.

Fourer, R. (1981), "Solving Staircase Linear Programs by the Simplex Method: 1. Inversion," In *Large Scale Linear Programming*, G.B. Dantzig et al, Eds., IIASA, 179-259.

Gelman, E. and M.A. Pollatschek (1986), "On Triangular and Nearly Triangular Structures in LP," Technical Report IE-32, Faculty of Ind. Eng. and Mgmt, Technion, Israel.

Gelman, E. and M.A. Pollatschek (1987), "NTLLP - Nearly Triangular Linear Programs", In Preparation.

Gille, P. and E. Loute (1981), "A Basis Factorization Technique for Staircase Linear Programs," In *Large Scale Linear Programming*, G.B. Dantzig et al, Eds., IIASA, 261-285.

Hellerman, E. and D. Rarick (1972), " The Partitioned Pre-Assigned Pivot Procedure (P4)," In *Sparse Matrices and Their Applications*, D.J. Rose and R.A. Willoughby, Eds. Plenum Press, N.Y., 67-76.

Kron, G. (1963), *Diakoptics*, McDonald, London.

Lasdon, L.S. (1970), *Optimization Theory for Large Systems*, McMillan, N.Y.

McBride, R.D. (1980), "A Bump Triangular Dynamic Factorization Algorithm for the Simplex Method," *Math. Progr. 18*, 49-61.

Murty, K.G. (1983), *Linear Programming*, Wiley, N.Y.

Polya, G. (1962), *Mathematical Discovery; On Understanding, Learning and Teaching Problem Solving*, Wiley, N.Y.

Wagner, H.M. (1954), "A Linear Programming Solution to Dynamic Leontief Type Models," RAND Rep. RM-1343, The Rand Corporation, Santa Monica, Calif.

APPENDIX A

Underlying Problems Structure.

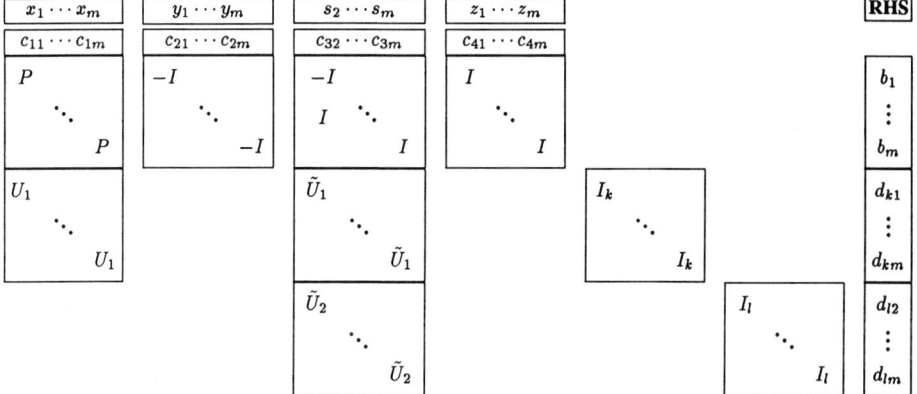

- $P, I \in R^{n \times n}$, $U_1, \tilde{U}_1 \in R^{k \times n}$, $\tilde{U}_2 \in R^{l \times n}$, $I_k \in R^{k \times k}$, $I_l \in R^{l \times l}$
  $\forall i, j : x_i, y_i, s_i, z_i, b_i, c_{ij} \in R^n$, $d_{ki} \in R^k$, $d_{li} \in R^l$
- either $\tilde{U}_1$ or $\tilde{U}_2$ is vacuous
- if U_1 and $\tilde{U}_1$ are vacuous then $d_{ki} = 0$ $(i = 1, \ldots, m)$
- if $\tilde{U}_2$ is vacuous then $d_{li} = 0$ $(i = 2, \ldots, m)$

APPENDIX B

Memory Allocation

\multicolumn{2}{c}{HEAP}	
Array	Dimension
β_{new}^{-1}	$|V|^2$
β_{old}^{-1}	$|V|^2$
Work Space 7	$m \times (n + k + l)$
$\vdots$	$m \times (n + k + l)$
Work Space 1	$m \times (n + k + l)$
RHS (b_{new})	$m \times (n + k + l)$
Pi (π)	$m \times (n + k + l)$
Row Link List	$2 \times m \times (n + k + l)$
Col Link List	$2 \times m \times (4n + k + l)$
RHS (b_{old})	$m \times (n + k + l)$
Price (c)	$4 \times m \times n$
$\tilde{U}_2$	$l \times n$
$\tilde{U}_1$	$k \times n$
U_1	$k \times n$
P	$n \times n$

⇑
Bottom

OPTIMIZING EXCHANGE AGREEMENTS IN THE REFINING INDUSTRY

TERRY P. HARRISON AND JACK L. MARTIN
Department of Management Science
Penn State University
University Park, PA 16802

ABSTRACT

We describe the successful design and implementation of a system to assist United Refining Company in determining how to best "trade" petroleum products with competing firms to minimize procurement and distribution expenses. A parallel implementation of our model with the existing manual system indicates a recurring annual savings of $150,000 to $200,000.

We employ a standard network optimization code, GNET, to solve problems with hundreds of sources and thousands of distribution lanes in a matter of seconds on a desktop computer. We believe that this application is representative of an important new class of management science uses; namely, modeling in the personal computing environment for users who have not previously implemented the techniques of management science.

1. INTRODUCTION

Decisions regarding supply and distribution are often a major factor in the ultimate profitability of many firms. This is especially true in the petroleum refining industry. Here the cost of crude oil and the transportation charges to distribute refined products are the major costs of production.

To defray distribution costs, many refiners execute "exchange agreements", where two refiners agree to trade products. For example, refiner A may have a large retail demand in one region but have no local terminal to supply that demand. Similarly, refiner B may have a large retail demand near refiner A's supply, while having a large supply near refiner A's retail demand. The two refiners may agree to exchange a fixed amount of product, resulting in lower unit costs for both firms. Since certain types of retail products are quite similar regardless of refiner, exchange agreements are especially common. These exchange agreements, in our case negotiated on a monthly basis, contain a provision for the "terminal differential cost", which is the cost to refiner A of "lifting" (removing) one gallon of a particular product at a given location of refiner B. Refiner A executes an exchange agreement by informing an exchange partner of its intention to draw certain amounts of product at various terminals of the exchange partner. A key management decision then is to determine *how to best draw against these exchange agreements*.

A number of prior applications of management science have been reported from the refining industry (Zierer and White[1976] and Durrer and Slater[1977] discuss representative examples). Some recent applications that were of especially significant impact are Brown and Graves[1981], Brown, Ellis, Graves, and Ronen[1987], and Klingman, Phillips, Steiger, and Young[1987]. All of these applications are quite extensive in scope, and deal with national and multi-national firms already well acquainted with management science.

In this paper we describe the successful development and implementation of a management support system to optimize exchange draws for United Refining Company. Our ability to provide fast solutions to complex allocation problems in a desktop computing environment was one of the key elements in the overall success of the project.

Another factor contributing to the success of the project is the ability of our model to determine optimal exchange agreements. That is, given a set of exchange partners and a fixed exchange cost structure, what levels of exchange should we attempt to obtain? This information allows the user to become more competitive by negotiating trade agreements that decrease total supply and distribution expenses.

Finally, we believe that this type of application is an indication of a class of new uses for management science techniques. With the lower cost and increasing performance of desktop computers, many applications are now feasible that were not previously possible, even in the recent past. The trend of increasing power in desktop computing is likely to continue unabated in the foreseeable future. For example, Carver Mead, a preeminent researcher in the design of computer chips and the Gordon and Betty Moore Professor of Computer Science at the California Institute of Technology stated in a recent interview that we can expect "... a 10,000-fold increase in the cost effectiveness of computing in the next decade. ... These developments open opportunities for entrepreneurial creativity and invention unprecedented in the entire history of technology." [Gilder 1988]. We believe that the impact of this new technology will be particularly significant for the new users of management science. It will permit the wealth of tools and experience developed over the past 40 years to be transferred to these new users in a much more effective fashion.

2. THE ENVIRONMENT AT UNITED REFINING COMPANY

United Refining Company refines and sells petroleum products primarily throughout New York, Ohio, and Pennsylvania. The company currently owns and operates a refining plant in Warren, Pennsylvania as well as approximately 285 retail gasoline stations throughout the tri-state area.

The primary goal of the managers of supply and distribution is to meet retail demand at a minimal cost. The supply available to meet demand comes from two sources: 1) product resulting from the refining process, and 2) product traded for or purchased from competitors. Trade agreements afford United the opportunity to be flexible in the location of its supplies since many companies operate multiple terminals. When exchanging with a company that has multiple terminals, United can "lift" different percentages of the total exchange amount at each terminal. These exchange percentages need not be specified a *priori* in the exchange agreement. Thus, flexibility exists in both supply location and volume.

Product distribution costs are comprised of two components: 1) terminal differential costs, and 2) transportation costs. The optimal method of supplying retail demand must consider both components in order to minimize total expenditures.

The terminal differential costs are a direct result of the exchanges made with competitors. These differentials reflect the relative pipeline transportation costs at each terminal. For example, if the pipeline tariff is $0.01 per gallon at Harrisburg and $0.025 per gallon at Rochester, then the location differential is $0.015 for a company lifting product at Rochester with an exchange supply in Harrisburg. The differentials may be either positive or negative depending on the source of supply of each company's product at the time of the exchange agreement.

Transportation costs reflect the price paid to ship a gallon of product from a supply location (terminal) to a demand location (station). The company currently uses a small internal truck fleet and ten external carriers for transporting product. Transportation costs for using a common carrier are independent of routing sequence since costs are a function only of the distance from a terminal to a retail customer and a negotiated cost per mile of transporting product. Each carrier has a variety of locations from which to load, and a specific set of retail stations to supply.

Prior to the use of our model, the method to determine lift volumes and transportation assignments was a two part process. First, the Supply Group assigned the amount to lift by terminal based on past experience and manual cost calculations. After the lift volumes were specified, the Transportation Group assigned retail stations to supply terminals. Our model is an uncapacitated transshipment approach that jointly considers the cost of supply (terminal differential costs) and the cost of distribution. Since gasoline comprises 90 percent of the distribution costs of United's retail product line, the management at United chose to have us focus on gasoline supply and distribution.

3. MODEL DEVELOPMENT

The objective of our model is to minimize the expenses associated with supply and distribution of gasoline. The objective function reflects both the terminal differential costs and the distribution costs. The constraints are a result of the supply and demand at the various terminals and stations respectively.

We use the following notation.

Index Sets
$\mathcal{T} \equiv$ terminals, $\mathcal{T} = \{t \mid t=1,...,T\}$
$\mathcal{P} \equiv$ exchange partners, $\mathcal{P} = \{p \mid p=1,...,P\}$
$\mathcal{S} \equiv$ stations, $\mathcal{S} = \{s \mid s=1,...,S\}$
$\mathcal{T}_p \equiv$ set of terminals for exchange partner p
$\mathcal{T}_s \equiv$ set of terminals available for servicing station s
$\mathcal{S}_t \equiv$ set of stations available for service from terminal t

Data
c_{ts} = transportation cost for shipping one gallon of product from terminal t to station s
d_{pt} = terminal differential cost per gallon for exchange partner p at terminal t
e_p = gallons of product available from exchange partner p
h_s = gallons of product required at station s

Decision Variables

x_{pt} = gallons to be lifted from exchange partner p at terminal t

y_{ts} = gallons shipped from terminal t to station s

Our formulation for this problem is:

$$\text{minimize} \sum_{p \in \mathcal{P}} \sum_{t \in \mathcal{T}_p} d_{pt} x_{pt} + \sum_{t \in \mathcal{T}} \sum_{s \in \mathcal{S}} c_{ts} y_{ts}$$

subject to

$$\sum_{t \in \mathcal{T}_p} x_{pt} = e_p \quad \forall \; p \in \mathcal{P} \qquad \{\text{supply}\}$$

$$\sum_{s \in \mathcal{S}_t} y_{ts} - \sum_{p \in \mathcal{P}} x_{pt} = 0 \quad \forall \; t \in \mathcal{T} \qquad \{\text{transshipment}\}$$

$$\sum_{t \in \mathcal{T}_s} y_{ts} = h_s \quad \forall \; s \in \mathcal{S} \qquad \{\text{demand}\}$$

$$x_{pt}, \; y_{ts} \geq 0$$

Terminal T is a dummy terminal connected to all exchange partners and stations (at a high cost) to ensure a feasible flow. Also, United's own refining facility is simply treated as another exchange partner with the exchange volume fixed at production capacity and the terminal differential cost set to zero.

Figure 1 illustrates the network structure. Note that this formulation permits modeling of multiple commodities through the use of a pure network formulation since all arcs are uncapacitated. This is accomplished by replicating the product network for each commodity, starting at the exchange partner nodes.

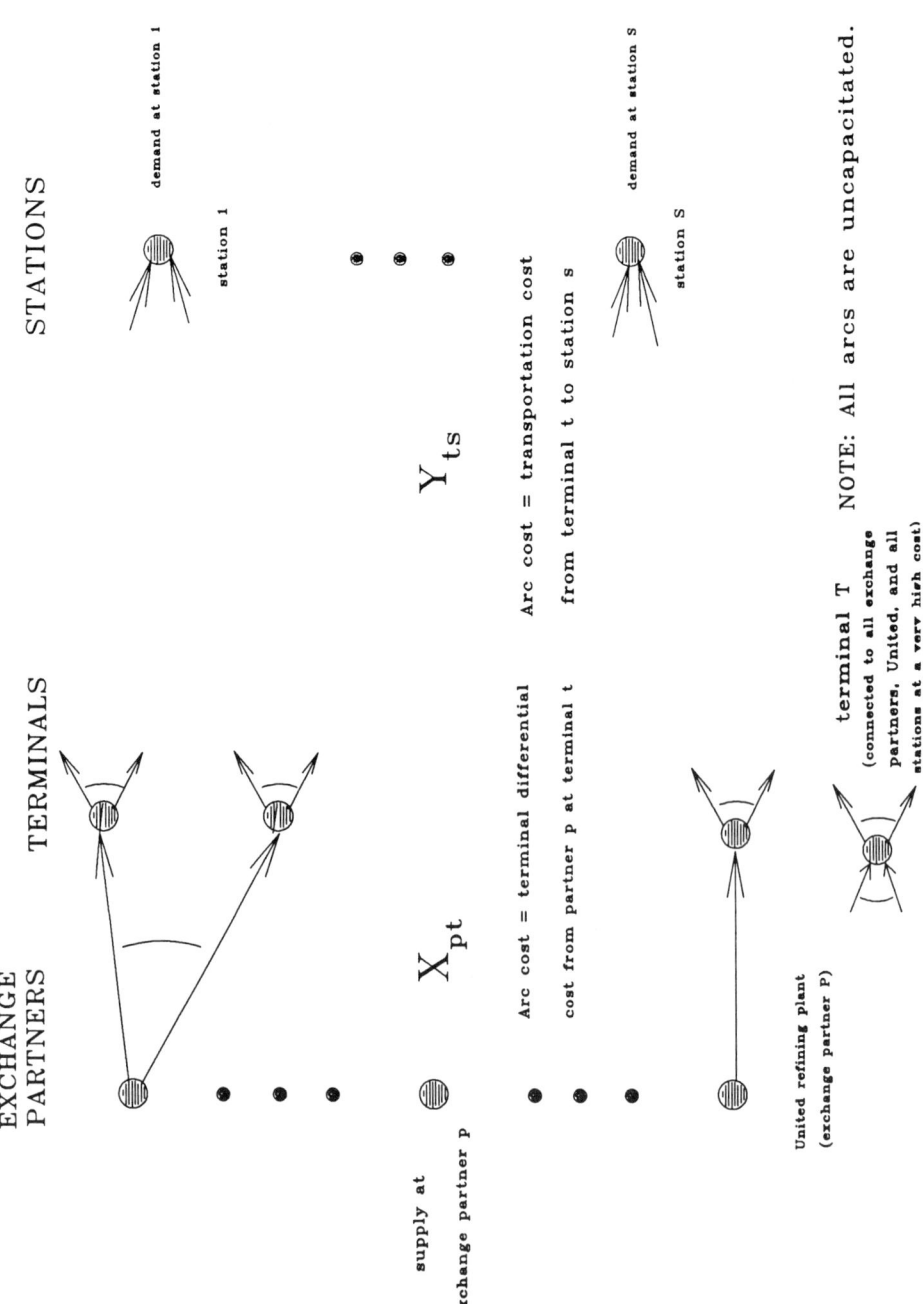

FIGURE 1 Network structure for determining levels of use in exchange agreements.

4. IMPLEMENTATION

An integral part of the implementation was the selection of an appropriate network optimization package. After examining several alternatives, we decided to use GNET, a pure network code written in FORTRAN [Bradley, Brown, and Graves 1977]. The main reasons for selecting this package were 1) its availability in a microcomputer version, 2) modest storage requirements, and 3) its performance on a set of sample problems. For example, for a typical problem instance with over 450 nodes and more than 1,900 arcs, execution time was only 10 seconds on a 6 megahertz IBM AT.

The next phase of the implementation process was to analyze the current method of decision making at United in an effort to determine the benefits available through our model. Prior to implementing the network model United followed a policy of negotiating exchanges and specifying the supply locations in advance of making the distribution assignments. Once the exchanges were set, a manager manually evaluated the distribution patterns and made assignments in the manner that was judged to be best. The process of making the assignments alone, typically took six to eight hours.

Our model allows for one person to negotiate the exchanges, and immediately evaluate the optimal assignment patterns and supply locations. This is done by accessing a corporate database with the appropriate cost and demand data, and subsequently generating and solving the model. In this fashion the analysis can be performed by a single person in a matter of minutes as opposed to the existing method which requires several employees over a period of days. The entire software package consists of a matrix generator, GNET, and a report writer. This results in a turnkey system that is easy to learn and use.

A number of advantages of our approach were immediately recognized. First, a reduction in the person hours necessary to make assignments. Secondly, there was an increased ability to react quickly to changes in the data, such as a change in volume negotiated with an exchanged partner or the addition of a new retail outlet. Lastly, the network model was ruthlessly efficient in "finding" bad data, such as incorrect shipping costs or terminal differentials. Although these benefits have a significant impact in terms of improved decision making, we have chosen to use the dollar savings as a more quantifiable measure of our success.

One measure of the potential savings was determined by comparing actual company decisions with recommendations of our model using a historical dataset. This network consisted of 8 exchange partners, 28 terminals, and 286 retail stations. Total demand for the month was 25 million gallons. Our model produced a solution with roughly a two percent savings.

After three months of parallel testing, the savings had dropped to approximately $5,000 per month. This was a result of the schedulers making use of some unintuitive savings found by the model in the first month. Since there were not any significant changes to the data during the test period, the schedulers quickly learned from the model's prior solutions and incorporated this information into their own recommendations. It is expected that the $5,000 per month represents the "steady state" savings that result from the network model reacting to minor changes in supply and distribution costs.

5. CONCLUSIONS

Our development of a management support system to identify optimal exchange levels and transportation assignments has provided United Refining Company with a valuable tool for reducing the costs associated with product supply and distribution. Continuing annual savings are expected to be over $150,000.

Although this is a relatively unsophisticated model, it has proved to be the "right tool" for the situation. An important success factor was "just enough" use of management science techniques. Too much technical infusion would have been overwhelming. Now with credibility established and a basic understanding of the modeling process, more complex models may be considered.

Other key components contributing to the overall success of the project were the modest resource requirements, the speed at which solutions are obtained, and the ability to exercise the model in a desktop computing environment, without the need for technical assistance outside of the Supply and Transportation Groups.

Lastly, we believe that this application is representative of a sizable new market for uses of management science -- namely the introduction of MS methods into organizations that have not been traditional users. The ease-of-access, flexibility, computational power, and low cost of desktop computing is the key factor to creating this new market. We expect that this segment will be a major source of growth for management science practice over the next decade.

REFERENCES

Bradley, G., Brown, G. and G. Graves. (1977), "Design and Implementation of Large Scale Transshipment Algorithms," *Management Science,* Vol. 24, No. 1, pp:1-34.

Brown, G. and G. Graves. (1981), "Real-Time Dispatch of Tank Trucks." *Management Science,* Vol. 31, No. 1, pp:19-32.

Brown, G., Ellis, C., Graves, G. and D. Ronen. (1987),"Real-Time, Wide Area Dispatch of Mobil Tank Trucks," *Interfaces,* Vol. 17, No. 1, pp:107-120.

Durrer, E. and G. Slater. (1977), "Optimization o Petroleum and Natural Gas Production rr A Survey," *Management Science,* Vol. 24, No. 1, pp:35-43.

Gilder, G. (1988), "You Ain't Seen Nothing Yet," *Forbes,* Vol. 141, No. 7 (April 4), pp:89-93.

Klingman, D., Phillips, N., Steiger, D., Wirth, R. and W. Young. (1986), "The Challenges and Success Factors in Implementing an Integrated Products Planning System for Citgo," *Interfaces,* Vol. 16, No. 3, pp:1-19.

Klingman, D., Phillips, N., Steiger, D. and W. Young. (1987), "The Successful Deployment of Management Science Throughout Citgo Petroleum," *Interfaces,* Vol. 17, No. 1, pp:4-25.

Zierer, T., Mitchell, W. and T. White. (1976), "Practical Applications of Linear Programming to Shell's Distribution Problems," *Interfaces,* Vol. 6, No. 4, pp:13-26.

NONPROCEDURAL IMPLEMENTATION OF MATHEMATICAL PROGRAMMING ALGORITHMS

JAMES K. HO
Management Science Program, University of Tennessee
Knoxville, Tennessee 37996

ABSTRACT

It is shown that the implementation of many mathematical programming algorithms using spreadsheet software can be described as instances of a nonprocedural approach to computer programming. This concept is generalized to an abstract computing environment called HYPERCELLS. Its significance in view of rapid development in parallel computation is discussed.

1. INTRODUCTION

With the widespread use of microcomputers in academia, business, industry and government, spreadsheet software has become the most popular general purpose quantitative tool for numerical computation. It is essentially a two dimensional array of cells. Each cell may contain text for documentation, numerical values from data, or a formula dependent on values in other cells. Whenever the value in a cell is changed, the content of cells with formulas depending on it can be recalculated automatically. A simple example is given in Figure 1. Cells B1 through B4 contain quarterly revenues. Cell B6 contains a formula for the sum of the values in B1 through B4. It therefore represents the total revenue for the year. When the quarterly values are entered or altered, the total is updated accordingly.

Most commercial spreadsheet packages provide a substantial set of mathematical functions with which complex formulas can be written for nontrivial computational models. Specifics of a design include the order of computation and the ability to resolve circular references. For this reason, while the initial thrust has been in finance and accounting applications, there is a growing interest in this type of computing environment in science and engineering.

In this paper, we demonstrate and generalize certain abstract properties of modeling and computing in the spreadsheet environment. They can be interpreted as a nonprocedural approach to the implementation of numerical methods in general and mathematical programming in particular. A nonprocedural approach to computer programming is one that relies more on the characterization of the solution than on the description of every step

Copyright 1989 by Elsevier Science Publishing Co., Inc.
Impacts of Recent Computer Advances on Operations Research
Ramesh Sharda, Bruce L. Golden, Edward Wasil, Osman Balci, William Stewart, Editors

required in the computation. The distinction from conventional computer programming is shown in Section 2. The cases of dynamic and linear programming are presented in Sections 3 and 4 respectively. Section 5 introduces the concept of Hypercells as a general abstraction of the spreadsheet and discusses the potential of parallel processing within this framework.

The purpose of this paper is to formalize to some extent the departure from conventional implementation of mathematical programming afforded by the spreadsheeet environment. Its significance draws from both the ever increasing popularity of the latter as well as the potential for generalization. At present it is difficult to project future development in this direction and hence no attempt will be made to compare the absolute effectiveness of the different approaches.

	A	B
1	First Quarter	$125,000.00
2	Second Quarter	$145,000.00
3	Third Quarter	$137,000.00
4	Fourth Quarter	$158,000.00
5		
6	Total Revenue	$565,000.00

Figure 1. Simple Example of a Spreadsheet Model

	A	B	C	D	E	F	G	H	I	J	K	L
1	1	3	-2	-1		3	3	0		3	-4	1
2	0	-1	0	3	x	0	-1	2	=	6	1	7
3	2	4	1	2		-1	2	1		9	4	15
4						2	0	3				

Figure 2. Nonprocedural Implementation of Matrix Multiplication

2. NONPROCEDURAL IMPLEMENTATION OF NUMERICAL METHODS

To illustrate the nonprocedural environment provided by spreadsheet software, we use the simple example of matrix multiplication. In Figure 2, the range of cells from A1 to D3 contains a 3 by 4 matrix A. The range of cells from F1 to H4 contains a 4 by 3 matrix B. The product C is in the range from J1 to L3.

In conventional computer programming, a procedure can be coded to compute the coefficients of the product matrix. Indeed, by looping over i from 1 to 3 and j from 1 to 3, C_{ij} is given by the inner product of row i in A and Column j in B. The formula for the inner product is specified once with generic indices i and j and executed repeatedly as i and j take on different values over the appropriate ranges.

Consider next the situation on a spreadsheet. The value of C_{11} is given by a formula in cell J1: +$A1*F$1+$B1*F$2+$C1*F$3+$D1*F$4. The "$" sign indicates an absolute address and its absence indicates a relative address. Since all commercial spreadsheet packages include such feature, this formula can be copied to all the other cells in C using typically a single operation. Each cell in C will then contain a formula for the appropriate inner product. When entries in A or B are altered, the values in C will be recalculated. Note that ultimately, the values in C are computed "procedurally" in some well defined sequence specific to the particular spreadsheet environment. What we mean here by a nonprocedural approach is that there is no explicit code in some computer language for the implementation of the algorithm for matrix multiplication. Instead, the spreadsheet in Figure 2 contains the essence of the operation, namely, that every coefficient in the result is the inner product of a row and a column. It is quite obvious that this nonprocedural approach implies redunduncy and requires more memory than conventional programming. However, this redunduncy can be exploited in parallel computation with multiprocessors. In our example, each inner product for the coefficient of the product matrix can be computed independently.

Using the same principle, many numerical methods can be implemented on a spreadsheet. Examples of significant potential include finite difference methods for the solution of partial differential equations. In the following, we focus on mathematical programming and illustrate the nonprocedural approach for both dynamic and linear programming.

3. DYNAMIC PROGRAMMING

Consider the simple example in Figure 3. There are two stages. Stage 2 has two states: C and D. State C has a single choice with resulting state E and immediate payoff of 3 units. State D has a single choice with resulting state E and immediate payoff of 2 units. Stage one has two states: A and B. State A has two choices: one with resulting state C and immediate payoff of 2 units; the other with resulting state D and immediate payoff of 5 units. State B has two choices: one with resulting state C and immediate payoff of 3 units; the other with resulting state D and immediate payoff of 4 units. The DP problem is to find an optimal policy which prescribes a sequence of choices from each starting state in Stage 1 to termination that will maximize the total payoff.

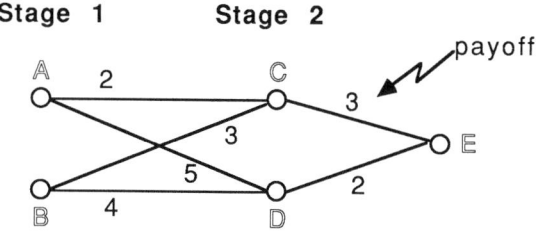

Figure 3. A Simple Example in Dynamic Programming

	A	B	C	D	E	F	G
1	# of stages		STAGE	1	# of states	2	
2	2		State	# of decisions	Opt. Policy	Opt. Value	
3			A	2	D	7	
4			B	2	alternatives…	6	
5							
6			Stage	1	State	A	
7			Decision	Payoff now	Payoff later	Total Payoff	
8			C	2	3	5	
9			D	5	2	7	*
1 0							
1 1			Stage	1	State	B	
1 2			Decision	Payoff now	Payoff later	Total Payoff	
1 3			C	3	3	6	*
1 4			D	4	2	6	*

	H	I	J	K	L
1	STAGE	2	# of states	2	
2	State	# of decisions	Opt. Policy	Opt. Value	
3	C	1	E	3	
4	D	1	E	2	
5					
6	Stage	2	State	C	
7	Decision	Payoff now	Payoff later	Total Payoff	
8	E	3	0	3	*
9					
1 0	Stage	2	State	D	
1 1	Decision	Payoff now	Payoff later	Total Payoff	
1 2	E	2	0	2	*
1 3					
1 4					

Figure 4. Spreadsheet Implementation of a Dynamic Programming Model

The method of recursion is assumed well known and will not be described here. To implement this method on a spreadsheet, it is necessary to design a format for the DP model. Figure 4 represents the above example in the format used in [Ho 1987]. There is a section with five columns for each stage. The top part of such a section contains the optimal policy for the stage. For instance, from State A at Stage 1, the optimal choice is to go to State D in the next stage with an optimal value of 7. Whereas from State B there are alternative optimal choices with a value of 6. The rest of the section contains the choices for each state. A decision is specified by the resulting state at the next stage. The payoff now is problem data. The payoff later is given by the optimal value of the resulting state. The total payoff is the sum of payoff now and payoff later. The optimal value for the state is the maximum of the total payoffs among the choices. An asterisk indicates an optimal choice. The optimal policy is the optimal choice if unique, otherwise there are alternatives indicated by multiple asterisks.

The above relations in the DP model are constructed recursively from the last stage backwards. The actual formulas may depend on the particular spreadsheet environment. In any case, it is possible to implement the DP method nonprocedurally so that when immediate payoffs are changed, the solution will be recomputed automatically. Dynamic programming recursion is perhaps the simplest and most natural example of the nonprocedural implementation of optimization algorithms on spreadsheets.

4. LINEAR PROGRAMMING

Both the algebraic formulation of linear programs and the simplex method [Dantzig 1963] have natural tabular formats. On a spreadsheet, one can encode the definition of the simplex tableau. Using a considerably more intricate and elaborate design of a recursive system than that for DP, the tableau can be updated automatically until the stopping criterion is met. In the following, we will describe a particular implementation in some detail.

Consider the following linear programming problem.

$$
\begin{aligned}
\text{Maximize} \quad & 8A + 11B + 9.5C \\
\text{Subject to} \quad & 3A + 2B + 4C \leq 74 \\
& A + 2B \leq 40 \\
& 2A + 3C \leq 50 \\
& B \leq 10 \\
& A, B, C \geq 0
\end{aligned}
$$

	A	B	C	D	E	F	G	H	I	J	K	L	M
1	0	Step:	0	Status:	Phase 2								
2										If Piv	PIVC		
3	PIVC:		0	0	0	0	0	1	0	1	6		
4	j:		1	2	3	4	5	6	7	8	Basis		
5													
6	Pivot Row		0	0	0	0	0	0	0	10			
7													
8	i:	PivCol								RHS		Ratios	Dj
9	-1	0	0	0	0	0	0	0	0	0			0
10	0	11	0	0	0	0	8	11	9.5	0			11
11	1	2	1	0	0	0	3	2	4	74	1	37	0
12	2	2	0	1	0	0	1	2	0	40	2	20	0
13	3	0	0	0	1	0	2	0	3	50	3	*****	0
14	4	1	0	0	0	1	0	1	0	10	4	10	4
15													
16												MinRat	PIVR
17												10	4
18												PIVOT	1

Figure 5. Initial Tableau for LP Example

	A	B	C	D	E	F	G	H	I	J	K	L	M
1	1	Step:	3	Status:	Optimal								
2										If Piv	PIVC		
3	PIVC:		0	0	0	0	0	0	0	0	None		
4	j:		1	2	3	4	5	6	7	8	Basis		
5													
6	Pivot Row		0.25	0	0	-0.5	0.75	0	1	13.5			
7													
8	i:	PivCol								RHS		Ratios	Dj
9	-1	0	0	0	0	0	0	0	0	0			0
10	0	-1.16	-2.66	0	0	-5.66	0	0	-1.16	-254			0
11	1	1.333	0.333	0	0	-0.66	1	0	1.333	18	5	13.5	1
12	2	-1.33	-0.33	1	0	-1.33	0	0	-1.33	2	2	*****	0
13	3	0.333	-0.66	0	1	1.333	0	0	0.333	14	3	42	0
14	4	0	0	0	0	1	0	1	0	10	6	*****	0
15													
16												MinRat	PIVR
17												13.5	1
18												PIVOT	1.333

Figure 6. Final Tableau for LP Example

Figure 5 illustrates a spreadsheet implementation of the simplex tableau. Initially, this represents the original problem in standard form. However, the formulas involved are defined in such a way that subsequent recalculations lead eventually to the final tableau shown in Figure 6. The required formulas are tabulated below in generic, pseudo-code format so that we are not confined to the specifics of particular software.

Cell Range	Content	Formula
A1	Mode	0 to initialize; 1 thereafter
C1	Iteration Count	If Mode=0 then 0, else Iteration Count+1
F1	Solution Status	If SumOfInfeasibilities>0 then
		if pivot then "Phase 1"
		else "Infeasible"
		else if MaxReducedCost≤0 then "Optimal"
		else if pivot then "Phase 2"
		else "Unbounded"
C3..I3	Pivot Column Selector	If SumOfInfeasibilities>0 then
		if Phase1ReducedCost of Column =
		MaxPhase1ReducedCost and
		MaxPhase1ReducedCost > 0 then
		Value=1
		else Value=0
		else if Phase2ReducedCost of Column =
		MaxPhase2ReducedCost and
		MaxPhase2ReducedCost > 0 then
		Value=1
		else Value=0
J3	Pivot Column Indicator	Max(C3..I3)
K3	Pivot Column Index	If PivotColumnIndicator=0 then
		Value="None"
		else Value=index of first column with Pivot Column Selector of 1
C4..J4	Column Indices	j=1,...,8
C6..J6	Pivot Row	A vertical look-up of the pivot row
A9..A14	Row Indices	i= -1 for Phase 1 Objective
		i= 0 for Phase 2 Objective
		i = 1,...,4 for constraints
B9..B14	Pivot Column	A horizontal look-up of the pivot column
C9..F9	Phase 1 Reduced Costs for Logical Variables	If Mode>0 then NewValue=Simplex Pivot Update of OldValue (using the pivot and appropriate entries in the pivot row and pivot column)
		else if Logical Variable is in an " =" row

		then Value=0
		else Value=Partial Sum of column corresponding to pivoting on artificials
G9..I9	Phase 1 Reduced Costs for Structural Variables	If Mode>0 then NewValue=Simplex Pivot Update of OldValue
		else Value=Partial Sum of column corresponding to pivoting on artificials
J9	Sum of Infeasibilities	Same as above
C10..F10	Phase 2 Reduced Costs for Logical Variables	If Mode>0 then
		if Logical Variable is in an " =" row
		then Value=0
		else NewValue=Simplex Pivot Update of OldValue
		else Value=0
G10..I10	Phase 2 Reduced Costs for Structural Variables	If Mode>0 the NewValue=Simplex Pivot Update of OldValue
		else if Minimization then Value= - Objective Coefficient of Structural Variable
		else Value=Objective Coefficient of Structural Variable
J10	Phase 2 Objective Value	If Mode>0 then NewValue=Simplex Pivot Update of OldValue
		else Value = 0
C11,D12,...,F14	Diagonal entries in Tableau for Logical Variables	If Mode>0 then
		if Row is Pivot Row then NewValue = OldValue/Pivot
		else NewValue=Simplex Pivot Update of OldValue
		else if RightHandSide$\geq$0 then
		if not "$\geq$" constraint then Value=1
		else Value= -1
		else if "$\leq$" constraint then Value= -1
		else Value=1
C11..F14 except above		

| | Off-diagonal entries in Tableau for Logical Variables | If Mode>0 then
    if Row is Pivot Row then NewValue = OldValue/Pivot
    else NewValue=Simplex Pivot Update of OldValue
else Value=0 |
| G11..I14 | Tableau for Structural Variables | If Mode>0 then
    if Row is Pivot Row then NewValue = OldValue/Pivot
    else NewValue=Simplex Pivot Update of OldValue
else if RightHandSide>0 then
    Value=Matrix Coefficient
    else Value= - Matrix Coefficient |
| J11..J14 | Right-Hand-Side of Tableau | If Mode>0 then
    if Row is Pivot Row then NewValue = OldValue/Pivot
    else NewValue=Simplex Pivot Update of OldValue
else Value=Absolute Value of RightHandSide |
| M9 | Maximum Phase 1 Reduced Cost | If Max(C9..I9)>0 then
    Value= Max(C9..I9)
else Value=0 |
| M10 | Maximum Phase 2 Reduced Cost | If Max(C10..I10)>0 then
    Value= Max(C10..I10)
else Value=0 |
| K11..K14 | Basis Indices (Index of Column basic in Row) | If Mode>0 then
    if row is Pivot Row then
        NewValue=Index of Pivot Column
    else NewValue=OldValue
else if RightHandSide$\geq$0 and "$\leq$" constraint
    then Value=Row Index
else if RightHandSide<0 and "$\geq$" constraint then Value=Row Index
else Value= -Row Index |

L11..L14	Pivot Ratios	If nonbinding row then Value=Infinity else if TableauEntry>Pivot Tolerance and 　　RightHandSide≥0 then Value= 　　RightHandSide /TableauEntry else if TableauEntry< Zero Tolerance 　　and basic column is artificial 　　and RightHandSide< Zero 　　Tolerance then Value=0 else Value=Infinity
M11..M14	Min Ratio Indicator	If Ratio=MinRatio and MinRatio<Infinity 　　then Value=Row Index else Value=0
L17	Min Ratio	MIN(L11..L14)
M17	Pivot Row Index	MAX(M11..M14)
M18	Pivot	If PivotRow=0 then Value="none" else Value=Pivot Coefficient in Tableau

Note that the above spreadsheet template is a complete implementation of the two-phase simplex method for general LP problems with any type of constraints and right-hand-sides. A similar approach that is less compact and less general first appeared in [Carroll 1986]. To gain this compactness in the present design, it is necessary to recalculate various ranges of the spreadsheet separately. This can be automated by a few lines of macro instructions of the following form.

```
While PivotColumnIndex≠"None" and PivotRowIndex≠"None"
    Recalculate (A1..M18)        {Update Tableau}
    Recalculate (C3..K3)         {Find pivot column}
    Recalculate (B9..B14)
    Recalculate (L11..L17)       {Find pivot row}
    Recalculate (M9..M18)
```

The basic difference between the spreadsheet implementation and, say, a conventional Fortran code of the simplex method, or one coded in a spreadsheet macro language [Ho 1987] is that the former emphasizes the actual definition of the important concepts whereas the latter deals with their translation into computational procedures.

Essentially the spreadsheet in Figure 5 says that the simplex tableau is the update of itself. The definition of the update is incorporated directly into the formulas for the cells holding the tableau, just like the defintition of matrix multiplication is expressed in our earlier example. The process of constructing the entire LP spreadsheet can also be automated with e.g. macro programs that define all the appropriate ranges and formulas according to given dimensions. Functional versions of such software using Lotus 1-2-3 [Lotus Development Corporation 1985] are used in this work. While we are not concerned with direct comparisons of computational efficiency at this stage, it is clear that memory usage in the nonprocedural approach is going to be high because of the replication of formulas. However, such redunduncy may be exploited eventually in parallel computations as we shall discuss in some generality in the next section. In terms of solution speed, it is significantly more efficient than a macro program for the simplex method [Ho 1987]. To date, our initial experience has been with small textbook problems with less than 50 constraints.

5. HYPERCELLS AND PARALLEL COMPUTATION

The spreadsheet belongs to a new paradigm in computing environments that is still in its infancy. Our effort is to illustrate its implications in mathematical programming rather than to extol its actual efficacy. Critics who hasten to challenge the significance of this association should be reminded of the case with parallel computing. There too, one often found it difficult to justify radical approaches for incremental improvements. However, as multiprocessor computers become prevalent, a constructive rethinking of computational methodology begins to take shape. Along such lines, we conclude the paper with a vision of the nonprocedural environment.

Consider the n-dimensional generalization of the two-dimensional spreadsheet. It is an array of n-tuples that we shall call hypercells. Each hypercell may contain text, a value or a function in values in other hypercells. Functions are defined in a given library and should include all the usual mathematical and logical operations. A protocol for the recalculation of functional values is also given.

As an example of the possible application of such a computing environment, we can extend the above optimization models and have a third dimension representing changes in parameters as a function of discrete time points. The nonprocedural implementation of linear or dynamic programming can then provide time-phased solutions to a sequence of related problems. At this writing, the forthcoming version of a popular spreadsheet software package is already slated to be three-dimensional.

With the rapid development of parallel computer architecture (see e.g. [Fox and

Messina 1987]), it will also become attractive to distribute the tasks of recalculating the hypercells over an array of processors. The fact that formulas are explicitly associated with each hypercell in the nonprocedural implementation of numerical methods makes it especially suitable for parallel processing. The main concern with programming in this environment will be the control of the interdependencies of data with respect to the given protocol for recalculation. In cases where most of the hypercells can be updated independently and concurrently, like most entries in our LP tableau, this parallel nonprocedural approach should be very efficient. While the performance of single processors are bounded by physical limits, their costs are continuing to lower. For this reason, a multiprocessing hypercell computing environment should become viable in the foreseeable future.

Acknowledgement

The author wishes to thank T. Owen Carroll for a stimulating discussion. This research was supported in part by the Office of Naval Research under grant N00014-87-K-0163.

References

Carroll, T.O. (1986), *Decision Power with Supersheets*, Dow Jones-Irwin, Homewood, IL.

Dantzig, G.B.(1963), *Linear Programming and Extensions*, Princeton University Press, Princeton, NJ.

Fox, G.C. and P.C. Messina (1987) "Advanced Computer Architectures", *Scientific American* Vol 257, No 4.

Ho, J.K. (1987), *Linear and Dynamic Programming with Lotus 1-2-3* , MIS Press, Portland, OR.

Ho, J.K., T.C. Lee and R.P. Sundarraj (1988), "Decomposition of Linear Programs using Parallel Computation", *Mathematical Programming* (in press.)

Lotus Development Corporation (1985), *Lotus 1-2-3 Reference Manual*, Cambridge, MA.

CLOSED QUEUEING NETWORK ANALYSIS OF INDIRECT LABOR REQUIREMENTS

ROBERT TERRY, DAVID DeBALD, AND RAMESH CHIKKALA
Industrial and Systems Engineering, Ohio University
278 Stocker Center, Athens, Ohio 45701-2979

ABSTRACT

In the development of cost reduction plans for a production system, determination of the optimum number of various indirect support personnel such as material handlers, repair persons, and setup personnel is critical. Since the size of any of these categories affects the expected number of machines that are running, the optimal size of each of the categories of indirect labor are dependent. This paper utilizes a closed queueing network model to represent the stochastic behavior of the production system. This queueing network is then used to formulate the problem of determining the optimal sizes of the various indirect labor categories as a constrained discrete nonlinear programming problem, which is solved by the sectioning search method.

1. INTRODUCTION

The approach to be described in this paper was applied to a well-established manufacturing system in one of the most profitable Fortune 500 Companies. This application resulted in a savings of almost one million dollars (measured in 1987 dollars) in the first year alone. Unfortunately, the name of the company cannot be mentioned due to their desire for confidentiality.

Production systems require various types of indirect labor support such as repair persons, material handlers, and setup personnel in order to function properly. Reducing the cost of each of these indirect labor categories is critical for reducing the overall production cost. Due to the high cost of both machinery and its related indirect labor requirements, a trade-off exists. Levels of indirect labor which are too low will result in unnecessary machine down time, and thus reduce the overall output from the production system. On the other hand, levels which are too high will result in unnecessarily high indirect labor costs and idle indirect manpower.

The problem of determining the optimal levels for each of the m different categories of indirect labor cannot be solved by breaking the total problem into m subproblems and solving them independently. This is due to the dependency between the expected workloads for any given indirect labor category and the sizes of each of the other indirect labor categories. This suggests that it will be necessary to develop a model of these dependencies prior to developing a model of the optimization problem.

The remainder of this paper is organized as follows. Section 2 presents a closed queueing network model of the dependencies between the expected workloads for each of the indirect labor categories and the size of each of the category's workforce. Since the associated state transition equations for the closed queueing network representation are far too complex to be solved analytically to obtain a useful closed form solution, the third section discusses a numerical algorithm which may be used to solve the closed queueing network problem. Section 4 presents a model of the optimization problem and a prototype system for solving this problem. The fifth section presents a numerical example which illustrates the methodology.

2. QUEUEING NETWORK REPRESENTATION

The dependencies between the category sizes and the workloads for the various indirect labor categories can be represented by the closed queueing network shown in Figure 1. In this figure, the nodes corresponding to each of the indirect labor categories are assumed to be single queue, multi-channel service facilities. The node, referred to as a "Support Requirement Generating" (SRG) facility, serves machines which are currently running to convert them into machines which need to be serviced by indirect labor. It is further assumed that the number of channels in the SRG service facility is sufficiently large to prevent the formation of a queue at that facility.

When the SRG node generates machines which need assistance from indirect labor, it is assumed that a probability distribution is used to randomly determine the specific type of indirect labor which is required. These probabilities are denoted by the symbols shown above the arcs leading from the SRG node to the indirect labor nodes in Figure 1. It is assumed that machines which are receiving indirect service will be in a state which precludes them from generating additional indirect labor requirements. Also the arcs leading from the indirect labor nodes to the SRG node signify that machines are returned to the pool of running machines after they have received the required indirect labor.

Service times for each of the parallel channels in an indirect labor node are assumed to be independent, identically distributed, exponential random variables. Since the locations of the machines are assumed to be fixed, the indirect support personnel are therefore required to visit the machines in order to perform the required service. Thus, it can be assumed that each of the indirect labor nodes has unlimited queueing capacity.

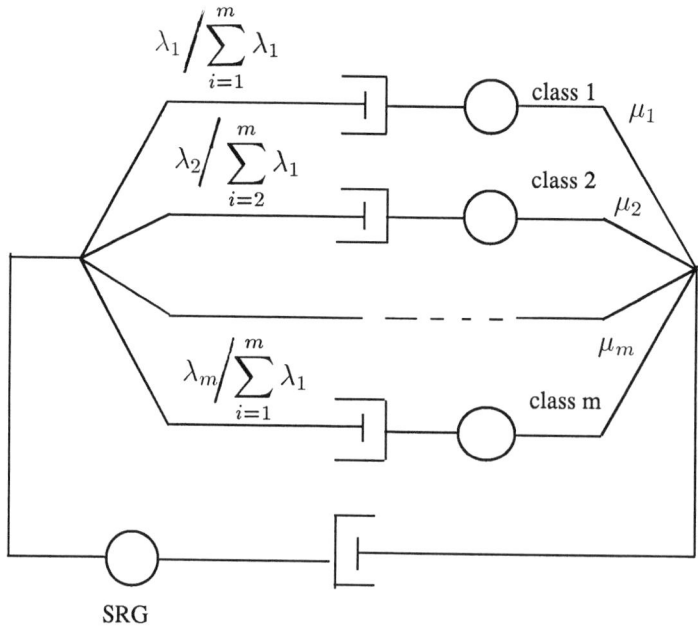

Figure 1: Closed Queueing Network Representation of Indirect Labor Support Problem

Each of the machines at the SRG node is assumed to independently generate indirect labor requirements in a Poisson fashion. The SRG node is assumed to operate as an infinite server facility, i.e. each of the machines at the SRG facility, regardless of the number of machines currently there, captures an SRG server immediately after its release from an indirect support service facility. The service rate for each of the SRG servers is calculated as the sum of the rates at which the machines are serviced by each of the categories of indirect labor, as shown in the Figure 1.

As an illustration, consider the following general case in which a given set of machines require support from m categories of indirect support labor at a rate of $\sum_{i=1}^{m} \lambda_i$, as shown in Figure 1.

Each of the machines which are running is served within the SRG facility with a service time distribution equivalent to that at which the machines require indirect support. When the machine leaves the SRG facility, the sub-population of machines currently capable of generating indirect support requirements is decreased by one.

When a machine goes down, it is routed to indirect support queue k with probability $\lambda_k / \sum_{i=1}^{m} \lambda_i$. Here the machine is serviced at a rate of μ_k, and returns to the pool of running machines at the SRG facility after being served.

3. CLOSED QUEUEING NETWORK SOLUTION METHODOLOGY

At any given moment, the total number of machines which are down will be a random variable. Increasing the number of persons in any given indirect labor category will cause the expected value of this random variable to decrease.

In the next section, the focus will be on developing a mathematical model for determining the sizes of the indirect labor categories which minimize the sum of both the cost associated with lost production and the cost of providing the indirect labor. In order to accomplish this objective, it will be necessary to first have a mathematical model which describes the functional relationship between the expected number of machines which are down and the sizes of the various indirect labor categories. Accordingly, the objective of this section will be to develop such a model.

The problem of solving for the expected number of machines which are down, given the sizes of the various indirect labor categories, can be approached by utilizing the well known conservation of flow principle. Here, the rate of flow out of each feasible network state is equated to the flow into the same state in order to develop steady state global balance equations. Since a multi-dimensional variable will be necessary to denote the state of the network, we will let the vector

$(n_1,n_2,...,n_m)$ denote n_1 machines waiting for or receiving category 1 service, n_2 machines waiting for or receiving category 2 service, etc. The following set of steady state global balance equations (1) result when the conservation of flow principle is applied to each of the feasible network states.

$$(\lambda_1+CAP_1(n_1)\mu_1)P(n_1,n_2,...,n_m) +(\lambda_2+CAP_2(n_2)\mu_2)P(n_1,n_2,...,n_m)$$
$$\vdots$$
$$+(\lambda_m CAP_m(n_m)\lambda_m)P(n_1,n_2,...,n_m)= \quad (1)$$

$$CAP_1(n_1+1)\mu_1 P(n_1+1,n_2...n_m)+\lambda_1 P(n_1-1,n_2,...,n_m)$$
$$+CAP_2(n_2+1)\mu_2 P(n_1,n_2+1,...,n_m)+\lambda_2 P(n_1,n_2-1,...,n_m)$$
$$\vdots$$
$$+CAP_m(n_m+1)\mu_m P(n_1,n_2,...,n_m+1)+\lambda_m P(n_1,n_2,...,n_m-1)$$

With this notation, $CAP_i(n_i)$ denotes the number of machines which are being serviced, at queue i, when n_i machines are down and require service by indirect labor category i. These multidimensional finite difference equations differ from the one-dimensional finite difference equations encountered in elementary queueing theory in that the latter can be solved recursively, while the former must be solved simultaneously.

Since these equations are linearly dependent, the fact that the sum of the state probabilities equals unity must be used in order to achieve a closed set of equations. The closed queueing network described in the preceding section is a special case of the queueing networks described by [Jackson 1957]. [Gordon and Newell 1967] were able to show that closed Jackson networks yield the following closed form solution, where s_i is the number of servers at node i, n_i is the number of machines being serviced at node i and $G(n)$ is the normalizing constant.

$$a_i(n_i) = \begin{cases} n_i! & \text{for } n_i \leq s_i \\ n_i-s_i \\ s_i & \text{for } n_i \geq s_i \end{cases} \quad (2)$$

$$P(n_1,n_2,...,n_m) = \frac{1}{G(n)} \Pi_{i=1}^{m} \frac{(\lambda_i/\mu_i)^{n_i}}{a_i(n_i)} \quad (3)$$

$$G(n) = \sum \Pi_{i=1}^{m} \frac{(\lambda_i/\mu_i)^{n_i}}{a_i(n_i)}. \qquad (4)$$

[Chandy 1972] decomposed the global balance equations for the closed Jackson networks into a number of subsystems of equations, called local balance equations, which can be solved recursively. The algorithm based upon the local balance equations is called the Local Balance Algorithm for Normalizing Constants (LBANC).

4. OPTIMIZATION PROBLEM

The objective is to determine the sizes for each of the indirect labor categories which will minimize the sum of the opportunity cost of lost production due to machine down time and the cost of providing the various types of indirect labor. In the following discussion, it will be assumed that m categories of indirect labor are required.

The cost of providing type i indirect labor will be equal to the product of the number of persons in that indirect labor category, s_i, and the cost per unit time of providing each of the persons in this category, c_i. If the value of s_i is specified for each of the m different types of indirect labor then the expected value of machine down time can be obtained by using the LBANC algorithm referred in the preceding section to solve the closed queueing network model described in section 2. The cost associated with this quantity, which is a multi-variate function of the sizes of the indirect labor categories, will be denoted by $E(s_1,s_2,...,s_m)$.

The s_i are assumed to be integer decision variables which must obey two constraints. First, all $s_i \geq 0$ since having a negative number of indirect labor category size will be meaningless. Second, $s_i \leq u_i$ where u_i denotes the upper limit for the size of the type i indirect labor category.

The problem described above can be formulated as the following constrained discrete nonlinear optimization problem:

minimize $E(s_1,s_2,...,s_m) + \sum_{i=1}^{m} c_i s_i$

subject to $\quad s_i \leq u_i \qquad\qquad \forall \quad i$

$$s_i \geq 0 \qquad \forall \; i$$

$$s_i = 0, 1, 2, \ldots u \qquad \forall \; i$$

The next section illustrates how a discrete, nonlinear search of the above solution space can be combined with an appropriate numerical algorithm for solving the closed queueing network to yield a system for solving the above problem.

5. ILLUSTRATIVE EXAMPLE

The optimal mix of indirect labor personnel can be obtained by combining the method for solving the closed queueing network problem with a systematic routine to search over the possible combinations of indirect labor category sizes. This will be illustrated with the following problem.

A manufacturing system contains 25 CNC milling machines which require attention from material handlers, repair persons, and setup persons. The mean rates at which these indirect support persons are required are 0.05, 0.10, and 0.08 per hour per machine which is running, respectively. The mean rates at which these three categories of indirect labor service the machinery are 1.2, 0.06, and 1.4 per hour, respectively. The hourly costs for each of the three categories of indirect support are $7.00, $8.00, and $9.00, respectively. The hourly cost associated with a machine which is off-line is $10,000 due to lost production time.

This example was approached in two steps: The coding of an appropriate solution algorithm for the closed queueing network model described in Section 2, and the application of a constrained discrete nonlinear search routine. As for the former, a modified version of the Local Balance Algorithm for Normalizing Constants (LBANC) described by [Sauer and Chandy 1987] was used. This algorithm was chosen because of its property of high numerical stability, and the fact that cases in which the algorithm fails (overflow and underflow due to small values of the normalizing constant) are readily apparent. The choice of an algorithm for a given application depends upon a trade-off between numerical accuracy, execution time, and ease of implementation.

The process for determining the optimal sizes of the indirect labor categories involved searching the space of possible combinations of sizes for each of the three

Number within repair class			Expected	
Material Handlers	Repair Persons	Set up Persons	Number of Machines Down	Total Cost
3	3	3	8.1774	81846.23
4	3	3	8.1738	81817.44
5	3	3	8.1734	81820.41
4	4	3	6.1500	61587.31
4	5	3	5.5422	55517.25
4	6	3	5.3620	53722.73
4	7	3	5.3095	53206.35
4	8	3	5.2953	53071.90
4	9	3	5.2918	53044.95
4	10	3	5.2910	53045.35
4	9	4	5.2536	52672.39
4	9	5	5.2479	52624.12
4	9	6	5.2471	52625.40
5	9	5	5.2466	52617.62
6	9	5	5.2464	52623.26
5	10	5	5.2458	52617.89
5	10	6	5.2450	52619.16
5	10	4	5.2515	52666.20
6	10	5	5.2457	52623.52
4	10	5	5.2471	52624.39

Repair class	Optimum number	Cost
Material Handlers	5	
Repair Persons	9	52617.62
Set up Persons	5	

Table 1

indirect labor categories. In this example, the sectioning search algorithm [Glankwahmdee, Liebman, and Hogg 1979], which was developed for solving unconstrained discrete non-linear problems, was modified to handle the linear constraints.

This particular optimization problem, conducted with sectioning search and using a micro computer with a 4.77 MHz clock speed, took about 10 minutes. Results of the optimization example are given in Table 1. A copy of the prototype system used for this example, written in Pascal for the IBM PC, can be obtained by writing to the first author.

6. CONCLUDING REMARKS

As manufacturing facilities move towards higher levels of automaton, indirect support costs will also become increasingly more important. Companies that fail to optimize their indirect labor system will be at a competitive disadvantage. This paper has presented a systematic procedure which utilizes closed queueing networks and discrete nonlinear optimizations models to determine optimal sizes for the various categories of indirect labor.

So far, the discussion in this paper has assumed that there are only three categories of indirect support: setup, repair, and material handling, each of which is performed by a manually paced system. However, the methodology can be readily utilized to handle more general situations. In particular, it may be used in situations in which one or more of the indirect support activities are performed by automated devices. For example a system of automated guided vehicles (AGV's) and robots could be used instead of manual material handlers. It is also capable of handling situations in which the repair activity is subdivided into a number of specialities such as electricians, mechanics, machinists, plumbers, etc.

REFERENCES

Chandy, K.M. (1972). The Analysis and Solutions for General Queueing Networks, *Proc. 6th Annual Princeton Conference on Information Science and Systems,* Princeton University, 224-228.

Glankwahmdee, A., Liebman, J.S., and Hogg, G.L. (1979). Unconstrained Discrete Nonlinear Programming, *Engineering Optimization,* 4, 95-107.

Gordon, W.J., and Newell, G.F. (1967). Closed Queueing Networks with Exponential Servers, *Operations Research 15,* 244-265.

Jackson, J.R. (1957). Networks of Waiting Lines, *Operations Research 5,* 518-521.

Sauer, C.H. and Chandy, K.M. (1981). *Computer Systems Performance Modeling,* Prentice-Hall, Inc., Englewood Cliffs, New Jersey.

A MICROCOMPUTER-BASED MARINE GEOGRAPHIC INFORMATION SYSTEM WITH MARKETING APPLICATION

MARIA LUISA VILLANUEVA, NANCY A. WITTPENN, C. BRUCE AUSTIN AND EDWARD BAKER

Boating Research Center, Division of Marine Affairs,
Rosenstiel School of Marine and Atmospheric Science, University of Miami,
Miami, FL 33149

ABSTRACT

The Boating Research Center, a non-profit organization located within the Division of Marine Affairs at the University of Miami's Rosenstiel School of Marine and Atmospheric Sciences has developed a computer-based Marine Geographic Information System. This system is designed to manage and analyze large marine-based data files the attributes of which can be linked to specific geographic locations.

One of the BRC's main goals is to become a repository for marine information gathered by government, academic and business institutions for the main purpose of advancing all types of research related to boats and boating activities.

This paper describes the Boating Research Center's Marine Geographic Information System and how it is being utilized for studies with marketing application.

1. INTRODUCTION

The introduction of mapping and graphics programs into the microcomputing environment has extended the application and benefits of Geographic Information Systems. The Boating Research Center (BRC), a non-profit organization located within the Division of Marine Affairs at the University of Miami's Rosenstiel School of Marine and Atmospheric Sciences currently maintains a variety of marine-based data in a Geographic Information System. This Marine Geographic Information System (MGIS) enables data attributes to be linked to specific geographic locations on maps in addition to performing a variety of practical statistical analyses. The BRC MGIS is presently in operation for Florida and is in the process of expanding to other states.

2. BRC COMPUTER FACILITY

2.1 Computer Hardware

The BRC MGIS is maintained on a WELLS AMERICAN IBM AT Clone. The microcomputer has two internal hard disk drives of 80 and 30 mb capacities and a 1.2 mb floppy disk drive. The hard disk drives contain all of the application programs utilized for daily data maintenance and analysis. They also contain a variety of marine-based data files.

The BRC utilizes a WORM (write once read many) drive which has a 240 mb compact disc cartridge capacity. Although it can be directly accessed for data manipulation, its primary purpose is to archive historical data.

A 20 mb tape drive is used for backup purposes. Completed studies and other smaller size databases are backed up in the tape drive for future reference.

An HP Colorpro plotter is used to plot maps, graphs and charts. A EPSON letter quality printer is used to produce reports and mailing labels necessary for mail surveys.

Data exchange with the RSMAS Computer Facility (VAX System) is accomplished with the use of an ETHERLINK [3Com Corporation 1985] board for hard-wire connection and the use of a 2400 baud rate internal modem for phone line connection.

2.2 Computer Software

The BRC uses dBASEIII-plus [Ashton-Tate 1986] and FOXBASE-plus [Fox Software 1986] for its relational database management. These software packages are used to maintain and manipulate BRC files, to import data for use in LOTUS 123 [Lotus Development Corp. 1985] and ATLAS*GRAPHICS [STSC, Inc. 1987] and to export data to formats used by other interested parties.

A LOTUS 123 spreadsheet is used as a tool in tabular data presentation. It is also used to do simple data manipulations for small sized databases. An important use of LOTUS 123 is the conversion of FOXBASE or dBASE files into DIF files for use with ATLAS*GRAPHICS.

ATLAS*GRAPHICS is a software package which provides mapping capabilities through prepared boundary files. It can also import custom boundary files digitized by the MAP EDIT [STSC, Inc. 1986] software. For statistical analysis, STATGRAPHICS [STSC, Inc. 1987] software is currently in use. The BRC can also access the VAX resident SPSS-X [SPSS Inc. 1987] and VMS SAS [SAS Institute, Inc. 1988] through modem use with KERMIT [Columbia University, N.Y.] software.

3. MGIS DATABASES

The BRC MGIS currently maintains different databases which when combined together provide the opportunity to do research on boat ownership and boating activities. When used with the existing computer facilities, the database of the MGIS can provide a great service in advancing research for the boating industry, academia and government agencies.

3.1 Florida Vessel and Title Registration Files (1982-1988)

The Florida Vessel and Title Registration File (VTR) is gathered by the Florida Department of Natural Resources [FDNR 1982-1988] primarily to meet the federal requirements of the 1971 Federal Boating Act, to collect revenue, for law enforcement and for ownership verification and title transfer. The file contains the following information:

3.1.1 Information on Boat Owner

1. Name
2. Address
3. City
4. State
5. Zip
6. Residency

3.1.2 Boat Characteristics

1. Brand
2. Model Year
3. Hull Identification Number
4. Registration Number
5. Decal Number
6. Length
7. Title Number
8. Title Issue Date
9. Hull Material
10. Propulsion
11. Fuel Use

3.1.3 Boat Use

1. Type of Use (Pleasure, Commercial, Dealer, Etc.)
2. If Commercial Use, type of commercial fishing done (shrimp, conch, baitfish, etc)

3.1.4 Other Information
   1. Registration Date
   2. Status of Lien and Title
   3. Additional Owners

The VTR files are provided by the Florida DNR in 6250 bpi ASCII format tapes. These tapes are downloaded to the PC from the VAX mainframe via hardwire connection. The data are then imported to dBASE and copied to the laser disk cartridges. The BRC separates the VTR master file into county subfiles for easier and faster access of data at the county level.

3.2 US Census Data, Demographic, Housing and Socioeconomic Indicators

The BRC maintains US Census Data by census blocks and can access estimates of current year and 5-year projection of demographic, housing and socioeconomic indicators at the zip code level through the National Planning Data Corporation's MAX LINK [1987]. The data is accessed by modem on a need basis. Examples of these indicators are as follows:

3.2.1 Demographic Indicators:
   1. Population
   2. Median Age
   3. Households
   4. Families
   5. Migration

3.2.2 Housing Indicators:
   1. Number of Housing Units
   2. Mean Gross Rent
   3. Mean Value of Owner Occupied Units

3.2.3 Socioeconomic Indicators:
   1. Household Income
   2. Education
   3. Civilian Labor Force

3.3 USCG Boating Accidents and USCG Manufacturer's Identification Codes (MIC)

The USCG Boating Accident file [U.S. Dept. of Transportation 1969-1986] consists of all reported boating accidents in the United States by state, county, date and location of accident. It also includes some characteristics of the boats involved in the accident, the type of injury sustained, weather and water conditions and cause of accident.

The USCG MIC file [U.S. Dept. of Transportation 1986] contains the MIC assigned to manufacturers. It also contains data on manufacturer's address, telephone number, date business started and date it expired. It is especially useful for cross referencing the Hull Identification Number (which contains MIC codes) in the FL VTR files.

3.4 Other Data

Other data maintained by the BRC are Florida Manatee Mortality [FDNR 1975-1988] from 1975 to present, Florida marina locations [Bureau of State Lands Management 1984] and marina survey data.

4. MARKETING STUDIES

The Boating Research Center has done a number of studies for businesses and government agencies. The following section of this paper presents some of these studies which have various marketing application.

4.1 Market Share/Facility Location

A study was done by the BRC for a manufacturer of Brand "A" boats. The manufacturer was interested in obtaining data in a form which would help him in his decision to open a service center in Dade County, Florida and in evaluating possible locations for this service center. This manufacturer was particularly interested in servicing their brand of 16'-34' outboards although they had expressed a desire to service other brands as well.

Boat manufacturers are interested in knowing the location of their customers for market share purposes. Most often, manufacturers can only track a few of their

Fig. 1 Brand A 16'–34' Outboards
Relative Market Share
Dade Co., 1986

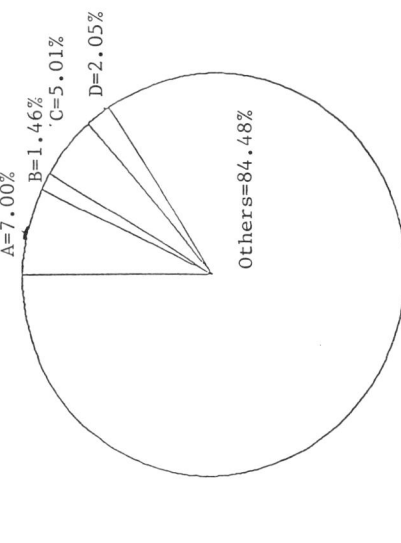

Fig.2
Distribution of Brand A Outboards
16–34' in length
Dade Co., 1986

1 Dot = 5 Boats
1122 Total
(P.O. Boxes not included)

★ Centroid

A=7.00%
B=1.46%
C=5.01%
D=2.05%
Others=84.48%

16'–34' Outboards in Dade Co.

	Number	Percent Share
Brand A	1122	7.00%
Brand B	234	1.46%
Brand C	803	5.01%
Brand D	328	2.05%
Others	13539	84.48%
Total	16026	100.00%

Fig. 3 1986 Ave. Household Income (Dade Co.)

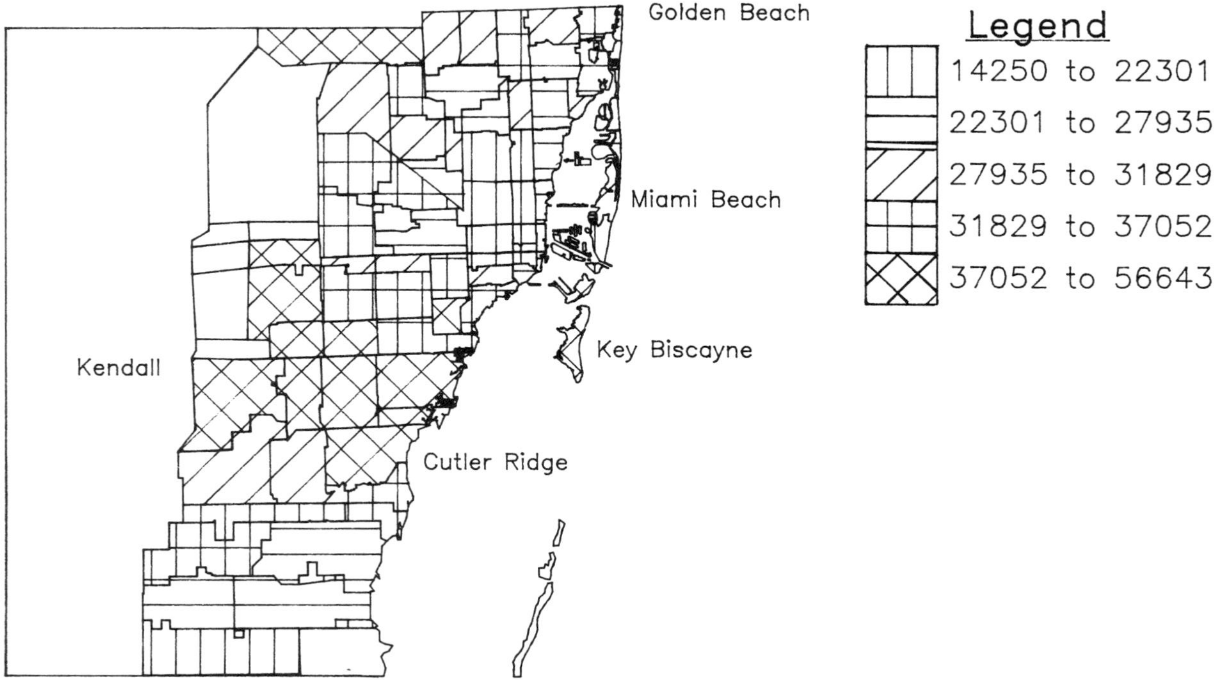

Legend
14250 to 22301
22301 to 27935
27935 to 31829
31829 to 37052
37052 to 56643

Table 1. Boat Ownership Trends by Selected Categories, Dade Co. 1982-1987

Year	Total (Dade)	All Outboards	All Inboards	All 16' - 34' Length	Brand A Total	Brand A Sales of New Boats
1982	29373	18010	6988	21863	773	59
1983	35037	21555	8025	25897	834	61
1984	37081	22859	8147	27302	960	115
1985	37755	23211	7879	27684	1023	117
1986	40750	24449	8023	28346	1152	130
1987	40395	24690	7928	27787	1234	156

new boat customers through their warranty card returns. In addition, a large fraction of boat owners are used boat owners. Thus, after the first sale, manufacturers do not necessarily have a complete history of who owns their product(s).

The information contained within the Florida VTR files makes the evaluation of boat ownership possible. In this case, the first task of the BRC was to obtain a clear picture of Brand "A" boat owners and their market share in the 16'-34' outboard range. Using FOXBASE-plus, a search within the Dade County subfile for Brand "A" boats with the aforementioned attributes produced a file of Brand "A" boat owners and their locations. Figure 1, a chart produced by LOTUS Graphics, shows market share of Brand "A" boats in relation to total market as well as other top brands. Figure 1 also displays the total number of 16'-34' outboards for Brand "A", other top brands, and for Dade County. Figure 2 is a map of the distribution of Brand "A" boat owners of 16'-34' outboards in Dade County. This map produced from ATLAS*GRAPHICS reveals the location of boat owners at the zip code level. Other maps like the one in Figure 3 show the relationship between demographics, housing and socioeconomic indicators and boat ownership at the zip code level.

In the selection of service center locations, the use of boat ownership distribution centroids are considered. In this analysis, population centroids are merged with the distribution of boat owners to obtain a weighted centroid of boat owners. Figure 2 shows the calculated centroid. In lieu of population centroids, the geographic centroids for each zip code area were used. These geographic centroids in terms of latitude and longitude were merged with the number of boats per zip code in order to obtain the weighted centroid of Brand "A" boat owners. Using these data and evaluation criteria supplied by the manufacturer, various prospective sites are then compared and contrasted.

4.2 Boat Ownership Trends

The information on market trends of any industry is very vital in understanding current and future market behavior and ascertaining opportunities presented in the market. Individuals and/or businesses interested in entering a market always need to know how the market behaved in past years and its potential in the future. Businesses already in the market also need to know their performance in terms of their market shares. With market trends, they can compare their growth with the industry in general and with their competitors in particular.

The availability of the 1982-1987 Florida VTR files has enabled the analysis of market trends for the state's boating industry. Boat ownership trends in terms of boat use and boat characteristics (i.e. length, hull, propulsion) can now be determined. Studies of trends in boating activities by geographic levels (e.g. county, zip code, etc.) is now a possibility. Table 1 shows trends in boat ownership in Dade County, Florida by selected categories. The data from this table were extracted from the Dade County subfile searching for records with the required attributes. Column 4 of this table shows an estimate of new boat sales of Brand "A" boats. Although the Florida VTR files do not contain a field for new boat sales, these values can be estimated by comparing the current calendar year with the boat's model year. These data have been supplied to various manufacturers for use in their market research plans.

5. MARINA SITE DEVELOPMENT

The increase in boat ownership in Dade County has opened new opportunities to enter the boating market. One of these opportunities is the development of marinas to serve the needs of owners of berthed boats. At the same time, this growth in boating activity has also increased concerns on the impact of recreational boating on the environment.

A study recently undertaken by the BRC involved a proposal to add 212 wet slips to an already existing 99 slips in a marina owned by a private condominium complex in Northeast Dade County. In order to evaluate the need for this addition and its possible impact on the environment, the BRC conducted a survey to identify already existing facilities in the vicinity of the proposed site, studied boat traffic, analyzed boat ownership in the general area and examined the mortality of manatees, an endangered species in the state of Florida. In its survey of existing facilities, a telephone survey of condominiums with wet slips was done. The study of boat traffic required the collection of the registration numbers of boats using the waters in the area at different times and days. These numbers were merged with the current Florida VTR file in order to locate boat owners and identify the characteristics of their boats. Boat ownership patterns were also studied by extracting records of boat owners in Dade and Broward County subfiles with zip codes near the vicinity of the marina. Figure 4 shows the distribution of owners of one type of berthed boats. Here, an assumption that inboard boats over 25 feet are berthed boats was made to facilitate the determination of demand for wet slips in the area.

The manatee mortality in Dade Co. was also considered in the study. Fig. 5 shows the distribution of manatee kills in Dade Co. from 1975 to 1985. The map sites the geographical occurrences of manatee kills in relation to the proposed site for the additional wet slips.

The use of the MGIS greatly enhanced the process of evaluating the feasibility of a marina site development. With the data gathered and analysis done in the MGIS along with the other guidelines observed by the state in marina development, the BRC can now make a recommendation on the development of a marina on a specific site.

6. CUSTOMER RETENTION

Customer loyalty to brands and repeat purchase have been subjects of several studies in the past [Morrison 1966; Ehrenberg and Goodhardt 1968]. This is because repeat purchase and customer loyalty are good indicators of a company's overall performance.

The BRC is currently undertaking a study relating to customer retention and brand loyalty. The primary purpose of the study is to obtain with a Customer Retention Index (CRI) from which an individual manufacturer's CRI can be compared with the industry CRI. The basic concept of this index is to measure the company's ability to capture eligible repeat customers.

The primary data to be used in the study is within the MGIS database. The 1982-1987 FL VTR files provide the necessary observations on customers purchasing habits in terms of brand selection and length of product retention.

Table 2 presents a working table of preliminary data that are used in obtaining the customer index. The data were taken by manipulating and sorting the 1982 to 1987 Dade County subfiles to estimate new boat sales for, say generic Brand "A". The cells in the table display the various customer retention and sales categories for the indicated years. At this point in time, the results obtained from the analysis are preliminary. The data has been found to contain many types of errors. Misspellings in names and addresses can cause errors in tracking boat owners year to year. Migration in county and state levels can greatly affect both the attrition and retention estimates for boat owners. These weaknesses should be considered in the analysis to achieve a relevant conclusion on customer retention.

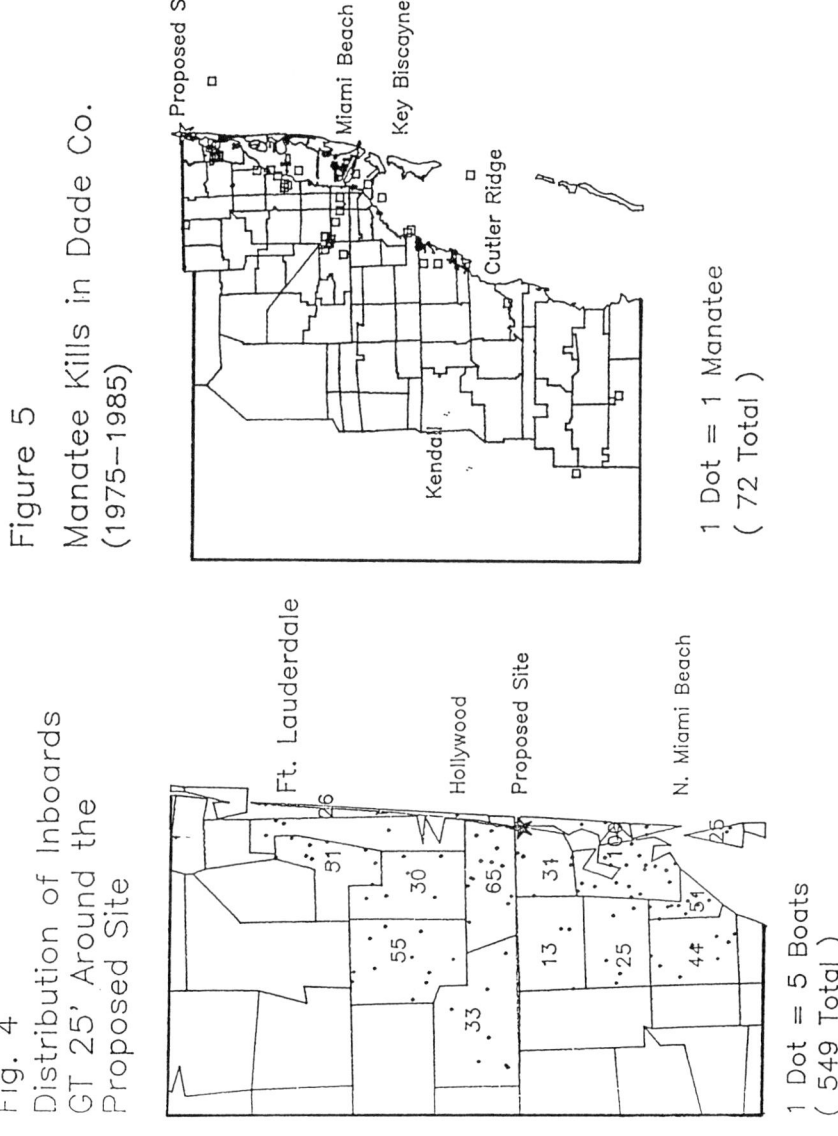

Fig. 4
Distribution of Inboards
GT 25' Around the
Proposed Site

1 Dot = 5 Boats
(549 Total)

Figure 5
Manatee Kills in Dade Co.
(1975–1985)

1 Dot = 1 Manatee
(72 Total)

Table 2. Customer Retention Worksheet

	1982	1983	1984	1985	1986	1987
1982	NC= RC= TC=59	RN 47 AN 12	RN 42 AN 17	RN 37 AN 22	RN 27 AN 32	RN 24 AN 35
1983	PC=0	NC 61 RC 0 TC 61	RN 54 AN 7	RN 43 AN 18	RT 42 AN 19	RN 40 AN 21
1984	PC 1	PC 0	NC 114 RC 1 TC 115	RN 92 AN 23	RN 73 AN 42	RN 64 AN 51
1985	PC 0	PC 0	PC 0	NC 117 RN 0 TC 117	RN 94 AN 23	RN 82 AN 35
1986	PC 1	PC 0	PC 1	PC 0	NC 128 RC 2 TC 130	RN 125 AN 5
1987	PC 0	PC 0	PC 1	PC 1	PC 2	NC 152 RC 4 TC 156

TC = Total new boat sales in sales year
NC = New customer
RC = Repeat customer
RN = Retention number
AN = Attrition number
PC = Prior customer

7. CONCLUSION

Recreational boating has enormous economic impact in many states [Milon et al. 1983; Gilmore Research Group 1984]. The concept of BRC is to provide analytical support to this industry by collecting, processing, and disseminating information on that industry. With the advances in microcomputer processing capabilities, the BRC has established a marine geographic information systems accessible to all levels of the marine industry and government agencies.

The direct and easy access to the marine-based data files contained within the BRC's MGIS has provided opportunities for valuable research involving boats and boating activities. The studies which have been presented in this paper are those with marketing application. In addition, the type of data contained within the MGIS can allow further analysis in the environmental, engineering, economic and recreational fields.

REFERENCES

"An Inventory of Multi-Slip Docking Facilities in Florida, 1984", Division of State Lands, Bureau of State Lands Management, Submerged Lands Section.

ATLAS*GRAPHICS, STSC, Inc., Strategic Locations Planning, Inc., 1987.

dBASEIII-plus, Ashton-Tate, 1986.

Ehrenberg, A.S.C. and G.J. Goodhardt (1968), "A Comparison of American and British Repeat-Buying Habits", *Journal of Marketing Research*, 5 (Feb.), 29-33.

ETHERLINK, 3Com Corporation, 1985.

Florida Manatee Mortality (1975-1988), Bureau of Marine Research, Division of Marine Resources, Florida Department of Natural Resources.

Florida Vessel and Title Registration (1982-1988), Bureau of Vessel Titling and Registration, Florida Department of Natural Resources.

FOXBASE-plus, Fox Software, 1986.

Gilmore Research Group (1984), "Recreational Marine/Boating Industry, 1984 Economic Impact Study for Northwest Marine Trade Association", Seattle, Wash.,

KERMIT, Columbia University, N.Y.

LOTUS 123, Lotus Development Corporation, 1985.

"Manufacturers Identification Codes", (1986), Office of Boating, Public and Consumer Affairs, Management Information Service Branch, U.S. Coast Guard, Dept. of Transportation.

MAXLINK, National Planning Data Corporation, 1987.

Milon, J.W., D. Mulkey, P.H. Riddle and G.H. Wikowske (1983), "Economic Impact of Marine Recreational Boating on the Florida Economy", Report No. 54, Florida Sea Grant College, Tallahassee, Fla.

Morrison, D.G. (1966), "Testing Brand Switching Models", *Journal of Marketing Research*, 3 (Nov.), 401-409.

SPSS-X, SPSS Inc., 1987.

STATGRAPHICS, STSC, Inc., Statistical Graphics Corporation, 1987.

U.S. Census Data, National Planning Data Corporation, 1987.

U.S. Coast Guard Boating Accidents (1969-1986), Office of Boating, Public and Consumer Affairs, Management Information Service Branch, U.S. Coast Guard, Dept. of Transportation.

VMS SAS, SAS Institute, Inc., 1988.

MATHEMATICAL PROGRAMMING SOFTWARE FOR THE MICROCOMPUTER: RECENT ADVANCES, COMPARISONS, AND TRENDS

EDWARD WASIL

Kogod College of Business Administration, The American University
Washington, D.C. 20016

BRUCE GOLDEN

College of Business and Management, University of Maryland
College Park, Maryland 20742

RAMESH SHARDA

College of Business Administration, Oklahoma State University
Stillwater, Oklahoma 74078

ABSTRACT

In this paper, we present the state-of-the-art in mathematical programming software for the microcomputer. Previous studies and package summaries are reviewed and several currently-available, high-quality LP and NLP systems are described. Package features, trends, and future directions are discussed.

1. INTRODUCTION

In the early 1980s, commercial software developers introduced mathematical programming systems for the desktop microcomputer. These first-generation systems generally contained powerful solution procedures that were capable of handling linear programs (LPs) and nonlinear programs (NLPs); some could also solve systems of simultaneous linear and nonlinear equations. For the most part, this software resembled its mainframe counterparts. Data entry and editing were cumbersome and report-writing features were unsophisticated. Many systems were reasonably quick and accurate when solving medium-size problems but slowed considerably when large-scale problems were attempted.

Copyright 1989 by Elsevier Science Publishing Co., Inc.
Impacts of Recent Computer Advances on Operations Research
Ramesh Sharda, Bruce L. Golden, Edward Wasil, Osman Balci, William Stewart, Editors

In the last two years, a number of second-generation LP and NLP packages have emerged. These packages can operate on powerful microcomputers (such as 80386-based machines) and contain sophisticated new features that allow users to model, manage, and solve problems more efficiently and effectively.

In Tables 1 and 2, the evolution of NLP systems and LP systems is traced. Although these tables are not encyclopedic, the articles cited do contain a wealth of information regarding mathematical programming packages, features, and related computational experiments.

Table 1. Overview of Recent Advances in NLP Software

Author	Year	Comments
Harrison	1985	The author compares the GRG2 code on the IBM 4381 vs. the IBM PC/XT using 30 test problems. The ratio of running time on PC to running time on mainframe is about 41. All problems are solved to optimality on both machines. Results are viewed as encouraging.
Golden & Wasil	1986	A survey of 11 micro-based software packages for solving NLPs and simultaneous equations is presented. Package features are discussed in greater detail for 8 of these. These packages are compared with respect to accuracy and efficiency.
Waren, Hung & Lasdon	1987	This article updates a 1979 survey of mainframe-based NLP software. In general, micros were not used to solve NLPs back in 1979. Now we can solve medium-size problems on micros. Six micro-based packages are reviewed briefly. The major focus of this paper is not on micros; rather it is on mainframe systems and new algorithmic developments.
Wasil, Golden & Liu	1988	The authors present a comprehensive survey of the capabilities and features of six state-of-the-art NLP packages. Modeling languages, mathematical programming features, and user-interface and user-control capabilities are discussed. The packages are tested on 27 problems for accuracy and efficiency.

Table 2. Overview of Recent Advances in LP Software

Author	Year	Comments
Sharda	1984	LP packages are summarized via tables and categorized. A directory of software publishers and prices is included.
Sharda	1985/6	The focus here is on spreadsheet optimization and on how spreadsheets can be used for LP modeling. Two commercially-available systems are considered in detail.
Sharda & Somarajan	1986	New LP packages are summarized. Then four of the more powerful and advanced LP packages are compared along several dimensions. These packages are run on 14 test problems and compared with the MPSX solutions. Five packages having mixed integer programming capabilities are tested on three small MIPs.
Ho	1987	Macro programs for solving LPs and DPs, using Lotus 1-2-3 on the IBM PC and Microsoft Excel on the Apple Macintosh, are introduced. These electronic spreadsheet programs are slow, but extremely easy to use.
Greenberg	1987	A micro-based version of ANALYZE, an interactive system that aids in the analysis and solution of LPs, is described.
Sharda	1988	Recent advances in LP software are highlighted. New microcomputers and more memory motivated a fresh look at the field. Twenty LP packages are reviewed (15 of these were introduced since the 1984 Interfaces article). Recent advances are noted.
Sharda & Guha	1988	A handful of LP packages were run on an 80386 machine and tested against 49 benchmark problems. Accuracy and running times are reported.

Our goal in this paper is to provide an up-to-date discussion of packages that solve LPs and NLPs and report on the user-interface, user-control, and mathematical programming capabilities of this software. On the basis of functional performance and other characteristics (such as ease-of-use), we will focus on a small number of standout systems and comment on trends and future directions in mathematical programming software for microcomputers.

2. LP and NLP SOFTWARE

2.1 Software Review

A comprehensive review of the commercial marketplace for mathematical programming software reveals that potential users have a substantial number of systems from which to choose. Currently, over 24 LP packages and 8 NLP packages that operate primarily on an IBM PC are available (very few systems run on the Apple Macintosh). Over the last three years, developers have included a wide variety of new features and capabilities that allow users to model, manage, and solve linear and nonlinear programs more easily, efficiently, and accurately. In this section, we review the current status of LP and NLP software with respect to mathematical programming features, user-interface and user-control capabilities, and modeling languages. Our overview is meant to be representative of the "best" in commercial LP and NLP systems. We limit the discussion to popular packages that contain highly-regarded implementations of mathematical programming features and capabilities.

To begin the review, we give the following brief description of this software class. It is useful to note that LP and NLP packages

- o cost from $50 to $2,500 for a single copy to as much as $13,000 for a corporate site license,
- o can handle at most 8,000 rows and 16,000 columns (LPs) and 300 rows and 500 columns (NLPs),
- o offer limited integer programming support (about 10 packages also solve IPs ranging in size from 25 to 1,600 integer variables),
- o access math coprocessors (8087, 80287, 80387) to improve processing speed, and
- o model problems in a spreadsheet, in a natural format similar to an actual formulation, and in matrix form.

Table 3. Representative LP and NLP Software

Package	Problem Type	Max. Problem Size Rows	Cols	Integer	Price*	Hardware	Minimum Memory**	Distributor
HYPER LINDO	LP	2000	4000	1000	$1000	IBM MAC	640K 8087	LINDO Systems, Inc. P.O. Box 148231 Chicago, IL 60614
LINDO/386	LP	5000	15000	14900	$1500	Compaq 386	3Mb 80287 80387 Weitek W1167	LINDO Systems, Inc. P.O. Box 148231 Chicago, IL 60614
WHAT'S BEST!	LP	2000	4000	400	$995	IBM MAC	556K 8087	General Optimization 2251 N. Geneva Ter. Chicago, IL 60614
EUREKA: THE SOLVER	NLP	20	20	NA	$99.95	IBM MAC	384K	Borland International 4585 Scotts Valley Dr. Scotts Valley, CA 95066
GAMS/MINOS	LP NLP	300+	500+	NA	$1600	IBM	512K hard disk 8087	The Scientific Press 507 Seaport Court Redwood City, CA 94063
SUPER GINO	NLP	50	100	NA	$650	IBM MAC	512K 8087	LINDO Systems, Inc. P.O. Box 148231 Chicago, IL 60614

* Single copy price, educational version
\+ Approximate limit with 640K for LPs, smaller limit for NLPs
** IBM version

MAC Apple Macintosh
NA Not applicable

In Table 3, we list six packages that are representative of state-of-the-art LP and NLP systems for the microcomputer. The packages that we selected for inclusion in this table are dedicated commercially-available systems as opposed to packages that are designed primarily for instructional use or that contain several MS/OR techniques on one disk, i.e., "smorgasbord" software. The interested reader is referred to [Assad and Wasil 1986] and [Yurkiewicz 1988] for comprehensive reviews of educational OR software. For the most part, these six packages are stand-alone systems. They are sufficiently easy to use (i.e., menu or command driven) so that users are not required to write computer code to access their algorithms. We point out that WHAT'S BEST! is a spreadsheet-compatible program. It uses a spreadsheet program such as Lotus 1-2-3 (supplied by the user) for data input and LINDO as the optimizer. GAMS/MINOS is really two packages in one: GAMS is the modeling language and MINOS is the optimizer capable of solving both LPs and NLPs. EUREKA and SUPER GINO can also solve a system of simultaneous nonlinear equations. In addition to single copies, many software distributors offer site license agreements and educational discounts. For example, the student edition of GAMS costs $75 and can solve LPs, NLPs, and MIPs.

In the last few years, developers have increased both the capacity and speed of LP and NLP systems. From Table 3, we see that this group of LP packages can handle as many as 5,000 rows and 15,000 columns (which matches the limits of the LINDO mainframe code), while the upper limit for NLP packages is 300 rows and 500 columns (in contrast, the mainframe version of GINO handles a 200 x 400 matrix). Most systems can access a math coprocessor chip such as the 8087 to substantially decrease the solution time. As an example, LINDO Systems, Inc. reports that LINDO/386 running on a Compaq 386/20, 32 bit, with a Weitek W1167 floating point coprocessor has close to 50% of the speed of a VAX 8650. LINDO/386 required 12 seconds to solve a 516 x 1,035 LP, while LINDO/Mainframe took 5 seconds. In contrast, HYPER LINDO requires nearly 8 minutes on a PC/XT with an 8087 coprocessor.

While most systems run on MS DOS-based PCs, a few can operate on the Apple Macintosh. Several versions of both LINDO and GINO are available for the Macintosh, as well as a version of EUREKA. An industrial version of WHAT'S BEST! that costs $1,995 is available for the Macintosh II. It requires Microsoft Excel 1.5, HyperCard, and 2-4 Mb of memory and can solve problems with as many as 8,000 rows and 16,000 columns.

Finally, many LP packages now have the ability to solve integer programming problems. For example, HYPER LINDO supports both zero/one and general integer variables with an upper limit of 1,000 integer variables. The industrial version of WHAT'S BEST! can handle 1,600 zero/one variables. Mixed-integer models created with GAMS can be solved with ZOOM (Zero/One Optimization Method). The GAMS/ZOOM system (which also contains the XMP optimizer) is now available from The Scientific Press and can handle 200 zero/one variables. Integer variables are automatically converted by GAMS/ZOOM into sums of zero/one variables.

In the remainder of this section we focus on two key areas of software development: (1) user-interface and user-control features and (2) modeling languages.

2.2 User-Interface and User-Control Features

Over the last three years, developers of mathematical programming software have included new features that allow users to easily enter, edit, and output problem data. The approaches adopted by developers range from full-screen, interactive data input to batch-oriented entry that requires an external text editor. For example, EUREKA contains a sophisticated full-screen editor that has many standard features found in word processing packages. With this editor, it is easy to copy, move, or delete a block of text as well as search for a string of characters and replace it with another. The data entry functions of LINDO and GINO are completely embedded within the software; that is, the user can create, review, and edit a model while "inside" each program. With these packages, it is also possible to externally create a model (say, using the text editor EDLIN) and then import the model for solution. This capability is desirable for modeling and editing large problems since the text editors in LINDO and GINO contain few features associated with up-to-date text editors.

Many LP packages can now read problems saved in the widely-accepted MPS format. This capability allows users to easily transfer problems that were stored on a mainframe to the microcomputer or to exchange problems from different LP systems. In addition, several packages (LINDO is an example) can save an MPS format file for an LP developed with another format.

We point out that many NLP packages appear to have been designed for a wide range of users. This range extends from technically advanced analysts who may wish to exercise a high degree of control over the model input and solution process to occasional users who want a fully automatic package that makes all of the necessary optimization decisions. To accommodate the wide range of software control needs, many packages include features that allow the user to override automatic operation. For example, GINO lets the user select a starting point, specify the number of iterations at various stages, and select values for 15 different algorithmic parameters (which are comprehensively discussed in the GINO manual). Similarly, the user's guide to GAMS/MINOS devotes about 15 pages to explaining key parameters and the choice of settings.

Some LP systems also allow users to control the solution process. Users can set tolerances, interrupt the algorithm, save the basis, and restart from that basis. In addition, a few LP systems can be incorporated as subroutines in custom-designed programs. For example, LINDO can be purchased as Fortran linkable object code.

2.3 Modeling Languages

Recently, much attention has focused on the development of general purpose mathematical modeling languages that have the ability to represent LPs and NLPs easily and efficiently. There are three different ways that packages use to represent a problem: (1) natural, (2) compact, and (3) spreadsheet.

A package that uses the natural form produces a model that closely resembles the traditional "paper and pencil" formulation that lists the objective function and constraints. LINDO and GINO allow the user to represent problems in this way but they don't use subscripts and superscripts. Although the natural form is visually appealing (especially for instructional purposes) and is generally easy to learn, it is probably best suited for representing small problems.

With the compact style of representation, problem data can be stored in tabular form (e.g., a matrix of coefficients) and summation and product notation can be used to model the constraints and objective function. The compact form lends itself to modeling large-scale problems efficiently, although users are required to learn a new, sophisticated modeling language. GAMS (General Algebraic Modeling System), LINGO (Language for INteractive General Optimization), and MPL (Mathematical Programming Language) are examples of new PC-based modeling languages that have been designed to interface with commercially-available LP optimizers. Recall that GAMS can also interface with NLP and MIP optimizers.

Perhaps the most significant achievement in LP software over the last few years has been the development of spreadsheet-compatible programs. The convenient data entry and editing features of spreadsheets make it easy for a user to develop the LP matrix. Since these packages allow blocks of numbers or relationships to be copied from one location to another, it is easy to construct LPs that have blocks of similar structure. The report generation and graphics features of these programs can be used to generate final reports that incorporate results derived from the optimal solution stored in a spreadsheet data file. A few LP packages offer only spreadsheet-like input and data editing while several systems can only read a problem from a spreadsheet file and write the optimal solution to such a file. Three packages (VINO, WHAT'S BEST!, and XA) offer the most complete integration within a spreadsheet. The user creates an LP in a spreadsheet file and presses one or two keys to solve the problem. The optimizer is hidden from the user (LINDO in WHAT'S BEST!) making it appear that the spreadsheet program contains optimization capabilities.

3. CONCLUSIONS

In the last few years, developers of LP and NLP packages for the microcomputer have included a wide variety of new software features and options that help users model, manage, and solve mathematical programming problems easily and efficiently. Systems now contain high-powered modeling languages that allow management scientists to represent problems in a compact, understandable way. Many contain sophisticated optimizers that "automatically" solve LPs or NLPs and also allow users to set key algorithmic parameters.

In the future, we think that micro-based LP and NLP packages will develop along several directions. Expert systems will be used to help solve NLPs and micro-based NLP codes will be available as subroutines that can be incorporated in user-designed mathematical programming systems. In late 1989, we expect a microcomputer version of Karmarkar's algorithm that is capable of solving LPs and NLPs to be released.

REFERENCES

Assad, A. and E. Wasil (1986), "Microcomputers and the Teaching of Operations Research," *Computers & Operations Research 13,* 2/3, 211-229.

Golden, B. and E. Wasil (1986), "Nonlinear Programming on a Microcomputer," *Computers & Operations Research 13,* 2/3, 149-166.

Greenberg, H. (1987), "ANALYZE: A Computer-Assisted Analysis System for Linear Programming Models," *Operations Research Letters 6,* 5, 249-255.

Harrison, T. (1985), "Micro versus Mainframe Performance for a Selected Class of Mathematical Programming Problems," *Interfaces 15,* 4, 14-19.

Ho, J. (1987), "OptiMacros: Optimization with Spreadsheet Macros," *Operations Research Letters 6,* 2, 99-103.

Sharda, R. (1984), "Linear Programming on Microcomputers: A Survey," *Interfaces 14,* 6, 27-38.

Sharda, R. (1985/6), "Optimization Using Spreadsheets on a Microcomputer," *Annals of Operations Research 5,* 599-612.

Sharda, R. (1988), "The State of the Art of Linear Programming on Personal Computers," *Interfaces 18,* 4, 49-58.

Sharda, R. and A. Guha (1988), "Microcomputer LP Systems: A Performance Comparison," Working Paper, College of Business Administration, Oklahoma State University, Stillwater, OK.

Sharda, R. and C. Somarajan (1986), "Comparative Performance of Advanced Microcomputer LP Systems," *Computers & Operations Research 13,* 2/3, 131-147.

Waren, A., M. Hung, and L. Lasdon (1987), "The Status of Nonlinear Programming Software: An Update," *Operations Research 35,* 4, 489-503.

Wasil, E., B. Golden, and L. Liu (1988), "State-of-the-Art in Nonlinear Optimization Software for the Microcomputer," forthcoming in *Computers & Operations Research.*

Yurkiewicz, J. (1988), "Educational Operations Research Software: A Review," *Interfaces 18,* 4, 59-71.

PROJECT MANAGEMENT SOFTWARE FOR THE MICROCOMPUTER: RECENT ADVANCES AND FUTURE DIRECTIONS

EDWARD WASIL

Kogod College of Business Administration, The American University
Washington, D.C. 20016

ARJANG ASSAD

College of Business and Management, University of Maryland
College Park, Maryland 20742

ABSTRACT

Developers of project management software for the microcomputer have been very busy over the last four years including new features and capabilities that are designed to help users represent, organize, and report project information easily and effectively. In this paper, we highlight the trends underlying most of the recent major changes that have occurred to this software in areas such as scheduling, reporting, progress tracking, and costing, and pay special attention to the resource management features of these packages.

1. THE MARKET FOR PROJECT MANAGEMENT SOFTWARE

During the six or so years since the introduction of the first commercial project management (PM) software packages for the microcomputer, PM software has secured a firm position as a constituent of most microcomputer software libraries. While mainframe PM systems were traditionally limited to a narrow class of sophisticated users, the microcomputer revolution has propelled PM into a position of widespread visibility and usage that is unparalleled among quantitative techniques rooted in operations research. A recent survey cited in PC Week (9/19/88) estimates that PM accounts for 3 to 4 per cent of all end-user requests among corporations, as compared to 17 to 20% for spreadsheets. According to another study (see PC Week, 8/22/88) the proportion of sites that have installed PM software increased from 16% in October 1986 to 31% by December 1987 among those corporations owning 500 PC's or more.

The initial rapid growth of the market for PM software has led to some over-optimistic projections. In 1985, one source projected that the size of the market would grow to $228 million by 1990, while a more conservative estimate cited $82 million. However, by 1987, even this latter estimate was reduced to about $70 million by lowering the projected annual growth rate from 24% to 20%. In fact, it is hard to find reliable estimates for the annual sales of PM software. One estimate places the annual sales of one of the leading packages in the 15,000-25,000 range, while another package claimed 60,000 users worldwide in 1987. In any case, it is important to note that even modest estimates point to widespread sales and use of PM software.

The PM software market exhibits wide product diversity and no sign of a clear market leader. Currently, the market offers PM packages for the microcomputer that range from $200 to over $6000. However, about 85% of the sales is captured by four packages in the $500-$800 price range -- Time Line, Harvard Total Project Manager, SuperProject, and Microsoft Project. In the order stated, their annual sales are estimated at 30%, 25%, 15%, and 15% of the market while by December 1987 their installed market shares were placed at 14%, 40%, 13%, and 16%. Currently, these well-known "mid-range" packages can handle projects with 500-1000 activities and 200-300 resources.

From its inception, the development of PM microcomputer software has been faced with the conflict between offering more features and retaining ease of use. New releases or entirely new packages are introduced in an effort to balance these two considerations while responding to market needs. In this sense, PM software has to compete in a more dynamic market than, say, spreadsheets. As shown in Figure 1, in the course of three years or so, the mid-range packages have all gone through three releases (or more) that have substantially increased their range of features and power. The increased sophistication of the mid-range packages has created a niche for "low-end" packages that focus on ease of use and cost under $300.

The prices for the high-end of PM software run between $2000 and $6000. The project size handled by these packages can exceed thousands of activities or be subject to memory limitations alone. They generally offer extensive customization and user-defined options that elaborate upon the basic features found in mid-range packages. The developers of some high-end packages, such as Artemis Project,

Prestige PC, and Primavera Project Planner, had established records as providers of mainframe PM software prior to entering the PC market. Clearly, such high-end packages target the sophisticated user. Accordingly, the PC-based PM packages often allow communications with compatible PM software for mini or mainframe machines. The more sophisticated packages in this group have started to exploit advanced features such as relational databases, fourth generation languages, LAN-specific versions, and multi-user capabilities.

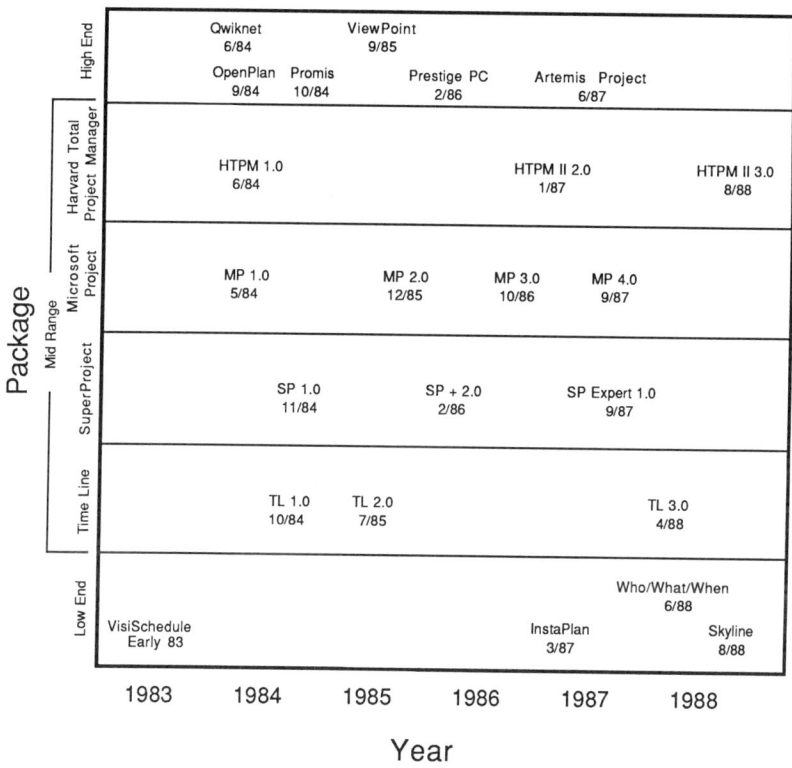

Figure 1. Timing of PM Software Releases

In this paper, we focus on project management software for the microcomputer alone and report on recent developments since the publication of our earlier studies [Assad and Wasil 1986] and [Wasil and Assad 1988]. Section 2 provides a broad overview of the basic components of current PM packages while Section 3 enters a more detailed discussion of resource management by focusing primarily on the four mid-range packages mentioned earlier. These four packages not only account for over 80% of sales of PM software, but also illustrate most of the important changes PC-based PM packages have undergone in the last four years. Indeed, our goal throughout this paper is to highlight the trends underlying such changes, of which Section 4 gives a brief summary.

2. UPDATE ON BASIC PM FEATURES

The essential features of a PM software package have gradually stabilized over the last four years. A package may be expected to perform scheduling, costing and resource management, progress tracking, and generate a variety of associated reports. This section reviews recent developments in these functions.

2.1 Scheduling

The main output showing the project schedule in early PM packages was the Gantt chart, which displayed horizontal activity bars and highlighted the critical tasks. While an enhanced Gantt chart remains the primary display of the project schedule in many current packages, the enhancements are indicative of the recent trend in customizing output in PM software.

An example of a Gantt chart produced by a recent version of Time Line appears in Figure 2. First, the task name can be followed by up to 16 different columns of activity-related information. The columns selected and displayed in Figure 2 are activity work breakdown codes, task names, assigned resources, and per cent of work completed. Other choices of fields include start date, duration, and total slack time. Second, tasks can be filtered according to some user-defined criterion (e.g., all tasks using a particular resource) with the resulting subset highlighted on the chart. Third, the display can include up to five resource histograms allowing the user to view the schedule and the associated resource usages simultaneously.

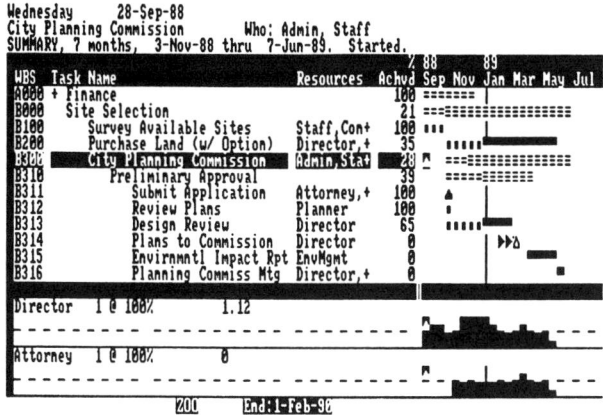

Figure 2. Gantt Chart from Time Line 3.0

Most packages also produce the project network as an activity-on-node PERT chart. Figure 3 shows the project network from SuperProject Expert that highlights the critical path. In this package and some others, the user can control the layout of the network to produce a "natural" diagram, while the networks generated automatically by other packages (with no user input) may have an awkward appearance. The issue of project network representation for large networks has not been settled in PM software: Automatic network generation is useful for larger projects but inflexible in its layout. Some high-end packages designed to handle large projects have de-emphasized on-screen displays in favor of hard-copy network diagrams produced by specialized plotters. For small projects, however, the PERT chart remains the most convenient vehicle for showing dependencies. For this reason, even a low-end package such as InstaPlan offers a "classic PERT option" as an $80 add-on to its basic package. Finally, in the time-scaled PERT chart, the nodes of the project network are activities drawn as bars in a Gantt chart. This hybrid representation attempts to combine the benefits of PERT and Gantt charts and is used in several high-end packages (e.g., Promis and ViewPoint).

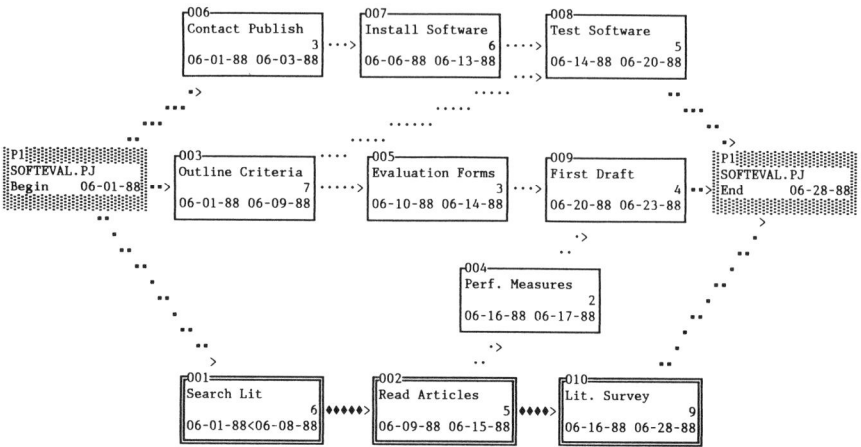

Figure 3. PERT Chart from SuperProject Expert

2.2 Generating Reports and Tracking Progress

A clear trend in PM software is the increasing variety of options for report generation. While some packages still include standard reports (Artemis Project has 50 and Qwiknet has 25), many produce customized reports designed by the user directly on the screen. The user simply selects possible headings and decides upon the layout of the selected columns of information. Alternatively, the user may modify standard reports by adding or deleting certain fields or selecting subsets of activities. The tracking of progress for a project is also a standard feature of most high-end packages. Over time, actual schedule information has to be input and compared with the original plan -- a process that was laborious in early PM releases. High-end packages now facilitate such updating and allow different planned or updated versions to be stored simultaneously.

2.3 Costing and Managing Resources

The ability to develop cost schedules is now a standard feature of PM software but especially developed in high-end packages. Planned and actual costs can be computed for each activity and aggregated at various levels. Earned value reports can be generated to track the expenditures based on the portion of the project completed to date. As costs are generally attached to resources allocated to project activities, there is a clear link between resource and cost management. Early packages that kept these two modules separate were cumbersome to use as a result. Current packages have integrated the two more fully and offer a variety of costing options that may differ according to the resource utilized. The ability to combine information from multiple projects is important to both cost and resource management. Indeed, one could argue that the attention paid to cost and resources is an important factor in separating mid-range and high-end packages. Section 3 returns to resource leveling that forms the algorithmic heart of resource management.

2.4 The User Interface

Given the general evolution of PC software, it is not surprising that PM packages currently offer many user-oriented conveniences such as extensive help menus, data-entry shortcuts, and flexible calendar and time unit definitions. In addition, however, PM software is now providing outlining features to help users in organizing project information. Using work breakdown structures, the user can easily create an initial outline of the project and then divide these broad categories into more specific tasks. In Time Line, this hierarchical structure is reflected in indented task names on the Gantt chart and a series of nested boxes circling subsets of activities on the PERT chart. Harvard Total Project Manager II and SuperProject Expert also use a graphic work breakdown structure. Moreover, recent upgrades now permit the user to keep notes related to the project. Time Line can store about two pages of notes for individual tasks or resources which may be collected into a project journal created by the user. The "note text" in SuperProject Expert serves a similar function. One may surmise that the primitive word processing capabilities used in such note-taking may be enhanced substantially in the future.

2.5 Interfacing

Interfaces between PC-based PM packages and other software have become more common. Time Line can import ASCII files and export data to Lotus 1-2-3 and dBASE III and also to CA-TELLAPLAN. Microsoft Project can share data with Primavera Project Planner (a high-end package that costs $2500 and handles 10,000 tasks). Such interfaces are advertised as important features of some high-end PM packages. For example, Artemis Project links up with its mainframe counterparts and Prestige PC can upload data to CUE on minicomputers and PREMIS on mainframes.

The preceding discussion does not exhaust the list of new features in PM software. The user can now store multiple project schedules and effect global changes (e.g., delay all tasks using resource A by 2 days). Time Line has an Undo/Redo command that spans up to 99 steps. These features are making sensitivity analysis more accessible. SuperProject Expert has finally introduced the three-estimates approach of PERT into its product. In short, there has been a dynamic increase in the number and sophistication of PM features as this software has evolved in the direction of more flexibility and increased user control.

3. RESOURCE LEVELING

Leveling the usage of resources across a single project or multiple projects lies at the core of the resource management problem. Once an option on only a few packages, automatic resource leveling now appears in at least 40 PM packages listed in a recent article of PC Week (8/29/88). High-end packages advertise the capability of leveling 100-500 resources simultaneously to appeal to the sophisticated user. Since the leveling algorithms have received much attention in the project management literature, this section discusses the leveling feature in some greater detail.

In PM software, resource leveling generally refers to the problem defined in Figure 4. In the resource-constrained problem, the availability of a resource in each time period is fixed. The goal is to produce a feasible schedule that does not overcommit resources beyond their availabilities. This problem has been studied in the operations research literature: Comparisons of exact and heuristic solution techniques for this problem can be found in [Davis and Patterson 1975], [Patterson 1984], and [Russell 1986] while [Davis 1973] provides its historical background.

Notation

Project network with tasks and dependencies

m resources are required and availability of resource k is R_k

Task i -- duration t_i

resource utilization rate r_{ik} of resource k (k = 1,2,...,m)

$r_i = (r_{i1},...,r_{im})$

Resource-Constrained Scheduling Problem

In each time period, we must have the sum of the amounts of resource k used by all tasks less-than-or-equal-to R_k (k = 1,2,...,m). Tasks are scheduled to minimize delays subject to the resource constraints. The goal is to minimize the project duration.

Figure 4. Resource-Constrained Problem

The user can employ a manual or automatic procedure to obtain a feasible schedule for the resource-constrained problem with PC-based software. The manual approach relies on graphical displays of resource usage histograms or loading diagrams (recall that Time Line can display up to five such histograms simultaneously). With the aid of these histograms, the user can identify the over-allocated resources and manually shift certain activities to reduce or eliminate the violations. This approach may work for small projects with only a few resources. In the presence of many resources, however, the simultaneous tracking of usages over time could severely tax the user's interactive abilities. Consequently, an automatic leveling feature becomes very attractive for larger projects.

As mentioned before, automatic leveling features have migrated from the high-end to the mid-range packages. Many packages (such as Time Line) can automatically resolve all resource conflicts, possibly at the expense of lengthening the project duration, to produce a feasible project schedule. This is known as resource-limited leveling in the popular literature. Other packages (such as Microsoft Project) fix the project duration and try to reduce resource violations by shifting activities only within their slack times. Of course, such a procedure may not remove all of the violations, thus requiring the user to manually adjust the schedule. We point out that SuperProject Expert can perform both types of leveling. A few high-end packages (including Open Plan and Artemis Project) offer a time-limited leveling procedure. This procedure produces a schedule that meets the project completion date by allowing some resource usages to exceed the maximum amount specified by the user.

Some systems allow the user to influence the automatic algorithm by assigning task priorities and also extend the automatic solution feature across projects (i.e., these packages solve the resource-constrained problem for several projects that share a set of resources over the same time period). Time Line also performs resource-driven scheduling, i.e., the length of a task is calculated based on the number of assigned resources.

To test the power of the algorithms employed by current PM packages to solve resource-constrained problems, we applied Primavera Project Planner (version 2.60), SuperProject Plus (version 2.0), and Time Line (version 2.0) to 35 test problems taken from the problem set described in [Patterson 1984]. The problems ranged in size between 7 and 51 activities and each contained 3 resources. The length of the schedule produced by each package was compared against the known optimal solution and against the project duration produced by the min slack rule procedure (this heuristic has been extensively studied and has been shown to perform well). Aggregate statistics for these packages are presented in Table 1.

Table 1. Summary of Computational Results

	PPP	SP+	TL	MSR
Average Percent Over Optimal	12.4	5.2	3.8	5.9
Number of Times Optimal	3	11	13	11

PPP Primavera Project Planner TL Time Line
SP+ SuperProject Plus   MSR Min Slack Rule

From Table 1, we see that Time Line was the best performing package over the entire set of 35 problems. It produced the largest number of optimal schedules (13) and had the smallest average percent deviation over optimal (3.8%). It also outperformed the min slack rule.

4. TRENDS IN PM SOFTWARE

From the previous discussion, we have seen that over the last two years, developers of high- and low-end project management packages for the microcomputer have been very busy including new features and capabilities that are designed to help users represent, organize, and report information easily and effectively. This highly dynamic market environment ensures that this class of software will continue to evolve along several new directions. In this section, we identify some of the software trends that have recently emerged.

4.1 Standardization of Basic Features

Essentially all mid-range and high-end packages now offer project managers a fairly comprehensive set of basic PM tools in the areas of scheduling, costing/budgeting, resource management, progress tracking, and reporting. Features such as network diagrams, resource histograms, automatic resource leveling, and actual vs. planned reports, which were previously found only in mainframe software and a few expensive PC packages, now constitute the core of most packages' "standard PM options."

In the last two years, software developers have recognized that an off-the-shelf package (even a feature-laden system) cannot address all users' needs. Many packages now contain a large number of options especially in the areas of project representation and reporting that allow users to customize forms, charts, and reports. A few packages are even designed to let users perform in-house software modifications. For example, users of Artemis Project can purchase a fourth generation programming language to develop their own applications with. Still other packages are moving in the direction of becoming "full feature" integrated products that offer word processing, database management, outlining, scheduling, and graphics capabilities in a single system. (A new package called Skyline attempts to combine these and other applications and even offers a version in French).

4.2 Powerful Hardware - Software Combinations

The recent emergence of powerful new microcomputers (such as the IBM Personal System/2) along with anticipated dramatic operating system and user interface changes over the next few years (especially for the IBM PC) will impact the way in which future PM packages manage, display, and distribute project information. For example, new multi-tasking operating systems will give users the capability of performing several project management functions simultaneously. Software will be redesigned to take advantage of very fast PC's equipped with state-of-the-art numeric coprocessors (many packages currently do not access this chip). This software revision will increase the processing speed of most PM packages allowing project managers to analyze very large projects in a short amount of time.

4.3 Mainframe and Interpackage Links

One of the areas that has received the attention of both software developers and users is the ability to exchange project information residing within a given package with a mainframe system, other micro-based PM packages, or business productivity software on the PC. Many packages can now export data to word processors and spreadsheets and a few have import/export links to high-end PM systems. Only a handful of packages can interface directly with a mainframe system but the number of packages with this capability is steadily increasing. There are many advantages of connecting the micro-based package to the mainframe system: Users can develop and update projects on the PC and then upload the data to the mainframe where it can be quickly collated, merged, and analyzed with information from company-wide applications. For example, the ability to effectively manage a large number of resources across multiple projects (a difficult, time-consuming task on the PC) is greatly facilitated with this link.

REFERENCES

Assad, A. and E. Wasil (1986), "Project Management Using a Microcomputer," *Computers & Operations Research 13,* 2/3, 231-260.

Davis, E. (1973), "Project Scheduling Under Resource Constraints-Historical Review and Categorization of Procedures," *AIIE Transactions 5,* 4 (Dec.), 297-313.

Davis, E. and J. Patterson (1975), "A Comparison of Heuristic and Optimum Solutions in Resource-Constrained Project Scheduling," *Management Science 21,* 8 (Apr.), 944-955.

Fersko-Weiss, H. (1987), "Master Plans: Project Management Software," *PC Magazine 6,* 16 (Sept.), 153-209.

Patterson, J. (1984), "A Comparison of Exact Approaches for Solving the Multiple Constrained Resource, Project Scheduling Problem," *Management Science 30,* 7 (July), 854-867.

Russell, R. (1986), "A Comparison of Heuristics for Scheduling Projects with Cash Flows and Resource Restrictions," *Management Science 32,* 10 (Oct.), 1291-1300.

Wasil, E. and A. Assad (1988), "Project Management on the PC: Software, Applications, and Trends," *Interfaces 18,* 2 (Mar.-Apr.), 75-84.

V.

ARTIFICIAL INTELLIGENCE AND EXPERT SYSTEMS

ARTIFICIAL INTELLIGENCE BASED APPROACHES FOR SOLVING HIERARCHICAL OPTIMIZATION PROBLEMS

G. ANANDALINGAM
Department of Systems
University of Pennsylvania

R. MATHIEU
Department of Systems Engineering
University of Virginia

C. L. PITTARD
Department of Systems Engineering
University of Virginia

N. SINHA
Department of Systems
University of Pennsylvania

ABSTRACT

This paper reports on the use of artificial intelligence based techniques to solve hierarchical optimization problems. In particular, we use modifications of the genetic algorithm and simulated annealing, techniques that belong to the generate-and-test paradigm of AI, to solve bi-level linear programming (BLLP), a special hierarchical optimization problem. These techniques are used to generate the leader's decision vectors, and the follower's reaction is obtained from the solution of a linear program. Results show that, while it takes more cpu time, the AI based techniques gets closer to the global optimum than one of the more successful BLLP algorithms for problems of most sizes.

1. INTRODUCTION

The artificial intelligence (AI) and operations research (OR) communities approach their problem solving tasks from different perspectives. OR tends to tackle problems using what might be called the hill-climbing paradigm, in which new sets of solutions are obtained from old ones by ascending (or descending) a relatively smooth surface (the hill) in a manner that is mathematically rigorous. On the other hand, AI researchers tend to prefer a generate-and-test approach to problem solving, in which candidate solutions are created in some reasonable way and then checked for goodness. The key to the AI approach is the use of significant amounts of domain-specific knowledge to direct the process of solution generation (Pearl, 1984).

The advantage of using OR techniques is that they facilitate the development of theoretical guarantees on the performance of these algorithms, especially convergence. However, np-hard problems, such as job shop scheduling and travelling salesman problems, have resisted solution by these precise search methods. AI search techniques, on the other hand, provide a possible approach to finding good solutions to these np-hard problems. By incorporating randomness and domain specific knowledge, AI search methods have the potential to obtain good solutions to many of these problems most of the time.

This paper explores the use of the AI-based search techniques, simulated annealing (SA) and the genetic algorithm (GA), for solving a class of np-hard hierarchical optimization problems called bi-level linear programming (BLLP). Our results show that both AI-based methods get closer to the global optimal solution than a well known method in BLLP, namely Bard's [1983] grid search method. This result holds true for problems of all sizes. However, both methods take much longer to satisfy the stoppping criterion.

The rest of the paper is organized as follows: In Section 2, we provide an overview of simulated annealing and the genetic algorithm, and discusss how they solve optimization problem. In Section 3, we present the bi-level linear programming problem. In Sections 4 and 5, we present GABBA and SABBA, respectively the genetic algorithm and simulated annealing based algorithms that we use for solving BLLP. We discuss convergence in Section 6. Section 7 presents our computational results.

2. AI BASED OPTIMIZATION TECHNIQUES

We consider simulated annealing and the genetic algorithm to belong to the generate-and-test paradigm of artificial intelligence. Both techniques capture the gross features of the solution domain before homing in on the optimal (or acceptable near optimal) solution. This 'domain specific knowledge' is essential for the techniques to solve the optimization problems. As such, they also cannot be classified along with other traditional OR techniques for solving the BLLP.

Simulated Annealing (Kirkpatrick et al., 1983) operates in a manner similar to pure random search. However, new solutions need not always be improvements. Some worse solutions are accepted at random with nonzero probability according to a specific parametrized distribution, usually called the *temperature*. In optimization, Simulated Annealing works as follows: At relatively high temperatures, many solutions are accepted, even if they are bad. This allows the search to jump from mode (peak) to mode in the search space; if only improved solutions were accepted, the search would seek a local optima, but in general would be precluded from seeking the global optima. Successively lower temperatures identify more and more detail while solutions become more and more localized. Ultimately, the intent of Simulated Annealing is to obtain a very good solution on a very good mode of the search space.

The Genetic Algorithm (GA) bases the search for better solutions on Darwinian principles of looking for fitter genes, where the genes are analogous to admissible solutions to the problem, and 'fitness' is the objective function value. Unlike simulated annealing, instead of maintaining a single solution at any one point in time, the GA maintains a population of solutions. When going from one iteration to the next, only the best overall population is considered. The initial population of solutions is usually generated at random. Each succeeding population of solutions is created from its predecessors using genetic operators, *cross over* and *mutation*, which seek to preserve and combine the good characteristics of the better members of the preceeding population of solutions. Solutions are usually represented as a string of ones and zeroes: Cross-over replaces part of one string with the corresponding part of another, and mutation arbitrarily changes the value of a character on a string to another member of its alphabet (another of its possible values).

From an optimization perspective, the Genetic Algorithm works as follows: The first generation of solutions, generated at random, is uniformly distributed over the search space. Succeeding generations, due to the 'survival of the fittest' of their ancestors, tend to be increasingly localized around the best modes in the search space. The final generation usually is concentrated around one or at most few very good modes of the search space.

3. THE BI-LEVEL LINEAR PROGRAMMING PROBLEM

Let us consider a two-level hierarchical system where the higher level decision maker (hereafter the "leader") controls decision variables $x \in X$ and the lower level (hereafter the "follower") controls $y \in Y$ respectively. The leader is assumed to select his decision vector first, and the follower select his decision vector after that. Using this notation, the bi-level linear programming problem is formulated as:

P1

$$Max_x F(x,y) = ax + by \tag{1}$$

where y solves

$$Max_y f(x,y) = cx + dy \tag{2}$$

subject to

$$g(x,y) = Ax + By - p \leq 0 \tag{3}$$

$$x \in X, \quad y \in Y \tag{4}$$

Note that once x is given, the follower's objective is simply $\text{Max}_y dy$ and cx can be dropped from (2).

Definition The follower's *rational reaction set* is given by the set

$$RR(x) = [y^* \in Y : f(x, y^*) \geq f(x, y), \quad \forall y \in Y, \quad x \in X \quad and \quad g(x, y) \leq 0] \quad (5)$$

Note that it is usual to replace the sets X and Y by the positive real spaces of the appropriate dimension. So equation (4) will usually be given by $x \geq 0, y \geq 0$.

Hierachical optimization problems are more complex than familiar mathematical programming problems. Bialas and Karwan [1984] showed that even the bi-level linear programming (BLLP) problem is *non-convex*. Solutions to BLLP problems were based on either vertex enumeration (Candler and Townsley [1982], Bialas and Karwan [1984], and Anandalingam and White [1987]), or the Kuhn-Tucker approach (Bard, [1983], Anandalingam [1988]). None of these have attempted to solve large size problems or even to address the issue of multiple local optima. It is clear that there is considerable room for efficiency in the solution to the BLLP and other hierarchical optimization problems.

4. THE GABBA ALGORITHM
4.1. Basic Parameters

GABBA, the Genetic Algorithm Based Bi-level programming Algorithm is best described as an adaptive reproductive plan based on some principles of the genetic algorithm. In order to solve the bi-level linear program, the leader's decision vector is reproduced according to a modification of the GA, and the follower's decision vector is obtained by solving the second level linear programming problem. The fitness test also involves a modification of traditional GA tests.

GABBA's reproductive plan is controlled by the operators: population size, number of structures in the previous generation's population to reproduce, percentage of alleals in each structure to reproduce, number of new structures to produce randomly every generation, and selection strategy. It does not exploit cross-over. It could be argued that cross-over is a special case of mutation, since it could be reduced to multiple mutations. Also, unlike most pure genetic algorithms, GABBA does not encode its structures as 0-1 bit strings, but rather as a string of base-10 digits. The new code is more intuitive for adapting reproductive plans to mathematical programming.

In GABBA, all structures are defined by alleals of base-10 numbers. Each alleal is defined to have a head and a tail. The point that separates the head from the tail is determined by a parameter, SCALE, where

$$\text{SCALE} = 10^n, n \in I$$

where I is the set of positive real integers. For example, if our alleal is 12345.67, and SCALE = 10.0, the head of the alleal is 1234*.**, and the tail of the alleal is ****5.67.

When optimizing a function using this base-10 scheme, the information to be passed on to the next generation is contained in the head. When creating a new species from an old species, the head of the previous generation is kept, and a random number, generated using a uniform distribution on the interval (0, SCALE) becomes the new tail. For example, if 1234*.** is passed to the new generation, and a random tail of 9.81 is generated, the new species becomes 12349.81. Thus, we keep generating tails at a given SCALE level until 'good' solutions are obtained. After we determine what are "good" solutions based on the problem objective, the SCALE value is modified so that new solutions are more precise than the old ones.

The population is generated within feasible lower and upper bounds. Thus the *alphabet* for each alleal is all base-10 numbers between the lower and upper bounds; this is different from traditional uses of GAs, where the alphabet is made up of the binary code (0, 1).

The *selection strategy* is based on obtaining, at each generation, the N most fit structures (i.e. solutions with the highest value of F(x, y), the leader's objective). Candidates for selection include the N structures from the previous generation, NP offspring structures newly created by mutation of structures in the previous generation, and NR new structures produced randomly.

4.2. The Algorithm

The reader should note that, as given in the Definition, equation (5), whenever we refer to the follower's rational reaction set RR(x), we mean that the following linear program is solved, *for given* x, (say x^*), using a standard algorithm:

P2

$$Max_y dy \qquad (6)$$

subject to

$$By \leq p - Ax^* \qquad (7)$$

$$y \geq 0 \qquad (8)$$

Note that in the following, although we suppress k, the generation index, in the case of the decision vectors and their components, it should be understood that we are considering these vectors at the appropriate generation.

The GABBA algorithm proceeds as follows:
Step 0:(Initialization)
    Let k = 0, F*(-1) = -∞.
    Set parameters
      (a) N - population size;
      (b) NP - number of current solutions (i.e. structures) in population P(k) to undergo mutation;
      (c) NX - number of decision variables (i.e. alleals) x to undergo mutation;
      (d) NR - number of new random solutions created during each iteration;
      (e) e - degree of accuracy required.

    Generate upper and lower bounds $\forall x_i \in x$ where $x = (x_1, ...x_{n1})$ by solving:

$$Max_{x,y}/Min_{x,y} \quad x \tag{9}$$

subject to
$$Ax + By - p \leq 0 \tag{10}$$
$$x, y \geq 0 \tag{11}$$

Set SCALE = $10^n, n \in I$, such that SCALE $\geq$ Max $(x_1, ..., x_{n1})$.

    Generate population P(k) which contains N pairs [x, y(x)] such that $\forall\ x_i \in x$, $x_i \sim$ U[min x_i, max x_i], and y(x) $\in$ RR(x).

Step 1
    Let F(k) = ax + by(x)
    (Note that there are N objective values F, one each for each member of the population.)
    Let $F^*(k)$ = Max F(k), and $[x^*, y(x^*)] = \arg F^*(k)$.

Step 2(SCALE Change)
    If $F^*(k) = F^*(k-1)$ and
      the average performance of the top 60$\geq 0.85 F^*$,
      Then SCALE = SCALE/10

Go To Step 3.

Otherwise, Go To Step 4.

Step 3(Stopping Criterion)

If SCALE < e, then Stop, Optimal Solution = [x*, y(x*)]

Otherwise go to Step 4.

Step 4(Mutated Structures)

Mutate the NP pairs [x, y(x)] from P(k) with the largest level 1 objectives as follows:

For each pair [x, y(x)], create a new pair [x', y(x')] where x' is obtained by mutating NX randomly selected elements of x such that

$$x_i' = \text{int}(x_i/\text{SCALE})*\text{SCALE} + z$$

with

$$z \sim U[0, \text{SCALE}]$$

and y(x') ∈ RR(x') if it exists.

If y(x') ∈ RR(x') does not exist,

the mutation process moves to the next [x, y(x)] pair.

Step 5(New Random Structures)

Generate NR pairs [x", y(x")] such that Ax" + By(x") ≤ 0, and x" and y(x") ≥ 0, where $\forall x_i \in x, x"_i \sim$ U[Min x, Max x], and y(x") ∈ RR(x").

Step 6(Selection)

Set k = k + 1

From the N, [x, y(x)] pairs from the previous solution, the NP or less [x', y(x')] pairs obtained from mutation, and the NR, [x", y(x")] new random pairs, SELECT the N pairs with the largest value of F to form P(k).

Go To Step 1

5. SABBA ALGORITHM

SABBA the Simulated Annealing Based Bi-level programming Algorithm proposed in this paper makes use of a special property of the BLLP: given x, the follower's rational reaction is obtained by solving the linear program P3. Thus, we need only generate vector x randomly. In fact, we use Step 0 of GABBA to generate the admissible range for the x's, and then generate x's by letting them be distributed uniformly in the admissible range. The main differences are the selection criterion, and the tests of acceptability.

We will now present the algorithm. In order to keep the description concise, we will adopt the following notation:

F : the objective of the leader as defined by Eq.(1) for current solution

F*: the optimum value of F at current iteration.

z* : array that stores the optimal solution.

k* : the maximum allowable iterations with no change in optimal solution.

α : temperature reduction parameter.

T*: the minimum temperature allowed for annealing schedule.

Statement of the algorithm:

Step 0(Initialize):
> set $F^* = -\infty$; temperature T=T_{max}.
> Let k = 0.

Step 1
> Generate x ~ U(x_{min}, x_{max}) as in Step 0 of GABBA.

Step 2
> Solve P3 for x generated in Step 1; obtain [x, y(x)] and estimate F.

step 3
> Compute Δ F = F - F*

> If Δ F > 0, Then F* ←F, and z* = [x, y(x)].

> If Δ F < 0, let z* = [x, y(x)] with probability exp(-Δ F/T)
> F* ← F

> If Δ F = 0,   k = k + 1
> If k > k*, Go To Step 4.
> Else Go To Step 1.

Step 4
> k = 0
> Lower Temperature, T → α T,

If $T < T^*$, Stop, z^* is the Optimal Solution.
Else Go To Step 1.

6. CONVERGENCE

In most search techniques, the problem is considered solved if, for some $\epsilon > 0$, an element of the following set has been identified:

$$A_z(\epsilon) = [z \in Z : \| z - z^* \| \leq \epsilon] \qquad (12)$$

$$A_F(\epsilon) = [z \in Z : \| F(z) - F(z^*) \| \leq \epsilon] \qquad (13)$$

where, as before, $z = [x, y(x)]$, z^* is the optimal solution, and Z is the feasible region. In GABBA we use a variation of the set $A_z(\epsilon)$ for stopping the algorithm, and in SABBA, we use a variation of $A_F(\epsilon)$.

Generally one cannot guarantee *absolutely* that probabilistic search methods would provide a solution. Under conditions on the sampling distributions and the curvature of F(.), it can be proved that an element of optimality set A is sampled *almost surely* as the sample size increases. One option to absolutely guarantee success would be to use the probabilistic technique in the first stage for locating regions where good local optima exist, and to use traditional OR techniques at the second stage to find the actual optima. We do not do this in this paper.

7. COMPUTATIONAL RESULTS

7.1. Preliminaries

A random bi-level linear programming problem generator was constructed in order to test GABBA and SABBA against other algorithms. The problems generated were of size (3, 7, 4), (5, 10, 6), (6, 14, 8), and (8, 17, 10), where (n1,n2,m) represents the number of the level 1 decision variables, the level 2 decision variables, and the constraints respectively. The problems contained both positive and negative coefficients in the objectives and constraints. The coefficients matrix was kept full by allowing only a small percentage of 0's. In all 15 random problems were generated for each problem size. The problems were run on an ATT PC6300 Plus microcomputer with Intel 80286 microprocessor, and 80287 math coprocessor.

7.2. Bard's Grid Search Technique

The performance of the AI-based techniques was tested against Bard's [1983] grid search technique. The choice of the grid search technique was based on the fact that it has had much publicity in the literature, and is generally acknowledged as an efficient algorithm. Also like the AI-based techniques, it does not guarantee global optimality.

Bard [1983] showed that bi-level linear programs can be solved by obtaining a maximal λ that solves the following straightforward linear program:

$$P(x, y, \lambda) = Max \quad \lambda(ax + by) + (1 - \lambda)(dy) : s.t. \quad Ax + By \leq p \qquad (14)$$

and provides a y $\geq$ 0 that is feasible for the problem:

$$Q(y) = Max \quad dy : s.t. \quad By \leq p - Ax \qquad (15)$$

Bard's procedure is to iteratively solve the problem P(x, y, λ) for varying values of λ, where new values of λ are found from sensitivity analysis concepts, and arranged on a grid. (See Bard [1983] for details). The modified grid search (MGS) algorithm used in this paper follows the general principle in Bard's [1983] paper, but uses upper and lower bounds on λ at each iteration so as to converge quickly. The algorithm is stopped when there is no change in the λ.

7.3. Computational Results

Performance was measured on the basis of computational effectiveness, measured by CPU time, and quality of solution, measured by two means: (i) the percent of time that one of the algorithms succeeded in producing a better solution (i.e. a higher level 1 objective at the end of it's execution), and (ii) the sum of absolute deviation of the best solutions of each defined by

$$D = \sum_{m=1}^{M} [F^*_{MGS}(m) - F^*_{AI}(m)] \qquad (16)$$

where $F^*_i(m)$ is the best value of F obtained from the i-th method (i = Modified Grid Search, MGS or one of the AI-based methods), for the m-th problem, and M is the total number of problems. Note that if the absolute deviation D is positive, it means that the solutions produced by the Grid Search technique were better than those produced by the AI-based methods in an overall sense. Conversely, if D was negative, the specific AI-based method under investigation was better.

Table 1
GABBA versus Grid Search

Problem Size	Grid Search mean cpu	GABBA mean cpu	GABBA dominates Grid Search (%)	D
(3,7,4)	4.23	24.81	40.0%	0.181
(5,10,6)	13.69	80.48	66.6%	-0.057
(6,14,8)	27.27	699.45	73.0%	-0.135
(8,17,10)	63.99	3281.59	60.0%	-0.593

Table 2
SABBA versus Grid Search

Problem Size	Grid Search mean cpu	SABBA mean cpu	SABBA dominates Grid Search (%)	D
(3,7,4)	4.23	508.74	33.3%	0.137
(5,10,6)	13.69	645.42	51.2%	-0.009
(6,14,8)	27.27	923.00	61.4%	-0.111
(8,17,10)	63.99	1879.25	62.2%	-0.504

For problems of two sizes, GABBA was run for varying settings of NR and NX (See Step 0 in Section 4.2. for Definitions). The settings of NP, N, and SCALE modification heuristic were held constant. (These results are not shown, but are available upon request). The results do not easily lead to a choice of the best GABBA to use. The trade-off was between choosing a method that had a low average cpu time (in seconds), or in choosing one that yielded a better near optimal solution. We decided that the probability of reaching a near optimal solution was more important than cpu time. Hence the GABBA, with NP = 0.50N, NX = 0.50n1, NR = 0.40N, and N = 2*n1 was chosen for all subsequent analyses.

It should be noted however, that we have not optimized GABBA in the sense of Grefenstette's [1986] paper. The vast number of computer runs required for optimizing parameters was beyond our research budget. Also experimentation seemed to show that the optimal parameter setting were very sensitive to problem size, and other problem characteristics. Thus, a strict optimization of parameters may not have been possible.

The fairly simple bi-level linear programming technique based on Genetic Algorithms provided reasonably good results. Although the grid search algorithm took less time to solve the problems of different size, GABBA yielded a better solution most of the time. (Table 1). In problems of size (6, 14, 8), GABBA was 73 out of 100 times better than the grid search technique. This means that GABBA would be more likely to reach a global optimum than would grid search, or, since grid search is considered to be one of the most efficient BLLP algorithms, any other technique proposed to solve bi-level linear programs.

In the case of SABBA, we experimented with a number of values for k^*, α, and T^*. Here the trade-off was between being too far away from the optimum, and taking too long for convergence. We finally settled in on allowing no change in the F^* for 5 iterations (i.e. $k^* = 5$), the lowest temperature, T^*, to be 0.01 degrees, and $\alpha = 0.1$.

Results in Table 2 shows that, similar to GABBA, SABBA dominates Grid-Search in the larger problems. Again, the mean time taken to achieve satisfactory near-optimal solutions was longer than the grid-search algorithm. However, SABBA got closer to the global optimum more times in all larger problems than grid-search. GABBA dominates SABBA in both measures for problems of all sixes.

9. REFERENCES

Anandalingam, G. (1988), 'A Mathematical Programming Model of Decentralized Multi-Level Systems', *Journal of the Operational Research Society*, vol. 39, no. 11.

Anandalingam, G. and D. J. White (1988), 'A Penalty Function Approach to Solving Bi-Level Linear Programming Problems', Working Paper, Dept. of Systems, University of Pennsylvania, August.

Bard, J. F. (1983), 'An Efficient Point Algorithm for a Linear Two-Stage Optimization

Problem', *Operations Research*, vol. 31, July-August, pp 670-684.

Bard, J. F. and J. E. Falk (1982), 'An Explicit Solution to the Multi- Level Programming Problem', *Computers and Operations Research*, vol. 9, no. 1, pp 77-100.

Bialas W. F. and M. H. Karwan (1984), 'Two-Level Linear Programming', *Management Science*, vol. 30, no. 8, August, pp 1004-1020.

Fortuny-Amat, J. and B. McCarl (1981), 'A Representative and Economic Interpretation of a Two-Level Programming Problem', *Journal of the Operational Research Society*, vol. 32, pp 783-792.

Glover, F. (1986), 'Future Paths for Integer Programming and Links to Artificial Intelligence', *Computers and Operations Research*, vol 13, pp 533-549.

Glover, F. (1987), 'Tabu Search', mimeo, Center for Applied Artificial Intelligence, Graduate School of Business, University of Colarado, October.

Grefenstette, J. (1986), 'Optimization of Control Parameters for Genetic Algorithms', *IEEE Transactions on Systems, Man, and Cybernetics*, vol. 16, January-February, pp 122-128.

Kirkpatrick, S., C. D. Gelatt, and M. P. Vecchi, (1983), 'Optimization By Simulated Annealing', *Science*, 220 (4598), May, pp 671-680.

Kumar, V. and Kanal, L. N. (1983), 'Some new insights into the relationships among dynamic programming, branch and bound, and heuristic search procedures', *Proceedings*, IEEE International Conference on Systems, Man, and Cyberneics, pp 19-23.

Pearl, J. (1984), *Heuristics: Intelligent Search Strategies for Computer Problem Solving*, Addision Wesley, Reading, MA.

IMPACT OF NEUROCOMPUTING ON OPERATIONS RESEARCH

James W. Denton
College of Business Administration, Kent State University
Kent, Ohio 44242

Gregory R. Madey
Loral Corporation
Akron, Ohio 44315
and
College of Business Administration, Kent State University
Kent, Ohio 44242

ABSTRACT

A survey of neurocomputing and its potential implications to selected operations research problems is provided. These implications include the use of neurocomputing to solve traditionally difficult OR problems and the application of classical OR techniques to the improvement of neurocomputing methods. Neurocomputing may solve difficult OR problems including 1) the traveling salesman problem, 2) problems with fuzzy data, 3) problems with missing data, 4) problems requiring machine learning, and 5) ill-structured pattern matching problems. Experiments on a credit approval problem using actual consumer credit application data from a major international firm are described. The use of nonlinear optimization techniques to improve the learning algorithm of the feedforward back-propagation neurocomputing architecture is explored.

1. INTRODUCTION

Neurocomputing, also known as connectionism, neural networks, or parallel distributed processing, is regarded by some as a revolutionary new approach to problem solving. Others remain skeptical, waiting for neurocomputing to produce some results that cannot be duplicated by traditional methods. It has received much attention in the popular media, probably due to its analogy to the processes and structure of the brain. Beneath the hype, however, evidence is beginning to show that this emerging technology can prove to be useful in a variety of fields. Research publications in cognitive psychology, electrical engineering, neurophysiology, and other fields report that neurocomputing has been used in solving problems in those fields. Interest in neurocomputing has grown to the extent that it now has its own professional organization, the International Neural Network Society (INNS), with a membership of more than 2000.

Copyright 1989 by Elsevier Science Publishing Co., Inc.
Impacts of Recent Computer Advances on Operations Research
Ramesh Sharda, Bruce L. Golden, Edward Wasil, Osman Balci, William Stewart, Editors

The OR community also has begun to recognize the potential of neurocomputing. Evidence of interest in the field can be found in the number of presentations at recent OR/MS conferences [Baum 1988; Greenberg 1988; Madey 1988a; Mort 1988; Pao and Sobajic 1988]. OR practitioners are interested in neurocomputing because it has demonstrated the ability to solve problems that have historically proven difficult for traditional methods. These problems are characterized by their inability to be defined in concise terms [Abu-Mostafa and Psaltis 1987].

Proponents point to the potential of neurocomputing in this type of problem as an indication that this new technology offers promise. It has already been demonstrated successfully in pattern recognition and natural language processing applications [Sejnowski and Rosenberg 1987; Kinoshita and Palevsky 1987; Jorgenson and Matheus 1986]. The skeptics point out, however, that neural networks have not yet been proven to be better than traditional sequential computing, and that very few applications have made it out of the laboratory and into daily use [Williamson 1988]. We examine the field of neurocomputing from the perspective of OR in two ways: 1) the use of neurocomputing to solve OR problems, and 2) the use of OR techniques to speed up the learning phase of neurocomputing.

2. NEUROCOMPUTING AS AN OR TOOL

In the operations research area, computationally difficult problems such as the traveling salesman problem exhibit the same type of characteristics as pattern recognition problems and natural language processing. The vast number of possible solutions overwhelms the ability of algorithmic procedures to find an optimal solution in reasonable time. It has been shown that neurocomputing offers a quick method to find a good, although not necessarily optimal, solution to this problem [Hopfield and Tank 1986].

One valuable property of neural networks is called spontaneous generalization. This property allows the network to capture general properties of patterns which it has learned [McClelland, et al. 1986]. It is possible, therefore, to "teach" a neural network to classify patterns into groups through a supervised learning process. An example of a real-world application of this ability would be to use a neural network to accept or reject consumer loan applications. The network is trained using existing applications that have already been classified as "accept" or "reject". The training process defines the interconnective strengths between nodes in the network so that the closest match between actual and target output patterns is achieved.

Neurocomputing methods were evaluated on this type of problem by the authors using data obtained from consumer credit applications from a large corporation [Madey and Denton 1988b]. The network used was a layered feedforward network with three layers. In this architecture, the input patterns of training data are assigned as the activation states of the nodes in the first layer of the network. Activation states of the nodes in the second and third layers are then determined. For this problem, the third and final layer contains one node, and the activation state of that node indicates whether the application is accepted or rejected. See figure 1.

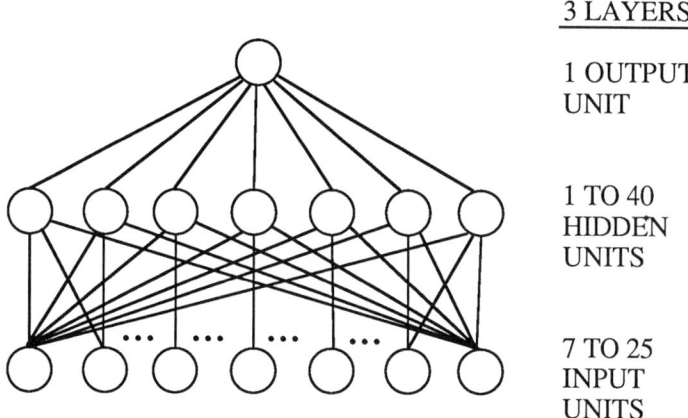

3 LAYERS

1 OUTPUT UNIT

1 TO 40 HIDDEN UNITS

7 TO 25 INPUT UNITS

Figure 1. The network architecture used in the consumer credit model [Madey and Denton 1988b]. The layered feed-forward network requires a layer of input units, a layer of output units, and at least one layer of hidden units. The set of patterns of activation of the output units are associated with a set of input patterns by defining an appropriate set of weights for the interconnections and threshold values for the units. These weights and threshold values are learned by the network through repeated presentation of the associated input and output patterns and gradually changing the values according to some learning algorithm.

Back-propagation was used to train the network to associate the correct response (accept or reject) with each input pattern (coded data from credit applications). During the training phase, the training data set is presented to the network repeatedly, and the interconnective strengths between the nodes are adjusted so as to minimize the difference between the actual and target output values.

The resulting network performs qualitatively like a discriminant analysis. Based on some input vector, the observation is classified into one of two groups. The performance of the network was determined by evaluating loan application data that the network had never seen before. A typical experimental run used 30 observations for training and 150 observations for testing. Often, the training set was not completely learned due to possible inconsistencies in the data. During the learning phase, the performance of the network was periodically tested by presenting the testing data to the network and assessing the degree of agreement between the network's classification and the actual classification.

Performance of the network in replicating the actual classifications given were consistently in the 85% to 95% range for both accepted and rejected applications. A discriminant analysis run on the same data yielded performance of 89% correctly classified (95% for accepted applications and 68% for rejected applications).

The raw data was coded into variables that took values from 0.1 to 0.9. The coding scheme used depended on the type of data contained in the field. Sometimes the data field contained a binary (yes/no) data element. In this case, a "no" was assigned the value of 0.1, a "yes" was assigned the value of 0.9, and missing data was assigned the value of 0.5. Categorical data was handled similarly, but with one variable resulting from each possible category. For example, if a data field consisted of three valid entries (A, B, and C), along with missing data, three input variables to the network were set up. The first took a value of 0.9 for "A", 0.1 for "not A", and 0.5 for missing data. The second took a value of 0.9 for "B", 0.1 for "not B", and 0.5 for missing data. The third took a value of 0.9 for "C", 0.1 for "not C", and 0.5 for missing data. The final type of data to be represented in the data fields was continuously variable data. For these fields, the minimum value over all applications was assigned 0.1, the maximum value over all applications was assigned 0.9, and intermediate values were determined by linear interpolation. Missing data points were assigned a value of 0.5.

In all cases, the input value to the network for missing data is 0.5. The intention is to represent a non-committal value to the network. It is hoped that by representing missing data in this way, we can take advantage of another valuable property of neural networks, default assignment. This is the ability of the network to fill-in missing information for one item based on similarities to other items. For example, let us assume that two of the data fields in the record are income and number of credit cards currently held. Let us also assume that low income individuals usually have very few credit cards held, and that our teaching data tends to reject applicants with low incomes. Default assignment will aid in classifying applicants even if the income field is missing by recognizing the relationship between income and credit cards held. Since the network was trained to reject low income applicants, and low income applicants tend to have fewer credit cards held, the network will also tend to reject applicants with few credit cards held in the absence of income information. In this way, the network is attempting to find a close match to the data upon which it was trained, even though the exact pattern was never explicitly learned.

Another approach to the credit evaluation problem would be to develop a set of rules in an expert system. Through knowledge engineering with human experts in credit evaluation, knowledge engineers could develop a knowledge base, or set of rules to be followed in order to decide whether an application is to be accepted or rejected. The neural network is essentially internalizing its own "rules", in the form of interconnective weight and threshold values, through an examination of existing data. Thus neural networks offer a means of developing expert systems without going through the time consuming knowledge engineering required for the development of explicit rules.

The raw data contained roughly 80% accepted applications. Initial attempts at training consisted of using this proportion in the training data. It was found that this resulted in a tendency for the network to accept everything, since it was getting reinforced 80% of the time when it accepted an application. Later training, using training data equally representing accepted and rejected records corrected this tendency.

It was also noted that performance on the testing data increased at first, as expected, as training progressed. However, if training continued, network performance gradually got worse. Figure 2 shows a typical relationship between training time and performance.

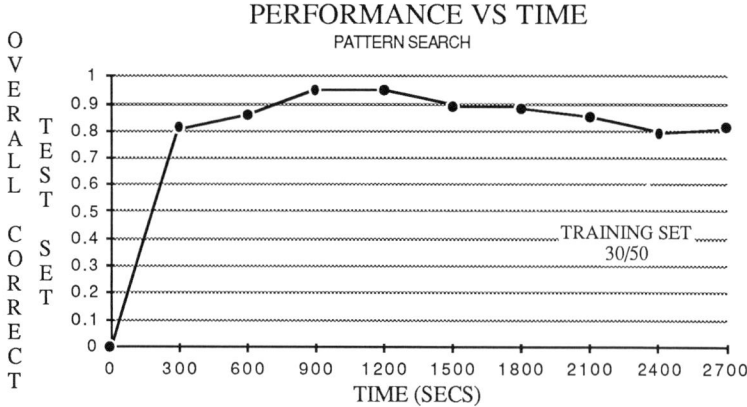

Figure 2. A typical learning curve for the credit evaluation problem. The performance of the network, in terms of the percentage of applications in a testing set correctly classified, first increases rapidly to a maximum, and then gradually tails off. The testing set contains applications which have not been used to train the network.

3. OR TOOLS APPLIED TO NEUROCOMPUTING

One popular neural network architecture is the semi-linear feed-forward network, which was used in the credit evaluation problem discussed above. The usual learning method used in this type of network is back-propagation [Rumelhart et al. 1986a; Jones 1987]. Back-propagation has been shown to implement a gradient descent in weight-space, reducing the total error between the actual and desired output patterns as the presentations of the input patterns continue. However, most examples of networks that have successfully learned these patterns involve very small problems, such as the exclusive-or

(XOR) logic problem, binary addition, simple encoding problems, and recognition of simple characters [Rumelhart et al. 1986a]. The learning time for larger real-world problems may prove to be prohibitive. For this reason supercomputers such as the Cray X-MP/24 may be useful in the learning phase of neural network implementation. After this computationally difficult phase, the resulting network produces its output quickly and can be moved to a PC for stand alone use. It can also be called as a subroutine by another program, or used as a form of knowledge representation or knowledge chunking within an expert system.

In an attempt to decrease the learning time, which can be significant, the learning problem is expressed as a non-linear optimization problem. Various operations research techniques exist to solve this type of problem, and some of them are attempted in this new context. One method, due to Hooke and Jeeves [1961], has been applied by the authors and resulted in up to an five-fold reduction in learning time in the XOR problem.

The Hooke and Jeeves algorithm is a searching technique for optima in unconstrained multidimensional space. The objective function used in our evaluation is the sum of the differences between the actual activation states of the output units in the final layer of the network, and their target values over all training presentations. See the appendix for the mathematical representation of the objective function. The solution space has one dimension for each interconnective weight and threshold value to be learned in the network.

The algorithm begins by randomly assigning a value to each weight or threshold, and then evaluating the value of the objective function at this point, which becomes the first base point. An exploration of solution space then takes place around the base point. This is accomplished by checking each dimension, in turn, for improvement in the objective function value. The weight or threshold value represented by one dimension is increased by a small amount (called the step size), and the objective function is evaluated. If improvement is found, the new value of the weight of threshold in question is adopted, and the exploration is continued on the next dimension. Otherwise, the weight or threshold value in question is decremented by the step size, and the objective function is evaluated. If an improvement is found, the new value of the weight or threshold is adopted. Otherwise the original value is kept. In either case the exploration procedure continues with the next dimension.

Once all dimensions have been explored in this manner, a new base is established at the final point in the exploration (assuming an improvement has been found in the objective function). At this point the algorithm employs a heuristic in an attempt to speed up the search. A pattern move is made in order to identify one particular point to evaluate for potential objective function improvement. This point is determined by first determining the vector from the next to last base point to the last base point and multiplying it by the pattern move size. If the move does indeed improve upon the objective function value, further exploratory moves are undertaken around the improved point. If not, exploration takes place around the last base point. The rationale is that further improvement is likely to be found in the same direction that has yielded past improvement.

The algorithm continues in this manner, a succession of explorations and pattern moves, until the explorations fail to identify any improvement in the objective function. At this point the exploratory step size is decreased, and the algorithm continues. When the exploratory step size reaches some preset minimum value, the algorithm terminates unsuccessfully. When the maximum error (difference between the activation of any output unit in any presentation and its target value) becomes less than a preset value, the algorithm terminates successfully.

The Hooke and Jeeves algorithm was tested against the standard back-propagation method on the well-studied XOR problem. Figure 3 shows the network structure used, and the patterns to be learned.

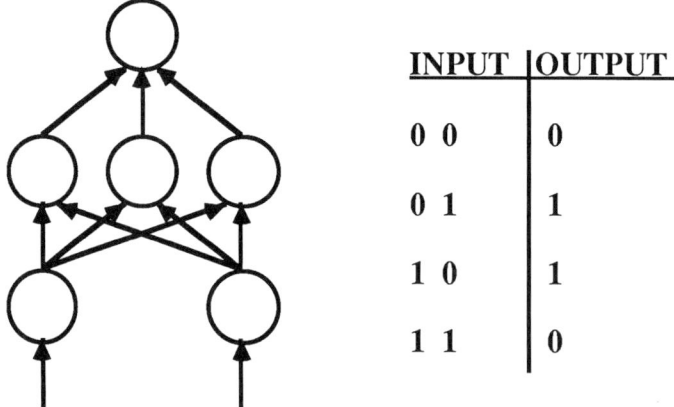

Figure 3. The network and patterns to be learned with for the Exclusive-OR problem.

Table 1 gives the results of one hundred runs of the exclusive-OR problem using back-propagation to learn weights. The number of iterations of the algorithm is reported. When the iteration count reached 2600, the algorithm was terminated unsuccessfully. This is denoted by an asterisk in the table. Table 2 shows the result of using the Hooke and Jeeves algorithm on the same problem, using the same random starting points. Here the number of objective function evaluations are reported for each trial. Again, unsuccessful trials are denoted by an asterisk.

The number of successful terminations in the Hooke and Jeeves version was 79 out of 100 trials. In order to have an equal basis for comparison, the termination condition for the back-propagation algorithm was set to 2600 iterations. This yielded an equivalent number of successes. Timings were done so that the iteration count of the back-propagation method could be compared to the evaluation count of the Hooke and Jeeves algorithm. The back-propagation method required an average of 5.96 seconds per successful solution. The 99% confidence interval for this mean is plus or minus 0.58 seconds. The Hooke and Jeeves algorithm required 1.09 seconds per solution, with a 99% confidence interval of plus or minus 0.14 seconds. On this problem, the Hooke and Jeeves searching method was 5.47 times faster in finding a set of weight and threshold values to represent the exclusive-OR network. For larger problems (e.g., the consumer credit problem described above), the Hooke-Jeeves method fails to scale up and doesn't perform as well as the standard pack-propagation model. Nonetheless, more efficient nonlinear minimization methods (e.g., conjugate gradient methods) may provide improvements over the gradient methods currently used in standard back-propagation models.

Table 1. Learning the Exclusive-OR problem through back-propagation.

Run	Iter	Run	Iter	Run	Iter	Run	Iter
1	999	26	1153	51	889	76	1479
2	2560	27	1351	52	903	77	2355
3	1087	28	*	53	1780	78	1705
4	990	29	1560	54	1234	79	1494
5	1698	30	1515	55	1120	80	*
6	*	31	732	56	2580	81	*
7	906	32	*	57	*	82	1087
8	1069	33	1507	58	2511	83	*
9	1186	34	1243	59	910	84	1653
10	1655	35	1180	60	1101	85	1476
11	2152	36	1623	61	1687	86	1524
12	1237	37	*	62	1779	87	*
13	916	38	1038	63	*	88	1214
14	*	39	*	64	1778	89	1458
15	868	40	1490	65	1547	90	1362
16	887	41	1253	66	*	91	*
17	1744	42	1006	67	2506	92	1007
18	*	43	1390	68	2253	93	737
19	*	44	1162	69	1471	94	*
20	969	45	997	70	970	95	*
21	1320	46	1203	71	896	96	921
22	1028	47	1456	72	1034	97	2479
23	1388	48	*	73	2425	98	*
24	1391	49	1615	74	919	99	1520
25	*	50	1713	75	832	100	871

Neurocomputing will have an impact on operations research because it offers the operations research practitioner a new tool that may be useful for solving problems that have been historically very difficult. Computationally difficult problems and problems that contain fuzzy data fall into this category. Neurocomputing also represents a new area of application for operations researchers since better algorithms are needed to implement learning if real-world problems are to be solved through neurocomputing.

Table 2. Learning the Exclusive-OR problem through Hooke and Jeeves.

Run	Eval	Run	Eval	Run	Eval	Run	Eval
1	225	26	497	51	438	76	349
2	108	27	401	52	178	77	554
3	89	28	334	53	247	78	676
4	261	29	758	54	486	79	186
5	178	30	491	55	565	80	700
6	106	31	340	56	642	81	551
7	118	32	*	57	300	82	521
8	*	33	1014	58	*	83	445
9	519	34	387	59	*	84	*
10	437	35	*	60	448	85	311
11	*	36	474	61	*	86	293
12	167	37	360	62	*	87	*
13	*	38	455	63	385	88	*
14	262	39	535	64	410	89	288
15	277	40	898	65	300	90	355
16	393	41	455	66	268	91	716
17	864	42	281	67	411	92	297
18	527	43	299	68	374	93	600
19	285	44	442	69	256	94	*
20	443	45	*	70	495	95	591
21	189	46	218	71	310	96	*
22	621	47	*	72	357	97	*
23	*	48	231	73	*	98	*
24	371	49	391	74	530	99	222
25	313	50	424	75	*	100	627

REFERENCES

Abu-Mostafa, Yasser S., and D. Psaltis (1987), "Optical Neural Computers," *Scientific American 256*, 3, 88-95.

Baum, E. (1988), "Neural Nets and Combinatorial Optimization," TIMS/ORSA National Meeting (Washington, D.C., Apr.)

Greenberg, H. (1988), "Tutorial on Learning Models in Optimization," TIMS/ORSA National Meeting, (Washington, D.C., Apr.)

Hooke, R. and T.A Jeeves (1961), "'Direct Search' Solution of Numerical and Statistical Problems," *Journal of the Association for Computing Machinery 8*, 2, 212-229.

Hopfield, J.J. and D.W. Tank (1986), "Computing with Neural Circuits: A Model," *Science, August 8*, 625-633.

Jones, W.P. and J. Hoskins (1987), "Back-Propagation," *Byte*, (Oct.), 155-162.

Jorgensen, C. and C. Matheus (1986), "Catching Knowledge in Neural Nets", *AI Expert*, (Dec.), 30-38.

Kinoshita, J. and N. Palevsky (1987), "Computing with Neural Networks", *High Technology*, (May), 24-31.

Madey, G. (1988), "The Use of Multiattribute Utility Theory in Rule Based Systems and Neural Networks", TIMS/ORSA National Meeting, (Washington, D.C., Apr.)

Madey, G. and J. Denton (1988), "Implications of Neurocomputing on OR/MS/IS," TIMS/ORSA National Meeting, (Washington, D.C., Apr.)

Madey, G. and J. Denton (1988), "Credit Evaluation with Missing Data Fields," In *Abstracts of First Annual INNS Meeting* (Boston, Mass., Sept. 6-10), Pergamon Press, New York, p. 456.

McClelland, J.L., D.E. Rumelhart, and G.E. Hinton (1986), "The Appeal of Parallel Distributed Processing," In *Parallel Distributed Processing: Explorations in the Microstructure of Cognition*, D.E. Rumelhart and J.L. McClelland, Eds. MIT Press, Cambridge, Mass.

Mort, M. (1988), "A Neural Network Architecture for the Management of Limited Resources", TIMS/ORSA National Meeting, (Washington, D.C., Apr.)

Pao, Y-H and D. Sobajic (1988), "Neural-Net Engineering and Applications", TIMS/ORSA National Meeting, (Washington, D.C., Apr.)

Rumelhart, D.E., G.E. Hinton, and R.J. Williams (1986), "Learning Internal Representations by Error Propagation", In *Parallel Distributed Processing: Explorations in the Microstructure of Cognition*, D.E. Rumelhart and J.L. McClelland, Eds. MIT Press, Cambridge, Mass.

Rumelhart, D.E. and J.L. McClelland (1986), "PDP Models and General Issues in Cognitive Science," In *Parallel Distributed Processing: Explorations in the Microstructure of Cognition*, D.E. Rumelhart and J.L. McClelland, Eds. MIT Press, Cambridge, Mass.

Sejnowski, T.J. and C.R. Rosenberg (1987), "Parallel Networks that Learn to Pronounce English Text," *Complex Systems 1*, 145-168.

Williamson, M. (1988), "Neural Networks: Glamor and Glitches," *Computerworld*, (Feb. 15), pp. 89-92.

APPENDIX

The learning problem in the feedforward network can be formulated as an unconstrained minimization problem in which threshold values and interconnective weights are the decision variables to be determined in order to minimize the sum of the squared error between the actual network output and the desired network output for all training presentations. Thus we seek to

$$\text{Minimize } E = \sum_p \sum_{i=1}^{n_k} (t_{pi} - a_{ki})^2 \quad (1)$$

where a_{ki} is computed recursively as

$$a_{ki} = \frac{1}{1 + e^{-\left(\theta_{ki} + \sum_{j=1}^{n_{k-1}} w_{kij} a_{k-1,j}\right)}} \quad (2)$$

with

$$a_{1i} = I_{pi}. \quad (3)$$

Also,
- t_{pi} is the desired output at node i in the final layer for training presentation p,
- I_{pi} is the training input at node i in the first layer for training presentation p,
- a_{ki} is the activation state of node i in layer k,
- θ_{ki} is the threshold of node i in layer k,
- w_{kij} is the weight from node i in layer k to node j in layer k - 1
- p is the index of the training presentation,
- i is the index of the node in layer k
- j is the index of a node in layer k - 1,
- n_k is the number of nodes in layer k
- k is the index of the layer in the network.

Evaluation of the objective function for a given set of weights and thresholds begins with the assignment of the training inputs to the activation states of the nodes in the initial layer, as shown in equation (3). Then equation (2) is recursively used to compute the activation states of the succeeding layers until the activation states of the nodes in the final layer are determined. The objective function value can then be computed from (1).

NEURAL NETWORKS FOR AN INTELLIGENT MATHEMATICAL PROGRAMMING SYSTEM

HARVEY J. GREENBERG
Mathematics Department
University of Colorado at Denver
Denver, CO 80204

ABSTRACT

This paper gives preliminary results on the application of neural networks to the design of an intelligent mathematical programming system. Three applications considered here are: model completion, discourse and rulebase generation.

1. INTRODUCTION

What is an *intelligent mathematical programming system*? What is a *neural network*? How does the latter apply to the former? These are the questions we shall answer here, beginning with some background.

For 40 years mathematical programming has been a powerful technique to support operational and planning decisions. Because of its wide scope of applications, linear programming (LP) is used by most major industries – petroleum, steel, forestry, manufacturing, communications, and banking – to support its decision-making. It became clear by the late 1950's that optimizers had to expand into database management and related support for modeling and analysis. This is when the *Mathematical Programming System* (MPS) took shape.

Due to the explosive growth of inexpensive computer power and to the highly successful applications during the 1960's, we can solve far larger problems that we can understand. The *Intelligent Mathematical Programming System* (IMPS) [Greenberg 1987a] is aimed at reconciling this deficiency and markedly extending computer assistance for model formulation, management and analysis.

To develop a truly new role for the computer as an *intelligent* participant in applied mathematical programming it has become necessary to return to basics and rethink what we mean by a model. At the simplest level a model is a collection of *objects* and *relations* among those objects. Without going further here, it suffices to note investigations into structural methodologies that deal exclusively with relational concepts, notably *structured modeling* [Geoffrion 1987], *graph inversion* [Greenberg, Lundgren and Maybee 1988], and the direct use of *expert systems* [Murphy and Stohr 1985]. All of these approaches have similar aims, but they are distinctly different. Collectively, they contribute to a foundation for creating an artificially intelligent environment to formulate and apply large-scale mathematical programming models.

The IMPS extends the traditional role of formulation, derived from a matrix-driven vantage, to interacting with some knowledge-bases. Its output includes rules and other representations of knowledge that can be used to support model management and analysis, especially in the problem domain. We thus begin to see the emergence of a system with multiple constituencies, and the interfaces comprise the *discourse module*.

Discourse is how the human communicates with the computer, and our objective is to orient this towards the human's problem domain rather than the traditional computer language. Natural language (English text) plus iconic-based graphics are the foundation upon which we have built both a syntactic and semantic translator, which is used in the ANALYZE rulebase development [Greenberg 1987c] and in the MODEL ASSISTANT.

Many argue that a system is not performing intelligent reasoning unless it has the capacity to *learn*. Indeed, this is an important break with traditional mathematical programming systems, and it is one of our most vital frontiers. Learning comes in different forms, depending upon what we wish to learn. A rulebase system can use logical methods, notably *generalization* and *specialization*, to revise its rulebase. This applies to some of the analysis we want an IMPS to do. Another learning model, which is really a family of models, is the *neural network*, inspired by how we believe our brain functions. That approach is the subject of this study.

A *neural network* is defined as a network, $N=[V,A]$, where V is a (finite) set of nodes and A is a set of arcs - i.e., an ordered pair of the form $<v_i, v_j>$ in $V*V$. We say the nodes represent *neurons*, or groups of neurons; and, the arcs represent a pattern of *connectivity* among the neurons. Associated with each node is a *state*, which may be continuous or discrete, usually called the *activity level*. Associated with each arc is a *weight*, which is one of the parameters we can control. With roots in the seminal works of [McCulloch and Pitts 1943; Rosenblatt 1959; Widrow and Hoff 1960; Grossberg 1976], we see by the recent works in [Rumelhart and McClelland 1986; Post 1988; Gallant 1988] (for examples) that neural networks provide a formal basis for associative memory.

Whereas the network defines the *structure* of the neural model, the associated values (node activity levels and arc weights) change according to the model's *dynamical equations*. Each activity level changes according to a function of not only its own current level, but also of its neighbors' levels and associated weights. The defining equation, usually expressed as a differential equation, is called an *activity rule*.

A *neural model* is the specification of the network, the initial states and weights, and the dynamical equations that govern the system's evolution. In addition, there may be a *learning equation*, which describes how weights change as a function of the current system state and, typically, some error feedback.

Each arc may be typed according to whether it is *excitatory* (i.e., increases the activity level of the head node) or *inhibitory* (i.e., decreases the activity level of the head node). Sometimes this distinction may be simply modeled by letting an arc weight become positive (excitatory), negative (inhibitory) or zero (no effect). There are cases, however, where it is useful to separate explicitly the arcs into types subjected to different learning equations or activity rules.

The general idea is to seek an *equilibrium state* – that is, where the state no longer changes. During learning, associations form, perhaps by the dynamics alone without explicit evaluation of the stimulus-response pairings. Such is *associative learning* [Kohonen 1987]. When an evaluation function is explicitly present, such as during *training*, learning is forced – that is, particular associations are formed, such as for pattern recognition. Once learning ceases, a process of *forgetting* may begin, followed (perhaps) by *relearning*.

One of the simplest neural networks is a bipartite graph with one set of n nodes representing input stimuli by its n-vector of activity levels, say x; and, the other set of m nodes representing output responses by its m-vector of activity levels, say y. Then, the $m*n$ weight matrix, W, is used to associate the pair by $y = Wx$. The problem is to specify W such that certain stimulus-response pairs, say $\{(x^i, y^i)\}$ for $i=1, \ldots, k$, are associated – i.e., $y^i = Wx^i$. In general, this set may be overdetermined (many i's) or underdetermined (few i's), so a least squares or distance criterion is used to choose W. This problem can be solved simply by computing the generalized inverse of $X = [x^1, \ldots, x^k]$ to obtain $W = YX^+$ (a projection). In neural computation we want to use dynamics to obtain convergence to this W. That is, the learning rule has the form: $DW = (y^i - Wx^i) + x^i$, where + means outer product, upon presentation of the i-th training pair (x^i, y^i). In words, we perform iterative improvement using the *error vector*, $y^i - Wx^i$, moving in a path driven by the negative gradient of the least squares function.

It is typical when specifying an energy function, whose stationary points correspond to equilibrium points, for there to be many local minima. In some cases the local minima are desirable, notably when they represent memory of patterns and we want an unknown pattern to propagate from its input specification to a *nearest* local minimum for classification. In other applications we seek a global minimum, thus requiring a procedure that does not simply converge to a local minimum (or, even worse, another type of stationary point). This can be achieved in theory by employing the Boltzmann Theorem for diffusion, relying on the physical analogue in thermodynamics.

Briefly, a neural model has the following ingredients.

Structure

+ A set of processing units, which comprise the *nodes* of the network.
+ A pattern of connectivity, which comprise the *arcs* of the network.

Spaces for control
+ A *state* of activity levels (for each node).
+ A knowledge of associations vested in arc *weights*.

Functions for Dynamics
+ An *activity rule*, which combines the level of a node with outputs of neighbor nodes and weights across respective arcs to produce a new activity level of the node and its firing value (output for next cycle).
+ *Learning equations*, which determine changes in arc weights as functions of the two levels of its endpoints and its current weight.

There are additional ingredients, such as constraints on activity levels, typically modeled with reflecting barriers or sigmoid functions. Another specification is whether to update states synchronously or asynchronously. A synchronous update means all equations use the current state, which inherently exploits an analog computer architecture. Asynchronous updates must further specify a rule for the order of making changes. One rule is by random selection, another is by most active node (ties broken randomly). The asynchronous dynamics take less advantage of massively parallel architecture, and neural computing tends to mean analog.

The pattern of connectivity may also specify *layers*, which is a grouping of nodes that restricts connections, and *clusters* within layers that have mutual inhibitory intra-cluster connections, which [Grossberg 1976] has shown how to achieve with *lateral inhibition*. Such added structure helps to design and analyze neural models for a wide variety of applications, including those for the IMPs, which we shall describe in the next section. The competitive learning models, like [Rumelhart and Zipser 1985], was a starting point for our use of *Adaptive Resonance Theory* (ART) [Carpenter and Grossberg 1988].

Almost all aspects of neural modeling are in a young stage, requiring a great deal of research. Even the meaning of a solution is questionable. Does the system converge? If so, to what does it converge, and how long does it take? Can we improve upon its convergence properties, particularly with a neural computer architecture? Are some equilibrium states unreachable? What are stability properties of equilibria? Such questions remain to be answered, even in the present context.

Now we consider the application of neural networks to three problems in the IMPs. The research is still in progress, so only the basic approach is described. Substantive results are expected after the preliminary experiments are concluded.

2. NEURAL NETS FOR IMPS

Model completion is the problem of finding a model that best fits partial information provided by the user. It can be viewed as essentially the same problem as in vision, described by Kohonen. In that case the neural model is designed for content-addressability - that is, a model library accessed by matching certain patterns in the partial specification. We shall modify this in two ways. First, unlike the recall problem, we want the model assistant to be able to form new models, not in the library. Second, we include a category feature, which is an index value with no meaning to scale.

To elaborate, consider a grid, as in an electronic blackboard, where each grid point is described by 2 state values: the *type* of icon and the *level* of its activity. This is mapped into an initial state of a neural network using t-node clusters to represent the 1 of t types (competitive neurons) and its activity level to represent the (continuous-valued) level. To illustrate, suppose there are 3 icons to represent production, conversion and marketing of some materials. With the null icon added we have 4-icon clusters in each grid location. Allowing for a grid of 12 *40, we have an input layer with 480 clusters, each having 4 nodes. (In graph-theoretic terms the cluster is K_4 with inhibitory arcs between distinct nodes and loops as excitatory arcs (i.e., laterally inhibitive).) Between clusters there are arcs whose weights reflect training of what types of icons (and level) tend to precede other types.

The combinatorial explosion is controlled in the use of associative mappings, but there is no apparent escape from the largeness of the neural network. Returning to Kohonen's model, we can remove the category index and have a network with $n*m$ nodes (1 per grid point) and represent the type of icon with activity levels. Kohonen has demonstrated that this (and modern descendants) are very effective for pattern recall, but little is known whether it can generate new patterns (i.e., models) as a rulebased system could do. The work of Gallant should prove especially valuable with the experiments in progress.

Discourse mappings may include icon-to-algebra mappings, as in the model completion problem. More generally, the problem is purely associative: how can we separate some mixture of text, icons and algebra into a triple of pure text, pure icons and pure algebra that comprise different representations of the same problem? Some of this is done presently when we map a structure-driven representation, which uses a mixture of text and algebra, to a matrix (that is, the standard input to an optimizer), which is purely algebraic. The Graphics-Based Modeling System (GBMS) [Jones 1988a,b] is another example of mapping one form of discourse to another. Text composition, already a part of ANALYZE, stems from the syntax that has been a part of linear programming for 30 years, and one semantic model, based on economic activity analysis for closed, simple exchange, was considered by [Greenberg 1987b]. No system currently solves the complete problem of discourse mappings.

One possible neural model is to let the network be composed of three layers, representing icons, text and algebra as follows. In the icon layer, define clusters with t+1 nodes in each cluster (as before, to represent t types of icons plus the null icon) over some grid, which is now 3-dimensional to account for pages (i.e., adjacent screens). Connections between clusters reflect modeling rules, such as *production feeds materials into either conversion or marketing*. In other words, if we take a node from each cluster (possibly the null icon), we can apply causal analysis to create links that then give a graphic representation of a model.

In the text layer we can use schema theory [Rumelhart, Smolensky, McClelland and Hinton 1986; Gelman and Hirst 1987; Beaver and Pope 1988] to represent elements of an MBA vocabulary (for example) and sentence structures to describe a problem. (An early example of this is PLANETS [Lucas 1974].) Key words, like *production, marketing* and *process*, may be linked to their counterparts in the icon layer. Inter-text links reflect a natural language model, like in [Sowa 1984].

Finally, the algebraic layer has a node for each activity class in the linear program and for each constraining row. This layer is a bipartite graph that represents the fundamental digraph of the LP. Its nodes are connected with those of the icon and text layers through training. In other words, the algebraic connections are *learned* for a particular modeling environment.

Rulebase generation is the problem of generating rules (context free) to support analysis or model management. A first effort is simply to attach this to the library, and use model completion. Potentially, however, it may be possible to create new rulebases for models not yet resident in the library. Exactly how this might be done is under study.

3. CONCLUSIONS

Neural networks are possible models for associative mappings to give intelligence support for modeling and discourse. Its potential for analysis support, such as diagnosing infeasibility, remains uncharted. Recent efforts in the IMPS Project have focused on its value in the MODEL ASSISTANT, notably for model completion. For discourse mappings, there is already a sharply growing literature for natural language processing (text and speech). The present efforts, together with the major thrust taken by hundreds of others, suggest the future is in associative, massively parallel architecture and in training, rather than conventional programming, to achieve a substantial part of our goal. All of these characteristics distinguish the neural network and related connectionist models (like cellular automata).

REFERENCES

S. Beaver and M. Pope (1988), "Applying a Neural Network to Goal Relaxation," In *Mathematics Clinic Final Report: Neural Networks and Artificial Intelligence*, H.J. Greenberg (Ed.), University of Colorado at Denver, Denver, Colo., Dec.

G. Carpenter and S. Grossberg (1988), "The ART of Adaptive Pattern Recognition by a Self-Organizing Neural Network," *IEEE Computer* 21, 77-88.

S.I. Gallant (1988), "Connectionist Expert Systems," *Communications of the ACM* 31:2, 152-169.

B. Gelman and G. Hirst (1987), "Parsing as an Energy Minimization Problem," In *Genetic Algorithms and Simulated Annealing*, L. Davis (Ed.), Morgan Kaufmann, pp. 141-154.

A.M. Geoffrion (1987), "An Introduction to Structured Modeling," *Management Science* 33, 547-588.

F. Glover and H.J. Greenberg (1987), "Netforms Provide Powerful Tools for Enhancing the Operations of Expert Systems," *Proceedings of the Rocky Mountain Conference on Artificial Intelligence*, Boulder, CO, 259-265.

H.J. Greenberg (1983), "A Functional Description of ANALYZE: A Computer-Assisted Analysis System for Linear Programming Models," *ACM Transactions On Mathematical Software* 9, 18-56.

H.J. Greenberg (1987a), "Development of an Intelligent Mathematical Programming System," WORMSC *Proceedings*, Washington, D.C., Nov.

H.J. Greenberg (1987b), "A Natural Language Discourse Model to Explain Linear Programs," *Decision Support Systems* 33, 333-342.

H.J. Greenberg (1987c), "ANALYZE: A Computer-Assisted Analysis System for Linear Programming Models," *Operations Research Letters* 6, 249-255.

H.J. Greenberg, J.R. Lundgren and J.S. Maybee (1988), "Extensions of Graph Inversion to Support an Artificially Intelligent Modeling Environment," *Annals of Operations Research* (to appear).

S. Grossberg (1976), "Adaptive Pattern Classification and Universal Recoding Part I: Parallel Development and Coding of Neural Feature Detectors," *Biological Cybernetics* 23, 121-134.

C.V. Jones (1988), "An Introduction to Graph-Based Modeling Systems," Technical Report 88-10-02, The Wharton School, University of Pennsylvania, Philadelphia, Penn.

C.V. Jones (1988), "Applications of a Graph-Based Modeling System (GBMS)," Technical Report 88-10-03, The Wharton School, University of Pennsylvania, Philadelphia, Penn.

T. Kohonen (1987), *Self Organization and Associative Memory* (2nd ed.), Springer-Verlag, Berlin, FRG.

J. Lucas (1974), "PLANETS," Technical Report, General Motors, Troy, Mich.

W.S. McCulloch and W. Pitts (1943), "A Logical Calculus of the Ideas Immanent in Nervous Activity," *Bulletin of Mathematical Biophysics* 5, 115-133.

F.H. Murphy and E.A. Stohr (1985), "An Intelligent System for Formulating Linear Programs," *Decision Support Systems* 2, 39-47.

R. Rosenblatt (1959), *Principles of Neurodynamics*, Spartan Books, New York.

D.E. Rumelhart and J.L. McClelland (eds.) (1986), *Parallel Distributed Processing: Explorations in the Microstructure of Cognition*, Volume 1: *Foundations*, MIT Press, Cambridge, Mass.

D.E. Rumelhart and D. Zipser (1985), "Feature Discovery by Competitive Learning," *Cognitive Science* 9, 75-112 (see also Chapter 5 in [Rumelhart and McClelland 1986]).

H.A. Simon (1959), *Models of Thought*, Yale University Press, New Haven, Conn.

J.F. Sowa (1984) *Conceptual Information Processing*, North-Holland, Amsterdam, Holland.

B. Widrow and M.E. Hoff, Jr. (1960), "Adaptive switching Circuits," *IRE WESCON Conv. Rec.*, Part 4, 96-104.

THE COMPUTER AS A PARTNER IN ALGORITHMIC DESIGN: AUTOMATED DISCOVERY OF PARAMETERS FOR A MULTI-OBJECTIVE SCHEDULING HEURISTIC

MICHAEL R. HILLIARD AND GUNAR E. LIEPINS
Oak Ridge National Laboratory[*]
Bldg 4500N, P.O. Box 2008
Oak Ridge, TN 37831-6179

MARK PALMER AND GITA RANGARAJEN
University of Tennessee
Knoxville, TN 37996

ABSTRACT

Many scheduling problems are so complex that optimization techniques cannot be used; an heuristic approach is required. Additionally, the problem is often multi-objective: minimize distance travelled and delay. Using a military airlift scheduling heuristic as an example, we show how the machine learning branch of artificial intelligence provides a technique to discover the settings of the parameters that control the heuristic search and lead to non-dominated solutions. The technique is a modification of the genetic algorithm and evolves a population of parameter vectors suited to various combinations of the objectives. The research highlights the usefulness of artificial intelligence and parallel processing in algorithm design.

1. THE ROLE OF HEURISTICS

As we expand the role of computers in society, the need for algorithmic procedures specific to individual problems increases. Real world problems involve numerous constraints and objectives which cannot be easily modeled using classic optimization techniques. These problems are best solved by heuristic procedures specifically tailored or significantly modified for the particular application.

[*] *Operated by Martin Marietta Energy Systems for the Department of Energy under contract No. DE-AC05-84OR21400*

Developing useful heuristics is difficult when they are "tuned" by parameters and when the solutions generated by the heuristic are evaluated on multiple criteria.

Many heuristics consider problem solving as a search guided by approximate evaluations of solutions or partial solutions. Consider the class of heuristics which search a tree of partial solutions using an evaluation function f() to provide an approximate value for exploring a particular branch of the search tree. While the function f() may not be an accurate bound on the best solution in the sub-tree with which it is associated, it is expected to provide a "good guess" at the value. The "guess" should be good enough to allow the system in most cases to choose the better branches to explore. This heuristic search procedure is popular in game playing programs as well as in algorithmic formulations for problems that defy analytical evaluation. In the case of the scheduling algorithm for the Military Airlift Command, the function f() involves numeric parameters which the designer has no analytical method to determine. In this situation the parameters are typically either left for the user to set, based on little guidance, or the parameters are set using constants which seem to work well based on the designer's experience with (often limited) test sets.

Many algorithms leave parameters to be chosen by the user. For example, some hill climbing techniques require step size and desired accuracy, simulated annealing requires initial temperature and a cooling schedule, and the genetic algorithm requires parameters such as population size and crossover rate to be set by the user.

2. MULTI-OBJECTIVE EVALUATIONS

In most applications, the solution determined by any algorithm will be evaluated on multiple objectives. Since different values of the algorithm parameters may result in different solutions for a given data set, the problem becomes how to find a collection of parameter settings which produce "good" solutions. Assuming that the user's decision is based solely on the values of the objectives, producing "good" solutions implies choosing undominated solutions. If we can produce such a collection of parameter settings, then the user can choose among the parameter settings based on the subjective criteria involved in multi-objective decision making. If the collection of parameters has been derived by using a representative set of problems, and the user wants to increase one objective and decrease another, selection of the appropriate parameters from the collection should produce a new solution meeting that criteria.

3. THE MAC PROBLEM

The Military Airlift Command (MAC) uses scheduling algorithms to manage the deployment of military forces. A schedule may require hundreds of planes moving thousands of troops and hundreds of thousands of tons of cargo over a three month period. Solving these scheduling problems requires an heuristic approach since it involves an airlift system model that exceeds the range of practical applications of known optimization techniques. The scheduling problem is also complex in that it is multi-objective: distance travelled and the lateness of any delayed forces must both be minimized with different emphases during different scenarios. The Oak Ridge National Laboratory (ORNL) is developing a new generation scheduling system called the Airlift Deployment Analysis System, ADANS, to meet MAC's needs in planning such deployments.

3.1 The Need for Multi-objective Evaluation

A schedule for a deployment may be a war plan used for analysis, an exercise schedule carefully worked out in advance, or a schedule for an actual military crisis. Planners evaluate each of these types of plans using several objectives including such measures as percent of requirements delivered on time, percent of aircraft capability used, total cost, and smoothness of the delivery profile. The relative importance of the various objectives depends upon the particular scenario being supported. Cost and lateness are of primary interest in an exercise, but a crisis situation will require emphasis on timely delivery and smoothness of the delivery profile. We have chosen two major objectives to illustrate the parameter tuning technique, total delay, and total cost (which is proportional to distance flown). These two criteria capture the objectives of efficiency and effectiveness--the fundamental tradeoff in many multi-objective problems.

3.2 The ADANS Scheduling Algorithm

The ADANS scheduling algorithm requires as input, information on the aircraft available, the capabilities of the airfields to be used, and movement requirements (the amount of equipment and number of troops to be moved, the origin and destination of the move, available to load date, and required delivery date). The algorithm uses an insertion based heuristic similar to one developed for scheduling urban dial-a-ride systems [Jaw, 1986]. The movement requirements are ordered by priority and timing and are considered sequentially. For each requirement, the system may determine several ways to insert the pick-up and delivery into the itinerary for a plane. The collection of all possible insertions on all suitable planes constitutes the set of candidate insertions.

The system must then decide which candidate is the "best" choice. To measure the relative goodness of the insertions, the system measures the following four quantities:

f_1 - The additional distance flown

f_2 - The additional delay incurred

f_3 - The percentage of the requirement which can be carried on this plane (some requirements may necessitate the use of multiple aircraft)

f_4 - The percentage of the available aircraft space used.

Each insertion possibility is scored by a weighted sum of the four factors $f=(w_1f_1 + w_2f_2 - w_3f_3 - w_4f_4)$, and the insertion with the lowest score is chosen. By repeating this process, and never backtracking, the algorithm schedules all the requirements.

3.3 Controlling the Heuristic

One method of "tuning" the heuristic to a particular trade-off between objectives is to modify the four weights influencing the heuristic's insertion choice. A user trying to set the weights to achieve a particular trade-off between efficiency and effectiveness can easily become frustrated by the sometimes seemingly inconsistent relationship between the weights and the total distance travelled or the total delay. The discovery of the relationship between the four dimensional weight space (three dimensional if the weights are normalized) and the one dimensional trade-off curve in the objective space is therefore essential. An automated discovery technique provides a method for creating a linear ordering of weight vectors progressing from sets which emphasize minimal cost to those emphasizing minimal delay.

4. THE MULTI-OBJECTIVE GENETIC ALGORITHM

The genetic algorithm is a "pseudo-random" search operator which provides a means to search poorly understood, irregular spaces. John Holland developed the genetic algorithm and provided its theoretical foundation in *Adaptation in Natural and Artificial Systems* (1975). Holland's formulation was motivated by the observation that reproduction in conjunction with the pressure of natural selection has developed species remarkably well adapted to their environment. The breakthrough contribution that set his formulation apart from those of predecessors was the central role played by the crossover operator as the discovery mechanism; mutation is an infrequent operator, used primarily to preserve population diversity. Although Holland was not able to prove convergence theorems for genetic algorithms, he did prove one theorem about the efficiency of the technique--the genetic algorithm optimally allocates trials to the hyperplanes of the search space and, in this sense, it is optimal.

4.1 The Genetic Algorithm Cycle

Although there are many possible variants of the basic genetic algorithm, the fundamental underlying mechanism is relatively standard and consists of three basic operations: (1) evaluation of individuals in the population, (2) formation of a gene pool, and (3) recombination and mutation. The individuals resulting from these three operations form the next generation's population (see figure 1). The process is iterated until the system ceases to improve. (Usually at this time, the population has converged to a few well performing individuals.) Generally, each individual in the population is represented by a binary string which encodes a solution to the problem. The population size remains fixed from generation to generation and is typically between 50 and 200 individuals. Individuals contribute to the gene pool in proportion to their relative merit (function evaluation divided by average evaluation) on the function being optimized, that is, well performing individuals contribute multiple copies, and poorly performing individuals contribute few (if any) copies (see figure 2). The recombination operation is the crossover operator, which selects two parents at random from the gene pool and a crossover position within the binary encoding. The parents exchange tails, the portion of the string to the right of the crossover point, to generate two offspring (see figure 3). Mutation is a probabilistic operator which changes each position on a string with a small probability, usually in the .01 range (see figure 4). The strings generated by crossover and mutation form the new population. A thorough introduction to genetic algorithms is provided in [Goldberg 1988], and public domain code is available [Grefenstette 1984]. The proceedings of two international conferences provide a useful overview of current research [Grefenstette 1985, 1987].

4.2 An Example of the Genetic Algorithm

As a simplistic example of a genetic algorithm application, consider maximizing the function $f(x) = 1-x^2$ where the variable x is restricted to belong to the interval [0 , 1]. Assume that the population size is fixed at four and that a four-bit binary representation is chosen. Then one possible cycle is illustrated in Figure 5.

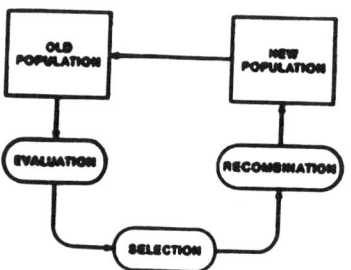

Figure 1. The Genetic Algorithm Cycle

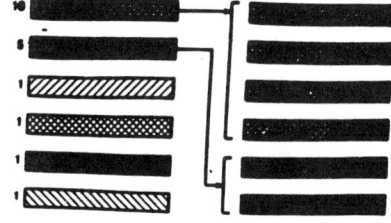

Figure 2. Selection is proportional to relative merit.

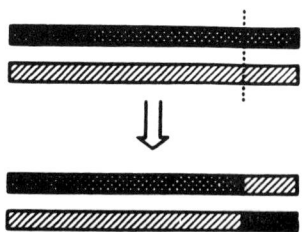

Figure 3. Pairs of strings exchange tails in crossover.

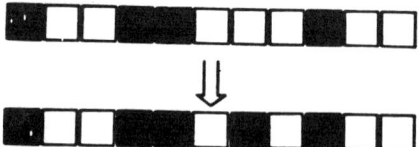

Figure 4. Mutation preserves population diversity.

X-Value	Old Population	Function Evaluation	Relative Merit	Gene Pool	New Population
1/16	0 0 0 1	.996	1.27	0 0 I 0 1	0 0 0 0
1/4	0 1 0 0	.938	1.20	0 1 I 0 0	0 1 0 1
3/16	0 0 1 1	.965	1.23	0 I 0 1 1	0 0 1 1
7/8	1 1 1 0	.234	0.30	0 I 0 1 1	0 0 1 1
		Average = .7833			

Function Evaluation at $X = 1/16$.
$1-(1/16)^2 = .966$

Relative Merit at $X = 1/16$
$.966/.7833 = 1.27$

Figure 5. One Genetic Algorithm Cycle for $f(x) = 1 - x^2$

4.3 Multi-objective Genetic Algorithms

There are two multi-objective implementations of the genetic algorithm. The first implementation was VEGA, the vector evaluated genetic algorithm [Schaffer, 1985]. The VEGA formulation partitions the gene pool into equally sized subpools, one for each objective, and fills each subpool by selecting from the current population based on that subpool's objective function. The VEGA methodology is equivalent to using an adaptive linear combination of the objective functions for evaluation.

In contrast, the Pareto genetic algorithm selects individuals based on the dominance relationships in the population. If we assume each of the objectives is to be minimized, then $z=(z_1,z_2,...,z_n)$ is undominated if there does not exist a $z'=(z'_1,z'_2,...,z'_n)$ such that $z'_i \leq z_i$ for all i and $z'_j < z_j$ for some j. The set of all undominated population members constitute the first Pareto front. If those members on the first Pareto front are removed from the population, the population members undominated by the remaining members of the population form the second Pareto front. This process is continued until all members of the population have been placed on fronts. Each of the fronts is given a decreasing function evaluation, and the process of selection continues as in a standard genetic algorithm with each population member being selected based on the evaluation associated with its front. This method prevents the linearization of the comparison and relies on the objective values only through the dominance relationship. We have also conducted experiments using this technique to deal with constrained optimization problems by considering the satisfaction of constraints as one objective [Liepins, et. al., 1988].

5. EXPERIMENTS WITH THE ADANS SCHEDULER

5.1 A Parallel Implementation of the Genetic Algorithm

We implemented a parallel version of the genetic algorithm to determine undominated fronts of weight vectors for the ADANS scheduler. The population consisted of 32 bit binary strings representing weight vectors. During evaluation, the system decomposed each population member into four 8-bit strings, producing the four weight values w_1, w_2, w_3, and w_4 each ranging from zero to 255, and the ADANS algorithm was used to schedule a test set of requirements using the ranking function determined by the four weights. The scheduling code was implemented in FORTRAN on each node of an Intel iPSC/2 Hypercube parallel processing computer, providing simultaneous evaluation of up to sixty- four members of the population. The genetic algorithm was implemented in C on the host machine and used the results of the scheduler (delay and cost) as input.

Occasionally a set of weights created a schedule which would not deliver all of the requirements. To maintain the partial information provided by these individuals yet discourage their appearance in the population, the scheduler returned the values:

$$delay = D + pUD/S$$
$$cost = C + pUC/S$$

where D = delay of scheduled cargo
          C = cost of scheduled cargo
          U = amount of unscheduled cargo
          S = amount of scheduled cargo
          p = penalty factor.

It is important to create such a function since the genetic algorithm can profit from the partial information provided by the values if the penalty function is not too severe [Liepins et. al., 1988].

5.2 Comparison of Techniques

To provide a comparison, three techniques were used--the Pareto genetic algorithm, VEGA, and a random search through the weight vector space. The system maintained a front representing the undominated weight vectors found so far, and these fronts are represented in Figures 6, 7 and 8. Each of the three techniques were run until 1000 new individuals had been evaluated. Since the random search

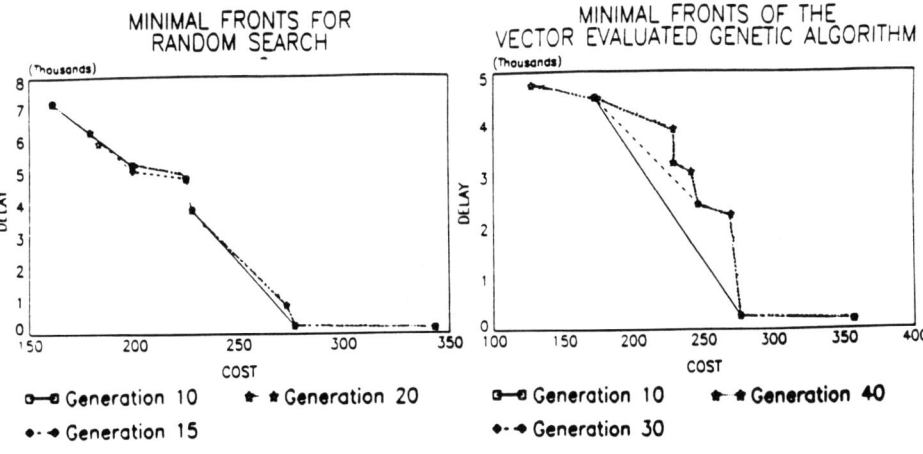

Figure 6. Evolution of minimal front through random search.

Figure 7. Evolution of minimal front using VEGA.

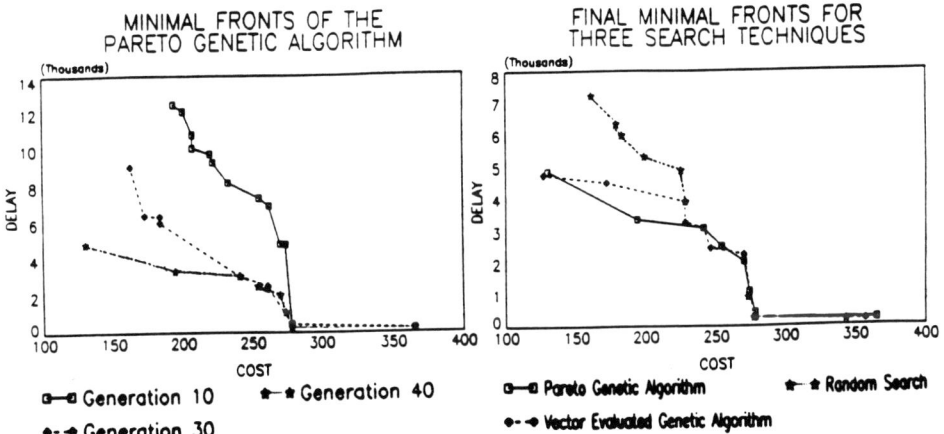

Figure 8. Evolution of minimal front using Pareto genetic algorithm.

Figure 9. Comparison of minimal fronts for the three techniques.

generated a completely new population at each generation, that technique ran for 30 generations. The VEGA and Pareto formulations do not replace the entire population at each generation, and thus ran for 56 generations. Figure 9 provides a comparison of the final fronts generated by the three search techniques. The graph shows that both of the multi-objective techniques perform better than random search. Judging qualitatively, based on this and other experiments, the Pareto technique seems to be comparable or slightly dominant to the VEGA technique, but this cannot be quantified until further experiments are conducted.

While encouraging, our results merely provide a preliminary proof of concept. In application, the weight vectors on the undominated front would have to work well over an entire class of problems, rather than a single test problem.

6. SUMMARY

The use of the genetic algorithm as a tool for discovering good parameters for heuristics seems to be promising. The technique provides a means for the computer to become a partner in the development of heuristic algorithms where the setting of parameters is often one of the most critical design decisions. This pairing of the novel discovery mechanism of the genetic algorithm with the parallel processing architecture provides an interesting tool to assist the algorithm developer.

ACKNOWLEDGEMENTS

The authors wish to express their sincere appreciation to Charles Bowman for assisting in the modifications to the ADANS scheduling code to provide the interface to the genetic algorithm. The concept of the Pareto genetic Algorithm arose during discussions with David Goldberg of the University of Alabama, and we appreciate his contribution to the formulation of the concept.

REFERENCES

Goldberg, D.D. (1989), *Genetic Algorithms in Search, Optimization, and Machine Learning*, Addison-Wesley, Reading, Mass.

Grefenstette, J.J. (1984), *A User's Guide to Genesis*, Technical Report CS-84-11, Computer Science Department, Vanderbilt University, Nashville, Tenn.

Grefenstette, J.J. (1985), (ed.), *Proceedings of an International Conference on Genetic Algorithms and Their Applications* (Carnegie-Mellon Univ., Pittsburg, Penn., July 24-26).

Grefenstette, J.J. (1987), (ed.), *Genetic Algorithms and Their Applications: Proceedings of the Second International Conference* (MIT, Cambridge, Mass., July 28-31) Lawrence Erlbaum Associates.

Holland, J.H. (1975), *Adaptation in Natural and Artificial Systems*, University of Michigan Press, Ann Arbor, Mich.

Jaw, J.J., A.R. Odoni, H.N. Psaraftis, and N.H.M. Wilson (1986), "A Heuristic Algorithm for the Multi-Vehicle Advance Request Dial-A-Ride Problem with Time Windows,"*Transportation Research B, 20B, No. 3*, 243-257.

Liepins, G.E., M.R. Hilliard, J. Richardson, and M. Palmer (1988), "Genetic Algorithms as Pseudo Random Search Operators" (to appear).

Schaffer, J.D. and J.J. Grefenstette (1985). "Multi-objective Learning via Genetic Algorithms," in *Proceedings of the Ninth International Joint Conference on Artificial Intelligence*, (Los Angeles, CA, Aug. 18-23), Morgan Kaufman, 593-595.

FLEXIBLE SYSTEMS FOR THE DESIGN OF HEURISTIC ALGORITHMS IN COMPLEX OR DOMAINS

JEAN-YVES POTVIN AND STEPHEN F. SMITH
The Robotics Institute, Carnegie Mellon University
Pittsburgh, Pennsylvania 15213

ABSTRACT

Over time, a rich corpus of heuristic strategies has been developed to solve complex OR problems. However, the design of heuristic strategies that perform well in complex problem domains remains a difficult problem. The performance of a specific strategy (or collection of strategies) can vary considerably from one problem to the next, and the designer must somehow acquire knowledge relating characteristics of the problem at hand to the appropriateness of various alternatives. To facilitate this process, this paper advocates a "design through experimentation" methodology based on the use of flexible interactive software tools. With such tools, it becomes possible to quickly configure different heuristic strategies and examine their performance in different problem solving contexts. The expertise gained in this experimentation can then be encoded to produce systems capable of automatically constructing resolution strategies well suited to the problems to be solved. We describe two systems offering facilities for the design of new heuristic algorithms: OPIS, a factory scheduling system and ALTO, a system for the design of vehicle routing heuristics.

1. INTRODUCTION

It is well known that many problems considered by the field of Operations Research (OR) are NP-complete and therefore cannot be solved optimally in polynomial time. This is a major obstacle, particularly in addressing "real world" instances of these problems. As a matter of fact, in factory scheduling and vehicle routing, the domains of interest in our work, specific problems are typically large, complex, and involve the satisfaction of idiosyncratic sets of constraints. To solve such problems, researchers have developed over time a rich corpus of heuristic strategies [Bodin et al. 83, Panwalker and Iskander 77]. Some of these heuristics perform very well, particularly when they are designed to solve loosely constrained problems. There exist, for example, many heuristics for the Traveling Salesman Problem (TSP) and some of them produce optimal or near-optimal results most of the time (apart from some pathological "worst case" problems) [Rosenkrantz et al. 77]. However, the availability of good heuristic resolution strategies drops quickly when the complexity of the problem increases. For example, few

Copyright 1989 by Elsevier Science Publishing Co., Inc.
Impacts of Recent Computer Advances on Operations Research
Ramesh Sharda, Bruce L. Golden, Edward Wasil, Osman Balci, William Stewart, Editors

heuristics are known to solve a TSP problem with single time windows, and those heuristics are very sensitive to specific characteristics of the problem (e.g. the distribution of the time windows over the time line and their width) [Bodin et al. 83].

The major difficulty here stems from an inability to deduce the kind of heuristic strategies that will perform well given the characteristics of the problem at hand. Indeed, even two distinct instances of a given generic problem can in some way be so "different" that a heuristic strategy that performs well on one instance will fail when applied to the other. This is the case, for example, in capacity-constrained vehicle routing problems. If the constraints are very tight, then the sparseness of feasible solutions requires an assignment-like type of approach. On the other hand, if capacity constraints are loose, there is no need for such an approach since feasible solutions can easily be identified.

The lack of the basic expertise needed to deduce an appropriate resolution strategy from the characteristics of the problem at hand, particularly for complex, real world problems like the routing of transportation vehicles or the scheduling of jobs in a factory, impairs the development of expert systems in those areas. A necessary first step toward this ultimate goal is the creation of flexible interactive tools facilitating the design and experimentation of new heuristic strategies. With these tools, researchers can quickly configure new heuristic strategies and evaluate their effectiveness on different instances of a given generic problem, thus enabling development of the expertise necessary to derive a good heuristic strategy. The expertise, once collected, can then be incorporated into the final expert system, allowing it to automatically construct appropriate heuristic strategies in particular problem solving contexts.

The idea of allowing an expert user to be part of the problem solving process is not a new one and has already provided some interesting results in the field of OR [Cullen et al. 81, Krolak et al. 72, Muller et al. 87]. However, the state of the computer technology has always been a major obstacle for further progress. The breakthrough of new technologies and techniques in the field of Artificial Intelligence (AI) now allows OR researchers to work with the types of hardware and software environments needed to implement sophisticated and flexible interfaces between the user and the computerized system. Hence, it is now possible to widen the involvement of the user during the problem solving process and to allow him/her to dynamically orient the resolution process as partial solutions are built up.

2. FLEXIBLE SYSTEMS FOR THE DESIGN OF HEURISTIC ALGORITHMS

2.1 An Incremental Methodology for Heuristic Algorithm Design

Historically, the design of heuristic resolution strategies for specific problems has been treated as a problem analysis task carried out well in advance of any experimentation. An attempt is made to understand the structure of the problem, and on the basis of this analysis a specific solution procedure is formulated. In complex, real-world problems, this often implies commitments as to how the problem is to be decomposed (or partitioned) into subproblems and in what order the subproblems will be solved as well as the specific heuristic procedures to be employed [Ferland et al. 85, Rousseau and Blais 85]. It is only after these commitments have been made that implementation of the actual problem solving system and experimentation with the heuristic strategy takes place.

While we are certainly not in disagreement with the need for initial problem analysis, we can identify several difficulties with this traditional problem solving methodology:

- In complex problem domains, it is difficult to anticipate the behavior of a specific heuristic procedure across the full range of problems that it must address, let alone a larger heuristic strategy that combines problem decomposition assumptions and several heuristic procedures.
- It is quite often the case that no single heuristic procedure or strategy is adequate in all situations, and the differential use of distinct procedures/strategies, driven by characteristics of the problem at hand, is required to achieve a good solution. Such context-dependent heuristic strategies are even more difficult to analytically realize, and are rarely even considered.
- A priori commitment to a completely specified resolution procedure advocates a "closed design" implementation philosophy. Systems are developed to function as "black box" solutions to the end user, with no provision for subsequent extension or revision of the resolution procedure. Given the first two problems identified above, this implementation philosophy further exacerbates the design problem.

In large part, reliance on a sequential "design/implement" approach to problem solving has been due to the lack of adequate support for alternative design methodologies. However, recent advances in the field of AI have changed this situation, and it is now possible to consider other alternatives. Of particular interest in overcoming the difficulties identified above is a methodology for heuristic strategy design that emphasizes experimentation *during* the design process. Under this approach, heuristic strategies are determined incrementally as problem solving experience in the application domain is accumulated. Such a "design through experimentation" methodology is enabled by the development of interactive software environments (or tools) that facilitate specification and analysis of design alternatives relative to a particular problem domain. We refer to such tools as *Strategy Design Systems* (SDS).

In considering the concept of SDSs in more detail, we can identify two distinct levels at which decision-making support for incremental heuristic strategy design is required:

- *heuristic procedure level* - At the heuristic procedure level, the designer's concern is to specify the behavior of the basic heuristic procedure or procedures to be used in solving the problem at hand. To this end, a SDS provides support in the form of a set of basic building blocks which can be instantiated to realize different heuristic behaviors. The identification and definition of appropriate building blocks within the SDS is obviously not an easy task, depending both on the application under consideration and the degree of generality that is intended. At one extreme, instantiation might simply require parameterization of a well-defined set of procedures. This is the case within the OPIS scheduling system described in Section 3. Other design applications require greater flexibility in the specification of heuristic procedures. The ALTO system described in Section 4 provides general templates that enable the definition of a wide variety of vehicle routing heuristics.

- *resolution planning level* - At the higher resolution planning level, the designer's concern is to construct a problem solving plan that will confront the problems to be solved in the most effective way (i.e. make the most effective use of the basic heuristic procedures that have been specified). In the vehicle routing domain, for example, a plan might be (1) generate seed nodes using *heuristic 1*, (2) generate node clusters centered around these seed nodes using *heuristic 2*, and (3) resequence the nodes in each cluster using *heuristic 3*. Of course, the plan may be more complex, specifying actions that are contingent on characteristics of the current problem solving state. At this level, the SDS provides a flexible environment for interactive problem solving, enabling the user to examine the behavior of both individual heuristic procedures and composite heuristic strategies while solving specific instances of the problem under consideration. The current problem solving state can be examined at any point to better understand the context sensitivity of different procedures to problem characteristics and incrementally determine which procedure or set of procedures should be applied next.

SDSs, then, provide a set of building blocks (i.e. a set of primitives for specifying basic heuristic procedures), that are instantiated and composed by the user to create different resolution strategies. The nature of these building blocks can range from specific parameterized heuristic procedures to general templates providing guidelines to the user in creating specific heuristic procedures. The development of a composite heuristic strategy (a resolution plan dictating the manner in which specified procedures are to be employed) is viewed as the outcome of a learning process. This is accomplished through experimentation with different alternatives in the context of solving particular problems. The results of this experimentation then provide the basis for implementation of the final problem solving system. In some cases (e.g. the OPIS system), the SDS itself provides a framework for directly encoding the final resolution plan in an executable form.

2.2 Benefits of the incremental methodology

The flexibility introduced in the incremental approach to problem solving can be exploited either by a human user or by a control module embedded in the computerized system. The aim of this paper, as well as the examples provided in the following sections, concerns SDSs intended to human users as a vehicle for extending their problem solving expertise in complex problem domains. To our knowledge, there do not yet exist computerized systems capable of automatically designing new heuristic strategies. Nonetheless, the coupling of SDSs with automatic learning mechanisms is an intriguing future possibility. Current research in the area of learning from examples and experimentation (e.g. [Mitchell et al. 83]) is relevant in this regard.

The extent to which the user can take advantage of the flexibility of such systems depends on his/her level of expertise in the domain as well as his/her knowledge of the basic heuristic procedures embedded in the system. Using the terminology of coupled systems where a symbolic process must cooperate with various symbolic/numeric processes [Kitzmiller and Kowalik 87], we get a "deep coupling system" when the user has extensive knowledge of the internal structure and behavior of the heuristic procedures and a "shallow coupling system" when the user has no such knowledge (the main symbolic process being a human user and the other symbolic/numeric processes being the basic heuristic procedures). Since deep coupling is known to be more powerful than shallow coupling, it is desirable to have expert users with extensive knowledge of the basic heuristic procedures in order to take full advantage of the system. Thus, we envision researchers engaged in heuristic algorithm design to be the principal users of such systems, as opposed to the final "end users" of specific problem solving systems.

With the support of SDSs, it becomes possible to more efficiently formulate new heuristic algorithms and analyze their behavior. This provides several new opportunities:

- SDSs can improve the productivity of organizations (e.g. research centers) engaged in producing solutions to particular problems for use by various industrial and government clients. Specialized software can be developed as a result of multiple experimentations done with the system on different instances of a problem, thus reducing unpredictability in the final outcome as well as overall development time.

- SDSs also provide a means of acquiring a finer level of problem solving expertise in various fields of OR, particularly with respect to state-dependent resolution strategies. This offers the promise of solution procedures that are more robust across the full range of problems that must be solved and more sensitive to the idiosyncratic characteristics of specific real-world problems.

- Ultimately, we can foresee SDSs as providing a framework for automated acquisition and refinement of expertise in particular application domains. In this light, heuristic strategy design is viewed as an open ended activity, where systems are "seeded" with available problem solving expertise but are capable of revising/extending this knowledge as subsequent problem solving is performed.

In the following sections, we illustrate the concept of a SDS in the context of two specific systems, OPIS and ALTO, which offer flexible design capabilities in the areas of factory scheduling and vehicle routing respectively. These systems are actually used to design and experiment with new heuristic strategies in their respective domains.

3. OPIS

OPIS [Smith 87] is a factory scheduling system developed at Carnegie Mellon University as a vehicle for investigating the potential of constraint-based scheduling techniques for coordinating actual factory floor decision-making. It is motivated by earlier work in this area with the ISIS scheduling system [Fox and Smith 84]. OPIS is implemented in CRL, a frame-based language developed by Carnegie Group, and runs on both Texas Instruments Explorer and Symbolics hardware.

Broadly speaking, the factory scheduling problem concerns the allocation of resources to manufacturing activities over time so that the orders for parts received by the factory are produced in a timely and cost-effective fashion. The problem is further complicated in actual manufacturing environments by the unpredictability of factory operations. Thus, a realistic solution requires integration of two broad capabilities: (1) generation of production schedules that accurately reflect the constraints and objectives of the actual manufacturing environment, and (2) incremental revision of these schedules as unanticipated events on the factory floor force deviations from planned activities.

The OPIS scheduling system is predicated on a common view of predictive and reactive scheduling as an opportunistic problem solving process, dynamically focused by characteristics of current solution constraints [Ow and Smith 88]. Under this view, schedules are generated and revised incrementally through the combined use of a collection of distinct scheduling methods (or heuristic procedures). Each method offers different capabilities relative to resolving particular constraint conflicts and optimizing according to specific scheduling objectives. The resolution planning problem (i.e. which method to apply next at any point) is thus one of trading off the strengths and weaknesses of each method vis a vis characteristics of current solution constraints. This view is realized by a "blackboard" system architecture [Erman et al. 80] (depicted in Figure 1), wherein scheduling methods are implemented as independent knowledge sources (KSs) that may be applied to extend and revise the globally accessible current schedule. All changes to the schedule, whether the result of KS application or the result of external updates in factory status, are managed by an underlying schedule maintenance system, which infers the consequences of each change and recognizes any constraint conflicts

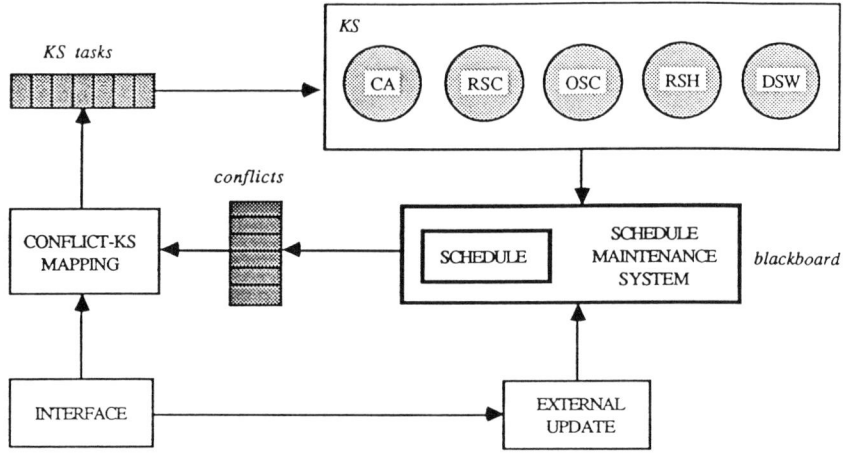

Figure 1: OPIS architecture

that have been introduced into the schedule (e.g. capacity constraint conflicts resulting from indication of a machine breakdown). Resolution planning decisions are based on analysis of these detected conflicts, or, in the absence of actual conflicts, predictions of the conflicts that are likely to arise relative to those portions of the schedule that have yet to be specified. For example, the capacity analysis (CA) KS identified in Figure 1 predicts areas of resource contention as a means of focusing problem solving activity.

Underlying principles of constraint-based scheduling [Smith and Ow 85] and experience in different manufacturing environments have led to implementation of the following scheduling methods within the OPIS architecture:

- **Order Scheduler (OSC)**. The OSC provides a method for generating or revising the scheduling decisions relating to some contiguous portion of a given order's production plan. Given its focus, the OSC emphasizes resolution of *order-centered* conflicts (e.g. precedence violations) and achievement of order-centered objectives (e.g. minimizing work-in-process time).
- **Resource Scheduler (RSC)**. The RSC provides a method for generating or revising a designated resource's schedule. In contrast to the OSC, the RSC emphasizes resolution of *resource-centered* conflicts (e.g. capacity violations) and achievement of resource-centered objectives (e.g. minimizing tardiness).
- **Right Shifter (RSH)**. The RSH implements a less sophisticated reactive method which resolves conflicts by simply "pushing" the scheduled execution times of specific operations forward in time.

- **Demand Swapper (DSW)**. Demand swapping is a specialized reactive method that tries to solve or lessen the severity of a time conflict caused by an unexpected delay to an order. It attempts to exchange the remaining portion of the problematic order's schedule with the correspondent portion of another order's schedule.

Given the commitment to these scheduling methods, the primary focus of strategy design within OPIS is at the resolution planning level. Specification of a resolution plan in this context requires definition of a mapping from the set of conflicts (actual or anticipated) that can arise during problem solving to the set of scheduling methods, dictating which scheduling action(s) should be taken in any given problem solving state. Problem solving proceeds within the OPIS architecture by repeatedly applying this mapping to the current set of conflicts (see figure 1). Consider the reactive problem of responding to a time conflict introduced into an order's schedule as a result of an external update indicating that extra rework operations are required. Since scheduling methods define local scheduling actions that may be taken, resolution of this conflict (e.g. revision of the order's schedule) may introduce new conflicts into the schedule (e.g. capacity conflicts in the schedules of resources just allocated to the order). Problem solving continues until a consistent (i.e. conflict free) overall production schedule is produced.

OPIS provides a sophisticated graphical interface for specifying and experimenting with alternative resolution strategies [Matthys and Potvin 88]. Within this interface, the user works interactively at solving specific scheduling problems (e.g. revising a pre-existing schedule in response to a simulated machine breakdown), designating which scheduling action(s) to take on each resolution planning control cycle. At each choice point, the user is provided with an *analysis report*, which characterizes potentially relevant features of the current control state. These features include the type and severity of the current conflicts as well as indicators of the flexibility in the time and capacity constraints imposed by the schedule in the "vicinity" of these conflicts. As choices are made, user selected scheduling actions are stored, along with the context in which each was selected, for later retrieval of the full resolution plan. Facilities are also provided for restoring a particular scheduling state, which enables comparison of alternative scheduling actions and resolution strategies. Finally, interactively determined resolution strategies may be encoded as *meta-level* heuristics to produce specific automated schedulers and enable more extensive testing of alternatives.

The OPIS system was developed to provide a framework for investigating opportunistic, constraint-directed scheduling strategies. It is currently configured with a model of a computer board assembly and test line located at the IBM manufacturing facility in Poughkeepsie, NY. Using the reactive scheduling problems that arise in this manufacturing environment, current use of OPIS is aimed at the development of strategies for incrementally revising the pre-existing production schedule when unanticipated events occur. Some initial results in this regard are reported in [Ow et al. 88].

4. ALTO

ALTO is an interactive and graphic system built at Montreal University to facilitate the development and experimentation of routing algorithms for transportation vehicles. The system is written in LOOPS, a frame based language, and implemented on the 1108 Xerox Lisp Machine. ALTO is actually designed to solve a class of transportation problems known as "node routing problems". In these problems, the demand is located on the nodes of a transportation network and the fleet of vehicles, starting from a central depot, must collect this demand at minimal cost.

In contrast to OPIS, which commits to specific constraint-based problem solving methodology and provides strategy design capabilities relative to a fairly specific set of heuristic procedures, the ALTO system [Potvin et al. 87] emphasizes the design of such heuristic procedures. Hence, the focus of strategy design is at the heuristic procedure level *and* resolution planning level, thus supporting development of a wider range of resolution strategies.

Basically, the problem solving methodology advocated by ALTO is based on a set of templates that are instantiated by the user (at the heuristic procedure level) and then combined to create complete resolution strategies (at the resolution planning level). The templates model basic operators, that is, general heuristic procedures commonly used to build economic routes for transportation vehicles. More precisely:

- **INIT** is an operator allowing the creation of new routes. For each new route, one "seed" node is selected and used for initialization purposes (i.e. each route produced will contain only the selected seed node). Hence, this operator provides a way to define a general orientation for each new route.
- **ADD** is a general iterative procedure for insertion of nodes into existing routes. At each iteration, a new node is selected and added to one of the existing routes. This operator provides a general structure allowing the user to specify which nodes should be considered next for insertion and where they should be inserted.
- **MERGE** is a general iterative procedure allowing fusion of existing routes. At each iteration, two new routes are selected and merged together. This operator provides a general structure allowing the user to specify which routes should be merged and how they should be merged.
- **EXCHANGE** is an operator that modifies the sequence of nodes in the routes using the well known 2,3-opt exchange procedures [Lin 65]. This operator integrates multicriteria decision analysis and allows the introduction of various optimization criteria to guide the exchange procedures (e.g. minimizing the total length of the routes, equalizing the repartition of demand among vehicles, etc.).

Each operator takes into account three different types of constraints: maximal vehicle capacity, maximal vehicle travel time and single time windows for demand pick-up at the nodes. Operator ADD, for example, only inserts nodes into routes when all the "active" constraints (as specified by the user) are satisfied. Individual constraints can be turned on or off at each step during the resolution process. It is thus possible to build routes in a "constraint free" context, and then to modify these routes with the constraints turned on to attain feasibility.

a)
$$\text{INIT}$$
```
N = <number of routes>
While N > 0 do
       SEED = <selection formula for a seed node>
       initialize a new route with SEED
       N    = N - 1
```

b)
$$\text{INIT}_1$$
```
N = 1
While N > 0 do
       SEED = (MAXOBJ SET_nodes DIST_depot,node )
       initialize a new route with SEED
       N    = N - 1
```
$$\text{SEED} = (\text{MAXOBJ SET}_{nodes} \text{ DIST}_{depot,node})$$

Figure 2: Operator INIT

To illustrate how the user can provide his/her own specifications during the instantiation process, a simplified version of the template for operator INIT is shown in figure 2. Figure 2a shows the basic structure of the operator INIT, which is meant to initialize routes with "seed" nodes (it is then possible to add more nodes to the routes with operator ADD). This template allows the user to specify the number of new routes to be created and their associated seeds. In figure 2b, we can see a specific instantiation INIT_1 of operator INIT where the user asks for the creation of only one new route and identifies the farthest node from the depot as the seed. In general, the templates are filled with numeric arguments and "selection formulas", that is, formulas allowing selection of objects from predefined sets (in our example, the selection of a given seed from the set of all nodes). The selection formulas can be easily created by the user via use of a system-provided specification language.

The user is then able to dynamically design new resolution strategies on an operator-by-operator basis. In other words, the user has the opportunity to examine the current status of the routes before deciding which instantiated operator to apply next. Such an

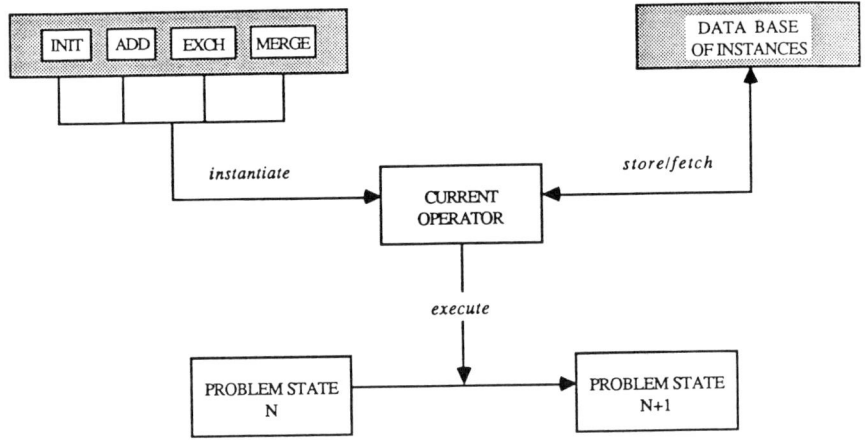

Figure 3: The incremental resolution methodology of ALTO

instantiated operator can be generated just before its application to the current solution or it can be selected from a data base previously created by the user (see figure 3). Extensions are foreseen to also provide the means to specify at once a complete resolution strategy (i.e. a complete sequence of instantiated operators leading to the final solution).

ALTO is actually used to design resolution strategies for complex mail pick-up problems with time windows at the nodes and maximal travel time for the vehicles. It is also used to compare the behavior of many well-known heuristic algorithms, since the four basic operators can be instantiated to reproduce a large class of routing heuristics already described in the literature [Lapalme et al. 88]. Some interesting results related to the use of ALTO are reported in [Potvin et al. 87].

5. CONCLUSION

In this paper, we have advocated an incremental approach to the design of heuristic algorithms in complex OR domains, and have emphasized the use of flexible strategy design systems to support this activity. The emergence of new technologies, particularly in the field of AI, now provides the OR community with the kind of computer environments needed to develop such systems.

Among the benefits afforded by these flexible systems, we should mention:

- The ability to generate many different solutions for any given problem, using different resolution approaches. This feature is very interesting, since for real problems there can be many "good" solutions depending on various subjective qualitative criteria.

- Rapid development of new heuristic algorithms in face of complex real problems, thus allowing research centers to be more productive and to release better software.
- Acquisition of problem solving expertise, allowing the creation of knowledge-based systems able to appropriately analyze a given problem and take decisions about the way to solve it.

OPIS and ALTO are two examples of this new trend in the design of OR systems. Both provide interactive facilities for the design of new heuristic strategies in face of problems exhibiting different characteristics. The use of such tools provides opportunities for the development of problem solving systems that are better equipped to handle the complexity of real world problems. Future developments can also be foreseen in the area of automatic learning, allowing such systems to learn from previous experimentation in order to improve their problem solving behavior.

ACKNOWLEDGEMENTS

Stephen Smith's research has been funded in part by International Business Machines Inc. under contract number 71223046 and by CMU Robotics Institute. Jean-Yves Potvin's research has been funded in part by the National Sciences and Engineering Research Council of Canada and by CMU Robotics Institute.

REFERENCES

Bodin L., B. Golden, A.Assad and M. Ball (1983), "Routing and Scheduling of Vehicles and Crews: The State of the Art", *Computers and Operations Research 10*,2.

Cullen F., J. Jarvis and D. Ratliff (1981), "Set Partitioning Based Heuristics for Interactive Routing", *Networks 11*, 2, 125-143.

Erman L.D., F. Hayes-Roth, V.R. Lesser and D.R. Reddy (1980), "The Hearsay-II Speech-Understanding System: Integrating Knowledge to Resolve Uncertainty", *Computing Surveys 12*, 2, (June), 213-253.

Ferland J.A., J.M. Rousseau and L. Chapleau (1985), "Clustering for Routing in Densely Populated Areas", *European Journal of Operational Research 20*, 2, 48-57.

Fox M.S. and S.F. Smith (1984), ISIS: A Knowledge-Based System for Factory Scheduling", *Expert Systems 1*, 1 (July), 25-49.

Kitzmiller C.T. and J.S. Kowalik (1987), "Coupling Symbolic and Numeric Computation in Knowledge-Based Systems", *AI Magazine 8*, 2 (June), 85-90.

Krolak P., W. Felts and J. Nelson (1972) "A Man-Machine Approach Toward Solving the Generalized Truck Dispatching Problem", *Transportation Science 6*, 2 (May) 149-170.

Lapalme G., J.Y. Potvin and J.M. Rousseau (1988), "A General Heuristic for Node Routing Problems", In *Advances in Optimization and Control*, H.A. Eiselt and G. Pederzoli, Eds., Springer-Verlag, 124-143.

Lin S. (1965), "Computer Solutions of the Traveling Salesman Problem", *Bell System Technical Journal 44*, 10 (Dec.), 2245-2269.

Matthys D. and J.Y. Potvin (1988), "Interactive Configuration of Scheduling Strategies in OPIS", Working Paper, Robotics Institute, Carnegie Mellon University, Pittsburgh, Penn.

Mitchell T.M., P.E.Utgoff and R.B. Banerji (1983), "Learning by Experimentation: Acquiring and Refining Problem-Solving Heuristics", In *Machine Learning*, R.S. Michalski, J.G. Carbonell and T.M. Mitchell, Eds., Tioga Publishing Co., Palo Alto, pp. 163-190.

Muller H., S. De Samblanckx and D. Matthys (1987), "The Expert System Approach and the Flexibility-Complexity Problem in Scheduling Production Systems", *International Journal of Production Research 25*, 11, 1659-1670.

Ow P.S. and S.F. Smith (1988), "Viewing Scheduling as an Opportunistic Problem Solving Process", In *Annals of Operations Research 12*, R.G. Jeroslow, Ed., Baltzer Scientific Publishing Co., 85-108.

Ow P.S., S.F. Smith and A. Thiriez (1988), "Reactive Plan Revision", In *Proceedings 7th National Conference on Artificial Intelligence*, (St. Paul, Minn., Aug. 21-26) AAAI, Menlo Park, Calif., pp. 77-82.

Panwalker S.S. and W. Iskander (1977), "A Survey of Scheduling Rules", *Operations Research 25*, 1 (Jan.), 45-61.

Potvin J.Y., G. Lapalme and J.M. Rousseau (1987), "ALTO: A Computer System for the Design and Experimentation of Routing Algorithms", Publication No. 616, Departement IRO, Universite de Montreal.

Rosenkrantz D., R. Sterns and P. Lewis (1977), "An Analysis of Several Heuristics for the Traveling Salesman Problem", *SIAM Journal of Computing 6*, 3 (Sept.) 563-581.

Rousseau J.M., and J.Y. Blais (1985), "HASTUS: An Interactive System for Buses and Crew Scheduling", In *Computer Scheduling of Public Transport 2*, J.M. Rousseau, Ed., North-Holland, 45-60.

Smith, S.F. (1987), "A Constraint-Based Framework for Reactive Management of Factory Schedules", In *Intelligent Manufacturing*, M.D. Oliff, Ed., Benjamin-Cummings Publishing, Menlo Park, pp. 113-130.

Smith S.F. and P.S. Ow (1985), "The Use of Multiple Problem Decompositions in Time-Constrained Planning Tasks", In *Proceedings 9th International Joint Conference on Artificial Intelligence* (Los Angeles, Calif., Aug. 18-23), pp. 1013-1015.

VI.

VEHICAL ROUTING AND SCHEDULING APPLICATIONS

SCAN:
A DECISION SUPPORT SYSTEM FOR RAILROAD SCHEDULING

DEJAN JOVANOVIĆ AND PATRICK T. HARKER
*Decision Sciences Dept., The Wharton School, University of Pennsylvania
Philadelphia, Penna. 19104-6366, U.S.A.*

ABSTRACT

This paper presents an overview of a decision-support model for the tactical scheduling of railroad traffic which is meant to support the medium-term issues facing a railroad. This initial version of the *Schedule Analysis (SCAN)* system is based upon notions from both simulation and combinatorial optimization, and is designed to provide schedulers with a tool for scheduling which provides real-time response. After describing the conceptual and algorithmic underpinnings of the SCAN system and its associated user interface, examples taken from a major railroad are used to illustrate the capabilities and limitations of the current system. Preliminary results from the use of this system at a major railroad are also discussed.

1. INTRODUCTION

Recent years have seen a renaissance of North American railroads, both in terms of economic indicators (ton-miles, revenues) and the development of new "space age" communication, information, navigation, and electronic control systems [Welty 1987,1988]. Increased traffic volumes, new technologies and stronger competition have put pressure on railway companies to rethink their management strategies and operating practices in order to make use of the wealth of information and control capabilities provided by new systems and, in turn, to increase the level of service offered. It became apparent that decision-makers need new methodologies and tools in order to make better decisions from a system-wide perspective. The model described in this paper is designed to fill the gap in the area of operations research (OR) models applicable to the problem of medium-term (tactical) scheduling of trains.

1.1 Tactical Rail Scheduling Problem and OR Models

Tactical train scheduling is defined as the determination of planned (scheduled) train arrival and departure times at important points (yards, terminals, junctions) along a train's route; these times are then published in timetables intended both as marketing information for railroad customers and official guidelines (or goals) for the railroad employees. Train routes, car-blocking and yard polices are determined at a higher (longer term) planning level, and they are assumed as given inputs to the tactical scheduling process, along with marketing considerations (i.e., the train arrival/departure times most attractive to the customers).

The main issue involved in tactical train scheduling is a trade-off between the train arrival/departure times desired from the marketing point of view, and the reliability of actual schedule performance (i.e., on-time train arrivals) as influenced by over-the-line and yard delays incurred by trains. Shorter transit times are more attractive to the customers and can result in better equipment utilization; however, these gains can be more than offset by the resulting higher frequency of late train arrivals and the deterioration of the reliability of the transportation service offered. It is hard to overemphasize the importance of on-time shipment arrivals in today's transportation market, and the fact that the trains' schedule performances play a vital role in the overall reliability of railroad services [Bouley 1987]. In practice, train schedulers have almost no means (aside from their past experience) to predict the on-time performance of their new or revised schedules. The adjustments of schedules are usually myopic in nature and dictated by historic train performance; in other words, rather than setting goals, the tactical scheduling function is simply a summary of the actual train operating practices defined by the oftentime uncoordinated actions of train and yard dispatchers and engineers. The methodology embedded in the SCAN system takes a somewhat different perspective; namely, the basis for reliable rail operations are achievable goals set at the tactical scheduling level. The main purpose of SCAN is to enable schedulers to produce schedules which are consistent with the physical constraints of over-the-line train operations or, in other words, to produce *robust* schedules that contribute to reliable operations.

1.2 Current State-of-the-Art in Railroad Scheduling

No existing model of rail operations was appropriate for task of tactical rail scheduling; however, we can learn from the shortcomings of the existing models. A large number of models developed to support railroad operations (for comprehensive, though somewhat dated review see [Assad 1980]) can be categorized as either *goal-* or *action*-oriented, borrowing the classification given by [Morlok 1970]. Representative of the goal-oriented models are optimization models which, in the context of rail operations, are either network oriented models (the most recent and successful example is described in [Crainic 1984]), or focus on the real-time operations of a single railway line. While network optimization models are useful in determining yard and blocking policies and train routes, these models do not implicitly deal with schedules; they instead use train frequences. In the real-time category, there are few operational models of optimal line operations (or train dispatching) to date (see, for example, the description of the Norfolk Southern Railroad's proprietary dispatching system described in [Sauder *et al* 1983]). Even if more such real-time systems were available, the short-term scope of such a model would make it impractical for planning purposes. Another problem with the optimization models, both network- and line-oriented, is that they are usually based on relatively rigid and simplified mathematical formulations of the problem; at present it is a challenge just to understand and define all the intricacies involved in the tactical train scheduling problem, let alone produce a detailed mathematical formulation of the problem.

Action-directed models are usually discrete-event simulation models and are used to assess the impacts of various proposed actions. These models, depending on their scope, can accomodate a great level of detail. Network-oriented simulation models, however, either ignore or use overly simplified representations of over-the-line train interference; this interference is one of the main sources of delays that trains incur and thus, directly influences schedule performance. Simulation models of line operations, on the other hand, are usually stochastic and incorporate train interference — meets and overtakes — in great detail (a somewhat dated review of these models can be found in [Bongaardt *et al*]). However, because of the level of detail incorporated and the large number of iterations required to get a statistically significant sample, these models are too slow and cumbersome to be used interactively; e.g., so as to allow the analyst to make iterative improvements to the alternative plans being evaluated within a reasonably short period of time. An additional shortcoming of most simulation models in the area of rail transportation is that, besides being data intensive, they require extensive preparation and knowledge of the software from their users; the final output must be processed by the technical people with a thorough understanding of the particular simulation package *and* rail operations before it can be presented to a decision maker.

2. SCAN SYSTEM DESIGN

Although the SCAN decision support system is being developed within the scope of a broader research effort aimed at the optimal control of railroad operations [Harker 1986], it was designed so that it can serve as a useful stand-alone tool for railroad management, independent from any real-time control systems which may be implemented on the railroad. In order to achieve this goal, several design objectives were chosen:

- **Ease of use and user independence.** The system was intended to be used directly by the decision-makers, without extensive training requirements and without need for technical consultants, such as programmers and MIS experts, to process system input and output. Both the inputs to and the outputs from the model should be easily and quickly comprehended by the users. This goal prompted the use of the interactive-graphics and menu oriented user interface.

- **The system should be interactive.** Closely connected to the ease of use, the realization of this objective is necessary in order to make the system truly useful in supporting the decision-making process. After the invocation of any command, the user should receive a meaningful response from the system in a reasonable amount of time (e.g., before he forgets what he asked from the model). This objective required the use of fast-response algorithms and adequate computational power.

- **Modular design.** The algorithms used in the model, data input-output to the algorithms, initialization routines and user interface should be designed and coded as relatively independent modules. This goal allows different algorithms to be added or substituted in the model as the research progresses and the users' needs and enviroment change.

The choice of the computing enviroment for the SCAN system was dictated by the above objectives; we needed more computational power than a PC could offer and better graphics and real-time response capabilities than a time-sharing mainframe could offer. Therefore, we chose a graphics-oriented, multiple-window, mouse-controlled Apollo DN 3000 workstation.

3. SCAN METHODOLOGY

3.1 Model Philosophy, Scope, Assumptions and Data Needs

As discussed in the Introduction, the purpose of this model is to *help* in the design of robust (reliable) train schedules, not to provide an "optimal" schedule. Accordingly, the model starts with given train schedules and evaluates their feasibility; if a given set of schedules is found to be infeasible, the system offers interactive or automatic procedures to modify the given schedules until they are feasible. Once the set of schedules are proven feasible, their reliability can be estimated. All the remaining objectives (besides reliability) imbedded in the tactical scheduling process are the domain of the user; the scheduler follows these objectives through the proposed initial set of schedules and by controlling the subsequent interactive modification of that set.

Reliability of train schedules is a system-wide issue; i.e., because of interactions among trains, it is not possible to consider the reliability of a single train's schedule while ignoring the schedules of the other trains. Consequently, the SCAN methodology has a system-wide scope. However, in order to ensure the fast model response required for the interactive nature of the SCAN system, the railway network over which the schedules are analyzed was disaggregated into basic units of analysis called *traffic lanes*. A lane is defined as a railway line between two points on the network termed *reporting stations* (usually yards, terminals and junctions) where trains are scheduled to arrive and/or depart at a certain time.

This methodology incorporates two basic assumptions: (a) all trains are scheduled, and (b) all the trains going through a reporting station are scheduled at that station. The first assumption is a major one and does not mirror the current practice of North American railroads: there is a substantial number of regional and local trains that are not scheduled at the tactical level. However, the philosophy embedded in the SCAN system maintains that on-time performance is a system-wide issue and thus, in order to improve it, planners at the tactical level should have some control over the operation of unscheduled trains rather than leaving it to the discretion of train dispatchers. A system of scheduled slots, similar to those employed by the airline industry, could be used for this purpose so that unscheduled trains can be incorporated within the SCAN system using the slots allocated to them.

The 24 hour time horizon of the model was chosen as natural for a tactical scheduling model since that represents the practical cycle of most train schedules (viewed from a particular reporting station, not from a train).

The data required by the model can be classified into three basic categories: track description, train travel times, and, of course, proposed train schedules (for a detailed description of all the information required by SCAN I package see [Harker *et al.* 1987]). The track description for a given traffic lane lists all points, termed *meetpoints*, where trains can meet or pass (i.e., overtake) each other; such points are side tracks, yards, and points at the ends of double-track sections. Travel time files list free-running (i.e., without interference from other trains) transit times between adjacent meetpoints for various train types classified according to their performance. Statistical distributions of stochastic input parameters are also needed for the schedule reliability estimation (e.g., variance of free-running times influenced by locomotive health, etc.).

3.2 SCAN Algorithms

There are three algorithms incorporated within the SCAN I system: one that evaluates the feasibility of a given set of schedules over a given lane, one that modifies the infeasible schedules until feasibility is achieved, and one that estimates a measure of reliability of a given set of schedules. The schedule feasibility evaluation algorithm attempts to find a feasible meet-pass plan that satisfies given schedules (i.e., that enables all trains to arrive on time to their reporting stations within the lane). A feasible meet-pass plan specifies the time-space coordinates (when and where) of train paths and their interactions in such a way that no physical constraints of the train motion and interaction are violated; e.g., two trains travelling in opposite directions cannot meet on a piece of single track, only at a siding, yard or double-track section.

The feasible meet-pass plan generation problem can be formulated as a mixed-integer mathematical programming problem, where the integer binary variables determine the location of train meets and continuous variables represent train arrival and departure times at each meetpoint in the lane. There is no explicit objective function in this problem; i.e., the goal, as described by Jovanović and Harker [1988], is to find a feasible solution(s) that meets the schedule. This problem is NP-complete, and in many ways is similar to a job-shop scheduling problem. However, some features of the problem enabled the design of an efficient implicit enumeration algorithm. The special structure of the problem allows, for fixed binary variables, the resulting problem in the continuous variables to be solved trivially. This characteristic allows for the design of an implicit enumeration-like rather than an LP-based branch-and-bound technique. Node generation is performed using process-interaction simulation techniques to actually move the trains over the lane in a manner which ensures that only feasible nodes are generated. Thanks to the availability of 32-bit integer variables in the Apollo workstation enviroment, there is no need for floating point operations; in fact, only integer addition and comparison were used in the implementation of the algorithm. Computationally inexpensive node evaluation (200 nodes/sec on Apollo DN 3000), coupled with a strong initial bound (no train can be late) and depth-first search resulted in satisfactory running times for most real-world data sets encountered. Typically, it takes under 10 seconds on the Apollo DN 3000 for the SCAN I system to derive a meet-pass plan that satisfies the schedules or to prove that the given set of schedules is infeasible. However, for some rare test data sets involving a substantial number of overtaking trains, the problem size was so large that it required almost 30 minutes of Apollo DN 3000 CPU time for the algorithm to prove that the schedules are infeasible.

If no feasible meet-pass plan that meets the schedules can be found, the schedule modification module returns the "best" partial meet-pass plan with indication of the unresolved train conflict (cf. Figure 2); the "best" in present version of SCAN is defined as that plan which corresponds to the deepest node generated in the search tree before the schedules were proved to be infeasible. The scheduler may then choose to let the heuristic embedded in the schedule modification algorithm render given schedules feasible or he may do it interactively by resolving infeasible train conflicts one by one.

Finally, if the set of schedules is feasible, the scheduler can invoke the reliability estimation module to obtain a measure of the 'robustness' of the schedules. In SCAN I, this measure is defined to be probability that all trains in the given set will arrive on time. This probability is estimated by a Monte Carlo simulation where each sample point represents one run of the feasibility evaluation routine with different values of the stochastic input parameters. In the present version, the stochastic parameters are limited to free-running train travel times.

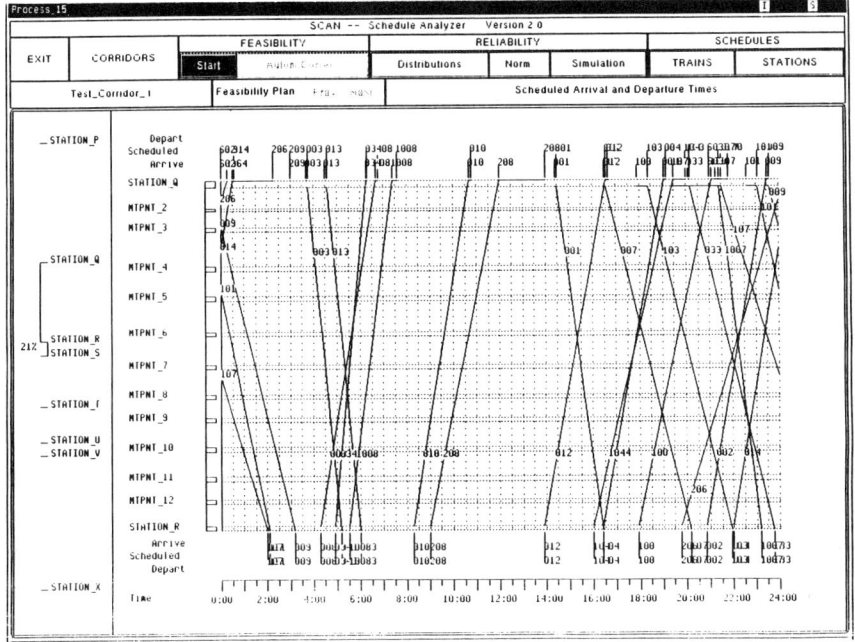

Figure 1: Station_Q–Station_R schedule diagram.

4. SCAN USER INTERFACE

The SCAN user interface was designed to be mouse-controlled and menu driven, with some elements of graphics-oriented direct manipulation [Jones 1987]. The menu system allows a novice user to start using the system immediately, eliminating syntax errors or the need to memorize the commands, without inhibiting the expert user (due to the relatively small number of commands available in SCAN I). Examples of direct manipulation include the choice of a traffic lane to be analyzed (the user positions the cursor on the desired lane on the railway line diagram in the left window shown in Figure 1 and clicks on the mouse button) and the input of statistical distributions for the stochastic parameters (the user positions the cursor at the desired coordinates on the frequency histogram). An illustration

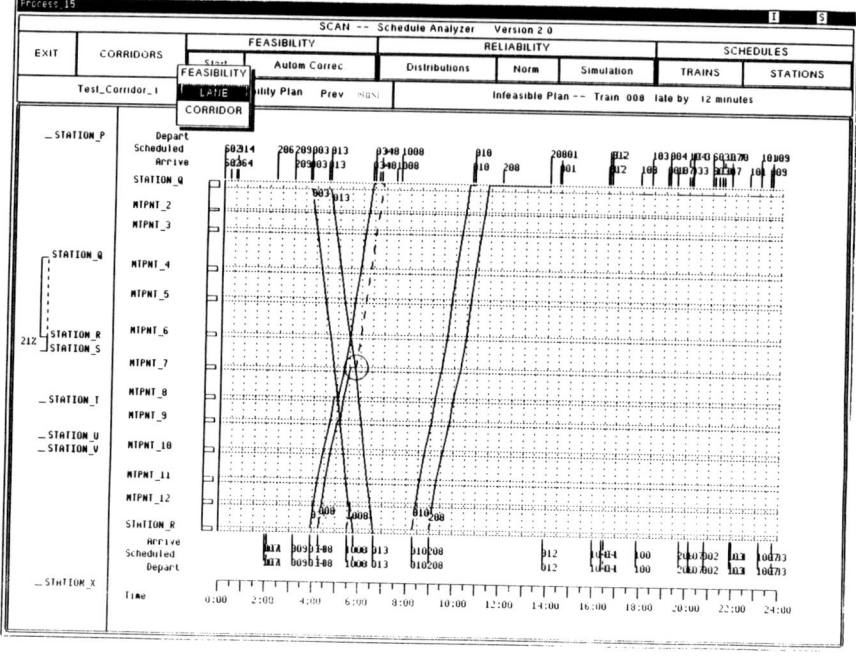

Figure 2: Station_Q–Station_R: an infeasible meet-pass plan.

of the success of the interface is that when the prototype SCAN system was delivered to a major railroad for field testing, it was not accompanied by a user manual and none of the users seemed to require one.

For the presentation of output, we continued the railroad tradition of using time-distance diagrams to represent the movement of trains. SCAN I uses two types of diagrams: schedule diagram (Figures 1 and 5) in which the scheduled (desired) train departure and arrival times at the reporting stations are connected by a straight line, and the meet-pass plan diagrams (Figures 4 and 6) which represent one possible realization of the schedule or show why it is not possible to achieve the given schedule (Figure 2). All meetpoints on the analyzed traffic lane and their names are displayed on the vertical axis alongside the track schematic. Color is used to differentiate among various types of trains in the diagram, with red reserved

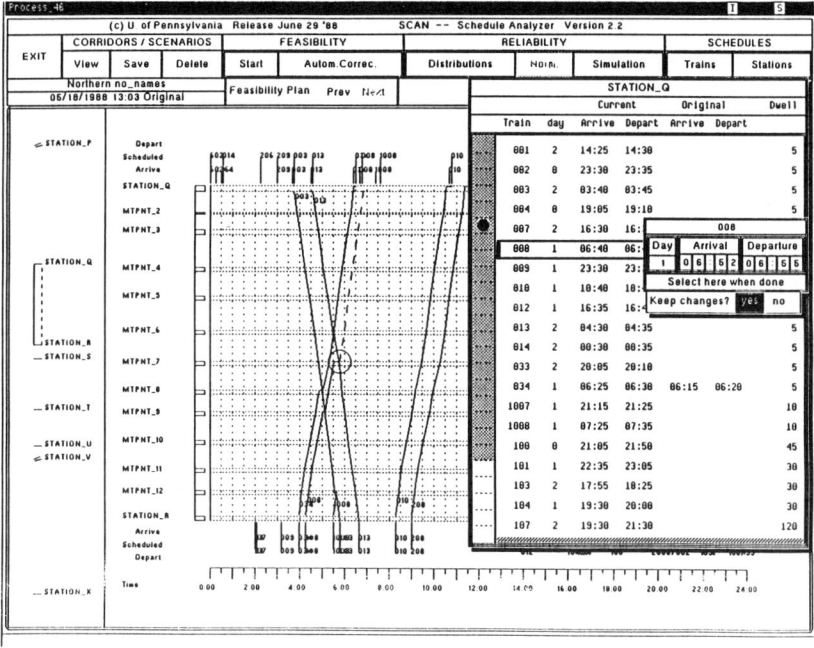

Figure 3: Menu-controlled modification of train's 008 schedule.

for late trains. An important asset of the graphical output of the algorithmic results is that it proved to be an invaluable tool not only for the end users, but also for the algorithm developer during the testing and debugging of the code.

Coding of the interface was substantially accelerated through the use of Apollo Domain *Dialogue* user interface management system (UIMS). Dialogue provides a library of menu building and control routines that can be called from a standard procedural language such as Pascal (the entire SCAN system was coded in standard Pascal augmented by the procedures from Dialogue and Domain 2D-graphics libraries).

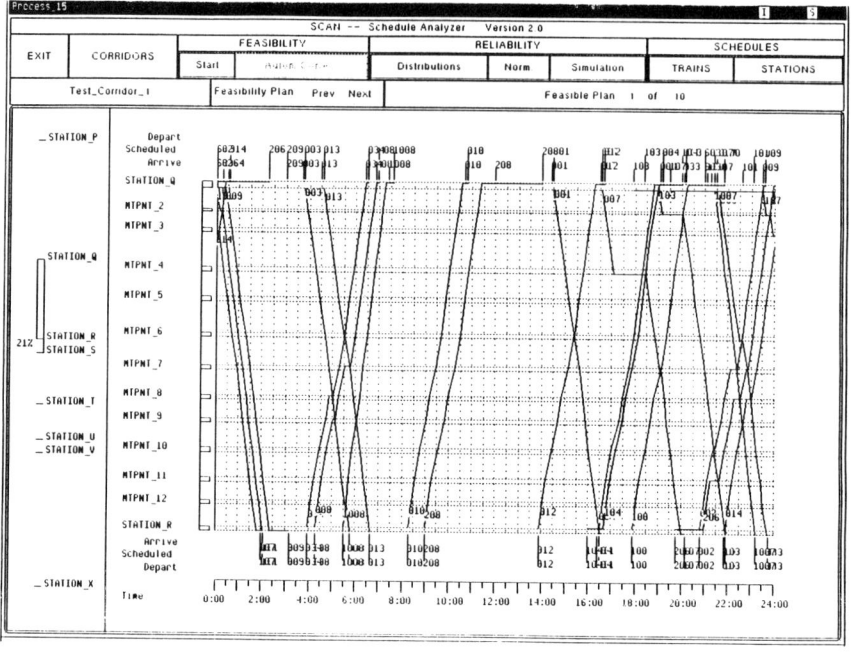

Figure 4: Station_Q–Station_R: a feasible meet-pass plan.

5. EXAMPLES

In this section we present examples of the evaluation of the proposed schedules over two traffic lanes. Figure 1 presents a schedule diagram for the Station_Q-Station_S lane; note a straight line connecting these two stations in the left window which indicates which lane is being analyzed. By simply looking at the diagram, one would be tempted to conclude that this set of schedules would be easy to meet since there are several 'holes' in the schedule and the majority of trains seem to meet or pass each other at a meetpoint (i.e., a siding). However, invocation of the feasibility checking option reveals a series of infeasible train conflicts. One such conflict is shown in the Figure 2. The conflict can be resolved by the schedule-modification procedure or by manually changing the scheduled arrival or departure time of one of the trains involved in the meet; manual modification of a train schedule is illustrated in Figure 3. Finally, after the schedules of eight trains have been interactively modified by the analyst, the given set of schedules has been rendered feasible, as illustrated by a feasible meet-pass plan in Figure 4.

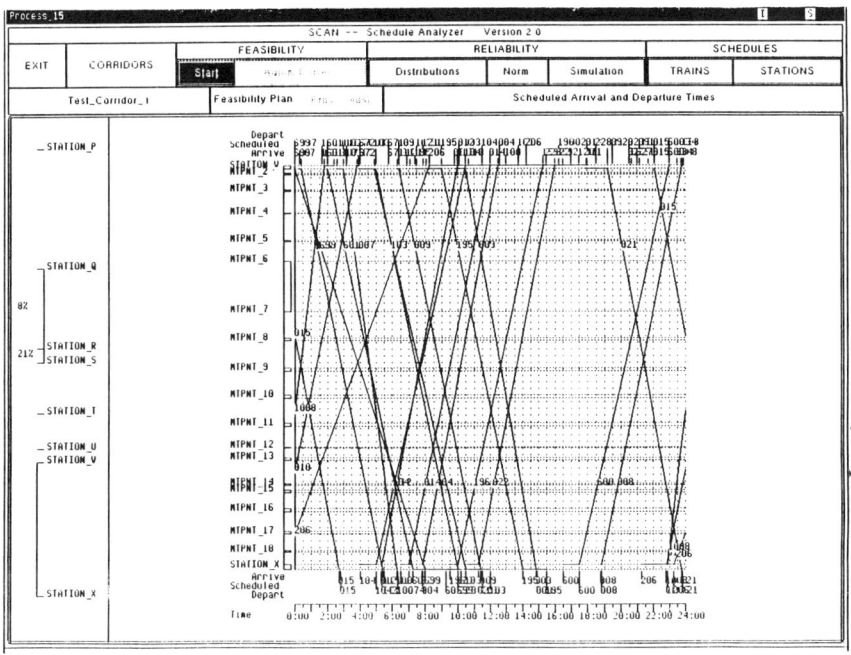

Figure 5: Station_V–Station_X schedule diagram.

The schedule diagram for a second example, the Station_V-Station_X lane in Figure 5, on the other hand, suggests a barely achievable set of schedules since the train paths are dense and interconnected, and many of them do not intersect at a siding or a double track section. The feasibility algorithm, however, discovers over 500 meet-pass plans that can achieve the given set of schedules; one is presented in Figure 6.

The above examples illustrate the type of added information that the SCAN system

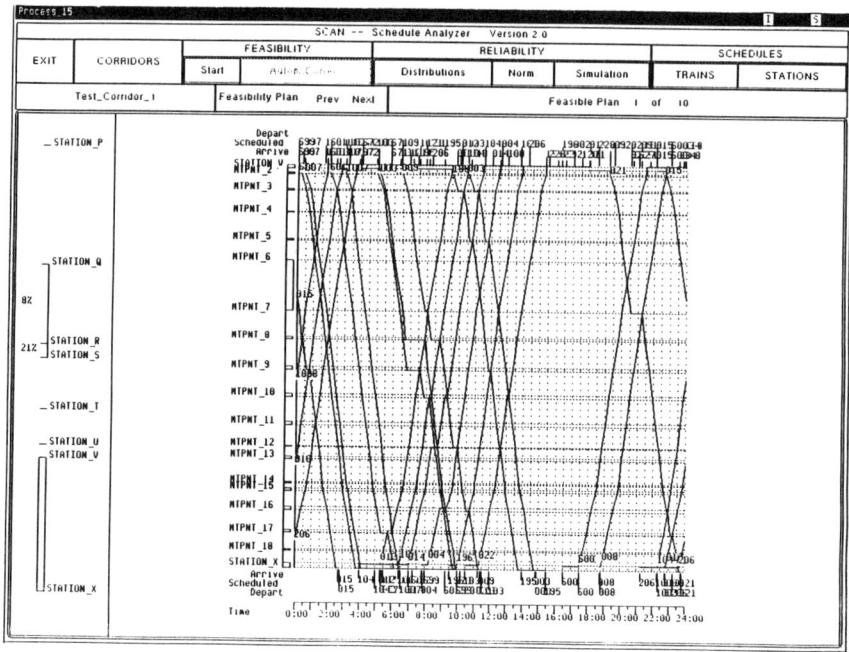

Figure 6: Station_V–Station_X: a feasible meet-pass plan.

presents to the decision-maker; simply collecting data and presenting it in a nice graphical form can often be misleading if it is not accompanied by adequate analysis.

6. SCAN I IN PRACTICE

The SCAN I system is currently being used at a major U.S. railroad in order to obtain achievable schedules. SCAN has refocused this railroad's efforts on increasing the level of service offered to their customers by highlighting the role of proper scheduling of trains. As is preached in Operations Research classes but oftentime not believed, it was the *act of modeling* more than the model itself that has made the biggest impact on the railroad: they are beginning to believe in scheduling! In this sense, SCAN has already been a success, given its acceptance by the schedulers. This can be illustrated by quoting one of the SCAN users:

> "...calling up the software, running feasibility checks and changing the schedule data... was accomplished with minimal effort and confusion. This is very important as we would like to see '**non-programmer types**' able to access the system and use it for analyzing and improving operations. Many non-analysts were eager to '*try it for themselves*'. ... The graphic representation of the schedules is a strong asset. Without it, the analysis would essentially produce *just a bunch of numbers that don't mean anything to me and don't allow me to get any real work done*."

As for the quantitative measures of the impact of SCAN I, statistics are being collected to provide the numerical evidence of the system's impact on the operations of the railroad as the system is being used to analyze larger and larger portions of the network.

7. FUTURE DIRECTIONS

In order to provide the scheduler with even greater sophistication in the support of tactical scheduling, several research issues concerning the methodology employed in SCAN I remain to be solved. Among these are the issues of cyclic schedules, introduction of the *measure* of schedule infeasibility rather than just stating that the given set of schedules is infeasible, and better measures of the reliability of schedules. Improved, faster algorithms are required in order to accomodate these new methodologies and enable the system to be used over larger, aggregated, traffic lanes, while retaining interactive nature of the system.

Besides these algorithmic and methodological issues, one of the challenges for the future development of SCAN system will be to retain the positive features of the existing user interface while supporting the more sophisticated flow of information between the user and SCAN which will be required by the new methodologies. For example, the user should be given greater control over the feasibility evaluation algorithm in the fashion of the interactive optimization: results of each iteration of the algorithm should be displayed immediately with the user having the option to stop the algorithm, examine the 'best' solution so far, and either accept that one or restart the algorithm with the option of directing the algorithm towards better solution. The "Dialog" type of UIMS has the necessary flexibility for the concurrent package architecture where both the algorithm modules and UIMS can concurrently control the display, as opposed to the current SCAN architecture where an external UIMS has control over the display and invokes algorithmic modules as necessary; however, this architecture is not only difficult to implement but may also compromise the modularity of the package. Another challenge lies in increasing the role of direct manipulation as the mode of user interface. An obvious example would be to allow the user to modify schedules directly in the time-distance diagram by moving the path of the train using the mouse.

REFERENCES

Assad A.A. (1980), "Models for rail transportation," *Transportation Research 14A*, 205–220.

Bongaardt H.L. Jr., E.L. Clausing, G.F. List, S.A. McEvoy, and H.G. Ramp (1980), "Railroad network modelling: recent practical applications," *Proceedings of the Transportation Research Forum* pp. 499–512.

Bouley, J. (1987), "Just in time," *Railway Gazette International 2* (February) 93–95.

Crainic, T. (1984), "A comparison of two methods for tactical planning in rail freight transportation," *Operational Research '84: Proceedings of the 10th International Conference on OR*, Elsevier Publishing Co, NY, pp. 707–720.

Harker, P.T. (1986), "Use of Global Positioning Information for Real-Time Control of The Rail Network", A research proposal submitted to Burlington Northern Railroad, Decision Sciences Department, The Wharton School, University of Pennsylvania, Philadelphia, Penna.

Harker, P.T. (1987), D. Jovanović and S.F. Hallowell, "Data Needs for The SCAN System", Report NSF-87-3-1, Decision Sciences Department, The Wharton School, University of Pennsylvania, Philadelphia, Penna.

Jones, C. V. (1987) "User Interfaces," Working Paper 87-11-10, Decision Sciences Department, The Wharton School, University of Pennsylvania, Philadelphia, Penna.

Jovanović, D. and P.T. Harker (1988), "Railroad Schedule Validation and Creation: The SCAN I System," Working Paper 88-03-04, Decision Sciences Department, The Wharton School, University of Pennsylvania, Philadelphia, Penna.

Morlok E.K. (1970), "A goal-directed transportation planning model," *Transportation Research*, 4, 199–213.

Sauder, R.L. and W.M. Westerman (1983), "Computer aided train dispatching: decision support through optimization," *Interfaces 13*, 24-37.

Welty, G. (1987), "ATCS: On time, on target," *Railway Age 6*, (June),39–40.

Welty, G. (1988), "ATCS: More than 'train control'," *Railway Age 8*, (August), 45–49.

AN INTERACTIVE DECISION SUPPORT SYSTEM FOR VEHICLE ROUTING

Kendall E. Nygard, Paul Juell and Kadaba Nagesh
Department of Computer Science and Operations Research
North Dakota State University
Fargo, North Dakota 58105

ABSTRACT

ROUTE is a Decision Support System (DSS) that uses state-of-the-art vehicle routing models and algorithms, yet provides an interactive environment that allows human expertise to be utilized in powerful ways. The system runs on large-screen high-resolution SUN and Hewlett-Packard desktop workstations. ROUTE amplifies the power of the user by providing simple and consistent tools for quickly and accurately providing input data, invoking alternative algorithms, comparing results, editing routes, and producing output reports and plots. Several types of graphics displays and multiple windows help the user evaluate and edit routing plans. These facilities allow the user to easily evaluate answers, make changes, and experiment with various models until good routes are developed.

1. INTRODUCTION

Efficient routing of vehicles is of fundamental importance in our society. Cars, trucks, busses, trains and airplanes constantly pickup and deliver people, materials, finished products and foods, all at considerable cost. Operations researchers have devoted person-centuries to developing vehicle routing models and algorithms (Bodin et al. 1983; Assad and Golden, 1988). Although recent advances in mathematical modeling tools for vehicle routing problems are impressive, it is typical for practical vehicle routing problems to be complicated by factors which are only partially captured by existing models. Among these elusive factors are time constraints for visiting stops, blending pickups and deliveries, splitting loads, tour length limits and many others (Ronen 1988). As a result, many organizations use a great deal of human input and expertise to route their vehicles, and expend considerable effort adapting computerized models which are not ideally suited to their needs.

In this paper we describe ROUTE, a decision support system designed to take maximum advantage of state-of-the-art vehicle routing models and algorithms, yet provide an interactive interface which allows human expertise to be utilized in powerful ways. Basic interaction with the user is with a mouse, pop-up menus, multiple windows, and graphical displays. The system presently runs on both Hewlett-Packard series 320 and SUN 3/260 workstations running the UNIX operating System. Both systems use a Motorola 68020 CPU and 19 inch high resolution color monitors, ideal for graphics-oriented interaction with the user. Input to the system can be provided from data files, or from actual maps by using a digitizing tablet with a 24 x 36 inch active area. Output maps of the routes can be directed to a large size D plotter.

Section 2 of this paper describes the user interface of the ROUTE system, including details of the graphics interface for specifying input, viewing, comparing and editing the routes. Section 3 contains an evaluation of the effectiveness of the system and presents conclusions.

2. USER INTERFACES IN THE ROUTE SOFTWARE SYSTEM

To develop a set of routes from raw data, a user of ROUTE would typically carry out three major steps corresponding to the INPUT, ROUTE DEVELOPMENT TOOLS and OUTPUT options in the main menu illustrated in the screen print of Figure 1. The main menu items are always present on the top of the screen in "button" style as they appear in the Figure. All the menu options in ROUTE are invoked by pointing and clicking with the mouse. ROUTE is a totally integrated package. Great care was taken to assure that non-creative work is hidden from the user. For example, the mathematical models and other tools require somewhat different formats for input data (radial vs cartesian coordinates, etc). The conversions are all handled internally by ROUTE. Each of the three major steps is described below.

2.1 The INPUT process.

The primary input data is the location of the stop points, typically provided either as data files or as marked locations on paper maps of the geographical area. Stop addresses, services required (quantities of goods to pick up or deliver, time constraints, etc.), and vehicle information (number available, capacities, etc.), are usually provided in tables. When using maps, there are pop-up menu options to digitize the data from the screen or from a digitizing tablet. When a digitizing tablet is used, the paper map is physically taped to the surface and tapping a key on a puck with crosshairs transmits the coordinates to the computer. Visual feedback is provided by displaying the evolving map on the screen as it is digitized. Usually the background map is digitized first, fol-

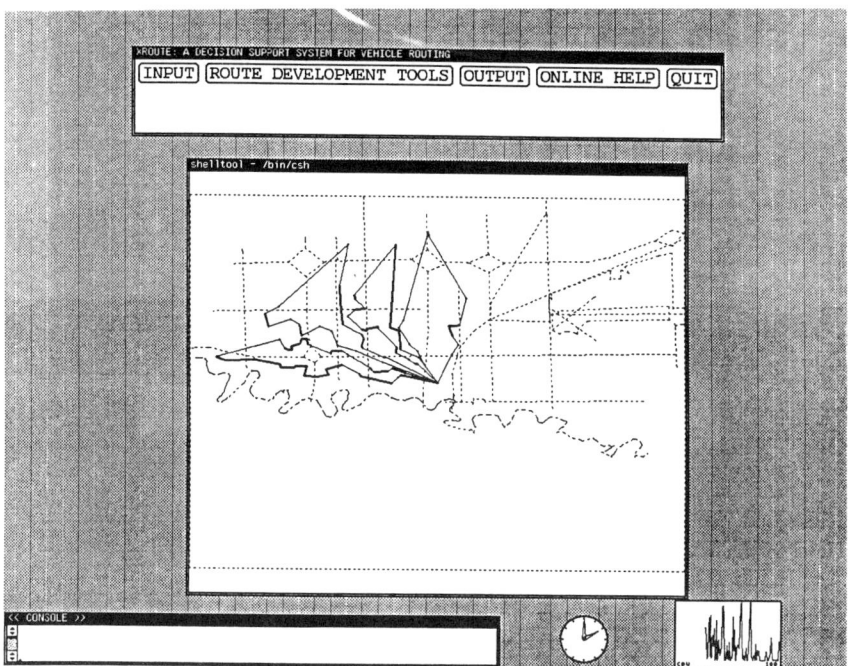

Figure 1. Windows Open to the Main Button Menu and a Plot in the ROUTE System.

lowed by the actual stop locations. The background map is important for two reasons: i) it provides a context and orientation for the stop points and ii) it helps the user make manual adjustments for rivers, coastlines, mountains and other geographical barriers that most of the algorithms ignore. The digitizing process is fast and accurate, with most background maps digitized in less than an hour. As stop locations are digitized, they are graphically displayed as small yellow circles, with the background map fully displayed in light gray for reference. When a stop location is displayed, a screen prompt requests keyboard input of a stop ID and address (used in report writing) and information about quantities of goods to pickup or deliver. As they are keyed, stop IDs are displayed on the screen in yellow next to their locations. Characteristics of vehicles are entered from the keyboard in response to prompts. To visually verify that the information is accurate and complete, the user can invoke the plotter with scaling identical to that of the input map, and produce a plot on translucent vellum to physically overlay onto the original map.

The SCREEN option of INPUT allows the user to enter stops by pointing on the screen and clicking with the mouse. This is useful when the user is well along in the route development process and wishes to experiment with the possibility of expanding the routes to include stops that may be added in the future.

After digitizing is complete, the user selects a meaningful name for the data, e.g., ZONE1. An underlying routine converts the information to a standard form usable by the ROUTE DEVELOPMENT TOOLS and uses the supplied name (ZONE1) to label the data file in a special directory. As explained below, the ROUTE DEVELOPMENT TOOLS concatenate model-specific extensions to these user-chosen file names to provide a basic way of keeping track of which algorithms and other procedures have been applied to the basic data.

2.2 The ROUTE DEVELOPMENT TOOLS.

The second step is creating the vehicle routes. Since several vehicles are usually required, route development typically involves assigning stops to vehicles as well as sequencing the stops served by each vehicle. In this system, route development is expected to be a highly interactive process in which people choose and invoke various heuristic algorithms, evaluate results by viewing reports and graphical displays, and make changes to routes and the parameters that drive the available algorithms. The interactive nature of the ROUTE software encourages experimentation and allows a user to easily combine the use of algorithms with experience. The work of the available algorithms is usually controlled either by human setting of the input parameters or tailoring of the output. This is almost always necessary because some real world problem constraints cannot be included in the algorithms. For example, stops that are on opposite sides of a river or a controlled access highway might be reassigned by a human if an algorithm that primarily used Euclidean distance placed them on the same route.

The ROUTE DEVELOPMENT TOOLS submenu is illustrated in Figure 2.

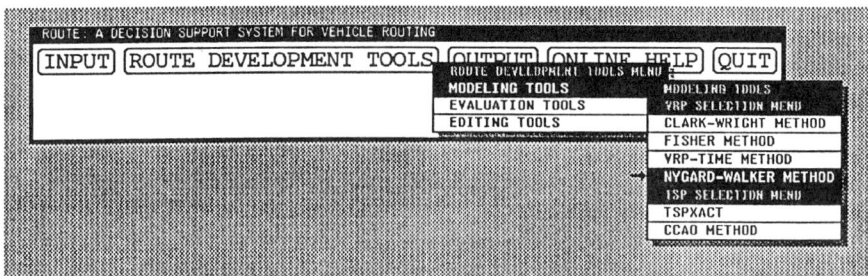

Figure 2. The Modeling Tools Submenu. The VRP and TSP options are multiple vehicle and single vehicle algorithms respectively.

The ROUTE DEVELOPMENT TOOLS subcategories are MODELING TOOLS, EVALUATION TOOLS and EDITING TOOLS, and each is described in more detail below.

MODELING TOOLS. The MODELING TOOLS are all algorithms for creating routes. At present, the MODELING TOOLS include

- Clarke-Wright, a venerable heuristic algorithm capable of producing fast solutions to large scale problems with multiple vehicles and an objective of minimizing total distance (Clarke and Wright 1964)

- FISHER, a heuristic for the multiple vehicle problem that uses a generalized assignment model and produces high-quality solutions to small and medium size problems (Fisher and Jaikumar 1981)

- VRPTIME, an adaptation of the Fisher algorithm that accommodates problems with time deadlines for the stops (Nygard et al. 1988).

- NYGARD-WALKER, a heuristic that uses spacefilling curves and Lagrangian relaxation to obtain solutions to very large-scale multiple vehicle problems (Nygard and Walker 1988).

- TSPEXACT, an exact branch and bound algorithm for the TSP that uses assignment problem relaxations

- CCAO, a heuristic that can quickly produce high-quality solutions to large-scale TSPs (Golden and Stewart 1985)

The algorithms differ somewhat in the types of problems they can handle (number of stops and vehicles, time constraints, characteristics of stops and vehicles), and their adaptability to the specific problem offered through parameter setting. All the multiple vehicle algorithms allow user control of the number of vehicles and their capacities. Options for algorithm-based and human setting of seed point locations are available in FISHER and VRPTIME. Seed movement methods can be selected in VRPTIME. Grid sizes and perturbation methods are user-selectable in NYGARD-WALKER.

The ability to use the EVALUATION TOOLS and EDITING TOOLS to quickly compare routes generated by the same model with different parameter settings is critically important to the user, because the solutions generated by vehicle routing models are sensitive to many user controlled factors.

When several algorithms are used on a given problem, the underlying user-transparent routines that convert standard data to the formats expected by these models provide a valuable basic service.

When an algorithm is invoked, a pop-up menu showing data files that are available for input appears on the screen. After an algorithm has been run on a file of problem data, the output file is named by attaching an extension to the data file name that identifies the model and run number that produced the routes. For example, running the CCAO, CLARKE-WRIGHT and VRPTIME algorithms on an input data file named Zone1 would produce solution files named Zone1.ccao, Zone1.clrk and Zone1.vrpt. If the same algorithm is run more than once on the same input data file, a run number is also attached to the extender. For example, if the CLARKE-WRIGHT algorithm was run twice on Zone1 data, the route files Zone1.clrk---1 and Zone1.clrk---2 would be created. This feature helps keeps the work orderly when the user wishes to experiment with using several sets of parameters for an algorithm being applied to same data. In the example above, the CLARKE-WRIGHT algorithm may have been run the first time with a number-of-vehicles parameter set at six, and the second time set at five. This file naming convention is used in all of the MODELING, EVALUATION and EDITING TOOLS. Use of this internal naming convention means that few "undo" facilities are needed, and that valuable work is seldom accidently lost.

EVALUATION TOOLS. The EVALUATION TOOLS provide text and graphical displays for determining the performance of single routing plans and comparing sets of routing plans. When an EVALUATION TOOL requires a data file, the user is automatically provided with data and route files in pop-up menus.

ROUTE runs on computers with large rapidly refreshed high resolution color displays and software support for multiple windows. Several of the EVALUATION TOOLS use multiple windows to provide the human user with a collection of reports and pictorial displays that work symbiotically. Within ROUTE, there are examples of distinct windows providing information about a given routing plan in different ways, contrasting alternative routing plans, and overlapping to conveniently record a sequence of activities that have been carried out.

Figure 3 shows a screen with 2 windows that illustrates the work of the SHOW REPORT and VIEW SINGLE ROUTE EVALUATION TOOLS. In the left window is a standard written report that lists the stop sequence with distances travelled, arrival times, stop demand (draw), ID and an address or a location description. The method used to calculate the distances is also reported. All the methods can use a distance matrix, or calculate distances from the Euclidean or Taxicab metric. The right window in Figure 3 shows

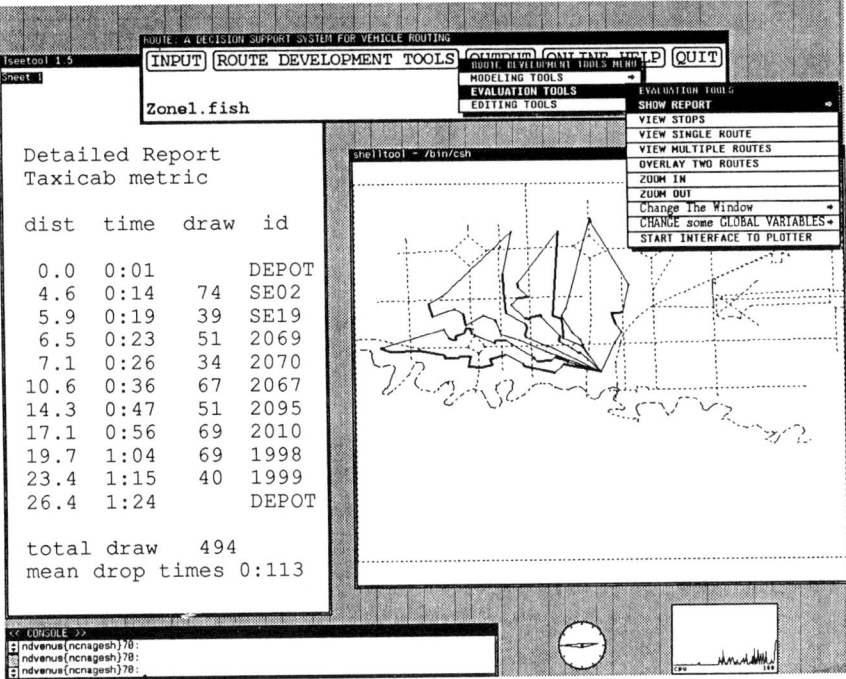

Figure 3. An illustration of a written report and accompanying plot, shown in multiple windows that were located and sized by the user.

a plot of a routing plan obtained by clicking on the VIEW SINGLE ROUTE option. The window cans be positioned and sized with the mouse by using the CHANGE WINDOW option, followed by clicking on the upper left and lower right corners of the desired location on the screen. Clicking on the VIEW STOPS tool would produced a pop-up menu of data files, and selecting one would produce a screen plot of just the stop locations. The VIEW MULTIPLE ROUTES option automatically places windows precisely in each of the 4 quadrants of the screen. The 4 quadrants were chosen because several users said that they liked the symmetry, and that one-fourth of a 19 inch high-resolution screen still provides enough size and detail in the plots to be useful. The OVERLAY ROUTES feature is the most powerful graphical comparison tool provided by this system. With this tool, 2 routing plans are selected from the pop-up menu for graphical comparison. The first is plotted with dashed lines, and the second is plotted with solid lines. The result is that links in common between the routing plans are shown as solid, and links on the first plan but not the second appear dashed. Figure 4 is an illustration of the OVERLAY feature, produced with a laser printer plot for clear presentation.

Other options control the level of detail of the screen plots. The ZOOM IN and

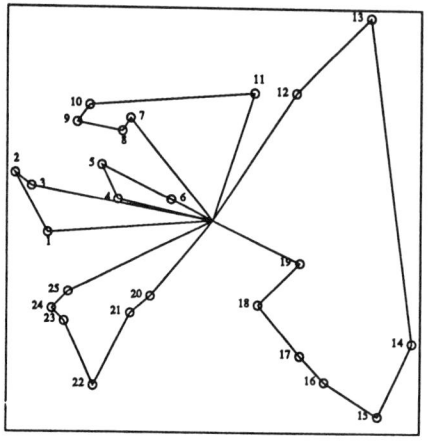
Tours generated usind Model A

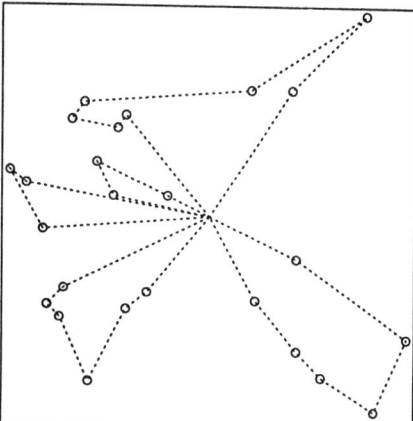
Tours generated using Model B

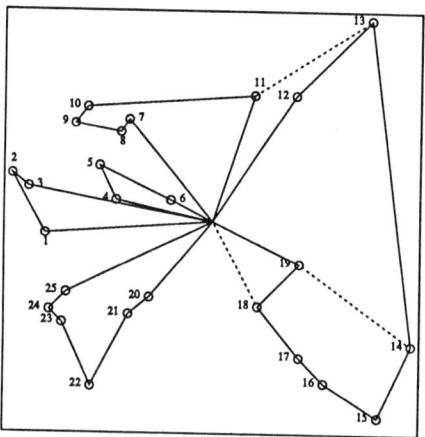
Tours after OVERLAYING Tour A and Tour B

Figure 4. Use of the OVERLAY TWO ROUTES option to visually identify the three links in Model B that are not in Model A.

ZOOM OUT capabilities use an automatic 2-power magnification change referenced on the center of a plot. They can be used successively to achieve higher powers of 2. The CHANGE COORDINATES option allows the user to graphically select world coordinates within a window, providing an arbitrary zoom capability. With this option, the user simply uses the mouse to click on the upper left and lower right corners of an area within a window, and that area is magnified to fill the window.

EDITING TOOLS. The EDITING TOOLS, shown in Figure 5, support user experimentation with the problem data and routing plans.

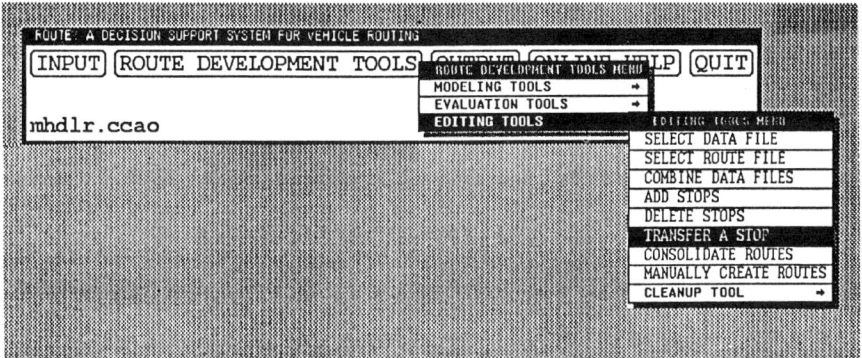

Figure 5. The EDITING TOOLS menu. All of the options are designed to facilitate human involvement in route development.

The SELECT DATA FILE and SELECT ROUTE FILE options have their natural meanings of providing the selection menus of data and route files respectively.

The COMBINE DATA FILES, ADD STOPS and DELETE STOPS options provide support for editing the data files. The COMBINE DATA FILES option is used for human control in partitioning the stops into zones. Upon invoking this option, the user chooses 2 data file names, then uses mouse pointing and clicks to select stops that are to be moved from one data set to the other. The new data files are stored separately from the old, and can be used in development of alternative routing plans. The ADD STOPS option allows the user to expand a data file by pointing and clicking on a screen location. The DELETE STOPS option is a good example of graphical feedback. With this option, when the user clicks on a stop which is to be deleted, the circle representing the stop "blinks" on the screen plot before deletion, assuring the user that the choice is correct. DELETE DATA FILE and DELETE ROUTE FILE accomplish file deletion when selected. Regularly deleting files is important in ROUTE, because the MODELING and

EDITING TOOLS only create new files, never altering an old file in place. Thus, files can easily proliferate during the analyses.

The TRANSFER A STOP, CONSOLIDATE ROUTES and MANUALLY CREATE ROUTES are tools for human control of the routes. With the TRANSFER A STOP option, the user selects 2 routing plans, clicks on a stop on one of the routes, then moves the pointer to the other route and clicks on a stop that the person wants the first stop to follow. Figure 6 illustrates the process.

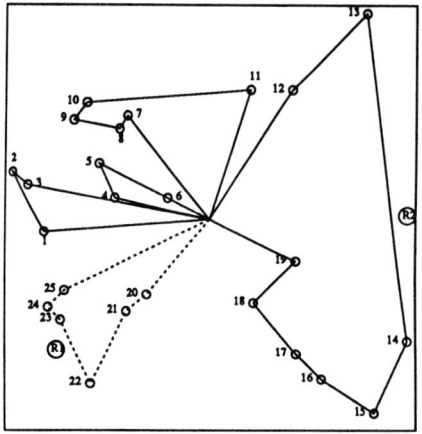 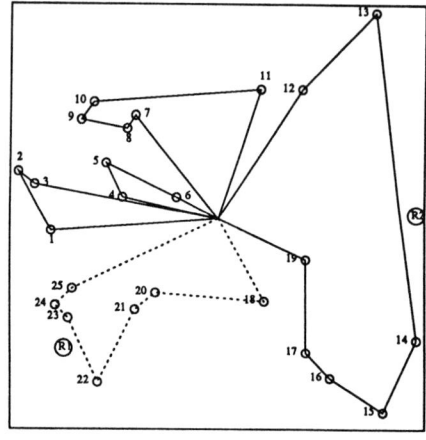

A. Tours generated by using Model A   B. Tours generated by transfering Stop 18 from R2 to R1

Figure 6. An illustration of the TRANSFER A STOP option in the EDITING TOOLS. The most common use is to tailor routing plans to avoid rivers and other geographical barriers.

The CONSOLIDATE ROUTES option simply combines collections of distinct route files into one. This is useful in routing systems where the problem was partitioned into zones, as commonly happens in practice. In such cases, CONSOLIDATE ROUTES is always used in preparation for final hardcopy printed reports and plots, in order to provide a complete and unified set of results. When a routing plan is built up from many zones, the user may spend considerable experimental time examining trial consolidations, in making zoning decisions, and and consolidating to simplify the set of active route files as progress is made. When the user wishes to manually input a route from scratch with no algorithm involvement, the MANUALLY CREATE ROUTE option is selected. The route is specified by sequentially clicking on stops with the mouse in the desired order. Studying the currently used routes can help the analyst understand subtleties of the real problem, and provide basic guidance into algorithm selection. Thus, once the stop data is entered, it is usual to proceed by using the MANUAL CREATE ROUTES option to input the current routes. In actual routing applications, we find that it is common for a person using the ROUTE system to quickly produce sets of routes on the order of 10%-15% shorter than current practice. In addition, ways to operate with fewer vehicles than current practice can often be identified.

2.3 The OUTPUT Process

After INPUT and ROUTE DEVELOPMENT are complete, the final major step is producing the output reports. The basic output consists of large paper plots of a background map with stops and routes shown in colors, tables of the sequences in which the stops are visited, and performance information. To accomplish the output process, the user consolidates the route files for any separate zones, then selects the OUTPUT button on the main menu. PRINT REPORT and PLOT ROUTES options are then offered. The PRINT REPORT selection triggers a submenu for options of producing hardcopy of an individual route plan report, or a unified report for the entire routing plan. The PLOT ROUTES option prompts the user for a scaling factor, then produces a 24 X 36 plot of the routes, either on paper complete with background map, or on vellum for overlaying onto a conventional map of the roads and streets. A stable of 14 different color pens in 2 different widths allows the final paper plots to show the background map, stop locations and adjacent routes in different colors, with wide lines used for the recommended routes for good contrast.

3. EVALUATION, SUMMARY AND CONCLUSIONS

Within their research groups, the authors have been developing vehicle routing software since 1979. This software has been used to develop over 40 routing systems for school busses, grain trucks and trains, newspaper distribution vehicles and Air Force cargo planes, as well as to support basic research. In each major routing project, the work began with the preparation of a Gantt chart to schedule the activities, and a log book was kept until project completion. To evaluate the effectiveness of the ROUTE software system, these log books were consulted to determine the proportion of project time spent on activities other than operations research analyses and modeling. Although the projects are diverse enough to rule out valid statistical analyses, we estimate that about 80% of the time in these projects was spent on non-OR aspects of the work. The non-OR time was spent primarily in 4 ways: i) digitizing the raw input data from maps manually with transparent grid paper, ii) coding and invoking special programs to reformat data for use with alternative algorithms and report writers, iii) coding and running specialized report generators to compare output from diverse procedures, and iv) customizing plots to overlay onto maps for route comparison and to supply to clients.

When ROUTE is used, the time required to carry out the digitizing process, although still not trivial because of the need to tap stops with the mouse and to enter information from the keyboard, has been dramatically reduced and is much less error prone. Time spent on the other 3 activities has been virtually eliminated. We conservatively estimate that non-creative time now consumes no more than 20% of the time expended on a project. The remaining 80% is now spent the way we prefer: thinking, fitting mathematical models to the problem at hand, evaluating and experimenting with alternative routing plans.

We conclude that ROUTE is extraordinarily successful software; and that much of the reason lies in the integration of different functions and tools into one interactive environment, facilitated by powerful user interface techniques.

REFERENCES

Assad, A. and B. Golden, Eds. (1988) *Vehicle Routing: Methods and Studies,* North Holland, Amsterdam.

Bodin, L., B. Golden, A. Assad, and M. Ball (1983), "Routing and Scheduling of Vehicles and Crews: the State of the Art," Computers and Operations Research 10, 63-211.

Clarke, G. and J. W. Wright (1964), "Scheduling of Vehicles From a Central Depot to a number of Delivery Points," Operations Research 12, 568-581.

Fisher, M. and R. Jaikumar (1981), "A Generalized Assignment Heuristic for Vehicle Routing," Networks 11, 109-124.

Golden, B. L. and W. Stewart, "Empirical Analysis of Heuristics," in *The Traveling Salesman Problem,* E. Lawler, J. Lenstra, A. Rinooy Kan and D. Shmoys, eds. Wiley-Interscience, New York 1985, pp. 207-249.

Nygard, K. E., P. Greenberg, W. Bolkan, and E. Swenson (1988), "Algorithms for the Deadline Vehicle Routing Problem," in *Vehicle Routing: Methods and Studies,* A. Assad and B. Golden, Eds, North-Holland, Amsterdam, pp. 107-125.

Nygard, K. E. and R. Walker (1988), "A Vehicle routing Algorithm Based on Spacefilling Curves", Technical Report, Department of Computer Science and Operations Research, North Dakota State University, Fargo, N.D.

Ronen, D. (1988), "Practical Aspests of Vehicle Routing and Scheduling," The European Journal of Operations Research 35, 137-145.

VEHICLE ROUTING AND SCHEDULING FOR HOME DELIVERY

JOANNE R. SCHAFFER AND PAMELA K. PEARL

Ryder Truck Rental, Inc., 3600 N.W. 82 Avenue
Miami, Florida 33166

ABSTRACT

This paper examines the development of a computerized routing and scheduling system for home delivery. This problem involves not only the delivery of goods to homes, but also must allow for pickups and exchanges of goods. Locating customers must be fast and relatively efficient as there is no stable customer base. Routes must be developed to meet customer time windows, but also allow the drivers to return to a home when the customer was not there on the initial visit. The routes constructed by the computer must resemble the routes the dispatcher would have developed in order for these routes to be accepted. Last minute changes and modifications must be handled easily and efficiently as the home delivery environment is very dynamic.

1. INTRODUCTION

The dispatcher for a home delivery routing and scheduling system (HDRS) must develop routes that allow for the delivery, pickup, and/or exchange of goods to customers' homes or places of business. These goods can include furniture, refrigerators, washers, dryers, etc. and they must be delivered within a time period specified by the customer; that is, within a time window. Vehicles are dispatched and returned to the home depot on the same day.

A major problem in home delivery is that the number of stops for a large distributor may vary between 400 and 1000 stops per day. The demand is greatly influenced by such things as seasonal factors, sales, and promotions and can change without warning. There is no stable customer base in home delivery, and hence routes are not stable over time. The problem is then to maintain a constant driver force. Additionally, since drivers are paid by the number of stops they make, the dispatcher must react quickly to these changes in demand and balance the numbers of stops on the routes for full time drivers.

The HDRS is an application of the vehicle routing and scheduling problem with time window constraints (VRSPTW). Golden and Assad [1986] present an overview of this problem and Assad [1988] discusses vehicle routing from a practical standpoint. Both provide excellent sources of references for this and related routing and scheduling problems.

In the VRSPTW, routes must start and end from a common depot. This is usually a distribution center or a warehouse. Customers may require the delivery, pickup, or exchange of goods. These services may be defined by measures such as: the number of pieces, the weight of the items, and/or the volume. Vehicles set capacity restrictions on these measures. Each stop's service must begin no earlier and end no later than the open and close times set by the time window.

In addition to the above constraints, the HDRS requires that the drivers satisfy rules for the number of hours that they are allowed to drive and the number of hours that they are allowed to be on duty each day. The Department of Transportation (DOT) restricts drivers to driving ten hours per day or working fifteen hours per day for drivers operating beyond designated commercial zones. On duty time includes drive time, time spent loading the truck for delivery, and the time spent making the delivery, pickup, or exchange. In home delivery, the driver is a delivery man and as such spend most of their time loading and unloading the truck. As this is a more strenuous activity than driving, the on duty time can be restricted to be less than fifteen by the HDRS system.

The manual routing system for home delivery starts with the dispatcher sorting all of the sales tickets for the day by zip code. He/she next takes the sorted tickets and groups them by pre-defined route areas. The dispatcher then begins forming routes using his/her knowledge of the areas and knowledge of the drivers' experience in making deliveries (i.e., knowing how many deliveries each driver can reasonably make in one day's work). The routes are formed one at a time, starting from the farthest point away from the depot and working inward. Tradeoffs between routes are made after routes have been constructed in order to balance the numbers of deliveries. This manual process takes the dispatcher at least four hours.

2. ROUTING ALGORITHMS

The object of routing algorithms for HDRS is to develop routes quickly and efficiently, therefore freeing up human resources for more meaningful, analytical tasks. Also, since drivers will sequence stops according to their own expert knowledge of areas, fine tuning of routes is left to the drivers and the routing algorithm's main purpose is to group stops together into routes. Even the dispatchers respect the drivers knowledge of local areas in the actual sequencing of routes.

Routing algorithms for the VRSPTW in the literature have largely been confined to the development of heuristics. This problem has shown not only to be NP-hard, but much more difficult to solve than the vehicle routing problem without time window constraints (Savelsbergh [1984] and Solomon [1986]).

Another consideration for the routing algorithm is that the problem must be solvable in a reasonable amount of time on a micro-computer, such as an IBM - PS/2 Model 60. Typically, home delivery operations do not have a mainframe or suitable mini computer that can be used for routing and scheduling and the use of a personal computer reduces the expense. The logistics portion of a business (i.e., transportation, distribution, warehousing, etc.) is the last frontier of cost minimization and as such is the most resistant to attempts to involve computerized routing and scheduling.

In the literature, many of the heuristics for the VRSPTW are adapted from the Clarke and Wright [1964] savings procedure originally proposed for the VRP. Initially, each stop forms its own route. Two routes are combined if the resulting route is feasible and produces a savings (i.e., reduced miles). Solomon [1987] compares several of these route construction procedures modified for the VRSPTW.

Routes obtained from a routing model must be shown to be driveable from a practical standpoint. "Computerized algorithms" can make "bad" decisions when dispatchers know some information not available to the computer. This may be knowledge of local areas, road construction, drivers' work habits, etc. The advantage is that the computer can test many more possibilities than the dispatcher and arrive at solutions not readily apparent. The problem then becomes to convince the dispatcher that the resulting routes are workable.

Routes can be categorized into three different types: "tear drop" or "petal shaped" routes, "lollipop" routes, and "stick" routes. Figure 1. depicts these route types. Petal shaped routes are the routes traditionally made by routing models. These are the routes that minimize miles. Stops are made by the truck all along a loop starting and ending from the depot. Lollipop routes tend to have a long stem, where no stops are made, with a condensed or concentrated loop at the end of the stem. Stick routes are long straight routes with deliveries on the way out from and way in to the depot.

From a dispatchers perspective, petal shaped routes are only desirable when the route is close in to the domicile. This is due to the problem in home delivery of the customer not being home when the driver reaches their home. The routes must be such that the driver has the ability to return to missed stops later in the day without adding too many extra miles. Missed deliveries is a major problem in HDRS and hence is one that is important to try to minimize, if possible, from a routing standpoint. Thus, stick routes become the most practical overall, with lollipop routes practical in remote areas or areas far from the depot, and petal shaped routes only for routes near to the depot.

3. HOME DELIVERY ROUTING HEURISTIC

The routing algorithm for the HDRS was designed more as an aid to the dispatcher rather than as an end result. The major emphasis is to group stops into feasible routes that meet time window constraints, load restrictions, driver rules, and other time constraints. The objective of the route building is to minimize the miles driven without making excessive waiting time on the routes with the fewest number of trucks. The routes must also allow for drivers to service areas where it is possible to return to missed stops without adding an inordinate amount of time to the route.

This was accomplished by allowing the user of the system (the dispatcher) to define routing areas. These are regions that have traditionally formed routes and are, in fact, currently being used to build the routes manually. Once these areas have been defined, basic routing algorithms can be used to route to them. An objective here is to initially have the computer form routes that the dispatchers are "used to" seeing and gradually wean them away from these routing areas to more

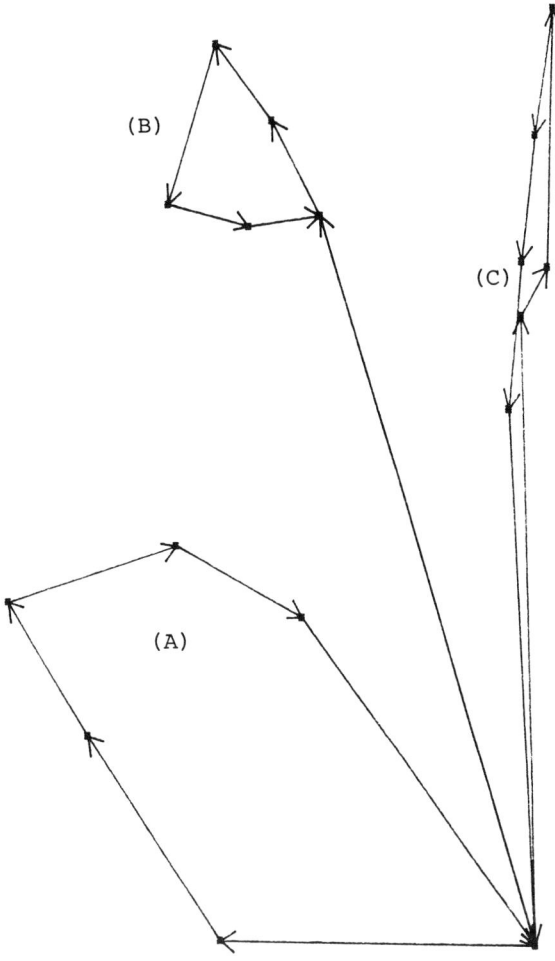

Figure 1. Route Types: (A) Petal Shaped,
(B) Lollipop,
(C) Stick

efficient groupings. Early acceptance of the computerized system is of a primary concern.

Another means of requiring stops from the same neighborhood to be placed on the same route is to form "super" stops. These super stops are formed by stops that have the same characteristics (i.e., they are from the same small neighborhood and have the same time window) and redefining them as a single stop. This is possible since time windows for home delivery are generally defined as A.M. or morning stops, P.M. or afternoon stops, after 5:00 P.M. stops, or stops that can be serviced any time. Very few stops are allowed narrow windows. The forming of super stops not only forces the stops from the same local neighborhood to be on the same route, but it also greatly reduces the computer time required for a solution since it condenses the problem.

A major issue in routing algorithms is deciding when it is time to end a route and start a new route. From a manual perspective, the dispatcher can take an overview and using his/her judgment will make decisions as to when a route is full or when there are no more stops that can be added efficiently to the route. Computerized algorithms do not have this intuition and base the termination decision on predetermined rules such as time and capacity restrictions. Thus there are times when these algorithms will make poor decisions in order to fill a truck.

To help alleviate this problem, route groups can be either designated as exclusive or as nonexclusive. Stops in an exclusive group will only be routed with stops in that same group. Stops in a nonexclusive group (A) can be routed with stops in another nonexclusive group (B) only when: (1) there are no more unrouted stops in group A that can be feasibly inserted on the route, (2) group B is the closest area to the stops from group A on the current route, and (3) there are one or more stops from group B that can be feasibly inserted on the route. The dispatcher can of course override the exclusive group restrictions when modifying routes (as he/she can override any of the other constraints of the model). In this way routes that more closely resemble routes that the dispatcher is used to seeing can be formed and hence can lead to a higher probability of having the routes being accepted by this dispatcher.

After the initial route building is complete, the routes may be optimized in order to reduce the number of miles driven without increasing the waiting time. Since driving time is determined by the number of miles driven, the total time for the routes can be made as a function of miles driven and waiting time.

Baker and Schaffer [1986] present computational experience with branch exchange heuristics for the VRSPTW using time and distance in a weighted objective function. These heuristics look at breaking two or more links in one route or between two or more routes and then reconnecting the nodes in the route(s) differently. The procedures that seemed to yield the most improvement for the time spent looking for exchanges were: a two-optimal within route (breaking two links within a single route), three-optimal within route (breaking three links within a single route), two-optimal between two routes, and a three-optimal between two routes.

These optimizers were adapted in the context of the home delivery algorithm. Optimizing is done with respect to the super stops and to the route group definitions. Two routes are optimized together only if they are from the same exclusive group or both routes contain stops from the same nonexclusive group. This again greatly reduces the time for the optimizers to run and has been shown not to alter the quality of the solution.

4. RESULTS AND CONCLUSIONS

The HDRS system described was written and tested for a home delivery operation. As the routing and scheduling portion is to be a small portion of an entire computerized home delivery system (complete with payroll, accounting, customer pre-calling, etc. functions), it has not yet been implemented. This means that only preliminary results and predictions are available at this time.

Benchmark testing has shown a 7% reduction in the number of miles for the initial optimized routes formed by the computerized HDRS when compared with the routes actually routed by the dispatcher. After the dispatcher has manually modified these routes the percentage reduction is much higher.

To illustrate the results of the heuristic, seventy-three stops which comprised five routes, manually built by the dispatcher (out of the twenty-five routes for May 3, 1988) were selected. These routes are displayed in Figure 2. For the manually built routes, the total system mileage was 411 miles. Figure 3. displays the routes formed by the heuristic. Improvements included a savings of 39 miles (from 411 to 362 miles) and one truck was eliminated. Thus one driver could also be

Figure 2. Dispatcher's Manually Built Routes

Route Summary Information

Rt	#St	Miles	Load 1	Load 2	Load 3	Start	End	Drive	Wait	Total
1	15	138	30	15	0	7:53 Thu	16:34 Thu	3:41	0:00	8:41
16	13	80	23	13	0	7:34 Thu	14:13 Thu	2:19	0:00	6:39
21	13	65	24	13	0	7:38 Thu	14:14 Thu	2:16	0:00	6:36
24	16	60	28	16	0	10:59 Thu	18:33 Thu	2:14	0:00	7:34
25	16	68	41	16	0	7:38 Thu	15:22 Thu	2:24	0:00	7:44

Total System Miles   411
Customers In Model   73
Number Of Routes   5

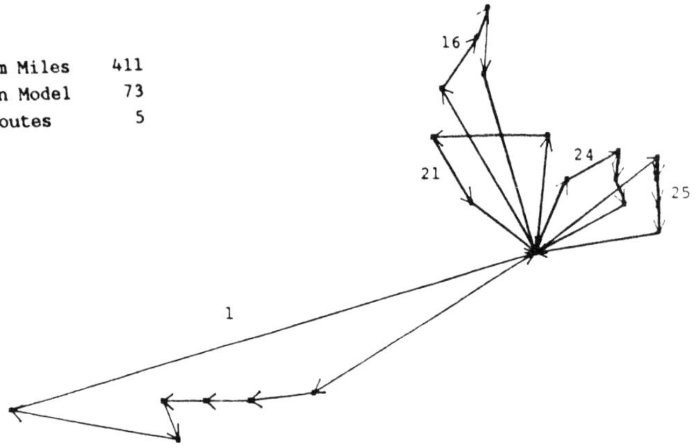

Figure 3. Heuristically Constructed Routes

Route Summary Information

Rt	#St	Miles	Load 1	Load 2	Load 3	Start	End	Drive	Wait	Total
1	19	138	37	19	0	7:26 Thu	17:45 Thu	3:59	0:00	10:19
2	22	100	40	22	0	7:39 Thu	18:19 Thu	3:20	0:00	10:40
3	12	50	21	12	0	8:14 Thu	14:02 Thu	1:48	0:00	5:48
4	20	74	48	20	0	7:48 Thu	17:11 Thu	2:43	0:00	9:23

Total System Miles   362
Customers In Model   73
Number Of Routes   4

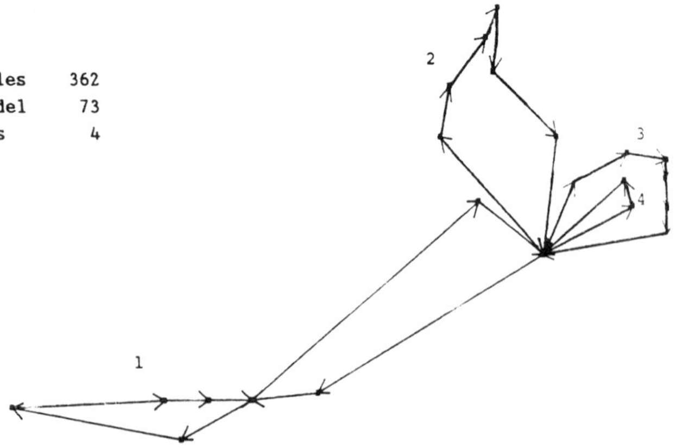

eliminated.

Instead of having the dispatcher sort sales tickets by route area and "rough route," which takes approximately 8 hours per day, the ticket information will be keyed into the system. A rough first draft of routes will be presented to the dispatcher at the beginning of their shift. This will allow refinement of automated routes which will make the routing function more efficient. The data which has been keyed into the system will be used not only to provide route information, but will also be used for printing the load manifest.

Currently these load sheets are being typed manually after the dispatcher has determined the routes and before the customers are called to confirm the delivery time. As many changes must be made to the routes after the pre-notification stage, the load sheets are filled with handwritten changes by the time the driver actually gets them and are very difficult to read. Also, these sheets are used after the route has been run for billing and payroll purposes.

In the computerized HDRS system, these last minute changes can be entered manually and the routes could even be rerun before the final load sheets are printed. Thus, having the final load sheets printed directly from the routing program is seen as a major advantage of this HDRS system. On an IBM PS - 2 Model 60 a problem with 800 stops has been shown to run and optimize in about fifteen minutes. The home delivery environment is continuously dynamic. It is rare to find many repeat customers in the day to day routine. Routing and scheduling is the heart and driving force of the entire home delivery system (HDRS, billing, payroll, claims and damages, accounting, etc.). Ultimately this system will provide management the information it requires to make informed decisions on a daily and weekly basis in order to manage their entire operation.

REFERENCES

Assad, A.A. (1988), "Modeling and Implementation Issues in Routing," *in Vehicle Routing: Methods and Studies,* B.L. Golden and A.A. Assad, Eds. Elsevier Science Publishers B.V., Amsterdam, Netherlands, pp. 7-45.

Baker, E.K. and Schaffer, J.R. (1986), "Computational Experience with Branch Exchange Heuristics for Vehicle Routing Problems with Time Window Constraints," *American Journal of Mathematical and Management Sciences 6*

(Nos. 3 & 4), pp. 261-300.

Clarke, G. and Wright, J. (1964), "Scheduling of Vehicles from a Central Depot to a Number of Delivery Points," *Operations Research 12,* pp. 568-581.

Golden, B.A., and Assad, A.A. (1986), "Vehicle Routing with Time-Window Constraints," *American Journal of Mathematical and Management Sciences 6* (Nos. 3 & 4), pp. 251-260.

Savelsbergh, M.W.P. (1984), "Local Search in Routing Problems with Time Windows," Report OS-R8409, Centre for Mathematics and Computer Science, Amsterdam.

Solomon, M. (1987), "Algorithms for the Vehicle Routing and Scheduling Problem with Time Window Constraints," *Operations Research 35,* pp. 254-265.

Solomon, M. (1986), "On the Worst-Case Performance of Some Heuristics for the Vehicle Routing and Scheduling Problem with Time Window Constraints," *Networks 16,* pp. 161-174.

VII.

SIMULATION

SIMULATION MODEL DEVELOPMENT: THE MULTIDIMENSIONALITY OF THE COMPUTING TECHNOLOGY PULL

OSMAN BALCI AND RICHARD E. NANCE

Department of Computer Science and Systems Research Center
Virginia Polytechnic Institute and State University, Blacksburg, Virginia 24061

ABSTRACT

Recent computing advances in artificial intelligence, computer graphics, human-computer interface, networking, parallel processing, and software engineering pull simulation model development in different directions. This paper discusses the impacts of significant advances in these areas on simulation model development, overviews how our Simulation Model Development Environment design is influenced by the recent advances, and speculates on the impacts of predicted future advances in these areas on simulation model development. The paper concludes that the computing advances in the six areas can be integrated under a simulation environment to provide an extremely powerful platform for simulation model development and execution.

1. INTRODUCTION

Systems design in technology sensitive applications is often characterized as advanced by "needs push" or "technology pull". The reality of the latter descriptor is that a need can be difficult to recognize, and the perception of entirely different forms of meeting that need can prove nearly impossible. For example, one who had used only batch processing systems prior to 1972 could not envision how programming productivity could be enhanced through interactive time-sharing. Frequently, only after experiencing particular technical innovations can the definition of the need for them be formulated. This paper is motivated by the recognition that the "pull" of computing technology has caused the needs for simulation model development to undergo significant redefinition.

The early development of discrete event simulation models assumes one of two forms: (1) the use of functional routines to assist in the production of a model in a general purpose language, typically FORTRAN, or (2) the employment of one of the specialized simulation programming languages, which often entails a significant learning commitment. Both approaches characterize model development activities in the early to mid 1960s, and both continue to dominate the current scene. The former, or simulator, approach has persisted largely because of the predominance of FORTRAN as an instructional language in engineering curricula; the latter, because of strong advances in simulation programming language (SPL) capabilities in the 1970s. A weakness of both the simulator and SPL approaches is the inherent limitation of a model representation that must also serve as a model implementation. The 1980s mark a transition in the understanding of what is needed to cope with the size and complexity of models that are no longer bound by execution time constraints.

Since June 1983 our MDE project has addressed a complex research problem: prototyping discrete-event Simulation Model Development Environments (SMDE) following the automation-based software paradigm [Balci and Nance 1987a]. The major research goal has been to provide an integrated and comprehensive collection of computer-based tools to: (1) offer cost-effective, integrated, and automated support of model development throughout the model life cycle, (2) improve the model quality by effectively assisting in the quality assurance of the model, (3) significantly increase the efficiency and productivity of the project team, and (4) substantially decrease the model development time. The SMDE prototype is being developed on a Sun color computer workstation. The reader is referred to [Balci and Nance 1987b] for details of the SMDE prototype.

In this paper we review the impact of significant recent advances in several important areas of computing technology on simulation model development. While computing technology has experienced notable advances across a broad front, the following selected areas certainly must rank among the most significant: (1) artificial intelligence, (2) computer graphics, (3) human-computer interface, (4) networking, (5) parallel processing, and (6) software engineering. In every section devoted to each of the six areas, we: (a) review the impact of substantial recent advances in that area on simulation model development, (b) overview how our SMDE design is influenced by the recent advances in that area, and (c) speculate on the impact of predicted future computing advances in that area on simulation model development. Concluding remarks are presented in Section 8.

2. ARTIFICIAL INTELLIGENCE

Two "schools of thought" are apparent in the attitude toward the AI/discrete event simulation interaction in simulation model development: one ascribes to the primacy of AI as the fundamental basis for development; the other, sees AI as only a contributor. Because of space limitations, we confine the discussion to the former "school", and review the impact on simulation model development in five categories: (1) knowledge-based simulation, (2) intelligent simulation environments, (3) intelligent front ends for model generation, (4) goal-directed simulation, and (5) introspection.

The Rule Oriented Simulation System (ROSS) [McArthur et al. 1986], developed at the Rand Corporation, is an English-like, object-oriented, interactive, and visual language implemented in Lisp. Relying on recently developed AI techniques and expert systems technology, ROSS provides a simulation environment in which users can conveniently design, test, and modify large knowledge-based simulation models. It has been successfully applied to a strategic air penetration simulation and a tactical ground-based combat simulation. ROSS has significantly impacted the manner in which simulation models of soft problems are developed with its integration of the object oriented paradigm, visual interactive simulation, and AI techniques.

The Knowledge-Based Simulation system (KBS) [Reddy et al. 1986] is similar to ROSS; however, KBS stresses the automatic analysis of simulation results. All simulation models are descriptive in nature. They produce results with no indication of the "goodness" or "badness" of the results leaving the burden of analysis and interpretation to the simulationist. On the other hand, prescriptive models, like linear programming models, produce results (solutions) with a label such as "optimal", "feasible", or "infeasible", thereby facilitating the analysis of results. Analyzing and interpreting the results of a large and complex simulation model are very difficult. KBS tries to resolve this problem by way of providing prescriptive results.

The Knowledge-Based Model Construction (KBMC) system [Murray and Sheppard 1988] uses domain knowledge, extracts the necessary information from the modeler in a structured interactive dialog, and generates a complete model specification. A programmed model in the SIMAN language is automatically created by the KBMC system from this specification, utilizing modeling knowledge and SIMAN knowledge. Similarly, the Modeling Advisor for GEST programs (MAGEST) [Oren and Aytac 1985] uses knowledge about the GEST morphology, incremental knowledge about the user programs, and domain knowledge to generate a model specification in the GEST language. A programmed model in Simscript II.5 is then created from this specification. Representing the program generation approach, KBMC and MAGEST both exemplify ideas in the achievement of the automation-based paradigm for simulation model development [Balci and Nance 1987a].

Shannon [1986] provides an excellent overview and speculates that one of the major impacts of AI on simulation will be the creation of intelligent simulation environments to make the task of conducting simulation studies easier, faster and more accurate. The SMDE research project has been termed very ambitious by several colleagues although SMDE prototypes have been mostly "unintelligent." (The term "intelligent environment" is used as described in [Shannon 1986].) Building one that is intelligent under the objectives of the SMDE research project is simply not possible within the current technology. We speculate that it will be a long time (at least a decade) for domain-independent, generic intelligent simulation environments to be realized.

Doukidis and Paul [1986] describe their experiences in building a natural language understanding system to aid the formulation of simulation models. The success of developing a natural language interface for model generation is dependent upon the advances in translation devices, voice recognition systems, and synthetic voice reproduction devices. Recent advances have provided only encouragement for further research and significant impact on simulation model development will not be realized for at least another decade.

The Goal-Directed Simulation approach proposes a major shift from the traditional problem analysis view to solution synthesis view. It suggests the construction of a simulation model as a collection of goals decomposed into sub-goals. At the execution and experiment levels, the model seeks to achieve the goals given the knowledge by the user about the objectives, goals, performance criteria, and behaviors [Umphress and Pooch 1987]. Recent research in this area has attempted to demonstrate the feasibility of this approach.

Using the introspection AI technique, the simulation model is built to learn about itself and to gain knowledge by tracing the dynamics of its execution. Introspection is a common objective of many knowledge-based systems. If achieved, this technique should prove very beneficial especially for model verification and validation. Currently, existing as an idea only, introspection requires further developments to prove a workable approach.

3. COMPUTER GRAPHICS

Recent advances in computer graphics have made visual simulation possible. Visual simulation can now be conducted as post-simulation animation or simulation-concurrent animation on many workstations with graphics processors and on Personal Computers. Making visual simulation interactive requires more computing power than the already very demanding power required for noninteractive simulation. Thus the impact of recent advances in computer graphics on simulation is also dependent on the advances in the semiconductor (computer architecture) technology to provide more powerful hardware required for visual simulation.

Grant and Weiner [1986] review the following ten commercially available graphically animated simulation systems: AutoGram, BEAM, Cinema, Modelmaster, PCModel, RTCS, SeeWhy, SimFactory, SIMPLE1, and TESS. They indicate that "Collectively, about 500 animated simulation systems have been installed in the U.S. Four years ago there were less than ten such installations." Bell and O'Keefe [1987] present a short history of Visual Interactive Simulation (VIS), describe some recent developments, and suggest four future areas of research: (1) type and quality of visual display, (2) software and hardware for VIS, (3) the need for methodology, and (4) the role of expert systems.

In our SMDE research project, a general purpose traffic intersection visual interactive simulator is prototyped to gain some experience with VIS and to develop some expertise in using SunView and SunCore software packages for VIS. This work is being extended by the implementation of a new conceptual framework in the development of a visual interactive simulator, applicable to a large class of problems.

Predicted future advances in the high-speed computing technology and computer graphics should make the VIS a more viable approach. Computer graphics will play a crucial role in the development of models used for training and educational purposes.

4. HUMAN-COMPUTER INTERFACE

The research at Xerox's Palo Alto Research Center between 1978 and 1982 provides the underpinnings for the current state-of-the-art technology for human-computer interfaces. In 1982, Sun Microsystems developed a window management system, SunWindows (later its improved version was called SunView), around the technology developed by Xerox. Apple Computer has implemented a different version of Xerox's graphical interface technology in their Macintosh computers in 1984, opening the door for a whole new type of software. Recently, the Presentation Manager interface for Microsoft's new operating system, OS/2, incorporates a graphical interface which is very similar to the Macintosh's.

Today, all the major players in the microcomputer industry believe in graphical interfaces and appreciate the "what-you-see-is-what-you-get" benefit of these visual interfaces. Unfortunately, the simulation community has continued ignoring the potential benefits of this interface technology in simulation model development. Graphical interfaces have been provided by some vendors to extract information from the user to automatically generate SPL- and domain-specific models (e.g., Network II.5 for computer-communications network design and analysis, Comnet II.5 for telecommunication network analysis). The state-of-the-art interface technology has not yet been effectively utilized for simulation model development.

The SMDE research project is highly dependent on the Sun interface technology (specifically the usage of a mouse, a high-resolution monitor, icons, windows, scroll bars, buttons, pull-down menus, pop-up menus, and hierarchical menus). The technology has significantly facilitated the rapid prototyping of SMDE tools. The prototypes have been built in much less time and in a much better form expediting the experimentation with the prototypes. Clearly, productivity gains have been realized over the dumb-terminal interface technology used earlier in the research project. In continuation of the current research, a new conceptual framework is under development for simulation modeling using Sun's state-of-the-art interface technology.

The significant technological advances in the human-computer interfaces provided by operating systems will considerably change the manner in which information is extracted from a modeler, thereby facilitating simulation model development. An advanced interface can assist the modeler in representing a system at a level which is much closer to his conceptualization. Advances should hasten the transition from implementation-centered to specification-centered model development, the crux of the automation-based paradigm.

5. NETWORKING

In the past, computer networking has been divided into two subdomains: wide area networks (WAN) and local area networks. The criteria distinguishing the two – geographical separation, data rate, and ownership [Tanenbaum 1988] – have become blurred by rapid advances in communications technology.

Both practitioners and researchers draw direct benefits from the sharing of ideas through the Simulation Digest, an electronic bulletin board administered by Professor Paul Fishwick of the University of Florida. In general, WAN developments have spawned far wider and more frequent sharing of ideas and writings among members of the simulation community. The communication channels of The Invisible College for simulation now link terminals, workstations, microprocessors, and main frames across the world. The appearance of communications products based on the Open System Interconnection model is now moving into the session and presentation layers [Stallings 1985, pp. 385-394], which assures the expansion of data sharing and a more open, progressive research community.

Since the early 1970s, following Farber and Larsen's [1972] seminal report, the advance of local network technology has appeared confused, sometimes even chaotic. Initially, the perception of an intimate tie with distributed processing added to the confusion. However, as concepts have become more clearly defined and distinctions more apparent, local network design and operation looms as a research and an application domain related to WAN, distributed systems, and even network operating systems. As the IEEE Local Network standards have evolved and the new technology has matured, the impact of network computing has become discernible.

Simulation modeling is already feeling the effect of workstations replacing large mainframes as the principal development engines. Yet, the computational requirements of some simulation models far surpass the capabilities of current microcomputers. A solution lies in the networking of microcomputers with super computers and mainframes. The modeler will develop the simulation model on a microcomputer but its execution will take place on a super computer or mainframe in such a way that the usage of the supercomputer or mainframe will be transparent to the user. This technology is now made possible by the development of the X window system at MIT. Sun Microsystems has proposed an improved version, Network extensible Window System (NeWS), based on the PostScript language with powerful graphics primitives. NeWS provides a platform on which highly diverse user interfaces and window applications can be built independently of any computer hardware or operating system.

We anticipate a much more detailed solution to this problem in the near future with the availability of Mach – a multiprocessor oriented operating system and environment. Mach is currently being developed at Carnegie Mellon University with the objective of providing an extensible kernel that supports an integrated, networked, and UNIX compatible computing environment consisting of both large and small multiprocessors and uniprocessors. It provides a binary compatible 4.3BSD UNIX interface to include: (1) multiple threads of control per address space, (2) extremely flexible memory sharing, (3) capability-protected, network-transparent interprocess communication which has been integrated with the virtual memory system, and (4) support for both loosely-coupled and tightly-coupled multiprocessors.

6. PARALLEL PROCESSING

Since the earliest perceptions of parallel processing as offering the next major source of computational speedup, discrete event simulation has proved a fertile domain both for theoretical and practical interest. The explanation of this interest most likely lies in the inherent preoccupation of simulation models with time and the underlying conceptual insistence on some global indexing attribute, usually labeled "system time." Such a view seems contrary to a perceived basic tenet of parallel processing: abandonment of centralized control of program execution.

Clearly, the emphasis of research in parallel (concurrent or distributed) simulation has been on model execution: how to reduce the time (and cost) of obtaining samples of model behavior. This point notwithstanding, the implications for model development, although indirect, are significant.

A recent result of research in this area is to categorize the execution of simulation models on different processors, perhaps with no motivation for speedup, as distributed simulation. Parallel or concurrent simulation is the attempt to exploit non-sequential execution to achieve speedup. Using this definitional distinction, distributed simulation is more closely related to computer networking, and the treatment in this paper follows that distinction.

The earliest treatments of parallel model execution focus on the consequent problems in eliminating global control, problems of immense concern in the operating systems research community as well. Loss of computational integrity – assuring the correctness of a computational process – and deadlock – the inability to exchange data necessary to complete a computation – are the challenging problems. Dominating these early works are the mechanisms for guaranteeing the conclusion of a correct computational process [Bryant 1977; Peacock et al. 1979]. Algorithms to accomplish this guarantee are described in various works [Chandy and Misra 1981; Reynolds 1982; Nicol and Reynolds 1984]. These algorithms have been classified as the conservative approach to exploiting parallelism. Underlying this approach is the a priori guarantee that permitting two events to occur simultaneously has no effect on the occurrence of future events [Chandy and Misra 1981, p. 205].

Another approach, typified by Jefferson [1985] and Sokol et al. [1987], is deemed the optimistic approach. The "optimism" is expressed in the philosophy of letting individual processes proceed in an independent fashion until the discovery of incorrect behavior, then roll back all affected processes to regenerate the correct behavior.

In addition to the a priori versus a posteriori distinction, note that the early optimistic approach has an event perspective while the optimistic approach takes a process view. The process view is also taken in the later development of conservative algorithms [Nicol and Reynolds 1984].

An entirely different exploitation of parallelism is to allocate simulation support functions, e.g. events list management, random number generation, etc., to separate processors [Comfort 1982; Wyatt et al. 1983]. Such an approach proves simpler to develop and more robust (less subject to inherent model dependencies). The model development task remains essentially impervious under this approach since the functional partitioning is model independent. Exploitation of parallelism at this high level, compared to the potentially very low level when dealing with model decomposition, could lead to diminished returns in execution time (cost). The level of parallelism is termed the granularity, which could be extremely important in the speedup realized from parallel execution.

The speedup obtained through parallelism is also a key to utilizing AI techniques in model representation that do not impose an excessive penalty on model execution. This observation assists in judging the feasibility of approaches to intelligent simulation environments described in Section 2.

To date, the SMDE prototypes have been unconcerned with the challenges of parallel simulation in either the effect on model development or model execution. However, this is likely to change in the near future, prompted by a recognition of some promising relationships between world views and granularity.

7. SOFTWARE ENGINEERING

Quite expectedly, the initial impact of software engineering is seen at the program level: the use of structured programming and top-down design techniques in a simulation programming language (Simscript II.5) [Heimberger 1976]. Early efforts to relate software engineering to discrete event simulation view the latter as simply an applications programming domain. Within the research community in software engineering, Lehman emerges as one of the few early contributors to characterize the programming task as inherently a modeling activity [Lehman 1980, pp. 4-8]. This small group includes Zurcher and Randell, colleagues of Lehman at IBM T.J. Watson Research Center. The modeling characterization underscores a major linkage between computer science and operations research: both are essentially problem solving disciplines.

The perception of influence is often slow to materialize. For example, Simula, originally introduced in 1963 as a discrete event language extension of Algol, embodies several major conceptual advances for that time (and for today): implementations of the process mechanism, co-routine concept, abstract data type (class) concept, and inheritance (class concatenation). The advanced capabilities of Simula only now are beginning to be appreciated, stimulated by the popularity of the object oriented paradigm (OOP), primarily associated with Smalltalk. Simula is now recognized as the first language to exhibit the OOP principles.

The enunciation of the automation-based paradigm [Balzer et al. 1983] has served to elevate program specification and the attendant modeling concerns in the consciousness of the software engineering community. In fact, a much earlier work, depicting program development as a procession of (simulation) model developments [Zurcher and Randell 1969], presents a design prototyping approach (without the throwaway aspect of rapid prototyping). Perhaps the combined legacy of OOP and the automation-based paradigm is the credibility of the assertion that development of a program should initiate with development of a model.

The SMDE Project has resulted in a confluence of simulation and software engineering concepts. Tools promoting model specification can be viewed as the response to development needs for programmers under the automation-based paradigm. Hopefully, the future impact shows results contributing to support environments that enhance productivity in modeling activities beyond simulation and in system development projects that transcend the software domain.

8. CONCLUDING REMARKS

Clearly, recent and continuing advances in the six areas reviewed exert different directional "pulls" on simulation model development. The challenge is to meld these technological advances so as to mold a powerful environment for simulation model development and execution. This environment development should exploit these six areas to achieve complementary rather than competitive influences.

The OOP provides a desirable conceptual framework for simulation modeling and produces much needed reusable and maintainable models; however, because of the overhead involved, OOP-based models have relatively poorer execution speeds. The use of computer graphics significantly amplifies the need for more CPU power. As for AI, the need for computational power is so high that special computer hardware is manufactured to try to meet the demand (e.g., Lisp workstations). Simulation is also known to be extremely CPU intensive. Hence, combining OOP, computer graphics, and AI for the development and execution of simulation models poses a phenomenal demand for CPU power.

Advances in the semi-conductor technology (computer architecture), parallel processing, and networking jointly contribute to meeting the ever-increasing demand for CPU power. The Mach environment integrates parallel processing and networking at a low level, providing a promising platform for simulation model development and execution.

Finally, the "bottom line" of this review can be succinctly stated for the SMDE project: In the rapidly changing technological context of today, rapid prototyping is a necessity not an alternative.

ACKNOWLEDGMENTS

This research was sponsored in part by the U.S. Navy under contract N60921-83-G-A165-B03 through the Systems Research Center at VPI&SU. We thank Professor James D. Arthur for reading the manuscript and his suggestions for improvement.

REFERENCES

Balci, O. and R.E. Nance (1987a), "Simulation Support: Prototyping the Automation-Based Paradigm," In *Proceedings of the 1987 Winter Simulation Conference* (Atlanta, Ga., Dec. 14-16). IEEE, Piscataway, N.J., pp. 495-502.

Balci, O. and R.E. Nance (1987b), "Simulation Model Development Environments: A Research Prototype," *J. of the Operational Research Society 38*, 8 (Aug.), 753-763.

Balzer, R., T.E. Cheatham, Jr., and C. Green (1983), "Software Technology in the 1990's: Using a New Paradigm," *IEEE Computer 16*, 11 (Nov.), 39-45.

Bell, P.C. and R.M. O'Keefe (1987), "Visual Interactive Simulation – History, Recent Developments, and Major Issues," *Simulation 49*, 3 (Sept.), 109-116.

Bryant, R.E. (1977), "Simulation of Packet Communication Architecture Computer Systems," MIT LCS/TR-188, MIT, Cambridge, Mass.

Chandy, K.M. and J. Misra (1981), "Asynchronous Distributed Simulation via a Sequence of Parallel Computations," *Communications of the ACM 24*, 11, (Apr.), 198-206.

Comfort, J.C. (1982), "The Design of a Multi-Microprocessor Based Simulation Computer - 1," In *Proceedings of the Annual Simulation Symposium* (Tampa, Fla., Mar.). pp. 45-52. (Note: Companion papers appear in the 1983 and 1984 Proceedings.)

Doukidis, G.I. and R.J. Paul (1986), "Experiences in Automating the Formulation of Discrete Event Simulation Models," In *AI Applied to Simulation*, E.J.H. Kerckhoffs et al. Eds. SCS Simulation Series, Vol. 18, No. 1, (Feb.), 79-90.

Farber, D.G. and K.C. Larsen (1972), "The System Architecture of the Distributed Computer System – The Communications System," In *Proceedings of the Symposium on Computer Networks* (Brooklyn Polytechnic Institute, New York, Apr.)

Grant, J.W. and S.A. Weiner (1986), "Factors to Consider in Choosing a Graphically Animated Simulation System," *Industrial Engineering 18*, 8 (Aug.), 36-38,40,65-68.

Heimberger, D.A. (1976), "Structured Programming Using SIMSCRIPT II.5," Presentation at the Simulation and SIMSCRIPT Conference, Washington, D.C., Sept. 21.

Jefferson, D. (1985), "Virtual Time," In *Transactions on Programming Languages and Systems 7*, 3 (July), pp. 404-425.

Lehman, M.M. (1980), "Programs, Programming and the Software Life Cycle," Report No. 80/6, Department of Computing and Control, Imperial College of Science and Technology, London, Apr.

McArthur, D., P. Klahr, and S. Narain (1986), "ROSS: An Object-Oriented Language for

Constructing Simulations," In *Expert Systems – Techniques, Tools and Applications*, P. Klahr and D.A. Waterman, Eds. Addison-Wesley, Reading, Mass., pp. 70-94.

Murray, K.J. and S.V. Sheppard (1988), "Knowledge-Based Simulation Model Specification," *Simulation 50*, 3 (Mar.), 112-119.

Nicol, D.M. and P.F. Reynolds, Jr. (1984), "Problem Oriented Protocol Design," In *Proceedings of the 1984 Winter Simulation Conference* (Dallas, Tex., Nov. 28-30). IEEE, Piscataway, N.J., pp. 471-474.

Oren, T.I. and Z.K. Aytac (1985), "Architecture of MAGEST: A Knowledge-Based Modeling and Simulation System," In *Simulation in Research and Development*, A. Javor, Ed. North Holland, Amsterdam, pp. 99-109.

Peacock, J.K., J.W. Wong, and E. Manning (1979), "Distributed Simulation Using a Network of Processors," *Computer Networks 3*, 44-56.

Reddy, Y.V.R., M.S. Fox, N. Husain, and M. McRoberts (1986), "The Knowledge-Based Simulation System," *IEEE Software 3*, 2 (Mar.), 26-37.

Reynolds, P.F., Jr. (1982), "A Shared Resource Algorithm for Distributed Simulation," In *Proceedings of the Ninth Annual International Computer Architecture Conference* (Austin, Tex., Apr.). pp. 259-266.

Shannon, R.E. (1986), "Intelligent Simulation Environments," In *Proceedings of the Conference on Intelligent Simulation Environments* (San Diego, Calif., Jan. 23-25). Published as Simulation Series 17, 1 (Jan.), 150-156. SCS, San Diego, Calif.

Sokol, L.M., D.P. Driscoe, and A.P. Wieland (1987), "MTW: A Strategy for Scheduling Discrete Simulation Events for Concurrent Execution," MP-8700018, The MITRE Corporation, McLean, Va., Oct.

Stallings, W. (1985), *Data and Computer Communications*, Macmillan, New York.

Tanenbaum, A.S. (1988), *Computer Networks*, 2nd edition, Prentice-Hall, Englewood Cliffs, N.J.

Umphress, D.A. and U.W. Pooch (1987), "A Goal-Oriented Approach to Simulation," In *Proceedings of the Conference on Methodology and Validation* (Eastern Simulation Conferences, Orlando, Fla., Apr. 6-9). Published as Simulation Series 19, 1 (Jan. 1988), 44-49. SCS, San Diego, Calif.

Wyatt, D.L., S. Sheppard, and R.E. Young (1983), "An Experiment in Microprocessor-Based Distributed Digital Simulation," In *Proceedings of the 1983 Winter Simulation Conference* (Arlington, Va., Dec. 12-14). IEEE, Piscataway, N.J., pp. 271-277.

Zurcher, F.W. and B. Randell (1969), "Iterative Multi-Level Modelling – A Methodology for Computer System Design," In *Information Processing 68*, North-Holland, Amsterdam, pp. 867-871.

LOCATING P MOBILE SERVERS ON A CONGESTED NETWORK: A SIMULATION ANALYSIS

REX K. KINCAID

Department of Mathematics, College of William and Mary
Williamsburg, Va. 23185

KEITH W. MILLER AND STEPHEN K. PARK

Department of Computer Science, College of William and Mary
Williamsburg, Va. 23185

ABSTRACT

We investigate meaningful measures of system response time and analyze the robustness of algorithms which determine optimal home locations of mobile servers on congested networks. The result of this effort is a microcomputer-based simulation model that allows a decision maker to compare and contrast home locations for mobile servers with respect to a variety of network performance measures.

1. INTRODUCTION

In the last five years there have been dramatic developments in personal computers and high-performance workstations. The computational capability that these systems now provide make it both practical and desirable for operations researchers to consider simulation-based models as a cost and time effective companion to more traditional analytic procedures. Indeed, we submit that in today's technological environment, mathematical analysis and simulation modeling should be used together as complementary activities and, by so doing, synergistic results can be achieved. There is a need to dispel the dogma that simulation models are necessarily expensive to run, always time consuming to build, and that they should be used only as an *alternative* to mathematical analysis. In an age of inexpensive, high-performance, readily available personal computing, an operations researcher who chooses to rely exclusively on traditional mathematical analysis tools and thereby limits the scope of his research, is a one-dimensional analyst living in a multi-dimensional world.

Experience has shown that simulation models can be used effectively to solve real-world stochastic operations research problems for which traditional assumptions about homogeneous arrival processes and steady-state behavior are not valid. Building on this experience, we have used a combination of contemporary microcomputer-based simulation modeling techniques and traditional mathematical analysis methods to study the problem of determining the optimal home locations of p mobile servers on a congested network. The net result of this effort is a microcomputer-based decision support tool which is described in Section 4.

Network location theory is generally concerned with the problem of locating a fixed set of points to optimize a specified network objective. Historically, two types of location problems have been studied—deterministic and stochastic. The seminal paper in deterministic network location theory is generally attributed to Hakimi [1964]. In this paper he formulated both center and median location problems. Stochastic location problems represent a natural extension of the earlier deterministic analysis. A stochastic formulation allows for the random nature of requests for service and provides a more meaningful characterization of a congested system's operational effectiveness. Two early key references for stochastic location problems are Carter, Chaiken, and Ingall [1972] and Larson [1974]. In the last 15 years many publications have appeared addressing stochastic location problems.

The motivation for the research in this paper arose from congested network models in Berman and Larson [1982], Berman, Larson and Chiu [1985], and Berman, Larson, and Parkan [1987]. In particular the last reference formulates a mobile server location problem called the Stochastic Queue p-Median (SQPM) problem which we discuss further in Sections 2 and 4.

2. FORMULATION

In this section we generalize the SQPM problem by formulating the Mobile p-Server Home Location (MPSHL) problem. Let $G(V, E)$ be a congested transportation network where V is the vertex set denoting demand centers with $|V| = n$ and E is the edge set denoting transportation arteries. Travel between points on the network is assumed to occur along shortest paths. The shortest path distance (in terms of travel time) between any two points x and x' on G is denoted $d(x, x')$.

There are p distinct mobile servers on G which respond to calls for service from of the n demand centers. When *available*, the mobile servers reside in fixed home locations denoted $X = (x_1, \ldots, x_p)$ on G. The home location of server i is x_i. A server is available only when it is idle at its home location. Service calls are generated in a random, possibly non-homogeneous, Poisson manner from within each demand center. (By *within* we imply that some level of aggregation of demand has occurred.) Whenever a call for service arrives, the closest available server is dispatched. Calls that find no servers available enter a queue and wait for service by the first available server. When a queue develops, the result is a *congested* network.

The *service time* for any mobile server is the sum of two components. The non-travel time component is the on-scene service time (at the location of the call) plus the off-scene service time (at the home location of the server). Typically this component is stochastic. The travel time component is the round-trip travel time to the location of the call and back again to the server's home location.

The *response time* associated with each call for service is the sum of any delay in the queue plus the travel time to the call. An *optimal* solution to the MPSHL problem is a location vector X^* which minimizes some measure of *system* response time. Our primary interest is to investigate meaningful measures of system response time and to analyze the robustness of algorithms which determine optimal home locations for the service units.

2.1 Measures of Transient Response Time

Algorithms for locating servers on a congested network typically assume that the service call process is homogeneous, that the queueing system will achieve steady state, and that the steady-state *average* behavior of the queueing system sufficiently characterizes its operation. All of these assumptions are necessary if the methods of traditional queueing theory are to be applied. However, in a simulation environment these assumptions are neither necessary nor enlightening.

A simulation model provides the capability to use both time averaged and ensemble averaged statistics to evaluate network performance as a function of the home locations of the mobile service units. Let T denote a finite interval of simulated time. The *time averaged* response to a call for service, given a server home location vector X, is the sum of two components

$$\tilde{R}(X,T) = \tilde{t}(X,T) + \tilde{W}_q(X,T) \qquad 2.1$$

where $\tilde{t}(X,T)$ denotes the average time spent in travel by a server from its home location to the location of a call for service and $\tilde{W}_q(X,T)$ denotes the average time a call for service spends waiting in the queue. These *finite horizon, transient* statistics will have a natural run-to-run variability. However, the *ensemble average* of $\tilde{R}(X,T)$, along with a corresponding confidence interval, can be estimated using traditional statistical techniques applied to data generated by replicated runs of a simulation model.

In addition to these average statistics, a simulation model provides a wealth of other descriptive statistics that are not readily available in an analytical model. Specifically, since each network event is simulated, frequency distributions (histograms) can be easily generated for any event of interest.

A performance measure commonly used to specify the performance of mobile servers in a congested network is the *maximum* response time of a service unit. This statistic can be estimated from a response time histogram. From this histogram the percentile of responses that are less than a given threshold value $\mathcal{R}$ is readily available for any value of $\mathcal{R}$.

It is intuitive that if the network is rarely congested then the home location of the servers should be at the p-medians. That is, if the servers are frequently idle they will usually be available to serve those demand centers to which they are closest. However, if the system is frequently congested, then servers may be sent to distant vertices; in that case it would be better if the home location of all servers is at the 1-median. In any case, a transient system statistic of significant interest is the relative frequency of times a demand center is serviced by a mobile server other than that one whose home location is closest. This statistic is strongly correlated with system response time and it is easily produced by a simulation model.

2.2 A Measure of a Steady State Response Time

A special case of the MPSHL problem occurs when the demand for service is assumed to be an independent homogeneous Poisson process with rate $lambda$ and the queueing system is assumed to be in steady state. In this case, as T approaches infinity the experimental (simulated) statistics $\tilde{R}(X,T)$, $\tilde{W}_q(X,T)$, and $\tilde{T}(X,T)$ will approach the expected (theoretical) steady state values of average response time $\bar{R}(X)$, waiting time in the queue $\bar{W}_q(X)$, and travel time to a call $\bar{t}(X)$ respectively.

If the demand at each vertex k is viewed as an independent Poisson process with mean rate λh_k where h_k denotes the fraction of service calls generated at vertex k, then $\bar{R}(X)$ can be expressed in closed form. Let the state of the system be represented by a p component binary vector. A 0 in component i signifies that mobile server i is free at its home location and a 1 signifies that it is busy. Let the p component vector F denote any of the (free) states of the system for which at least one service unit is available and, by definition, the queue is empty. There are $2^p - 1$ possible values of F. Similarly, let the p component vector B_j denote the (busy) system state in which no service units are available and $j \geq 0$ calls are waiting in the queue. Then

$$\bar{R}(X) = \sum_F P(F) \sum_{k=1}^{n} h_k D(F,k) + \sum_{j=0}^{\infty} P(B_j)\bar{R}_j. \qquad 2.2$$

The term $P(F)$ is the steady state probability that the system is in the free state F, and $P(B_j)$ is the steady state probability that the system is in the busy (congested) state B_j. The term $D(F,k)$ is the shortest path time to vertex k from the closest available service unit when the system is in state F, and $\bar{R}_j$ is the expected response time when the queue length is j.

If enough traditional queueing theory type assumptions are made, then all the terms in Equation 2.2 can be determined. Specifically, Berman et al. [1987] discuss this special case of the MPSHL problem and point out that it is an $M/G/p$ queueing system (Poisson arrivals, general service times) with p distinguishable service units. They call a home location vector X^* that minimizes Equation 2.2 a Stochastic Queue p-Median. Unfortunately, there are no exact analytic results for distinguishable server $M/G/p$ queueing systems. In fact, good approximate closed form expressions do not even exist for such a system. Berman et al. [1987] circumvent this difficulty by using the well established hypercube model as the basis for two *heuristic* solutions to the SQPM problem.

The hypercube model (see Larson and Odoni [1981] for a detailed discussion) assumes that an $M/M/p$ (*not* $M/G/p$) queueing system is in operation and uses the steady-state probabilities of the $2^p - 1$ possible states. This is an expedient approach for providing (hopefully) reasonable answers to the SQPM problem. However, as Berman et al. [1987] point out the approximation of an $M/G/p$ queueing system by an $M/M/p$ queueing system is a poor one, particularly if travel time is the major component of the service time. Moreover, we feel that the essentially transient nature of the queueing environment is not captured by a steady-state approach.

In the next section we provide several examples that illustrate the importance of the transient behavior of a queueing network and the need to account for non-homogeneities in arrival processes. These simulation examples illustrate that when analyzing a single queue—or a network of queues—steady-state is usually a convenient fiction.

3. STATISTICS

Figure 3.1 illustrates the simulated performance of an $M/M/1$ queue operating for 100 (normalized) units of time in "steady-state" at a relatively high loading ($\rho = 0.8$). Requests for service (customers) are arriving as a homogeneous Poisson process with rate 1 and being served with an exponential distribution at a rate of 1.25. Time is increasing along the horizontal axis and the vertical axis represents the number of customers in the system (server + queue). Three statistics are shown. The open circles represent the actual number in the system—based on one replication of the simulation and sampled each unit of time. The closed circles represent this snapshot (time sampled) statistic averaged over an ensemble of 10 replications. If the snapshot statistic were averaged over *infinitely many* replications, the steady-state dotted line would be the result. (In steady state, the number in an $M/M/1$ queue is a Geometric random variable with mean $\rho/(1-\rho)$.)

It is clear from Figure 3.1 that there is a large amount of natural variability about the steady-state mean. This is true for an $M/G/p$ queue as well. However a comparable figure for an $M/G/p$ queue is not easily constructed because there is no closed form (or approximate) expression for the steady-state mean. Because a large variability about the steady-state mean is present in either queueing environment, any steady-state network analysis must be viewed with healthy skepticism.

Figure 3.2 is similar to Figure 3.1 except that the *first* 100 units of time are illustrated. Because the system is assumed to be initially in an idle state, some time is required for the system to respond to the step increase in arrival rate at $t = 0$. The initial transient in this case is seen to persist for a significant number of customers (approximately 40) and steady-state analysis is (by definition) not applicable during this period. This observation is particularly relevant when queueing theory is used to model systems with a small number of customers.

Because of their transient, stochastic nature, congested networks represent examples of systems which are difficult to analyze using traditional techniques, particularly if the service

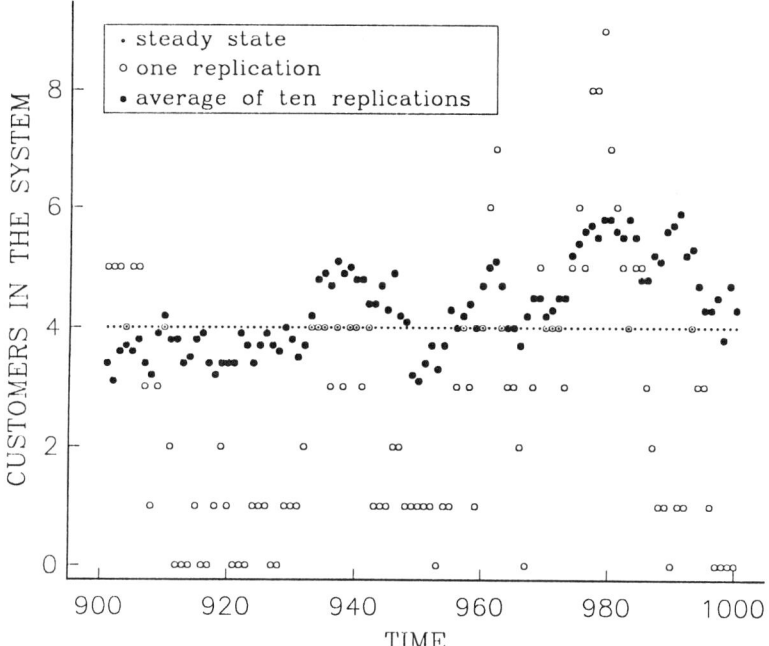

Figure 3.1. Steady-state behavior of an M/M/1 queue ($\rho = 0.8$).

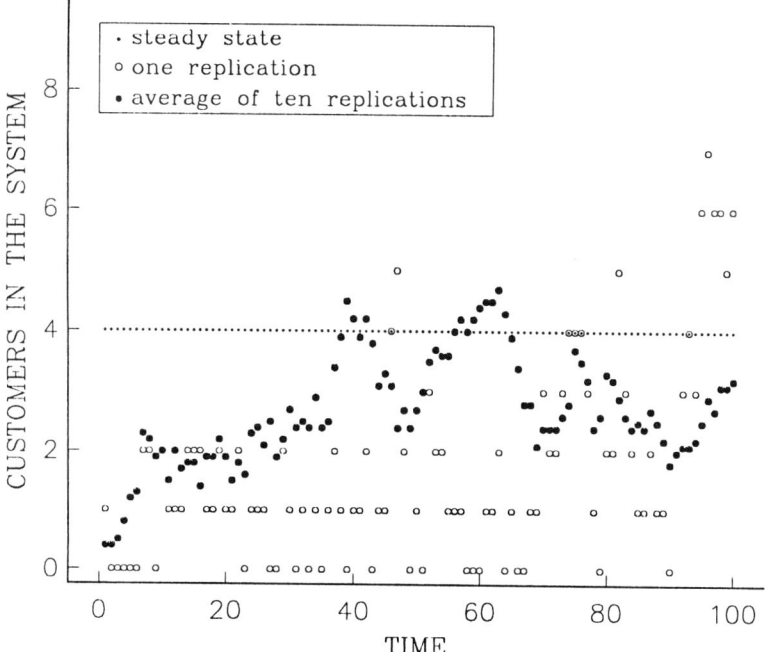

Figure 3.2. Initial transient behavior of an M/M/1 queue ($\rho = 0.8$).

process is non-homogeneous. Congested networks display this type behavior when calls for service are generated by emergencies. We have analyzed the frequency of calls to 911 for the Richmond, Virginia area in 1986. Figure 3.3 is a graph of a typical *daily* (24 hour) demand pattern. The mean is 3 calls per hour. However, the non-homogeneous demand pattern is periodic and returns to a nearly idle state every 24 hours, thereby underscoring the importance of the initial transient behavior of the queue.

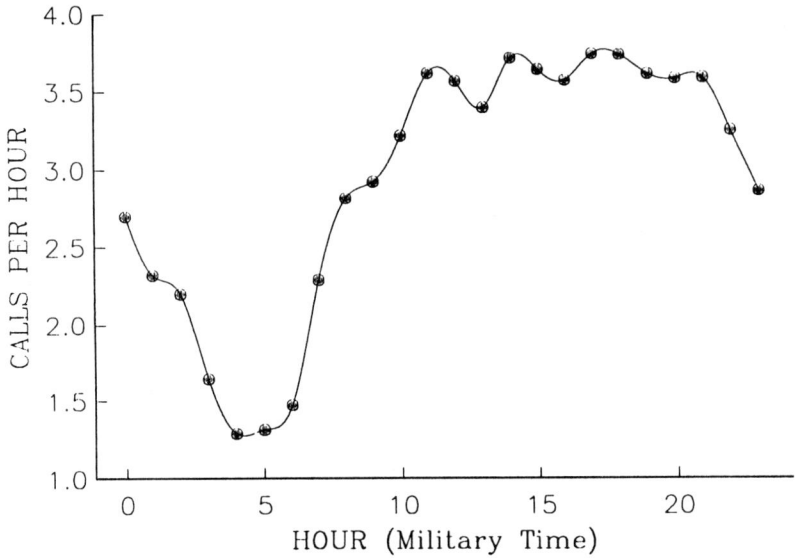

Figure 3.3. Daily demand distribution for calls to 911.

A similar phenomenon can be observed if the 911 data is aggregated on a *weekly* level. This weekly non-homogeneity has been observed by several authors. Baker and Fitzpatrick [1986] report a similar finding when tabulating data for ambulance calls by day of the week for 46 counties in South Carolina. Each of the 46 counties exhibited a similar trend where demand peaked at the end of the week. The distribution of calls for service from the 911 data also exhibits a non-homogeneous seasonal pattern (peaks on holidays, etc.).

4. SIMULATION MODEL

In this section we demonstrate the inconsistencies that can arise when a steady-state average response model is used to determine the home location of mobile servers in a congested network. In addition the benefits of a microcomputer based simulation model of the MPSHL problem are presented.

Throughout this section we refer to the 3-server, 10 demand center network pictured in Figure 4.1. This example is from Berman et al. [1987]. The numbers on the edges of the network are the travel times between demand centers. The fraction next to each demand center k is h_k, the fraction of service calls generated within k. If a call for service is generated and no server is available a FIFO queue is formed. The mean (exponential) service time for each server is 1.

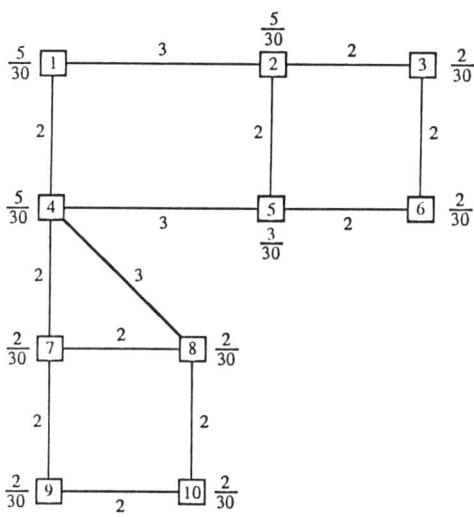

Figure 4.1. 3-server congested network model

We have constructed a simulation model, MPSS, of the 3-server network in Figure 4.1. MPSS is written in Pascal and is implemented on an IBM-AT class microcomputer. Simulated requests for service are processed by MPSS at the rate of approximately 8000 customers per minute. Hence, a decision maker (user) running MPSS is operating in an interactive environment in which mobile server home locations can be analyzed in minutes. To initialize MPSS a user must enter home locations for the three servers (X, restricted to the vertices), the mean service time for each server, the time interval to be simulated (T), parameters characterizing the rate of requests for service rate (λ), and a random number seed. At the end of a simulated period of operation the statistics generated by MPSS are summarized on the screen. A response time histogram is displayed along with a bar graph showing the number of calls for service generated at each demand center as well as the percentage of calls that are not serviced by their closest server. Several traditional time averaged statistics are displayed as well. The user may save this summary statistics screen and then simulated network performance with a different set of home locations for the three servers. The summary statistics screen for this alternative set of server home locations can be saved as well and the user may toggle back and forth between the two screens to compare the network performance. This allows a user to employ his/her judgement as to what criteria are most important in selecting mobile server home locations.

It is not surprising that the MPSHL problem is a sensitive socio-political decision problem involving multiple criteria. Savas [1978] provides an excellent discussion of appropriate performance measures for determining the location of public services. He divides them into three types of measures—efficiency, effectiveness, and equity. Average response time is an example of an *efficiency* measure and is often considered the primary objective (as in the SQPM problem). The effectiveness of a solution to the MPSHL problem can be gauged by mortality or morbidity rates. A 95th percentile response time provides a convenient measure of *effectiveness* since a smaller 95th percentile response time is likely to increase the chances that all patients will survive. It is possible, however, that a solution to the MPSHL problem is efficient and effective and still be perceived as *inequitable* if all segments of the population are not treated similarly. We think that it is essential to integrate efficiency, effectiveness and equity considerations into a solution methodology for the MPSHL problem.

Consider the difficulties that can arise when an efficiency measure—average response time—is used *exclusively* to determine solutions to the MPSHL problem. For the network in Figure 4.1, vertices 2, 4, and 9 comprise the 3-median solution while vertex 4 is the 1-median solution. A solution to the SQPM problem for this network will be located at the 3-medians whenever the system is lightly loaded (small λ) and at the 1-median whenever the system is heavily loaded (large λ). In Figure 4.2 we plot the net (homogeneous) request for service rate, λ, versus the steady-state average response time, $\bar{R}(X)$, for $X_1 = (2, 4, 9)$ and $X_2 = (4, 4, 4)$. At the value $\lambda \approx 0.2$ X_1 ceases to be better than X_2 with respect to average response time. At $\lambda = 0.18$ MPSS produces values of 3.3 for $\bar{R}(X_1)$ and 3.8 for $\bar{R}(X_2)$ and we conclude, for this value of λ, that $X_1 = (2, 4, 9)$ is a better solution than $X_2 = (4, 4, 4)$. However, when we examine the corresponding response time histogram, the 95th percentile response times for X_1 and X_2 are 10.1 and 7.9 respectively, and X_2 is better. How then do we decide which location is "best"?

One approach is to treat the MPSHL problem as a multi-objective optimization problem. Then we must either generate nondominated solutions from which a decision maker can choose or we must assess the decision maker's utility function apriori and solve the resulting single objective problem. The literature on both of these approaches is large and we make no attempt here to advocate one approach over the other. Instead, we point out that a decision maker using MPSS can compare a variety of home locations for mobile servers as possible solutions to the MPSHL problem. In addition the summary statistics screens give values for several efficiency and effectiveness measures (others can be added). The decision maker can then pick whatever solution seems best. We do not provide any specific measures of equity. However, one possibility is to determine average response

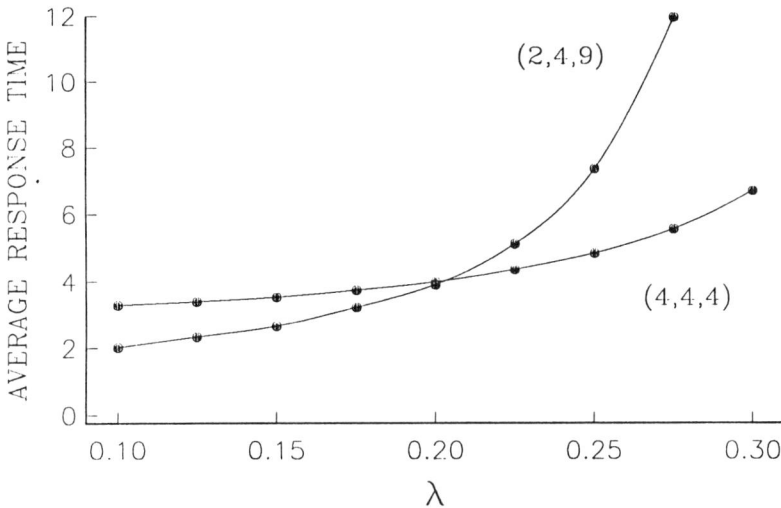

Figure 4.2. Arrival rate versus average response time.

time and 95th percentile response time for subnetworks (areas of a city) and thereby identify subnetworks that have poorer service than others.

CONCLUSIONS

Our objective in this paper was to investigate meaningful measures of system response time for the MPSHL problem, and show the importance of relaxing the restrictive assumptions required by traditional steady-state analytic models. In so doing we have studied the impact of transient statistics and we have demonstrated the difference between home locations with small average response time and home locations with small 95th percentile response time. By removing the restrictive assumptions imposed by a steady-state analytic queueing model we have provided a better approximation, in our opinion, to the observed behavior of congested networks in which mobile servers are to be located. With the advent of extremely fast microcomputers and workstations, a simulation model like ours gives a decision maker the ability to compare network performance measures for different sets of home locations and provides a rich environment for studying solutions to the MPSHL problem.

ACKNOWLEDGEMENTS

We wish to thank the Department of Public Safety in Richmond, Virginia for providing us with data on calls to 911 and in particular we gratefully acknowledge the helpfulness of Albert F. Vincent, the Emergency Medical Services Coordinator.

REFERENCES

Baker, J.R. and K.E. Fitzpatrick, (1986), "Determination of an Optimal Forecast Model for Ambulance Demand Using Goal Programming," *Journal of Operational Research Society,* 37, 1047-1059.

Berman, O. and R.C. Larson, (1982), "The Median Problem with Congested Facilities," *Computers and Operations Research,* 9, 119-126.

Berman, O., R.C. Larson, and S. Chiu, (1985), "Optimal Server Location on a Network Operating as an M/G/1 Queue," *Operations Research,* 33, 746-771.

Berman, O., R.C. Larson, and C. Parkan, (1987), "The Stochastic Queue p-Median Problem," *Transportation Science,* 21, 207-216.

Carter, G.M., J.M. Chaiken, and E. Ignall, (1972), "Response areas for two emergency units," *Operations Research,* 20, 571-594.

Chiu, S., O. Berman, and R.C. Larson, (1985), "Stochastic Queue Median on a Tree Network," *Management Science,* 31, 764-772.

Hakimi, S.L., (1964), "Optimal Locations of Switching Centers and Medians of a Graph," *Operations Research,* 12, 450-459.

Larson, R.C., (1974), "A Hypercube Model for Facility Location and Redistricting in Urban Emergency Services," *Computers and Operations Research,* 1, 76-95.

Larson, R.C. and A.R. Odoni, (1981), *Urban Operations Research,* Prentice Hall, Englewood Cliffs, N.J.

Lubicz, M. and B. Mielczarek, (1987), "Simulation Modeling of Emergency Medical Services," *European Journal of Operational Research,* 29, 178-185.

Savas, E.S., (1978), "On Equity in Providing Public Service," *Management Science,* 24, 800-808.

THE DESIGN AND DEVELOPMENT OF AN ANALYZER FOR DISCRETE EVENT MODEL SPECIFICATIONS

ROBERT L. MOOSE, JR.
BNR
Research Triangle Park, North Carolina 27709

RICHARD E. NANCE
Virginia Polytechnic Institute and State University
Blacksburg, Virginia 24061

ABSTRACT

The Model Analyzer is a utility that renders automated and semi-automated support of the model development process. A prototype of this tool, demonstrating the capability for diagnostic analysis of non-executable model representations, is described from the user perspective. Key concepts affecting design decisions are discussed in the context of an underlying theory of model representation and analysis. The importance of world-view-independent model representation is stressed as a precursor to the early employment of model diagnosis and analysis.

1. INTRODUCTION

Advances in computing technology have contributed to ever-increasing expectations for application systems and precipitous increases in the complexities associated with development of such systems. Development models, like the systems represented, have exceeded the capabilities of their designers and users. The rational response to such a potentially dangerous situation is to utilize the same technology in coping with the problems of understanding, validating, maintaining, and using large complex models. A Model Development Environment (MDE) [Balci 1986] is an example of utilizing computing technology in this way. The subject of this paper is a tool within the MDE that has the objective of assisting users in coping with the development of models that could surpass the comprehension of their creators: the Model Analyzer.

A Model Analyzer is a required element of a Minimal Model Development Environment (MMDE) tool set (see [Balci 1986]). Within the integrated, automated support of simulation model development, provided by the MMDE, the Analyzer performs diagnostic analyses on non-executable model representations. These analyses are based on both static (attribute-based) and dynamic (graph-based) aspects of model representations.

This paper describes an initial prototype of the Model Analyzer. The reader interested in the implementation details should consult a companion report [Moose and Nance 1987]. Background and contextual information to provide a relatively self-contained treatment is included in Section 2, which discusses the underlying theory of model representation and analysis. This discussion addresses the topics of world-view-independent model representation, graphical representation of model dynamics, and model diagnosis.

Section 3 outlines the primary conceptual contributors: the role of UNIX ‡, the **lex**, and **yacc** utilities, and the implementation decisions to employ a hierarchy of abstract data types. Together, discussion of these elements sets forth the design philosophy for the Analyzer.

Section 4 describes the state of the Analyzer prototype in terms of the functionality perceived by the moduler. A brief summary and conclusions are provided in Section 5.

2. MODEL ANALYSIS

Balci [1986] stipulates the requirements for *Model Development Environments* (MDEs) in terms of the following objectives:

(1) offer cost-effective integrated support continuously throughout the entire life cycle of model development,
(2) improve the model quality by effectively assisting in the quality assurance of the model,
(3) significantly increase the efficiency and productivity of the project team, and
(4) substantially decrease the model development time.

To achieve these objectives, he proposes a layered structure that progressively details the requirements for *Minimal Model Development Environments* (MMDEs). The functional requirements of each tool are defined, and tool integration is accomplished through a *Kernel Model Development Environment* (KMDE) augmented by a *Kernel Interface* supplying communications support.

This report is concerned with a prototype version of the Model Analyzer (or Analyzer, for short), an element of the proposed MMDE toolset. The Model

---

‡ UNIX is a trademark of AT&T Bell Laboratories.

Analyzer is intended to provide the functionality for [Balci 1986, p. 63] †

1) diagnosing the model specification created using a tool called the Model Generator, and

2) assisting in communicative model verification.

The prototype tool described herein is intended to partially satisfy the first of these requirements.

The functionality provided by the Model Analyzer prototype resides in its ability to perform several of the attribute- and graph-based diagnostics (including complexity [Wallace 1985] defined in [Overstreet 1982; Overstreet and Nance 1984]. The Analyzer, the primitive model representation language on which it operates, and the diagnostics it performs are described in the remainder of this report.

2.1. Primitive Representation Using the Condition Specification

Overstreet and Nance [1985] propose the *Condition Specification* (CS) as a nonexecutable representational form especially amenable to diagnostic analysis. Use of the CS, which is a rule-based semantic specification formalism, enables the realization of the following benefits:

(1) Model specifications (MSs) that are independent of the three traditional world-views and automatic translation of such MSs to their world-view dependent equivalents.

(2) Diagnostic analysis of MSs before the model implementation stage is reached. Among other advantages, this facilitates the verification of models earlier in the modeling effort [Overstreet 1984, p.3].

(3) Automatic derivation of graphical representations that permit model simplification through diagnostic assistance prior to an executable model form (program) [Nance and Overstreet 1987].

(4) Automatic production of documentation from MSs.

Further, the CS formalism leads to establishment of the unsolvability of various general diagnosis problems and other theoretical results [Overstreet and Nance 1985, p. 200]. (Details and proofs are contained in [Overstreet 1982]. The remainder of this section is a condensation of material taken from [Overstreet and Nance 1985].)

A *model specification* is defined as a quintuple:

---

† The reader is referred to [Nance 1981] for a discussion of the role of communicative models in a MDE, to [Balci 1986] for the requirements for the Model Generator, and to [Hansen 1984] for details on a Model Generator prototype.

< input specifications,
    output specifications,
    object definition set,
    indexing attribute,
    transition specification >.

The input and output specifications jointly define the interface between the model and its environment. The indexing attribute, commonly called "system time," provides the means for depicting temporal relationships so fundamental in discrete event simulation.

Objects are defined in terms of attributes, which must be typed by the modeler. The enumeration of values for all attributes of an object at a particular value of system time defines the *state of that object* at the particular *instant* (value of system time). The transition specification for a model defines: (1) an initial state, (2) termination conditions, and (3) the dynamic structure — how each attribute value (and object) affects every other attribute value (and object).

The transition specification could take several forms. The choice of semantic and syntactic form is influenced by two competitive goals: (1) the desire for generality in model description and (2) the advantages of formal specification in reducing ambiguity and accommodating verification and validation techniques. The condition specification, summarized in Table 1, is an attempt to strike a balance between descriptive generality and an instructive formalism.

The primitive semantic construct is the Condition-Action Pair (CAP): (1) a condition, (2) a boolean expression or time-based signal, and (3) an associated action, which is taken when the condition is evaluated as "true." Specification using the CAP construct requires the modeler to prescribe: (1) the condition(s) under which defined attributes change value and (2) the expression effecting the change. CAPs with identical conditions are grouped into an action cluster (AC). Figure 1 explains and illustrates the relationships among the object specification (definition stage), the CAP (specification stage), and the action cluster.

Although both static and dynamic representations are produced in the generation process, the current version of the Model Analyzer addresses the model dynamics exclusively. Accordingly, the context free grammar on which the Analyzer is based (given in Backus Normal Form in Appendix A of [Moose and Nance 1987]) describes the detailed syntax of object definitions and Condition-Action Pairs. The reader is referred to [Overstreet 1982] for an in-depth discussion of the CS grammar.

2.2. Translation to Action Cluster Incidence Graphs

Many of the model diagnostics presented in [Overstreet and Nance 1984] and implemented in the Analyzer depend on a graphical representation known as an *action cluster incidence graph* (ACIG). The ACIG is derived from the *action cluster attribute graph* (ACAG) that maps the attribute (object) description into a dynamic description in terms of action clusters.

Table 1. Syntax and Function of Condition Specification Primitives (Reprinted with permission of the ACM from [Overstreet and Nance 1985, p. 197]).

Name	Syntax	Function
Value change description	Not specified	Assign attribute values
Set Alarm	SET ALARM(< alarm name > [(< argument list >)] , < time delay >)	Schedule an alarm
When Alarm	WHEN ALARM(< alarm name exp > [(< parameter list >)])	Time sequencing condition
After Alarm	AFTER ALARM(< alarm name > & < Boolean exp > [(< parameter list >)])	Time sequencing condition
Cancel Alarm	CANCEL ALARM(< alarm name > [, < alarm id >])	Cancel scheduled alarm
Create	CREATE(< object type > [, < object id >])	Generate new model object
Destroy	DESTROY(< object type > [, < object id >])	Eliminate a model object
Output	Not specified	Produce output
Stop	Not specified	Terminate simulation experiment
Comment	{ < any text not including a "}" > }	Comment

An *action cluster* (AC) is defined as "a collection of model actions that must always occur concurrently. It may involve attribute changes for several objects, but these changes are 'atomic' in the sense that they must always occur as a unit". [Overstreet 1982, p. 3.45]. Given a set of CAPs, the equivalent set of ACs is formed by combining (the actions of) each subset of CAPs whose conditions are equivalent. The common condition within each subset of CAPs becomes the condition of the resultant AC.

"An action cluster is *determined (DAC)* if its condition is determined (purely time-based), *contingent (CAC)* if its condition is contingent (based on state attributes), and *mixed* if its condition is mixed (both time and state)" [Overstreet 1982, p. 3.46]. The importance of distinguishing between time- and state-based attributes is explained in [Nance 1981].

The following definitions are taken from [Nance and Overstreet 1987, p. 44]:
"An attribute x is a *control attribute* of an action cluster if x appears in a condition expression of the action cluster.
An attribute x is an *output attribute* of an action cluster if the action cluster can change the value of attribute x.
An attribute x is an *input attribute* of an action cluster if the value of x affects the output attributes of the action cluster."

An ACIG provides a graphical representation of the dynamics of a model by showing possible interaction between AC pairs. The arcs in an ACIG represent cause/effect relationships between AC occurrences. An ACIG is defined (roughly) as follows: (See [Overstreet and Nance 1984, pp. 14-15] for a more precise statement.)

Let $ac_1, ac_2, \ldots, ac_n$ be the ACs of a CS. For each i, let

C_i = set of control attributes for ac_i and

O_i = set of output attributes for ac_i.

Then for each i, j, the ACIG contains a directed arc from ac_i to ac_j iff $O_i \cap C_j \neq \phi$. Arcs may be classified as time-based or non-time-based depending on the nature of the associated attribute(s).

2.3. The Forms of Diagnostic Assistance

Overstreet and Nance [1984, p.2] identify the following as the purposes of model diagnosis:

(1) to assist in the identification of conceptual errors (misperceptions) or descriptive errors (misrepresentations) as early as possible in the modeling effort,

(2) to suggest alternatives that might be less prone to errors or might offer more efficient model development and experimentation, and

(3) to provide guidance and checks on the modeling effort.

They categorize diagnostic assistance as follows:

- *Analytical diagnosis:* "determination of the existence of a property..."
- *Comparative diagnosis:* "measures intended to depict differences among multiple representations of a single model or between representations of different models."
- *Informative diagnosis:* "includes assistance in the form of characteristics extracted or derived from model representations."

Table 2, extracted from the source cited above, is included here to illustrate diagnostics in each category and exemplify the targeted capabilities of the Analyzer.

Given the requirements for the Analyzer, in terms of both general requirements and diagnostics to be provided, the primary factors influencing its design are:

(1) Use of the UNIX operating system in general and **lex** and **yacc** (yet another compiler compiler) in particular.

(2) Treatment of Condition Specifications, both the components and the graphical representations, as abstract data types.

3. DESIGN APPROACH

3.1. Support Provided by UNIX

Lex LESM75 and **yacc** JOHS78 are two well known and widely recognized utilities provided by the UNIX operating system. Both **lex** and **yacc** can be considered meta-tools in the sense that they generate language recognizers. **Lex** generates recognizers for type 3 (regular) languages; **yacc** generates parsers for LALR(1) languages. A common practice (intended by the authors of **lex** and **yacc**) is to use a **lex** produced scanner in conjunction with (to supply tokens for) a **yacc** produced parser.

A brief introduction to these two tools is given here. The reader is referred to [Lesk and Schmidt 1975] and [Johnson 1978] for further details.

The main components of a **lex** specification are regular expressions and associated actions. Each regular expression describes a set of possible tokens. The action associated with a regular expression specifies, in C programming language statements (or in Ratfor statements [Lesk and Schmidt, p.1], the steps to be executed when an element of the corresponding set is recognized.

Regular expressions and actions may be modified independently, and regular expression/action combinations may be added or deleted as necessary. Due to possible order dependencies, caution must be exercised in cases where the sets denoted by two or more regular expressions have elements in common. The mutual independence and extensibility readily support incremental development and implementation of a lexical analyzer and the underlying **lex** specification.

An action may be as simple as returning a token type when a keyword is recognized, such as

```
signal   {
          return( SIGNALSYM );
       }
```

or an action may perform a certain amount of processing before returning.

The philosophy underlying **yacc** is similar to that underlying **lex**. A **yacc** specification is centered on a set of rules and associated actions. The **yacc** generated parser executes actions as it matches pieces of a stream of tokens with designated components of rules. As with **lex**, the ease with which a **yacc** specification may be modified,

---

Object Specification Extract

    repairman: status   :(avail, travel, busy)
                                       location   :(idle, i:1..n)

Condition Action Semantics

    (<condition> , <action set>)

Condition Action Pair Examples {and Explanations}

    (WHEN ALARM arr_facility (i:1..n), status :=busy)
    {When the repairman arrives at a facility, he is immediately
       busy repairing the facility.}

    (WHEN ALARM arr_idle, status :=avail)
    {When the repairman arrives at the idle location, he is
       available to repair failed facilities.}

    (WHEN ALARM arr_facility (i:1..n), location :=i)
    {When the repairman arrives at a facility, his location is
       that facility.}

Action Cluster Formation

    WHEN ALARM arr_facility (i:1..n);
       SET ALARM (end_repair (i), neg_exp(mean_repairtime));
       status :=busy;
       location :=i;
    END WHEN

Figure 1. Illustration of the Relationships in Attribute Definition and Specification. (Reprinted from [Nance and Overstreet 1987, p.41.])

Table 2. Categorized Summary of Diagnostic Assistance
(Reprinted from [Overstreet and Nance 1984.])

Category of Diagnostic Assistance		Properties, Measures, or Techniques Applied to the Condition Specification (CS) (*Implemented † Under Development)		Basis for Diagnosis
1)	Analytical: Determination of the existence of a property of a model representation.	a)*	Attribute Utilization: No attribute is defined that does not affect the value of another unless it serves a statistical (reporting) function.	Action Cluster Attribute Graph (ACAG)
		b)*	Attribute Initialization: All requirements for initial value assignment to attributes are met.	ACAG
		c)	Action Cluster Completeness: Required state changes within an action cluster are possible	ACAG
		d)	Attribute consistency: Attribute Typing during model definition is consistent with attribute usage in model specification.	ACAG
		e)†	Connectedness: No action cluster is isolated.	Action Cluster Incidence Graph (ACIG)
		f)†	Accessibility: Only the initialization action cluster is unaffected by other action clusters.	ACIG
		g)†	Out-complete: Only the termination action cluster exerts no influence on other action clusters.	ACIG
		h)	Revision Consistency: Refinements of a model specification are consistent with the previous version.	ACAG
2)	Comparative: Measures of differences among multiple model representations.	i)	Attribute cohesion: The degree to which attribute values are mutually influenced.	Attribute Interaction Matrix (originates with the ACAG)
		j)	Action Cluster cohesion: The degree to which action clusters are mutually influenced.	Action Cluster Interaction Matrix (originates with the ACAG)
		k)†	Complexity: a relative measure for the comparison of a CS to reveal differences in specification (clarity, maintainability, etc.) or implementation (run-time overhead) criteria.	ACIG
3)	Informative: Characteristics extracted or derived from model representations.	l)*	Attribute Classification: Identification of the function of each attribute (e.g. input, output, control, etc.)	ACAG
		m)	Precedence Structure: Recognition of sequential relationships among action clusters.	ACIG
		n)	Decomposition: Depiction of subordinate relationships among components of a CS.	ACIG

expanded, or contracted facilitates an incremental design and implementation strategy.

The capabilities of **yacc** are necessarily more sophisticated than those of **lex**. Rules for a **yacc** specification constitute the production rules of an LALR(1) grammar (see, for example, [Aho and Ullman 1977]) that describes the language to be accepted. Actions may be placed at the beginning, end, or between any two elements (terminals and nonterminals) of the right hand side of a rule. A single rule may contain multiple actions in different right-hand-side positions. **Yacc** also provides a simple mechanism for error recovery.

At its lowest level, the **yacc** specification for the Analyzer depends on the following types of data structures:

(1) List.
(2) Queue.
(3) Hash table.

Higher level data structures are defined in terms of these primitive ones. Support routines included in this specification include the following:

(i) Base level list, queue, and hash table management routines.
(ii) Routines that handle the internal representation of a CS and its components, which include an object table, attribute tables, a condition-action pair list, and an action cluster table.
(iii) ACIG construction and management routines.
(iv) Complexity and other graph based diagnosis routines.
(v) Input/output routines.

3.2. Abstract Data Types

Viewing a CS and its components as abstract data types (ADTs) is a key decision in the design and implementation of the Analyzer. Thus, for each of the structures mentioned in (1) to (3), (ii), and (iii) in Section 3.1 a set of operations exists by which the structure is created, modified, and accessed. Conceptually, no other operations on the structures are allowed. In general, the potential benefits of the ADT approach include increased modularity, reduced complexity, and increased modifiability of the resultant program.

4. THE MODELER'S VIEW OF THE ANALYZER

The typical user views the Model Analyzer as a combined interactive/non-interactive tool that:

(1) Takes as input a Condition Specification of a simulation model.
(2) Parses the representation, halting with the message "syntax error" if it detects an error.
(3) Compiles diagnostic information on the model representation.
(4) Allows the modeler, through menu selections, to view components of the model representation and pieces of the diagnostic information.
(5) Produces and (if possible) displays a graphical form (an ACIG) of the model representation.

4.1. Condition Specification Input

The Analyzer expects input in the form of a CS model representation following a prescribed syntax. According to this grammar, a CS representation is arranged as explained informally in the following paragraphs. (The formal grammar is given in Appendix A of [Moose and Nance 1987].)

Following the name of the CS, one or more objects are defined. Each object definition consists of the name of the object and zero or more attribute declarations. The name of the first object must be **environment**. This object represents the environment component of the model and also acts as a repository for *global* attributes. Attribute declarations follow a Pascal-like syntax [Jensen and Wirth 1974]. Valid attribute types are **real, integer, boolean,** (time-based) **signal**, and modeler-defined enumerated types. Numeric types may be preceded by one of the qualifiers **positive, nonnegative, nonpositive,** or **negative**.

After the object definitions, the model dynamics are specified in the form of a nonempty list of condition-action pairs. Each CAP may be prefixed by the name of an action cluster. The effect of these prefixes follows:

(1) If a CAP is preceded by an *owner (AC) prefix*, it becomes part of that AC.
(2) If a CAP is not prefixed, and if x is the most recently named owner prefix, the CAP becomes part of AC x.
(3) All CAPs that are given before the first prefixed CAP become *unowned CAPs*.

The purpose of owner prefixes is to enable a straightforward mechanism for the transformation of a list of CAPs to a set of ACs. It is desirable to have the transition specification read as a list of CAPs. However, various diagnostics (including complexity) require the existence of the corresponding set of ACs and an ACIG (action cluster incidence graph). Use of owner prefixes enables automatic production of ACs and an (unsimplified) ACIG without having to resort to more knowledge-oriented algorithms [†].

[†] AC production and various operations involving ACIGs have been identified as candidates for future applications of artificial intelligence techniques.

The condition and action component of each CAP can be either *simple* or *compound*. A simple condition is an arbitrary, boolean-valued expression, a **when** expression, an **after** expression, or the initialization condition (**start**). A compound condition is a simple condition preceded by one of the keywords **forall** or **forsome**. A simple action is an assignment statement, an **input/output** operation, a **set_alarm/cancel** operation, a **create/destroy** object operation, a function call, or the temination action (**stop**).

Within conditions and actions, the following syntactic conventions govern attribute references. An attribute name may be given in parenthesis with a valid object name preceding the left parentheses. In this case, the reference is interpreted as a reference to an attribute of the designated object, whose declarations must contain one for the named attribute. If an attribute is named without an associated object, the reference is bound to an attribute declaration, if one exists, in the environment object. In either case, a syntax error is indicated if an appropriate declaration does not exist.

A CAP may also contain references to *local variables*. A local variable name consists of a percent character followed by any (Pascal-like) identifier name (except keywords that have special meanings to the Analyzer). Local variables are not declared, and references to them may appear in many places where attribute references are expected.

4.2. Error Detection

Currently, the Analyzer contains no provisions for error recovery or reporting and also lacks some error detection capabilities (most notably, those associated with type checking). Two primary implications of these shortcomings are

- Detection of a syntax error causes processing to halt without any diagnostic messages.
- Attributes may be intermixed freely in CAPs without regard for type compatibility. (The type **signal** represents an exception to this statement.)

4.3. Compilation of Diagnostic Information and Post-parsing Operations

During parsing, the entire CS representation is saved internally in a composite data structure. The specifics of this data structure are generally transparent to the modeler. In addition to saving objects and CAPs as read, the Analyzer also constructs and saves ACs and records sets of input, output, and control attributes for each AC. Further, the Analyzer augments the data structure with three pieces of diagnostic information for each attribute. This information indicates whether the attribute is:

(1) referenced,

(2) used as a control or input attribute, or

(3) initialized (before being referenced, for example, on the right hand side of an assignment statement).

Immediately following the successful parsing of a CS representation, the Analyzer initiates an interactive session during which the modeler may view various components of the model as well as the previously noted attribute-based diagnostic information. The modeler determines the information to be displayed by making selections from the menu of Figure 2. Some selections require additional input, such as an AC or attribute name, from the modeler. Note that the attribute-based diagnostic information is contained in the attribute and object displays.

```
Display information for:
    (0 to exit)
    1) entire condition specification
    2) all objects
    3) single object
    4) single attribute
    5) all condition action pairs
    6) all action clusters
    7) single action cluster
```

Figure 2. Model Analyzer Menu

The final actions of the Analyzer are the construction and display of an ACIG and the computation and display of a measure of complexity. As previously discussed, the ACIG depicts cause/effect relationships between action cluster occurrences. The Analyzer displays the ACIG in two forms if possible. Irrespective of the output device, an adjacency matrix representation of the graph is displayed first. If the output device is a Ramtek 6221 color graphics terminal, the traditional graphical representation is also displayed. Between these two displays, the Control and Transformation (CAT) complexity measure [Wallace 1987] for the CS model respresentation is computed and displayed.

Currently, other graph-based diagnostics are under development and not available to the modeler. These diagnostics, to be provided in future prototypes, include:
- Connectedness.
- Reachability.
- Additional complexity measures.

5. CONCLUSIONS

The experience of designing and implementing a Model Analyzer prototype has confirmed the utility of the Condition Specification as a model representation which permits the extraction of world-view independent diagnostic information. This research has also illustrated the ease with which diagnostic tools may be created within the UNIX environment.

A number of issues are yet to be addressed, and a number of diagnostics remain to be implemented. Issues remaining to be addressed include the form and utility of diagnostics, such as attribute and action cluster cohesion, that are based on adjacency matrix representations of component interactions, and the application of artificial intelligence techniques in various areas of model analysis. For example, the ability to establish the semantic equivalence of textually different conditions can eliminate the need for constructing both a condition-action pair (CAP) list and an action cluster (AC) table. The AC table then can be derived automatically.

The diagnostics remaining to be implemented consist primarily of graph based information such as AC reachability and action cluster incidence graph (ACIG) connectedness. Future developers of Analyzer prototypes may include these diagnostics in a straightforward, incremental fashion by following the design strategy outlined in this report.

Acknowledgments

This research was supported in part by the Office of Naval Research and the Naval Sea Systems Command under Contract No. N60921-83-G-A165 through the Systems Research Center at Virginia Tech. Design and implementation of the ACIG construction and display routines are due to Jack C. Wallace. Implementations of the generalized list, hash table, and queue routines are due to Matt Humphrey. Karen Kaster provided assistance with the text and table formatting. Table 1 was taken from [OVEC85], Copyright 1985, Association for computing Machinery, Inc., reprinted by permission.

REFERENCES

Aho, A.V. and J. D. Ullman (1977), *Principles of Compiler Design*, Addison-Wesley, Reading.

Balci, O. (1986), "Requirements for Model Development Environments," *Computers and Operations Research* 13(1), 53-67.

Hansen, R.H. (1984), "The Model Generator: A Crucial Element of the Model Development Environment," Technical Report CS84008-R, Department of

Computer Science, Virginia Tech Blacksburg, Va., Aug.

Jensen, K. and A N. Wirth (1974), *Pascal User Manual and Report, Second Edition*, Springer-Verlag, New York.

Johnson, S.C. (1978), "Yacc: Yet Another Compiler-Compiler," In *UNIX Programmer's Manual, 2B*, Bell Laboratories.

Lesk, M.E. and E. Schmidt (1975), "Lex - A Lexical Analyzer Generator," In: *UNIX Programmer's Manual, 2B*, Bell Laboratories.

Moose, Jr., R.L. and R.E. Nance (1987), "Model Analysis in a Model Development Environment," Technical Report SRC-87-010, Systems Research Center, Virginia Tech, Blacksburg, Va., July.

Nance, R.E. (1981), "Model Representation in Discrete Event Simulation: The Conical Methodology," Technical Report CS81003-R, Department of Computer Science, Virginia Tech, Blacksburg, Va.

Nance, R.E. and C. M. Overstreet (1987), "Diagnostic Assistance Using Digraph Representations of Discrete Event Simulation Model Specifications," *Transactions of the Society for Computer Simulation*, 4(Apr.), 33-56.

Overstreet, C.M. (1982), "Model Specification and Analysis for Discrete Event Simulation," Ph.D. Dissertation, Department of Computer Science, Virginia Tech, Blacksburg, Va.

Overstreet, C.M. and R. E. Nance (1984), "Graph-Based Diagnosis of Discrete Event Model Specifications, Revised Draft," Technical Report CS83028-R, Department of Computer Science, Virginia Tech, Blacksburg, Va., June.

Overstreet, C.M. and R. E. Nance (1985), "A Specification Language to Assist in Analysis of Discrete Event Simulation Models," *Communications of the ACM 28,* (Feb.), 190-201.

Wallace, J.C. and R. E. Nance (1985), "The Control and Transformation Metric: A Basis for Measuring Model Complexity," Technical Report TR-85-15, Department of Computer Science, Virginia Tech, Blacksburg, Va., Mar.

Wallace, J.C. (1985), "The Control and Transformation Metric: Toward the Measurement of Simulation Model Complexity," In *Proceedings of the 1987 Winter Simulation Conference* (Atlanta, Ga., Dec. 14-16). IEEE, Piscataway, N.J., pp. 597-603.

VISUAL SIMULATION: SEEING IS BELIEVING?

RAY J. PAUL

London School of Economics & Political Science
Houghton Street, London WC2A 2AE, England

ABSTRACT

Visual simulation is an increasingly popular method of problem solving. There are a wide variety of graphical symbolisms, movement representations, and screen layouts available. Visual modelling can assist both the analyst and the decision maker. However, there are problems associated with visual interpretation which need to be understood and handled by the analyst. Seeing should not be believing. These issues are discussed in this paper, and some suggestions for improvement made based on research and development undertaken on the VS6 simulation modelling system.

1. INTRODUCTION

Recent advances in microcomputer technology have had a major impact on simulation modelling and the use of graphics in particular. Associated improvements in the ease of use of computer software, because of the power of mass purchasing, have also had a significant influence on these areas. Birtwhistle [1985] contains a number of papers illustrating the growing interest in, and variety of, graphics simulation systems. The Computer Aided Simulation Modelling (CASM) research project at the LSE has attempted to incorporate these advances in its software developments.

The CASM research objectives are to automate as much of the simulation modelling process as possible in order to make the use of simulation modelling efficient and inexpensive [Balmer and Paul 1986]. Recognising that many simulations involve the progressive development of a model in order to comprehend a complex problem, CASM have developed systems that are easy to use, quick to modify, and which provide a working model at all times. In other words, systems for rapid prototyping. The latest version of these systems, VS6 [Paul et al 1988, and VS6 1988], will be used to illustrate the themes of this paper.

Visual representation in simulation modelling comes in a variety of forms, and these are discussed in the next section. The reasons why such representations have become almost obligatory in simulation modelling are examined in the following section. However, the use of visual simulation is relatively new and untried, and many problems are being uncovered. Some of these problems are outlined in the fourth section, followed by conclusions concerning the future use of visual methods.

2. VISUAL METHODS

2.1 Graphics Representations

There are a number of ways of visually representing the logic of a simulation model whilst it is running. The simplest form is to use keyboard characters to represent model objects. The advantage of this approach is that no special graphics hardware or software needs to be purchased. The disadvantages are that screen design is extremely limited, and that keyboard characters are generally not versatile enough to convey to the onlooker which objects are which.

More visually appealing representations rely on icons, pre-defined symbols or shapes, generated in some automated or semi-automated fashion. Icons can readily be constructed to look like the objects being modelled. For example, VS6 has a graphics editor which allows for a shape of variable size to be constructed from circles, boxes, lines, and cursor controlled drawing (for drawing single pixels, for example). The shape can be filled or painted-in, and with the appropriate graphics card, can be multicoloured. Iconic representations tend to be more expensive than keyboard characters (in terms of analyst time, speed of running the model, and computer memory). They also tend to be heavily machine dependent. For example, VS6 can only run on IBM PC compatibles and upwards.

Further sophistication can be provided by animation. The icons can be made to move on the screen at a speed and distance representative of the real life object. Such methods require more overheads in terms of system control, particularly in timing, and of parallel movements of many icons. The effort required to add animation is therefore considerable. There is also some debate as to whether animation, whilst visually appealing, hides the logic of the model in a mass of visual detail.

Greater realism can be obtained from a three dimensional rendering of objects on the screen [Wyvill 1985]. Objects can be projected in perspective with the hidden surfaces removed. Shading, reflection and shadows can be introduced to simulate light effects. However, these methods can not be used for real time applications and are not generally available on inexpensive machines. Angell and Griffith [1987] and Foley and Van Dam [1983] examine these wider aspects of computer graphics.

The presentation of simulation results is another important aspect of modelling to benefit from colour graphics. Apart from the obvious ability to show results in the form of histograms, pie-charts, and a variety of graphs, these diagrams can also be shown dynamically. As the simulation model progresses through its run, the development and maturing of the statistic(s) under observation can be observed. Maivald [1985] discusses the use of colour presentation graphics as a teaching aid, simulating the behaviour of solutions to sets of equations.

2.2 Visual Simulation Techniques

There are a variety of ways of combining graphics into a simulation model. Bell and O'Keefe [1987] argues that visual interactive modelling systems are alternative solution techniques to more traditional methods. One can choose between adding a visual display to an existing modelling method, or redesigning the modelling method entirely around the visual interface.

The obvious approach is to code the graphics into the model itself. This has the advantage of tying the visual movement directly to the model logic. Its disadvantage, however, is that model development becomes more intricate as the logic and movement instructions are intertwined. Since most real applications go through a considerable development cycle, this is quite a disadvantage.

An alternative is to set-up the graphics for the model in an independent suite of routines that can be called as appropriate by the simulation model, and can easily be switched on or off. VS6 is a good example of this approach. The problem and its associated visual representation(s) are constructed in an interactive interpretive system. VS6 will automatically generate a Pascal program for the problem on request, similar in style to that described by Paul and Chew [1987]. The graphics for the generated code are handled by a library of routines controlled by a graphics file. Fast results from the model, when the model is considered to be working satisfactorily, can be obtained by switching the graphics routines off. The generated program can be amended, for example to handle more complex conditions, without the graphics being affected. Any change to the model logic flow will, though, require the respecification of the problem.

Visual interactive simulation usually implies that the graphical interface is constructed interactively. The term interactive is sometimes applied to the running of the model, whereby the user can interrupt a program run, graphically redesign the model, and then continue the run. This form of interaction is considered desirable, for example, when testing the use of dynamic scheduling rules. The simulation problem is typically modelled in a generic simulation system which is driven by data representing the problem specification.

Another form of user control is provided by systems that drive a graphics screen from an output file of a simulation model. This enables the picture to be run backwards or forwards under user control. Its obvious advantage is the ability to check back when a query arises. Such systems usually incorporate speed control. Its main disadvantage is that two independent systems must usually be tested and altered as the model develops.

2.3 Screen Layout

There are a variety of ways of using graphics on a screen. Buzzell et al [1985] describes the use of a pair of very high resolution (1024 x 1280 pixels) colour graphics displays to model the command/control function in a battlefield simulation. The displays provide map type images for battle manoeuvre and command/control. The background image is very detailed and significant, with movement overlaid and relatively crude. Most simulation applications are concerned with the flow and position of objects, with the background as a secondary or irrelevant item.

The most common type of screen layout is the placing of icons representing objects on screen positions which indicate their current state. Movement is then represented in a number of ways. State change to state change can be depicted by simultaneous change of position of all objects that change their state at that time. Alternatively, animation, as described above or with icons, can be used to represent movement. The latter has the advantage of appearing more 'natural' to the layman. The former has the advantage of showing the model control in its simplest form.

Many simulation systems handle increasing model complexity by greater resolution, enabling more information to be packed on the screen. An alternative, as used by the VS6 system, is to allow the construction of a number of parallel screens, or scenes, which can be switched whilst the model is running. There are a number of ways such scenes can be designed. A large problem can be turned into a grid, where each scene is a grid cell. The scenes can then be switched to enable the appropriate part of the system to be viewed. Another approach is to develop a series of hierarchical scenes, with an aggregated version of the whole problem on one scene, and more detailed layouts of some of the more complex model interactions on separate scenes. It has also proved useful to have several scenes of the same part of the model, each with different mixtures of objects and state positions illustrated. This has aided user understanding of a complex interaction. The power of the available variety of screen designs is not yet matched by a universal knowledge of how to use this power. This problem will be addressed below.

CADmotion [1988] is an example of an icon based visual simulation system that incorporates true computer aided design features. For example, it incorporates true zoom and pan features, true-to-scale drawing, and an automatic sketching tool for drawing. These features are particularly appropriate for manufacturing and other physical models.

Pidd [1988] describes the use of logical displays, where on-screen block diagrams show the aggregated state of play of the system. The blocks do not need to represent objects, but can designate complete processes made up of many different object types.

Dynamic presentation graphics have already been mentioned above. Some systems incorporate such graphics in interactive windows to an iconic visual display. The user can interrupt a run of the model, select a histogram from a pre-specified set of diagrams, and see the histogram being updated dynamically on a small window on the screen.

2.4 Model Specification

Colour graphics are also beginning to play an important role in model construction and development. CADmotion and its associated PCModel simulation system allow the specification of a model by designing a screen display. Systems such as this work well on a certain restricted class of simulation problem. It would be difficult to design a system that could handle any conceivable problem in this way. An alternative approach, illustrated by VS6 as described above, is to generate program code from a specification of a simpler problem, and then add the particular complexities to the code. VS6 handles the specification part of the modelling with a colour graphics pull down tile or tablet system. A problem can be entered into the interface in a structured fashion, but with the added facility of easy modification as necessary. The user is effectively given a three dimensional matrix in which to specify the problem, with pull-down colour tiles enabling the third dimension.

3. THE PURPOSES OF VISUAL METHODS

Many authors have described the virtues of visual simulation [Wyvill 1985, and Bell and O'Keefe 1987]. Enhancement of simulation results via presentation graphics has already been mentioned. The other two commonly extolled virtues are the facilitation of debugging and testing of the model, and a visual analogue of the problem for communication purposes.

3.1 The Analyst

The obvious attraction for the analyst of a visual model is that it can often easily be seen when the model is not working. A printed numerical output may contain the information required to detect an error, but it usually has to be searched for, and then traced (sometimes painfully). An error displayed visually is usually obvious and the reason self evident. However, the power of visual modelling is restricted to the extent that the model logic is covered by the visual display(s). Visual modelling can introduce undue over confidence in the analyst because the models look 'alright'.

Some aspects of the model logic are often difficult or impossible to display visually. For example, in a recent port simulation model the movement of the model entities (ships and berths) was relatively straightforward [El Sheikh et al 1987]. However, the rules of engagement of the entities were very complex, based on ship cargo characteristics, berth handling capabilities, and a variety of priority rules for ship types, which varied by berth type. Any attempt to represent visually such rules would probably be self-defeating, in that the screen would be too difficult to comprehend.

3.2 The Modelling Process

'Seeing is believing' aids the customer/analyst relationship as the simulation modelling technique ceases to appear to be a black box. The ubiquitous cliche 'a picture is worth a thousand words' certainly seems to apply. With a careful design of the visual display(s), the customer(s) can appreciate that the model does indeed mimic the real problem. Some belief in model validity may even be induced. Better suggestions for the alternatives to be modelled might be catalysed.

The advantage of visual simulation is further enhanced if the systems used are flexible and fast, so that rapid visual prototyping in collaboration with the customer becomes a possibility. For example, VS6's specification windowing interface enables a working model to be easily constructed with graphics in a short period of time. Interaction between analyst and customer can then proceed, with customer corrections being rapidly handled, and enhancements added and tested dynamically. Such a modelling system also encourages 'first-cut' modelling, whereby a simple version of the problem is modelled, tested, and understood before further development. Development using this staged approach, in collaboration with the customer, can lead to the cessation of unnecessary development as the problem reaches the required level of understanding. Adding more and more detail to a simulation model, in the belief that this is a move towards 'realism', is probably the chief cause of models becoming too large, unwieldy, and eventually incomprehensible. This is true for any form of modelling, not just graphics.

4. PROBLEMS WITH VISUAL SIMULATION

4.1 Characteristics of Human Vision

It is not the purpose of this paper to give a discourse on human psychology. In simple terms, visual interpretation is influenced by inherited information (genetics), personal experience, and cultural or environmental factors. Vision is interpreted by the brain, which does not remember all the visual detail. Selectivity takes place, so that only parts of the picture are taken in. Vision is not like a camera, anymore than memory is like a tape recorder. Memory is reconstructive, and is not just storage.

Vision is biased by preconceptions, personal subjectivity, current temperament, and one's personal involvement or commitment. It is quite common to seek confirmation of some previously held view. Dreams, wishes, desires and thoughts affect what one thinks one knows or sees. Lastly, and importantly in this discussion, clarity, speed, presentation and colour all affect interpretation of vision.

These factors are exemplified by contradictory or even physically impossible eyewitness evidence. Watching a film the second time around does not encourage belief in one's memory! Two of the most popular colours in visual simulation are red and green. Something of the order of 10% of people are colour blind to these colours! Some schools of thought proclaim that black and white systems are the best, since they are easily understood without colour confusion.

Of course, most if not all of these factors affect communication in whatever form it takes. The written presentation of material is commonly interpreted in many ways. Numerical information in a report is usually condensed, and assumptions underlying the modelling process are often forgotten. This is especially true as the number of people involved in handling the information increases. Visual information may be more reliable, but it is relative reliability, not absolute. Seeing should not be believing!

4.2 The Customer

There is an obvious need to educate the customer as to the purpose of simulation. Horror stories abound of customers viewing a snapshot of the model and assuming that the problem always has these characteristics. Customers need to be aware of the difference between weather, the state of the atmosphere at any one time, and climate, the average of weather. Even if the customer is aware of the nature of a statistical experimental tool, there is still the danger that seeing is believing. An alternative problem arises when a customer sees a sampled value that is considered to be unrealistic, and then decides the whole analysis is false.

These observations are particularly pertinent to those systems that claim to make the analyst redundant. Smith [1986] points out that there are three problems associated with the simulation version of statistical modelling. It is difficult enough, and very important, for an analyst to convey these correctly to a customer, let alone the customer using the model without analyst support. The first is the combined question of steady states, run lengths and multiple runs, especially for terminating simulations. The second is the problem of interactions among variables, whereby some combinations can be rare and important. The third is to have some experimental model for determining good and bad results, and for generating sensible strategies.

Presentation graphics, whilst an improvement on textual results, require a great deal of thought. For example, in the author's experience, statistical distributions, and their measures of spread, are not universally understood in the health community. So simulation modelling of patient queueing time has to be presented in simple ways. In such environments scaling of diagrams and selection of axes can have a significant impact on interpretation.

4.3 The Analyst

Graphics do not verify a model, they enhance it. Visual modelling is slow. It is impossible to test all model interactions visually for a complex model. However, a customer not educated in the modelling process may be witness to an unknown error, thereby undermining analyst credibility. Whilst a visual representation may indicate some faults in model logic, new ones can be introduced by the extra graphical components of the system.

The ability to build larger, more complex, impressively visual models can tempt the analyst away from the modelling purpose. As mentioned above, systems like VS6 encourages the staged development of simulation models. The analyst must resist the temptation to increase detail unless the justification exceeds that of providing 'look-alike realism'.

Visual modelling is a new process, requiring experience and education. Other disciplines can and should be applied, such as graphics design and psychology.

5. CONCLUSIONS

Visual modelling is a powerful complement to an analyst's problem solving capabilities, but it has new problems to overcome as well. In time, the development of visual interactive modelling techniques may produce its own methodology as Bell and O'Keefe [1987] suggests.

One area of interest to the CASM research group is the use of graphical and textual techniques for model formulation. Several systems exist that work from a graphical specification of the problem [for example, Granda and Pourrahimi 1985]. Attempts have been made to construct textual systems that aid the analyst and the customer formulate the problem [Doukidis 1987, and Paul and Doukidis 1986]. The latter systems resort to artificial intelligence methods, which are increasingly being used in conjunction with simulation [Paul 1989a and 1989b]. The way forward would appear to be some form of graphical artificial intelligence system [Knox 1988].

The most important potential benefit of visual simulation is the increasing ability to help a decision maker by working together in a collaborative effort. Graphics is the way forward. In spite of the problems outlined above, humans 'think' visually. Text is a poor approximation, being only one dimensional, and is even more unreliable.

REFERENCES

Angell, I.O. and G. Griffith (1987), *Higher-resolution Computer Graphics using FORTRAN 77*, Macmillan, London.

Balmer, D.W. and R.J.Paul (1986), "CASM- The Right Environment for Simulation," *Journal of the Operational Research Society 37*, 5 (May), 443-452.

Bell, P.C. and R.M. O'Keefe (1987), "Visual Interactive Simulation - History, recent developments, and major issues," *Simulation 49*, 3 (Sept.), 109-116.

Birtwhistle, G, Ed. (1985), *AI, Graphics and Simulation*, The Society for Computer Simulation, San Diego, CA.

Buzzell, C.A., R.G. Ransom, J.J Rhoades, and D.P. Wiltzius (1985), "Using interactive color graphics to model the command/control function in a battlefield simulation." In *AI, Graphics and Simulation*, G.Birtwhistle, Ed. The Society for Computer Simulation, San Diego, CA.

CADmotion. (1988), *CADmotion and PCModel*. Simulation Software Systems. San Jose, CA.

Crookes, J.G., D.W. Balmer, S.T. Chew, and R.J. Paul (1986), "A Three-phase Simulation System Written in Pascal," *Journal of the Operational Research Society 37*, 6 (June), 603-618.

Doukidis. G.I. (1987), "An Anthology on the Homology of Simulation with Artificial Intelligence," *Journal of the Operational Research Society 38*, 8 (Aug.), 701-712.

El Sheikh, A.A.R., R.J. Paul, A.S. Harding, and D.W. Balmer (1987), "A Microcomputer Based Simulation Study of a Port," *Journal of the Operational Research Society 37*, 8 (Aug.), 673-681.

Foley, J.D., and A. Van Dam (1983), *Fundamentals of Interactive Computer Graphics*, Addison Wesley, Reading, Mass.

Granda, J.J. and F. Pourrahimi (1985), "Computer Graphics Techniques for the Generation and Analysis of Physical System Models." In *AI, Graphics and Simulation*, G.Birtwhistle, Ed. The Society for Computer Simulation, San

Diego, CA.

Knox, P.M. (1988), Automated Graphically-Based Discrete-Event Simulation Systems, Unpublished Ph.D thesis, University of London, England.

Maivald, O. (1985), "Simulation as a Teaching Method using Interactive Computer Graphics in Color," In *AI, Graphics and Simulation*, G.Birtwhistle, Ed. The Society for Computer Simulation, San Diego, CA.

Paul, R.J. (1989a), "Artificial Intelligence and Simulation Modelling," in *Computer Modelling for Discrete Simulation*, M. Pidd, Ed. Wiley, London. In press.

Paul, R.J. (1989b), "Combining Artificial Intelligence and Simulation," in *Computer Modelling for Discrete Simulation*, M. Pidd, Ed. Wiley, London. In press.

Paul, R.J. and S.T. Chew (1987), "Simulation Modelling using an Interactive Simulation Program Generator," *Journal of the Operational Research Society 38*, 8 (Aug.), 735-752.

Paul, R.J., S.T. Chew, and P.M. Knox (1988), 'An Integrated Automated Visual Simulation System,' CASM report, Department of Statistics, L.S.E. In progress.

Paul, R.J., and G.I.Doukidis (1986), "Further Developments in the Use of Artificial Intelligence Techniques which Formulate Simulation Problems," *Journal of the Operational Research Society 37*, 8 (Aug.), 787-810.

Pidd, M. (1988), *Computer Simulation in Management Science*. 2nd Ed. Wiley, Chichester.

Smith, V.L. (1986), "Visual Interactive Modelling," Letter in *the Journal of the Operational Society 37*, 10 (Oct.), 1017-1020.

VS6. (1988), *The VS6 Simulation Package and User's Guide*. Syspack Ltd, London, England.

Wyvill, B. (1985), "Current Trends in Graphics and Animation," In *AI, Graphics and Simulation*, G.Birtwhistle, Ed. The Society for Computer Simulation, San Diego, CA.

SIMULATING A MARINE CONTAINER TERMINAL ON THE MACINTOSH II

MICHAEL B. SILBERHOLZ
Computer Sciences Corporation
Beltsville, Maryland 20705

BRUCE L. GOLDEN
College of Business and Management, University of Maryland
College Park, Maryland 20742

EDWARD K. BAKER
School of Business Administration, University of Miami
Coral Gables, Florida 33124

ABSTRACT

In recent years, the marine container terminal has become the focus for potential productivity improvements. We have developed a sophisticated simulation model to address some of these issues, on a Macintosh II microcomputer. This paper introduces the simulation model and highlights the special features used in the development and documentation phases.

1. INTRODUCTION

This paper describes a marine port simulation model for marine container terminals (see the reference list for related work), which since the adoption of container technology by worldwide shipping interests in the 1960s, has become a critical nexus of world trade. Consequently, as ocean freight traffic has increased, the marine container terminal has become the focus for potential productivity improvements. Our simulation model is, in some sense, an outgrowth of several discussions with individuals affiliated with the ports in Baltimore and Miami. This computerized simulation model analyzes the impact of work rules on the productivity and costs of these ports. The convenience, environment for development and documentation, and the computational speed of the Apple Macintosh II made it an ideal choice for our model-building effort.

2. HARDWARE CONFIGURATION

The port simulation model was built and tested on an Apple Macintosh II microprocessor with one megabyte of memory. The central processor of the Macintosh II is a Motorola MC68020 which utilizes a 32-bit architecture and operates at a 15.6672 megahertz clock frequency. The Macintosh II also utilizes a MC68881 floating point device. The MC68881, when accessed by the software, increases the speed of floating point arithmetic operations up to 200 times. The one megabyte of memory provided on the basic Macintosh II system was sufficient for the model's execution but limited the use of software tools. This problem could be alleviated, however, since memory on the Macintosh II is expandable to eight megabytes on the processor board, and up to two gigabytes using Apple NuBus slots.

The Macintosh II is equipped with two 800-kilobyte double-sided disk drives and an internal 40-megabyte hard disk drive. The system utilizes a 13-inch Apple Color High Resolution RGB monitor. This monitor provides a 640-by-480-pixel display for the presentation of text and graphics. Operator input is received either from a 105-key keyboard or from a mouse. Hardcopy is generated using an ImageWriter II dot matrix printer which displays text and graphics outputs at resolutions of up to 160-dots per inch. High quality output, when required, is generated by copying the target output documents to 800-kilobyte disks and then transporting them to a system equipped with an Apple LaserWriter printer.

The documentation of this research was greatly enhanced by the ability to scan photographs from other sources by using a digitizer. This product, ThunderScan for Macintosh, allows photographic images to be digitized into one of 32 shades of gray, using a scanning device attached to an Image Writer II printer. Images may be enlarged up to 800 percent or reduced to 25 percent when scanned.

3. SOFTWARE CONFIGURATION

Six major software packages were used to develop and document the port simulation model. The model was developed using the first of these packages, Borland's Turbo Pascal. Pascal was chosen as the programming language as it is a structured language, it was relatively inexpensive, and was readily available. Pascal's data constructs, such as record and pointer structures, were readily adapted to the model, especially in the management of queues and statistics.

Unfortunately, the version of Turbo Pascal employed for the simulation was developed for earlier models of the Macintosh and occasionally causes system crashes during program execution. This phenomenon is primarily due to architectural differences between the earlier Macintosh systems and the Macintosh II. The severity and frequency of these processing interruptions was reduced by configuring the RGB monitor as a two-shade black and white monitor. Another problem with Turbo Pascal is that it does not use the MC68881 floating point coprocessor. Instead, it uses the Standard Apple Numerics

Environment for all arithmetic operations, thereby ignoring the increased speed of the MC68881 and lengthening execution times.

Another major software package used in the development of the model was the Macintosh Programmer's Workshop (MPW) software environment. The MPW package provides a complete, professional-level, integrated programming environment for the Macintosh and it was developed by Apple Computer, Incorporated. MPW provides many utilities which aid in software development on the Macintosh as well as upgrades to the system subroutine libraries to make use of the MC68881 floating-point coprocessor. In addition, the MPW package provides examples of programming in the Macintosh environment using Pascal, C, or Assembler language. These examples are very useful for learning to manage menus, files, and screens on the Macintosh. This package, although highly integrated, is difficult to learn.

Another software package used in the development of the model is the Extender GrafPak subroutine library. The capabilities of this set of compiled libraries allow multiple curves to be generated using one of seven different types of graph formats, such as bar plots and log-log plots. Titles and labels as well as user defined tick marks and grid patterns may be added to these plots using any letter font or style.

The majority of the documentation for this paper was entered and edited using the Microsoft Word word processing program for the Apple Macintosh. Microsoft Word allows all of the standard steps of document generation, namely outlining, entering, formatting, revising, proofreading, and printing, to be exercised by the editor. Normal text, mathematical formulas, or graphics output from other applications may be incorporated in a Microsoft Word document. All commands are entered via menu selection or by typing the appropriate command at the keyboard. Special features available in Microsoft Word are hyphenation, spelling correction, table of contents generation, and indexing, all easily requested using a menu selection. Another feature, recently provided to Microsoft Word users at no cost, is a desk accessory called Word Finder. Word Finder adds a thesaurus capability to Microsoft Word.

Another software package, MacPaint allows perfectly structured shapes or freehand designs to be incorporated into drawings. MacPaint was used to generate several descriptive figures, such as Figure 1, depicting a sample port . MacPaint provides five basic drawing shapes, three of which, the rectangle, the rectangle with rounded edges, and the oval, are structured, following the grid lines contained in the graphics window. The remaining two shapes, the free hand border and the polygon follow the design of the user. The pen size, pen pattern, and fill pattern may all be set by the user. In addition, various tools are provided to free hand draw, paint, spray paint, erase, and letter, to mention a few.

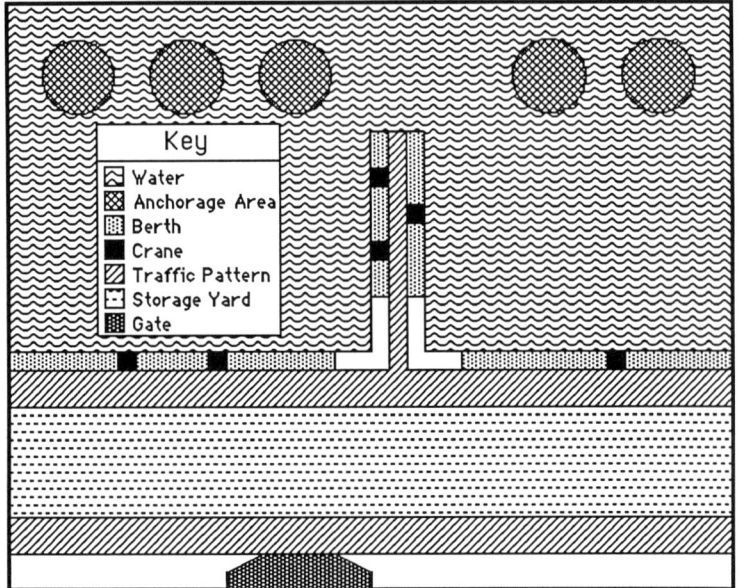

Figure 1 - MacPaint Example of a Sample Port

The final software package, MacDraw, is another package which allows structured shapes or freehand designs to be incorporated into drawings. MacDraw was used to generate many of the remaining figures in the documentation. The major difference between MacPaint and MacDraw is that MacDraw does not provide any of the free hand paint features of MacPaint. The same basic structured shapes and freehand shapes are provided. In addition to normal straight line drawing, an arc is provided to connect two points. These features can be seen in Figure 2 which depicts the storage yard at a sample port. In this figure, curved lines, various line types, various pen sizes and pen patterns are used to define the different features in the storage yard.

The above mentioned software packages and hardware are available from a variety of vendors. Macintosh related publications, such as MacUser, occasionally offer reviews of various hardware and software products, and sources for those products.

The overall software configuration used in our modeling effort is summarized in Figure 3.

4. MODEL APPLICATIONS

The port simulation model is composed of two application programs, the simulation program and the graphics support program, which are described below using data flow diagrams. The sample data flow diagram in Figure 4 highlights the basic features of such a structure. Five symbols are used to describe any process. A triangle signifies the start of a process, a circle references a lower-level process, a directed line defines the flow of data, a split line defines a decision path, and a square defines the end of a process.

All of the circled subprocesses, as well as the name of the overall process which is being defined, are contained in the key. The "S" and the "E" define the start and end of the process whose name is included in their descriptions. The lower-level processes are defined by the process number included in the process symbol of the data flow diagram. If these processes are complex, they are expanded on subsequent data flow diagrams. Otherwise, they are described in the associated text.

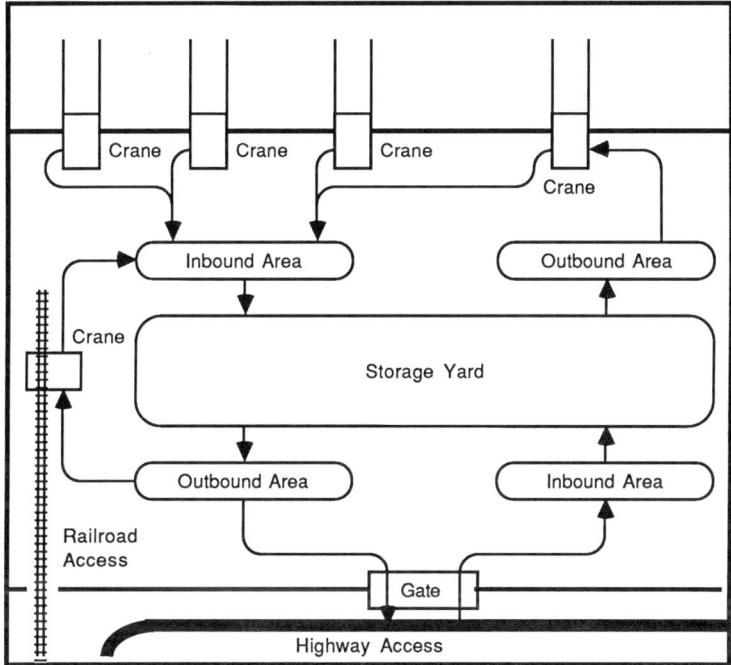

Figure 2 - MacDraw Example of a Sample Storage Yard

Package	Application
Extender GrafPak	Subroutine library for plot generation
MacDraw	Figure generation using predefined shapes
MacPaint	Editing scanned pictures
Microsoft Word	Documentation generation
MPW	Programming environment and sample programs
Turbo Pascal	Basic simulation programming language

Figure 3 - Overview of Software Package Used in Simulation

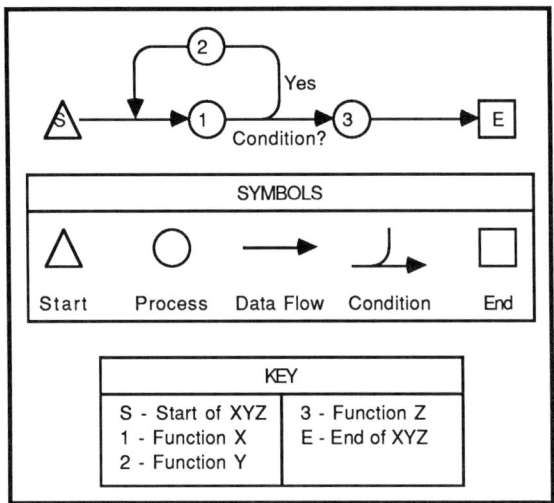

Figure 4 - Sample Data Flow Diagram

The major portion of the port simulation model, the simulation program, is illustrated in the processes of the next two figures and this will be discussed next. Each figure depicts a high-level process, and is described by lower level processes and data flows. The highest level of the simulation program is depicted in Figure 5. In this diagram, once the simulation program is activated, the simulation control parameters are read and verified by the 'read simulation parameters' process.

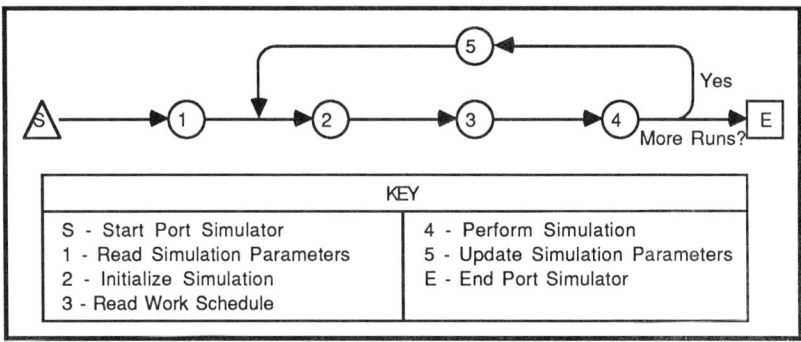

Figure 5 - Port Simulator Process

If the control parameter specification is error free, various queues and statistics are initialized. This is accomplished by executing several low-level simulation queueing procedures and clearing all appropriate status variables within the program. After initialization is completed, the schedule control parameters, if requested, are read and verified. If this operation is also error free, the requested simulation is carried out by the 'perform simulation' process. If additional simulation runs are required, as indicated by control parameter looping structures or additional work schedule definitions, the appropriate simulation parameters are updated and control is passed back to the 'initialize simulation' process.

The 'perform simulation' process is further defined in Figure 6. When this process is executed, the first work event, namely the arrival or departure of a work crew, at the first berth is initialized by the 'schedule first work event' process. This process is repeated until all work events at the berth have been scheduled. After all work events have been scheduled for the first berth, a ship arrival is scheduled by the 'schedule first arrival at berth' process. If additional berths are present at the port, control is returned to the 'schedule first work event' process so that the next berth can be initialized.

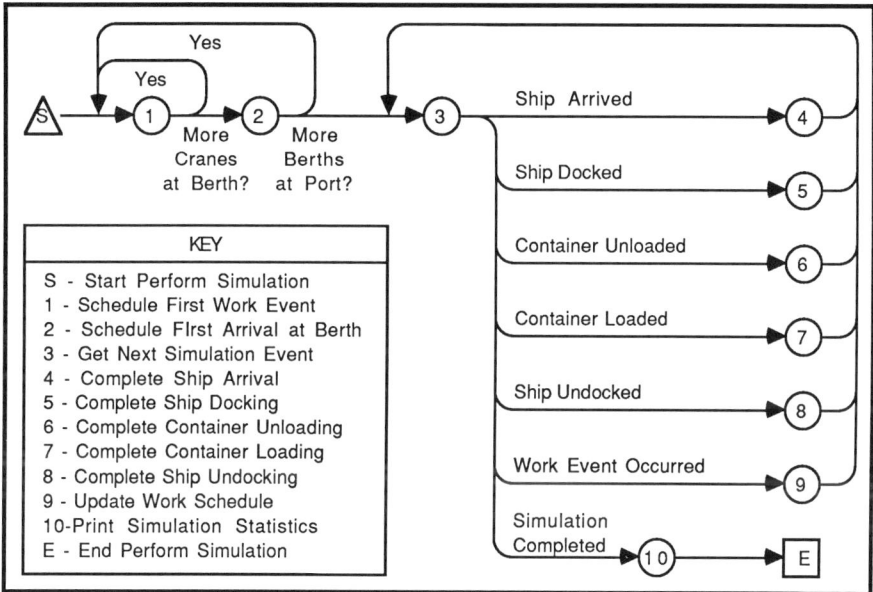

Figure 6 - Perform Simulation Process

Upon completion of the work event and ship arrival scheduling, the actual simulation is performed. The 'get next simulation event' process retrieves the next scheduled event from the simulation event queue. These events are stored in ascending time order. When an event is retrieved, the simulation clock is updated to the time of the event. Initially, only a work event or a ship arrival can occur. After the first ship arrives, a ship docked event is possible. Likewise, after a ship docked event has occurred, container loaded and unloaded events are possible. Finally, ship undocked events can occur.

When a simulation event is retrieved from the event queue, one of seven processes is executed. These processes correspond to ship arrivals, ship docking, container loading and unloading, ship undocking, work events, and simulation completion. With the exception of simulation completion, all of these processes generate statistics and schedule one or more future events, and then return to the 'get next simulation event' process. After a sufficient number of ships have departed the port, the simulation completion event is scheduled. This event signifies the completion of the simulation run and causes the simulation statistics to be output. After the output is generated, the perform simulation process exits.

The 'complete ship arrival' process, when entered, immediately places the ship on the queue of ships awaiting a berth. The next ship arrival at the berth is then scheduled. If a berth is not available for use, the 'complete ship arrival' process exits. If a berth is available, the ship is assigned to the berth and the state of the shipping channel is checked. If the ship can maneuver at the current time, the completion of the maneuver operation is scheduled. Otherwise, the ship is placed on the end of the maneuver queue. Upon completion of these operations, the 'complete ship arrival' process exits.

After an arriving ship has completed its maneuver operation, the 'complete ship docking' process determines the characteristics of the ship. The initial payload of the ship and the number of containers to be loaded and unloaded from the ship are all determined using simulation control parameters. The 'complete ship docking' process next attempts to schedule the unloading of a container by each of the cranes allocated to the ship. It starts by checking if a work crew is currently staffing the first crane at the berth. If it is, the completion of a container unload operation is scheduled for the crane. Otherwise, the unload request is placed on the work crew queue at the crane. This scheduling operation is repeated for the remaining cranes at the berth. Upon completion of the unload scheduling, the complete ship docking process exits.

The 'complete container unloading' process may be unable to reach completion. This occurs when the required work crew's shift has ended, or the work crew is on a break when the unload completion event would have occurred. When this is the case, the unload request is placed on the appropriate work crew queue and the process exits. If the required work crew is operating the crane when the unload completion occurs, appropriate unload statistics are collected and the number of containers to be unloaded by the crane is decremented. If additional containers are to be unloaded by the crane, the unload completion of the next container is scheduled and the process exits. Otherwise, the number of containers to be loaded by the crane is checked. If any containers are to be loaded, the load completion of the first container is scheduled and the process exits. If all required containers have been transferred, the ship is readied for departure. If the ship can maneuver at the current time, the completion of the maneuver operation is scheduled.

Otherwise, the ship is placed at the end of the maneuver queue. After the departure is scheduled, the process exits.

The 'complete container loading' process is similar to the 'complete container unloading' process. After the work crew schedule is checked, the appropriate load statistics are collected and the number of containers to be loaded by the crane is decremented. The remainder of the process is identical, except that container unloading is not checked.

The 'complete ship undocking' process collects the final statistics for the ship and records them. After the statistics are recorded, the queueing data structures used to represent the ship are released. Following departure processing, the maneuver queue is checked. If any ships are waiting to maneuver to or from a berth, the first ship in the queue is removed and its maneuver completion time is scheduled. The length of time that the ship was in the maneuver queue is calculated and combined with any other maneuver wait time for the ship. Upon completion of the collection of statistics, the process exits.

The 'update work schedule' process is the final 'perform simulation' process to be described in detail. When a work event occurs, this process is entered and the next work event is immediately scheduled. If the work event is a break start or end of shift event, the process exits. Otherwise, the first transfer request for the specified work crew is removed from the work crew queue. Based on the type of transfer request, either an unload completion or a load completion is scheduled. If any containers remain on the queue for the work crew, control is passed to the remove work request from queue process. Otherwise, the 'update work schedule' process exits.

The other portion of the simulation model, the 'graphics support' process, is depicted in Figure 7. When activated, the process immediately reads the data selection criteria from the operator. Prior to accepting the operator's criteria, the simulation program report is analyzed and the operator is notified of the number of report entries which match the specified criteria. This allows the operator to edit the selection criteria prior to the generation of any plots.

After validation of the selection criteria, the operator selects the information to be included in the first plot. The simulation report is scanned using the selection criteria, and all requested data are retrieved. The expected value and variance of the data are determined and plotted. The operator must accept this plot before generating the next plot. If the first plot is rejected by the operator, it is deleted from the graph. After accepting or rejecting the plot, the operator may request the generation of another plot. If so desired, control may be transferred so that another plot request can be specified.

Once plot generation is completed, the operator has the ability to discard the graph, save it, print it, or quit. If the operator specifies the generation of a new plot, the existing graph and selection criteria is cleared, and control is transferred to the read selection criteria process. If a save is requested, the name of the graph is read and the graph is permanently stored. If a print is requested, the graph is printed on the attached print device. Otherwise, quit is specified and the graphics support process exits without saving the operator's work.

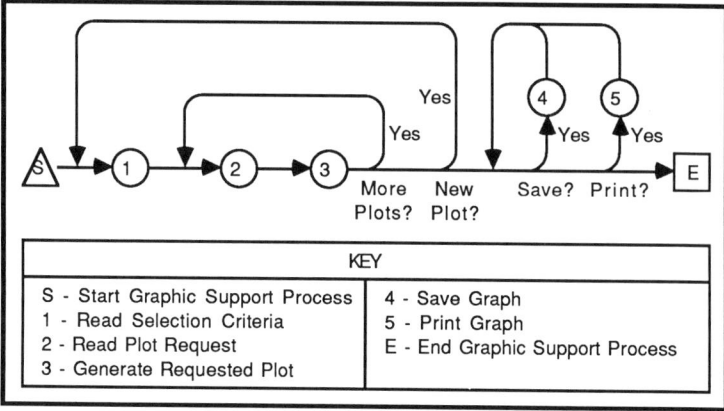

Figure 7 - Graphics Support Process

Work is still progressing on the graphics support program. When completed, it will allow the operator to enter commands by using the mouse to select them from the menu bar. One of the MPW sample programs for Pascal will be used as the basis for the graphics support program. Apple Computer Incorporated grants users of the Macintosh Programmer's Workshop a royalty-free license to incorporate MPW sample programs into their own programs provided that use is exclusively on Apple computers.

With the simulation model, the user can configure the container terminal to be simulated. The number of berths at the terminal, the number of cranes per berth, as well as the cycle time of the cranes and the interference among cranes at a berth may all be specified. Loading at the port may be specified by defining the ship arrival rate and the number of containers exchanged per ship. In addition, the occurrence of storms and the rules governing operations during storms may be specified. Various cost parameters allow the wait cost for ships, the wait costs for containers and their contents, and the operation costs of the port to be generated. The operation costs include both the cost of container transfer between the ship and the berth and the cost of idle resources during times of insufficient demand on the terminal.

The user of the simulator may operate the port in one of several modes. A simplistic 24 hour-a-day, 365 day-a-year mode of operation may be used to calibrate the model against models which use queueing theory. The user may also operate the port by defining the actual daily hours of operation and by specifying the work gang schedules, rate schedules, and number of crews available. In addition, the user may specify whether crews may be moved between berths and whether the crews may work overtime. If crews work overtime, the user may also specify the minimum number of hours for which the crew is guaranteed pay.

Each of these parameters may either be defined as a stochastic variable from one of several random distributions or as a fixed number. The output of the model and a detailed description of the simulation experiment will be discussed in a sequel paper.

5. CONCLUSION

The various Macintosh applications, Microsoft Word, MacDraw, and MacPaint, provide an excellent support structure for the generation of documentation. Programming of the simulation program portion of the model, which does not use the Macintosh screen interface was, with the exception of the detection of several deficiencies in Turbo Pascal, relatively easy. On the other hand, the programming of the graphics support portion of the simulation model, which does use the Macintosh screen interface, proved to be a challenge. This interface would have taken a long time to develop if the sample MPW Pascal programs had not been available. These programs used many of the features which were required by the graphics interface.

There are many software packages available for the Macintosh II. Some of the packages provide applications which may have been adaptable to the graphics support program. Other packages provide subroutine libraries, some in source format, others in object format, which offer some of the screen manipulation interfaces required in the Macintosh environment. It would behoove anyone planning to develop software to fully examine these products. Due consideration should also be paid to the Macintosh Programmer's Environment. It provides many tools which are very useful in the development of a Macintosh program.

REFERENCES

Frankel, E. G. (1987), *Port Planning and Development*, John Wiley and Sons, N.Y.C.

Schonfeld, P. and Sharafeldien, O. (1985), "Optimal Berth and Crane Combinations in Containerports," *Journel of Waterway, Port, Coastal and Ocean Engineering 111*, 6, 1060-1072.

van Hee, K. M. and Wijbrands, R. J. (1988), "Decision Support System for Container Terminal Planning," *European Journal of Operational Research 34*, 262-272.

VIII.

MODEL DEVELOPMENT AND ANALYSIS SYSTEMS

MATHEMATICAL PROGRAMMING MODELING PROJECT - OVERVIEW

GORDON H. BRADLEY

Operations Research Department, Naval Postgraduate School
Monterey, CA 93943

ABSTRACT

The Mathematical Programming Modeling Project (MP2) was initiated at the Naval Postgraduate School in the Spring of 1988. Its goal is to design and then prototype a comprehensive and integrated system to support optimization experts as they build models and develop algorithms. The system supports model building, optimization, access to literature, model libraries, high level solution algorithms, and construction of interactive documents. The design incorporates several important computer science ideas: hypertext, inheritance, typing and abstraction. The system is unique in its focus on support for the conceptual activities of these experts. The functional capabilities that support these conceptual activities operate on a potentially huge dynamic structured knowledge base.

1. INTRODUCTION

The MP2 system is integrated in the sense that it supports most activities associated with optimization experts within a single system that has a uniform interface to the user. The system supports many tasks performed by optimization experts including:
- model building including construction, validation, analysis, reformulation, documentation
- access to literature including capabilities to search, construct bibliographies, annotate
- construction of libraries of validated models with support for building integrated models
- construction of solution algorithms including solution control of optimization software with a high level language, capabilities to support the design, development and testing of algorithms
- evaluation, simulation, optimization of models
- development and organization of textual materials including models, documentation, reports, lecture notes, comments, critiques
- communications with colleagues, collaborators

The scope of the tasks shows that in addition to model building and algorithm development the system supports as many knowledge based activities as possible.

2. MOTIVATION

Over the last few years a number of computer based tools have been built to support people in building models and developing algorithms. A few of these tools, especially GAMS [Bisschop and Meeraus 1982; Kendrick and Meeraus 1987], have had a major and widespread impact on the way that experts construct and solve models. Many additional tools are being built and even more are proposed. These tools use the increased power of computer hardware, more capable software and high quality graphics to produce more effective and efficient ways to model and do optimization. These tools automate mechanical tasks that are done by people; a natural question is whether it is possible to build tools to support conceptual activities. My opinion is that this is possible. Other researchers share this view, for example [Dolk 1986a, 1986b: Geoffrion 1986, 1987; Greenberg 1988; Murphy and Stohr 1985] are each working on different approaches to this challenge. My particular perspective is that new concepts from the very active research in the cognitive sciences can be combined with some exciting ideas in computer science to use the increased hardware assets to offer the possibility of a dramatic change in the way optimization is conducted.

The proposal is to build a database of virtually all the facts an expert works with. This would include models, model libraries, solution strategies, solution algorithms, all relevant literature (journals, books, reports), databases of optimization problems and a wide variety of original textual material (documentation, papers, lecture notes, comments, ideas, exams, problems, answers). For most of us, more and more of this material is being stored electronically. This data is clearly necessary to conduct research because it is the basis of the person's expertise - but just as clearly the data itself is not sufficient. It is also necessary to structure this data by capturing the extensive and complex relationships among all its elements. This is still not sufficient to be able to support conceptual activities; there need to be a variety of processes that operate on this structured data. Basic processes include the ability to add, delete and modify data and relations. Optimization specific processes to optimize, analyze, validate, integrate, etc. are needed. Research is necessary to design and develop processes to construct textual objects from the (evolving) structured database and to provide support to dynamically restructure this data as the expert gathers new data, develops new results and gains new insights. Thus any system to support the conceptual activities of the expert must include a huge store of facts, complex relationships among the facts and powerful processes to operate on it. The project focuses on supporting the *conceptual activities* of the human with the *functional capabilities* of the system that uses the *structured knowledge base*. There are reasons to believe that a system can be designed and built that will dramatically increase the support of optimization experts.

MP2 is a high risk potentially high payoff project to explore this exciting possibility by designing and then prototyping a system with these capabilities.

3. TECHNOLOGY BACKGROUND

In computer hardware there has been a continuous decline in price and increase in capability that has put within the reach of individual optimization experts computers with the speed and memory to solve production size optimization problems. This same capability makes it possible to develop personal computer systems to do model formulation, symbolic algebraic calculations, syntax analysis and other sophisticated operations that only a few years ago required major size computing facilities. The increased power has also allowed fast enhanced graphics that can provide high productivity user interfaces.

The technology is also at hand for fast low cost access to huge databases. High density magnetic storage devices and the emerging write-once optical disks make practical the storage of the thousands of books, journals and papers that are used by optimization experts. Low cost scanners with character recognition software make it relatively easy to transfer typed materials to a computer where it can be read, searched, modified, printed, etc. It is of course not necessary to have personal copies of all this material, access through a network is sufficient for many tasks. A more pressing issue is the logical and software problem of how to organize and structure this much local and global information. MP2 addresses this problem directly.

Present technology (that is continuing to drop in price) is adequate to store the large quantity of data and represent the relationships among its elements in sufficient detail to provide real time support for the cognitive tasks that MP2 supports. See [Mel et al. 1988] for a prediction of the capabilities of low cost personal computers in the year 2000. One feature that impacts MP2 is the prediction of high density read-write storage cards using optical laser technology. They predict that a credit card size unit will store a gigabyte (equivalent to 20,000 books). They predict network access to huge quantities of data with the ability to do fast matches using keywords.

4. USERS OF THE SYSTEM

The description of the system refers to optimization experts as the users of the system. The system is intended for modeling and algorithm experts in universities, industry and government who are doing research or applications. The system is not intended for a casual user; a level of involvement is assumed that would justify the effort to construct a highly individualized knowledge base and then keep it current. The system is also intended for intense use by students learning modeling and algorithms regardless of whether after their education they intend to be casual or intense users of optimization. An expected side benefit of the project is the identification of a subset of capabilities that do not require a level of intense involvement and thus can support users who are only occasionally involved in optimization.

5. FOCUS ON CONCEPTUAL CAPACITIES

The MP2 focus is on the expert's conceptual activities and the operations to support them. The system is designed to contain a potentially enormous number of facts and a rich variety of methods to support the structuring of these facts. The system is dynamic in that facts are continuously added, deleted and modified, but more importantly, the system has capabilities to dynamically restructure the facts in order to make them more accessible and more useful. These structured facts together with the processes that operate on them is referred to as a knowledge base [see note 1]. The project avoids using the term "information" for the contents of the knowledge base. Taking the definition that "information is the meaning that humans assign to data," we reserve information generation to humans and thus can talk about the capabilities of the system to facilitate the construction (by humans) of information from the knowledge base. The distinction between knowledge (data, relations, processes) and information allows us to focus on the conceptual activities of the human.

Since the project uses terms, definitions, results and insights from the cognitive sciences [Gardner 1985; Stillings et al. 1987], it is important to establish a position on whether the system is intended to yield results on and insights about human information processing. It is not. Although the project is directed toward identifying human problem solving needs so the system can effectively support them, there will be no attempt or claim that the structures of the system have any psychological validity. Further in identifying human cognitive activities the project avoids making any assumptions about possible human mechanisms to achieve them. Thus we avoid taking any position on the mercurial and controversial issues surrounding the cognitive sciences. The project takes an engineering approach to building a system to support humans in the problem solving tasks involved in optimization modeling and algorithm development. The project uses ideas which have their roots in the cognitive sciences (especially cognitive psychology and artificial intelligence), but design decisions to incorporate them into the system are based solely on their ability to support the project goals rather than on any belief that they are the same mechanisms used by humans. We argue at several points in the development that the system automates things that humans now do, but assiduously avoid any claims that the system does or does not do this in the same way or even with the same data as humans. The techniques that have been used thus far come almost exclusively from the symbol system view of the cognitive sciences (rather than from the more recent connectionism view) but this reflects the greater maturity of these ideas and their easy implementation on conventional digital computers rather than on any position on which has more psychological validity.

The goal of the project is to design and prototype a system that assists humans rather than one that models human processes, therefore anthropomorphic terms are avoided. The terms that refer to the system use words that are as neutral as possible with respect to human capabilities and that are different from the terms that refer to the human using the system. The system is tightly connected to human problem solving capabilities but the goal is to complement rather than simulate human capabilities; the resulting system can give only limited insight into human information processing in the same way that a glove reveals the form but none of the substance of the human hand.

6. STATIC VIEW OF THE SYSTEM

The derivation and restructuring actions of the system are the most innovative and provide the most support for the conceptual activities of the experts that the project is intended to support. However, until the prototype is built, the easiest way to introduce a reader to the system is first to describe the static features.

The system represents optimization models in an executable modeling language (EML). There are production EML systems, e.g. GAMS [Bisschop and Meeraus 1982; Kendrick and Meeraus 1987], and prototype systems e.g. [Clemence 1984; Day and Williams 1986; Dolk 1986; Fourer et al. 1987; Geoffrion 1986, 1987; Lucas and Mitra 1988]. There are a variety of different features in these systems but all provide a single algebra notation in which the modeler conceives, records, and validates the model; this notation also documents the model. The model in this notation is read by a computer, translated into a form for optimization, solved and its solution returned for analysis - all without manual intervention. This is illustrated by Figure 1 using a "generic" EML described in [Clemence 1988] and used in [Bradley and Clemence 1987, 1988]. This is the lowest level representation of the model that the modeler deals with.

The text in Figure 1 enclosed in <<..>> represents what is called typing information [Bradley and Clemence 1987, 1988; Clemence 1988]. The modeler assigns each variable, coefficient, constant, function, constraint, input and output of the model a type that consists of its concepts, qualities and units of measurement with optional scale factors. The typing system checks the composition of functions, constraints, input and output. The system performs unit conversions where appropriate. The system allows a hierarchy of concepts that provide inheritance of quantities and automatic concept conversion. The typing data allows the system to perform validity checks to determine if the model correctly

```
<< CONCEPT GRAPH
  @* <- @OBJECTIVE[COST]
  @* <- @BUTTER[WEIGHT_PER_PERIOD] >>

<< UNIT SYSTEMS
  WEIGHT_PER_PERIOD : AvoirdupoisWeight/StandardTime
  COST : USCurrency >>

SETS
  DAIRIES i ; << nominal >>
  WAREHOUSES j; << nominal >>
  PATHS(i, j) := {DAIRIES} X {WAREHOUSES};

VARIABLES
  SHIPMENTS(i, j) {PATHS}; << WEIGHT_PER_PERIOD of @BUTTER
  # [100]POUNDS/DAY # >>

PARAMETERS
  SCOST(i, j) {PATHS}; << COST of @OBJECTIVE/WEIGHT_PER_PERIOD of
  @BUTTER # DOLLARS/( [100] POUNDS/DAY # >>
  SUPPLY(i) {DAIRIES} ; << WEIGHT_PER_PERIOD of @BUTTER
  # [100] POUNDS/DAY # >>
  DEMAND(j) {WAREHOUSES}; << WEIGHT_PER_PERIOD of @BUTTER
  # TONS/WEEK # >>

FUNCTIONS
  OBJECTIVE := SUM(i, j) {PATHS} ( SCOST(i, j) * SHIPMENTS(i, j) );
    << COST of OBJECTIVE # DOLLARS # >>

CONSTRAINTS

  OUTBOUND(i) {DAIRIES} := SUM(j) {PATHS} ( SHIPMENTS(i, j) =L=
  SUPPLY(i) ); <<WEIGHT_PER_PERIOD @BUTTER # [100] POUNDS/DAY # >>
  INBOUND(j) {WAREHOUSES} := SUM(i) {PATHS} ( SHIPMENTS(i, j) =E=
  DEMAND(j) ); <<WEIGHT_PER_PERIOD @BUTTER  # [100] POUNDS/DAY
  # >>

ASSERTION
  SUM(i) {DAIRIES} (SUPPLY(i) ) =G= SUM(j) {WAREHOUSES} (DEMAND(j) );

SOLVE
  MIN : OBJECTIVE;  SUBJECT TO ALL;

REPORT
  PRINT := SHIPMENTS(i, j) {PATHS}; <<  WEIGHT_PER_PERIOD of @BUTTER
  # [1000 POUNDS/DAY # >>
```

FIGURE 1 BUTTER SHIPMENT MODEL IN TYPED EML

represents the modeler's intentions. The example does not show the full range of checks that the typing system performs, see [Bradley and Clemence 1987, 1988; Clemence 1988].

This particular EML separates model and data, so we can refer to Figure 1 as the model; Figure 1 together with a data file that specifies the sets and parameters for the model is referred to as a problem. The model can be viewed as an abstraction with all the possible problems viewed as instances of this model. There are higher levels of abstraction, for example, Figure 1 can be viewed as a special case of (that is, derived from) the class of all transportation models which in turn is derived from the class of all transshipment models, and so on. This view of abstraction and derivation is important for several reasons:

1. It is a parsimonious way to "store" the model because the system need not store Figure 1 and all the other instances of the class of transportation models, it need only store how Figure 1 is derived from its parent model.
2. Based on its derivation a model inherits attributes and properties from its parents. Examples are validation, documentation, solution algorithms, report formats, and many other objects that are inherited (possibly with modification) from the abstraction.

Modelers know the relationships among their models and the properties that are inherited. MP2 provides mechanisms to embed this in the knowledge base. In the computer science literature this kind of inheritance is usually called "object-oriented."

This representation of models together with a library of models and their relationships is central to the design of MP2. The derivation of a model from its parent is a special case of the derivation of an integrated (or composite) model from two or more component models. [Bradley and Clemence 1988; Clemence 1988] describe a LIBRARY process for EML's that captures in the model representation the derivation of the integrated model from its components. Figure 2 shows the model specification of the integration of two transportation models. The sink nodes of the first equal the source nodes of the second. (other integration examples are developed in [Clemence 1988]). A process of derivation replaces the LIB calls in Figure 2 with the model from the library modified as specified in the parameters of the LIB statement. This is not just to save typing. It is important for the system to have and retain knowledge of the derivation of the model because when the user develops the properties of the integrated model (like validation, documentation, output formats) they are derived as inherited properties from the component models (with possible modifications). This process cannot be wholly automated because the modeler, not the knowledge base, assigns meaning to objects. When building composite objects the modeler uses as many of the properties of the components as possible and creates as little new as possible. The system supports this activity.

```
LIB  % := &TRANSPORT WHERE
   ELIM ( DEMAND(j), INBOUND(j), ASSERTION, SOLVE );
   END

LIB  %EAST := &TRANSPORT WHERE
   ELIM ( SUPPLY(i), OUTBOUND(i), ASSERTION, SOLVE );
   WAREHOUSES <- CUSTOMER;
   j <- k;
   DAIRIES <= WAREHOUSES;
   i <- j;
   END

FUNCTIONS
   TOTAL_OBJECTIVE := OBJECTIVE + EAST.OBJECTIVE;
   << COST of @OBJECTIVE # DOLLARS # >>

CONSTRAINTS
   TRANSSHIP(j) { WAREHOUSES } := SUM(i) { PATHS } ( SHIPMENTS(i, j) )
     =E= SUM(k) { EAST.PATHS } EAST.SHIPMENTS(j, k);
   << WEIGHT_PER_PERIOD @BUTTER # [100]POUNDS/DAY # >>

SOLVE
   MIN: TOTAL_OBJECTIVE; SUBJECT TO ALL
```

FIGURE 2   DERIVATION OF A TYPED INTEGRATED MODEL

Although the introduction of EML's is relatively recent, the choice of a specific EML is already difficult because of the lack of a standard. Although almost every model can be represented in each of the EML's, the translation from one notation to another is not straightforward. Because MP2 is concerned with building model libraries, collaboration among experts and the construction of integrated models (possibly with components from different sources) this issue is troublesome. One possible solution is the development of a new standard for the interface between EML's and solvers that would be at a high enough level that the conversion of model notations would be easier. A model in one EML would be automatically converted to the standard representation and then this would be automatically converted to a second EML. This second conversion is potentially very difficult particularly if the standard is at such low level (like MPS SHARE format) that information needed for the second conversion is lost in the first conversion. This is a very difficult issue and will require diligent work and cooperation among researchers and developers to develop a good high level standard. This effort is critical in order to avoid the problems associated with having incompatible EML's.

In addition to the capability to solve models, modelers need the ability to perform a variety of other operations on models. There is a rich literature on pre-solver operators that, for example, identify extraneous variables and constraints [Bradley et al. 1983; Greenberg 1981], identify gub, network and other special structure [Brown and Wright 1981], etc. There are also post-solver operators that, for instance, write reports, analyze solutions, identify the cause of solver failures [Greenberg 1983b, 1988], etc. The results of some of these operators is seem only by the solver, others need to be presented to the modeler and thus must be in terms of the EML. Much of the previous work has been done on very low level representations of the model/problem (e.g. MPS SHARE format) and thus it is very difficult to create the EML representation of the result. Many of these algorithms must be redeveloped so they can operate on an EML or other high level representation of the model/problem.

7. DYNAMIC VIEW OF THE SYSTEM

The dynamic aspects of the system are built on several important computer science ideas: hypertext, inheritance, typing and abstraction. The most evident feature of the dynamic system is the hypertext organization of all the objects of the system. The hypertext system will include a rich set of link and node types of contemporary hypertext systems plus a new group from optimization including nodes of value, table, function, expression, constraint, model, etc. The link types will also be extensive and extended to include unique support for modeling.

Hypertext (also called nonlinear text or hypermedia) is an active area of development and research [Conklin 1987; Communications of the ACM 1988; Yankelovich et al. 1985]. The current state of the art is that the robust commercial products like HyperCard have only a few of the features of the sophisticated research and prototype products. The MP2 prototype can use the limited feature products but the final MP2 system will also need features like version control, links to and from words and phrases, user specified typing for links and nodes and automatically generated maps to support browsing.

MP2 also requires some features that have not thus far been associated with hypertext. An expanded idea of derivation for models and text is necessary. As with models, documents are derived from other text. In this view, the specification of a document is a description of the process of constructing it from its components. Thus a document is viewed as a process that operates on a knowledge base. This leads to another benefit of derivation:

> 3. As the knowledge base evolves over time, documents can be updated by again applying their derivation process to the new knowledge base.

The initial goal is that MP2 derivations produce only rough documents that are then reviewed and polished by the expert. Through the derivation processes, the knowledge base is an active agent (not passive as a database) in the propagation of new facts throughout the knowledge base. As the expert gains new facts, ideas and insight through reading, talking, running tests, etc. the knowledge base nodes and links are modified. This is done in a myopic fashion by only modifying the parts of the knowledge base that are directly effected by the new data. The MP2 system supports the distribution of this new data and the implications of the interactions with existing data. Thus derivation is a mechanism for the MP2 system support of the expert's conceptual activity of integrating new information.

Locating results in the optimization literature is important for experts. The extensive typing of nodes and links in the hypertext will support algorithms that will provide literature searches, build bibliographies and allow the user to analyze and annotate the literature.

8. RESTRUCTURING THE KNOWLEDGE BASE

The capability of the system to derive models and documents demonstrates the active role that processes under human control can take in a knowledge base. The processes are the active agents that act on the evolving contents of the knowledge base. The MP2 project will also investigate the feasibility of having new data become an active agent in the integration of new data into the knowledge base. The relationships in the knowledge base can be bi-directional; this admits the possibility that processes can be developed that would propagate the effects of new data to other elements in the knowledge base. Since the system has no intelligence and unlike humans cannot assign meaning to the facts in its knowledge base, this process must be human directed and controlled. The hypothesis to be tested is whether the rich structures of typed relationships among the typed nodes of the system make possible significant restructuring of the knowledge base with relative little human direction. This is not a modest proposition.

9. OPTIMIZATION CONTROL LANGUAGE

The capabilities of MP2 described thus far have focused on modeling. The system supports the experts who develop new solution algorithms with a language for controlling the optimization process using the EML representation of the model. Since the EML is the lowest level representation of the model that the expert uses, the solution control language is applied to it. This language allows a variety of possibilities that range from automatic operation to the design of new solution algorithms. This should be viewed as the next logical step in a long term trend to move the user interface from the solution algorithm to the model. The earliest optimization algorithms had very crude interfaces; the user was required to provide the data in the exact form the algorithms needed to operate on it. Matrix generators were the first step to make the interface reflect more closely the way the user viewed the data and allowed the computer to translate into the needed data structures. Modeling languages like GAMS brought an equality between model and solution algorithm by making the computer rather than the modeler meet the solver interface [Fourer 1983].

MP2 is taking the next step which is to bring the solver under the direct control of the modeler through directions that are applied to the EML representation. This is not just a superficial change with the system hiding the solver interface. This is a new view of the solver as "optimization engine" controlled from the EML level. The design of optimization software will have to be rethought because control of the trajectory of computation that has been viewed as an integral part of the solver is now viewed as separate from the computational parts that do pivoting, reinversion, etc. This will lead directly to levels of the solver with the modeler able to have as much control as he can effective exercise. There will emerge a hierarchy of control from the automatic (basically what we have today with only limited static choices of parameters) to extreme situations where new algorithms will be developed and tested. MP2 envisions a rich set of controls and relationships that will open up a new field of research on the construction of automatic controls for solving optimization problems. This will include the development of sophisticated control algorithms that will monitor and control the numerical properties and solution trajectory of the fundamental building blocks such as pivoting, inversion, reformulation, etc. These control algorithms will have a wealth of data about the computation and will have a variety of powerful high level techniques like reformulation of the model or even remodeling as the computations unfold.

10. SYSTEM ARCHITECTURE

The final product of the project is not a knowledge base that is the union of everything known in optimization. Rather the goal is to design an architecture and basic operators that will allow each user to build and maintain a highly individualized system. The design goals include providing methods for experts to add modules from other experts. Indeed, the project envisions that this will be become a major mechanism for experts to communicate. The final product will be an architecture and an initial knowledge base together with facilities to add the work of others and most importantly the capability for the user to continually restructure the knowledge base as new facts are added.

11. COMMENTS

MP2 is focused on the support of optimization experts. The definition of optimization is broad enough to include evaluation and simulation of optimization models. Thus the system capabilities include those of spreadsheets. The project could be extended to include stochastic operators and thus at least partially support other operations research modeling. The capabilities of the system that deal with textual materials and the analysis of literature can be used by a wide variety of people who use and construct documents.

The project will use all relevant ideas, procedures, software, etc. from fields like artificial intelligence and databases. There is at least one aspect of our approach that distinguishes it from much of the work in these other areas. The usual approach to developing useful systems is to take the available and emerging technology and apply it to the most realistic task possible. This results in insights and demonstrates potential for the ideas, but often constructs systems with relatively little benefit for the practicing professionals it is suppose to support. The MP2 approach is the opposite: the aim is to support the full range of tasks facing the optimization expert - any and all available technology will be brought to bear on this problem but no feature of the system that compromises the effectiveness of the system will be introduced just to use a new technology. Where appropriate, manual effort, paper, pencil, human memory, etc. will be used. In addition, if the benefit of the computer feature is not more than the effort to use it, it will not be included in the system. MP2 is not technology in search of a problem, rather it is building the best possible man/machine system using (only if appropriate) some powerful emerging ideas and technology. Much that is done by optimization experts is already computer based (e.g. modeling, solving, problem analysis, documentation, word processing). MP2 focuses on determining if higher level human conceptual activities can be effectively and efficiently supported.

12. DEVELOPMENT PLAN

During the Fall of 1988 a seminar at the Naval Postgraduate School will be the focus of an effort to build a simulated prototype of the system. The prototype is simulated in the sense that scripts (or story boards) of how the system would operate will be constructed without the development of the hundreds of thousands of lines of code that the system will ultimately require. This will allow an evaluation in early 1989 of the potential benefits of the system. This approach will give only limited insight into the effort required from the user to maintain the dynamic knowledge base or the difficulty to build the final system. Contingent on the results of this evaluation, a strategy for the initial development will be constructed that will emphasize activities that can resolve the most uncertainty per unit investment. Capabilities to derive (for example, models from libraries of models, text from other text) will be developed before those to restructure the knowledge base because the former are more clearly understood and the later will be based on these capabilities.

13. CONCLUSIONS

The system has been described as consisting of *static*, *dynamic* and *restructuring* parts. The *static* system is the comprehensive and integrated union of existing and proposed capabilities. For most features envisioned there are production versions or prototypes of almost all of the capabilities needed. The others, for instance, the control of optimizer computation, appear straightforward. So while the integration of these diverse capabilities will present many challenging design choices, there are no obvious technical obstacles.

The *dynamic* capabilities are more challenging because there is not yet much experience building hypertext systems. There are some known problems, for instance, the problem of the user becoming disoriented ("lost in hyperspace") and the "cognitive overload" that comes with naming many objects and establishing many links [Conklin 1987]. These problems are being worked on by a wide variety of researchers and developers. They will hopefully develop new solutions at a faster rate than they encounter new problems. The project will be an active participant in this research because the derivation and restructuring processes have not previously been identified as needed capabilities.

It is primarily in derivation and *restructuring* that new ground is being broken and thus it is impossible to estimate without further research the feasibility, let alone the cost or the benefits, of such capabilities.

If it is feasible to build a system with significant automatic derivation and restructure capability, it would provide more support to the optimization expert than any existing system. The strongest indication that powerful results are possible come from experiences with typing and model integration in executable modeling languages [Bradley and Clemence 1987, 1988; Clemence 1988]. In modeling languages, typing gives the capability to check automatically the units, quantities and concepts of the objects in the model, problem and output. The result of this obvious and straightforward idea is a powerful mechanism to perform model validation. The motivation and intuition behind the Mathematical Programming Modeling Project is that when the complete system that is described above is built the richness of the structures with the many interrelationships and mutually supportive pieces will allow derivation and restructure operators of unexpected power. The hypothesis is that powerful capabilities can come from a set of relatively simple processes operating on a realistic size domain of human expertise and that the conceptual activities of users can receive significant support.

ACKNOWLEDGMENT

I would like to acknowledge the useful comments I received from Art Geoffrion on earlier drafts of this paper. I would also like to thank the participants in the Naval Postgraduate School Mathematical Programming Seminar, Fall 1988 (Jerry Brown, Fred Buoni, Dan Dolk, Eric Godat, Steve Goertzen, Mike Mayer, Mike Olson, Mike Puntenney, Rich Rosenthal, Mike Sagaser, Art Schoenstadt and Cheng Sim) for the significant contributions that they have made to the MP2 project. I would like to acknowledge the support of the Mathematics Group of the Office of Naval Research.

NOTE

1. The term knowledge base will be used to refer to the store of data, relationships and processes. The term was selected because it is descriptive and is superior to alternatives (e.g. database). The term comes from the artificial intelligence literature and its use there is suggestive of its meaning here. However, it is not possible to give a precise definition of the term because the purpose of MP2 is to understand what knowledge can be used by optimization experts and how that knowledge can be stored, structured and processed. Since the purpose of MP2 is the study of the knowledge base, its meaning must come from its context in optimization.

REFERENCES

Bisschop, J. and Meeraus, A. (1982), "On the development of a general algebraic modeling system in a strategic planning environment," *Mathematical Programming Studies,* Volume 20, pages 1-29.

Bradley, G. H. (1987), "Cognitive science view of software engineering," in *Software Engineering Education,* Norman E. Gibbs, and Richard E. Fairley, eds., Springer-Verlag, New York, N.Y., 1987, pages 35-51.

Bradley, G. H., Brown, G. G., and Graves, G. W. (1983), "Structural redundancy in large-scale optimization models," in *Redundancy in Mathematical Programming*, M. Karwan, et al., eds., Springer-Verlag, New York, N.Y., pages 145-169.

Bradley, G. H. and Clemence, Jr., R. D. (1987), "A type calculus for executable modelling languages," *IMA Journal of Mathematics in Management,* Volume 1, pages 277-291.

Bradley, G. H. and Clemence, Jr., R. D. (1988), "Model integration with a typed executable modeling language," *Proceedings of the 21st Annual Hawaii International Conference on System Sciences*, Volume III, IEEE Computer Society, Washington, D. C., pages 403-410.

Brown, G. G. and Wright, W. G. (1981), "Automatic identification of embedded structure in large-scale optimization models," in *Computer-Assisted Analysis and Model Simplification*, H. J. Greenberg and J. S Maybee eds., Academic Press, New York, N.Y., pages 369-388.

Clemence, Jr., R. D. (1984), "LEXICON: A structured modeling system for optimization," Master's thesis, Naval Postgraduate School, Monterey, Calif., 97 pages.

Clemence, Jr., R. D. (1988), "A type calculus for executable modeling languages," PhD Dissertation, Naval Postgraduate School, Monterey, Calif., (in preparation).

Communications of the ACM, Volume 31, Number 7, July 1988 (special issue on hypertext, the articles are available on HyperCard for MACs and Hyperties for IBM PC compatible)

Conklin, J. (1987), "Hypertext: An introduction and survey," *Computer*, Volume 20, Number 9, pages 17-41.

Day, R. E. and Williams, H. P. (1986), "MAGIC: The design and use of an interactive modeling language for mathematical programming," *IMA Journal of Mathematics in Management*, Volume 1, pages 53-65.

Dolk, D. R. (1986), "Data as models: An approach to implementing model management," *Decision Support Systems*, Volume 2, pages 73- 80.

Dolk, D. R. (1986), "A generalized model management system for mathematical programming," *ACM Transactions on Mathematical Software*, Volume 12, pages 92-125.

Dolk, D. R. and Konsynski B. (1985), "Model management in organizations," *Information Management*, Volume 9, pages 35-47.

Fourer, R. (1983), "Modeling languages versus matrix generators for linear programming," *ACM Transactions on Mathematical Software*, Volume 9, pages 143-183.

Fourer, R., Gay, D. M. and Kernighan, B. W. (1987), "AMPL: A mathematical programming language," Computing Science Technical Report No. 133, AT&T Bell Laboratories, Murray Hill, N.J., 63 pages.

Gardner, H. (1985), *The Mind's New Science: A History of the Cognitive Revolution*, Basic Books, Inc., New York, N.Y., 1985.

Geoffrion, A. M. (1986), Structured Modeling, (unpublished manuscript).

Geoffrion, A. M. (1987), "An introduction to structured modeling," *Management Science,* Volume 33, pages 547-588.

Greenberg, H. J. (1981), "The scope of computer-assisted analysis and model simplification," in *Computer-Assisted Analysis and Model Simplification,* H. J. Greenberg and J. S. Maybee, eds., Academic Press, New York, N.Y., pages 17-26.

Greenberg, H. J. (1982), "A tutorial on computer-assisted analysis," in *Advanced Techniques in the Practice of Operations Research,* H. J. Greenberg, F. H. Murphy and S. H. Shaw, eds., American Elsevier, pages 212 - 249.

Greenberg, H. J. (1983), "A Functional description of ANALYZE: Computer-assisted analysis system for linear programming models," *ACM Transactions on Mathematical Software,* Volume 9, pages 18 - 56.

Greenberg, H. J. (1983), "ANALYZE: A computer-assisted analysis system for linear programming models," *Operations Research Letters,* Volume 6, pages 249 - 255.

Greenberg, H. J. (1988), Foundations for an Intelligent Mathematical Programming System, (unpublished manuscript).

Greenberg, H. J. and Maybee, J. S, eds.(1981), *Computer- Assisted Analysis and Model Simplification,* Academic Press, New York, N.Y.

Kendrick, D. A. and Meeraus, A.(1987), *GAMS: An Introduction,* The Scientific Press, Palo Alto, Calif.

Lucas, C. and Mitra, G. (1988), "Computer assisted mathematical programming (modeling system: CAMPS)," *The Computer Journal,* Volume 31, pages 364 - 375.

Mel, B. W., Omohundro, S. M., Robison, A. D., Skiena, S. S., Thearling, K. H., Young, L. T. and Wolfram, S. (1988), "TABLET: Personal computer in the year 2000," *Communications of the ACM,* Volume 31, pages 639 - 646.

Murphy, F. H. and Stohr, E. A. (1985), "An intelligent system for formulating linear programs," *Decision Support Systems*, Volume 2, pages 39 - 47.

Schrage, L. (1981), *Linear, Integer, and Quadratic Programming with LINDO*, The Scientific Press, Palo Alto, Calif.

Stillings, N. A., Feinstein, M. H., Garfield, J. L., Rissland, E. L., Rosenbaum, D. A., Weisler, S. E. and Baker-Ward, L. (1987), *Cognitive Science: An Introduction*, The MIT Press, Cambridge, Mass., 1987.

Yankelovich, N., Meyrowitz, N. and van Dam, A. (1985), "Reading and writing the electronic book," *Computer*, Volume 18, Number 10, pages 15-30.

OPTIMIZATION WITH CONSTRAINT PROGRAMMING SYSTEMS

R.G. BROWN, J.W. CHINNECK, G.M. KARAM

Dept. of Systems and Computer Eng., Carleton Univ.,
Ottawa, Ontario, CANADA, K1S 5B6

ABSTRACT

Constraint programming systems (CPS) are computational tools that have potential applications in the automatic solution of constrained optimization problems. This paper reviews the constraint satisfaction mechanisms used by these tools, surveys currently available CPS, and examines the ability of CPS to solve a variety of problems associated with constrained optimization. We conclude that present CPS have limited (though important) uses in constrained optimization, but that they show great promise for the future.

1. INTRODUCTION

CPS are declarative: the user states a problem as a set of constraints, any variable being a potential input or output. The system automatically ensures that any values assigned to variables are consistent with the constraints. How this is done depends on the constraint satisfaction mechanisms that are built into the CPS. This in turn determines the effectiveness of the system in dealing with different classes of constrained optimization problems and constraint sets.

The constrained optimization problems of interest here are: (1) finding a single point in the feasible region, (2) defining the limits of the feasible region, (3) finding the optimum point in the feasible region, and (4) sensitivity analysis. The purpose of this paper is to examine the capabilities of CPS in the automatic solution of these problems.

Automated solutions to these problems have long been sought by OR researchers. The more sophisticated LP packages in fact provide these capabilities for the special case of continuous variables and linear constraints and objective functions. However, there is no automated solution in the general case which also includes integer or binary variables and nonlinear or logical constraints.

While OR researchers have applied the tools of mathematics in the search for an automated system, CPS have their roots in new developments in computer science and artificial intelligence, including logic programming, symbolic manipulation, object-oriented paradigms, and interval arithmetic. One of the first CPS appeared in 1963 [Sutherland 1963]. Little new was seen until the late 1970's when several researchers found new applications in engineering and computer science.

There are two broad classifications of CPS: *constraint systems* and *constraint programming languages*. Constraint systems are closed packages allowing input of the problem and producing solutions. Constraint systems do not provide any general programming capabilities.

Constraint programming languages are primarily general purpose logic programming languages augmented with arithmetic processing capabilities that are more powerful and logically cleaner than those of conventional logic programming implementations, notably Prolog [Sterling and Shapiro 1986].

There are no constraint systems which specifically address optimization problems, and their limited flexibility makes it difficult to modify them to do so. In contrast, the general purpose nature of the constraint programming languages suits them to optimization applications; accordingly we concentrate on the constraint programming languages in this paper.

Section 2 describes the methods normally used by CPS to satisfy sets of constraints. Section 3 discusses constraint systems, and in Section 4 several constraint programming languages are reviewed. Section 5 discusses how CPS can be applied to typical optimization problems.

2. CONSTRAINT SATISFACTION MECHANISMS

The heart of a CPS is the mechanisms which find values for the variables which are consistent with the constraints. Most CPS incorporate several mechanisms. The most common of these are reviewed below.

2.1 Local Propagation

Local propagation is the simplest and fastest mechanism for constraint satisfaction [Steele 1980]. It solves one simple equation in one unknown, such as $2 \times A = 6$, and then propagates the value of A to other equations, which may then be solvable. Local propagation is defeated by the simplest of simultaneous equations such as $A + B = 2$ and $A - B = 4$. Since each equation has two unknowns, neither can be solved. It is likewise defeated if the same variable appears twice in one equation, as in $A + A = 4$.

2.2 Relaxation

Relaxation [Sutherland 1963; Borning 1985] is a classic numeric technique that tries to satisfy a set of constraints of the form $f(x) = 0$, where x is a vector of variables. Using the actual $f(x)$ values as an indication of error and assuming that the error varies linearly with all variables, each x is adjusted in turn to minimize the sum of the error terms squared. The procedure terminates successfully when the total error converges to a value less than some tolerance.

Relaxation works only with continuous variables. Potential problems include the rate and dependability of convergence.

2.3 Term Rewriting

Term rewriting is a symbolic procedure in which one or more expressions are reduced by making a series of substitutions embodied in a collection of rewrite rules, each consisting of a head and a body [Leler 1988]. When an expression can be matched with a rule head using a substitution, the expression is replaced with that given by applying the same substitution to the rule body. The ordering of rules may influence the final answers, and since there is no undoing of rewritings, alternate solutions are not explored.

Term rewriting is a powerful technique, but is relatively slow, and it is difficult to ensure that the sequence of substitutions arising from a set of rules will always terminate.

2.4 Other Mechanisms for Constraint Satisfaction

Additional constraint satisfaction mechanisms are used by some existing CPS, but the details of most are proprietary. The constraint satisfaction mechanisms used in the languages described in section 4 are interval arithmetic heuristics (BNR-Prolog), a modified simplex algorithm (CLP($\mathcal{R}$)), and *decision procedures* (Trilogy).

2.5 Constraint Set Capabilities of Satisfaction Mechanisms

All of the constraint satisfaction mechanisms described above can handle linear equations, either singly or simultaneously, with the execution of local propagation. Most can also handle linear inequalities (with the exception of relaxation). Simultaneous nonlinear equations are more difficult. Only relaxation, term rewriting, and BNR-Prolog interval arithmetic can usually solve them (depending on the problem). When non-linear inequalities are added, only term rewriting and interval arithmetic have a possibility of arriving at a solution.

3. CONSTRAINT SYSTEMS

Constraint systems employ one of two approaches, as described briefly below.

3.1 The Object-Oriented Approach

The object-oriented approach provides an environment in which a model is created by assembling user-created "objects" which are software representations of elements in the real problem. This implicitly defines the constraints inherent in the real problem.

Steele [1980] created an object-oriented environment for the analysis of integrated circuit chips in his much-referenced Ph.D. thesis. The behaviour of the chips was embedded in Lisp procedures assigned to variables, and the chip inputs and outputs were not predefined. For instance, a logical AND gate could have its "output" pin set to TRUE. The chip would then force its "input" pins to TRUE, the only consistent values. The system used a local propagation constraint satisfaction mechanism.

No object-oriented systems are commercially available, but the code for implementing a local propagation system is available [Abelson et al. 1985].

3.2 The List-of-Equations Approach

Abstract concepts such as objective functions are stated more easily using a list of equations rather than by implicit object-oriented relationships. A number of list-of-equations systems are currently available. TK!Solver has met with some commercial success [Konopasek and Jayaraman 1984]. It uses local propagation as long as possible, then relaxation. Bertrand [Leler 1988] is a term rewriting system that allows users to provide their own rules and may be used for any symbolic processing, not just arithmetic equation solving. Gosling [1983] describes methods of generating local propagation procedures from a list of equations.

4. CONSTRAINT PROGRAMMING LANGUAGES

Constraint programming languages are an outgrowth of the need to provide logically clean arithmetic in logic programming languages [Lassez 1987]. The constraint features have eliminated many problems by allowing arithmetic expressions to be given without having to consider the order of value determination, thus X=Y+6, 6=X-Y, etc. are equivalent.

Although the built-in constraint satisfaction mechanisms in most of these languages can solve only simple systems, the general purpose nature of the languages allows algorithms for other cases to be programmed. The arithmetic constraint processing capabilities of three constraint programming languages are described and tested below.

4.1 CLP($\mathcal{R}$)

CLP($\mathcal{R}$) (Constraint Logic Programming, Real number domain) is a version of Prolog which recognizes arithmetic statements and processes them in the domain of real numbers using a version of the simplex algorithm that is separate from the logic programming search mechanism [Lassez 1987]. It can solve sets of linear equality and inequality expressions, but does not assign any values to the variables unless they represent a unique solution. An optimal value would be determined only if it were unique.

Evaluation of nonlinear expressions is delayed until instantiations of variables reduce them to linear form. For instance, X*Y=6 is not processed until a value for X or Y is determined. Once linearized, the constraint is checked for consistency with previously processed constraints, and any unique solutions are determined. Inconsistency will result in logical failure, causing the usual Prolog backtracking. "MAYBE" is returned rather than the usual "YES" or "NO" if any expressions remain unprocessed at the end of computation.

4.2 Trilogy

Trilogy [Complete Logic Systems 1987] is a commercially available language combining features of logic programming and conventional languages. It can handle integer equality and inequality expressions. A simple example given in the manual is: 8A+6B=46, A>=0, B>=0, for which Trilogy returns two solutions, A=2 and B=5, and A=5 and B=1.

Trilogy manages large problems by applying *decision procedures*. Where there are too many possibilities, a message is output, but no particular solution is produced.

Trilogy does not allow the combination of integer and floating point numbers in constraints, e.g. the query 5.5*X + 1.01*Y = 11 gives an error message, yet it will allow the equivalent 11/2*X + 101/100*Y = 11.

4.3 BNR-Prolog

Bell-Northern Research in Canada has developed BNR-Prolog [Bell-Northern Research 1988], a version of Prolog for the Macintosh II. BNR-Prolog supports the *interval* as a built-in data type, plus interval arithmetic constraint processing. An interval is a set of two floating point numbers representing the lower and upper limits of the values for a variable. Intervals overcome problems of exact number representation due to machine limitations, or due to insufficient information about the variable. When the lower and upper limits of an interval are the same, a *point interval* results.

Consider a variable A that is between 10 and 11, denoted A = [10, 11], a variable B = [2.5, 3], and the constraint C = A+B. The lowest and highest values of C are the sum of the respective A and B values, thus C = [12.5, 14]. Interval arithmetic operations of addition, subtraction, multiplication, and division are not invertable (calculating A from C, B, and A=C-B results in A = [9.5, 11.5], not [10, 11]). This precludes the direct use of common algorithms for solving simultaneous equations [Alefeld et al 1983], thus BNR-Prolog uses heuristics for interval constraint processing. To ensure numerical accuracy, BNR-Prolog always rounds down when calculating lower interval limits, and rounds up for upper limits.

Unknowns are initially assigned the widest interval possible, [-3.4e38,+3.4e38]. As the program progresses, each new constraint will tend to narrow the intervals, possibly to a point. A logical failure results if an inconsistency is found, e.g. an interval's lower limit exceeds its upper limit.

BNR-Prolog provides a special solve procedure to facilitate the narrowing of specific variable intervals. It subdivides the interval in question, and will generate non-contiguous intervals containing valid variable values, if necessary.

4.4 Other Constraint Programming Languages

Other constraint programming languages include Prolog-III [Colmerauer 1987] and

CHIP [Dincbas et al 1988]. Prolog-III uses a modified simplex algorithm to resolve numeric constraints in a manner similar to CLP($\mathcal{R}$). CHIP is limited to discrete variables, (such as natural numbers) but includes a built-in branch and bound optimizer. As we do not have copies of these languages, they were not included in our tests.

4.5 Testing the Constraint Programming Languages

We tested the three constraint programming languages described above using a series of problems. Table 1 summarizes a set of six simple example problems and the results returned by the languages.

Table 1 shows that each of the languages failed to provide a satisfactory solution under certain conditions. Other observations are given below.

BNR-Prolog demonstrated the unusual property that a "YES" response means only that IF there is a solution, it is within the ranges given. BNR-Prolog was the only system that provided a useful response to the last problem. The `solve` procedure, while not perfected in our prerelease version, was helpful.

CLP($\mathcal{R}$)'s "MAYBE" response is preferable to BNR-Prolog's "YES" with qualified values since it clearly indicates that an answer cannot be determined one way or the other.

Trilogy was the only system that could generate alternate solutions to a problem because it was the only system restricted to integer constraints. The refusal to compile a nonlinear constraint is unfortunate since run time inputs might make it linear.

5. OPTIMIZATION PROBLEMS AND CPS

The optimization capabilities of the various constraint satisfaction mechanisms and constraint programming languages are summarized in Table 2.

A striking feature of Table 2 is the columns for finding either a single point or the optimum point in the feasible region. Generally speaking, CPS are capable of finding such points only if the feasible region is a point. The only exception is CHIP, which applies a built-in branch and bound optimizer to discrete variables.

CPS have greater success in defining the limits of the feasible region. Term rewriting can potentially return a symbolically reduced set of equations that defines the feasible region, while Trilogy can define small integer feasible regions by returning all possible values. The multidimensional "boxes" defined by the BNR-Prolog intervals can approximate the feasible region.

Finally, current CPS are not capable of performing sensitivity analysis. However, the intervals in BNR-Prolog are helpful in that small deltas can be applied to parameters, simply by specifying intervals on the parameter values.

The conclusion to be drawn from Table 2 is that CPS are at present very poor at solving the kinds of problems associated with constrained optimization. However, existing CPS

Table 1: Example Problem and Results

Simple inequality and objective function (max. z). Solution: $z = 300$. $x_1 \geq 0, x_2 \geq 0, x_1 + x_2 \leq 100, z = 2 \times x_1 + 3 \times x_2$. CLP($\mathcal{R}$): "solution available", but no values returned. Trilogy: generated 66 possible solutions. BNR-Prolog: x_1 and $x_2 = [0, 100]$, $z = [0, 500]$. Applying **solve** to z reduced it to $[0, 313.29]$.
Linear equations with unique solution: $x_1 = 3, x_2 = 1, x_3 = -3$. $x_1 + x_2 + x_3 = 1, x_1 - x_2 = 2, x_1 - x_3 = 6$. CLP($\mathcal{R}$): correct solution. Trilogy: correct solution. BNR-Prolog: intervals not narrowed. Applying **solve** to x_1 gave $x_1 = [2.998, 3.001], x_2 = [0.99804, 1.001], x_3 = [-3.002, -2.999]$.
Parallel lines. No solution. $3 \times x_1 + 6 \times x_2 = 5, x_1 + 2 \times x_2 = 7$. CLP($\mathcal{R}$): "no solution". Trilogy: "no solution". BNR-Prolog: intervals narrowed slightly to $[-e37, e37]$ range. **solve** narrowed x_1 to $[-e38, -e6]$ and x_2 to $[e6, e37]$.
Linear equations with multiple solutions: $x_2 = x_3, x_5 = x_6, x_1 = x_4 = 0$. $x_i \geq 0, i = 1..6, x_1 + x_6 = x_5, x_1 + x_3 = x_2, x_2 + x_4 = x_3, x_4 + x_5 = x_6$. CLP($\mathcal{R}$): "yes". Trilogy: "too many choice points". BNR-Prolog: intervals narrowed slightly to $[-e37, e37]$ range. **solve** applied to x_1 did not return a solution after hours of processing.
Linear equations with unique solution of all $x_i = 0$. $x_i \geq 0, i = 1..15, x_1 = 5 \times x_7, x_2 = 4 \times x_7, x_8 = 2 \times x_7, x_9 = 2 \times x_7$, $x_3 = 7 \times x_{10}, x_4 = 4 \times x_{10}, x_{12} = 6 \times x_{10}, x_{13} = 2 \times x_{10}, x_5 = 3 \times x_{14}$, $x_{11} = 2 \times x_{14}, x_{15} = 4 \times x_{14}, x_6 = 2 \times x_{14}, x_7 = x_{10} + x_{11}, x_{12} = x_8 + x_{14}$, $x_{13} = x_9 + x_{15}$. CLP($\mathcal{R}$): correct solution. Trilogy: correct solution. BNR-Prolog: correct solution.
More complicated inequalities, including quadratic function. $x_2 = [0, 0.432]$. $x_1 \geq 0, x_2 \geq 0, x_1 + 2 \times x_2 \leq 2, 2 \times x_1 \geq x_2$ $x_2 \leq (x_1 - 1) \times (x_1 - 1)/2 + 1/8$. CLP($\mathcal{R}$): "maybe". Trilogy: "unable to compile: constraint too complex". BNR-Prolog: $x_1 = [0, 2], x_2 = [0, 0.625]$. **solve** narrowed x_2 to $[0, 0.439]$.

Constraint satisfaction mechanisms or language	Finding a single point in the feasible region (f.r.)	Finding the limits of the feasible region (f.r.)	Finding the optimum point	Sensitivity analysis
Local Prop.	if f.r. is point	if f.r. is point	if f.r. is point	no
Relaxation	if f.r. is point	if f.r. is point	if f.r. is point	no
Term Rewriting	if f.r. is point	potentially	if f.r. is point	no
CLP($\mathcal{R}$)	if f.r. is point	no	if f.r. is point	no
Trilogy[1]	yes	yes	if f.r. is point	no
BNR-Prolog	if f.r. is point	as interval "box"	if f.r. is point	helpful

[1] for natural numbers only.

Table 2: Summary of Capabilities of Mechanisms and Languages

were designed for other purposes, and little attention has yet been given to their potential for constrained optimization. CPS research is still in it's infancy; with only a little further work, CPS could become valuable tools for constrained optimization.

An obvious improvement to be made is in finding a single point where the feasible region is larger than a unique point. What is needed is the ability to recognize the existence of degrees of freedom, and the capability of fixing free variable values so as to determine a single point. These improvements should not be difficult.

Finding the optimum point is more difficult. There are really no alternatives beyond the mathematical approaches historically taken by OR researchers. Some of the CPS described above come very close to including an optimization facility, while CHIP (not tested) actually does so. CLP($\mathcal{R}$) and Prolog-III both use a modified simplex algorithm to resolve linear (or linearized) constraints; this could be easily converted to an ordinary simplex LP optimization. Trilogy uses *decision procedures* to manage the search space; it is reasonable to assume that a branch and bound algorithm could be incorporated without undue difficulty, though the problem of establishing a suitable bounding function remains.

The more general nonlinear optimization problem remains completely unaddressed by CPS. A good first step would be to include standard steepest descent algorithms as built-in functions. The problem remains of locating the global optimum, rather than local optima. The interval arithmetic paradigm used in BNR-Prolog shows great promise here. In conjunction with the `solve` procedure, the interval "boxes" gradually tighten around the feasible region from the outside. This has the effect of guaranteeing that the global optimum point will not be missed. However, the present version of BNR-Prolog is not able to tighten the box sufficiently.

Sensitivity analysis is also not a strength of current CPS, unless there is a point feasible region, in which case changes in a variable value are easily propagated to other variables. This is a strength of the object-oriented paradigm in which any variable can be treated as an input or an output, so that it is easy to change the value of a particular variable and observe the sensitivity of the other variables to the change.

Despite their inability to automatically solve optimization problems, current CPS are still valuable optimization tools. First, constraint satisfaction mechanisms such as local propagation and term-rewriting can be used to simplify large optimization problems before they are submitted to conventional solvers. This capability alone should be of great interest to OR researchers in computer-assisted analysis of models and model simplification.

Secondly, the constraint programming languages provide an excellent platform for the programming of more sophisticated algorithms. For example, it should be simple to program a branch and bound algorithm in Trilogy while taking advantage of the built-in solution generation and management schemes. Similarly, more advanced algorithms can be programmed in CLP($\mathcal{R}$) or BNR-Prolog which take advantage of the built-in constraint managers. These platforms also directly incorporate logical constraints which are sometimes difficult to handle in conventional solvers.

6. CONCLUSIONS

Our examination of existing CPS shows that they are, at present, of limited use in automatically solving constrained optimization problems. However, they do have other important uses in optimization problems. Local propagation and term rewriting mechanisms can be used to simplify large models prior to solution, and the constraint programming languages can be used as platforms incorporating useful built-in functions from which to program more sophisticated algorithms.

CPS are at an early stage in their development, and there are several hopeful indications for their future in optimization. The first is the ability of the logic-based languages to automatically track multiple solutions, eliminating an awkward problem for conventional solvers. The second is the promise inherent in interval arithmetic-based CPS of: (1) guaranteeing a global optimum, even in nonlinear problems with discontiguous feasible regions, or (2) at least narrowing the search space to a multidimensional box before conventional solvers are introduced.

The third is the potential increase in the solving power of CPS that may result from experiments in combining different constraint satisfaction mechanisms and optimization routines in a single package. While the extent to which this can be done depends on the amount of overhead and processing delay that the user will tolerate, the results may be worthwhile. Some combination of the constraint satisfaction methods described here (and possibly others) and one or more optimization routines may finally yield the automated solver that OR researchers have sought.

CPS, while only partially useful to optimizers at present, show great promise for the future. CPS research is a very worthwhile investment.

ACKNOWLEDGEMENTS

We gratefully acknowledge the financial support of Bell-Northern Research, and the Natural Sciences and Engineering Research Council of Canada (NSERC) through operating grants.

REFERENCES

Abelson, H. and G.J. Sussman with J. Sussman (1985), *Structure and Interpretation of Computer Programs*, The MIT Press, Cambridge, Mass.

Alefeld, G. and J. Herzberger (1983), *An Introduction to Interval Computations*, Academic Press, New York, N.Y.

Bell Northern Research (1988), *BNR-Prolog Reference Manual*, Ottawa, Ontario, Canada.

Borning, A. (1985), "Thinglab–A Constraint Oriented Simulation Laboratory", Ph.D. Thesis, Stanford University, Palo Alto, Calif.

Colmerauer, A. (1987), "Opening the Prolog-III Universe", *Byte Magazine 12*, 9.

Complete Logic Systems (1987), *Trilogy User's Guide*, North Vancouver, British Columbia, Canada.

Dincbas, M., Simonis, H., and Van Hentenryck, P. (1988), "Solving a Cutting-Stock Problem in Constraint Logic Programming", in *Logic Programming: Proceedings of the Fifth International Conference and Symposium*, R.A. Kowalski and K.A. Bowen, Eds., MIT Press, Cambridge, pp.42-58.

Gosling, J. (1983), "Algebraic Constraints", Technical Report CS-83-12, Carnegie-Mellon University, Pittsburgh, Penn.

Konopasek, M. and S. Jayaraman (1984), *The TK!Solver Book*, Osborne/McGraw-Hill, Berkeley, Calif.

Lassez, C. (1987), "Constraint Logic Programming", *Byte Magazine*, (Aug.), pp. 171-176.

Leler, Wm. (1988), *Constraint Programming Languages: Their Specification and Generation*, Addison-Wesley, Reading, Mass.

Steele, G.J. (1980), "The Definition and Implementation of a Computer Programming Language Based on Constraints", Technical Report AI-TR.595, MIT, Cambridge, Mass.

Sterling, L. and E. Shapiro (1986), *The Art of Prolog: Advanced Programming Techniques*, The MIT Press, Cambridge, Mass.

Sutherland, I.E. (1963), "Sketchpad: A Man-Machine Graphical Communication Interface", Ph.D. Thesis, MIT, Cambridge, Mass.

CONCEPT AND FIRST EXPERIENCES WITH AN OBJECT-ORIENTED INTERFACE FOR MATHEMATICAL PROGRAMMING

Manfred Grauer, Stephan Albers and Martin Frommberger
University of Dortmund
Computer Science Department
Postbox 50 05 00
D-4600 Dortmund, F.R.Germany

ABSTRACT

In this paper, we present the concept of, and first experiences with a software-system for linear and nonlinear, single and multiple criteria programming. The concept is to use the "WYSIWYG"-(What You See Is What You Get)-approach from desktop-publishing in combination with features from an object-oriented computer language. The system combines symbolic derivatives with numeric methods. The combination of several optimization methods (Scanning, Random Search, Direct Search, Sequential Quadratic Programming, Generalized Reduced Gradients) assures the robust solution of a broad class of nonlinear programming problems. The system as presented here is focuses mainly on the nonlinear aspect.

Using the idea of the reference-point-method multiple criteria problems can be analyzed. The system runs as ISAAC on MacIntosh-computers and as OPTIX on SUN-computers for more complex problems.

1. INTRODUCTION

In the last few years computer users in general have changed from computer experts to people who are interested in problem solving with computer assistance. In the same way computer interaction has changed from line-oriented terminals and technical oriented commands to graphic displays with sophisticated window- or desktop interfaces.

In the paper we will point out how the design (section 2.) and the implementation (section 3.) of an intelligent user-interface for mathematical programming in the single and multiple-criteria case (section 5) can be achieved. In the current version of the system we focus on nonlinear cases (section 4.) and present the combination of several nonlinear programming methods to assure robust solution procedures. The software-system as described here exists in the <u>Computer Science Department of the University of Dortmund</u> (I) as a student-version called ISAAC for use on MacIntosh-computers, mainly for educational purposes and (II) as a professional version called OPTIX for use on SUN-computers for large-scale problems. These systems belong to the so-called class of I^3-software (interactive, intelligent, integrated).

2. CONCEPT OF THE I^3-SOFTWARE DESIGN

The questions of designing a corresponding user interface are now investigated in some more detail. The main idea here is to use the "<u>WYSIWYG</u>" (What You See Is What You Get) - concept from desktop-publishing in combination with features of an object-oriented computer language. The Smalltalk System [Goldberg 1984] incorporates such a combination with a graphic user interface and various programming tools such as a debugger and a system-browser. Until today Smalltalk is the system with the best man-machine interaction so that when developing ISAAC and OPTIX this type of user interface was taken as the model. This concept, together with a multiple-criteria approach, stands for the first "I^1"(interactive).

In addition to this, the integration of several different linear and nonlinear programming methods stands for the second "I^2"(integrated). On the other hand the package is designed <u>to combine symbolic and numeric methods</u>, for instance, a knowledge-base is used for the choice of the most efficient combination of nonlinear programming techniques during a solution run or to compute symbolic derivatives ("I^3" - intelligent).

The <u>symbolic derivatives</u> computed by the system are simplified for faster evaluation before they are used. Algorithms can be changed at anytime during the optimization process; starting-points for new iterations can be chosen by clicking with the mouse at existing points. This is possible because all computed points are printed in a window called the history window.

Both systems (ISAAC, OPTIX) consist of a window interface, a language for problem definition and a combination of some optimization algorithms. Figure 1 which is a hardcopy from a Sun-computer shows all the currently implemented algorithms together with a problem description and a test run with some iteration values. Figure 2 presents another typical problem definition on a MacIntosh.

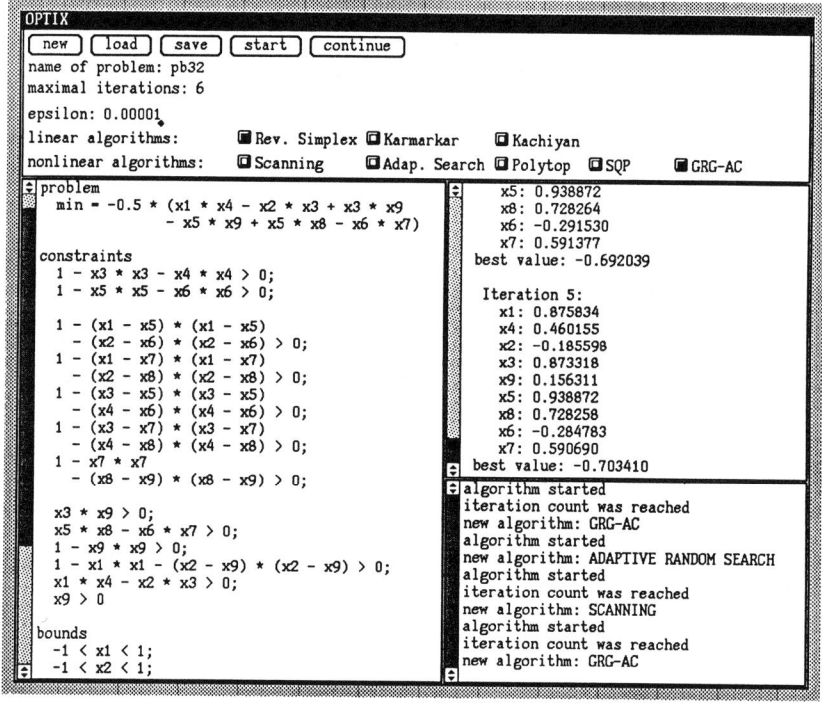

Figure 1 Problem formulation (problem Nr.32 from [Golden and Wasil 1986]) and solution with OPTIX on a Sun.

3. THE IMPLEMENTATION OF THE SYSTEM

Today most numerical engineering applications are written in FORTRAN. We decided however, to use the computer language C, for the reason that C is probably the fastest high level language necessary for a comfortable man-machine interaction; the user interface of the Apple MacIntosh was implemented in object-oriented Pascal. On the other hand C, in contrast to current FORTRAN, possesses structured data types which are the basis for a high abstraction level; without this it is very difficult to design systems of such a complexity. This is in our opinion one of the main reasons why numerical programs usually possess crude user interfaces.

Furthermore, some of the software tools like LEX, YACC and SunView which are needed for our interface design can only be used in combination with C or the operating system UNIX respectively. The use of C also allows high portability especially under the

UNIX system. Nevertheless we are able to combine existing FORTRAN programs with our optimization package.

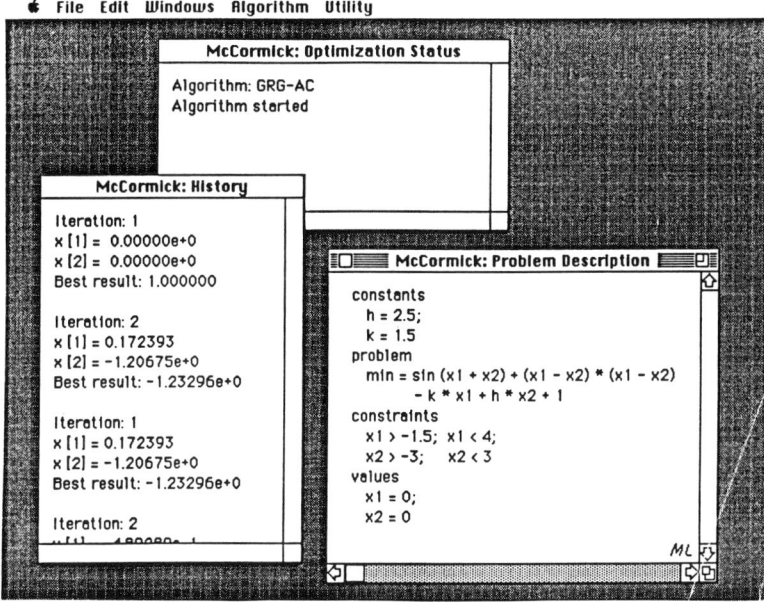

Figure 2 Problem formulation (problem Nr.3 from [Golden and Wasil 1986]) and solution with ISAAC on a Macintosh-computer.

This can be done in several ways, e.g. through interprocess communication, files and by linking routines from different computer languages; further investigations can be found in [Banares-Alcantara et al. 1988]. Here, the expert system environment OPS5 which is written in FranzLisp is presented in combination with FORTRAN-77.

It was decided to develop a context-free language for the problem description because this can be done in C very quickly using the scanner-generator LEX and the parser-generator YACC. The problem description language is descriptive rather than imperative so it is neither possible nor necessary to program the problem solving method. It seems worthwhile to mention that this problem description language also allows anything from basic mathematical to trigonometric functions. On the one hand a language like this is not the final step to a comfortable man-machine interaction. We are considering the problem input using non-modal menues [Goldberg 1984]. On the other hand the problem description could be extended to the automatic solution of ordinary differential equations as in [Shampine and Gordon 1973].

4. THE MATHEMATICAL PROGRAMMING METHODS

The system contains modules for mathematical programming methods for both linear and nonlinear cases. The revised Simplex method, the Kachiyan- and the Karmarkar-algorithm are available as solvers for the linear case. These methods are not yet integrated (no matrix-generator for the Simplex method and no automatic projective transformation for the Karmarkar-method exist in our system) and can be used only independently from the system. Work is at present being carried out in this area.

The main emphasis here is put on the solution of the nonlinear programming problem. A robust solver is therefore necessary for single and multiple-criteria problems.

More specifically, we are concerned with the solution of a nonlinear problem in its most general form:

$$\min f(x)$$
$$\text{s.t.} \quad 0 \leq g(x)$$
$$x_l \leq x \leq x_u \text{ and } x \in R^n.$$

To solve a broad class of problems of the above type we combine several methods which deal with most of the possible characteristics of these problems. To cope with the **multiplicity of solutions (multimodality)** to the problem the system provides the **Scanning** and the **Adaptive Random** search algorithms (see figure 1). These algorithms are normally used at the beginning of an optimum seeking process. To deal with **nondifferentiability**, a direct search method, the **Polytop**-algorithm, is used. We can usually assume that, in the vicinity of the solution, the constraints and the objective function(s) are **smooth**. In this case, and if in addition the problem is convex, then a quadratic approximation of the programming problem is the best model for a solution procedure.

The literature and the authors' own experiences [Grauer 1979] suggest that algorithms such as **Sequential Quadratic Programming (SQP)** and **Generalized Reduced Gradients** with active constraints strategy **(GRG-AC)** are most effective. Both of these algorithms are included in the library of available nonlinear programming tools for our system. Currently, as can be seen in Figure 3, one can switch from one method to another by hand. Under development is a knowledge base which either gives advice as to when to switch, or does it automatically. In Figures 1 and 2 one can see the solution of test problems taken from the list in [Golden and Wasil 1986].

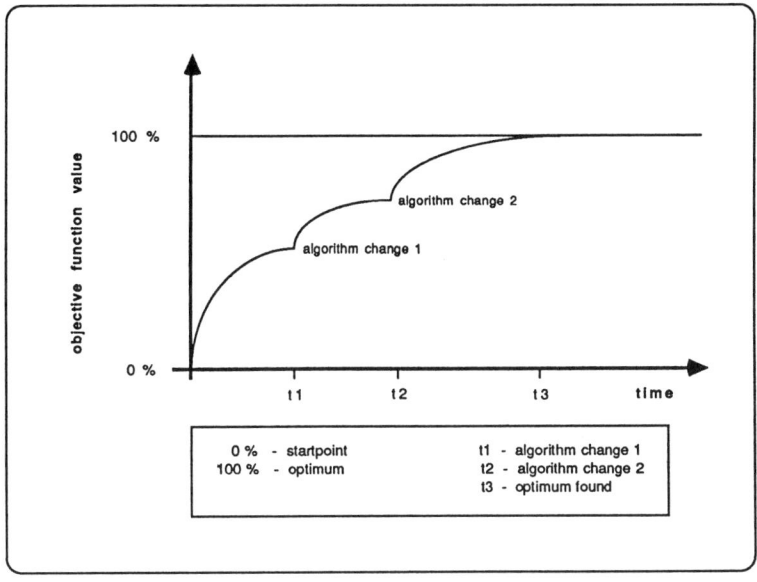

Figure 3. Combination of nonlinear programming methods by the user during a solution procedure.

5. THE MULTIPLE CRITERIA APPROACH

By multiple criteria decision making we mean here the interactive analysis of multicriteria (vector-valued) programming problems. First we define this problem, then we describe the scalarization method as a tool for generating efficient points which probably represent good decisions.

The multicriteria programing problem can be stated in the following way. Let Φ(open) be a subset of $\mathbf{R}^n$ and introduce the inequality constraints as in section 4

$$g(.) : \Phi \Rightarrow \mathbf{R}^m$$

and define the decision set (feasible set)

$$U = \{ \, u \in \mathbf{R}^n : u \in \Phi, 0 \leq g(u) \, \}.$$

The criterion functions are

$$q_i(.) : U \Rightarrow \mathbf{R} \, , \, i=1,2,...,r$$

with corresponding criterion map

$$q(.) : U \Rightarrow \mathbf{R}^r \, , \, q = (q_1,...,q_r)^T.$$

The subset
$$Y = q(u) = \{ y \in R^r : y = q(u), u \in U \}$$
is called the attainable set.

The problem statement (in the case of minimization) is defined thus: find the optimal decision(s) $\hat{u} \in U$ for $q(u)$ subject to $u \in U$.

For such a problem a decision $\hat{u} \in U$ is called optimal (Pareto-optimal) iff $u \in U$ and $q(u) \leq q(\hat{u}) \Rightarrow q(u) = q(\hat{u})$ for every $\hat{u}$-comparable $u \in U$.

This definition appears to be the natural extension of the optimization of a single criterion to the optimization of r criteria, in the sense that any further improvement in any one of the criteria values requires a worsening in at least one other criterion value. This usually infinite set of solutions is called the set of nondominated or efficient solutions.

A very common way to obtain efficient solutions is by parametrization of the Pareto-optimal set. This Pareto-set then, is the set of optima for a single criterion function or for a sequence of single criterion optimization problems which can be numerically solved by methods described in the previous section. For such a one-to-one correspondence the term "scalarization" is used in connection with scalar valued functions of the criteria whose minima happen to be members of the Pareto-optimal set. The choice of this scalar valued function is mainly influenced by (I) the context of the decision making process for which it serves and by (II) computational considerations.

We took the concept of "bounded rationality" in decision theory and satisficing behavior [Simon 1957 and 1958] as the base for designing a dialogue on the computer between the user and his multiple criteria problem. This means that the one-to-one correspondence (scalar valued function) in this aspect should meet certain features of the decision making paradigma being used, such as:

- it should be similar to utility functions as in normative decision theory and its maximization should lead to efficient nondominated decisions relative to the actual list of criteria q_i;
- it should depend on aspirations ($\hat{a}_i$) of the decision maker which satisfy certain target levels for his criteria, thus also expressing the current preference structure among his criteria;
- it should correspond to the minimization of the distance between the decision outcomes $q(\hat{u})$ and the aspiration levels $\hat{a}$, if the latter are not attainable, and to maximization of such a distance, if they are attainable;
- the test of attainability and efficiency of aspirations $\hat{a}_i$ should be numerically easy and
- it should be also usable in the case of dynamic outcomes, which is important in multicriteria planning and control problems.

A scalar valued function which meets these requirements is proposed in the reference-point-method [Wierzbicki 1982] (see also [Grauer et al. 1984]).
For the multicriteria nonlinear static programming problem a scalar valued function (s: $R^r \Rightarrow R$) which meets the above listed features could be of the following type

$$s(q,\hat{a}) = \{ \sum_{i=1}^{r} \mu_i [|q_i(t)-\hat{a}_i(t)|]^p \}^{(1/p)},$$

where $0 \leq \mu_\iota$ is a weighting factor which can include also normalization (scaling) of the criteria and $\sum_{i=1}^{r} \mu_\iota = 1$.

In the multiple-criteria dynamic case such a function can be written as:

$$s(q,\hat{a}) = \min_{t_0 \leq t \leq t_f} \min_{1 \leq i \leq r} \mu_\iota [q_i(t)-\hat{a}_i(t)] + \ldots$$

$$\ldots + \sigma \sum_{t=t_0}^{t_f} \sum_{i=1}^{r} \mu_i [q_i(t)-\hat{a}_i(t)],$$

where $\sigma > 1$, $0 \leq \mu_i$, $\sum_{i=1}^{r} \mu_i = 1$ and $t \in [t_0,t_f]$ is the time horizon of the planning or control problem.

This multicriteria planning or control problem will be transformed using the function s(.) in a general nonlinear static programming problem as presented in section 4 and all the numerical procedures can be reused. In this dynamic case the surrogate problem is characteristic in that it usually has an iterative procedure (normally the solution of a system of differential equations, see for instance [Grauer 1988]) in the constraints and in the objective function(s). To solve this problem in a reliable manner and fast enough in most cases (excluding academic examples) a combination of nonlinear programming methods as discussed in the previous section is needed.

In Figure 4 the formulation of a multicriteria problem using the input-language and the generation of an efficient point (the selfish optimum of q_1) is shown.

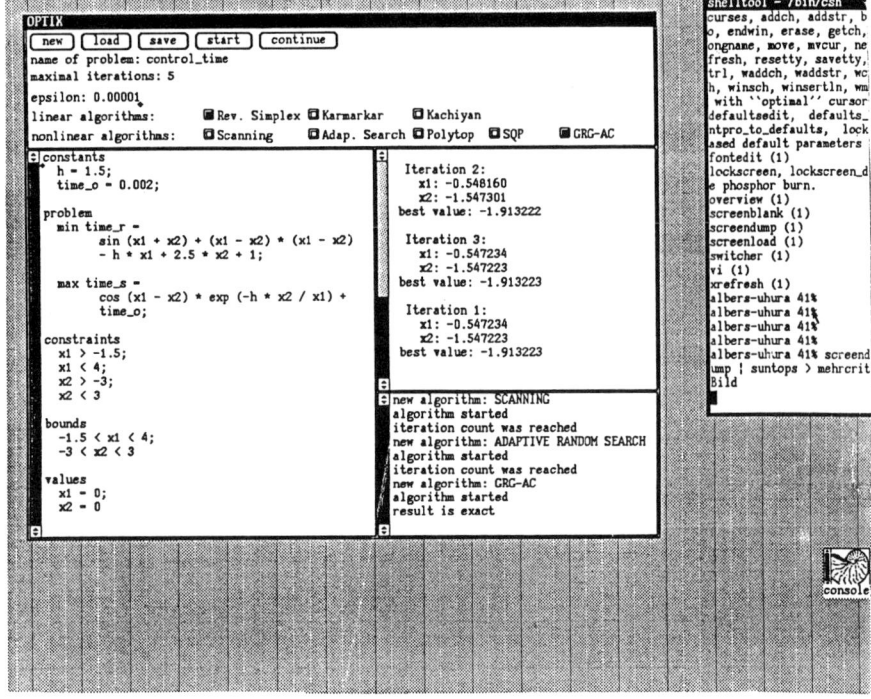

Figure 4 Formulation of a multicriteria problem and analysis of nondominated solutions with OPTIX on a SUN-computer

6. CONCLUSIONS

The future development of the presented system is planned along the following lines:

(I) To get a fast and robust problem solution the system allows the parallel and sequential use of different algorithms for one problem.

(II) To use a knowledge base with different patterns (multimodal, nondifferentiable or smooth) of the problem and by that to control the serial or parallel work of several algorithms from a higher level. The development of such a knowledge base is currently underway.

(III) Although the combination of different methods through a knowledge base was demonstrated in the paper mainly for programming problems, this idea can also be used for other numerical solution processes as for instance the solution of systems of differential equations.

AKNOWLEDGEMENT

We would like to thank F.Brueggemann, S.Kunze, M.Luis, K.Schuermann and S.Zaeske who supported the development of some of the modules of the system.

REFERENCES

Banares-Alcantara R.(1986), Edahl R., Biegler L., Talukdar S., Grossmann I., Joobani R.: An expert systems approach to on-line optimization, Proceedings of AIChE-Meeting, April 1986.

Goldberg, A.(1984): Smalltalk-80: The interactive programming environment, Addison-Wesley Publishing Company, Reading, 1984

Golden,B.L.(1986), Wasil,E.A.: Nonlinear Programming on a Microcomputer, Comp. & Ops.Res. Vol.13, No.2/3, pp.149-166, 1986

Grauer,M.(1979), Gruhn,G. and Pollmer,L.: Optimization of a complex plant by a GRG algorithm, Comp.& Chem.Eng.,3,597-602, 1979

Grauer,M.(1984), Lewandowski, A. and Wierzbicki, A. P.: DIDASS (Dynamic Interactive Decision Analysis and Support System)- Theory, Implementation and Experiences, in: Interactive Decision Analysis, Lecture Notes in Economics and Mathematical Systems, Vol. 229, Springer-Verlag, 1984, New York and Berlin.

Grauer,M.(1988): A case study in the use of mathematical models for decision support in production planning, in Mitra, G. et al: Mathematical models for decision support, NATO-ASI Series, Springer-Verlag 1988

Shampine,L.F. and Gordon,M.K.: Computer solution of ordinary differential equations: The initial value problem, Freeman, 1973

Simon,H.A.,(1957): Models of man. MacMillan, New York, 1957

Simon,H.A.,(1958): Administrative behavior. MacMillan, New York, 1958

Wierzbicki,A.(1982):A mathematical basis for satisficing decision making. Mathematical Modelling, Nr.3, pp.391-405

TOOLS FOR MODELLING SUPPORT AND CONSTRUCTION OF OPTIMIZATION APPLICATIONS

GAUTAM MITRA

*Department of Mathematics and Statistics, Brunel University,
Uxbridge, Middlesex, United Kingdom.*

ABSTRACT

We argue the case for an open systems approach towards modelling and application support. We discuss how the 'usability' and 'skills' analysis naturally leads to a viable strategy for integrating application construction with modelling tools and optimizers. The role of the implementation environment is also seen to be critical in that it is retained as a building block within the resulting system.

1. INTRODUCTION

Computer based methods for supporting optimization applications are of great interest to operational research workers and management scientists. In this paper we put forward an analysis of the scope as well as the goal of such systems set against our understanding of the methodological, technological and organizational issues. We describe the new direction of research that we have embarked upon and provide an outline definition of the software tools that we have set out to develop.

A number of workers [Geoffrion 1988], [Bisschop 1988] have indicated the importance of the recent developments which take us beyond the considerations of robust optimization routines, and languages and systems for constructing mathematical programming models. The real life use of mathematical programming optimization models is one of many important examples of applying mathematical modelling. It is now well established that mathematical modelling in turn is but a particular instance of knowledge representation [Geoffrion 1985], [Mitra 1988]. In the fields of computer science and data processing there is a strong movement towards convergence of research directions. Thus methods of AI, database technology and programming language design are coming together [Brodie, Mylopoulos et al, 1984]. In the field of decision support systems these trends go even further [Mitra 1988] and management science and OR specialists are discovering close connections between their work and the research and developments in psychology, computer science and database technologies, as addressed to this topic. Although our own research objectives remain focussed on the well defined and also narrow topic of constructing applications using optimization techniques, we feel compelled to take into account substantial research results and software tools which are coming out of these fields. The late seventies and early eighties have seen the developments of a number of modelling languages and systems for mathematical programming [Fourer 1983], [Bisschop and Meeraus 1982], [Ellison and Mitra 1982], [Fourer, et al 1987], [Schrage 1988], [Lucas and Mitra 1988]. We believe the real challenge has moved on from the question of modelling language design to that of an integrated environment for application construction, modelling and solving. Geoffrion [Geoffrion 1988] makes a strong case for such a modelling environment and lists a few desired characteristics which are (i) support of modelling life-cycle, (ii) equal access to policy makers and OR/MS analysts, (iii) a consistent vocabulary for model description, (iv) good management of key resources namely, data, models, and solvers within the system. Bisschop puts forward his assessment of the issues with the following diagram 1.1

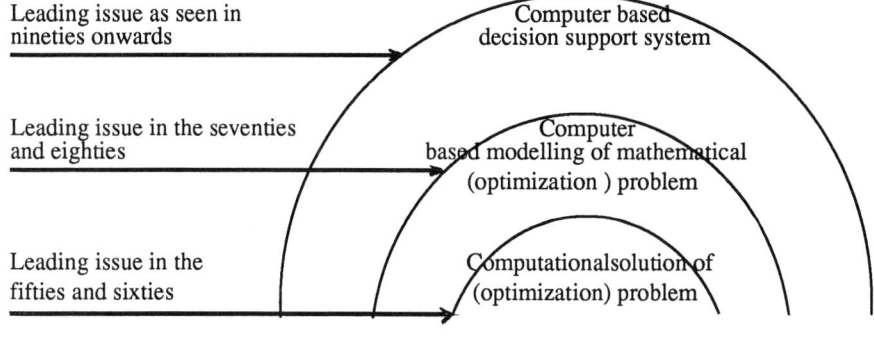

Diagram 1.1

This view is easy to explain and relate to. In his view the problems of optimization and modelling have been well addressed and many robust software tools for these can be found in the public domain. The development of an integrated Decision Support System is seen to be the leading research issue. We have also adopted a similar view of the software issues and put forward the argument that an 'open systems' approach should be adopted in the design of such systems. This approach also fits quite naturally with the layered view of the software items. For our purposes we define close and open systems in the following way. A close software system is one which has a well defined scope and applicability. It supports the user in his domain alone and it is difficult to extend its (re)use in other domains. In contrast, an open system is one which allows analysts, software engineer, end user, to make use of it for marginally different purposes and at different levels of competence. Although there exists a broad description of the scope of such a system, the system may be (re)used in application areas which were not originally conceived at the time of its initial design. Scientific software libraries, graphics libraries, with well defined communication and control interfaces are basic building blocks of open systems [Iles and Hague 1988].

2. REQUIREMENT ANALYSIS: SCOPE, USABILITY AND SKILLS

In order to derive an outline specification of the system we consider the technology of the systems components, usability of the system and the skills level of the intended users.

2.1 Technology:

The system is designed to incorporate upto date devices and software components and requires high resolution bit-mapped screens as in advanced work stations, with a mouse or an alternative pointing device; it also suports integrated text 2-D graphics (colour) and pictures. It can also access data through networked distributed database and although voice interface and animation displays and 3-D graphics are not immediately included, the design features allow their incorporation in future.

2.2 Usability and Skills Level:

Given that our objective is to define and implement an open system, we admit the very complex interaction between development and usage of the system. There are many constituents in these two roles and we categorize the constituents in four groups. We also introduce five different computer usage skills relevant to our analysis. In Table 2.1 we itemize these skills with a short code and in Table 2.2 we set out the constituents together with their relevant skills and their job focus. Eason and Harker [Eason and Harker 1988] in their paper on user orientated approach to design, discuss these issues of skill and usability. The concept of end user computing in its own right admits many criticisms. Yet the ETHICS approach of Mumford [Mumford 1983] follows product development through analysis, specification, design and prototyping, delivery and use. This methodology of systems development through user participation, is now well established. Set against this background the role and relevance of our constituents and our case for an open system, may be fully appreciated.

Skills	Short Code
Supply data for decision problem. Interpret computer solution and implement decision within organization.	DECSIMPL
Provide rules, regulations and requirements and define domain model.	DOMNMODL
Construct a general mathematical optimization model.	GENERALM
High level programming and customization of application.	APPLPROG
System development and programming	SYSTPROG

Table 2.1 An Analysis of Skills

2.3 An Outline of the System and Its Use:

In Diagram 2.1 we have illustrated how the layered software components make up the open system. There are four software layers which are optimizer/solver, modelling support system, application support system, and finally the application program.

Constituent	Skill	Job Responsibility
Problem Owner (End User)	DECSIMPL=Y DOMNMODL=N	Utilize the application (decision) support system and implement solution.
Domain Expert	DECSIMPL=? DOMNMODL=Y GENERALM=?	Work with the analyst/ knowledge engineer to create a domain specific application
Knowledge Engineer/ Analyst	DECSIMPL=N DOMNMODL=? GENERALM=Y APPLPROG=Y	Work with domain experts to create different applications
System Programmer	GENERALM=? APPLPROG=Y SYSTPROG=Y	Work with a variety of implemention vehicles to construct and integration application support, modelling and optimization tools.

Table 2.2 : Indication of skills: N = No, Y = Yes, ? = Question

The productivity and gearing achieved by such software tools is illustrated through Diagram 2.2. A discussion of the implementation environment which we wish to include as building blocks of the open system is postponed to section 5. The main players in the system are the analysts who use the modelling support system to create separate instances of models. The analyst, with a particular model instance then teams up with a domain expert to create an optimization application: crew scheduling, retail space planning are typical examples of these. Each application in turn serves a number of problem owners (end users).

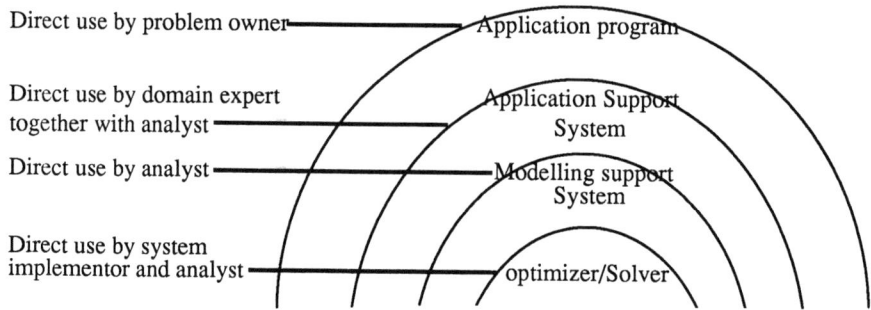

Digram 2.1

Application Domain	The Constituents	Description of Application
Bus Crew Scheduling	End User: Scheduling Team Domain Expert: Master Scheduler	Allocation of crews to bus time tables. Solution expected in extended bus timetable format with text and numbers.
Gasket Trim Minimization	End User: Shift Supervisors Domain Expert: Production Planner	Specify cutting of small rectangles out of large rolls or sheets to meet demand for parts. Solution required in report format with number, text and graphics.
Menu Formulation Problem	End User: Canteen Supervisor Domain Expert: Diet Planner	A varied and planned menu to meet client demand. Solution expected with 2-D or 3_D graphics, text and possibly picture.
Shelf space allocation in retail sector.	End User: Department Heads Domain Expert: Shop Manager	Allocate floor space and shelf space maximize selling of Solution in text, merchandize. graphics, 2-D, 3-D displays and possibly pictures.

Table 2.3: Representative Applications in Summary Form

In order to fix ideas and highlight the varying requirements we list a few well established applications of optimization models. These are set out in Table 2.3. Organizations which have made a commitment to the use of decision support systems usually have teams made up of analyst, domain experts and end users. Quite often a consultant or expert from the vendor company takes up the role of the analyst.

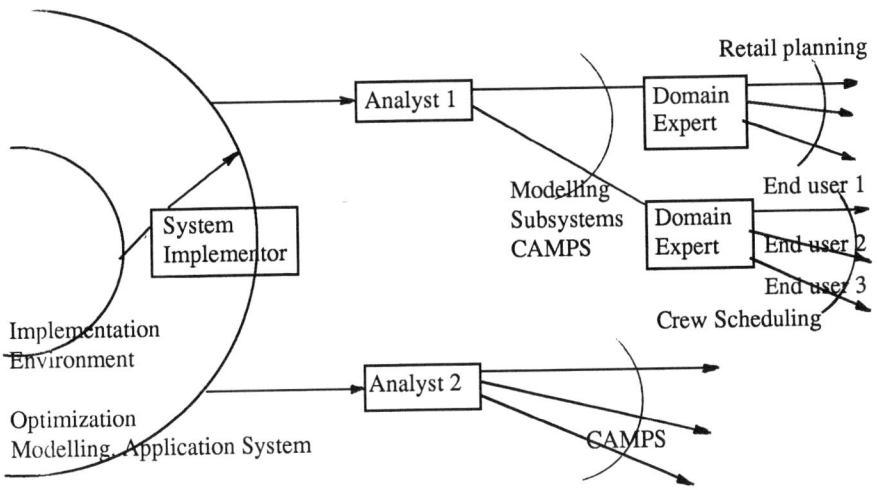

Digram 2.2

3. MODELLING SUPPORT

Substantial development has taken place in the definition of mathematical programming modelling languages and a number of features have been established as of great value in the modelling process. In this section we present those key features which we consider are important in aiding the analyst in his task to construct mathematical optimization models.

3.1 Model Description, Model Analysis and Solution Report.

In most of these systems the models are described through a series of progressive and structured definitions of : Sets and basic entities, Data tables , Groups of decision variables Groups of Constraints, Constraint relationships in linear form. In language based systems (UIMP, GAMS, AMPL) these are introduced using the language syntax and the keywords. Systems which make use of menus and screenforms, CAMPS, LPFORM, [Murphy et al 1986], the models are specified through interactive structured edit procedures. Most modelling systems also support simple reporting capabilities. The concept of model analysis, solution analysis, browsing and discourse are also pertinent at this level and has been well promoted by Greenberg [Greenberg 1983].

3.2 Model Reformulation and Model Integration:

Quite often it is simpler and more natural to describe a problem using logical variables and logical form for the relations. The methods of reformulating these into known MIP forms have been well discussed in [Darby-Dowman et al 1988], and [Williams et al 1988]. Many nonlinear programs can be also manipulated and reformulated into special ordered set type two form [Darby-Dowman et al 1988]. Murphy [Murphy et al 1986] makes a case for constructing and maintaining sub models such as production, inventory, transport and integrate these as and when appropriate. From an implementation viewpoint reformulation and model integration lead to the same issue of piecing together submodels. Automating this task provides great support to the analyst.

3.3 Model Validation:

Model validation can take place at symbolic level and also at data level when data items are supplied. Bradley [Bradley and Clarence 1987] has highlighted the importance of introducing units of measurement in the definition of coefficients, model variables and constraints. Given that a set of complete unit conversion rules are also supplied unit validation of the restrictions can be automatically carried out. The coefficients themselves can be symbolically analysed for solvability or otherwise of the model [Brearley et al 1975]. Data items themselves are first checked against specified limits as determined by the application. Data items can also be used to establish solvability of the model as a follow up of the symbolic analysis set out above.

3.4 Model Documentation:

Comparable with the requirement to document a computer program it is considered equally important to document a model. In a develpment environment it becomes necessary to communicate between analysts or between analyst and domain expert. Whereas in most language based systems the program with annotation is considered to be the documentation, in CAMPS we provide a separate utility to automatically document the model.

4. APPLICATION DEVELOPMENT

A customized system which supports a complete application with the model and the optimizer embedded in it, we call an application (decision) support system. We have identified application control, interface design (screens and menus), data and model management and discourse design, as essential aspects in the development of such a system. All these software features belong to the third layer of our system and they need to fit closely to the modelling layers.

4.1 Application Control:

This defines a complete set of end user commands by which the problem owner controls his application. These commands cover data entry and validation, error checking, model creation or revision, dispatch to the interactive or the batch queue to solve the model, and browsing of the solution returned by the solver.

4.2 Interface Design:

To start with we determine the nature of the interface and introduce text, graphics and other forms of communication. Specification of windows or screens, definition of structured edits or menu control by function keys, together with 'HELP' texts which are context specific, are the main tasks of interface design.

4.3 Data and Model Management.:

Within an organization for corporate purposes data may be held or prepared in more than one department. The organization is likely to use different models driven by a subset of data items. The organization may simply use submodels which are appropriate to support the functions of a given department. The importance of a combined scheme for data and model management for these purposes is well discussed by Palmer et al of Exxon [Palmer 1984], Lucas of EDS [Lucas 1986] and Dolk [Dolk and Konynski 1985].

4.4 Discourse Design.:

We see a convergence between the earlier generations concepts of diagnostic reports, exception reports, with the modern counterpart of diagnostic discourse, with full session summary and explanation procedure for decisions which are unclear to the problem owner. The discourse procedures are set out to convey through text, graphics, numbers and other communication vehicles many aspects of the model and solution to the end user. Greenberg has illustrated [Greenberg 1987] how end user discourse can be designed to explain LP models. We claim traditional solution reports often broken down into group requirements such as a financial report, production report and machine utilization report, can be similarly supported as sectoral views which Geoffrion calls Genus/module summary [Geoffrion 1987]. Since training an end user is genuinely a thorny issue we also plan to embed in the system a number of complete sessions of control and discourse as part of a training subsystem.

5. IMPLEMENTATION TOOLS

Our aim is to create an open system and for the first two software layers we have chosen standard (or at least well established) software items. We provide sufficient information concerning module definitions whereby different constituents can use these tools in their development tasks.

5.1 Implementation Tools for Optimizer and Modelling Support:

We have chosen FORTRAN, C and a low level screen package (CURSES) to implement FORTLP [Mitra and Tamiz 1988] and CAMPS respectively. Our choice is based mainly on efficiency and portability considerations. A complete statement of an LP model may be viewed as a declarative knowledge of the underlying physical problem. It is interesting to note that many combinatorial problems such as crew scheduling, vehicle routing and cutting stock problems, require activity generations (duties, routes, patterns, respectively) which can be only done by procedural methods. These examples also highlight the need to provide a programmer's interface to the generated code or at least the model generator statements of the modelling system. We are considering implementing such an interface. We would also like to highlight the work of Ladhelma and his colleagues [Ladhelma 1988] who have designed and implemented a mathematical modelling environment (MME) with a functional language MPL. They have created a very credible integrated modelling and optimization system.

5.2 Tools for Application Generation.

We have considered a number of Fourth Generation Languages and Knowledge Based Systems Shells as vehicles for implementing the outer layer of our application support software. We refer the readers to [Martland 1986], [Holloway 1988], and [Mettrey 1987] for over views of alternative 4GL and KBS products. 4GL and KBS both suffer from the drawback that there is a long learning time to make full use of these systems, execution, speed, and portability, are also problematical. On the other hand they provide powerful tools for display management and data management. The work of Markowitz [Markowitz et al 1984], EAS-E system seems highly relevant in this context. Since 4GL's do not support knowledge representation facility we have not considered them any further. We are, however, committed to use a suitable database system.

We are evaluating a number of knowledge based systems shells and our arguments for adopting a KBS product (or products) are set out below. Logic programming, production rules, frames, are perhaps the most useful knowledge representation method. In the MIP reformulation task, use of such an approach (PROLOG [Williams et al 1988]) has already been demonstrated. We also see very good use of production rules in validating data limits, consistency of units of measurement. CAMPS as a modelling tool uses the concepts of structured edit and program generation. The use of frames (structured objects with slots) at outer level can be used in a natural way to provide interface with the modelling system. Our target of dialogue support covers use of text, graphics, icons and even pictures. We expect to make use of frames and dialogue support tools of KBS shells. An example of application specific software architectures along these lines is already reported by Dempster [Dempster 1988] where he has used MINOS as the optimizer and KEE as the application as well as modelling of environment. Currently we are evaluating three such tools namely KEE (Knowledge Engineering Environment) [Fikes and Kehler 1985], ART (Automated Reasoning Tool) [Mettrey 1987], and LEONARDO [Jones and Graham 1988]. We also see the requirement for a separate PROLOG compiler and suitable interface definition as none of these tools support this facility. As structured objects and object oriented programming have emerged as an important method of knowledge representation, we are also considering whether or not SMALLTALK [Goldberg 1983] system can be introduced in this outer layer and used in the application development.

The two inner layers are concerned with mathematical description of the models and deriving computational solutions. The outer layer is concerned mainly with the domain expert and the end user. It has the primary requirement of capturing domain specific knowledge and supporting interaction and dialogue. As a result the possibility of using hypertext systems are also of interest to us. We find the facilities within KMS hypertext system [Akcscyn et al 1988] particularly attractive. Within this system it is possible to combine structured edit, navigation through the system, and also execution of images (program modules) at nodes. This might provide us with a rich implementation environment within which our software layers, along with the tools, may coexist.

We wish to conclude this section by justifying why we are evaluating such a variety of implementation tools with different focus and capability. Our main argument is that as hardware and software technology progress it becomes impossible to access them (e.g. natural language communication, multimedia systems) without defining a suitable control and interface structure. The only way to define such an interface is to learn and make use of the corresponding implementation vehicles. This observation also reinforces our case for an open system.

6. DISCUSSIONS

In this paper we have outlined the preliminary findings of our longer term research project of defining and constructing integrated tools which support optimization applications. We present requirement and usability analyses of the system and discuss our implementation strategy. There are many aspects of design and implementation that we are still exploring. Constructive criticisms on all aspects of this paper covering focus, definition and implementation strategy will be gratefully entertained and acknowledged in our future works.

ACKNOWLEDGMENTS

Our research in the field of modelling support system and optimization applications has been supported by the UK Science and Engineering Research Council, and US Army's European Research Office. Both these grants supported Dr C Lucas who implemented the CAMPS modelling system. NATO Scientific Affairs Division have supported our collaborative research with Dr H Greenberg. NAG Ltd have also maintained a strong interest in our work and are now working with us closely to define the next generation of software products. We have greatly benefitted from discussions with many colleagues. In particular we would like to mention H Greenberg, A Geoffrion, H P Williams, J Bisschop, P L K Jones, F Murphy, G Bradley, and M A H Dempster, whose innovative ideas have, in one way or another, been incorporated in our work.

REFERENCES

Akscyn, R M., McCracken, D L., and Yoder, E A., (1988). KMS: A Distributed Hypermedia System for Managing Knowledge in Organizations, *Comm ACM*, Vol 31, No 7, pp 820-8335.

Bisschop, J.J., (1988), A Functional Description of an Integrated Modelling Software for Mathematical Programming, (Aug), *presented to the 13th Internaitonal MathematicalProgramming Symposium,* TOKYO.

Bradley, G H., and Clarence, R D., (1987). A Type Calculus for Executable Modelling Languages. IMA Journal of Mathematics in Management, *Special Issue on Mathematical Programming Modelling Systems,* Guest Editor: G Mitra, Vol 1, pp 277-291.

Brearley, A L., Mitra, G., and Williams, H P., (1975). Analysis of Mathematical Programming Models Prior to Applying the Simplex Algorithm. Math Prog., Vol 8, pp 54-83.

Cunningham, K., (1986). Optimization Models with Spreadsheet Programs, Univ of Chicago, *Technical Report.*

Darby-Dowman, K., Lucas, C., Mitra, G., and Yadegar, J., (1988). Linear, Integer, Separable and Fuzzy Programming Problems: A Unified Approach TowardsReformulation. *Journal of the OR Society (GB),* Vol 39, No 2, pp 161-171.

Dempster, M.A.H., and Ireland, A.M., (1988). Expert Financial Systems for Debt Management in [Mitra 1988].

Dolk, D R., and Konynski, B., (1985). Model Management in Organizations, *Informationand Managemeent*, Vol 9, No 1, pp 35-47.

Eason, K.D., and Harker, S., (1988), The Supplier's Role in the Design of Products for Organisations, The Computer Journal (UK), vol. 31, No. 5, pp 426-430.

Fikes, R., and Kehler, T., (1988). The Role of Frame Based Representation in Reasoning, *Comm ACM, Vol 28, No 9,* pp 904-920.

Fourer, R., Gay, D M., and Kernighan, B W., (1987). AMPL: A Mathematical Programming Language. *Computing Science Technical Report No 133, AT & T Bell Labs,* Murray Hill, NJ, USA.

Geoffrion, A M., (1985), Private communication, *12th Internationa l Mathematical Programming Symposium, Boston.*

Geoffrion, A M., (1987). An Introduction to Structured Modelling, *Management Science,Vol 33,* No 5, pp 547-588.

Geoffrion, A M., (1988), Computer Based Modelling Environments: A Road to Greater Productivity, Quality and Popularity for Management Science/Operations Research, (May-Aug), *Keynote speech to Canadian Operations Research Society meeting, Montreal.*

Goldberg, A., and Robson, D., (1983). Smalltalk-80: The Language and Its Implementation. Addison *Wesley, Reading, Mass.*

Greenberg, H J., (1987). A Natural Language Discourse Model to Explain Linear Programs, *Decision Support System, Vol 33,* pp 333-342.

Greenberg, H J., Lucas, C., and Mitra, G., (1987). Computer Assisted Modelling and Analysis of Linear Programming Problems: Towards a Unified Framework, *IMA Journal of Mathematics in Management, Vol 1, pp* 251-265.

Holloway, S., (1988), Editor. Evaluation of Fourth Generation Systems, UNICOM Information Technology Report Series, Kogan Page, UK.

Iles, R., and Hague, S., (1988), Knowledge Based Front End Research Project: FOCUS, internal report NAG Ltd.

Jones, P L K., and Graham, I. Expert Systems: Knowledge, Uncertainty and Decision, Chapman and Hall, 1988.

Lahdelma, R., (1988). MME: A Mathematical Modelling Environment, presented to EURO IX, Paris. *Report of Nokia Research Center,* PO Box 780, 00101 Helsinki, Finland.

Lucas, J., (1986). Expert System/Mathematical Programming Applied to StrategicDecisions. *Paper presented at TIMS XXVII, Gold Coast, Australia, and runner up Franz Edelman Award, TIMS.*

Markowitz, H M., et al, (1984). The EAS-E Application Development System: Principles and Language Summary, *Comm ACM Vol 27, No 8, pp* 785-799.

Martland, D., (1986), Editor. Fourth Generation Systems, UNICOM - Technical Press Report Series, Gower Press, UK.

Mettrey, W., (1987). An Assessment of Tools for Building Large Knowledge-Based Systems, *AI-Magazine, winter 1987*, pp 81-89.

Mitra, G., (1987), Mathematical Programming Modelling Systems, Guest Editor Mitra, *Special Issue of IMA Journal of Mathematics in Management, vol 1*, No 3 & No 4.

Mitra, G., (1988), Editor, Mathematical Models for Decision Support, *Proceedings of NATO Advanced Study Institute, Springer Verlag.*

Mitra, G., and Tamiz, M., (1988). FORTLP: Linear and Integer Programming System, *User Reference Manual, Brunel University and NAG Ltd.*

Mumford, E., (1983), Designing Human Systems for New Technology; the ETHICS Method, *Manchester Business School.*

Murphy, F H., and Stohr, E A., (1986). An Intelligent System for Formulating LinearPrograms. Decision Support System, Vol 2, pp 39-48.

Palmer, K., et al (1984). A Model Management Framework for Mathematical Programming, Wiley, New York.

Williams, H P., and McKinnon, K I M., (1988). Constructing Intege Programming Models by Predicate Calculus, (Aug). *Presented to the 13th Internaional Mathematical Programming Symposium, TOKYO.*

THE GRG2 MODEL BUILDER

ALLAN D. WAREN AND MICHAEL PECHURA
College of Business Administration, Cleveland State University
Cleveland, Ohio 44115

LEON S. LASDON
School of Business Administration, University of Texas at Austin
Austin, Texas 78712

ABSTRACT

To facilitate the use of the GRG2 nonlinear optimization system, a program called the GRG2 Model Builder has been developed and is described herein. The Model Builder incorporates a model definition language, a context sensitive editor, an extensive help system, and various file utility capabilities. This program can significantly reduce the time needed to define a model to be optimized since it enables the user to write simple model definition language statements rather than having to code FORTRAN subroutines.

The Model Builder program translates the model definition language statements into FORTRAN statements which can then be compiled with any FORTRAN 77 compiler. It also creates either a GRG2 data file or a FORTRAN Main program which calls GRG2, whichever is requested. The Model Builder program itself runs on an IBM PC or equivalent, and is highly interactive.

1. INTRODUCTION

According to a recent article by Geoffrion [1987], one of the reasons that MS/OR is a low productivity activity is that current modeling capabilities are primitive in comparison to our abilities to analyze and solve the models once they have been created. He identifies four factors contributing to this imbalance:

i. at least three distinct representations are typically used for each model (a natural language one, a mathematical one, and a computer-executable one)

ii. interfacing models to optimizers and other advanced solvers requires technical skill and is laborious and time consuming

iii. most modelling software is specialized to one class of problems (e.g. linear programming or multi-period financial ones)

iv. modeling software supports only one or two of the many phases in the model life-cycle (determine requirements, design, build, test, use, revise, maintain, document, explain, analyze results, report findings, and evolve)

The fact that, in recent years, there has been considerable activity in the development of modeling languages for Linear Programming [Bisschop and Meeraus 1982; Burger 1982; Fourer 1983; Dolk 1986; Schrage 1986; Fourer et al. 1987; Welch 1987], indicates that many others have recognized shortcomings in the modeling process. However, although several of these modeling systems also provide (or plan to provide) support for nonlinear programming, their emphasis is on large, sparse, linear problems.

In terms of small to medium size, dense, nonlinear programming problems there has been substantially less activity although some efforts have been made [Schittkowski 1985; Liebman et al. 1986; Cunningham and Schrage 1987]. In this paper we describe a modelling system for such problems. This system uses GRG2 [Lasdon and Waren 1978], a widely used FORTRAN based nonlinear programming system, as its solver. This system is capable of solving linear and nonlinear equality and/or inequality equations as well as linear and nonlinear optimization problems. It has been designed to address the four low productivity factors enunciated by Geoffrion. In its current implementation it still requires the use of a FORTRAN compiler to translate its output into computer-executable form, although the next version will not.

2. SYSTEM OVERVIEW

The GRG2 Model Builder system is an interactive system for building, modifying, testing, and solving mathematical models. It also provides some support to the user in model organization, model documentation, and model management. Each model consist of its defining equations and variables, bounds for both, initial values for the variables, symbolic model constants and the current values of GRG2 parameters. The equations and variables should be continuous, but can be linear or nonlinear.

The system runs on a personal computer and is menu based. It incorporates file handling and printing utilities and includes a context sensitive, full screen editor. In addition to the usual editing functions, the editor supplies a skeleton model into which the user adds the specific model information needed.

With the Model Builder it is possible to write model equations in a simple and legible algebraic fashion. This model description is currently translated into FORTRAN code suitable for use with GRG2 (the output may include a GRG2 data file as well). To solve the model, the FORTRAN code must be compiled and linked to the GRG2 program, and the resulting EXE file must then be executed. Current work involves the development of an integrated compiler/linker which would permit bypassing these last steps, thus making the computer model the same as the mathematical one - at least from the perspective of the user. Even now, much of the compile and link process can be embedded in a batch file which can be executed from within this system.

Within the system, help is context sensitive. For example, in the edit subsystem, the initial help request provides help for cursor control and other edit functions. Requesting additional help from this help screen will provide help for the specific model section that currently contains the cursor.

3. SAMPLE MODEL

As a simple example of a model created with the system, consider the problem of designing an electronic components box [Liebman et al. 1986]. The box is to be rectangular in shape with its Height, Width, and Depth to be determined. Considerations in designing the box include the following:

(a) for reasons of heat dissipation the surface area, including the base, must be greater than or equal to 888 square inches.

(b) for marketing reasons the footprint of the box must be less than or equal to 252 square inches.

(c) in order to hold the required electronics, the volume of the box must be at least 1512 cubic inches.

(d) for aesthetic reasons, the Height to Width ratio must be close to the "golden mean" of 0.618.

(e) for profit reasons, the box must be as inexpensive as possible while satisfying the above requirements. The only costs we will consider are $0.05 per square inch for the sides, top, and bottom of the box and $0.10 per square inch for the front and back.

Since a primary objective of this system is to enable users with little experience in mathematical programming to build and use optimization models, it is important that only a single model representation be required and that this representation be as close as possible to a "natural" representation. To test whether this goal is at least partially realized, the reader is invited to examine the Box model on the next page and to compare it to the English language problem description above.

TITLE:
This is a model for an electronic components box.
;
CONSTANTS:
;
```
MinArea      = 888      ; the box must have a surface area larger than this.
MaxFootprint = 252      ; the box footprint must be less than this number.
MinVolume    = 1512     ; volume requirement for components
MaxRatio     = 0.718    ; for aesthetics the Height to Width ratio must lie
MinRatio     = 0.518    ;   between this pair of numbers.
CostSTB      = 0.05     ; cost of Sides, Top, and Bottom per square inch.
CostFB       = 0.10     ; cost of Front and Back per square inch.
```
;
LOCALS:
ARRAYS:
EQUATIONS:
;
```
Cost     =  2.0 * CostSTB * ( Depth * Width + Depth * Height ) +
            2.0 * CostFB * Width * Height
SurfArea =  2.0 * ( Height * Depth + Height * Width + Depth * Width )
Footprint = Depth * Width
Volume   =  Height * Depth * Width
Ratio    =  Height / Width
```
;
MINIMIZE:
Cost
;
BOUNDS:
;
;   Bounds for Variables
```
;Lower          Variable        Upper       Initial
;Bound          Name            Bound       Value
;--------       ----------      --------    --------
0.0             DEPTH           NONE        12      ;
0.0             HEIGHT          NONE        10      ;
0.0             WIDTH           50.0        15      ;
```
;
;   Bounds for Functions
```
;Lower          Variable        Upper
;Bound          Name            Bound
;--------       ----------      --------
NONE            COST            NONE
NONE            FOOTPRINT       MaxFootprint
MinRatio        RATIO           MaxRatio
MinArea         SURFAREA        NONE
MinVolume       VOLUME          NONE
```

4. MODEL STRUCTURE

Each model consists of up to eight sections. This separation of the various pieces of information describing the model is designed to help in updating, revising, and developing the model as well as in its documentation. These sections are briefly described below.

4.1 Title Section

This section is primarily intended to enhance the "self-documenting" capabilities of each model. Every model must include a title line, even if this line only contains a single character. This line is also the title that is used by GRG2 when it produces its reports. A maximum of one line (75 characters) can be used for GRG2 but the model description itself can contain any number of additional comment lines. A comment line is any line starting with a semicolon. Comments can also be appended to any line in the model since all characters from the first semicolon in the statement to the end of the statement are treated as a comment.

4.2 Constants Section

The constants section is included for documentation and model maintenance purposes. This section is optional, but again very useful. It enables the user to define symbolic constants which are eventually replaced by their actual numeric values when the model builder creates the FORTRAN programs for the GRG2 interface. Each constant is defined by specifying its name on the left, followed by an equal sign, and its value on the right. In order that meaningful names can be used, names consist of an alphabetic character followed by 1 to 31 alphanumerics. Capital and lower case letters are treated as the same but are useful for subdividing the name into more easily understood parts. Values are any legitimate FORTRAN 77 numeric integer or floating point constants.

4.3 Arrays Section

Frequently models contain groups of constants, variables, or equations which are closely related and for which it would be onerous to provide individual names and, in the case of such functions, individual definitions. Arrays are used to define lists of such items with a single statement and to identify a specific item from the list by specifying its position within that list by a subscript.

The constant array definition statement consists of a user provided array name, followed by at least one space and then the key word "CON" (lower or upper case as for all identifiers in GRG2 Model Builder) standing for "constant", followed by a space and the number of items for this constant array, followed by an optional comment. Currently only one-dimensional arrays are supported but the next version will support two dimensional array constants.

Values for array constants are provided in a subsection of the Bounds section, titled "Initial Constant Array Values" with one line allocated for each array element. Note that this section, including all the array identifiers, is automatically created for the user and only the actual values need to be filled in. Array constants must always be used with a subscript, usually a numeric integer value (between 1 and the array size specified) but the subscript may also be a local index variable (see the next section for examples).

In addition to constant arrays, the system also supports arrays of variables and arrays of functions. In terms of the definition of such arrays, in the ARRAYS section, the only difference from array constants is the use of the two key words "VAR" and "FUN" for variable and function arrays respectively. Bounds for array variables and array functions, as well as initial values for the array variables, are handled in a compatible fashion in the BOUNDS section.

4.4 Locals Section

In evaluating functions, it is often desirable to use temporary variables in order to save computational effort, or to make the model equations easier to understand, or as loop indexes or counters. The Model Builder supports both integer and real (floating point) local variables which are declared in this section. A declaration consists of the appropriate key word, either INT or REAL, followed by space, and followed by a list of variable names separated by commas.

4.5 Equations Section

This section is the fundamental part for every model. Each model equation is described in this section. However, the type of each equation (equality, inequality, or objective) is specified elsewhere, either in the Max/Minimize section or in the Bounds section. Here all equations look alike. Each equation consists of a left hand side (specifying the name, or range of names defined by this statement), followed by an equal sign, followed by an arithmetic expression.

The left hand sides of equations have two formats: simple and range. The simple format has a left hand side consisting of just an equation name. If the name is an array function name then it must be followed by a subscript. The range format has a left hand side consisting of a range specification followed by an array function name immediately followed by a variable subscript. This subscript must be a local integer variable and appears inside of paired parentheses. The range is specified by a FOR statement with the form: FOR index FROM start-value TO stop-value where 'index' is the local integer variable used as the function array subscript, 'start-value' is a symbolic or numeric constant specifying the first subscript value of the range of subscripts being specified, and 'stop-value' is the last subscript of the range.

Following the left hand side is an equal sign followed by the right hand side, which provides the algebraic definition for the equations. The range form of the left hand side specifies that this statement is the function definition for all of the functions in the specified range. The right hand side must be either an arithmetic expression or an array expression. An arithmetic expression can involve variable names, previously defined equation names, FORTRAN 77 generic functions, and symbolic constants - all appropriately combined with arithmetic operators and paired parentheses to group subexpressions. Array expressions have the following format: FOR index FROM start TO stop array-op arithmetic-expression where the 'array-op' is either SUM or PRODUCT.

The array operators, SUM and PRODUCT, cause the equation value to be initialized to zero and one respectively. Then 'arithmetic-expression' is evaluated, for each value of the iteration index in turn, and this resulting value is either added to or multiplies the current value of the function.

The arithmetic operators are +, -, *, /, and either ^ or ** representing addition, subtraction, multiplication, division and exponentiation respectively. Paired parentheses can include [], {}, and (). Constants are either previously defined symbolic constants or numeric constants (e.g. 123.456D3) and, except for exponents and subscripts, are treated as FORTRAN real values. The FORTRAN 77 generic functions are ABS, SQRT, EXP, LOG, LOG10, SIN, COS, TAN, ASIN, ACOS, ATAN, SINH, COSH, and TANH. Currently the system does not support user-defined functions but such support is also planned for the next version.

4.6 Maximize or Minimize Section

The system will automatically start each new model with a "MAXIMIZE:" section. To maximize an objective function then that function's name should appear in the first statement in this section. To minimize a function the section header need only to be replaced with the header "MINIMIZE:".

4.7 Bounds Section

Initial versions of both the Bounds and Options sections are automatically constructed when the Bounds and Options command is selected from the Main Menu. The system scans the current model and identifies the variables and equations and allocates one statement in the Bounds section for each. It is in this section that lower and upper bounds, and initial values are provided.

The system initially assigns the key word NONE as the appropriate upper and lower bound for all variables and equations. If possible meaningful bounds should be provided for all variables and constraint equations. If a variable must always be positive 0 should be inserted as its lower bound. Similarly, one should provide the best possible estimates of initial values for variables. Good estimates can substantially improve overall performance.

Equality equations are handled by specifying the same lower and upper bound for them. The objective function is the only one for which all bounds are ignored. Some intermediate quantities used within other equations may also be left without bounds.

4.8 Options Section

The GRG2 optimizer itself contains a fair number of options. These options enable the user to control the different print levels that are available, the limits on a variety of iteration processes, numerical tolerances used to determine if constraints are adequately satisfied and if various processes have converged, and to select among alternative methods that can be used to perform a variety of tasks. Fortunately, all of these options have default values assigned to them; values which have been found to work well in most cases.

However, since a specific problem may not fall into the "most cases" category then GRG2 may not solve it satisfactorily unless some of these default values are overridden. It is very easy to change the value of any of the GRG2 parameters simply by typing in its new value. In "overtype" mode, the system will automatically erase the entire existing entry when the first character is typed. This makes it particularly easy to set simple values such as 0 or 1.

5. FORTRAN OUTPUT

Recall that GRG2 is a FORTRAN based optimization system which requires that all equations be defined in a FORTRAN subroutine called GCOMP. In addition, all data values and parameter changes must be input either through a data file or passed through a complex calling statement, usually in a user provided FORTRAN Main program.

The current version of the GRG Model Builder creates the complete interface to GRG2 from the user defined model. It creates either a FORTRAN Main program and a FORTRAN GCOMP subroutine or a GRG2 data file and a FORTRAN GCOMP subroutine, whichever option is selected from the Compile menu. In the first case, both the FORTRAN Main and GCOMP routines will be in a file with a .FOR extension and with the same name as the model file.

When either Compile menu option, to generate an interface to GRG2, is selected, the Model Builder will always create a FORTRAN GCOMP subroutine. For the BOX model, it will be stored in a file called BOX.FOR. If the GRG2 data file option is selected, then only the GCOMP subroutine is contained in the BOX.FOR file. If the FORTRAN Main program option is selected, then this Main program is also contained in the BOX.FOR file. The resulting GCOMP routine for the Box model, for either case, is shown on the following page.

```
      SUBROUTINE GCOMP(F,X)
C     This is a model for an electronic components box.
      DOUBLE PRECISION F(5)
      DOUBLE PRECISION X(3)
      F(1)=2.0*5.0000000D-2.0*(X(1)*X(3)+X(1)*X(2))+2.0*1.000000
     >0D-001*X(3)*X(2)
      F(4)=2.0*(X(2)*X(1)+X(2)*X(3)+X(1)*X(3))
      F(2)=X(1)*X(3)
      F(5)=X(2)*X(1)*X(3)
      F(3)=X(2)/X(3)
      RETURN
      END
```

If the data file interface to GRG2 is selected, then the GRG2 Builder creates the GRG2 data file as well. In any case, the user does not need to know any of these GRG2 requirements.

6. CONCLUSIONS

The GRG Model Builder is our current attempt to provide easy access to the nonlinear optimization software system, GRG2. Since the modeling language statements have been designed to be as self explanatory as possible, the system minimizes the amount of optimization knowledge required by the user. It solves small to medium linear and/or nonlinear models and these models can include discrete values for such quantities as time or frequency. The required partitioning of model information into components is our approach to modularizing the model building process and, hopefully, simplifying model revision and maintenance.

Future plans include the development of an integrated model compiler/linker which would eliminate the difference between the mathematical and computer versions of the model as well as eliminating the need for a FORTRAN compiler. Other planned enhancements to the system include extending the language to incorporate two dimensional arrays and named sets of subscripts.

REFERENCES

Bisschop, J. and A. Meeraus (1982), "On the Development of a General Algebraic Modeling System in a Strategic Planning Environment," *Mathematical Programming Study 20* (Oct.), 1-29.

Brooke, A., A. Drud and A. Meeraus (1985), "High Level Modeling Systems and Nonlinear Programming," In *Numerical Optimization 1984*, P. T. Boggs, R. H. Byrd and R. B. Schnabel, Eds. SIAM, Philadelphia, Penn. pp. 178-198

Cunningham, K. and L. Schrage (1987), *The LINGO Modeling Language*, Technical Report, The University of Chicago, Chicago, Ill., Nov.

Dolk, D. R. (1986), "A Generalized Model Management System for Mathematical Programming," *ACM Trans. on Math. Software* 12, 2 (June), 92-126.

Fourer, R. (1983), "Modeling Languages Versus Matrix Generators for Linear Programming," *ACM Trans. on Math. Software* 9, 2 (June),143-183.

Fourer, R., D. M. Gay and B. W. Kernighan (1987), "AMPL: A Mathematical Programming Language," Computing Science Technical Report No. 133, AT&T Bell Labs, Murray Hill, N.J., Jan.

Geoffrion, A. M. (1987), "An Introduction to Structured Modeling," *Management Science* 33, 5 (May),547-588.

Lasdon, L. S. and A. D. Waren (1978), "Generalized Reduced Gradient Software for Linearly and Nonlinearly Constrained Problems," In *Design and Implementation of Optimization Software*, H. J. Greenberg, Ed. Sijthoff and Noordhoff, pp. 363-397.

Liebman, J., L. Lasdon, L. Schrage and A. Waren (1986), *Modeling and Optimization with GINO*, The Scientific Press, Palo Alto, Calif.

Meeraus, A. (1983), "An Algebraic Approach to Modeling," *J. of Economic Dynamics & Control* 5, 1 (Feb.), 81-108.

Schittkowski, K. (1985), "EMP: An Expert System for Mathematical Programming," *COAL Newsletter* 13 (Dec.), 19-21.

Schrage, L. (1986), *Linear, integer and quadratic programming with LINDO (Third edition)*, The Scientific Press, Palo Alto, Calif.

Welch, J. S. (1987), "PAM - A Practitioner's Approach to Modeling," *Management Science* 33, 5 (May), 610-625.

ON THE USE OF ADVANCED ARCHITECTURE COMPUTERS VIA HIGH-LEVEL MODELLING LANGUAGES

STAVROS ZENIOS, SOREN NIELSEN and MUSTAFA PINAR

Decision Sciences Department, The Wharton School
University of Pennsylvania, Philadelphia, PA 19104.

ABSTRACT

Advanced architecture computers are becoming increasingly attractive tools for large scale mathematical modeling. While such systems provide significant computing power, quite often they lack the user friendly operating environment necessary in the development and modification of large models. A two-machine configuration is proposed: a front-end for user interaction and a back-end number-cruncher for the compute intensive optimization. Such a link is developed here with the aid of a high level modeling language. We use the General Algebraic Modeling System (GAMS) to build links to a Floating Point Systems M64/60 minisupercomputer.

1. INTRODUCTION

This paper brings together two recent developments that each — in its own right— is having a significant impact on large scale modeling: advanced architecture computers (abbreviated: AAC) and high-level modeling languages (abbreviated: ML). The objective is to use ML to build a link between the user and an advanced architecture attached processor. In the arrangement we propose and implement in this study a user builds and modifies his model in the environment of the modeling language, using a familiar operating system such as VMS or Unix. The time consuming computations are executed on the attached high-performance computer. Interaction with the attached system is under the control of the ML and is transparent to the user. This configuration provides dual advantages for the implementation and solution of large scale systems. First, the high-level modeling language is endowed with the computing power that is characteristic of advanced architecture computers. Second, the AAC is made easily accessible to the modeler, bypassing the lack of interactive operating systems and the need to switch constantly between the front-end and the attached processor.

The need for a two-machine configuration when entering the realm of AAC has been emphasized elsewhere, see for example Gallo and Schatz [1988]. It is typified in the operating system design of computers like the CRAY X-MP, and the Floating Point Systems (FPS) M64 series. The CRAY Operating System (COS) is designed as a batch operating system. Users interact with the CRAY through a front-end by submitting batch jobs. The Floating Point Systems M64 series are attached array processors. Executable images of programs and the associated data sets are staged for execution through a front-end. Even compilation of a program can be executed on the front-end with cross-compilers. Both systems lack time-sharing capabilities. Multiple jobs are executed in a *rolled in/rolled out* mode: each job gets a fixed slot of time during which it uses all the resources available. If execution is not completed in this interval, it is rolled out to wait in queue for another time slot. More recently CRAY developed the Unix based operating system Unicos. Similar interactive operating systems are being developed for several commercially available parallel systems. However, a majority of AAC installations are set-up as batch environments.

While the batch environment of an AAC is quite useful for time consuming jobs, it is awkward from the users' point. The techniques we propose here aim at making the use of AAC easily accessible to users.

We implement a link between an attached array processor and a front-end through a high level modeling language. We use GAMS of Bisschop and Meeraus [1982] to control the execution of optimization problems arising from large scale mathematical models on an FPS M64/60. The ability of the ML to control several optimizers — like MINOS of Murtagh and Saunders [1983], ZOOM/XMP of Singal et al.[1989], or GENOS of Mulvey and Zenios [1987] — from within a common algebraic framework is now extended to the control of the attached array processor. The loosely coupled structure of GAMS — which functions as an integral system with the use of operating system procedures and external files — allows us to build this link with minimal changes to the overall ML system. We show through GAMS models borrowed from a wide spectrum of applications that our link maintains the transportability of GAMS models while resulting in significant gains in computational performance.

The manuscript is organized as follows. Section 2 is a technical description of the GAMS-FPS system. In Section 3 we illustrate the use of the integrated system with problems from financial modeling, chemical engineering, network optimization, matrix balancing, mathematical programming decompositions and several standard models from the GAMS library. Section 4 provides some conclusions.

2. THE GAMS-FPS MODELLING SYSTEM

The GAMS-FPS link provides modelers who wish to solve large-scale models with easy access to a minisupercomputer, the FPS M64/60, through an advanced modelling language, GAMS of Bisschop and Meeraus [1987]. This is done in such a way that the modeller works in a user-friendly environment using the operating system, editors, file management facilities etc. of the front end (in this case a DEC VAX 8700) to manipulate his models expressed in GAMS, yet have the AAC perform the time consuming computations involved in solving them. Modellers need not know anything about operating the AAC; GAMS provides a transparent interface. Modellers still have the choice of solving smaller models directly on the front-end to avoid waiting for a time slice on the attached processor. Potentially, even the choice of which computer to use for solving a given problem can be left to the modelling system, which would make its decision based on current usage statistics, problem size and so on.

2.1 The GAMS Modelling System

The components of the GAMS modelling system are the compiler and the solvers. The compiler is the main program of the system. It compiles the model written in the GAMS language, performs syntactic and semantic checks, generates reports aiding model documentation, and interfaces with the solvers. The solvers, which are typically FORTRAN implementations of mathematical programming algorithms, are executed through operating system procedure files by request of the compiler to perform the optimization of models.

The feature of GAMS which is of practical interest to us in this section is the way in which the individual components are linked together. GAMS is a loosely coupled system. After the compiler has compiled and analyzed a model, it generates a set of files containing a representation of the problem. The compiler then terminates, after having left a message for the operating system to start the solver chosen as suitable for solving the problem. The message left for the operating system requests that it execute an operating system procedure file. That file contains instructions to set up an environment suitable for the solver, and then to execute it. After execution of the solver, the compiler is restarted to process the results and to complete execution of the model.

The small set of files communicated from the compiler to a solver and vice versa constitutes an interface that makes GAMS an open system. The files represent a machine-independent snapshot of the solution process. This makes it possible to interrupt the solution process at this point, transfer the files representing the problem to a different computing environment, solve the model in the new environment, and transfer the solution back to the originating system.

2.2 The FPS M64/60 Array Processor

The FPS M64/60 is an attached array processor. While it is designed to process large arrays or vectors it does not support vector instructions. The high performance of the machine is achieved with innovations in the architecture design and with the aid of multioperation instructions and software pipelining for the execution of concurrent microoperations.

The Central Processing Unit (CPU) is designed with multiple functional units: two for floating point operations — a multiplier and an adder —, two memory access units — one for main and one for auxiliary memory —, a unit for address computation, four data registers, an address calculation unit and a conditional branch unit. A total of 10 distinct operations can therefore be initiated at every clock cycle. The floating point units operate on 64-bit words. The instruction word contains separate subinstruction parcels for each of the 10 functional units. It is thus possible to initiate a new operation for each unit during one cycle. Vector operations are executed using software pipelining. The CPU will operate in three modes depending on the characteristics of the problem. *Sequential programming* when operations follow one another without overlap, *overlap programming* when local parallelism is exploited by concurrent execution of individual arithmetic and memory operations and *pipelined programming* for vector computations.

The FPS M64/60 used in this study was accessed through a DEC VAX 8700. using the *SJE* (System Job Executive) mode of operation. The front-end process requests access to the AP, and, once this is granted, has exclusive use of it for the duration of the time-slice.

2.3 The GAMS-FPS link

Only a small fraction of the time spent in the GAMS compiler is used on floating point arithmetic, and the operations in the program are usually inhomogeneous. It is therefore expected that the gains from executing this program on the FPS would be small. Furthermore, users typically call the main program many more times than the solvers. In an environment with a heavily used attached processor without time-sharing facilities, such usage would be prohibitive for turn-around times. Finally, GAMS was written in Pascal and there is currently no Pascal compiler available for the FPS. On the other hand, the pipelined architecture of the FPS is well suited for the solvers, which are written in FORTRAN. It was therefore decided to execute the GAMS compiler on the front-end and the solvers on the AP. This design choice is not only dictated by the considerations mentioned above. It was also motivated by the need to carry out the modeling process in a user-friendly time sharing environment and leave out the time consuming computation for the AP.

The SJE mode of operation is well suited to the GAMS environment. In the GAMS-FPS link, operating system procedure files contain all the necessary commands needed to request use of the AP, copy data files, and to execute the solver. The modeller executes this version of GAMS exactly as he would the usual front-end version, and may in fact be totally oblivious to the fact that solving the models is taking place on the AP.

3. USE OF THE INTEGRATED SYSTEMS

The GAMS-FPS system was used to solve large scale optimization problems from several areas of application. We try to give a representative sample of models where a language like GAMS is typically used and to illustrate how the modeling approach we introduce here can improve the computational performance of the language by a significant factor. Appendix A provides details on the test problems.

The solvers were compiled for FPS execution with different levels of optimization. At level $OPT=3$ the software is optimized for vector and pipeline computing. In some instances we use $OPT=1$ to highlight the efficiency of FPS. All solvers were compiled at level $OPT=3$ in the results reported in subsequent tables unless otherwise stated. Results are stated in CPU seconds.

Financial Modeling. The use of optimization models for planning has gained widespread acceptance in the finance community over the last few years. They are used to build dedicated bond portfolios to finance specific projects or streams of liabilities, to select optimal stock portfolios to meet some desired specifications, management of cash flows for multinational transactions, in bond swapping, arbitrage and so on.

High-performance computers can be used in a wide variety of financial models to provide fast and accurate solutions to large problem instances. We solved a portfolio dedication model PORTFOL — built by two of us — using the GAMS-FPS link. The model specifies a portfolio of investment to meet a projected schedule of future liabilities over a long time horizon. The results obtained with a planning horizon of 15 and 20 periods are presented in Table 1.

Network Optimization. Optimization problems with network constraints appear in a

Problem	VAX time	FPS time
PORTFOL15	224.8	44.8
PORTFOL20	658.9	110.1

Table 1: Portfolio Dedication Models solved with MINOS

Problem	GAMS	VAX time	FPS time
CHINA	192.2	3.0	1.4
SAM10	2.8	1.4	0.5
SAMBO	39.5	304.2	120.3
SAMKE	8.2	3.0	1.2
MSM	715.0	2.4	0.5
PHOSDIS	1140.7	5.6	16.5

Table 2: Solving Network Models with GENOS

wide variety of applications: transportation, power scheduling, personnel planning, matrix balancing, cash flow management and others. Dembo et al. [1986] provide an update on the status of network optimization and several applications. Network solvers have been incorporated in GAMS, Zenios [1987], to form the GAMS/GENOS system. This system is part of the GAMS-FPS link and was used to solve linear problems drawn from transportation and nonlinear models developed for matrix balancing. Results are summarized in Table 2.

The SAM problems are matrix balancing problems; Zenios et al. [1988]. CHINA is a transportation study for China. MSM estimates the transport cost of different types of fertilizer in Morocco. PHOSDIS is a transportation model for phosphate fertilizer distribution. All transportation models are linear.

We used also the matrix balancing systems SAMBAL and MATBAL to solve test problems derived from development planning. The results are summarized in Tables 3 and 4. The subscripts q and e at the name of the problems indicate quadratic and entropy objective functions respectively.

Problem	GAMS time	VAX time	FPS OPT=1 time	FPS time
SAMBOq	5.3	22.4	13.8	7.4
SAMBOe	5.4	19.1	10.5	5.8
SAMKEq	1.8	1.6	0.9	0.5
SAMKEe	1.7	1.4	0.9	0.5
SAMMOe	41.4	10.6	5.2	3.0

Table 3: Solving Matrix Balancing with SAMBAL

Problem	GAMS time	VAX time	FPS time
IO10e	2.2	0.5	0.2
IOBOq	5.9	22.7	9.4
IOBOe	5.6	33.7	7.1

Table 4: Solving Matrix Balancing with MATBAL

Problem	VAX	FPS
SAMTUSD	6.10	3.23
HEAT4	703.7	123.1

Table 5: Solution of Decomposition Algorithms

Large Scale Decompositions. The integration of several optimizers through GAMS offers some interesting possibilities for the development and evaluation of algorithms. One may use the data management features of the language and control the execution of iterative decomposition algorithms where network problems and general linear or nonlinear programs are solved interchangeably. One would prototype algorithms within GAMS before proceeding with software implementations. This arrangement has been shown, Paules and Floudas [1989], to be a suitable vehicle for the solution of mixed integer nonlinear programs and has been used by Zenios [1987] for the development of decomposition algorithms for network optimization.

Within the GAMS-FPS system the performance of decomposition algorithms can be significantly improved. The data management and problem decomposition is carried out by GAMS on the front-end and subproblems are solved on the FPS. Results are summarized in Table 5.

SAMTUSD is a very small matrix balancing problem. It is set up as a nonlinear network program and it is in turn solved using simplicial decomposition, Mulvey et al. [1985]. HEAT4 is a mixed-integer nonlinear program for a heat integrated distillation sequence. It is solved using generalized Bender's decomposition.

Chemical Engineering Design. The application of mathematical programming methods to chemical engineering is a very active area of research. The chemical engineering models investigated in this paper are solved by using decomposition algorithms. The decomposition is formulated in GAMS, using the features of GAMS to manipulate data and iterate between nonlinear subproblems and mixed integer master problems.

The COMPLEX-D problem finds an interconnection pattern for mixing and merging among a number of separation columns. FULL62 models the synthesis of separation sequences. HEAT4 provides the optimal heat integrated distillation sequence for a 4 component separation. Only the data from the first decomposition iteration are included. Results are summarized in Table 6.

Other Applications. We finally tested a number of models from the GAMS library. INDUS is a linear programming model used by the government of Pakistan to analyze investment design and water policy issues. TURKEY is a sector model used to analyze Turkish agriculture. MEXSD is a dynamic model used in a study of the Mexican steel sector. WESTMIP is a small four sector mixed integer programming model used to illustrate the importance of economies of scale in a dynamic context. The CUBE is a toy combinatorial model. Finally, the network models SAMBO and PHOSDIS are solved again, but this time

Problem	VAX time	FPS time
COMPLEX-D	151.4	77.1
FULL62	9.2	4.9
HEAT4	703.7	123.1

Table 6: Models from Chemical Engineering Design

Problem	VAX time	FPS time
INDUS	39.9	17.2
TURKEY	118.5	43.6
MEXSD	3085.3	2258.6
WESTMIP	3781.6	1903.2
CUBE	1944.3	543.61
SAMBO	1063.0	278.5
PHOSDIS	393.9	84.0

Table 7: Models from the GAMS Library (using MINOS 5 or ZOOM)

as general nonlinear programming models using MINOS 5 instead of a network solver. Results are presented in Table 7.

4. CONCLUSION

In this report we have outlined an integrated modeling and computing environment for the solution of large optimization models. Advanced architecture computers like the FPS M64/60 provide significant computing power needed in several areas of application of optimization. At the same time developments in modeling languages facilitate the manipulation of very large models. By bringing together these two techniques we are able to solve efficiently and with ease several difficult classes of problems.

Acknowledgements: We would like to acknowledge the support of A. Meeraus and A. Brooke during our work on this project. C. Floudas and G. Paules provided test problems.

A TEST PROBLEM CHARACTERISTICS

Problem	Type	Equations	Variables	Discrete Variables
HEAT4				
— Subproblem	NLP	247	191	
— Master problem	MIP	284	274	80
COMPLEX-D	NLP	937	1433	
FULL62				
— Subproblem 1	NLP	270	567	
— Subproblem 2	NLP	270	251	
— Master problem	MIP	58	48	3
INDUS	NLP	275	404	
TURKEY	NLP	415	1159	
MEXSD	MIP	820	1808	112
WESTMIP	MIP	234	275	20
CUBE	MIP	100	77	26
PORTFOL15	LP	324	6792	
PORTFOL20	LP	329	17242	

Table 8: General Mathematical Programs

Problem	Type	Nodes	Arcs
CHINA	LP	816	2408
SAM10, IO10e		25	89
SAMKE, SAMKEq, SAMKEe	NLP	25	203
SAMBOq, SAMBOe, IOBOq, IOBOe	NLP	62	659
MSM	LP	66	2589
SAMMOe	NLP	232	1897
SAMTUSD	NLP	17	28
PHOSDIS	LP	912	9840

Table 9: Network problems.

Research partially supported by NSF grant ECS–8718971, CCR–8811135 and AFOSR grant 89–0145, and an award from the Wharton School University of Pennsylvania and Floating Point Systems.

REFERENCES

J. Bisschop and A. Meeraus. On the development of a general algebraic modeling system in a strategic planning environment. *Mathematical Programming Study*, 20:1–29, 1982.

R.S. Dembo, J.M. Mulvey, and S.A. Zenios. *Large Scale Nonlinear Network Models and their Application.* Report EES–86–18, Civil Engineering and Operations Research, Princeton University, 1986.

R. Fourer. Modeling languages versus matrix generators for linear programming. *ACM Transactions on Mathematical Software*, 9(2):143–183, June 1983.

K. Gallo and W. Schatz. The supercomputer breaks through. *Datamation*, 50–64, May 1988.

R. Hockney and C. Jeeshope. *Parallel Computers.* Adam Hilger Ltd., Bristol, England, 1981.

R. R. Meyer and S. A. Zenios, editors. *Parallel Optimization on Novel Computer Architectures. Annals of Operations Research*, A.C. Baltzer Scientific Publishing Co., Switzerland, Vol. 14, 1988.

J. M. Mulvey. *Nonlinear Network Models in Finance.* Advances in Mathematical Programming and Financial Planning, Vol. 1, pages 253-271.

J. M. Mulvey, S. A. Zenios, and D. P. Ahlfeld. *Simplicial Decomposition for Convex Generalized Networks.* Report EES-85-8, Civil Engineering Department, Princeton University, 1985.

J.M. Mulvey and S.A. Zenios. *GENOS 1.0: A Generalized Network Optimization System. User's Guide.* Report 87–12–03, Decision Sciences Department, the Wharton School, University of Pennsylvania, Philadelphia, PA 19104, 1987.

B. A. Murtagh and M. A. Saunders. *MINOS User's Guide.* Report SOL 77-9, Department of Operations Research, Stanford University, California, 1977.

G.E. Paules and C.A. Floudas. APROS: A discrete-continous optimizer for the automatic solution of mixed-integer nonlinear/linear programming problems. *Operations Research*, 1989 (to appear).

J. Singal, R. E. Marsten, and T.Morin. Fixed order branch-and-bound methods for mixed-integer programming: the ZOOM system. *ORSA Journal on Computing*, 1(1), 1989 (to appear).

S. A. Zenios. *Incorporating Network Optimization Capabilities into a High-Level Programming Language*. Decision Sciences Working Paper 87–08–04, The Wharton School, University of Pennsylvania, Philadelphia, 1987.

S. A. Zenios, A. Drud, and J. M. Mulvey. Balancing large social accounting matrices with nonlinear network programming. *Networks*, 1988 (to appear).

S. A. Zenios and J. M. Mulvey. Vectorization and multitasking of nonlinear network programming algorithms. *Mathematical Programming Study*, 1989 (to appear).

S.A. Zenios. Parallel Numerical Optimization: Current Status and an Annotated Bibliography. *ORSA Journal on Computing*, 1(1), 1989 (to appear).

IX.

TELECOMMUNICATIONS

EVALUATION AND DESIGN OF A VOICE TELECOMMUNICATIONS NETWORK

ANTHONY J. PERTICONE[†], JAMES P. JARVIS[‡], DOUGLAS R. SHIER[§]

ABSTRACT

Large, geographically dispersed companies often build voice telecommunications networks by leasing dedicated telephone lines. Procedures are developed here for determining the number and placement of such lines and the location of communications switches (exchanges). The procedures incorporate methods for approximating network congestion and minimizing costs associated with equipment purchase and lease. An application using data from a major textile company is presented.

1. INTRODUCTION

The practice of leasing dedicated telephone lines (tie lines) is common among companies with high telephone traffic between geographically separated plant locations. This paper examines various aspects associated with the design and analysis of such a voice telecommunications network. A procedure to approximate call congestion between sites and a network algorithm to generate low cost configurations are developed. Together, these models can be used to identify a set of good potential configurations, which can be further evaluated by decision makers. The approach has been applied to the telecommunications network of a major textile company and has produced a number of alternative configurations with improved operational characteristics. The two major contributions of this paper are in developing methods (1) to evaluate the grade of service for a given network configuration, and (2) to generate low cost configurations.

An important measure associated with any such communications system is its *grade of service*: namely, the probability that an attempted call cannot be completed over existing lines. Given telephone traffic data for a company, together with the costs associated with leasing tie lines and operating exchanges, our objective is to obtain network configurations (including the corresponding number of lines leased per link) that achieve near-minimum cost for a desired grade of service. Practical considerations for the situation being studied imposed two topological constraints on this general network problem (although costs could be reduced further without these

---

[†] AT&T Bell Laboratories, Holmdel, NJ 07733

[‡] Dept. of Mathematical Sciences, Clemson University, Clemson, SC 29634

[§] Dept. of Mathematics, College of William and Mary, Williamsburg, VA 23185

Copyright 1989 by Elsevier Science Publishing Co., Inc.
Impacts of Recent Computer Advances on Operations Research
Ramesh Sharda, Bruce L. Golden, Edward Wasil, Osman Balci, William Stewart, Editors

restrictions [Frank and Chou 1972]). First, only existing plant sites could be considered for the exchanges; second, only tree networks were considered.

2. BACKGROUND AND TERMINOLOGY

A communications network consists of various network *sites*, joined by *links*. The link (i,j) between site i and site j is composed of an integral number n_{ij} of telephone *lines*. A network site where a call can be switched from a line of one link to a line of another link is called an *exchange*. Two network sites are said to be *adjacent* if they are joined by a link. A given set of exchanges and links between sites define a network *configuration*. We restrict our attention to tree configurations, for which there is a unique path joining any two sites in the network.

The traffic generated between site i and site j is characterized by its *calling rate* λ_{ij} and its *service rate* μ_{ij}. The quantity $1/\mu_{ij}$ represents the average duration of a call and is referred to as the *mean service time* of a call. The quantity $a_{ij} = \lambda_{ij}/\mu_{ij}$, expressed in dimensionless units (*erlangs*), is termed the *offered load* between site i and site j. The *offered load to a link* is then the sum of all the offered loads between sites whose calls must use that link.

A line in the network is said to be *busy* if it is currently occupied by a call; otherwise it is *free*. Likewise, a link is said to be busy when all the lines in the link are busy. A call between two sites can be completed only if at least one line on each of the links in the path connecting the two sites is free. If any of the links are busy, the call is *blocked*. The proportion of time that a link is busy is referred to as the *blocking level* for the link. The *grade of service* associated with a network configuration is the probability that a randomly placed call in the network is blocked.

The most commonly used approach to compute the blocking on a link involves the standard Erlang Loss formula:

$$B(n,a) = (a^n/n!) / \sum_{k=0}^{n} (a^k/k!)$$

where B(n, a) denotes the probability of a call being blocked when calls arrive to a link consisting of n lines and the offered load is a. Theoretically, this formula is applicable only to links which service one type of call. Since a typical communications link services calls between several sites, the Erlang Loss formula does not apply. Independently, Whitt (1985), Kelly (1985), and Perticone (1986) have developed an approximation procedure to estimate the blocking on each link in a tree network. This procedure (the "reduced load approximation") is discussed further below.

The problem of determining a minimum cost configuration for a tree communications network is known to be a difficult one. In fact, a restricted version of this problem is known to be NP-complete, meaning that a heuristic procedure is therefore likely to be the only practical approach [Johnson et al. 1978]. Such a heuristic is presented in Section 4.

3. THE REDUCED LOAD APPROXIMATION

The blocking experienced on a particular link can be approximated by summing all the traffic intending to use this link (the offered load to the link) and using this value in the Erlang Loss formula. The resulting value is known to be an upper bound on the actual blocking experienced on that link [Whitt 1985]. In cases where very little blocking is present on the links, this approach is fairly reasonable. However, when blocking is at a practical level, such an approximation substantially overestimates the actual blocking.

One source of this discrepancy is the presence of blocking which prevents calls from being completed between non-adjacent sites in the network. Hence, we define a *reduced load*, $â_{ij}$, to be the effective load offered to link (i,j). In what follows, it is necessary to assume that blockings on the links are mutually independent. Define S_{ij} to be the set of all pairs of sites whose calls are routed over link (i,j), and define L_{km} to be the set of all links on the unique path joining sites k and m. Then the general form of the reduced load approximation for link (i,j) becomes

$$â_{ij} = a_{ij} + \sum_{\substack{(k,m) \in S_{ij} \\ (k,m) \neq (i,j)}} a_{km} \prod_{\substack{(p,q) \in L_{km} \\ (p,q) \neq (i,j)}} [1 - B(n_{pq}, â_{pq})],$$

where $B(n_{pq}, â_{pq})$ is obtained from the Erlang Loss formula. The product terms appearing in this formula incorporate the assumption of independent blocking along links.

Figure 1 illustrates the reduced load calculations. The reduced load estimate for link (1,2) is $â_{12} = a_{12} + a_{13}[1-B(n_{23}, â_{23})] + a_{14}[1-B(n_{23}, â_{23})][1-B(n_{34}, â_{34})]$, and the reduced load estimate for link (2,3) is $â_{23} = a_{23} + a_{13}[1-B(n_{12}, â_{12})] + a_{24}[1-B(n_{34}, â_{34})] + a_{14}[1-B(n_{12}, â_{12})][1-B(n_{34}, â_{34})]$.

The set of simultaneous nonlinear equations for the reduced loads can be most easily solved using an iterative technique. That is, the reduced loads are initialized to appropriate values, the blockings are calculated using the Erlang Loss formula, and the new reduced loads are then calculated as above. The process is repeated until the reduced loads (and thus the blocking values) on these links converge to within a specified tolerance. A variation on this approach has also been independently studied by Whitt (1985) and Kelly (1985).

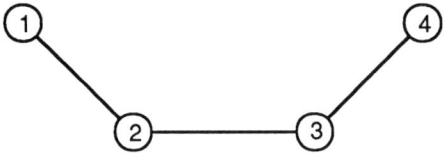

Figure 1. Network illustrating calculation of reduced loads.

Using the reduced load estimates of blockings between all pairs of sites, the grade of service for a network can be easily calculated. Namely, let p_{ij} denote the fraction of all calls in the network placed between sites i and j, and let L_{ij} be the set of links on the path joining sites i and j. Then the overall grade of service for the network is computed as

$$\begin{aligned} \text{Grade of Service} &= 1 - \sum_{i,j} p_{ij} \left[1 - \Pr(\text{i-j path blocked}) \right] \\ &\approx 1 - \sum_{i,j} p_{ij} \prod_{k \in L_{ij}} \left[1 - \Pr(\text{link k blocked}) \right] \end{aligned}$$

That is, the grade of service is one minus the sum, over all pairs of sites i and j, of the product of the fraction of calls between i and j and the probability that the route between i and j is available. It is in computing this latter probability that the independence assumption is again used. The blocking values produced by the reduced load approximation procedure compare favorably with the exact values determined by small scale models, especially for blockings on links [Perticone 1986].

4. GENERATION OF LOW COST NETWORK CONFIGURATIONS

In addition to the grade of service, another major factor in evaluating a voice communications network is its cost. The "network improvement algorithm" is a heuristic procedure that systematically alters the network configuration in order to reduce the overall cost without greatly changing its grade of service. In view of the obvious tradeoff between network cost and grade of service, the network improvement algorithm attempts to keep the grade of service relatively constant by setting a target level of blocking p applicable to every link. Keeping the blocking level of links near this target level tends to keep the grade of service (the average blocking experienced by any call) relatively constant.

Certain terminology is useful in describing the network improvement algorithm. A network consists of *exchanges* and *outlying* (non-exchange) sites. The *backbone configuration* of a network is the set of links used to connect the exchanges. An outlying network site is said to be *assigned* to a particular exchange if a link exists between the site and the exchange. In general, the set of sites assigned to exchange j is denoted by *cluster(j)*, with j also being an element of this set. (See Figure 2.)

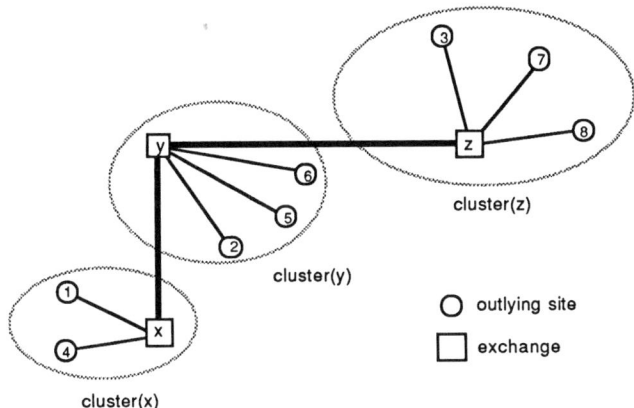

Figure 2. Terminology for the network improvement algorithm.

Let T_i represent the total traffic to and from site i, and let $T_{i,cl(k)}$ represent all traffic offered between site i and the sites of cluster(k). C_{ij} will denote the cost of leasing a line between sites i and j, and $N_p(a)$ will denote the number of lines required to achieve a blocking level of p given offered load a as per the Erlang Loss formula. The *assignment cost*, associated with assigning a site to a particular exchange, can be thought of as being composed of two elements: the *direct cost* and the *indirect cost*. The direct cost is the cost of the link connecting the site to its assigned exchange. The indirect cost is the cost of the additional number of lines needed in the backbone configuration to support this site's traffic to other clusters. Site i is said to be *locally balanced* if, based on the current assignment of sites to exchanges, it is assigned to the exchange producing the minimum assignment cost; otherwise, site i is *locally imbalanced*.

The inputs to the network improvement algorithm are the network sites, a set of candidate exchange locations, the traffic generated between each pair of sites, and the target blocking level p. The algorithm begins by determining an initial backbone configuration and an initial assignment of sites to exchanges. A "switching phase" is then applied in an attempt to find the lowest cost assignment of sites to exchanges for the fixed backbone configuration. A "backbone improvement" phase is then applied in an attempt to route the traffic between the exchanges in a more cost effective manner. If the cost of the network is reduced, the switching phase is again applied to see if any further cost reduction is possible, again followed by the backbone improvement phase. This process continues until no further reduction in the cost of the network can be achieved.

4.1 Assignment of Sites to Exchanges

The switching phase itself consists of two steps: a "local improvement" step and a "break-away" step. The local improvement step examines all sites which are locally imbalanced. Independently, the assignment of each such site is switched from the current exchange to the exchange that causes the site to become locally balanced; the costs of these new configurations are then calculated. The assignment producing the lowest cost network is selected, and this configuration becomes the current configuration to be evaluated for locally imbalanced sites. (Note that this new assignment may force a previously balanced site now to become imbalanced, or vice versa.) This process is repeated until a network is reached in which all sites are locally balanced or a previously examined network is encountered. The configuration produced during this step with the lowest cost is then considered by the break-away step.

The objective of the break-away step is to permit escape from a local, but not global, optimum. In this step, a particular site is selected (whether locally imbalanced or not), its current assignment is (randomly) switched to another exchange, and the local improvement step is then reapplied. If a lower cost network is found, the same site is selected once again and its assignment switched; if not, a different site is selected. This process continues until each site has in turn been selected and the break-away step has failed to produce an improved network.

4.2 Determining the Linkage between Exchanges

The objective of the backbone improvement phase is to reduce the cost of the network by reconfiguring the backbone configuration (assumed fixed in the switching phase). The linkage between exchanges is influenced by both the traffic between associated sites and the distances between exchanges. Several heuristic procedures were devised to incorporate both these traffic and distance considerations. The most satisfactory one involved the calculation of a minimum spanning tree for the backbone network, where the edge weights for the minimum spanning tree are given by the cost of a line between exchanges divided by the number of lines required to support the traffic between the sites assigned to those exchanges. Specifically, if $T_{cl(i),cl(j)}$ denotes the traffic between sites in cluster(i) and sites in cluster(j), the weight assigned to a potential link between exchanges i and j is defined by

$$\text{weight}(i,j) = C_{ij} / N_p(T_{cl(i),cl(j)}) .$$

Using such link weights, a minimum spanning tree for the exchanges is determined and this yields a potentially new backbone configuration. Since the link weights are directly related to distance and inversely related to traffic, a minimum spanning tree tends to include links between exchanges which are either a short distance away or have sufficient traffic to justify such a link. Note that there is no guarantee that the network cost is reduced by implementing the new backbone configuration.

4.3 Operation of the Network Improvement Algorithm

In testing the performance of the network improvement algorithm, several methods were examined for constructing an initial configuration for the network (the initial backbone as well as the initial assignment of sites to exchanges). The number of iterations required by the algorithm to reach a low cost configuration appears to be influenced more by the initial backbone configuration than by the initial assignment of sites to the exchanges. However, a variety of different initialization schemes all produced the same (optimal) solutions. (In general, using a minimum spanning tree based on distance to determine the backbone configuration and assigning sites to the nearest exchange produced a reasonable initial configuration.)

It was found that performance of the algorithm was enhanced if the heuristic was altered to increase the number of sites characterized as locally imbalanced. This alternative approach defines the indirect cost as the cost of lines needed in the backbone configuration to support only the traffic involving that site rather than the actual change in cost associated with the slightly altered traffic patterns associated with switching a site between two exchanges. Using this alternative characterization of local imbalance, the network improvement algorithm was applied to a number of randomly generated examples as well as a subset of the actual system which was the object of this study.

5. AN EXAMPLE APPLICATION

The techniques described above were applied to the design of a voice telecommunications network for a major textile company. The company's facilities consist of 46 sites located primarily in the Southeast, but also including sites in Los Angeles, Chicago, Dallas, Atlanta, and New York. After consultation with company engineers, it was determined that the design should incorporate at most three exchanges at nine potential locations. Data from over 500,000 calls generated during a four-week period were analyzed to determine call rates and service times. The data used in the network design was restricted to those calls from five peak-traffic hours on weekdays (9–12 am and 2–4 pm, Monday–Friday). This period encompassed approximately 200,000 calls.

To develop some confidence in the model, the current network configuration was analyzed using the reduced load approximation to estimate blocking levels. These estimates were compared with estimates of blocking derived from the historical call data. The historical data indicated a grade of service of 3.38%; the model estimate was 3.28%. Figure 3 compares model and historical estimates for blocking on individual links. The close agreement between these estimates lead us to proceed with the analysis.

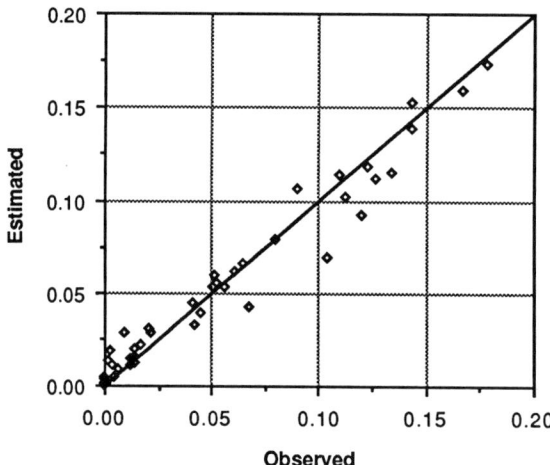

Figure 3. Comparison of model and historical blocking on links.

A number of alternative scenarios were evaluated. These included the current configuration as well as networks having from one to three exchanges and target grades of service from 1% to 7%. Examination of these results revealed that the alternative configurations were dominated by 1- or 2-exchange systems with the exchanges being located at two particular locations. The results are summarized in Figure 4. Note that the current configuration had an overall blocking level of 3.28% and a variable cost of almost $85,000 per month. (The variable cost includes line but not exchange costs.) This configuration is dominated by several others, including one with the same grade of service and a cost reduction of roughly $5000 per month (representing a 6% cost reduction).

One final consideration in network design is equity of service. That is, even though the grade of service is satisfactory, is this performance shared by individual links? Figure 5 compares the blocking estimates by link for the current and an alternative configuration (having the same grade of service but lower cost). It is evident from these data that system performance on a local level has been smoothed by the network design algorithm.

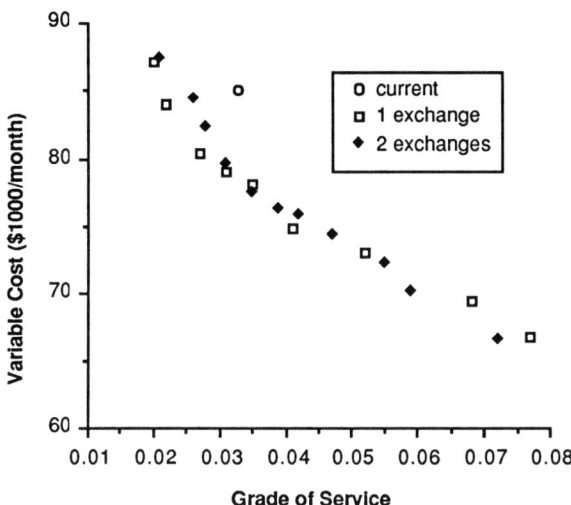

Figure 4. Evaluation of alternative versus current network configuration.

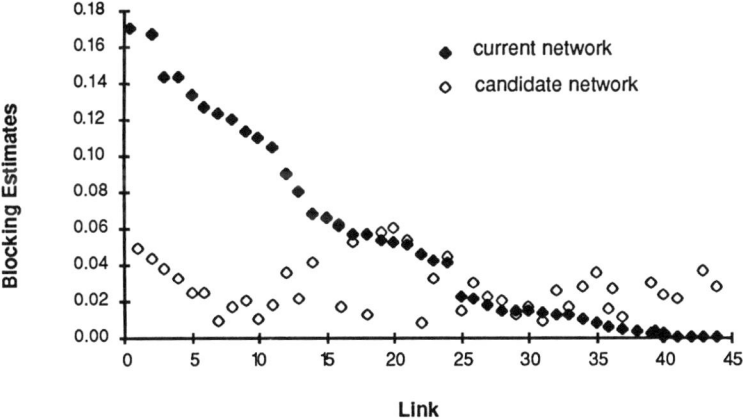

Figure 5. Comparison of blocking levels on individual network links.

6. CONCLUSIONS

This paper describes an approach for analyzing and designing voice communications networks. In particular, we develop models to evaluate the grade of service experienced by a network and to generate low cost network configurations. The reduced load approximation method was used to evaluate system congestion. In addition, a heuristic algorithm was developed to generate low cost network configurations, while maintaining the same approximate grade of service. By varying the target blocking level p and the set of candidate exchange locations in the network improvement algorithm, a variety of networks (differing in both cost and grade of service) can be generated. Therefore, a useful feature of this approach is in identifying, through repeated runs, a set of good configurations for further study. From such a set, decision makers can more easily select a desirable network for implementation in a voice communications setting.

These models have been used in evaluating the telecommunications network of a major textile company composed of 46 sites. The blocking estimates provided by the reduced load approximation turned out to compare favorably with historically observed blocking values. After applying the network improvement algorithm, several configurations emerged as strong candidates for the voice network studied. Configurations were produced which had the same grade of service as the current configuration, but which lowered monthly costs by approximately $5000 (6%). In addition, the alternative networks provided a more equitable distribution of service level throughout the network, compared to the existing telecommunications system.

REFERENCES

Frank, H. and W. Chou (1972), "Topological Optimization of Computer Networks," *Proceedings of the IEEE 60*, 1385–1397.

Johnson, D. S., J. K. Lenstra and A. H. G. Rinnooy Kan (1978), "The Complexity of the Network Design Problem," *Networks 8*, 4 (Apr.), 279–285.

Kelly, F. P. (1985), "Blocking Probabilities in Large Circuit-Switched Networks," Statistical Laboratory, University of Cambridge, England.

Perticone, A.J. (1986), "Design and Analysis of Telecommunications Networks," Ph.D. Dissertation, Dept. of Mathematical Sciences, Clemson University, Clemson, SC.

Whitt, W. (1985), "Blocking When Service is Required From Several Facilities Simultaneously," *AT&T Bell Laboratories Technical Journal 64*, 8 (Aug.), 1807–1856.

X.
NUMERICAL ANALYSIS

INTERVAL ARITHMETIC METHODS FOR NONLINEAR SYSTEMS AND NONLINEAR OPTIMIZATION: AN OUTLINE AND STATUS

R. BAKER KEARFOTT
Dept. of Mathematics, Univ. of Southwestern Louisiana U.S.L. Box 4-1010, Lafayette, Louisiana 70504

ABSTRACT

In operations research, we often try to to find the global optimum of a nonlinear function subject to constraints on the variables. Where applicable, methods of interval arithmetic can do this with *mathematical certainty*, despite the fact that the algorithms execute on conventional computers. This is because such methods perform a (seemingly contradictory) exhaustive but efficient search, and take account of all rounding errors through *directed roundings*.

We have transportable interval software to find all solutions to a nonlinear system of equations within a given region; minor modifications allow this software to solve the global optimization problem. The impact of this on operations research will be to enable certain such problems to be solved with *total reliability*.

Future development will increase the range of problems for which these methods are practical.

1. INTRODUCTION

An important problem in operations research is to find global optima of nonlinear functions subject to constraints. Recent progress in interval mathematics and interval software can impact operations research by providing solutions to the following specific instances of these problems.

Find, *with certainty*, approximations to all solutions of the nonlinear system

(1.1) $$f_i(x_1, x_2, ..., x_n) = 0, 1 \leq i \leq n,$$

where bounds l_i and u_i are known such that:

$$l_i \leq x_i \leq u_i \text{ for } 1 \leq i \leq n;$$

and, related to (1.1),

find, *with certainty*, the global minimum of the nonlinear objective function

(1.2) $$\phi(x_1, x_2, ..., x_n),$$

where bounds l_i and u_i are known such that:

$$l_i \leq x_i \leq u_i \text{ for } 1 \leq i \leq n.$$

An interval algorithm will produce a list of solutions whose coordinates x_i are given as small intervals of uncertainty. If the proper algorithm (cf. Section 3 below) is correctly implemented with directed roundings (cf. Section 2 below), completion of this algorithm constitutes a computational but *mathematically rigorous proof* that all solutions of (1.1) are within the intervals given in the list.

We have transportable software which will in practice solve many small to moderately sized polynomial systems of the form (1.1) without computer programming, and which will solve more general systems if we program the objective function [Kearfott and Novoa 1988]. The only way such software can fail is by not completing within a given time. (Nonetheless, on some problems, it completes in much less time than alternate methods.)

In this paper, we review facts about interval arithmetic and a class of algorithms of use to members of the operations research community. Section 2 contains elementary definitions and information on computer implementations of interval arithmetic. In Section 3, we discuss interval algorithms for solving nonlinear algebraic systems and for nonlinear optimization. In Section 4, we summarize strengths and weaknesses of these algorithms.

2. ELEMENTARY FACTS AND COMPUTER IMPLEMENTATIONS

Thorough introductions to interval mathematics are given in the books [Alefeld et al. 1983; Moore 1979]. In particular, one can find details for this section in chapters 1, 2, and 3 of [Moore 1979] or in chapters 1, 2, 3, and 4 of [Alefeld et al. 1983]. Also see [Rall 1981] and [Ratschek 1987] if they are available.

Numerous references facilitate advanced study. The bibliographies [Garloff 1985; Garloff 1987] list approximately 2000 books, journal and conference proceedings articles, and technical reports. In [Moore 1988], general interval and non interval numerical methods are compared. Additional proceedings include [Hansen 1969; Miranker 1986; Nickel 1980; Nickel 1986a].

Here, interval quantities will be denoted by boldface. We will also denote the n-vector whose i-th component is x_i by X and the n-vector whose i-th component is f_i by $F(X)$.

Interval arithmetic is based on defining the four elementary arithmetic operations on intervals. Let $a = [a_l, a_u]$ and $b = [b_l, b_u]$ be intervals. Then, if $op \in [+,-,*,/]$, we define

(2.1) $\qquad a \ op \ b = [x + y \mid x \in a \ and \ y \in b\,]$

For example,

$$a + b = [a_l + b_l, a_u + b_u].$$

In fact, all four operations can be defined in terms of addition, subtraction, multiplication, and division of the endpoints of the intervals, although multiplication and division may require comparison of several results. The result of these operations is an interval except when we compute a/b and $0 \in b$. In that case, we use *extended interval arithmetic* [Moore 1979, pp. 66-68] to get two semi-infinite intervals or else the whole real line.

Much of interval mathematics' power lies in the ability to compute *inclusion monotonic interval extensions* of functions. If f is a continuous function of a real variable, then an inclusion monotonic interval extension f is defined to be a function from the set of intervals to the set of intervals, such that, if x is an interval in the domain of f,

$$[\,f(x) \mid x \in x\,] \subset f(x)$$

and such that

$$x \subset y \text{ implies } f(x) \subset f(y).$$

Inclusion monotonic interval extensions of a polynomial may be obtained by simply replacing the dependent variables by intervals and replacing the additions and multiplications by the corresponding interval operations [Moore 1979].

We emphasize here that the result of an elementary interval operation is precisely the range of values that the usual result attains as we let the operands range over the two intervals. However, the value of an interval extension of a function is not precisely the range of the function over its interval operand, but only contains this range; it is an art to devise interval extensions whose values differ little from the actual range. For example, the values of an interval extension of a polynomial depend on the form in which the polynomial is written. See Kearfott [1988c] for an example, and see Ratschek and Rokne [1984] for a discussion of efficient ways of formulating interval extensions.

We may use the mean value theorem or Taylor's theorem with remainder formula to obtain interval extensions of transcendental functions. See Kearfott [1988c] for an elementary example. Alternate extensions are also possible; see Ratschek and Rokne [1984].

Several software packages [Bleher et al. 1987; Bundy 1984; Yohe 1979] are available for interval extensions of the elementary functions.

Mathematically rigorous interval extensions can be computed in finite precision arithmetic via the use of *directed roundings*. Let x and y be machine-representable numbers, and assume op is one of the four elementary operations +, -, *, or /. Normally, $x\ op\ y$ is not representable in the machine's memory, and there are various schemes of rounding. For example, we may always *round down* to the nearest *machine number less than $x\ op\ y$*, or we may always *round up* to the *nearest machine number greater than $x\ op\ y$*. In interval arithmetic with directed rounding, if

$$x\ op\ y = [c, d],$$

then we always round the value for c down, and we always round the value for d up.

Machine interval arithmetic with directed rounding does not involve deep concepts, but it can be quite powerful. For example, if interval arithmetic with directed rounding is used to compute an interval extension f of f,
$$[c,d] = f([a,b]),$$
and $[c,d]$ does not contain zero, then this is a rigorous proof (regardless of the machine wordlength, etc.) that there is no root of f in $[a,b]$.

The IEEE floating point standard, and hence hardware on many personal computers and mainframes, include support for directed roundings.

Various precompilers and compilers support the interval datatype. An early, reasonably portable one consisted of interval arithmetic packages of the Mathematics Research Center [Yohe 1977; Yohe 1979] in conjunction with the AUGMENT precompiler [Crary 1976]. ACRITH is a high-quality multiple precision and interval package for IBM mainframe equipment [Bleher et al. 1987], which has been used with AUGMENT in the past. More recently, researchers at IBM-Germany have developed the modern precompiler Fortran-SC [Walter and Metzger 1988] to access the ACRITH routines.

PASCAL-SC supports an interval data type directly in the compiler [Rall 1987]. There is much literature on using PASCAL-SC, even though it has until recently only been available on CPM-based personal computers. (There is now a version of PASCAL-SC for IBM PC-compatibles.)

L. A. Liddiard, E. J. Mundstock, and W. Walster wrote the "M-77" Fortran *compiler* which supports the interval data type. This compiler runs only on CDC equipment, but is available from CDC or from the University of Minnesota.

Clemmesen has described pseudocode outlining implementation of interval arithmetic [1984].

The speed of interval arithmetic operations varies greatly depending on implementation. Our experience is, however, that even the slowest implementations allow certain practical problems to be solved.

3. INTERVAL METHODS IN SOLVING NONLINEAR SYSTEMS OF EQUATIONS AND IN NONLINEAR OPTIMIZATION

Here, we discuss solution of (1.1) and (1.2), done via generalized bisection in conjunction with interval Newton methods. This general technique is described in chapters 19 and 20 of [Alefeld et al. 1983] and in chapters 5 and 6 of [Moore 1979]. An early paper on the technique is [Hansen 1968]. Other papers are (but are not limited to) [Hansen 1978; Kearfott 1987a; Kearfott 1987b; Moore 1977; Moore and Jones 1977; Neumaier 1985; Nickel

1971; Nickel 1986b; Schwandt 1985a].

In what follows we denote by X_0 the box in n-space described by
$$[\, X = (x_1, x_2, ..., x_n) \mid l_i \leq x_i \leq u_i \, \text{for} \, 1 \leq i \leq n \,].$$
In interval Newton methods, we find a box $\overline{X_k}$ which contains all solutions of the interval linear system

(3.1) $$F'(X_k)(\overline{X_k} - X_k) = -F(X_k),$$

where $F'(X_k)$ is a suitable interval extension of the Jacobian matrix of F over the box X_k, and where X_k is some point in X_k. We then define the next iterate X_{k+1} by

(3.2) $$X_{k+1} = X_k \cap \overline{X_k}.$$

The scheme based on solving (3.1) and performing (3.2) is termed an *interval Newton* method. The *convergence rate* of an interval Newton method is determined by the ratios of the *widths* of the component intervals of X_{k+1} to the corresponding widths of X_k.

If each row of F' contains all possible vector values that that row of the scalar Jacobian matrix takes on as X ranges over all vectors in X_k, then it follows from the mean value theorem that all solutions of (1.1) in X_k must be in X_{k+1}. If the coordinate intervals of X_{k+1} are smaller than those of X_k, then we may iterate (3.1) and (3.2) until we obtain an interval vector the widths of whose components are smaller than a specified tolerance.

If the coordinate intervals of X_{k+1} are not smaller than those of X_k, then we may *bisect* one of these intervals to form two new boxes; we then continue the iteration with one of these boxes, and push the other one onto a *stack* for later consideration. After completion of the current box, we pop a box from the stack, and apply (3.1) and (3.2) to it; we thus continue until the stack is exhausted. As is explained in [Moore and Jones 1977; Kearfott 1987a] and elsewhere, such a composite *generalized bisection* algorithm will reliably compute all solutions to (1.1) to within a specified tolerance.

The efficiency of the generalized bisection algorithm depends on

(1) the sharpness of the interval extension of the Jacobian matrix; and

(2) the way we find the solution $\overline{X_k}$ to (1.2).

In particular, iteration with formulas (3.1) and (3.2) should exhibit the quadratic local convergence properties of Newton's method, but repeated bisections are to be avoided if possible. We are thus interested in arranging the computations so that $\overline{X_k}$ has coordinate intervals which are as narrow as possible.

For many ways of solving (3.1), the following statement is true.

(3.3) if $\overline{X_k}$ is strictly contained in X_k, then the system of equations in (1.1) has a unique solution in X_k, and Newton's method starting from any point in X_k will converge to that solution. Conversely, if $X_k \cap \overline{X_k}$ is empty, then there are no solutions of the system in (1.1) in X_k.

See [Hansen and Walster 1988; Neumaier 1985; Qi 1982].

The Krawczyk method [Moore 1977] and an interval version of the Gauss-Seidel method [Hansen 1983] are popular ways of solving (3.1). See [Kearfott 1988b] for details, and see [Kearfott 1988c] for a detailed example of the interval Gauss- Seidel method. In both of these methods, it is usually necessary to first multiply (3.1) by a *preconditioner matrix* Y_k of real numbers. This matrix is often taken to be the inverse of the matrix whose entries are the midpoints of the entries of $F'(X_k)$.

For large, banded or sparse systems, multiplication by an inverse is impractical. Schwandt uses the interval Gauss-Seidel method without a preconditioner to solve systems like finite difference discretizations of Poisson's equation with a nonlinear forcing term [Schwandt 1984; Schwandt 1985b]. In such cases, an interval generalization of diagonal dominance ensures convergence of repeated iteration of the interval Gauss-Seidel method when Y_k is the identity matrix [Rall 1987].

Techniques for computing the rows of Y_k to minimize the widths of the intervals obtained via the interval Gauss-Seidel method (and thus maximize convergence rate) appear in [Kearfott 1988b]. These techniques involve solving linear programming problems for the elements of Y_k; these linear programming problems express optimality conditions for the width of each component interval of $\overline{X}$. The techniques are applicable to illconditioned and singular systems, and the linear programming problem can be altered to take account of structure or sparsity.

The solutions to the global nonlinear optimization problem (1.2) can be found by solving (1.1), where the f_i are the components of $\nabla \phi$. However, we may use the objective function directly to increase the algorithm's efficiency. If p and q are intervals, we say that $p > q$ if every element of p is greater than every element of q. Suppose that X and Y are interval vectors in the stack described below (3.2), and let ϕ be an interval extension to ϕ. Then, if $\phi(Y) > \phi(X)$, we may discard Y from the stack.

Papers and reviews on solution of the global optimization problem include [Baumann 1986; Hansen 1980; Hansen 1988; Ichida and Fujii 1979; Nickel 1986b; Rall 1985; Ratschek and Rokne 1987]. Walster, Hansen, and Sengupta report performance results on their global optimization algorithm in [Walster et al. 1985]. For performance results of a general interval nonlinear equation algorithm, see [Kearfott 1987b].

4. A SUMMARY OF STRENGTHS, WEAKNESSES, AND OPEN QUESTIONS OF INTERVAL OPTIMIZATION ALGORITHMS

4.1 Strengths and Weaknesses

Roughly, interval techniques work well for small and moderately sized polynomial and transcendental systems of the form (1.1) or (1.2). The performance is in general less predictable when there are larger numbers of variables, and it may not presently be practical to apply interval methods when the objective function is complicated (such as when its evaluation involves integrating systems of differential equations).

Interval methods *cannot* fail by identifying a point other than the global optimum of (1.2), or by terminating without finding all solutions to the system in (1.1). However, due to poor interval extensions or other reasons, they can take an excessive amount of computation time. On the other hand, they take considerably less computation time than alternate techniques (which also can, in theory, fail) for certain problems; see [Kearfott 1987b; Walster et al. 1985]. Regardless of relative efficiency, completion of a correct algorithm which employs interval arithmetic with correct directed rounding gives bounds on the solutions which are valid with the same certainty as a rigorous mathematical proof. This fact may be more important than computation time in some cases.

Interval methods for root-finding or for nonlinear optimization are well suited to constrained problems of the form (1.1) or (1.2), and should be seriously considered when the problems take that form.

4.2 Open Questions

First, apart from studies on certain special systems as in [Garloff 1986; Schwandt 1984; Schwandt 1985a; Schwandt 1985b; Thiel 1986], there is not much literature on the behavior of interval methods for large-scale systems. Indeed, the methods' practicality is less predictable for such systems. Nonetheless, we believe that special methods for structured problems can be developed which are predictably effective on wider classes of problems. These methods may involve variants of the preconditioner technique in [Kearfott 1988b] or of the subspace technique in [Kearfott 1988a].

Second, the question of singular and ill-conditioned systems is not fully resolved. These questions are addressed in [Kearfott 1988a; Kearfott 1988b], but additional work is desirable.

Third, it is not yet fully clear for what class of f_i these methods are presently practical. Often, if more operations are required to evaluate the f_i, then the resulting interval f_i will have a larger width and hence will be less useful. In our opinion, more studies need to be carefully done and reported.

We suggest that operations researchers explore the usefulness of interval techniques with the presently available software (e.g. [Kearfott and Novoa 1988]), and consult interval mathematicians as questions arise.

REFERENCES

Alefeld, G., and Herzberger, J. (1983), *Introduction to Interval Computations*, Academic Press, New York, etc.

Baumann, E. (1986), "Globale Optimierung stetig differenzierbarer Functionen einer Variablen," preprint, *Freiburger Intervall-Berichte 86*, 6, Institut für Angewandte Mathematik der Universität Freiburg, 1-89.

Bleher, J. H., Rump, S. M., Kulisch, U., Metzger, M., and Walter, W. (1987), "Fortran-SC – A Study of a Fortran Extension for Engineering Scientific Computations with Access to ACRITH," *Computing 39*, 2, 93-110.

Bundy, A. (1984), "A Generalized Interval Package and its Use for Semantic Checking," *ACM Transactions on Mathematical Software 10*, 397-409.

Clemmesen, M. (1984), "Interval Arithmetic Implementations Using Floating Point Arithmetic," *SIGNUM News 19*, 4, 2-8.

Crary, F. (1976), "The AUGMENT Precompiler," Technical Report 1470, Mathematics Research Center, University of Wisconsin, Madison, Wis.

Garloff, J. (1985), "Interval Mathematics: A Bibliography," preprint, *Freiburger Intervall-Berichte 85*, 6, Institut für Angewandte Mathematik der Universität Freiburg, 1-222.

Garloff, J. (1986), "Block Methods for the Solution of Linear Interval Equations," preprint, *Freiburger Intervall Berichte 86*, 3, Institut für Angewandte Mathematik der Universität Freiburg, 1-40.

Garloff, J. (1987), "Bibliography on Interval Mathematics, Continuation," preprint, *Freiburger Intervall Berichte 87*, 2, Institut für Angewandte Mathematik der Universität Freiburg, 1-50.

Hansen, E. R. (1968), "On Solving Systems of Equations Using Interval Arithmetic," *Mathematics of Computation 22*, 374-384.

Hansen, E. R., ed. (1969), *Topics in Interval Analysis*, Oxford University Press, London.

Hansen, E. R. (1978), "Interval Forms of Newton's Method," *Computing 20*, 153-163.

Hansen, E. R. (1980), "Global Optimization Using Interval Analysis – The Multidimensional Case," *Numerische Mathematik 34*, 3, 247-270.

Hansen, E. R., and Greenberg, R. I. (1983), "An Interval Newton Method," *Applied Mathematics and Computation 12*, 2-3, 89-98.

Hansen, E. R. (1988), "An Overview of Global Optimization Using Interval Analysis," In *Reliability in Computing*, R. E. Moore, Ed. Academic Press, New York.

Hansen, E. R., and Walster, G. W. (1988), "Nonlinear Equations and Optimization," accepted for publication in *Mathematical Programming*.

Ichida, K., and Fujii, Y. (1979), "An Interval Arithmetic Method for Global Optimization," *Computing 23*, 1, pp. 85-97.

Kearfott, R. B. (1987a), "Abstract Generalized Bisection and a Cost Bound," *Mathematics of Computation 49*, 179 (July), 187-202.

Kearfott R. B. (1987b), "Some Tests of Generalized Bisection," *ACM Transactions on Mathematical Software 13*, 3 (Sept.), 197-220.

Kearfott, R. B. (1988a), "On Handling Singular Systems with Interval Newton Methods," In *Proceedings of the Twelfth IMACS World Congress on Scientific Computation* (Paris, France, July 18-22), pp. 651-653.

Kearfott, R. B. (1988b) "Preconditioners for the Interval Gauss-Seidel Method," submitted to the *SIAM Journal on Numerical Analysis*.

Kearfott, R. B. (1988c) "Interval Arithmetic Techniques in the Computational Solution of Nonlinear Systems of Equations: Introduction, Examples, and Comparisons," *In Lecture Notes for the AMS-SIAM Summer Seminar in Applied Mathematics*, (Colorado State University, July 18-29).

Kearfott, R. B., and Novoa, M. (1988), "A Program for Generalized Bisection," submitted to the *ACM Transactions on Mathematical Software*.

Miranker, W. L., ed. (1986), *Accurate Scientific Computations*, Lecture Notes in Computer Science no. 235, Springer Verlag, New York, etc.

Moore, R. E. (1977), "A Test for Existence of Solutions to Nonlinear Systems," *SIAM Journal on Numerical Analysis* 14, 4 (Sept.), 611-615.

Moore, R. E., and Jones, S. T. (1977), "Safe Starting Regions for Iterative Methods," *SIAM Journal on Numerical Analysis* 14, 6 (Dec.), 1051-1065.

Moore, R. E. (1979), *Methods and Applications of Interval Analysis*, SIAM, Philadelphia.

Moore, R. E., ed. (1988), *Reliability in Computing*, Academic Press, New York, etc.

Neumaier, A. (1985), "Interval Iteration for Zeros of Systems of Equations," *BIT 25*, 1, 256-273.

Nickel, K. (1971), "On the Newton Method in Interval Analysis," Technical Report 1136, Mathematics Research Center, University of Wisconsin, Madison, Wis.

Nickel, K., ed. (1980), *Interval Mathematics 1980*, Academic Press, New York, etc.

Nickel, K., ed. (1986a), *Interval Mathematics 1985*, Lecture Notes in Computer Science volume 212, Springer Verlag, Berlin.

Nickel, K. (1986b), "Optimization Using Interval Mathematics," preprint, *Freiburger Intervall-Berichte 86*, 7, Institut für Angewandte Mathematik der Universität Freiburg, 55- 83.

Qi, L. (1982), "A Note on the Moore Test for Nonlinear Systems," *SIAM Journal on Numerical Analysis 19*, 4 (Aug.), 851-857.

Rall, L. B. (1981), "Interval Analysis: A New Tool for Applied Mathematics," Technical Report 2268, Mathematics Research Center, University of Wisconsin, Madison, Wis.

Rall, L. B. (1985), "Global Optimization Using Automatic Differentiation and Interval Iteration," Technical Report 2832, Mathematics Research Center, University of Wisconsin, Madison, Wis.

Rall, L. B. (1987), "An Introduction to the Scientific Computing Language Pascal-SC," *Computers and Mathematics with Applications 14*, 1, 53-69.

Ratschek, H. (1987), "Interval Mathematics," preprint, *Freiburger Intervall Berichte 87*, 4, Institut für Angewandte Mathematik der Universität Freiburg, 1-44.

Ratschek, H., and Rokne, J. G. (1984), Computer Methods for the *Range of Functions*, Horwood, Chichester, England.

Ratschek, H., and Rokne, J. G. (1987), "Efficiency of a Global Optimization Algorithm," SIAM Journal on Numerical Analysis 24, 5 (Oct.), 1191-1201.

Schwandt, H. (1984), "An Interval Arithmetic Approach for the Construction of an Almost Globally Convergent Method for the Solution of the Nonlinear Poisson Equation," SIAM *Journal on Scientific and Statistical Computing* 5, 2 (June), 427-452.

Schwandt, H. (1985a), "Krawczyk-Like Algorithms for the Solution of Systems of Nonlinear Equations,"*SIAM Journal on Numerical Analysis 22*, 4 (Aug.), 792-810.

Schwandt, H. (1985b), "The Solution of Nonlinear Elliptic Dirichlet Problems on Rectangles by Almost Globally Convergent Interval Methods," *SIAM Journal on Scientific and Statistical Computing* 6, 3 (July), 617-638.

Thiel, S. (1986), "Intervalliterationsverfahren für discretisierte elliptische Differentialgleichungen," preprint,*Freiburger Intervall Berichte 86*, 8, Institut für Angewandte Mathematik der Universität Freiburg, 1-72.

Walster, G. W., Hansen, E. R., and Sengupta, S. (1985), "Test Results for a Global Optimization Algorithm," In *Numerical Optimization 1984*, (Boulder, Colo., June 12- 14). SIAM, Philadelphia, pp. 272-287.

Walter, W., and Metzger, M. (1988), "Fortran-SC, A Fortran Extension for Engineering/Scientific Computation with Access to ACRITH," In *Reliability in Computing*, R. E. Moore Ed. Academic Press, New York, etc.

Yohe, J. M. (1977), "The Interval Arithmetic Package," Technical Report 1755, Mathematics Research Center, University of Wisconsin, Madison, Wis.

Yohe, J. M. (1979), "Software for Interval Arithmetic: A Reasonably Portable Package," ACM Transactions on *Mathematical Software 5*, 1 (Mar.), 50-63.

POLYNOMIAL CONTINUATION

ALEXANDER P. MORGAN
Mathematics Department
General Motors Research Laboratories
Warren, Michigan 48090-9057

ABSTRACT

Systems of polynomial equations come up in operations research in network flow and optimization problems. Polynomial continuation is a numerical method for computing all the isolated solutions to such a system. It is a "path tracking" or homotopy method, characterized by generating many paths, one for each solution to the system. It does not require the user to specify start points.

This paper gives an overview of the elementary aspects of polynomial continuation and also provides a summary of the more powerful m-homogeneous theory. The conclusions include suggestions for future research.

1. INTRODUCTION

Polynomial systems arise in a number of operations research activities and in related areas of engineering; for example, in traffic equilibrium problems and other network equilibrium problems [Magnanti 1982], in chemical process modeling (as chemical equilibrium systems [Meintjes and Morgan 1987]), and in nonlinear programming and optimization (e.g. solving the Kuhn-Tucker conditions). The applicability of homotopy methods to operations reseach is noted in [CONDOR 1988]; see, for example, p. 624.

Polynomial continuation is a numerical method for computing the full set of isolated solutions to a system of n polynomial equations in n unknowns. (A solution is *isolated* if the system has no other solutions nearby.) By way of introduction to this method, let us consider a simple example.

Suppose we wish to find all solutions to the system

$$x^2 + xy - 1 = 0$$
$$y^2 + x - 5 = 0 \tag{1}$$

The key "trick" of the method is to note that the related simplified system

$$x^2 - 1 = 0$$
$$y^2 - 5 = 0 \tag{2}$$

is easy to solve. The four solutions to (2) are $(x, y) = (\pm 1, \pm\sqrt{5})$. By defining the "homotopy"

$$h(x, y, t) = \begin{bmatrix} x^2 + txy - 1 \\ y^2 + tx - 5 \end{bmatrix}$$

the following strategy is developed:

We can solve

$$h(x, y, 0) = \begin{bmatrix} x^2 + 0xy - 1 \\ y^2 + 0x - 5 \end{bmatrix} = \begin{bmatrix} 0 \\ 0 \end{bmatrix}.$$

This is, in fact, equation (2). Beginning with a solution to $h(x, y, 0) = 0$, we can modify it to be a solution to $h(x, y, t_1) = 0$, where t_1 is a small positive number, using some local solution method. Then we can modify the solution to $h(x, y, t_1) = 0$ to become a solution to $h(x, y, t_2) = 0$ where $t_2 > t_1$, and by proceeding in this way, finally derive a solution to $h(x, y, 1) = 0$, which is equation (1). Such a sequence of solutions is called a "continuation path." The idea is that each solution to (2) yields a solution to (1) via continuation.

Certain technical issues not made explicit in the example must be overcome in general. Thus, we must recast the problem in complex arithmetic, because in general a polynomial system will have some complex solutions, even if its coefficients are real. We must take steps to assure that the continuation paths are well defined and do not bifurcate, turn back in t, "go singular," or get bogged down in some other way. We must devise fast and reliable numerical methods for path tracking.

Basically, we can distinguish two main steps:
(1) Define a homotopy, $h(z, t)$.
(2) Choose a numerical method for tracking the paths defined by $h(z, t) = 0$.

Step (1) is guided by results from algebraic geometry, while (2) is based on methods for the numerical solution of ordinary differential equations and local methods for the solution of nonlinear systems. Both parts are nontrivial and important.

Section 2 gives an overview of the elementary theory of both steps, while Section 3 summarizes a more advanced theory of homotopy construction. [Allgower and Georg 1980] and [Watson et al. 1987] provide additional information on path tracking. Section 4 gives conclusions and comments on future work.

The idea of polynomial continuation was first suggested in [Garcia and Zangwill 1977] and [Drexler 1977]. A number of papers have followed. There have also been significant physical applications. See [Morgan and Sommese 1987a] for many references.

2. A BRIEF INTRODUCTION TO POLYNOMIAL CONTINUATION

In this section we will sketch the theory of polynomial continuation in the simplest and most straightforward case: the number of continuation paths is equal to the total degree of the system. The first subsection treats paths in complex Euclidean space and the second paths in projective space. The results in this section are stated more precisely and are generalized in Section 3. The simple approach given here can be applied to any polynomial system, but the more sophisticated approaches can sometimes be much more efficient.

2.1 Paths in Complex Euclidean Space, C^n.

Let $f(z) = 0$ denote the system of n polynomial equations in n unknowns that we want to solve; e.g. $f(z) = 0$ could be the Kuhn-Tucker conditions for an optimization problem or the equilibrium conditions for a game, economic system, or transportation network. Call this the *target system*. The target system can have real or complex coefficients. Let $d_j = deg(f_j)$, the degree† of the jth equation of the target system, for $j = 1$ to n. Let $d = d_1 \cdot d_2 \cdots d_n$, the *total degree* of f.

We choose a system $g(z) = 0$ of n polynomial equations in n unknowns, the *start system*. Since g is the start system, we must know what its solutions are. In addition, g must obey the following conditions:

1. $deg(g_j) = d_j$ for $j = 1$ to n.
2. $g(z) = 0$ has d different isolated solutions. (Equivalently, all the solutions of $g(z) = 0$ are *nonsingular*; that is, if x^0 is a solution to $g(x) = 0$, then $dg(x^0)$ is nonsingular, where $dg(x^0)$ denotes the $n \times n$ Jacobian matrix of partial derivatives of g evaluated at x^0.)

The system defined by $g_j = z_j^{d_j} - 1$ for $j = 1$ to n is an acceptable choice, but if we choose g to match more of the structure of f, then the method will generally be more efficient. For example, g might equal f with a few terms deleted. Let Σ denote the set of solutions to $g(z) = 0$.

Define the *homotopy* (or *continuation system*) by

$$h(z,t) = (1-t)\gamma g(z) + tf(z) \qquad (3)$$

where $\gamma = e^{i\theta}$. Here $i = \sqrt{-1}$, e is the base of the natural logarithms, and θ is a real number "chosen at random." The theorem which justifies this homotopy (Theorem 1 in Section 3) states that, for each choice of f and g, there are a finite number of θ that lead to singular continuation paths; i.e., paths that cross, bifurcate, or explode into higher-dimensional components. We want to avoid these unknown "bad" θ, because the associated "paths" are more difficult (or impossible) to track effectively. Since there are only a finite number of bad θ, there is a zero probability of choosing one of them at random.

---

† The degree of a polynomial is the maximum of the degrees of its terms. The degree of a term is the sum of the exponents of the variables. Thus, the three terms of the polynomial $x^4 + x^2y^3 + 1$ have degrees 4, 5, and 0, respectively, and the degree of the polynomial is 5.

Geometrically, the solutions $U = \{(z,t) \in C^n \times [0,1) \mid h(z,t) = 0\}$ form d distinct smooth nonintersecting paths in $C^n \times [0,1)$, each an imbedding of a copy of $[0,1)$ in $C^n \times [0,1)$. These paths (with their righthand endpoints included, as discussed below) are called the *continuation paths* for the homotopy (3).

Let us consider one of these paths, $\alpha(s) = (z(s), t(s))$, parametrized by arc length, s. Thus $s \geq 0$ and, as s increases, t goes from 0 to 1. Further, t is strictly increasing as a function of s. Call $z^0 = z(0)$ the *lefthand endpoint* of the path. We have two cases:

- If the path has finite arc length, s^*, then $lim_{s \to s^*} t(s) = 1$ and $lim_{s \to s^*} z(s) = z^1$, the *righthand endpoint* of the path.
- If the path does not have finite arc length, then $lim_{s \to \infty} t(s) = 1$ and $lim_{s \to \infty} |z(s)| = \infty$. In this case, $f(z) = 0$ has a *solution at infinity*, noted below and discussed in the next section.

The proof that these cases exhaust the possibilities is based on the fact that $h^{-1}(0)$ is a 1-dimensional (real) smooth manifold for $t \in [0,1)$ and on the way complex Euclidean space imbeds in complex projective space. (See, for example, [Morgan 1986a], [Morgan 1986b], [Morgan and Sommese 1987a].)

Now, the d lefthand endpoints of the d paths are the points in Σ. Further, each isolated solution of $f(z) = 0$ shows up as a righthand endpoint of some path. Thus, if we track the paths numerically, beginning with the points in Σ, we can find all the isolated solutions of $f(z) = 0$. (As a part of this process, the diverging paths will have to be terminated. However, the projective transformation, described in 2.2, eliminates divergent paths.)

Path tracking is effected by solving a set of "initial value problems with energy function," as follows. Let $\dot{z}$ and $\dot{t}$ denote dz/ds and dt/ds, respectively. Denote by dh_z and dh_t the partial derivative matrices of h with respect to z and t, respectively. (See Note 3 below.) Then continuation paths are solutions to the initial value problem

$$\dot{z}(s) = -\delta[dh_z]^{-1} dh_t \qquad \dot{t}(s) = \delta \qquad (4)$$

where δ is a positive constant chosen so that $|(\dot{z}, \dot{t})| = 1$, with initial conditions

$$z(0) = z^0 \qquad t(0) = 0 \qquad (5)$$

for some $z^0 \in \Sigma$, having potential energy zero:

$$h(z(s), t(s)) = 0. \qquad (6)$$

Notes:

1. Since $|(\dot{z}, \dot{t})| = 1$, the paths are parametrized by arc length.
2. The fact that (6) holds as well as (4) and (5) gives us some options for path tracking not available if this path were merely defined by an initial value problem. Thus we may

augment standard ordinary differential equation solvers with special "path correction" devices (as described in [Watson 1979] and [Watson et al. 1987]), or we may use "predictor-corrector" methods (as described in [Allgower and Georg 1980], [Garcia and Zangwill 1981], [Morgan 1987], [Rheinboldt and Burdt 1983], and [Watson et al. 1987]) which require such additional information. (Simplicial path tracking strategies also require it. See [Allgower and Georg 1980] and [Garcia and Zangwill 1981].)

3. The dh_z is a $2n \times 2n$ real matrix, the "realification" of the $n \times n$ complex Jacobian matrix of partial derivatives of h, evaluated at $(z(s), t(s))$. If A is a $p \times q$ complex matrix, its *realification* is the $2p \times 2q$ matrix defined by replacing the entry $a_{i,j}$ by the 2×2 block $\begin{bmatrix} Re(a_{i,j}) & -Im(a_{i,j}) \\ Im(a_{i,j}) & Re(a_{i,j}) \end{bmatrix}$ where "Re" and "Im" denote the real and imaginary parts, respectively. Similarly, dh_t is the first column of the realification of the $n \times 1$ column matrix of partial derivatives of h with respect to t, evaluated at $(z(s), t(s))$. Further, for consistency with these conventions, we must interpret z and $\dot{z}$ as column vectors of real numbers; thus, $z = [Re(z_1), Im(z_1), \ldots, Re(z_n), Im(z_n)]^T$. This conversion of matrices via realification acknowledges that, while h is algebraically in complex arithmetic, we track real continuation paths in real space. Thus, for n polynomials in n unknowns, we end up tracking paths in $(2n + 1)$-dimensional real space. (See [Morgan 1987], Appendix 3, for more details.) Note that t and $\dot{t}$ are real numbers.

4. In most cases, to generate the right hand side of (4), we will solve the linear system

$$dh_z \, \dot{z} = -dh_t \qquad (7)$$

and not invert dh_z directly. Actually, (7) and (4) are derived from the $2n \times (2n + 1)$ linear system

$$[dh_z \mid dh_t] \begin{bmatrix} \dot{z} \\ \dot{t} \end{bmatrix} = 0. \qquad (8)$$

Some researchers recommend alternative ways to solve for $\dot{z}$ and $\dot{t}$ using (8). (See [Watson 1986].) However, we have had good results with (7).

5. The major computational challenge of the scheme we have outlined above is singular righthand endpoints. If all the solutions of $f(z) = 0$ are nonsingular, all the endpoints are nonsingular. This case is relatively routine to compute, but in practice it is the exception. Consequently, performance in the presence of singular endpoints is a major consideration for choosing a path tracker for polynomial continuation. See [Morgan et al. 1988].

2.2 Divergent Paths and the Projective Transformation

In the method described in 2.1 above, paths may diverge. Since $|z(s)| \to \infty$ as $t(s) \to 1$ for these paths, a test must be implemented to terminate the paths when $|z|$

gets too large or when too many steps have been taken. While this can be satisfactory (even *recommended* in some cases [Morgan 1987], Chapter 10), usually it is better to make a simple change of context to eliminate divergent paths altogether. This eliminates the heuristic element in the numerical method resulting from programming the decision to terminate paths that appear to be diverging.

The approach we recommend is to replace the system f by the *projective transformation* of f. (This idea was first proposed in [Morgan 1986b].) We will sketch the mechanics of this substitution here. Section 3 gives more detail. An alternative mechanism for eliminating divergent paths is suggested in [Wright 1985].

First, *homogenize* f via the substitutions $z_j \leftarrow y_j/y_0$ for $j = 1$ to n. This yields a new polynomial system (after we clear the powers of y_0 from the denominator): $\hat{f}(y_0, y_1, \ldots, y_n) = 0$ of n equations in $n+1$ unknowns. We can identify the solutions to $f(z) = 0$ with the solutions to $\hat{f}(y) = 0$ obeying $y_0 = 1$. In addition, there may be solutions to $\hat{f}(y) = 0$ with $y_0 = y_1 = \ldots = y_{k-1} = 0$ and $y_k = 1$ for some k between 1 and n. These do not correspond to solutions of $f(z) = 0$. (They, in fact, correspond to *solutions at infinity* of $f(z) = 0$. See Section 3.)

Now define $F(x_1, \ldots, x_n)$, a system of n polynomials in n unknowns, via $F(x_1, \ldots, x_n) = \hat{f}(x_0, x_1, \ldots, x_n)$ where $x_0 \equiv b_1 x_1 + \ldots + b_n x_n + b_{n+1}$ for some fixed complex numbers $b_1, \ldots, b_{n+1}$. This F is called the *projective transformation* of f.

We have the following facts about F (see [Morgan 1986b], [Morgan and Sommese 1987b], [Morgan and Sommese 1988]):

1. For random choices of $b = (b_1, \ldots, b_{n+1}) \in R^{n+1}$ and $\theta \in R^1$, the homotopy

$$h(x, t) = (1-t)\gamma g(x) + tF(x) \qquad (9)$$

has no divergent continuation paths, where $\gamma = e^{i\theta}$ and the start system, g, is as above. (It also suffices to choose random $b \in C^{n+1}$ and/or random $\gamma \in C^1$.)

2. If z^* is an isolated solution to $f(z) = 0$, then there is an isolated solution x^* to $F(x) = 0$ with $x_0^* \neq 0$, so that $z^* = \frac{1}{x_0^*} x^*$.

Thus, if we solve $F(x) = 0$ by path tracking the continuation curves defined by (9), then we can recover all the isolated solutions of $f(z) = 0$ from those of $F(x) = 0$. The advantage is that we don't have to decide when to truncate paths that seem to be diverging, since no paths diverge. Note that F has the same total degree as f, so the number of continuation paths is the same to solve $F = 0$ as to solve $f = 0$. There are additional computational advantages to the projective transformation. See [Morgan 1987, Chapter 5], [Morgan et al. 1988], and [Watson et al. 1987]. In the next section, we expand this idea somewhat by considering the projective transformation of h.

3. CONSTRUCTING HOMOTOPIES FOR POLYNOMIAL SYSTEMS

In this section we state the three theorems on which the m-homogeneous method of constructing polynomial homotopies is based. (These theorems are proven in [Morgan and Sommese 1987a] and [Morgan and Sommese 1987b].) Then we outline the steps in the homotopy construction process.

First, we need the definitions of a *geometrically isolated* solution and the *multiplicity* of a solution.

A solution to a polynomial system is called *geometrically isolated* (or simply *isolated*) if there is a ball around the solution that contains no other solution. A solution that is not geometrically isolated is singular, but an isolated solution can be singular also.

Let z^* be a geometrically isolated solution to the polynomial system $f(z) = 0$. Let U be a closed ball about z^* containing no other solution. We can perturb f by adding arbitrarily small complex numbers to each coefficient of f (including the zero coefficients) in such a way that the perturbed system has only nonsingular solutions. For all sufficiently small coefficient perturbations, the perturbed systems have a constant number, m, of solutions in U. This m is (by definition) the *multiplicity* of z^*. We note that a solution z^* to $f(z) = 0$ has multiplicity greater than one exactly when it is singular; that is, when the Jacobian matrix $df(z^*)$ is singular.

The algebraically proper context for generating the full solution list of a polynomial system is complex projective space rather than real or complex Euclidean space. This is because the structure of the solution set to $f(z) = 0$ is generic in projective space. (See, for example, Bezout's theorem in any algebraic geometry reference.) Homotopy continuation methods for generating the full solution list to $f(z) = 0$ have always implicitly acknowledged this by being formulated in complex Euclidean space and allowing paths to diverge to infinity. It is more numerically stable, however, to acknowledge projective space directly. We therefore follow the classical approach from algebraic geometry of homogenizing f and establishing our continuation process in projective space. In many cases it is advantageous to homogenize f so that it has an m-*homogeneous* structure (defined in this Section below). Then we view the solutions to $f(z) = 0$ as being in a Cartesian product of projective spaces. We will present our discussion in this generality. Since 1-homogeneous systems are merely homogeneous systems, the m-homogeneous approach includes all polynomial systems and does not limit us to special cases.

Complex projective space, P^k, consists of the lines through the origin in C^{k+1}, denoted $[(z_0, ..., z_k)]$, where $(z_0, ..., z_k) \in C^{k+1} - \{0\}$; that is, $[(z_0, ..., z_k)]$ is the line through the origin that contains $(z_0, ..., z_k)$. It is natural to view P^k as a disjoint union of points $[(z_0, ..., z_k)]$ with $z_0 \neq 0$ (identified with Euclidean space via $[(z_0, ..., z_k)] \rightarrow (z_1/z_0, ..., z_k/z_0)$) and the "points at infinity," the $[(z_0, ..., z_n)]$ with $z_0 = 0$.

We partition the variables $\{z_1,...,z_n\}$ into m nonempty collections. It will be notationally simpler here if we rename the variables with double subscripts. Thus, let $\{z_1,...,z_n\} = \bigcup_{j=1}^{m}\{z_{1,j},...,z_{k_j,j}\}$, where $\sum_{j=1}^{m} k_j = n$. Now choose homogeneous variables $z_{0,j}$ for $j = 1$ to m and define $Z_j = \{z_{0,j}, z_{1,j},..., z_{k_j,j}\}$ for $j = 1$ to m. Then evoke the substitution $z_{i,j} \leftarrow z_{i,j}/z_{0,j}$ for $i = 1$ to k_j and $j = 1$ to m, generating a system $\hat{f} = 0$ of n equations in $n + m$ unknowns (after we clear the denominators of powers of the $z_{0,j}$). Now $\hat{f} = 0$ naturally has solutions in $P \equiv P^{k_1} \times P^{k_2} \times ... \times P^{k_m}$. (See [Morgan and Sommese 1987a].) We say $\hat{f}$ is m-*homogeneous* because the variables are partitioned into m collections, $Z_1,...,Z_m$, so that $\hat{f}$ is homogeneous as a system in the variables of any one of the collections. We let $d_{j,l}$ denote the jth degree of the lth polynomial; that is, with all variables held fixed except those in Z_j, $\hat{f}_l$ has homogeneous degree $d_{j,l}$. Note that "1-homogeneous" is the same as "homogeneous," so theorems about m-homogeneous polynomial systems apply essentially to all polynomial systems.

The *Bezout number*, d, of an m-homogeneous polynomial system is defined to be the coefficient of $\prod_{j=1}^{m} \alpha_j^{k_j}$ in the product $D = \prod_{l=1}^{n} \sum_{j=1}^{m} d_{j,l}\alpha_j$. The significance of the Bezout number is that it is an upper bound on the number of homotopy continuation paths we will track in the space $P \times [0,1]$ (Theorem 1, below). The smaller d is, the better. Frequently, the m-homogenization of f for $m > 1$ has a (much) smaller Bezout number than the 1-homogenization. If $m = 1$, then $d = d_1 \cdots d_n$, the total degree of f. This is the "traditional" number of paths to track.

Consider the homotopy (3), where now we take g to be an m-homogeneous system of n polynomials in $n + m$ variables obeying the conditions given below. Let g be chosen so that its m-homogeneous structure matches that of f; that is, $Z_1,...,Z_m$ are specified and the $d_{j,l}$ for g are exactly the same as those for f. Naturally, many such g will exist. We can always choose $m = 1$ and g diagonal (e.g., $g_j = p_j z_{l,1}^{d_{1,l}} - q_j z_{0,1}^{d_{1,l}}$), but it is important to note that in practice we can often do better.

Let $S \subseteq P$ be a set of common solutions of $f(z) = 0$ and $g(z) = 0$. For each $s \in S$, we require that the following conditions hold. For $s \in S$ let K denote the full connected component of solutions of $g(z) = 0$ with $s \in K$.

If s is a geometrically isolated solution of $g(z) = 0$ (i.e., $K = \{s\}$), we assume that:
- s is a geometrically isolated solution of $f(z) = 0$, and
- the multiplicity of s as a solution of $g(z) = 0$ is less than or equal to the multiplicity of s as a solution of $f(z) = 0$.

If s is not a geometrically isolated solution of $g(z) = 0$, then we assume that:
- K is contained in S,
- K is the full solution component of $f(z) = 0$ containing s,
- K is a smooth manifold, and
- at each point $z^0 \in K$ the rank of $dg(z^0)$ is the codimension of K (that is, $n-$(the

dimension of K)).

Let Σ denote the solutions of $g(z) = 0$ in $P - S$. Then the following holds.

Theorem 1. Assume the points in Σ are nonsingular solutions of $g(z) = 0$. For any positive r and for all but a finite number of angles, θ, if $\gamma = re^{i\theta}$, then $h^{-1}(0) \cap ((P - S) \times [0, 1))$ consists of smooth paths and every geometrically isolated solution of $f(z) = 0$ not in S has a path in $(P - S) \times [0, 1)$ converging to it. In fact, if m_0 is the multiplicity of a geometrically isolated solution, z^0, that is not in S, then z^0 has exactly m_0 paths converging to it. Further, the paths are strictly increasing in t, and $dt/ds > 0$, where s denotes arc length.

This theorem is given in [Morgan and Sommese 1987b] as Theorem 1 (including the remarks after the statement of the theorem).

Let $L = (L_1, \ldots, L_m)$ with $L_j = \sum_{i=0}^{k_j} \beta_{i,j} z_{i,j}$ where $\beta_{i,j} \neq 0$ for some i, for each j. Then we say that $U_L = U_{L_1} \times U_{L_2} \times \ldots \times U_{L_m}$, is the *Euclidean coordinate patch defined by* L, where $U_{L_j} = \{[z] \in P^{k_j} | L_j(z) \neq 0\}$ is the Euclidean coordinate patch on P^{k_j} defined by L_j. Note that U_L, which is an open dense submanifold of P, can be identified with $C^n = C^{k_1} \times C^{k_2} \times \ldots \times C^{k_m}$ by identifying U_{L_j} with C^{k_j} via $[(z_{0,j}, \ldots, z_{k_j,j})] \to \frac{1}{L_j(z)}(z_{0,j}, \ldots, z_{i_j-1,j}, z_{i_j+1,j}, \ldots, z_{k_j,j})$, where $\beta_{i_j,j} \neq 0$ for $j = 1$ to m.

The following two theorems from [Morgan and Sommese 1987b] show us how to keep the continuation process in Euclidean space, even though our basic theorem (Theorem 1) is formulated in P, a Cartesian product of projective spaces.

Theorem 2. Let U_L be a given Euclidean patch on P defined by L, as above. If the solutions of $g(z) = 0$ in $P - S$ are all in U_L, then $h^{-1}(0) \cap ((P - S) \times [0, 1)) \subset U_L \times [0, 1)$, except for a finite number of θ.

Theorem 3. Assume the points in Σ are nonsingular solutions of $g(z) = 0$. Then $\overline{h^{-1}(0) \cap ((P - S) \times [0, 1))} \subset U_L \times [0, 1]$ for almost all U_L and all but a finite number of θ, where the overbar indicates topological closure.

Note that $\overline{h^{-1}(0) \cap ((P - S) \times [0, 1))}$ is the set of continuation paths, including end points. It equals $h^{-1}(0) \cap ((P - S) \times [0, 1])$ if and only if $f(z) = 0$ has only a finite number of solutions in $P - S$.

For computations, we need a convenient way to realize the U_L. We do this via "the projective transformation," as follows. (The projective transformation was introduced in [Morgan 1986b] and extended to the m-homogeneous case in [Morgan and Sommese 1987b].) With m-homogeneous h in the variables $z_{i,j}$ for $i = 0$ to k_j and $j = 1$ to m, we let

$$z_{0,j} = \sum_{i=1}^{k_j} b_{i,j} z_{i,j} + b_{0,j} \tag{10}$$

for $j = 1$ to m where the $b_{i,j}$ are constants and $b_{i,j} \neq 0$ for some i, for each j. The *projective transformation of* h (given by (10)) is the system H of n polynomials in the n variables $z_{i,j}$ for $i = 1$ to k_j, $j = 1$ to m (along with t) where $H_j = h_j$ for $j = 1$ to n with (10) defining the $z_{0,j}$ in terms of the other variables. By Theorem 3, $\overline{h^{-1}(0) \cap ((P - S) \times [0, 1))}$ (the homotopy paths, including end points) are completely represented in C^n as solutions to $H = 0$, for almost all $b = (b_{i,j})$ and all but a finite number of θ. Thus, for computations, we need not acknowledge projective space except by solving $H = 0$ with randomly chosen $b_{i,j}$ and θ. The finite solutions of $f(z) = 0$ are recovered via $z_{i,j} \leftarrow z_{i,j}/z_{0,j}$ for $i = 1$ to k_j and $j = 1$ to m. (If any $z_{0,j} = 0$, then the solution is at infinity.)

Here is a summary of the m-homogeneous solution process. We want to find all geometrically isolated solutions to $f(z) = 0$. The solution process described below finds all such solutions.

1. **Constructing the Homotopy.**
   a. Fix an m-homogeneous form for f. Usually, we choose an m-homogeneous form for f that minimizes the Bezout number.
   b. Choose the system g so that:
      - g has the same m-homogeneous form as f.
      - The solutions to $g(z) = 0$ are known.
      - The singular solutions to $g(z) = 0$ are also singular solutions to $f(z) = 0$. See Theorem 1 for conditions that must hold (i.e., restrictions on the set S).
      - If possible, $g(z) = 0$ and $f(z) = 0$ should share solutions and/or the coefficients of g should be "close to" the coefficients of f.
   c. Define H to be the projective transformation of h. Choose a set S of common solutions of $g = 0$ and $f = 0$. Let Σ be the solutions of $g = 0$ not in S. (Σ and S must obey the conditions of Theorem 1.)
2. **Numerical Path Tracking.** For each point in Σ, the associated path in $H^{-1}(0)$ will be tracked numerically from $t = 0$ to $t = 1$. This will yield the full list of geometrically isolated solutions to $H(z, 1) = 0$. No paths diverge to infinity, so the numerical path tracking will terminate in a finite number of steps without abandoning any path.

4. CONCLUSIONS AND FUTURE WORK

Section 2 summarizes the elementary theory of homotopy construction and path tracking for polynomial continuation, and Section 3 describes a more advanced m-homogeneous theory. On the one hand we have a very complete computational methodology, in the sense that we have an algorithmic method that works *in theory* for any polynomial system. In spite of this, it is not necessarily easy to carry out the computations in practice. Singular solutions and extreme scaling of coefficients can create catastrophic numerical problems. Further, the large number of paths that typically arise can be discouraging. The m-homogeneous theory improves this in a number of practical applications. One area for future work is to develop further techniques for customizing homotopies to the special structures that arise in applications. See [Morgan and Sommese 1988] and [Wampler et al. 1988] for some recent steps in this direction.

REFERENCES

Allgower, E.L. and K. Georg (1980), "Simplicial and Continuation Methods for Approximating Fixed Points and Solutions to Systems of Equations," *SIAM Rev.* 22, 28–85.

CONDOR (1988), "Operations Research: the Next Decade," *Operations Research 36*, 619–637.

Drexler, F. J. (1977), "Eine Methode zur Berechung sämtlicher Lösunger von Polynomgleichungessystemen," *Numer. Math. 29*, 45–58.

Garcia, C.B. and W.I. Zangwill (1977), "Global Continuation Methods for Finding All Solutions to Polynomial Systems of Equations in N Variables," Technical Report 7755, Ctr. for Math. Studies in Business and Economics, Univ. of Chicago, Chicago, Ill.

Garcia, C.B. and W.I. Zangwill (1981), *Pathways to Solutions, Fixed Points, and Equilibria*, Prentice-Hall, Englewood Cliffs, N.J.

Magnanti, Thomas L. (1982), "Models and Algorithms for Predicting Urban Traffic Equilibria," Sloan School of Management, MIT, Cambridge, Mass.

Meintjes, K. and A. P. Morgan (1987), "A Methodology for Solving Chemical Equilibrium Systems," *Appl. Math. Comput. 22*, 333–361.

Morgan, A. P. (1986a), "A Homotopy for Solving Polynomial Systems," *Appl. Math. Comput. 18*, 87–92.

Morgan, A. P. (1986b), "A Transformation to Avoid Solutions at Infinity for Polynomial Systems," *Appl. Math. Comput. 18*, 77–86.

Morgan, A. P. (1987), *Solving Polynomial Systems Using Continuation for Scientific and Engineering Problems*, Prentice-Hall, Englewood Cliffs, N.J.

Morgan, A. P. and A. J. Sommese (1987a), "A Homotopy for Solving General Polynomial Systems That Respects M-Homogeneous Structures," *Appl. Math. Comput. 24*, 101–113.

Morgan, A. P. and A. J. Sommese (1987b), "Computing All Solutions to Polynomial Systems Using Homotopy Continuation," *Appl. Math. Comput. 24*, 115–138.

Morgan, A. P. and A. J. Sommese (1988), "Coefficient Parameter Polynomial Continuation," *Appl. Math. Comput.*, accepted for publication.

Morgan, A. P., A. J. Sommese, and L. T. Watson (1988), "Finding All Solutions to Polynomial Systems Using HOMPACK," Research Publication GMR-6109, General Motors Research Laboratories., Warren, Mich. 48090.

Rheinboldt, W.C. and J.V. Burkardt (1983), "Algorithm 596: A Program for a Locally

Parameterized Continuation Process," *ACM Trans. Math. Software 9, 236–241*.

Watson, L. T. (1979), "A Globally Convergent Algorithm for Computing Fixed Points of C^2 Maps," *Appl. Math. Comput. 5, 297–311*.

Watson, L. T. (1986), "Numerical Linear Algebra Aspects of Globally Convergent Homotopy Methods," *SIAM Review 28, 529–545*.

Watson, L. T., S. C. Billups, and A. P. Morgan (1987), "HOMPACK: A Suite of Codes for Globally Convergent Homotopy Algorithms," *ACM Trans. Math. Software 13, 281–310*.

Wampler, C. W., A. P. Morgan, and A. J. Sommese (1988), "Numerical Continuation Methods for Solving Polynomial Systems Arising in Kinematics," Research Publication GMR-6372, General Motors Research Laboratories, Warren, Mich. 48090.

Wright, A. H. (1985), "Finding All Solutions to a System of Polynomial Equations," *Math. Comp. 44, 125–133*.

MODERN HOMOTOPY METHODS IN OPTIMIZATION

LAYNE T. WATSON

Department of Computer Science

Virginia Polytechnic Institute & State University, Blacksburg, VA 24061

ABSTRACT

Nonlinear systems of equations occur frequently in operations research, arising from game theory, nonlinear simulation models, statistical estimation, and nonlinear optimization. Probability-one homotopy methods are a class of algorithms for solving nonlinear systems of equations that are accurate, robust, and converge from an arbitrary starting point almost surely. These new techniques have been successfully applied to solve Brouwer fixed point problems, polynomial systems of equations, and discretizations of nonlinear two-point boundary value problems. This paper describes the impact of these new globally convergent homotopy algorithms on unconstrained and constrained optimization done in operations research.

1. INTRODUCTION

Continuation is a well known and established procedure in numerical analysis, and has recently become a powerful tool in operations research, beginning with the fundamental work of Scarf [1973] on economic equilibria. Continuation and homotopy methods have had enormous impact on some operations research problems such as economic equilibria, n-person games, combinatorial and complementarity problems, nonlinear statistical parameter estimation, nonlinear process simulation, and nonlinear programming. The purpose of this paper is to describe basic homotopy theory, state without proof the theoretical applicability of homotopy methods to nonlinear optimization, and give an example. Homotopy algorithms, in conjunction with parallel computers, offer a powerful mathematical tool to the operations research community.

The idea behind continuation is to continuously deform a simple (easy) problem into the given (hard) problem, while solving the family of deformed problems. The solutions to the deformed problems are related, and can be tracked as the deformation proceeds. The function describing the deformation is called a *homotopy map*. Homotopies are a traditional part of topology, and have found significant application in nonlinear functional analysis and differential geometry. Similar ideas, such as incremental loading, are also widely used in engineering.

These traditional continuation algorithms have serious deficiencies, which have been removed by modern homotopy algorithms. The differences, however, are subtle and mathematically deep, and the mathematical proofs of the statements in this article are beyond the scope of the presentation here. To explain the differences between the old and new homotopy techniques, a more detailed discussion is required. Suppose the given problem is to find a root of the nonlinear equation $f(x) = 0$, and that $s(x) = 0$ is a simple version of the given problem with an easily obtainable unique solution x_0. Then a homotopy map could be, e.g.,

$$H(\lambda, x) = \lambda f(x) + (1 - \lambda) s(x), \quad 0 \le \lambda \le 1.$$

The family of problems is $H(\lambda, x) = 0$, $0 \le \lambda \le 1$, and the idea would be to track the solutions of $H(\lambda, x) = 0$, starting from $(\lambda, x) = (0, x_0)$, as λ goes from 0 to 1. If everything worked out well, this would lead to a point $(\lambda, x) = (1, \bar{x})$, where $f(\bar{x}) = 0$. The "standard" approach is to start from a point (λ_i, x_i) with $H(\lambda_i, x_i) = 0$, and solve the problem $H(\lambda_i + \Delta\lambda, x) = 0$ for x, with $\Delta\lambda$ being a sufficiently small, fixed, positive number. The bad things that can happen are:

1) The points (λ_i, x_i) may diverge to infinity as $\lambda \to 1$.
2) The problem $H(\lambda_i + \Delta\lambda, x) = 0$ may be singular at its solution, causing numerical instability.
3) There may be no solution of $H(\lambda_i + \Delta\lambda, x) = 0$ near (λ_i, x_i).

The modern approach to homotopy methods is to construct a homotopy map $\rho_a(\lambda, x)$, involving additional parameters in the vector a, such that 1), 2), and 3) never occur or never cause any difficulty. The details of how this is done are given in Section 2. Section 3 summarizes basic homotopy results for optimization problems common in operations research, and makes the connection between operations research, optimization, nonlinear equations, and homotopies. An example of the globally convergent homotopy techniques applied to a common optimization problem is given in Section 4.

2. HOMOTOPY THEORY

The theoretical foundation of all probability one globally convergent homotopy methods is given in the following differential geometry theorem:

DEFINITION. *Let E^n denote n-dimensional real Euclidean space, let $U \subset E^m$ and $V \subset E^n$ be open sets, and let $\rho : U \times [0, 1) \times V \to E^n$ be a C^2 map. ρ is said to be transversal to zero if the Jacobian matrix $D\rho$ has full rank on $\rho^{-1}(0)$.*

PARAMETRIZED SARD'S THEOREM *[Chow et al. 1978]. If $\rho(a, \lambda, x)$ is transversal to zero, then for almost all $a \in U$ the map*

$$\rho_a(\lambda, x) = \rho(a, \lambda, x)$$

is also transversal to zero; i.e., with probability one the Jacobian matrix $D\rho_a(\lambda, x)$ has full rank on $\rho_a^{-1}(0)$.

The import of this theorem is that the zero set $\rho_a^{-1}(0)$ consists of smooth, nonintersecting curves in $[0, 1) \times V$. These curves are either closed loops, or have endpoints in $\{0\} \times V$ or $\{1\} \times V$, or go to infinity. Another important consequence is that these curves have finite arc length in any compact subset of $[0, 1) \times V$. The recipe for constructing a globally convergent homotopy algorithm to solve the nonlinear system of equations

$$F(x) = 0, \tag{1}$$

where $F : E^n \to E^n$ is a C^2 map, is as follows: For an open set $U \subset E^m$ construct a C^2 homotopy map $\rho : U \times [0, 1) \times E^n \to E^n$ such that

1) $\rho(a, \lambda, x)$ is transversal to zero,
2) $\rho_a(0, x) = \rho(a, 0, x) = 0$ is trivial to solve and has a unique solution x_0,
3) $\rho_a(1, x) = F(x)$,
4) $\rho_a^{-1}(0)$ is bounded.

Then for almost all $a \in U$ there exists a zero curve γ of ρ_a, along which the Jacobian matrix $D\rho_a$ has rank n, emanating from $(0, x_0)$ and reaching a zero $\bar{x}$ of F at $\lambda = 1$. This zero curve γ does not intersect itself, is disjoint from any other zeros of ρ_a, and has finite arc length in every compact subset of $[0, 1) \times E^n$. Furthermore, if $DF(\bar{x})$ is nonsingular, then γ has finite arc length.

The general idea of the algorithm is now apparent: just follow the zero curve γ emanating from $(0, a)$ until a zero $\tilde{x}$ of $F(x)$ is reached (at $\lambda = 1$). Of course it is nontrivial to develop a viable numerical algorithm based on that idea, but at least conceptually, the algorithm for solving the nonlinear system of equations $F(x) = 0$ is clear and simple. The homotopy map (usually, but not always) is

$$\rho_a(\lambda, x) = \lambda F(x) + (1 - \lambda)(x - a), \tag{2}$$

which has the same form as a standard continuation or embedding mapping. However, there are two crucial differences. In standard continuation, the embedding parameter λ increases monotonically from 0 to 1 as the trivial problem $x - a = 0$ is continuously deformed to the problem $F(x) = 0$. The present homotopy method permits λ to both increase and decrease along γ with no adverse effect; that is, turning points present no special difficulty. The second important difference is that there are never any "singular points" which afflict standard continuation methods. The way in which the zero curve γ of ρ_a is followed and the full rank of $D\rho_a$ along γ guarantee this.

The scheme just described is known as a probability-one globally convergent homotopy algorithm. The phrase "probability-one" refers to the almost any choice for a, and the "global convergence" refers to the fact that the starting point x_0 need not be anywhere near the solution $\bar{x}$. It should be mentioned that the form of the homotopy map $\rho_a(\lambda, x)$ in (2) is just a special case used here for clarity of exposition. The more general theory can be found in [Watson 1979a; Watson 1986; Watson et al. 1987a], and practical engineering problems requiring a ρ_a nonlinear in λ are in [Watson and Yang 1980] and [Watson and Wang 1981]. Below are some typical theorems for various classes of problems.

The computation of Brouwer fixed points represents one of the first successes for both simplicial [Allgower and Georg 1980; Scarf 1973] and continuous homotopy methods [Chow et al. 1978; Watson 1979a]. Brouwer fixed point problems can be very nasty, and often cause locally convergent iterative methods a great deal of difficulty.

THEOREM. *Let $B = \{x \in E^n \mid \|x\|_2 = 1\}$ be the closed unit ball, and $f : B \to B$ a C^2 map. Then for almost all $a \in \text{int } B$ there exists a zero curve γ of*

$$\rho_a(\lambda, x) = \lambda(x - f(x)) + (1 - \lambda)(x - a),$$

along which the Jacobian matrix $D\rho_a(\lambda, x)$ has full rank, emanating from $(0, a)$ and reaching a fixed point $\bar{x}$ of f at $\lambda = 1$. Furthermore, γ has finite arc length if $I - Df(\bar{x})$ is nonsingular.

Typically a mathematical problem (such as a partial differential equation) reduces to a finite dimensional nonlinear system of equations, and what is desired are conditions on the original problem, not on the final discretized problem. Thus the results in this section are used to derive, working backwards, useful conditions on the original problem, whatever it might be. The following four lemmas, which follow from the results of [Chow et al. 1978], are used for that purpose.

LEMMA 1. *Let $g : E^p \to E^p$ be a C^2 map, $a \in E^p$, and define $\rho_a : [0, 1) \times E^p \to E^p$ by*

$$\rho_a(\lambda, y) = \lambda g(y) + (1 - \lambda)(y - a).$$

Then for almost all $a \in E^p$ there is a zero curve γ of ρ_a emanating from $(0, a)$ along which the Jacobian matrix $D\rho_a(\lambda, y)$ has full rank.

LEMMA 2. *If the zero curve γ in Lemma 1 is bounded, it has an accumulation point $(1, \bar{y})$, where $g(\bar{y}) = 0$. Furthermore, if $Dg(\bar{y})$ is nonsingular, then γ has finite arc length.*

LEMMA 3. *Let $F : E^p \to E^p$ be a C^2 map such that for some $r > 0$, $x F(x) \geq 0$ whenever $\|x\| = r$. Then F has a zero in $\{x \in E^p \mid \|x\| \leq r\}$, and for almost all*

$a \in E^p$, $\|a\| < r$, there is a zero curve γ of

$$\rho_a(\lambda, x) = \lambda F(x) + (1 - \lambda)(x - a),$$

along which the Jacobian matrix $D\rho_a(\lambda, x)$ has full rank, emanating from $(0, a)$ and reaching a zero $\bar{x}$ of F at $\lambda = 1$. Furthermore, γ has finite arc length if $DF(\bar{x})$ is nonsingular.

Lemma 3 is a special case of the following more general lemma.

LEMMA 4. Let $F : E^p \to E^p$ be a C^2 map such that for some $r > 0$ and $\tilde{r} > 0$, $F(x)$ and $x - a$ do not point in opposite directions for $\|x\| = r$, $\|a\| < \tilde{r}$. Then F has a zero in $\{x \in E^p \mid \|x\| \leq r\}$, and for almost all $a \in E^p$, $\|a\| < \tilde{r}$, there is a zero curve γ of

$$\rho_a(\lambda, x) = \lambda F(x) + (1 - \lambda)(x - a),$$

along which the Jacobian matrix $D\rho_a(\lambda, x)$ has full rank, emanating from $(0, a)$ and reaching a zero $\bar{x}$ of F at $\lambda = 1$. Furthermore, γ has finite arc length if $DF(\bar{x})$ is nonsingular.

These theoretical algorithms have been implemented in sophisticated mathematical software packages such as PITCON [Rheinboldt and Burkardt 1983], CONKUB [Mejia 1986], and HOMPACK [Watson et al. 1987a]. The latter is an extensive collection of FORTRAN 77 routines implementing three different tracking algorithms for both dense and sparse problems, and containing high level drivers for special classes of problems.

3. BASIC OPTIMIZATION HOMOTOPIES

Consider first the unconstrained optimization problem

$$\min_x f(x). \tag{3}$$

THEOREM. Let $f : E^n \to E$ be a C^3 convex map with a minimum at $\tilde{x}$, $\|\tilde{x}\|_2 \leq M$. Then for almost all a, $\|a\|_2 < M$, there exists a zero curve γ of the homotopy map

$$\rho_a(\lambda, x) = \lambda \nabla f(x) + (1 - \lambda)(x - a),$$

along which the Jacobian matrix $D\rho_a(\lambda, x)$ has full rank, emanating from $(0, a)$ and reaching a point $(1, \bar{x})$, where $\bar{x}$ solves (3).

A function is called uniformly convex if it is convex and its Hessian's smallest eigenvalue is bounded away from zero. Consider next the constrained optimization problem

$$\min_{x \geq 0} f(x). \tag{4}$$

This is more general than it might appear because the general convex quadratic program reduces to a problem of the form (4).

THEOREM. *Let $f : E^n \to E$ be a C^3 uniformly convex map. Then there exists $\delta > 0$ such that for almost all $a \geq 0$ with $\|a\|_2 < \delta$ there exists a zero curve γ of the homotopy map*

$$\rho_a(\lambda, x) = \lambda K(x) + (1 - \lambda)(x - a),$$

where

$$K_i(x) = -\left|\frac{\partial f(x)}{\partial x_i} - x_i\right|^3 + \left(\frac{\partial f(x)}{\partial x_i}\right)^3 + x_i^3,$$

along which the Jacobian matrix $D\rho_a(\lambda, x)$ has full rank, connecting $(0, a)$ to a point $(1, \bar{x})$, where $\bar{x}$ solves the constrained optimization problem (4).

Given $F : E^n \to E^n$, the nonlinear complementarity problem is to find a vector $x \in E^n$ such that

$$x \geq 0, \quad F(x) \geq 0, \quad x^t F(x) = 0. \tag{5}$$

At a solution $\bar{x}$, $\bar{x}$ and $F(\bar{x})$ are "complementary" in the sense that if $\bar{x}_i > 0$, then $F_i(\bar{x}) = 0$, and if $F_i(\bar{x}) > 0$, then $\bar{x}_i = 0$. This problem is difficult because there are linear constraints $x \geq 0$, nonlinear constraints $F(x) \geq 0$, and a combinatorial aspect from the complementarity condition $x^t F(x) = 0$. It is interesting that homotopy methods can be adapted to deal with nonlinear constraints and combinatorial conditions.

Define $G : E^n \to E^n$ by

$$G_i(z) = -\left|F_i(z) - z_i\right|^3 + \left(F_i(z)\right)^3 + z_i^3, \quad i = 1, \ldots, n, \tag{6}$$

and let

$$\rho_a(\lambda, z) = \lambda G(z) + (1 - \lambda)(z - a).$$

THEOREM. *Let $F : E^n \to E^n$ be a C^2 map, and let the Jacobian matrix $DG(z)$ be nonsingular at every zero of $G(z)$. Suppose there exists $r > 0$ such that $z > 0$ and $z_k = \|z\|_\infty \geq r$ imply $F_k(z) > 0$. Then for almost all $a > 0$ there exists a zero curve γ of $\rho_a(\lambda, z)$, along which the Jacobian matrix $D\rho_a(\lambda, z)$ has full rank, having finite arc length and connecting $(0, a)$ to $(1, \bar{z})$, where $\bar{z}$ solves (5).*

THEOREM. *Let $F : E^n \to E^n$ be a C^2 map, and let the Jacobian matrix $DG(z)$ be nonsingular at every zero of $G(z)$. Suppose there exists $r > 0$ such that $z \geq 0$ and $\|z\|_\infty \geq r$ imply $z_k F_k(z) > 0$ for some index k. Then there exists $\delta > 0$ such that for almost all $a \geq 0$ with $\|a\|_\infty < \delta$ there exists a zero curve γ of $\rho_a(\lambda, z)$, along which the Jacobian matrix $D\rho_a(\lambda, z)$ has full rank, having finite arc length and connecting $(0, a)$ to $(1, \bar{z})$, where $\bar{z}$ solves (5).*

Problems of the form (3), (4), and (5) occur frequently in operations research. The above theorems show how these nonlinear optimization problems are converted to systems of nonlinear equations, which are then attacked by homotopy methods. The mathematical theory assures that, under reasonable hypotheses, the homotopy algorithms are globally convergent, i.e., they always converge to a solution from an arbitrary starting point. The above theory is more generally applicable than it might appear at first, because a general nonconvex nonlinear programming problem with both equality and inequality constraints is typically solved by reducing it to a series of quadratic programs of the form (4). The homotopy methodology has been successfully applied directly to the full constrained problem, but little supporting theory exists for that.

Homotopy algorithms for convex unconstrained optimization may not be computationally competitive with other approaches, but it is reassuring that the globally convergent homotopy techniques can theoretically be directly applied. For constrained optimization the homotopy approach offers some advantages, and, especially for the nonlinear complementarity problem, is superior to other algorithms. See [Watson et al. 1987b] for an application of homotopy techniques to the linear complementarity problem. Constrained optimization is addressed next.

4. EXPANDED LAGRANGIAN HOMOTOPY

The expanded Lagrangian homotopy method of Poore et al. [1988] is applicable to the general nonlinear programming problem

$$min \ \theta(x)$$
$$\text{subject to} \ \ g(x) \leq 0,$$
$$h(x) = 0,$$

where $x \in E^n$, θ is real valued, g is an m-dimensional vector, and h is a p-dimensional vector. In the most general situation the formulation and solution algorithm for the expanded Lagrangian homotopy are rather complicated. The method will be illustrated by applying it to a special case widely studied in the operations research literature, namely the linear complementarity problem:

$$w - Mz = q,$$
$$w \geq 0, \quad z \geq 0, \quad w^t z = 0,$$

where M is a given real $n \times n$ matrix and $q \in E^n$ is given; the unknowns are $w \in E^n$ and $z \in E^n$.

The expanded Lagrangian approach [Poore and Al-Hassan 1988] may be described as an optimization/continuation approach and has in its simplest form two main steps.

Step 1. (Optimization phase).

At $r = r_0 > 0$ solve the unconstrained minimization problem $\min\limits_{w,z} P(w, z, r)$ where

$$P(w,z,r) = \frac{1}{2r}\|w - Mz - q\|_2^2 + \frac{1}{2r}\langle w, z\rangle^2 - r\sum_{i=1}^n \ln z_i - r\sum_{i=1}^n \ln w_i.$$

Step 2A. (Switch to expanded system).

A (local) solution of $\min P$ must satisfy

$$0 = \nabla_{(w,z)} P = \begin{pmatrix} I \\ -M^t \end{pmatrix} \frac{(w - Mz - q)}{r} + \begin{pmatrix} z \\ w \end{pmatrix} \frac{\langle w,z\rangle}{r} - r\left(\frac{1}{w_1},\ldots,\frac{1}{w_n},\frac{1}{z_1},\ldots,\frac{1}{z_n}\right)^t.$$

Introduce the following variables:

$$\beta = \frac{w - Mz - q}{r}, \qquad \mu_i = \frac{r}{w_i}, \qquad i = 1,\ldots,n,$$

$$\theta = \frac{\langle w, z\rangle}{r}, \qquad \eta_i = \frac{r}{z_i}, \qquad i = 1,\ldots,n,$$

which ultimately represent the Lagrange multipliers. This helps to remove the inevitable ill-conditioning associated with penalty methods for small r and we thus obtain our equivalent but expanded system:

$$\begin{pmatrix} I \\ -M^t \end{pmatrix}\beta + \begin{pmatrix} z \\ w \end{pmatrix}\theta - \begin{pmatrix} \mu \\ \eta \end{pmatrix} = 0, \qquad \mu_i w_i - r = 0, \quad i=1,\ldots,n,$$

$$w - Mz - q - r\beta = 0, \qquad \eta_i z_i - r = 0, \quad i=1,\ldots,n.$$

$$\langle w, z\rangle - r\theta = 0,$$

(Remark. As a result of the optimization phase and the initial starting point with $r_0 > 0$, the solution $(w^{(0)}, z^{(0)})$ of $\min P(w, z, r_0)$ satisfies $z^{(0)} > 0$ and $w^{(0)} > 0$. As a consequence, $\mu^{(0)} > 0$ and $\eta^{(0)} > 0$ from the definitions of μ and η. They remain positive until $r = 0$ where we formally have

$$\begin{pmatrix} I \\ -M^t \end{pmatrix}\beta + \begin{pmatrix} z \\ w \end{pmatrix}\theta - \begin{pmatrix} \mu \\ \eta \end{pmatrix} = 0, \qquad \mu_i w_i = 0, \quad i=1,\ldots,n,$$

$$w - Mz - q = 0, \qquad \eta_i z_i = 0, \quad i=1,\ldots,n,$$

$$\langle w, z\rangle = 0, \qquad w, z, \theta, \mu, \eta \geq 0,$$

which implies that we have solved the problem.)

In practice we do not solve the optimization problem $\min P$ to high accuracy since a highly accurate solution may have only a digit or two in common with the final answer.

However, it is imperative that ∇P be reasonably small in magnitude, say less than $r_0/10$. The expanded system is converted to a homotopy map by letting $r = r_0(1 - \lambda)$ and modifying the first equation to obtain:

$$\begin{pmatrix} I \\ -M^t \end{pmatrix} \beta + \begin{pmatrix} z \\ w \end{pmatrix} \theta - \begin{pmatrix} \mu \\ \eta \end{pmatrix} - \frac{r}{r_0} \nabla P(w^{(0)}, z^{(0)}, r_0) = 0,$$

$$w - Mz - q - r\beta = 0,$$

$$\langle w, z \rangle - r\theta = 0,$$

$$\mu_i w_i - r = 0, \quad i = 1, \ldots, n,$$

$$\eta_i z_i - r = 0, \quad i = 1, \ldots, n.$$

Write this system of $5n + 1$ equations in the $5n + 2$ variables $\lambda, w, z, \beta, \theta, \mu, \eta$ as

$$\Upsilon(\lambda, w, z, \beta, \theta, \mu, \eta) = 0.$$

Step 2B. (Track the zero curve of Υ from $r = r_0$ to $r = 0$.)

Starting with arbitrary $r_0 > 0$, $w^{(0)} > 0$ and $z^{(0)} > 0$, the rest of the initial point $(0, w^{(0)}, z^{(0)}, \beta^{(0)}, \theta_0, \mu^{(0)}, \eta^{(0)})$ is given by

$$\beta^{(0)} = \frac{w^{(0)} - Mz^{(0)} - q}{r_0}, \quad \mu_i^{(0)} = \frac{r_0}{w_i^{(0)}}, \quad i = 1, \ldots, n,$$

$$\theta_0 = \frac{\langle w^{(0)}, z^{(0)} \rangle}{r_0}, \quad \eta_i^{(0)} = \frac{r_0}{z_i^{(0)}}, \quad i = 1, \ldots, n.$$

This approach requires careful attention to implementation details. For example, the linear algebra and globalization techniques with dynamic scaling are critically important in the optimization phase. For degenerate problems the path can still be long. One possible resolution is the use of shifts and weights as developed in the method of multipliers [Bertaekas 1982], but holding $r = r_0$ fixed. (This approach is currently under investigation in the context of linear programming [Poore and Soria 1988].) However, in keeping with the philosophy of the "pure" homotopy approach of the current work, we do not solve the optimization problem (Step A.), but instead use the above equations $\Upsilon(\lambda, w, z, \beta, \theta, \mu, \eta) = 0$ as a "pure" homotopy.

ACKNOWLEDGEMENT

This work was supported in part by AFOSR Grant 85-0250.

REFERENCES

Allgower, E. and K. Georg (1980) "Simplicial and continuation methods for approximating fixed points," *SIAM Rev. 22.* 28-85.

Bertaekas, D. P. (1982) *Constrained Optimization and Lagrange Multiplier Methods* Academic Press, New York, N.Y.

Chow, S. N., J. Mallet-Paret, and J. A. Yorke (1978) "Finding zeros of maps: Homotopy methods that are constructive with probability one," *Math. Comput. 32* 887–899.

Kreisselmeier, G. and R. Steinhauser (1979), "Systematic control design by optimizing a vector performance index", *In Proc. IFAC Symp. on Computer Aided Design of Control Systems* (Zurich, Switzerland) pp. 113–117.

Mangasarian, O. L. (1976), "Equivalence of the complementarity problem to a system of nonlinear equations," *SIAM J. Appl. Math. 31* 89–92.

Mejia, R. (1986), "CONKUB: A conversational path-follower for systems of nonlinear equations," *J. Comput. Phys. 63* 67–84.

Poore, A. B. and D. Soria (1988), "Continuation algorithms for linear programming," manuscript in preparation.

Poore, A. B. and Q. Al-Hassan (1988), "The expanded Lagrangian system for constrained optimization problems," *SIAM J. Control Optim.*, to appear.

Rheinboldt, W. C. and J. V. Burkardt (1983), "Algorithm 596: A program for a locally parameterized continuation process," *ACM Trans. Math. Software 9*, 236-241.

Scarf, H. (1973), *The Computation of Economic Equilibria*, Yale University Press, New Haven, Conn.

Watson, L. T. (1979a), "A globally convergent algorithm for computing fixed points of C^2 maps," *Appl. Math. Comput. 5*, 297–311.

Watson, L. T. (1979b), "Solving the nonlinear complementarity problem by a homotopy method", *SIAM J. Control Optim. 17*, 1 (Jan.), 36–46.

Watson, L. T. (1980), "Computational experience with the Chow-Yorke algorithm", *Math. Programming 19*, 92–101.

Watson, L. T. (1986), "Numerical linear algebra aspects of globally convergent homotopy methods", *SIAM Rev. 28*, 529–545.

Watson, L. T., S. C. Billups, and A. P. Morgan (1987a), "HOMPACK: A suite of codes for globally convergent homotopy algorithms", *ACM Trans. Math. Software 13*, 281–310.

Watson, L. T., J. P. Bixler, and A. B. Poore (1987b), "Continuous homotopies for the linear complementarity problem", Tech. Report TR–87–38, Dept. of Computer Science, VPI&SU, Blacksburg, Va.

Watson, L. T. and D. Fenner (1980), "Chow-Yorke algorithm for fixed points or zeros of C^2 maps", *ACM Trans. Math. Software 6*, 252–260.

Watson, L. T. and C. Y. Wang (1981), "A homotopy method applied to elastica problems", *Internat. J. Solids Structures* 17, 29–37.

Watson, L. T. and W. H. Yang (1980), "Optimal design by a homotopy method", *Applicable Anal.* 10, 275–284.

INDEX

A

Abstract, 497

Abstraction, 453

Action cluster, 412

Action-directed models, 349

Active objects, 30
  processor, 45

Actual network output, 312

Actual problem solving system, 334

Actual simulation, 439

ADANS algorithm, 328
  scheduling algorithm, 324

Adaptive Random, 478

ADD, 340

Advance modelling language, 509

Advanced Architecture computers (AAC), 507, 515

Algorithm design, 321

Algorithmic formulations, 322

Algorithmic parameters, 113

Alternative resolution stragedies, 339

ALTO, 340, 342

Analysis report, 339

Analytical diagnosis, 413

Application control, 491

Application program, 487, 488

Application support system, 487, 488

Appropriate parameters, 323

Approximation algorithms

Arc, 60, 63

Architecture design, 510

Array, 508
  expressions, 503
  index, 45
  processor, 510
  section, 501, 502

Artificial intelligence (AI), 289, 321, 386
  data base technology, 484
  search methods, 290
  search techniques, 290

Assignment problem, 23, 26, 27, 65, 170

Associative learning, 315

Associative mappings, 317

Asynchronous multiprocessor machine, 152

Asynchronous parallel algorithm, 150

Attached array processor, 508

Auction algorithm, 28, 172, 174, 176

Automated diagnosis

Automation-based paradigm, 389, 393

Average response time, 399

B

Back-propagation, 304

Backbone configuration, 524, 525, 527

Backbone improvement phase, 525, 526

Bard's grid search technique, 298

Basic genetic algorithm, 325

Basic network, 62

Basic optimization homotopies, 559

Batches, 84

Benders decomposition algorithm, 6

Best Fit (BF), 34, 38, 42

Best Fit Decreasing (BFD), 34, 42

Best known lower bound (BKLB), 151

Bi-level linear programming (BLLP), 290, 291, 295, 300

Bin, 35, 36
  packing, 33, 34
  problem, 33

Binary search, 122

Bitonic merge sorting algorithm, 51

Block structure, 83

Boating market, 257

Boating Research Center, 252, 258, 261

Bond strain energy, 92

Boolean, 417
  valued expression, 418

Bottom, 133

Boundary planes, 98

Bounds, 504
  section, 502

Bounds and Options sections, 503

Branch and bound algorithm, 131, 150, 471

Branch and bound tree, 132, 133

Branch and bound process, 132, 140

Brand loyalty, 258

Break-away step, 526

Build Solution Menu, 194

C

Candidate insertions, 324

Category sizes, 239

Child processes, 134

Cholesky Decomposition, 160

Closed queueing network, 241, 242, 246

CM time, 176

Coarse grain parallelism, 84

Color graphics, 190

Column Cholesky, 160, 162

Column Partition, 208

Column-wise storage, 96

Communicate, 100

Comparitive diagnosis, 413

Compiler, 509

Compiler vectorization, 77

Compilers, 72

Complementary problem, 560

Complexity analysis, 126

Computational effectiveness, 298

Computer Graphics, 388

Computer-impleted algorithm, 93

Computerized routing, 373

Conceptual activites, 450, 451

Conceptual capacities, 450

Condition Specification, 409
  primitives, 411

Condition-Action Pair, 410

Configuration, 507

Connection Machine (CM), 94, 169, 178
  system, 40, 44

Connectivity type, 191

Constants section, 501

Constrained discrete nonlinear optimization problem, 243

Constrained optimization, 463

Constraint programming languages, 463, 466, 467, 468

Constraint programmming systems, 463

Constraint systems, 463

Constraint-based scheduling techniques, 337

Consumer credit model, 304

Contigencies, 10

Continious homotopy methods, 558

Continuation, 544
  curves, 549
  path, 544
  paths, 546

Control algorithms, 457

Convergence, 87, 113, 297
  criterion, 73
  proofs, 110

Convex network problems, 176

Convex nonlinear problems, 178

Coordination, 85

Corner computations, 95

Cost management, 279

Counter, 100

Cray X-MP

Cross-over, 291

Crossover operator, 325

Crossover position, 325

Current configuration, 528

Current dual solution, 159

Current solution constraints, 337

Curve tracking

Customer retention, 258

Customers, 429

CYBER, 98

Cycle factor, 64

D

Dantzig-Wolfe primal decomposition approach, 16

Data graphics, 183

Data partitioning, 111

Decision Support System (DDS), 485, 489

Decision variables, 8

Decomposition, 3, 113
  algorithm, 17
  algorithms, 513, 514
  methods, 107

Decomposition routines, 161

Default assignment, 305

Demographic Indicators, 251, 256

Dense Assignment Problems, 171

Dependence relation, 163

Depth Cueing, 188

Depth-first search, 131, 132

Design variables, 8

Desired network output, 312

Deterministic algorithm, 92

Deterministic equivalent program, 107

Deterministic linear program, 5

Deterministic scenario subproblem, 108

Development models, 407

Development of heuristics, 375

Diagnostic analysis, 409

Diagnostic Assistance, 412, 415

Diagnostic messages, 418

Diagonal element, 52

Diagonalization algorithm, 74

Digitizing process, 363

Discourse, 313
  design, 491
  mappings, 317
  module, 314

Discrete nonlinear optimizations, 246

Discrete-event simulation models, 349, 385

Discrimination analysis, 305

Distributed memory multiprocessor, 132, 135

Distribution costs, 217

Distribution expenses, 217

Documentation phases, 433

Domain decomposition, 25

Dominance criterion, 50, 53

Dominance relation, 48

Dominance-based optimization, 53

Dominated solution, 51

Dominating diagonal, 141

Dual affine algorithm, 158, 160, 162

Dual algorithm, 59, 63

Dual-decomposition approach, 12

Dynamic, 459

Dynamic deterministic linear programs, 4

Dynamic linear programs, 4

Dynamic presentation, 426

Dynamic Programming (DP), 228, 229
  approach, 48
  programming equation, 120
  method, 230
  model, 230

Dynamic structured knowledge base, 447, 448

Dynamic task scheduling, 100, 112, 116

Dynamically assign tasks, 100

E

Early optimistic approach, 392

Edges, 187

Efficiency, 104, 128, 137

Electric power system planning, 3

Electronic components box, 499, 500

Elementary interval operation, 535

Elimination of constraints, 145, 148, 150

Empirical data, 120

Emulation software, 101

Enscapsulation, 24

Environment, 417

Equations section, 502

EREW paridigm, 44

EREW PRAM shared memory, 37

Error estimate, 52

EXCHANGE, 340

Exchange, 217
  agreements, 218
  partner, 218
  percentages, 219

Excitatory, 315

Exclusive-OR problem, 308

Expert systems, 313

F

Faces, 187

Fast-response algorithms, 350

Feasibility Algorithm, 357

Feasible solutions, 49, 53

Feedforward network, 312

Fiber optic network, 191

Fiber optic technology, 190

Field of View, 188

Final problem solving system, 335

Final resolution plan, 335

Financial modeling, 511

Fine-grain model, 164

First Fit (FF), 34, 37, 42

First Fit Decreasing (FFD), 34, 37, 42

Fixation of variables, 145, 148, 149

FLEX Algorithm, 85

Flexible, 205, 210
   memory management, 213

Flow, 73
   augmentation, 59
   conversation of, 57
   cost of, 57

Follower, 291

Forgetting, 315

Fork and join primitives, 134

Fractional block minimum, 123

Free flow, 73

Functual actual, 97

G

GABBA, 292, 294, 296, 299, 300

GAMS modelling system, 509

GATHER, 64

General algorithm, 52

General network problem, 521

Generalization, 314

Generalized bisection algorithm, 537

Generalized network problem (GNP), 57

Generic matrices, 209

Genetic algorithm (GA), 290, 291, 293, 300, 325
   application, 326

GENNET, 66, 67

Geographic information systems, 246, 248

Geometrical structure, 184

Geometrically isolated, 549, 550, 551

Global algorithm, 155

Global maximum, 94

Global nonlinear optimization problem, 538

Global optimality, 7

Global optimization, 92

Global software vectorization, 72

Globally convergant homotopy techniques, 556

Globally optimal solution, 172

GNET, 223

Granularity, 133, 138, 155, 392

Graph inversion, 313

Graphical interfaces, 389

Graphics interface, 362, 443

Graphics representation, 423

Graphics support program, 436, 442

Greedy algorithm, 45, 46, 51
   approach, 49
   heuristic, 195
   result, 55

H

Harmonic (H), 34, 42

HDRS, 381

Heap operations, 122

Hedging algorithm, 107, 111, 114, 118

Heirarchical optimization problems, 289

Heuristic, 324
   phase, 137
   procedure level, 334
   procedures, 321, 526
   stragedy, 334
   strategies, 332

High level modeling language (ML), 507

High-end packages, 278

Home delivery routing and scheduling system (HDRS), 373

Homotopies, 549

Homotopy 550, 552, 563
   algorithms, 561
   map, 556
   method, 557
   methods, 555, 560

Housing Indicators, 251, 256

Hypercells, 227, 236, 237

Hypertext system, 455

I

Implementation, 161
   environment, 484, 493
   tools 491, 492

Importance sampling, 3, 11, 15

Improve Solution, 195

Improve Solution Menu, 195

Inadmissible arc, 60

Increased user control, 280

Independence, 111

Indirect labor, 238, 243

Indirect labor categories, 241

Indirect support

Individual network links, 529

Inefficient program, 104

Infeasible, 51

Informative diagnosis, 413

INIT, 340

Initial heuristic, 138

Initial knapsack problem, 47

Initial problem analysis, 334

Initial test network, 77

Initial value problem, 546

Initialization phase, 48

Integer, 417

Integer knapsack problem, 44

Integrated model, 453, 454
   compiler\linker, 505

Integrated modeling, 515

Integrating application construction, 484

Intelligent Mathematical Programming System (IMPS), 313

574

Intelligent participation, 313

Interactive Network Design
    System (INDS), 190, 192

Interactive-graphics, 349

Interface, 493

Interface design, 491

Interfaces, 279

Interior point algorithms, 158

Interior point LP algorithms,
    167

Interior point methods, 158

International Neural Network
    Society, 302

Interprocess communication, 25

Interval algorithm, 534
    arithmetic, 534, 536
    methods, 533
    extensions, 535
    generalizations, 538
    methods, 536
    algorithms, 539

Introspection, 388

J

Juncture, 133

K

Knapsack capacity, 54

Knapsack problem, 144

Knowledge base, 455, 456, 475,
    482

Knowledge based systems, 492

Knowledge-Based Model
    Construction (KBMC), 387

Knowledge-Based Simulation
    system, 387

L

Large item computation, 53

Large optimization models, 515

Large scale optimization, 511

Large-grain model, 164

Leader, 291

Learning, 314
    equation, 314
    phase, 307
    problem, 312
    time, 307

Least function value, 123

Lift, 219
    volumes, 220

Lifting, 218

Line-oriented terminals, 474

Linear approximation, 89

Linear cost assignment
problem, 26

Linear problems, 498

Linear programming (LP), 205

Linear programming algorithm,
    184

Linear programming problem,
    230

Linear programs (LPs), 3, 14,
    263, 271
    lower block-triangular type,
    4

Linear programs, "Cont."
  modeling, 265
  packages, 265, 266, 269, 271
  problems, 235
  software, 267
  systems, 264, 266, 269, 270

Linear speedup, 128

Linearization, 89

Link flows, 73

Links, 77

List-of-Equations Approach, 466

Local Area networks, 389

Local propagation, 464

Local software vectorization, 72

Locals section, 502

Loosely Coupled, 30

Lower bounds, 145

Lower-level process, 437

M

Macintosh II microcomputer, 433, 434, 443

Mainframe PM software, 275, 284

Major key, 122

Manager, 132

Marine Georgraphic Information System (MGIS), 248, 258, 261

Market research plans, 257

Market share purposes, 252

Market trends, 256

Marketing application, 252

Massively parallel architectures, 55

Massively parallel computations, 176

Massively parallel systems, 84

Master Problem, 12

Mathematical analysis, 396

Mathematical modeling languages, 270

Mathematical modelling environment, 492

Mathematical models, 508

Mathematical programming, 475
  methods, 478
  software, 266, 269
  systems, 263

Mathematical Programming Modeling Project (MP2), 447

Mathematical Programming System (MPS), 313

Matrix balancing, 512, 513

Maximun flow augmentation, 64

Medium-grain model, 164

Memory requirements, 65

Menu oriented user interface, 349

MERGE, 340

Message-passing model, 33

MGIS Databases, 250

Military Airlift Command (MAC), 323

MIMD algorithms, 39, 42

MIMD distributed memory, 33

MIMD parallel bin packing algorithms, 35

Minimum cost configuration, 522

Minimum-degree algorithm, 165

Minor key, 122

Mixed integer programming model, 514

Model Analysis, 489

Model Analyzer 407, 408, 409, 410, 416
  Menu, 419

Model Builder, 504

Model completion, 313, 316

Model complexity, 425

Model definition language, 497

Model Description, 489

Model diagnosis, 407

Model diagnostics, 411

Model Documentation, 490

Model Integration, 490

Model logic, 427

Model management, 498

Model Reformation, 490

Model specifications, 409

Model Validation, 490

Model's dynamic equations, 314

Modeling capabilities, 497

Modeling Tools, 364, 365

Modelling, 484

Modifications, 61

Mother process, 134, 135

Mother-child relationship, 135

MPSHL problem, 404

Multi-objective problems, 323

Multi-stage stochastic planning problem, 8

Multiknapsack problem, 145

Multimodal urban transportation, 71

Multiperiod electric power system, 3

Multiperiod problems, 206

Multiperiod stochastic linear programs, 3

Multiple functional units, 510

Multiple Minimum-degree, 161

Multiple searching stragedies, 132

Multiple vehicle algorithms, 365

Multiplicity of solutions, 478

Multipliers, 68

Multistage stochastic programs, 110

Multitasked program, 100

Multitasking, 95, 98

Mutual exclusion access problem, 26

N

Near linear speedup, 116

Nearly Triangular, 205

Nearly Triangular Leontief Program NTLLP, 206, 207

Negative, 417

NETGEN, 65

NETGEN problem, 67

NETGENG, 65

Network configuration, 522, 527, 528, 529

Network connectivity, 191
 constraints, 191

Network design algorithm, 529

Network design problem, 71, 72

Network designs, 190

Network equilibrium assignment problem, 71

Network extensible Window System, 390

Network flow problem, 82

Network improvement algorithm, 524, 525, 527

Network location theory, 397

Network optimization, 169, 511
 algorithms, 170
 models 348, 349

Network planner, 190

Network problems, 57, 516

Network sites, 522

Network solvers, 512

Network Survivability, 197, 198

Network variables, 62

Neural network, 314

Neural network implementation, 307,

Neurocomputing, 302, 303, 306

New incumbents, 138

Next Fit (NF), 34, 42

NLP software, 267

NLP systems, 264, 266

Node processes, 35, 36

Non-commercial, 212

Non-committal value, 305

Non-creative time, 372

Non-linear optimization problem, 307

Non-null update

Non-optimal solution, 88

Nonbasic, 60

Nonlinear complementarity problem, 561

Nonlinear function subject, 533

Nonlinear minimization methods, 309

Nonlinear network problems, 170

Nonlinear networks, 177

Nonlinear optimization, 539

Nonlinear programming, 481, 498

Nonlinear programs (NLPs), 263, 271

Nonnegative, 417

Nonpositive, 417

Nonpreemptive, 137
  algorithm, 140

Nonprocedural approach, 228

Nonprocedural environment, 236

Nonprocedural implementation, 236

Novice user, 353

NP-Complete, 44, 332

Numerical computation, 226

Numerical engineering
  applications, 476

Numerical information, 429

Numerical path tracking, 552

O

Object paradigm, 32

Object-oriented approach, 465

Object-oriented programming, 23, 493

Objective function, 67, 312
  value, 307

Objects, 313

One-optimal, 196

Open system, 486

Operations research (OR), 289, 290, 332, 347
  problems, 302

OPIS, 337, 339, 343

Optimal assignment patterns, 223

Optimal exchange agreements, 218

Optimal policy, 230

Optimal primal solution, 159

Optimal solution, 7

Optimal values, 146

Optimistic evaluation, 121, 129

Optimistically, 120, 121, 123

Optimization, 468, 555
  control language, 456
  expert, 458
  literature, 456
  methods, 190
  models, 348, 451, 489, 499
  phase, 562
  problem, 190, 470, 545, 559, 562
  software, 457

Optimized, 497

Optimizing, 379

Options section, 504

OR models, 347

OR researchers, 463

OR specialists, 484

OR techniques, 302, 303

Order scheduler (OSC)

Origin-destination flows, 73

Original size, 147

Out-of-kilter algorithm, 58

Output reports, 371

Overall algorithm vectorization, 72

Overlaps, 87

P

Parallel algorithm, 123, 124, 151

Parallel algorithm's complexity, 126

Parallel algorithms, 33, 39, 42, 128

Parallel approximation algorithms, 44

Parallel computers, 39

Parallel decomposition algorithms, 118

Parallel execution, 132

Parallel greedy algorithm, 54

Parallel Harmonic algorithm, 38

Parallel Hedging algorithm, 115

Parallel hedging procedures, 114

Parallel implementation, 158, 165

Parallel knapsack approximation algorithms, 54, 55

Parallel Match Fit, 39

Parallel Model execution, 391

Parallel object-oriented implementation, 28

Parallel object-oriented program design, 24

Parallel phase, 133

Parallel prefix operations, 52

Parallel processing, 25, 32, 35, 126, 237, 321, 391
high-speed, 13

Parallel processors, 3, 5, 12

Parallel programming environment, 28

Parallel relaxation algorithm, 178

Parallel Segment Fit, 38

Parallel sparse implementation, 162

Parallel step, 125

Parallel variants, 113

Parallel version, 47

Parallel versions, 107, 111

Parallelism, 51

Parallelization, 92

Parallelizing, 38

Parameter settings, 322

Partial solutions, 322

Partition invariance, 208

Partitioning, 25
by object, 25
functional, 25
task, 25

Performance Ratio, 67

Path correction, 547

Penalty function, 328

Performance measures

Petal Fit (PF), 34, 35, 36, 42

Petroleum refining industry, 217

Piecewise-linear functions, 89

PLANES, 100

Planner, 192

Polynomial continuation, 543, 544

Polynomial equations, 543, 544

Polytope, 183

Port planning

Port simulation model, 434, 436

Positive, 417

PostScript Output, 188

Potential objective function improvement, 307

Predictor-corrector, 547

Preemptive algorithm, 140

Prefix operation, 49

Prefix summunation operation, 37

Prestractification, 15

Primal, 159

Primal algorithm, 59, 68

Primal simplex, 58

Primary input data, 362

Primary speed-up, 52

Primitives, 134

Probality distribution, 239

Probality-one globally convergent homotopy algorithm, 558

Problem formulation, 71

Problem menu, 193

Procedure, 521

Process synchronization, 25, 111

Processing nodes, 35

Processing time, 36

Processor self-address, 37

Processors, 8, 127

Product distribution costs, 219

Production variables, 8

Progam descriptive language, 477

Programming problems, 479

Progressive hedging algorithm, 107, 109

Project management software (PM), 273, 274, 276, 278

Project network, 277

Project schedule, 276

Project size, 274

Projective transformation, 548, 551

Proposed updates, 85

Pruning, 132

Pseudo-polynomial algorithms,

54, 55

Q

Quadratic assignment problem, 132

R

Random events, 9

Random heuristic, 195

Random networks, 77

Randomizes, 76

Real, 417

Real time, 184

Real-world problems, 198, 309

Real-world stochastic operations, 396

Recombination operation, 325

Reduced load approximation, 523

Reduced load estimates, 524

Reduced size, 147

Refined First Fit (RFF), 34, 36, 42

Refined Harmonic (RH), 34, 38, 42

Relations, 313

Relative reduction, 74

Relative vectorizing performance, 75

Relaxation, 464

Relearning, 315

Reliabilty estimation module, 352

Report generation, 278

Resolution planning level, 335

Resource leveling, 280

Resource management features, 273

Resource management problem, 280

Resource management, 279

Resource-constrained problem, 280, 281, 282

Resource-driven scheduling, 282

Resource-limited leveling, 281

Response time, 398

Restructuring, 459

Revised Simplex, 209

Right Shifter (RSH), 338

Robust (reliable) train schedules, 350

Robust schedules, 348

Rotation, 188

ROUTE, 361, 362, 370

Route construction procedures, 375

Route diversity, 197

Routing algorithms, 375

Routing heuristics, 376

Routing of vehicles, 361

Row Cholesky, 160, 162

Row Partition, 208

Rulebase generation, 313

S

SABBA, 295, 299, 300

Sample model, 499

Sampling approach, 15
  historical, 15
  procedure, 15

SAXPY, 162
  operation, 163

Scalar code, 96

Scaled profit group, 49

Scaling, 188

SCAN, 351, 354, 358
  decision support system, 349

Scan operations, 46

SCAN user interface, 353

Scanning, 478

SCATTER, 64

Scenario probalities, 109

Scenario subproblem, 109, 111

Scenario testing, 72

Schedule-modification procedure, 356

Scheduling, 276
  operation, 440
  problems, 323
  system, 373

Screen Layout, 425

SDSs, 336

Search tree, 132

Second order approximation, 89

Sectioning search

Sectioning search algorithm, 246

Semi-linear feed-forward network, 306

Sensitivity analyses, 80

Separability, 111

Sequential algorithms, 152

Sequential computers, 58

Sequential quadratic programming

Serial algorithm, 147

Serial reduction, 147

Serial Step, 125

Serialization, 126

Service times, 240

Shared class of objects, 29

Shared data structure, 131

Shared memory machine, 141

Shared memory multiprocessors, 135

Shared objects, 30

Shared-memory architecture, 167

Signal, 417

SIMD (single instruction multiple data), 94
  algorithms, 39, 42
  exclusive-read, 33
  packing algorithms, 40

Simplex algorithm, 211

583

Simulated annealing, 290

Simulated performance, 400

Simulation event, 440

Simulation model, 398, 402, 405, 424, 433
    development, 393

Simulation Model Development Environments (SMDE), 386

Simulation modeling, 390, 430

Simulation modelling system, 422

Simulation modelling technique, 428

Simulation models, 396

Simulation program, 436

Simulation programming language (SPL), 385

Simulation report, 441

Simulation-based models, 396

Simultaneous nonlinear equations, 523

Single block update, 85

Singular points, 557

Size reduction, 147

Socioeconomic Indicators, 251, 256

Software engineering, 392

Software trends, 283

Solid figure, 187

Solution algorithms, 16

Solution paths, 184

Solve models, 454

Solving capabilities, 451

Sparse linear systems, 213

Sparse network problems, 172, 173

Sparse problems, 199

Specialization, 314

Speedup, 101, 104, 128

Splitting, 140

Splitting process, 141

Spontaneous generalization, 303

Spreadsheet software, 226

Spreadsheet-compatible programs, 270

Stack, 537

Static, 459

Static task allocation, 112

Static task prescheduling, 111

Static task scheduling, 116

Statistical modeling, 429

Statistics, 400

Statistics Menu, 197

Steady state, 224

Stick-figure, 187

Stochastic assumptions, 126

Stochastic events, 11, 12

Stochastic input parameters,

Stochastic mathematical
  program, 3
Stochastic network models, 106
Stochastic planning problems,
  5, 12
Stochastic problem, 106
Stochastic programming, 106
Strategy Design Systems (SDS),
  334
Stratification, 15
Strip-mining, 98, 99
Structure, 314
Structured modeling, 313
Submatrix, 213
  Cholesky, 161
Subproblem, 11, 112
Supercomputer, 68, 80
Support system, 487
Surface Checking, 95
Survivability, 191
Symbolic factorization, 163
Synchronization and
  communication, 152
Synchronization phase, 133
Synchronization primitives, 165
Synchronized, 100
Synchronous update, 317
Synochronization, 166
System representation, 71

T

Tactical scheduling model, 351
Tactical train scheduling, 347
Tearing method, 213
Tentative function values, 123
Term rewriting, 465
Terminal differential, 218
  differential costs, 219, 220
The Master Problem, 6
The Sub Problem, 6
Three-dimensional, 187, 189
  polytopes, 184
Three-optimal, 196
Tightly coupled, 30
Time complexity, 46
Title section, 501
Totally Dense Assignment
  Problems, 31
Tracking of progress, 278
Transient system statistic,
  399
Translation, 188
Transportation, 512
  costs, 219, 220
  network, 76
  planning activities, 71
  problems, 65
Traveling Salesman Problem
  (TSP), 303, 332
Tree network, 200
Trilogy, 467

True times, 165

Two-connected, 191

Two-Connected Menu, 192, 193

Two-optimal cycle heuristic, 196

Two-phase simplex method, 235

Two-stage programs, 108

Two-stage stochastic programming, 5

Typical learning curve, 305

U

Unconstrained minization problem, 312

Upper bound constraint, 57

Upper Bounds, 145

Upper Limit, 101

User interaction, 190

User interface, 475

User interface changes, 284

User-control, 266, 269

User-defined abstract data type, 23

User-interface, 266, 269, 279

User-oriented conveniences, 279

User-transparent routines, 366

Utilization, 101

V

Vector algorithms, 158

Vector architecture, 166

Vector code, 96

Vector computer

Vector processing, 61, 65

Vectorize, 59, 163

Vectorized, 76
  algorithm, 66

Vectorized code, 65-68

Vectors, 63

VEGA vector evaluated genetic algorithm, 327

Vehicle routing and scheduling problem with time window constraints (VRSPTW), 374

Vertices, 183

Virtual processors, 165

Visual interactive simulation, 425

Visual model, 427

Visual modelling, 430

Visual representation, 423, 424

Visual simulation, 422, 426, 428

Voice telecommunications networks, 521, 530

W

Well-stated problem, 146

Wide area networks, 389

Workload distribution, 36

Workloads, 239

Z

Zooming, 188